Critical Acclaim for Australia's Argonauts

... an absorbing story of people, places and occurrences, spread over fifty years or more, where events pop-up and then fade away revealing information which will inform and indeed inspire the reader ... *Australia's Argonauts* is a remarkably rewarding tale ... a pleasure to read.

Dr Greg Gilbert, The Australian Naval Institute

... unrelenting research ... It is much more than a chronicle of the 1913 Entry, this is a window on the nation at war, societal attitudes and practises of our nation from the early days of Federation. Not only for old and young salts but also the nation's readers at large.

Vice Admiral Ian MacDougall, Chief of Naval Staff (1991-1994)

This is a story of what Australia was, what it wanted to be and what it became as the twentieth century advanced. *Australia's Argonauts* shows how the members of the first entry to the Royal Australian Naval College profoundly influenced our national life ... It is a fascinating book.

Rear Admiral James Goldrick, author of *Before Jutland*

... thoroughly engaging and deeply moving work is marked by painstaking research, nuanced analysis and sensitive handling of both brutalising events and human frailty. It will become a classic text in the RAN's evolving history.

Professor Tom Frame, author of *Where Fate Calls*

First published in 2016 by Barrallier Books Pty Ltd,
trading as Echo Books

Registered Office: 35-37 Gordon Avenue, West Geelong,
Victoria 3220, Australia.

www.echobooks.com.au

Copyright ©Peter Jones

National Library of Australia Cataloguing-in-Publication entry.

Author: Jones Peter, author.

Title: Australia's Argonauts : the remarkable story of the first class to enter the Royal Australian Naval College/Peter Jones.

ISBN: 9780995414716 (pbk)

Notes: Includes bibliographical references and index.

Subjects: Royal Australian Naval College--Students--Biography. Royal Australian Naval College--History. Naval education--Australia--History. Midshipmen--Australia--Biography.

Dewey Number: 359.50994

Book layout and design by Peter Gamble, Canberra.
Maps by Catherine Gordon
Set in Garamond Premier Pro Regular, 11/16.
www.echobooks.com.au

Front cover image: The fleet flagship HMAS *Australia* leading other units of the 2nd Battlecruiser Squadron out of the Firth of Forth on a sortie. Six of the 1913 Entry to the Royal Australian Naval College served in *Australia* during 1917-1918. (RAN)

AUSTRALIA'S ARGONAUTS

The remarkable story of the first class to enter the Royal Australian Naval College

Peter Jones

ECHO BOOKS

Dedicated to the memory of

The boys of the 1913 Entry to the Royal Australian Naval College

Captain Duncan Grant, CBE, RN
who did more than anyone to prepare them for their naval careers.

Commander Tony Grazebrook, RANR
who shone the lantern so I could follow.

Contents

Foreword	vii
Preface	ix
Acknowledgements	xiii
Officer Complements in RAN Ships	xx
Comparitave Naval Ranks	xxii
Scales of Measurement	xxiii
Chapter 1 – A Naval College for Australia	1
Chapter 2 – Geelong	19
Chapter 3 – Jervis Bay	55
Chapter 4 – Midshipmen At War	95
Chapter 5 – The Inter War Years	163
Chapter 6 – Captains at War	277
Chapter 7 – Sad Songs of the Death of Sailors	403
Chapter 8 – Road to Victory	513
Chapter 9 – These Have Been Men	567
Endnotes	643
Bibliography	705
Index	733

Foreword

War has been one of the central features of Australian history, and the two world wars defined the generations that participated. The Pioneer Class of the Royal Australian Naval College, joined their fledgling service in the glorious days of 1913, when the nation's ambitions were high and the new fleet was not only a widespread source of pride, but also seen as a sign of peace that came from being prepared for war. Preparations included those practical measures intended to ensure that the navy and its ships would eventually be commanded by Australian-trained officers. Through a regime of strict discipline, intense study and sporting pursuits, those who founded the Naval College sought to produce naval leaders ready and willing to serve their nation whenever and wherever required. How well the College performed is evident in the engrossing story told so well here by Peter Jones.

The creation of this narrative represents a significant achievement. Works on Australian naval social history are rare, and Peter has had to delve into areas of service and professional culture never previously examined. He has also needed to distil the essence of 28 very different careers, while at the same time balancing the attention given to the individual, class and the organisation to which they belonged. Moreover, these men were also an integral part of a wider Australia. Much more than a purely naval history, Peter has provided a lens through which we can view many aspects of national life and development across the twentieth century.

Despite the enormous amount of work, the writing of *Australia's Argonauts* has clearly been a labour of love. As one who has followed the manuscript's progress over many years, I can only admire Peter's patience, tenacity and thoroughness. That he himself joined the navy at an early age, has commanded ships in war, and rose to the highest ranks of the service, has allowed him unique insights into many of the issues discussed. Far more than a casual observer, he understands that none of these men were one-dimensional and the even-handed discussion of their varied strengths and failings is particularly noteworthy.

Australia's Argonauts makes an important contribution to our national and naval knowledge. I have no doubt that those who read it will better appreciate the contribution of 28 Australians, who lived out their lives against the backdrop of some of the most tumultuous times in our history. Not all achieved lasting fame, but their collective deeds, in no small measure built the national society that we continue to enjoy.

Dr David Stevens
Canberra, March 2016

Preface

> *Perhaps the hardest part of a naval career is that one's future hangs on a thread and there are more chances of that thread breaking than in most walks of life.*[1]
>
> John Collins

The idea for this book began with the passing of Rear Admiral Harry Showers on 31 July 1991. He was thought by the Navy to be the last survivor of the first class of twenty-eight 13-year old boys who joined the Royal Australian Naval College. Collectively known as the Pioneer Class, his passing was the end of the era. At the time, I was a young officer on the staff of the Chief of Naval Staff, Vice Admiral Ian MacDougall. In preparing Admiral Showers' obituary it became clear to me not only that his career was one of notable achievement, but that his entire class had made an astounding contribution to the Royal Australian Navy—both in war and peace. The idea for the book was formed. Admiral MacDougall embraced the idea and the search began for an author. The name we kept coming back to was Tony Grazebrook. He was the much respected naval correspondent to the then *Pacific Defence Reporter* who also had a deep knowledge of senior officer careers of both the Royal Navy and the Royal Australian Navy.

Tony readily accepted the assignment and approached the daunting task of retracing the lives in his typical methodical and comprehensive manner. The project became an increasingly absorbing one for Tony as he juggled the many facets of his life—family man, journalist, grazier and Commander in the Royal Australian Navy Reserve. The biggest surprise from his research was to find one of the class, Captain James Esdaile, very frail but still alive. He had though but months to live.

After nearly ten years of research Tony was diagnosed with advanced prostate cancer. With great courage Tony, supported by his devoted wife Phyllis, fought a losing battle against the disease. At Tony's funeral Admiral Michael Hudson presented Phyllis with a Chief of Naval Staff Commendation for Tony's distinguished service to the Navy through his carefully researched media reporting.

Two days before his death, I spoke to Tony about the book project. Tony, from his hospice bed, was still optimistic about beating the cancer and being able to tell the story of the Pioneer Class. It was therefore with a sense of duty to both Tony and the Pioneer Class that I proposed to Phyllis that I take on the book. When I examined Tony's folders and notes that were painstakingly gathered, I saw that the story was more remarkable than I appreciated. Tony's 'treasure trove' made me start to understand what had driven Tony for so many years. Like many part-time authors before me, I learnt the harsh lesson that it is exceedingly difficult to write a book when you also have another career. So began a period of some years where I undertook desultory research between sea postings and the demands of a young family. As the centenary of the 'Pioneer' Class in 2013 loomed I pressed on in earnest. What I found was that some leads in the research had maddeningly gone cold. If only I could have recovered a couple of years to find a particular individual still alive. In particular, I wished on more than one occasion I could talk to Tony about his thoughts, recollections from interviews or decipher his distinctive handwriting. But there was no turning back and on a positive note, the power of the internet had provided material that Tony could have only dreamed of accessing. Indeed, it allowed me to track down many more descendants to fill in the picture. In addition, my experience of sea command and then Flag rank had given me greater insight into the deeds of my subjects. Tony had been yet to commence writing the book before his death but it became clear my approach would be quite different based on the internet and my experiences.

What the research of Tony and I had laid bare was that the Pioneer Class were the most remarkable entry to the Royal Australian Naval College. When they joined in 1913 there was unparalleled idealism and hope in the new nation. There was unprecedented national interest in the progress of the young Cadet-Midshipman from the Governor-General to the broader Australian public. This was reflected in the frequent reports that appeared in national newspapers. The significant individual contributions of the Pioneer Class in a diverse array of undertakings within the Navy were never repeated by a subsequent group of midshipmen.

The story of the Pioneer Class is as much the saga of the Navy as it is about twenty-eight individuals. They share many of the same triumphs and tragedies. The sudden twists of fate, as well as fortune, have given their tale a universal human dimension.

A narrative history of a whole cohort gives the life of an individual their context and points of comparison. In writing about the lives of twenty-eight men I am conscious of the challenge I pose the reader in recognising, certainly early in the book, who were in the Pioneer Class. To assist the reader their names appear on page xxiv for ready reference. More importantly, however, I have used a device where if a member of the Pioneer Class is mentioned in a section of the book I have used both their first and family name, but then followed in subsequent references useby their first name. This differentiates them from others in the story.

Peter Jones
Canberra, 2016

Acknowledgements

The story of the Pioneer Class could not have been told without the tremendous support Tony Grazebrook and I received from their descendants, friends, old sailors and an array of people who are interested in preserving Australia's naval heritage. That support has ranged over more than two decades and thus some listed here have not lived to see the product of their assistance.

In the first rank are the families of those twenty-eight 13-year olds of the Pioneer Class. They have been most generous with access and use of family information, personal papers and photographs. I would like to thank and acknowledge the generous support of Mr Robert Albert, Ms Jane Albert, Captain Gordon Andrew, Mrs Caroline Armitage, Mrs Mary Backhouse, Mrs Gillian Bower, Commander Pat Burnett, Commodore Rory Burnett, Mr John Calder, Captain Mike Calder, Mr Robert Cliff, Lady Collins, Mr Peter Cowper, Mrs Barbara Crouch, Ms Claudia Esdaile, Ms Lucy Esdaile, Mrs Sandra Esdaile, Mrs Jean Farncomb, Mr Geoff Howells, Rev. John Howells, Mr George Kimlin, Mrs Betty Lee, Mr Peter Long, Mrs Marilou Long, Mrs Ursula Maffey, Mrs Deni McKenzie, Rev. Philip Newman, Mr James Newman, Mrs Lynette Newman, Mr Noel Ramsden, Mr Cy Sadleir, Ms Penny Tait, Mrs Sandra Trollope, Dr. Toni Trollope, Mr Howard Watts, Mr Merrick Watts,

Mrs Barbara Willingham, Mrs Beth Vallentine, Mrs Dorothy Vallentine and all their extended families.

Many in the Navy have been generous with their time, advice and support. I would like to particularly acknowledge Vice Admiral Ian MacDougall for his initial support for the book and for his comments on the draft. Vice Admirals Russ Crane and Ray Griggs also cast their green pens over early draft chapters. In the final stages Vice Admiral Tim Barrett has also been unstinting in his encouragement. Also greatly supportive over many years have been two Chiefs of Defence Force, His Excellency General David Hurley and that former naval person, Air Chief Marshal Mark Binskin.

My four naval class mates Rear Admiral James Goldrick, Dr. David Stevens, Paul Konings and Graeme Lunn, have been extremely generous and helpful in every stage of this project. In particular James and David spent considerable time commenting on the draft and answering my many questions about the Navy's history. Their deep knowledge of the RAN's past continued to amaze me. Paul was most helpful in providing his expert advice on maps and diagrams while Graeme, besides offering lodging during my UK research, went to considerable effort in researching the life of Harry Vallentine. My other classmates of Junior Entry 1974 have not only provided encouragement but gave me a first-hand appreciation of the life-long camaraderie that members of the Pioneer Class must have enjoyed. Rear Admiral Allan Du Toit also provided considerable support and encouragement. In Tony Grazebrook's early quest for information and descendants Norm Smith provided marvelous assistance.

Dr. John Reeve, the Osborne Fellow of Naval History, Professors Tom Frame and David Lovell at the University of New South Wales campus at the Australian Defence Force Academy have been great supporters of this project as has the Rector, Professor Michael Frater. That institution graciously provided invaluable support whilst I was a Research Fellow and then Adjunct Professor. In that vein the remarkable institution, Sea Power Centre – Australia, has also been unstinting in its support and I thank Captain Mike Macarthur, John Perryman and Commander Greg Swinden.

In this work I have particularly valued the assistance of other historians and writers who have given freely of their thoughts and offered advice and material. I would like to thank Mrs Barbara Poniewierski who first drew attention to the remarkable life of Rupert Long in *Intrigue Master*. Mr Tony MacDougall who like me found himself absorbed for many years in completing a book, and in his case *Collins of the Sydney*. He and I were able to share information and I valued his thoughts and friendship.

Among the quoted works in copyright I am grateful for permission to reprint excerpts. In particular I would thank Penguin Random House for permission to quote from *The Voyage of Argo*, the Imperial War Museum to quote from papers in their collection and The Hoyts Group to reproduce an example of Adrian Watts' artwork. For those literary heirs and original publishers I have been unable to trace, may I here record my acknowledgement. Similarly, I have tried where ever possible to trace the copyright of photographs. In particular some early photographs appeared in multiple collections and so their original copyright owner remained unclear.

Over the many years of its gestation, *Australia's Argonauts* has benefitted immensely from the information provided in letters, interviews and papers. Some people served with or knew the Pioneer Class, while others pointed Tony and then me in the right direction. These men and women included Rear Admiral Brian Adams, Mrs Mornay Bibby, Mr John Burgess, Captain WF Cook, Captain Peter Dechaineux, Ms Chris Degan, Commodore Vince Di Pietro, Captain Donald Dykes, Commander George Fowle, Captain Donald Fraser, Rear Admiral Steven Gilmore, Mrs Catherine Grant, Warrant Officer Allen Guthrie, Lieutenant Commander Henry Hall, Rear Admiral Simon Harrington, Mr Robert Hyslop, Captain Charles Huxtable,

The author interviewing the late former Warrant Officer Allen Guthrie.
(Peter Wilson)

Rear Admiral Geoffrey Loosli, Lieutenant Commander 'Mac' Gregory, Rear Admiral Guy Griffiths, Vice Admiral Sir Richard Peek, Captain Ian Pfennigwerth, Able Seaman Sandy Pearson, Mrs Elizabeth Pyment, Mr Michael Pyment, Michelle Ray, Mr Charles Reid, TJ Roberts, Commander Jason Sears, Lieutenant Syd Sharp, Lieutenant Commander Mark Shelvey, Mrs Pat Smith, Rear Admiral Michael Slattery, Admiral Sir Victor Smith, Dr. Rowan Stephens, Commander Arthur Storey, Mrs Joan Turnour, Commander Tony Vine, Rear Admiral Robyn Walker, Mr Peter Wilson, Lieutenant Commander Desmond Woods, Commander Graham Wright, Lieutenant Commander Ian Wrigley and Mr Allan Zammit. Even with such an honour roll I am sure I have missed many people and to that I apologise. I trust the book will do justice to their assistance.

The Royal Australian Naval College has been extremely generous in their support to both Tony and me. Commodore 'Toz' Dadswell and Lieutenant Commander David Jones, the successive custodians of the College museum have been strong supporters and a sounding board for the project. I would also like to thank the successive Commanding

Officers of the Naval College and their dedicated staff at the HMAS *Creswell* library. Mrs Toni Munday at the sister HMAS *Cerberus* Museum also provided invaluable support particularly in locating some of the Eldridge Papers.

Other institutions have been immensely helpful and I would like to acknowledge the assistance of the staff of the library at the Australian War Memorial, the Australian High Commission in Wellington, the National Library of Australia, the National Archives of Australia, the State Libraries of New South Wales, South Australia, Queensland and Victoria, Lisa Conti Phillips at the archives of the Australian Academy of Science, Mr Stephen Prince and the RN Naval Historical Branch, Mrs Barbara Gilbert and the RN Fleet Air Arm Museum, the Imperial War Museum, the National Archives United Kingdom; Registrar Ann Lambino and the State Coroner's Court of New South Wales; Rear Admiral Sam Cox, Joe Gordon and Glen Gray at the US Naval Historical and Heritage Command and finally the United Service Club, Queensland.

As this project reached the phase where I needed to secure a publisher I would like to acknowledge the assistance of Rear Admiral Raydon Gates in directing me to Ian Gordon and Echo Books. Ian has been immensely supportive of this book and his professional skill and that of his team are evidenced by its fine production. I would like to particularly thank my editor Mrs Kiri Mathieson for her skill and patience, artist Catherine Gordon for her excellent maps, Terry McCullagh for his work on the index and Peter Gamble for his meticulous work in typesetting the manuscript.

After I initially suggested this project to Tony Grazebrook, he grasped it in his typically methodical manner. It became an obsession and to his family I acknowledge their support and I trust this book will be another legacy of a great life lived.

I would like to also record my sincere thanks to my wife Rhonda and my boys Dion and Evan for their support and considerable understanding shown to me over the many years it took to complete *Australia's Argonauts*. Rhonda also provided most valued advice after reading the first draft. My extended family has also been most supportive and I have appreciated the input from my mother Patricia Matthews and mother-in-law Fiona Payget and sister-in-law Jasmine Payget in also reading the draft.

Finally, notwithstanding my debt to so many people, I take responsibility for any errors in this book. Indeed, I welcome additional information about the remarkable Pioneer Class for any future edition.

Peter Jones
Canberra, 2016

Officer Complements in RAN Ships

Representative ships with officer positions and their rank.

HMAS *Australia* Battlecruiser 1919	HMAS *Adelaide* Cruiser 1925
• Commodore Commanding HMA Squadron with a personal staff of 2 officers.	• Commanding Officer - Captain
• Commanding Officer & Flag Captain - Captain	• Commander - Commander
• Commander - Commander	• First Lieutenant - Lieutenant Commander
• Navigating Officer - Commander	• Engineering Lieutenant Commander
• Engineering Commander	• Paymaster Lieutenant Commander
• Paymaster Commander	• Gunnery Officer - Lieutenant
• 2 Chaplains	• Navigating Officer - Lieutenant
• Fleet Gunnery Officer - Lieutenant Commander	• 2 Engineer Lieutenants
• Torpedo Officer - Lieutenant Commander	• 2 Chaplains
• Fleet Wireless & Signal Officer - Lieutenant Commander	• Surgeon Lieutenant
• First Lieutenant - Lieutenant Commander	• Bridge watching-keeping, assistants to departmental officers or under training- 4 Lieutenants & 8 Sub-Lieutenants
• Surgeon Lieutenant Commander	• Paymaster Sub-Lieutenant
• Surgeon Lieutenant	• Instructor Lieutenant
• Bridge watching-keeping, assistants to departmental officers or under training - 8 Lieutenants & 7 Sub-Lieutenants	• 14 Warrant Officers serving roles such as Chief Gunner, Commissioned Shipwright & Warrant Electrician.
• 3 Engineer Lieutenants	• 6 Warrant Officers serving roles such as Gunner & Commissioned Shipwright.
• Paymaster Lieutenant	• Schoolmaster
• Instructor Lieutenant	• 13 Midshipmen
• 14 Warrant Officers serving roles such as Chief Gunner, Commissioned Shipwright & Warrant Electrician.	
• 11 Midshipmen	

HMAS *Tasmania* Destroyer 1926	HMAS *Toowoomba* Corvette 1942
- Commanding Officer - Lieutenant Commander - First Lieutenant - Lieutenant - Navigating Officer - Lieutenant - Engineer Lieutenant - Warrant Officer Gunner - Midshipman	- Commanding Officer - Lieutenant Commander - First Lieutenant - Lieutenant - Navigating Officer - Lieutenant - Engineer Lieutenant - Gunnery Officer - Sub-Lieutenant

HMAS *Shropshire* Heavy Cruiser 1945	
- Commodore Commanding HMA Squadron - Commodore Secretary - Commander - Flag Lieutenant Commander - Staff Officer Operations & Intelligence - Commander - Assistant to SO (O&I) - Lieutenant - Commanding Officer & Flag Captain - Captain - Commander - Commander - Squadron and ship's Navigating Officer - Commander - Engineering Commander - Supply Commander - 2 Chaplains - Squadron & ship's Gunnery Officer - Lieutenant Commander - Squadron & ship's Torpedo Officer - Lieutenant	- Squadron & ship's Radar Officer - Lieutenant - First Lieutenant - Lieutenant Commander - Engineering Lieutenant Commander - Surgeon Lieutenant Commander - Surgeon Lieutenant Commander (Dentist) - Radar Officers - 2 Lieutenants - Bridge watching-keeping, assistants to departmental officers or under training - 11 Lieutenants & 7 Sub-Lieutenants - 6 Engineer Lieutenants - 3 Supply Lieutenant - Surgeon Lieutenant - Schoolmaster - 13 Warrant Officers serving roles such as Chief Gunner, Commissioned Shipwright & Warrant Electrician. - 2 Midshipmen

Source: RAN Navy Lists

Comparative Naval Ranks

The Australian armed forces have a similar rank structure to their international counterparts and are detailed in the table below. To assist in reading *Australia's Argonauts*, the German and French naval ranks which vary from most navies are also outlined below.

Royal Australian Navy	Australian Army	Royal Australian Air Force	French Navy	German Navy
Admiral of the Fleet	Field Marshal	Marshal of the RAAF	Amiral	Grossadmiral
Admiral	General	Air Chief Marshal	Vice-Amiral d'escadre	Generaladmiral
Vice Admiral	Lieutenant General	Air Marshal	Vice Amiral	Admiral
Rear Admiral	Major General	Air Vice Marshal	Contre Amiral	Vizeadmiral
Commodore 1st Class	Brigadier	Air Commodore		Konteradmiral
Commodore 2nd Class				Kommodore
Captain	Colonel	Group Captain	Capitaine de vaisseau	Kapitän zur See
Commander	Lieutenant Colonel	Wing Commander	Capitaine de fregate	Fregattenkapitän
Lieutenant Commander	Major	Squadron Leader	Capitaine de corvette	Korvettenkapitän
Lieutenant	Captain	Flight Lieutenant	Lieutenant de vaisseau	Kapitänleutnant
Sub-Lieutenant	Lieutenant	Flying Officer	Enseigne de vaisseau de première classe	Oberleutnant zur See
Acting Sub-Lieutenant	Second Lieutenant	Pilot Officer	Enseigne deuxième classe	Leutnant zur See
Midshipman	Officer Cadet	Officer Cadet	Aspirante	Oberfähnrich zur See
Cadet Midshipman	Officer Cadet	Officer Cadet		Fähnrich zur See

Scales of Measurement

Australia's Argonauts uses in the text a mix of metric, imperial and nautical measures of length, distance and weight that were commonly used by the Pioneer Class and broader Australian society. The only variation is that terrestrial distances are expressed in kilometres. To assist the reader the following conversions are provided:

1 inch = 25.4 millimetres (mm) = 2.54 centimetres (cm)

1 nautical mile (nm) = 6,076 feet = 1.852 kilometres

1 knot = 1 nautical mile per hour

1 ton = 1016 kilograms

The Pioneer Class

Otto Edmund Albert
George William Thomas Armitage
Joseph Burnett
Norman Keith Calder
John Augustine Collins
Alfred Denis Conder
Ernest Semple 'Dick' Cunningham
James Claude Durie Esdaile
Harold Bruce Farncomb
Eric Augustus Feldt
Frank Edmond Getting
Lloyd Falconer Gilling
Paul Hugil Hirst
Elmer Benjamin Howells
Peyton James Kimlin
Frank Lockwood Larkins
John Valentine Stuart 'Jack' Lecky
Rupert Basil Michel Long
Hugh Alexander MacKenzie
Jack Bolton Newman
Edwin Scott Nurse
Winn Locker Reilly
Cyril Arthur Roy Sadleir
Henry 'Harry' Arthur Showers
Horace John Harold Thompson
Harry Bertram Vallentine
Adrian Joseph Beachleigh Watts
Llewellyn Leigh Watkins

Chapter 1
A Naval College for Australia

> *We do not regard the Navy as a toy – we regard it as a deadly instrument which may have to be used some day in the maintenance of our independence and liberty. We believe we can by building a local Navy render the best assistance to Empire interests everywhere.*
>
> Senator Hon. George Pearce

This is the story of a group of young Australian boys who were the first intake of cadet-midshipmen to enter the newly created Royal Australian Naval College. They were drawn from all states of the fledgling Commonwealth of Australia and were to leave an indelible mark on the Royal Australian Navy (RAN). From the outset they were known as the 'Pioneer' Class. History came to judge them as the most remarkable intake to ever enter the Royal Australian Naval College. Like the Argonauts of Greek mythology they faced both the dangers of the sea and violence from resolute foes. Through their courage and skill these boys became *Australia's Argonauts*. Like the Argonauts they suffered from the same human frailties that could lead to personal setbacks and tragedy. Before relating their tale, it is essential to describe the origins of their Navy and their naval college.

I

In 1901 the notion of an Australian Navy that was able to defend the continent, protect its trade and contribute to Imperial defence was one that was not universally supported. Indeed, amongst the main opponents of such a notion were the British Government and its Admiralty. Their preference was that Australia and other dominions continued to contribute funds to the maintenance of the Royal Navy (RN) for Imperial defence. In Australia, each colony had small navies for port and coastal defence. The drive for a more substantial Navy chiefly came from two dynamic men—a sailor and a politician. The sailor was Captain William Rooke Creswell; the politician was Alfred Deakin.

William Creswell joined the RN as a 14-year old cadet in 1865. After an eventful 13-year career including service against pirates off Zanzibar, Creswell resigned his commission to join his brother in a pastoral venture in the Northern Territory, then part of South Australia. In 1885 Creswell met an old shipmate Commander John Walcott, the then Naval Commandant of the South Australian Defence Force. That meeting led Creswell to become First Lieutenant of the small South Australian gunboat *Protector*. Over the next two decades Creswell served in ever more responsible positions in Colonial navies, including Commandant of the Queensland Naval Forces. From those vantage points he provided the intellectual arguments for an Australian Navy. Creswell wrote innumerable letters and articles on the subject, as well as giving speeches to various organisations and societies. Creswell later wrote:

> The undertaking I so lightly took in hand when I penned my articles for the *Adelaide Register*, thinking then only how I might convert unbelievers of the colony of South Australia, I subsequently discovered was Imperial in its dimensions. The small job I thought to accomplish in the twinkling of the eye turned out to be a mighty one, involving great protagonists and affecting the destiny of an Empire. My own small share in its accomplishments took me, as I have already observed, three and twenty years.[1]

In 1900 the limitations of Colonial navies were brought into stark relief by their participation in the efforts to quell the Boxer Rebellion in China. New South Wales and Victoria dispatched Naval Brigades each two hundred strong, while South Australia dispatched *Protector* under Creswell's command. For their part, British Admirals were lukewarm about the Australian naval involvement and would rather have employed RN warships than Colonial elements of unknown quality.

On Federation in 1901, the colonial navies merged into the Commonwealth Naval Force. The Fleet consisted of a motley collection of small warships and inshore craft with *Protector* and the old turret ship *Cerberus* the most imposing. The modest capabilities of the Commonwealth Naval Forces were such that the RN still maintained a squadron on the Australia Station.

For Creswell's naval aspirations to be realised they had to be promoted both in Australia and on the Imperial stage. A key gathering was the regular Imperial Conferences held in London. At the 1902 Imperial Conference the issue of naval defence was discussed. The outcome was a reaffirmation of the *status quo*. It perpetuated levies placed upon dominions or colonies for a definitive RN presence in their waters. Australia's annual contribution would not exceed £200,000.[2] There were however some more promising developments in Australia. In 1904 Creswell's stature was recognised when he became

The Father of the Royal Australian Navy Vice Admiral Sir William Creswell. He judged one of the key elements of an Australian Navy was a Naval College producing its own officers. (RAN)

the inaugural Naval Officer Commanding the Commonwealth Naval Forces. The following year the Australian Commonwealth Naval Board was constituted in Melbourne.

Creswell's vision of an Australian Navy received boosts during Alfred Deakin's three periods as Prime Minister (1903-04, 1905-1908 and 1909-1910). Deakin was one of the most remarkable politicians of his era. A barrister, accomplished journalist as well as an astute politician, he played a decisive role in the Colonies achieving Federation. Perhaps unique among his contemporaries, he had a well developed view of Australia's place in the British Imperial context. Not surprisingly, Deakin also shared Creswell's broad vision for a capable Australian Navy rather than one confined to coastal defence. In 1905 Deakin wrote:

> At present we are without evidence of our participation in the naval force towards which we contribute. Our £200,000 a year would seem in part repaid if we were enabled to take a direct and active part in the protection of our shores and shipping. But as we have no identification with the (RN) squadron ... there is so far nothing naval that be termed Australasian. No Commonwealth patriotism is aroused while we merely supply funds that disappear in the general expenditure of the Admiralty.[3]

Yet for Deakin it went even beyond that notion. An Australian Navy was potentially a major federal institution which could promote economic development and national identity. The Navy combined with the Army and universal military service, would serve to bind the states and their people into a nation. Deakin wrote in 1906 to the Governor General, as to the importance of a Navy:

> Nowhere are maritime communications more important than to Australia, seeing that our dependence upon sea carriage is certain to increase rather than diminish as population and production advance.[4]

Following a visit to Britain in 1906, Creswell and his staff developed a fleet plan of destroyer flotillas based at each of Australia's five major capitals. At the 1907 Imperial Conference in London, Deakin was the most dynamic of the dominion Prime Ministers and uncomfortably pushed the British Government under Sir Henry Campbell-Bannerman on a number of fronts. To meet future challenges Deakin advocated a more cohesive Imperial structure that included a permanent Imperial secretariat, greater dominion input into Imperial foreign policy and development of dominion navies. With his journalistic flair, Deakin appealed directly to British people through their newspapers. The support from the other dominions was, for differing reasons, lukewarm at best while the British Government was opposed to this radical partnering arrangement with the dominions. With regard to a Navy, Deakin pushed for support for the dominions to possess their own modest squadrons but with blue water capabilities. Lord Tweedmouth and his Admiralty advocated smaller coastal destroyers and submarines. The conference ended with the ball in the dominions' court. They had to submit their naval plans for consideration of assistance. This was at least some progress. Deakin recognised that Admiralty support was essential to building and supporting a new Navy with all its personnel, technical, industrial and operational complexities.

On his return to Australia Deakin's creativeness in policy development inspired him to look for opportunities to promote maritime awareness. In an action viewed with some unease in London, Deakin wrote to President Theodore Roosevelt inviting him to include Australian ports in the proposed world tour of a US battleship fleet. The subsequent 1908 visit of the 'Great White Fleet' was one of Australia's most memorable maritime events. The white-hulled battleships visited Sydney, Melbourne and Albany in succession. The public interest and enthusiasm in the visit has no parallel before or since. The Fleet's arrival in Sydney Harbour drew well over 500,000 spectators along the foreshore and in boats.[5] The social functions were seemingly unending and exhausting for the sailors. Parades were held, songs were composed to mark the occasion and the US Admirals were remembered with street names. Some of the future 1913 Entry boys, like Otto Albert then living on Sydney's harbourside, were caught up in the spectacle. The reception was equally

One of Australia's most remarkable maritime events: The 1908 visit of the US Great White Fleet. Here four of the Fleet's battleships enter Port Phillip Bay.
(State Library of Victoria)

overwhelming in Melbourne with one American midshipman writing, 'We have at last escaped from the hospitalities of Sydney only to be swallowed up in those of Melbourne'.[6] Deakin for his part gained much greater public and political support for an Australian Navy.

In November 1908 Deakin's government lost the election and was replaced by the Labor government under Andrew Fisher. While less eloquent on naval issues, Fisher nevertheless willingly and adeptly took the helm. In 1909 he ordered the first new warships for the Commonwealth Naval Force in the form of an initial batch of three destroyers. The following year the Admiralty provided, at Australia's request, Admiral Sir Reginald Henderson to conduct a study of Australia's naval defence requirements. The comprehensive report recommended a fleet of eight armoured cruisers, ten protected cruisers, 18 destroyers, 12 submarines and personnel strength of 15,000 men. This substantial fleet would be supported by 16 bases located around the coast. The Henderson Report was too grandiose for Australia's modest finances, industrial capacity and population. It also did not comprehend the remoteness of some of the locations designated for naval bases. These limitations were perhaps understandable. Henderson was an expert in dockyard administration. He had neither been a senior seagoing flag officer nor served on the Admiralty staff.[7] Despite its flaws the Henderson Report became the blueprint for much that was to follow. Within Navy Office it was referred to by some officers as 'the bible'.[8] More specifically for this story, the Henderson Report set in motion the construction of a naval college for the training of young officers to lead the new RAN.[9]

The final and unexpected twist in the birth of the Australian Fleet, came not from Australia but from a struggle of ideas within the Admiralty. On Trafalgar Day 1904, after breakfast with King Edward VII, Admiral 'Jacky' Fisher became the First Sea Lord at the Admiralty. He had a mandate to drastically prune and reform the RN. In the course of his sweeping reforms he introduced the revolutionary dreadnought battleships into service and scrapped innumerable small and slow warships that could neither 'fight nor run'. He faced considerable opposition to his views, particularly those around his 'battlecruiser' ships which had the firepower of a battleship but were lightly armoured and fast. Over time, Fisher developed the 'Fleet unit concept' in which battlecruisers, supported by a small number of cruisers, destroyers and submarines would be stationed around the globe. This concept was at complete odds to the accepted wisdom of concentrating a large battle fleet in British home waters. Fisher, mindful of both the financial strain being experienced by successive British governments and the growing dominion naval aspirations, successfully argued in the Committee of Imperial Defence that some Fleet units should in fact be dominion navies.[10]

On 2 June 1909 Deakin returned to power for the final time. Unable to attend the 1909 Imperial Conference, in his stead Deakin sent Colonel J.F. Foxton as Minister Without Portfolio. He was accompanied by Creswell to advise on naval matters. At the Conference Fisher tabled his innovative Fleet Unit Concept. To the Australian Delegation Admiral Fisher proposed an Australian Fleet of one battlecruiser, three cruisers, six destroyers and three submarines. This Fleet exceeded even Creswell's vision and he was concerned about the cost of the battlecruiser. The Admiralty countered by showing that the annual cost of the Fleet unit would be £600,000-£700,000 compared to £500,000 for the more modest Australian plans which had included providing some funds towards an RN dreadnought. In addition, the Admiralty would transfer to Australia its dockyard and shore establishment facilities and equipment in Australia. Foxton cabled Deakin with the proposal. Jackie Fisher's plan was warmly welcomed in Australia and Cabinet gave provisional approval on 27 September 1909. Events moved quickly. Following slight adjustments to the Fleet composition, the required naval loans were arranged and the order for the fleet flagship, the battlecruiser *Australia* was made in December 1909. She would be built at the John Brown shipyard on the Clyde. The Australian Fleet was born.

II

Creswell and Deakin recognised the need to train significant numbers of men as officers and sailors for the Australian Navy. How this was to be achieved coalesced into an increasingly coherent program with supporting public works in the years 1903 to 1912.

In respect to initial entry for sailors, the intent was to expand the modest colonial training facilities. The cruiser *Encounter* became a training ship which would allow sailors to achieve basic naval and specialist competencies. For the sailors that would man the Navy's new Fleet, they would receive further training on specific equipment in the UK. The manpower was to come from multiple sources, including sailors from the old Colonial navies, the merchant marine or fishing industry, fresh recruits and from the RN itself. The prospect of a new life in Australia with better pay and conditions provided sufficient attraction for a significant number of British officers and sailors to transfer to the fledgling navy. The RN also loaned officers and sailors to a significant degree. They were the only source of manpower for the RAN that had experience of operating a blue water navy and their contribution to the safe and efficient operation of the RAN Fleet cannot be underestimated.

In the longer term, a dedicated training establishment was needed. Admiral Henderson identified a site at Crib Point near the site for a future naval base on Westernport, Victoria. As events unfolded, the training establishment Flinders Naval Depot, or HMAS *Cerberus* it was later known, was commissioned in 1921, but the naval base was never constructed.

In 1906 Creswell, as part of his UK visit, had called on the distinguished physicist Professor James Ewing who was then the inaugural Director of Naval Education at Greenwich.[11] Ewing had in 1902, when Professor of Mechanics at Cambridge, advised Admiral Fisher on the new curriculum required for midshipmen of a modern navy.[12] Creswell's meeting was at the behest of the University of Melbourne which wanted the Commonwealth Government to fund a School of Naval Science on their campus. This would complement the new School of Military Science at the University of Sydney. The meeting would prove of immense value in shaping Creswell's ideas. He formed the view that while university training for some technical officers was essential, a naval college along the lines of the Royal Naval College at Osborne House on the Isle of Wight was the correct course of action.

In 1909 Creswell's able deputy, Captain Frederick Tickell wrote a memorandum which distilled the character and size of a naval college for the new navy. It was based on the RN model and would involve training 13-year old cadets for four years. Because of the cadet system in place in some Australian private schools the title 'cadet-midshipman' would be used in the RAN to avoid confusion. In 1913 Charles Bean wrote of RAN College training system:

> It will be a matter of fascinating interest to watch it develop, like watching an experiment from Plato's *Republic*. It is an attempt to obtain the best ability from the people, wherever it lies. The State realises that, for the sake of efficiency, it must catch young those who are to fill its higher posts ... Is there any reason why that experiment, if it succeeds, should end with the Army and the Navy?[13]

While Creswell and Tickell developed their plans for a Naval College, efforts were well underway to create a sister military college for the Army. On 30 May 1910 Colonel William Bridges who had been involved in the School of Military Science initiative was promoted to Brigadier General and appointed as Commandant to the new military college then under construction. The government had decreed that it was to be located on federal land where the new capital of Canberra would be built. There would be distinct differences in the Army and Navy college models. The new military college would be heavily influenced by the US Military College at West Point as well as the Canadian Royal Military College at Kingston at which Bridges had been a cadet. In contrast to their much younger naval counterparts the Army cadets would be from 17 years old on entry and would initially receive three years training before graduation. This would be extended to four years once the shortfall of officers was addressed.[14]

A question that both Bridges and Creswell had to grapple with was the size of their cadet population. Bridges concluded the Military College would eventually have a population of 150 cadets. For the Navy the planned Fleet size became the guide and it was estimated that about 30 cadet-midshipmen would be needed each year. Based on the eventual 120 cadet-midshipmen at the naval college, Tickell calculated the required facilities as well as naval and academic staff. The naval staff would comprise a Captain, three Lieutenants, a gunner, a boatswain, a carpenter and an artificer engineer. The academic staff would be five masters and five assistants.

While the case for the naval college was agreed, the more vexing question was its location. On 12 October 1909 the entrepreneurial Lord Mayor of Sydney, Sir Allen Taylor offered £40,000 from the Dreadnought Fund[15] if the naval college was situated in Sydney. Prime Minister Fisher accepted the offer and over coming months seven sites were inspected.[16] The Commander of the RN Australia Squadron, Vice Admiral Sir Richard Poore was then asked for his view and he recommended the Middle Head site. Despite Creswell's misgivings about a naval college close to and possibly constrained by a growing city, the Minister for Defence, Mr Joseph Cook agreed on 8 March 1910 to the Middle Head location. In April Andrew Fisher returned to power as Prime Minister and asked Admiral Henderson to examine the location of the naval college as part of his naval review. An increasingly restive Lord Mayor in May 1910 pressed for action on the matter. The issue had still some play in it.

The officer the RN had loaned to be the inaugural Captain of the naval college had recently arrived in Australia. He was Captain Bertram Chambers. An astute Londoner and navigation specialist, Chambers had himself joined the navy as a 13-year-old cadet. He had extensive sea service, most recently as Flag Captain to the Admiral commanding the Home Fleet. While commanding the flagship, the battleship HMS *Bulwark,* the ship was grounded. Fortunately, for Chambers the damage was minor and he was acquitted at a court martial.[17]

On his arrival in Australia Chambers was also asked his view on the location for the proposed naval college. His selections were in order, Barranjoey, Jervis Bay and then the Sutherland Shire area. A portion of Jervis Bay had been earmarked to become federal territory for the future port to the inland national capital of Canberra.[18]. After much consideration about sandflies, mosquitoes, playing fields and the heat of Sydney, Burraneer Point in Port Hacking on Sydney's southern outskirts became the new site for the College. Chambers wrote enthusiastically:

> ...in accepting Burraneer Point, the Commonwealth will have a site of which any nation might be proud and one not excelled by any existing naval college.[19]

A now satisfied Lord Mayor sent the Prime Minister a cheque for £20,000 with the balance to be sent before the end of the year. This however was not the end of the matter. In Federal Parliament, then in its temporary home in Melbourne, there was growing disquiet about the Sydney location. On 7 November as part of the debate over the Supply Bill, the Member for Eden Monaro Austin Chapman[20] argued that the naval college should be on federal land. He was an ardent federalist and successful advocate for the location of the national capital in his parliamentary seat. Dr. Earle Page went further and specifically argued for Jervis Bay. By happenstance, listening to this debate in the public gallery was a woman also with strong federalist views. She was Mrs Esther Collins and with her was her young son John. He would become a member of the Pioneer Class.[21]

Following the parliamentary debate on 16 November 1911 the Government announced that Jervis Bay would be the site for the naval college. To allow time for construction, a temporary site would be provided. This set in train another round of site selection, but mercifully more expeditious. Osborne House, Geelong with ready access to both rail and Port Phillip Bay was chosen. Its identical name with the Royal Naval College of Osborne House was both a coincidence and a good omen.

III

Having settled on the interim naval college, Captain Chambers had to gather around him a naval and academic staff, oversee the fit-out of Osborne House and recruit the first intake. In addition to all this, he was given command of the cruiser *Encounter*. The ship was ideally placed to provide him with much of the administrative support he needed and, when the time came, the mobile venue to interview young applicants in the different states.

Captain Chambers assembled a group of capable RN officers and sailors who brought considerable training experience and a desire for this, the first naval college beyond the shores of England, to be a success. Lieutenant Duncan Grant RN (retired) joined as the Executive Officer. Grant had been on the staff of both Osborne and Dartmouth colleges and was a physical training instructor by specialisation. Although quite deaf, this tall, lean and energetic officer was an outstanding youth leader and became universally admired. Grant was destined to have the most profound influence on the Pioneer Class and the College itself. The other two Executive or seaman officers were the First Lieutenant Charles Elwell and Lieutenant Cuthbert Pope. Both were well liked and with promising career prospects. Elwell, whilst in the RN, was actually Australian and his father was the Chief Electrical Engineer of New South Railways.[22] These officers were supported by the redoubtable Mr Thomas Dix, the Gunner, who would be responsible for parade drill. Dix was the epitome of an old salt who mixed a deep knowledge of the sea and adherence to naval discipline with a paternal regard for his young charges. One cadet-midshipman would later remark Mr Dix 'was a fine old gentleman and would have liked to have been more indulgent to us, but of course, the bonds of discipline prevented that.'[23]

A vitally important contribution to the naval college was made by the two engineering officers Engineer Lieutenant Commander William Monk and Engineer Lieutenant Ronald Boddie.[24] Their responsibilities ranged from assisting the Captain with establishing and maintaining Osborne House and then the new Jervis Bay site, but also providing some instruction in marine engineering. William Monk had been asked by Chambers to come from Osborne House and transfer to the young Navy. He brought with him details of the engineering equipment needed for the new College. Importantly Boddie, who would go on to the rank of Rear Admiral, was an insightful diarist. Assisting the two officers were three first-rate artificer engineers, Mr Marsden, Mr Creal and Chief Petty Officer Harefield. The Chief, along with Captain Chambers was one of the very few officers or sailors with a medal ribbon on their chests. Harefield had served in the steam and sail hybrid frigate HMS *Shah* when on 29 May 1877 she had fired the first torpedo in anger in an engagement against the Peruvian rebel-controlled armoured turret ship *Huáscar*. The torpedo missed, hampered by being slower than the *Huáscar*.

The naval staff were joined by a talented academic staff. In November 1911 notices appeared in the major Australian newspapers announcing the Navy was seeking a Director of Studies. Two of the three shortlisted applicants were Mr Frederick Brown, the first Principal of Perth Modern School and Mr Frederick Wheatley who had resigned the previous year

The Pioneer Officers & Senior Sailors. The early success of the Royal Australian Naval College can be traced the calibre of its officers. Captain Bertram Chambers is seated in the front and centre flanked on his right by Director of Studies Frederick Brown and on his left Lieutenant Commander Duncan Grant and the Reverend William Hall. Warrant Officer Thomas Dix is at the back right. (RAN)

as Headmaster of Rockhampton Grammar School. There were rumours the resignation followed Mrs Wheatley striking one of the academic staff.[25] Frederick Brown was a gifted mathematician with First Class Honours from London University and had been at Perth Modern for just a year. Wheatley had met Creswell and Henderson in 1910 when they visited Rockhampton. Over dinner Wheatley had expounded his views on naval education and Creswell reportedly said, 'You are the sort of man we should have as Headmaster. I will let you know when things develop'.[26] Wheatley would later maintain that he was told following the selection interview that he was the preferred candidate but that the Minister for Defence, Senator George Pearce had not accepted the recommendation and had decided upon fellow West Australian Frederick Brown.[27] The disappointed Wheatley arranged to undertake study at Lincoln College,

Oxford into the ionization of gases. Two days before his sailing from Port Adelaide, Wheatley received a telegram from Creswell to come to Navy Office. After taking the overnight train to Melbourne Wheatley was told that 'things were very unsatisfactory at Navy Office with the way Brown was acting'.[28] Brown at this time was undertaking various preparations which included finalisation of the syllabus and the entrance examination. After his meeting with Creswell, Wheatley saw Chambers onboard *Encounter* where according to Wheatley he was asked to take a position on the staff under Brown after his study in Oxford. This he agreed to do. On his return voyage from England he received a telegram in Colombo offering him the position of Senior Naval Instructor in physics and mathematics.[29] The seeds were sown for future difficulties.

Brown and Wheatley were joined by Chaplain and Naval Instructor the Reverend William Hall, RN. Educated at Durham School, Hall had been Master of the Navy Class at King's College Cambridge and was an expert at marine navigation. He invented the nautical slide rule, versions of which are still in use at sea.[30] The remainder of the academic staff, who were all Australians, were Senior Naval Instructors Stanley Smith, Charles Franklin and Leonard Morrison; and Naval Instructors Morton Moyes and Frank Eldridge. Moyes cut an impressive figure, a keen athlete, he had been with Sir Douglas Mawson in the Antarctic in 1911-12 and had been awarded the Polar Medal. Eldridge was destined to become Senior Master of the College and arguably its most influential academic. His outstanding *A History of the Royal Australian Naval College* was published in 1949. The staff were rounded out by Grant's bulldog, Bill.

IV

On 19 August 1912 a small article appeared in the *Sydney Morning Herald* headed 'NAVAL COLLEGE - THE FIRST ENTRIES'. It was the long awaited announcement that the Commonwealth Naval Secretary was seeking suitable boys whose 13th birthday fell that year to apply to join the first entry of the yet to be commissioned Royal Australian Naval

College. Similar announcements appeared in newspapers across the young nation. From September, an interviewing committee chaired by Captain Chambers, sat onboard *Encounter* as she visited all the state capitals except Hobart and Perth. Chambers was assisted by the District Naval Officer and the Director of Education in each state. In Perth and Hobart the District Naval Officer chaired the committee.

The successful boys would serve four years at the naval college before going to sea to complete their training. The newspaper article concluded with the statement that after entering the naval college, all expenses for the boys would be met by the Government. An exemplar exam was available on application and advertisements soon appeared in newspapers by enterprising tutors to coach for the exam.[31] In all, 138 applicants sat the educational examination.

The Government funding of tuition and uniform fees was a departure from the British practice where parents had to outlay up to £1,000 before their sons would be able to support themselves. Admiral Fisher had wanted to reform this aspect of officer recruitment because of the fear of 'drawing

The cruiser HMAS Encounter *sailed to four state capitals to enable boys to be interviewed by Captain Bertram Chambers for entry to the Royal Australian Naval College.* (State Library of Victoria)

our Nelsons from much too narrow a class'[32] This reform was seen as too radical for the RN. In contrast the Australian officers would have to serve until 30 years of age otherwise they would have to pay for part of their initial training.

In Melbourne James Watts read the article with interest. In late 1912 his son Adrian, rebelled against the Jesuit's religious education at Xavier College and of his own accord walked out in protest. Eddy Nurse was asked by his father, who had read *The Age* newspaper, would he like to join the Navy? Young Eddy:

> immediately thought of the white sailing boats I'd seen on the Bay while playing in the sand on the beach. I answered 'Yes!'[33]

That month variations of this conversation took place in homes ranging from a Sydney waterside mansion to a modest outback farm house. For the nation, the calling for the first intake of the Australia's naval college was an important step in forging its own Navy. Yet for twenty eight 13-year-old boys their decision would forever change their lives. Their careers in turn would decisively shape the course of the Royal Australian Navy.

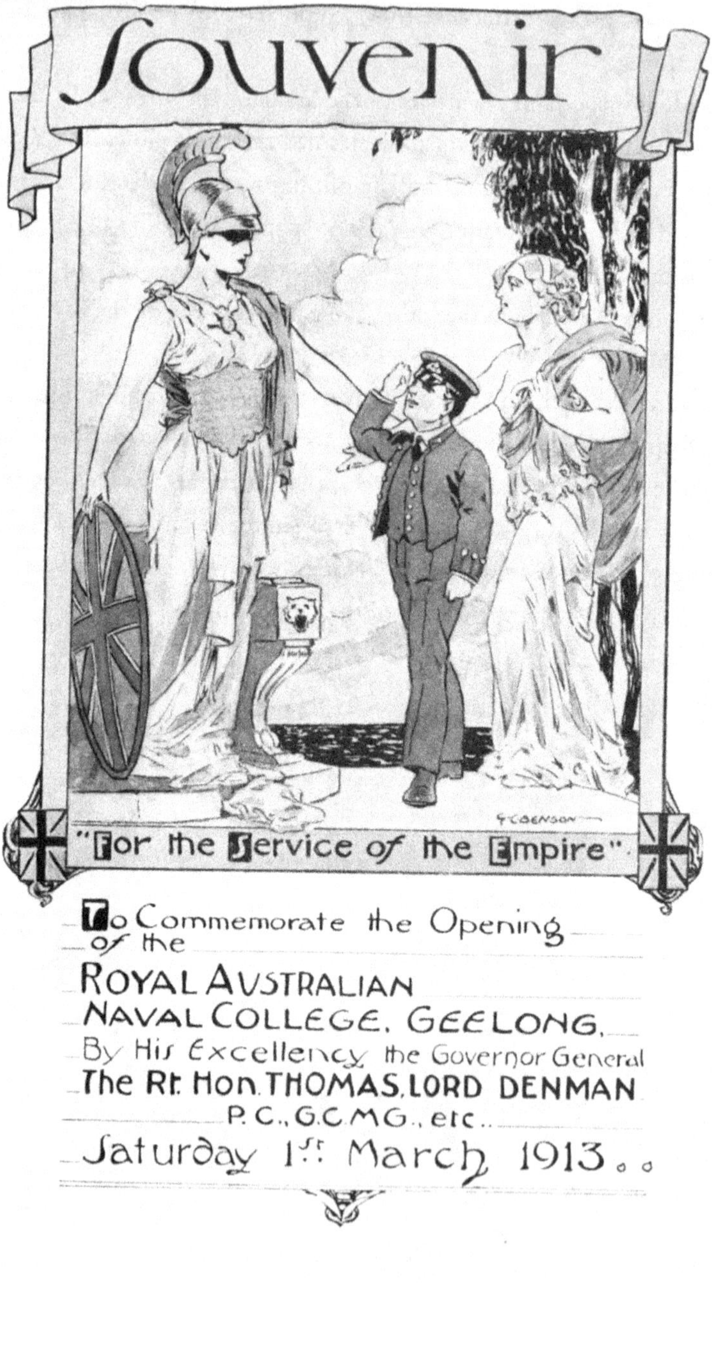
Souvenir
"For the Service of the Empire".
To Commemorate the Opening of the
ROYAL AUSTRALIAN
NAVAL COLLEGE, GEELONG,
By His Excellency the Governor General
The Rt. Hon. THOMAS, LORD DENMAN
P.C., G.C.M.G., etc.
Saturday 1st March 1913

Chapter 2
Geelong

Into the years that bring, to each one of us,
Measure for measure in pleasure and pain,
Step we unfaltering, sure there is none of us
Ever would barter his glory for gain.

Into the Years – A song for the RANC (1913)[1]

I

The interview process and eventual selection of the boys for the Royal Australian Naval College reflected its unique Australian character. Captain Chambers was at pains to ensure that social position had no influence on selection. Boys were each given a number and the interviewers or examination markers did not see the candidate's name. In addition, no questions were asked of their class background. Chambers declared that he would 'guarantee that after six months at the College it would be impossible to tell that the lad had lacked any social advantage'.[2] After completing the interviews Chambers wrote:

> Completed the interviews—a fine lot of boys. Some of those from the back blocks were a bit uncouth. For sorting out their intelligence we tried a variety of expedients. First we tried to get the boys entirely at ease. Then we gave them a bout at the jewel game with a dozen assorted

objects on the table, the boy being given so long to examine them was told to write a list. During the whole time I was doing the work I only found one boy who gave the whole dozen correctly. We had many who gave ten, but the average was seven or eight. Another test was to give the boy two minutes to look out of the port(hole) and take stock of all that he could see, then turning his back we would examine him— What colour was the steamer opposite? How many funnels? Had she any lighters alongside? etc. We would give the boy a message, the more cryptic the better, and then tell him to find the First Lieutenant who was somewhere about the ship. The lieutenant wrote down the message as he received it and gave the boys the reply to be brought back to us. To discover the First Lieutenant was itself a test. Still another test was to give the boy a pencil and a newspaper. Starting at the top of a column he was to put a dot above every a, capital or otherwise. At the end of two minutes we counted up how many he had dotted and how many errors and omissions he had made. This was an excellent test. Indeed, much character could be displayed. We also gave them an examination in what may be called 'General Knowledge'.[3]

On completion of the interviews around the country, the Naval Board met in Melbourne on 4 December 1912 to select the inaugural College entry. The Board was chaired by the Defence and Navy Minister, Senator George Pearce, who had himself made an early start in life. One of eleven children, Pearce left school as an 11-year old to help sustain the family. The Senator, a committed trade unionist, was to prove one of the nation's most accomplished and industrious Ministers for Defence. Also in attendance were Rear Admiral Creswell, Captain Constantine Hughes-Onslow, Captain Chambers and Paymaster-in-Chief Eldon Manisty.

Senator Pearce invited to the meeting a journalist from *The Argus* to report to the Australian public on the selection process. Pearce explained that a quota established for each state that roughly equated to its population. This resulted in New South Wales having nine places but with only seven boys suitably qualified; Victoria had seven places with sixteen qualified; Queensland had three places with one boy qualified; South Australia had two places but also with only one boy qualified; Western Australia had two places with three qualified, while Tasmania had one place with two qualified. Because the qualified candidates exceeded the vacancies, Pearce determined a ballot with candidate numbers would be held. Then for the first time the Naval Board would see candidate names when they were correlated to the numbers. *The Argus* reporter became an active participant in the proceedings by being asked to draw the numbers from the hat.

Captain Chambers outlined the examination and interview process and told the reporter that in selecting the boys:

> the board had borne in mind that something more than mere educational attainments and brains was required in a naval officer, who had to be a leader of men and capable of withstanding a sailor's arduous life.[4]

The reporter headlined his article in the next day's edition of *The Argus* with – 'ROYAL AUSTRALIAN NAVAL COLLEGE – FIRST SCHOLARS CHOSEN – INTERESTING BALLOT'.[5]

The selected boys for whom no ballot was required were the New South Welshmen Harold Farncomb, Ernest Cunningham, Joseph Burnett, Frank Getting, Lloyd Gilling, Hugh MacKenzie and Harry Vallentine; the Queenslander Eric Feldt, the South Australian George Armitage and the Tasmanian Paul Hirst.

For Victoria where qualified applicants exceeded the state allocation, the ballot was employed. The numbers pulled from the hat corresponded to Peyton Kimlin, Jack Lecky, Jack Newman, Eddy Nurse, Norman Calder, Adrian Watts and Harry Showers. The two Western Australians pulled from the hat were James Esdaile and Cyril Sadlier. Because some of the states did not meet the quota, there were then three more names pulled out the hat they were Victorians Ben Howells, Winn Reilly and Frank Larkins. Captain Chambers indicated the highest score for a candidate in the Commonwealth was that of James Esdaile, whilst Eddy Nurse was the highest scoring Victorian.

Finally, Senator Pearce announced that it was possible the numbers of cadets might need to be increased to meet Fleet manning requirements. If that was the case, then they would be chosen from the highest on the educational list. This proved necessary and Otto Albert (NSW), John Collins (Victoria), Alfred Conder (Tasmania), Rupert Long (Victoria), Horace Thompson (NSW) and Leigh Watkins (Victoria) were added to the inaugural class.[6] What appears to have been missed was a fully qualified Western Australian boy still in the hat who should arguably been in this supplementary group.

The only common denominator for the selected boys was that they were born in 1899. Eric Feldt born on 3 January was the oldest whilst Joe Burnett born on 21 December was the youngest. By coincidence the births of two boys Cyril Sadleir and Adrian Watts born on consecutive days appeared in the same birth announcement column of the *Western Mail* on 7 July 1899 whilst Peyton Kimlin and Jack Lecky shared birthdays.[7]

Chambers' egalitarian approach to selection had produced an inaugural class with only a quarter receiving private school education.[8] The profession of the fathers varied greatly in background. Among the mothers only those who were sole parents appeared to work outside the home. Otto Albert was the eldest son of Frank Albert who owned the well known and prosperous Sydney music and publishing business, J Albert and Son. Frank was a keen sailor who owned the majestic schooner *Boomerang* and he and his wife Minnie were leading figures in Sydney society. Eric Feldt's father was a Swedish born pioneering sugar cane producer from Ingham in Queensland. The families of Paul Hirst and Winn Reilly were also on the land.

The majority of the class members however, came from middle class backgrounds. Harold Farncomb's father was an accountant, Adrian Watts' an architect, Jack Newman's a doctor while Harry Showers' was a hotel keeper. Five boys, George Armitage, Dick Cunningham, Ben Howells, Peyton Kimlin and Rupert Long, were sons of teachers. Cyril Sadleir's father was soon to become Agent-General for Western Australia in London, Alfred Conder's father was Tasmania's State Mining Engineer while Frank Getting's Parisian father was the Superintendent of the Quarantine Station on Sydney Harbour after a period as a policeman. Hugh MacKenzie's father was also a policeman while Lloyd Gilling's father was a joiner. Two boys, Joe Burnett and John Collins were fatherless and had been brought up by hard-pressed mothers. John Collins was one of the few boys with a maritime connection with his late Irish father having been at one time a ship's doctor.

Jack Lecky was the son of marine engineer William Lecky, who had worked on the Western Australian gold fields and been the Resident Manager of the Penang Wharves Department in Malaya. While his older brother and sister had remained in Western Australia, Jack spent his early childhood in Penang. He was later sent to Scotch College in Melbourne to complete his education. Jack's life was altered to by the sudden death of his father in 1910 from appendicitis. Jack returned to Penang and to a step mother only eight years his elder, who also had a young son from her marriage with William to support. They soon returned to her native Victoria and Jack's acceptance into the Navy was a godsend.[9]

The 1913 Entry to the Royal Australian Naval College.
Known as the Pioneer Class. (RAN)
Back Row L to R: *Jack Newman, Eric Feldt, Paul Hirst, Adrian Watts, Ben Howells, Frank Getting, Leigh Watkins, Otto Albert, Frank Larkins, Eddy Nurse.*
Middle Row L to R: *Harry Vallentine, Winn Reilly, Harold Farncomb, James Esdaile, John Collins, Hugh Mackenzie, Peyton Kimlin, Norman Calder, Rupert Long.*
Front Row L to R: *Cyril Sadleir, George Armitage, Joe Burnett, Lloyd Gilling, Dick Cunningham, Harry Showers, Horace Thompson, Jack Lecky, Alfred Conder.*

II

On 1 February 1913 all the boys, with the exception of Eric Feldt, arrived at Osborne House. The boys and a few parents walked the grounds of the Naval College and took in the sweeping views of the bay. Before long each boy was ushered into an office where he was asked to swear an oath of allegiance to the King. That evening the tired but excited boys turned into their dormitory beds. John Collins recalled more than fifty years later that memorable first night:

> ...we heard the bugle sound the 'Still' and watched, for the first time, the procedure for nine o'clock rounds. Through the doorway came the drummer with his shining bugle, the Master-at-Arms carrying the candle lantern, the First Lieutenant in his mess undress with the Gunner bringing up the rear. The solemn procession marched briskly round and departed. Nobody wished us goodnight, which I thought rather mean, and the bugle sounded 'Lights out'.
> Our attention had earlier been drawn to a notice in the dormitory, 'No talking after lights out', but it was not long before the whispering started. The first day in the Navy had been an exciting one for a group of thirteen-year-old youngsters and there was a lot to talk about. Soon the volume grew until we were all chattering away and even joking about the notice. We were soon to learn an order in the Navy is to be obeyed.
> Fully dressed again, and sore from the whacks of the walking stick the First Lieutenant was wielding, we started to learn our lesson. Five minutes at the double round the lawn, five minutes marching, double again and march again, all the while being encouraged with the walking stick. After two hours even the most recalcitrant of us had long since given up wondering if the chatter had been worthwhile. The next night we tried it again; but at midnight, sore and weary, we admitted to ourselves that the Navy had won. Thereafter 'Lights out' meant silence'.[10]

On that second day the freshly-minted cadet-midshipmen were provided, to much excitement, with their naval uniforms. Their working uniform or rig was a pair of boots, gaiters, blue denim trousers and a dark blue flannel shirt and naval officers cap.

Eric Feldt arrived at Osborne House a couple of days late. In an eventful solo journey for a 13-year old, a cyclone and associated flooding had delayed his train and steamer from Ingham. His parents had been concerned that Eric was not cut out to be a sailor and thought that the law was a more likely profession for him on account of his great memory. His father told him, 'If after a year you find you don't like it and cannot fit in, I will pay the expenses of the year's education'.[11]

Eddy Nurse recalls, 'Slowly we came to know one another and learn our names and get nicknames. I think I got the name 'Mum'; inside a few days'.[12] Some of the other nicknames were 'Garge' Armitage, 'Joey' Burnett, 'Tusky' Calder, 'Chol' Conder, 'Bagger' Cunningham, 'Essy' Esdaile, 'Hal' Farncomb, 'Feltie' Feldt, 'Hungry' Getting, 'Hirsty' Hirst, 'Birdie' Howells, 'Flick' Larkins, 'Macka' MacKenzie, 'Nunky' Newman, 'Pate' Kimlin, 'Paddy' Reilly, 'Sadie' Sadleir, 'Thomo' Thompson and 'Flertie' Watkins. Harry Showers received the nickname 'Circus' because of his acrobatic skills while Rupert Long received his lifetime moniker of 'Cocky' because his adolescent voice would break into a 'squawk' at the most inconvenient of times.[13]

The height, weight and chest size of the boys were a source of fascination to both boys and staff. Their inevitable increases were the subject of articles in successive College magazines. The average age of the intake was 13 years 8.6 months with a weight of 98½ lb (45 kg). Their average expanded chest was 31 inches (78 cm) with a height of just under 5ft (152 cm). It led Otto Albert to write, 'Some cadets are born great: some have weightiness thrust upon them.'[14] The two tallest of the class at 5ft 6½ inches (167 cm) were Frank Larkins and Jack Newman. The Larkins family folklore has it that it was on this basis that Frank was made Cadet Captain.[15]

The focus of the first fortnight was preparing for the official opening of the Naval College by His Excellency the Governor-General, Lord Denman. The Prime Minister Andrew Fisher and

The Official Party arriving at Geelong onboard HMAS Warrego.
(Grant Collection)

Rear Admiral Creswell would also attend. On Saturday 1 March 1913, the official party took passage to Geelong from Melbourne in the torpedo boat destroyer HMAS *Warrego* accompanied by her sister ships *Yarra* and *Parramatta*. On arrival Captain Chambers led the party through a 200-strong Naval Reserve guard of honour from the jetty to Osborne House. They joined 200 guests who had journeyed in a special train from Melbourne as well as the Geelong public who were filled with civic pride. The Governor-General reviewed the 28 cadet-midshipmen who were paraded in front of the verandah. They were smartly dressed in traditional navy double-breasted 'monkey' jackets with three brass buttons on each sleeve to denote their rank and white cord lanyards around their neck which had a boatswains call (whistle) at the end. The last minute efforts of the staff to field all cadets in a complete uniform were in the end successful. In a speech introducing Lord Denman, the Prime Minister said 'Unlike other Naval Colleges, its doors were open to all. Intelligence and general fitness were the only qualities necessary. Happily all States were represented in it'.[16] The College would be the 'main route to the command of His Majesty's Australian Fleet'.[17]

Finally, Fisher paid tribute to 'the energy and ability of Senator Pearce to carry out the initial work of the foundation of the Australian Navy and Army'.[18]

For his part the Governor General said, 'the ceremony today makes it clear that the naval policy of this country was adopted in no reckless or ill-considered spirit – not as the result of an ephemeral phase of warlike enthusiasm – but it has been decided upon with care, thought and mature consideration'.[19] Lord Denman directed most of his remarks however to the young cadet-midshipmen:

> You cannot all be Admirals. You can all do your best to become efficient officers of the Royal Australian Navy. You are a picked lot of lads from every State of the Commonwealth and some day I hope you will be joined by comrades from New Zealand. You have advantage, which, so far as I know, no other country offers, in receiving this splendid education at the cost of the State. In this country people have been saying Australians will not make seaman, the same people will no doubt say that Australians will not make naval officers. You have got to prove that they are wrong, and in order to do that you have to attain to the standard of efficiency we are accustomed to associate with the British Navy, and as the British Navy is the greatest and most powerful the world has ever seen, to attain to its level of efficiency is no easy task ... Knowing as I do, what young Australians can perform in other walks of life, I have no doubt that you will succeed in the fine profession you have chosen'.[20]

The Governor-General was then presented with a tiny ship's bell. It was a replica made in the new College workshop of the original in the Victorian training ship *Nelson*. The speeches taken together were over-long and four cadet-midshipmen had to fall out of the parade while afterwards Ben Howells complained of a bad headache. On the completion of the formalities the official party adjourned to the Commandant's house for afternoon tea. For the young cadet-midshipmen it had been an exciting but exhausting experience. Despite this the day remained for them a treasured memory and their perspective was captured in the poem *Opening Day*.

Opening Day

You must wake and call me early,
Call me early, Bugler dear;
You must blow your little bugle,
Blow it loud and long and clear.

For the opening of a College
Doesn't happen every day;
And the chance of looking pretty
Doesn't often come our way.

The Gov'nor-General will be present,
And his Lady and his Aides;
And Noble Lords and Naval Members,
Gentle maidens, gushing maids.

There'll be the Captain and his Officers,
The Cadets all pert and smart,
The Stewards and Ship's Company,-
Just the sight to cheer your heart.

There'll be lots of beauteous ladies,
And flappers neat and trim,
And they'll turn their eyes upon me
And sweetly gurgle 'Yes that's him!'

For I'm sure that every optic
In that giddy, gaudy throng.
Will be turned on ME for certain,
As they see me march along.

Oh, I'm feeling most excited -
Almost up to fever heat;
Why, I don't know if I'm standing
On my head or on my feet.

When I have to be presented,
What shall I say or do or think?
Shall I murmur 'How d'ye do-dy,'
Or just 'Come and have a drink.'

Oh, I'm longing for tomorrow
With its pageant bright and gay,
so be sure and call me early
On the festal Opening Day

— 'Nemo'

The Official Party at the opening of the Royal Australian Naval College at Geelong. (RAN)
Front Row L to R: *Mrs Chambers, Lord & Lady Denman, Prime Minister Fisher and Mrs Pearce.*
Second R to L to R: *Lieutenant Commander Grant, Rev. Hall, Rear Admiral Creswell, Captain Chambers, Senator Pearce, Mrs Fisher & Mr Brown.*

III

The curriculum, daily routine and accommodation arrangements for the Naval College were modelled closely on the Royal Navy. In later years Eric Feldt reflected that:

> The scheme of training was exactly the same as that used at Osborne in the Isle of Wight, where the British cadets were trained. The object was to produce a naval officer who was interchangeable and, in fact, so far as possible, indistinguishable from the RN officer. That was all right. That was the only way they knew how to produce a naval officer when it comes to that. But it was rather a shock to us in its social implications. For instance, the difference between an officer and someone on the lower deck was something that was, well, very strange to me anyway. Where I'd been used to the farm where every employee was called by his Christian name. I once called a steward, when I first got there, 'Jimmy', which was his name. And you'd have thought I'd had called the King a dirty name by the lightning that flashed around my poor head as a result of it.[21]

The high degree to which the Osborne House model was adopted can be seen in the remarkable photographs taken by Duncan Grant and an examination of his surviving Division Officer logs from his tenure at Osborne House in 1905-06. Even the Naval College crest and the all-white rugby jersey were the same between the British and Australian colleges.[22] In the dormitories the spartan arrangements saw a locker at the foot of each bed for the cadet-midshipmen's uniform, books and personnel belongings. Ben Howells wrote to his parents:

> I have a bonza big chest, which doesn't look very nice from the outside, but as soon as you open it there is a great change. It is painted a bonza colour inside with a mirror fastened in the middle of the lid. Then there are two bonza little candle holders just like those you see on a piano, and down in one corner there is a place to keep your telescope. All these things are on the lid. Then before you can get to the inside of the box you have to pull up three tills. Each of these is divided into two, one half having a lid on it. Each of the lids has a bonza little catch on it. Underneath these are three compartments in which you stow your uniforms, etc. We have singlets, underpants, flannel trousers, serge trousers, shirts, pyjamas and everything you need provided.[23]

'I have a bonza big chest'. The dormitory at Geelong with the midshipmen's chests at the foot of each bed. (Grant collection)

At the same time however, the cadet-midshipmen were officers and there was one steward for each seven boys. The stewards prepare their uniforms and wait on them at meals. Familiarity with the stewards was frowned upon.

The academic subjects taught were extensive and demanding—English, French, German, mathematics, physics, chemistry, seamanship and gunnery (in the cruiser *Encounter*), navigation, history, geography, bible study and engineering. The latter was taught in a practice workshop. A visiting reporter from the *Sydney Morning Herald* wrote:

> You will see the cadets working in their own foundry and their own smithy, their own fitting shop and machine shop. They will cast a main bearing for a marine engine, or make a piston-ring—but their time is not wasted by manufacturing sets of engines for use. The one object is to make the work instructive. The college possesses a most elaborate perfect set of models—quite as elaborate as any at Osborne and Dartmouth, if not more so. There is a model of the battle-cruiser *Australia*'s interior, a model of her bows and cable flat, with ample chain for practising in miniature the process of letting go anchor, mooring, shackling, or shortening cable shackle by shackle. There are models of the old type of marine boiler, an exquisite model of HMAS *Australia*'s boilers, models of other water-tube boilers from the earliest to the most

modern, a wooden model of a turbine with the blades fitted—models of masts, signals, boats, casks, knots, model gear of all sorts—probably thousands of pounds' worth of models.[24]

The Engineering Workshop at Geelong.
L to R: *Harry Vallentine, Cyril Sadleir, Norman Calder, Alfred Conder & Ben Howells.* (Grant Collection)

The instruction however was a challenge in the very small classrooms at Osborne House. Some lessons had to be taught four times due to the classroom size. Lieutenant Boddie later wrote, 'I found I gave the second lecture best, at the third I became a little tired, and the fourth was monotonous'.[25] To accommodate these arrangements the class could be divided into four divisions—Starboard I, Starboard II, Port I and Port II. The divisions were filled in order of academic standing and this order would change following the annual examinations.

Sport figured greatly in the life of the cadets. They played rugby, soccer, Australian Rules, boxing, hockey and cricket against the staff, local teams as well as visiting schools and ships. Because of the small numbers of cadet-midshipmen, soccer was the predominant winter game until successive entries joined and rugby came to dominate sport. In addition, athletics and the 'Swedish' system of physical training were adopted from the Osborne House model. A Naval College brochure extolled the Swedish system which:

> ...is conducted not with the idea of 'putting on muscle' but the building up of a healthy and vigorous constitution. Particular attention is paid to the development of the chest, and thus of the heart and lungs, as health and therefore physical efficiency are largely dependent on the healthy action of these organs'.[26]

Naval discipline was ever-present, even on the sporting field, and on one occasion one of the boys refused to swap football jerseys with another ordered by the Sports Officer. The boy 'was marched off the playing field by a file of the guard, two six-foot sailors in gaiters and side arms.' John Collins wrote:

> I wondered aloud whether he would be hanged that night or in the morning. 'They always hang them at dawn' whispered the cadet next to me. Rather to our surprise he was not hanged. If I recall correctly he was awarded the most serious punishment other than dismissal, namely, a caning strapped over a box horse before the assembled cadets and ship's company. Grave offences were usually dealt with in this manner which had much to recommend it, so long as you were not the victim. Even for him it was soon over, and better in many ways than a long drawn-out period of extra drills.'[27]

A College officer recalled 'I have never met a man who remembered a cadet to whimper. Gasps and grunts were proper: but no blubbering'.[28]

The typical summer day for the cadets began with Reveille at 7 am followed by breakfast and a short parade before studies commenced at 9 am. Studies would continue after lunch until 4.30 pm when there would be sport until 6 pm. After dinner, the cadets' accommodation would be inspected and from 7.30-8.30 pm there would be homework followed by cocoa and biscuits with lights out at 9.15 pm. On Wednesday and Saturday afternoon sport would commence at 2.15 pm while Sunday there would be an hour of divinity studies followed by divine service. Sunday afternoon was set aside for recreation. Eddy Nurse recalled, 'Each day at the College was identical with the one before. The routine was cast iron and filled up to 90% of our working day ... At 9 o'clock we were really ready for bed.'[29] Eric Feldt later said:

> Well, it left no time for idle dreaming. It took every part of the day and took up all you can do. All the energy you had went into your living the ordinary life and carrying out the instructions that were given. It was, we realise since, a form of indoctrination.[30]

One of the four Roman Catholic cadet-midshipmen at the College spoke of the College routine and discipline to a correspondent from the Catholic Press. While expressing concern about the small numbers of Catholics at the College, the correspondent concluded that:

> For my part I think the boys are, if anything too well off, for with all my questioning I could not find out any hardships, or causes for grumbling. The discipline was strict, but not too much so, and when the boys see how necessary it is for the management of the college, and in future for the efficiency of the navy that they accept it as part of their training. The stewards make the beds, attend to the dormitories, and, if required, clean the boots. What, then is left for the boys to do? I must confess I should have liked to hear that they did some little things for themselves.[31]

Despite the almost all-consuming naval regimen the boys still found time to act their age. Ben Howells, Hugh MacKenzie and Eddy Nurse formed a secret society which involved writing stories and having secret signs. Ben would develop remarkably as a poet at the College with the guidance of his English teachers and would garner another nickname—'Ye olde scribe'.

A month after commencement the Naval College Canteen was officially opened by the effervescent Otto Albert. He was escorted by the First Lieutenant to a gathering of all the cadets. The *RANC Magazine* reported the occasion stating, that the cadets':

> ...pockets were overflowing with 6 weeks of back pay, and their rosy young faces beamed with the anticipation of consuming the large stock of delicious sweetmeats collected and displayed in tempting profusion before their eager gaze.[32]

Otto Albert's speech, no doubt influenced by the Governor General's recent opening address was recorded in full:

It is with very great pleasure that I take part in this great function today (Cheers). I thank you one and all for the honour you have conferred on me in asking me to open this Canteen, which I feel assured will be of lasting benefit and a source of great happiness to you Gentlemen and myself (Loud cheers). What can be more relaxing, after a very arduous day at Studies, than to exercise our mouths by stringing out some of the glorious stick-jaw and other edibles of a similar nature that I hear is to be sold? ... I feel that you will all do justice to it, especially on Saturdays, when your pockets are full to overflowing with money from the Paymaster's table. Not being accustomed to speech-making, Gentlemen, but, like some of you, more able to enter into the pleasure of eating some of the very enjoyable edibles that I see before me, I have great pleasure in declaring this Canteen open. (Loud and prolonged cheering). I would ask you all, being Sunday, to refrain from too much shouting, which I know is the only means of relieving your pent-up feelings, due to the excitement caused by this ceremony, which will be marked, I feel sure, as an epoch in the history of this College. (A great outburst of cheering, which lasted several minutes.)[33]

The Cadet-Gunner presented Otto with a jam tart served on a silver tray. 'A rush was then made for the Canteen, and Chief Steward Pearman had the busiest five minutes of his life.'[34]

The other memorable event in that first March was a sea-day in the old *Encounter*. The ship was to rendezvous off Port Phillip Bay with the sleek new four-funnelled cruiser, HMAS *Melbourne* before she visited her namesake city for the first time. The excited cadets mustered at the college jetty at 6.30 am under the charge of Engineer-Lieutenant Weeks. Three sailors brought 200 sandwiches and 120 rock cakes in baskets for the day. In an inauspicious start, the motor in the cutter 'refused duty' and the cadets had to row to *Encounter* after 'sundry crabs and minor mishaps'.[35]

Otto Albert formally opening the Naval College Canteen. (Grant Collection)

On embarking in *Encounter,* 'We were then told to look round the ship, but "not" to get in the way of the men working or touch the guns etc. We at once proceeded to look round the ship, to get in the way of men working, to touch the guns etc'.[36]

As *Encounter* shaped course for the entrance to Port Phillip Bay she was joined by *Yarra, Parramatta* and *Warrego.* Meanwhile, the boys toured the engine room and they were 'particularly struck by the compactness of everything, and the great amount of machinery crammed into such a small space'.[37] In a choppy sea the four ships joined *Melbourne* who led them in a ceremonial entry to the city of Melbourne. Once alongside, the cadets were taken to *Melbourne* to meet her Captain and the Governor-General. With formalities over:

> As soon as the G-G left we were once more turned loose in the ship, and several of us managed to find either a sister-brother-father-mother-uncle-aunt-nephew or niece, who asked leave to take us away. We did not expect it to be granted, but I suppose our relations looked trustworthy, so off we went. The unlikely ones, who could produce no relations, were fallen in on the Pier and marched to the station, and took a train to Melbourne, where we joined them in time to catch the Geelong train. We reached North Geelong in safety, after sundry inter-carriage scraps, and back to the College at 8.30 pm. It had been a long and interesting day for us - we had tea and so went to bed well nigh tired.'[38]

The following month the Naval College played *Melbourne* at cricket. The cadets feared 'a rare hiding' from a ship that came with a sporting reputation. The cruiser's team however was bowled out for 40 runs compared to the Naval College's 132 runs. Lieutenant Commander Grant top scored with 79 runs while Harry Showers took two wickets.[39]

The Naval College First XI which was known as the *Super-Dreadnoughts*[40], was led by Frank Larkins and regularly played private schools with Melbourne Grammar its chief rival. In a keenly anticipated match at year's end the cadets soundly beat the College officers, led by Grant.[41] The first cross-country race involved the cadet-midshipmen being taken by boats five miles along the bay and having to run back to

The sleek new four-funnelled cruiser, HMAS Melbourne *on arrival in Melbourne. The ship was the first modern warship the Pioneer Class had an opportunity to tour.* (Green Collection/State Library of Victoria)

the College. Jack Newman, a Geelong 'native' was the inaugural winner. Sport was balanced somewhat by other pursuits. Alfred Conder defeated James Esdaile in the inaugural chess championship. Throughout the year there were concerts and sing-alongs. Peyton Kimlin's musical talents on the piano were invariably drawn upon.

The new Australian Fleet, led by the battlecruiser *Australia*, arrived in spectacular fashion into Sydney Harbour on 4 October 1913. Among those to witness the scene were Duncan Grant and Frederick Brown. On the previous morning they had been at Jervis Bay inspecting the building construction and witnessed the battlecruiser slip into the bay. A pinnace came inshore with officers wanting to view the new College. The boat took Grant and Brown onboard *Australia* where they found a flurry of activity as sailors prepared the flagship for the fleet entry. In the subsequent mid-term leave the Naval College organised a visit for the New South Wales cadets to the new Australian Fleet. They returned to the College with 'every hair of their heads a spun yarn and every drop of blood stockholm (tar)'.[42]

The Naval College First XI - The Super-Dreadnoughts. The Captain is Frank Larkins with Bill the Bulldog standing between his legs (Grant Collection)

By the last term of 1913 it became clear that the new college at Jervis Bay would not be ready for occupation. On 17 December the cadets took the train to Melbourne and onward journeys to their homes with return tickets back to Geelong for their second year. For the cadet-midshipmen from Queensland and Western Australia this was their first time home because term breaks had not been long enough for a return journey. At the urging of Lieutenant Commander Boddie and others the term dates were eventually changed to recognize the vastness of the continent. The year had been emotionally draining on many of the young cadet-midshipmen. The surviving diaries and letters of the class frequently express feelings of homesickness and unhappiness. Eric Feldt reflected that:

> So we went on to the end of the first year, and I confess, I was very unhappy most of that time. The discipline, the strangeness, the lack of friends outside the college and what, really, was a certain amount of loneliness and, well, being cut off from the rest of the world was a bit trying. But, like the young, I was adaptable, and I slowly adapted myself

to it. My closest friend all this time was John Collins, and we always got around together and shared our hopes and fears, as small boys do. During that year leave was given, but those of us who lived too far away couldn't go on leave, because you couldn't get home and back in time, so we spent it at the college itself. But we all went home for Christmas, and that was a great break.[43]

On arrival at Ingham, Eric told his parents that he wanted to stay in the Navy 'as he had found nice mates, and one especially—Jack Collins'.[44] Whilst on Christmas leave Eric and two sisters Lucy (Tommy) and Emma and another girl took two horse sulkies down to Forest Beach near Ingham.[45] After some hours in the water and on the beach all except Tommy decided on one more dip. Instead she sat in shallows. While waiting something grabbed Tommy's leg. Momentarily she thought Eric was playing a trick until she felt a 'slimy thing' down her leg and rolled back in a faint. Fortunately, Eric had turned back and seen his sister. He recalled:

> It looked so odd, I couldn't make head or tail of it, but I put my hand out to grab her by the arm, and she yelled, 'Pull, pull!' My other sister grabbed her other arm, and we pulled. For a while, nothing happened, it held fast. Then it gave way, and we came up and stepped backwards on to the beach, dragging my sister with me with a crocodile holding on to her thigh where he'd grabbed her. At the time, I thought the crocodile was about 12 or 14 feet, but having seen a lot more crocodiles since, I would say it was really 10 to 12. It was the first crocodile I had ever actually seen, but it held on to her leg, and we held on to her for quite a minute – quite an appreciable time, it seemed, and I had just got the idea that I might kick him in the eye to make him let go, when, fortunately, he let go and slid back into the sea. I'm very glad he did. If he'd grabbed me, there would have been nobody to pull me out. Then we took my sister up, bandaged her up as best we could, put her in the bottom of one of the traps, and my sister took her back into town to the hospital. Then the other girl and I packed up the gear and we drove back in the other trap.[46]

Tommy received 34 stitches, a month in hospital and a life-long scar to remember her lucky escape and the cool headedness of her brother. An account of the incident was reported in the newspapers and there was talk of a lifesaving medal to be awarded to Eric. Duncan Grant suggested to Eric that a medal ribbon on a cadet-midshipman's uniform would give him unwanted attention. For whatever reason nothing more came of it.

IV

On 11 February 1914 the boys returned to Osborne House. In a wise move that became tradition, Chambers had the new 1914 entry of thirty boys arrive the day before the older boys. Ben Howells succinct first entry in his diary for the year was, 'Arrived at the College and found it overrun with the new lot'.[47] Later that week Ben recounted:

> Lieutenant Grant told us that the new lot were becoming too cheeky. He explained that if we found any of them in our mess room with their hats stuck on the back of their heads (or on their heads at all) or if they rushed around a corner and bundled into us, etc, we were to give them a dammed good kick in the behind. Today we have been obeying orders to the detriment of the new fellows' high spirits.[48]

Later that month the two entries played against each other in cricket with the 1913 Entry winning by just two wickets. Sport became the primary means for the classes to get to know each other and prevent unwanted bullying. The need to field representative teams in many sports drew heavily on both classes. In one memorable cricket match Norman Calder was struck by a cricket ball in the mouth with some force. In the jingoistic book *Glorious Deeds of Australasians in the Great War* the incident was lionised because of Norman's stoic approach:

> One youngster, during a game of cricket, was injured so seriously by the ball that an operation was immediately necessary. The lad walked into surgery, and saluted the doctor, who informed him that an anesthetic would be necessary. The boy drew himself up proudly. 'For the credit of the service, sir,' he said, 'I must decline.'[49]

Because some of his teeth were missing and others protruding, his class seized on his appearance and gave Norman his lifelong nickname of 'Tusky'. In January 1915 he was hospitalised for nearly three weeks for corrective surgery on his mouth.[50]

On 3 March to much anticipation, all the cadet-midshipmen and many of the officers took passage in the tender HMAS *Protector* to Melbourne to inspect the gleaming battlecruiser *Australia* on her first visit to the city. As 'old hands' on a sea day the Pioneer Class took possession of the bridge and quarterdeck and excluded the First Years from these more comfortable vantage points. John Armstrong,[51] a member of the 1914 Entry wrote to his parents:

> About eleven o'clock a box of buns was placed on the quarterdeck for the cadets. The 2nd year promptly got hold of it. It seemed as if the 1st year was not going to have any but when one of them went away we made a rush and captured the box and all.[52]

On arrival in Port Melbourne the cadet-midshipmen were taken around the ship in batches by the junior officers and Ben Howells wrote in his diary that evening:

> We had a bonza time down in the gunroom. The snotties (French for middys) shouted us to lime-juice, and fruits, also offered cigarettes. They seem to be a jolly merry lot. They have a bonza canteen aboard the *Australia*.[53]

Eric Feldt viewed *Australia's* gunroom as a 'quite a strange world indeed'.[54] This visit was eclipsed later that month by the departure of Captain Chambers to a sea command.[55] To mark the occasion, both the First and Second XI cricket teams played those of Geelong Grammar and these matches were followed by a farewell dinner and sing-song.

Chambers' contribution to the development of the Naval College and the 1913 Entry was substantial. It was he who helped ensure that the boys were drawn from all social classes. His faith in a more egalitarian approach was vindicated by the excellent academic progress and the cohesion of the 1913 Entry. The Naval College itself under Chambers' and Grant's leadership had developed a distinctive character. While the Royal Navy colleges were clearly their guide, the differences at Geelong were significant. It was chiefly the absence of entrenched bullying and frequent beatings that so characterised the life of Royal Navy cadets at the time. Chambers' approach was in part due to his own experiences in 1881 at *Britannia* Naval College where he was beaten so often that he and some fellow classmates regularly hid in an old boat shed.[56] Chambers also had great empathy for the less naturally gifted cadet-midshipmen. In introducing his memoirs Chambers wrote:

> My apology for putting this story of my life on paper is the desire to show that a person of average ability, and in a profession for which by constitution and mentality he has by no means well fitted, may still score a modified success provided he tries his best.[57]

Chambers' humanity and ability to glean the potential of the boys of the first Naval College intake was to have a long lasting impact on the RAN.

V

With Chambers' relief yet to arrive from England, the newly promoted Lieutenant Commander Grant took charge of the Naval College. During the Easter leave of 1914, Grant received a telegram on 28 April from Frank Albert seeking to delay Otto's return to the Naval College due to illness. On 1 May Frank telegrammed, 'Doctor reports my son's condition unsatisfactory suffering acutely from ear and high temperature. Please extend leave another week'. On the same day Commander Grant wrote:

> Dear Sir,
>
> Sick leave to your son may be extended until such time as the Doctor deems him fit to resume his work, without further application. I was very sorry to hear of your son's illness and shall be glad if you will kindly inform me at the end of each week of his condition.[58]

On 11 May 1914, Frank Albert telegrammed, 'My son's condition still unsatisfactory for college' and then on 15 May, 'Otto died this morning eight o'clock meningitis send any papers you wish me to sign. Frank Albert.' Then in a flurry of telegrams. Grant replied, 'Deepest sympathy from officers and cadet midshipman. Please advise date of funeral.' The reply arrived a couple of hours later, 'Many thanks for sympathy funeral Saturday two thirty. Frank Albert'.[59]

Duncan Grant was stunned by the news. Otto, with his ebullient good humour, had emerged as one of the personalities in the Pioneer Class. Grant sought the immediate assistance of his colleague Commander

A French Play – Ice on parle Francaise.
L to R: *Dick Cunningham, Harold Farncomb, Horace Thompson, John Collins, Otto Albert, Cyril Sadleir & James Esdaile.* (Grant Collection)

Frederick Brownlow, District Naval Officer Sydney. Brownlow led the naval mourners and organised a firing party from *Australia* to attend Otto's funeral at Waverley Cemetery, supported by the Royal Australian Artillery Band and a contingent of eighty officers and men. Brownlow later reported that the Alberts 'fully appreciated the last honours to their son'.[60] A substantial black marble column would soon mark Otto's grave with the signatures of his classmates inscribed on the monument. The column was stylistically 'broken' to symbolise a young life cut short.

The boys were also shocked by the news of Otto's death. On the very day Grant received the tragic telegram, the boys had thought Otto would be returning to the College on the Melbourne train. In a melancholy duty Cadet Captain Larkins and the paymaster mustered Otto's belongings at the College and forwarded them to Geelong railway station for transit to Sydney. They included a bugle, stamp album, morse key, five volumes of Harmsworth self educator (*A Golden Key to Success in Life*), a telescope, camera, Kodak developer and enlarger, a gramophone and 15 records.

The death of Otto Albert forged a long-standing association between his father Frank and the Naval College. In the first instance, he established the Otto Albert Prizes for Seamanship and Engineering. The Albert residence, *Boomerang*, became a home away from home for interstate cadets of Otto's class. Frank would also invite successive graduating classes to a dinner in Sydney to celebrate their achievement as well as regularly entertaining Otto's classmates and their wives throughout their careers. Grant became firm friends with Frank through the course of this association. In 1924 Frank gifted the yacht *Triton* to the College for sail training and went on to replace her with the newer *Sabrina* in 1960.[61] This association with the Naval College was to continue until Frank's death in 1962. Frank would be buried alongside his beloved son Otto at Waverley Cemetery.

The following month the class lost another of their number. Harry Vallentine had struggled with his studies and the regimen of the College. In his first year Harry had been put on probation for talking to Harry Showers in a physics examination.[62] He was subsequently placed on formal warning. The procedure for a formal warning was that the parents were given a term's notice that unless their son's performance improved to satisfactory level then he would be discharged from the Navy. Despite Harry's best efforts and improvements in the 1914 first term, the Director of Studies wrote:

> Should Vallentine be dismissed, as I think he should be, I venture to suggest that his parents be informed there is nothing against him except sheer unsuitability for the Service. He has had a sound training for a certain period free from all expense, and is being discharged at an age when he can choose any other walk of life without being handicapped.[63]

Harry left following the mid-year examinations by train to his parents' home in Sydney. The rumour went around the cadet-midshipmen that Harry had to leave because of a weak heart.[64]

The progress of three other cadet-midshipmen was viewed by Grant with concern for differing reasons. He wrote to the Naval Board on 9 June 1914 to propose Jack Lecky, Leigh Watkins and Adrian Watts all receive formal warnings for unsatisfactory performance. He wrote of Jack that he 'has always suffered from physical weakness. He is undoubtedly improving,

Harry Vallentine, his father and four of his brothers. (Vallentine Family)

but is hardly of the type that can 'take charge'. Being physically unequal to concentrated effort, he delays the class.'⁶⁵ Grant wrote of Leigh that he 'occupies a place in his year quite incommensurate with his abilities. He apparently does not take a sufficient interest in his work, and I consider his general conduct unsatisfactory'.⁶⁶ Of a different nature was Grant's assessment of Adrian in which he wrote he 'has good ability but is too lazy to use it. He exercises a bad influence, morally, on the other Cadets, and is, in my opinion, the only Cadet in the College (with the possible exception of Mr Watkins) who does not take a keen interest in his profession.'⁶⁷

The Naval Board considered Grant's proposal but felt in the case of Jack Lecky a formal warning would 'dishearten him and be counterproductive'.⁶⁸ Admiral Creswell agreed to the other cadets receiving warnings. In the case of Adrian Watts this should be given unless means were found to remove him on the basis of his bad moral influence. Creswell did note his concern that a proportionally large number of second year cadets were being recommended for warnings and whether this reflected poorly on the Selection Committee.⁶⁹ Perhaps if Captain Chambers had remained at the Naval College these young boys would have been given more time to develop before such judgements were made. In regard to Adrian Watts, for the next month there was an exchange of correspondence as to his suitability and character. His Year Officer, Lieutenant Commander Elwell wrote:

> From my experience of Cadet-Midshipman Watts during this half-year, I am of the opinion that his withdrawal under Article 109 of the College Regulations would be a benefit to the College. His conduct has never been wholly satisfactory and he exercises a pernicious influence on certain other Cadet-Midshipmen. I consider that the defects in his character are radical, and it is unlikely that any permanent change could be affected.[70]

The Reverend Hall went further when he wrote:

> Mr Watts is Roman Catholic, and therefore I do not meet him as Chaplain, but I am morally convinced, from close observation dating from early in 1913 when I began to suspect him of bad habits and bad influence, that his presence in the College is entirely undesirable. I consider that those Cadets with whom he forms temporary friendships, degenerate in character quite visibly, and know they recover themselves when his influence is removed.[71]

In summing up Grant wrote:

> I quite agree with these reports. I have personally long suspected Mr Watts of immoral habits, but he is too 'cunning' to allow himself to be caught red-handed. He is not a boy I would trust. There is not the slightest doubt of his bad influence, and I submit that his parents be required to withdraw him at the end of the term.[72]

In a subsequent memorandum to the Naval Secretary, Grant expanded on Adrian's conduct:

> For the past year I have taken much trouble in endeavouring to obtain some actual proof of Mr Watts' immoral habits and general bad influence, but such proof is extremely difficult to come by. A case of immoral behaviour was brought to my notice some six weeks ago in which Mr Watts was implicated although only as an eye witness. This fact coupled with the strong suspicion I already held, caused me to forward the report contained in my letter of 9 June. I drew Captain Chambers' attention to Mr Watts, from a moral point of view, some time ago, but did not consider I had enough evidence to justify me in making a request that a 'Warning' should be given. I suspect one or two cadets in the last entry, of immoral habits, but I would like to submit their names for a 'Warning' on suspicion only. From the report forwarded to me by Mr Hall, I gather that Mr Watts exercises a bad influence on study as well as out of study. Personally, I do not think he will improve in the next six months, and he may do incalculable harm.[73]

It is not clear what were the alleged 'immoral habits' of Adrian. During the 1910s this term could cover a wide gamut of what was deemed socially unacceptable behaviour. The euphemism provides a veil that remains in place to this day.

On 4 July Mr Watts was sent the formal warning.[74] Despite the advice of the Naval Secretary that the warning should state that Adrian Watts 'lack of progress in his studies is not the principal cause of this warning',[75] the approved warning stated the principal reason was poor performance in studies. Adrian's father wrote in reply to the Naval Secretary in defence of his son by stating Adrian had been in hospital in Geelong for three weeks with an ear infection and at home under care of a specialist for another three weeks. This had dulled his interest in studies.[76] In response the Naval Secretary shifted ground by stating: I am desired by the Naval Board to inform you that your son's case will receive careful consideration, but the Board wish me to state that your son's lack of progress in his studies was not the principal reason for the warning being issues to you.[77]

The two warned cadet-midshipmen noticeably improved their performance in their studies with their fledgling naval careers in the balance.

VI

To the Naval College staff, the citizens of prosperous Geelong extended a warm welcome and the Geelong Club granted honorary membership to the officers, while the Geelong Yacht Club extended honorary membership to the cadet-midshipmen as well. Melbourne was also within reach on weekends. Of the wives of the Naval College staff, Mrs Wheatley was notable in arranging numerous social events. In the process she introduced Lieutenant Commander Boddie to a young Melbourne beauty Lalla Watson. Boddie escorted Lalla to her home in a hansom cab and recalled:

> My generation and its predecessor owe Mr Hansom a debt of gratitude for inventing this incomparable vehicle. The man who has never been

The 1914 winning cutter crew. (Grant Collection)
L to R: *Rupert Long, Hugh MacKenzie, Leigh Watkins, Ben Harry Howells, Horace Thompson, Harry Showers.*
Centre L to R: *Eric Feldt, Eddy Nurse, John Collins, Lieutenant Commander Elwell, Jack Newman, Frank Larkins, Frank Getting.*
Front: *Winn Reilly.*

driven along a cobbled street, at night, in a hansom, with a glamourous young lady beside him, has missed a great experience and is to be pitied. The hansom was as swift as an Irish Jaunting Car, but more cosy, and more private, with the driver discreetly out of sight and out of mind. In these congenial circumstances, I was suddenly surprised to hear myself uttering a proposal of marriage. It sounded incongruous at the time. I was even more surprised to hear my offer accepted. At parting for the night, we agreed to meet next morning in the wide open spaces of Melbourne Park. No sooner had we parted than I realised I had made an impetuous mistake, and I spent a sleepless and restless night worrying over some kind of honourable withdrawal, but without finding any solution ... We met punctually at 11 am. As arranged, and a few moments later Lalla, to my great relief, told me she had made a mistake last night, and that everything was off. My reply was polite and dishonest, and we parted good friends and I hoped wiser.[78]

The Naval College staff however were not altogether happy. Boddie wrote:

> When I arrived a number of vendettas were going on in the college. Brown versus Hall was one, Wheatley versus Brown and Hall another, and these parties gathered supporters. Poor Grant had a thin time trying to remain neutral, but by the end of the year something had to be done and Brown got the sack. For a time things were better, until Mrs Hall an aggressive type of female, came out from England to join her husband, whereupon feuds broke out afresh followed by threatened law suits. Being a bachelor, I managed to remain on good terms with all parties, but Grant and later his successor Captain Charles Morgan and Mrs Morgan competed with the general strife by remaining aloof and visiting no married couples.[79]

The boys appeared oblivious to it all. On the morning of 4 August 1914 there was an unexpected parade. One of the cadets recounted:

> Duly assembled and reported correct, the Captain addressed the Ship's Company briefly and to the point. 'His Majesty the King has declared war against Germany. Three cheers for the King.
> Following the cheers Number One (Lieutenant Commander Elwell) took over and, for what I am sure the first time of hearing by almost all present, read the Articles of War. '... cowardice, shall suffer death or such other punishment as is hereinafter mentioned.' It was all thrilling stuff and awe-inspiring and little more work was done that day except to talk of when we would get away—would we be in time for anything? Would we get to the other side? And underlying all, 'Death or other such punishment'.[80]

Even to the normally sanguine Boddie it was a 'great and impressive occasion'.[81] There was considerable uncertainty in the Naval College as to its future. Rumours abounded about both the College and the war in general. Among the cadet-midshipmen there was a general rush for the newspapers whenever they arrived. John Armstrong in the junior class wrote to his parents, 'I suppose Sydney has not been bombarded yet. A rumour reached us that heavy firing had been heard outside the Heads'.[82]

There was a proposal for the Naval College to close for the duration of the war and the officers and sailors be assigned to the Fleet and in staff positions. The reality was less dramatic. During coming months some of the staff were indeed reassigned to more important war-related work. Wheatley and Hall were transferred to Navy Office in Melbourne. Wheatley was to head the equivalent of the Royal Navy's Room 40 to decipher German coded signals. At last Wheatley had a challenge to match his Oxford degree and command of the German language. His work in helping break the cypher key used by Vice Admiral Maximilian von Spee's Pacific Squadron prior to its destruction off the Falklands on 8 December 1914 drew the worthy appreciation from the Admiralty.[83]

Lieutenant Commander Elwell for his part joined the Fleet and participated in its capture of German New Guinea. Tragically, he had the distinction of being the first naval officer killed in World War I RAN service when he was shot while leading a charge in the landing at near Rabaul.[84] Eric Feldt later related, 'It was a shock. We didn't think that war would be like that—having someone killed who you knew quite well and liked. But that was the pattern, as the whole world was to know'.[85]

Lieutenant Pope was appointed Navigating Officer of *Sydney* and sent a vivid account of her successful engagement with the German cruiser SMS *Emden* off the Cocos Islands which was published in the College magazine. As a result of the shortage of officers Duncan Grant gave greater responsibility and authority to the cadet-captains which they generally used with discretion.[86] Now that Australia was at war, Grant also directed that the cadet-midshipmen would wear their uniform at all times except when playing sport. This also extended to when they were at home on term leave.

By virtue of the older age of the cadets and the ability to employ them in active service, the impact of the war on the Royal Military College at Duntroon was in stark contrast to the Naval College. Within three days of the declaration of war, the New Zealand Government had ordered their senior year cadets (18 to 20 years old) to be removed from Duntroon for war service. The Australian Government followed suit within the week. In October the next senior class of both nations were also 'specially commissioned' to join Australian Imperial Force (AIF) and the New Zealand Expeditionary Force respectively. In addition, by the end of August only one of the officers, the Adjutant, remained at Duntroon. The remainder, including Brigadier-General William Bridges, had left to join the AIF or their old regiments in Britain. Similar to the Naval College they would be replaced by older officers or reservists.[87]

VII

Grant and Boddie paid several visits to Jervis Bay to inspect progress on the new Naval College at Jervis Bay. Its situation on Captain's Point was stunning, with an outlook across the bay to Point Perpendicular and Bowen Island. To the north and south of the Naval College were white sandy beaches and virgin bush in the hinterland. The nearest town of any note was Nowra which was 37 kilometres of rough road distant. There was a population of 500 workmen and their dependants living on the site in tents, where they remained in these rough conditions, until the cadets had been in residence there for six months.[88] Despite the outstanding work still to be completed, Grant decided that the Naval College would move to Jervis Bay for the First Term of 1915.

Duncan Grant used boxing to resolve any simmering disagreements between the cadet-midshipmen. On 20 September Jack Newman and Ben Howells had just such a bout. After seventeen hard fought rounds Grant had them shake hands although Jack Newman wanted to continue the fight. John Armstrong wrote to his parents, 'Howells face is still a wonderful sight, two very black eyes, a swollen nose, very thick lips and sundry bumps.'[89]

On the last weekend of November, 22-year old Able Seaman Hugh Hollywood, one of the Naval College sailors and bugler, tried unsuccessfully to commit suicide by swallowing the contents of a bottle of iodine. This followed him getting drunk on news his girlfriend had jilted him. On the Monday morning parade the cadet-midshipmen were most impressed that while he appeared 'very white' he was still able to blow his bugle.[90] Hugh was posted from the College the following week.[91]

As the year neared its end the results from the term examinations were assessed. Leigh Watkins had shown a marked all round improvement and his parents were advised his warning had been removed.[92] For Adrian Watts, the outcome was very different with the Naval Secretary informing John Watts that his son must be withdrawn at the end of term.[93]

Once the cadet-midshipmen had left Geelong on 12 December, the staff set about to move the Naval College to Jervis Bay, 960 kilometres distant. Most of the staff left on 17 December. It would take four shiploads to move the Naval College effects. They ranged from heavy machinery, stores and boats to the more fragile furniture, crockery and laboratory equipment. Also embarked for the nominally two day voyage were Bill the bulldog and several of the officers' dogs. The last voyage which had some of the families embarked was the roughest and required the ship to seek shelter in bays on two occasions.[94]

One staff member would not be travelling to Jervis Bay. That was the Director of Studies Frederick Brown. Five months earlier, friction that existed between Brown and Dr Wheatley had come to the attention of the Naval Board and the Second Naval Member was given carriage of the matter to resolve. This proved easier said than done. On New Year's 1914 a meeting of the Naval Board including Senator Pearce was devoted to the matter. Brown, awkwardly in the presence of Wheatley who was now attached to Navy Office for cryptographic work, gave his account of 'what in his opinion had caused the friction and whether it was avoidable and if so how'.[95] Wheatley then gave a brief statement and both men retired from the room. The Reverend Hall was then admitted into the room. The outcome of the following discussion was that the position of Director of Studies would be disestablished and a Board of Studies of the Senior Instructors would be established under the Presidency of the Commanding Officer.

On Australia Day 1915 the Naval Board formally terminated the appointment of Frederick Brown, giving him six months paid leave to enable him to secure employment.[96] Two days later it appointed Dr

Dr Frederick Wheatley who was a most influential, but at times divisive figure at the Royal Australian Naval College.
(Mrs Mornay Bibby)

Wheatley as Chief Naval Instructor at the Naval College on a salary of £550 per annum.[97] In effect Dr Wheatley had become the de facto Director of Studies. In response to these developments Brown, as a Senior Naval Instructor unsuccessfully sought a court martial to clear his name. He then secured the services of Adrian Knox, KC as his legal counsel.[98] Following advice from the Crown Solicitor, the Naval Board Minutes of 3 October 1916 recorded that, 'It was decided to recommend that the Crown Solicitor be authorised to settle this case to the best advantage of the Department'.[99] Brown was subsequently paid a substantial but undisclosed compensation for wrongful dismissal without the case coming into court.[100]

In other unfinished business, correspondence continued into January and February between John Watts and the Naval Secretary. Following a meeting with the Naval Secretary John Watts wrote:

> [Adrian] has brains they stated but lacked application, this can be accounted for by the fact of his growth as a boy of 15 years of age, and also from an affliction of the ears which was endemic in the College, but appeared to dull his ambitions, he has now recovered from this, another reason given was that there was a suspicion of a boyish indiscretion, only a suspicion for he was never warned or accused of any offence, surely a boy of that age should be first warned and quickly spoken to if he was suspected, and in all British fairness be told the reason for his withdrawal, after two years in the College.
>
> As the father of a little boy I saw in Naval costume at the opening of the College you can appreciate the feeling of a parent in those conditions. My son is strong and healthy, fond of the sea and good at engineering for which

branch he should be well suited, boys of his age often lack ambition, but in a little time grow out of that state, realise their responsibility and turn their brains to good account, he has grown more than any other boy in the College.

If his case could be reconsidered and he be reinstated I feel sure that in the future he would apply himself and become an efficient officer.

I must apologise for taking up your valuable time in these turbulent and strenuous days with what may appear to you a small matter, but means so much to my son's future career. Trusting that you will give this your consideration.[101]

The final letter was sent from the Naval Secretary to John Watts on 10 February, nearly two months after Adrian's naval service had ended:

I have enquired into this matter and find that the decision that your son should be withdrawn was arrived at only after careful consideration of reports from the various Officers and Masters responsible for the tuition at the Naval College, and it is regretted that his re-instatement cannot be considered. I sympathise very much with you in the closing of your son's career at the Naval College, but I am sure there are other avenues of employment in which his abilities can be utilised to good purpose.[102]

In a pen script note on the file by the Minister for the Navy, Mr Jens Jensen wrote 'I would be glad if you would grant a short interview as there are matters which could be explained better than by writing'.[103] It is unclear whether this meeting ever took place.

The Pioneer Class looked forward to both Christmas leave and the prospect in the new year of training in the new purpose built Naval College on the shores of Jervis Bay.

CHAPTER 3
JERVIS BAY

> *When you leave the old schools for the RAN,*
> *They'll quickly change you from boys to men;*
> *You'll wield the sword as well as the pen*
> *At Jervis Bay.*
> 'All About It – To the 13-year-old of Australia' (1917)[1]

Late in the evening of 10 February 1915 a tired group of thirty-two 13-year old cadet-midshipmen arrived by bus at the new Naval College at Jervis Bay. They had travelled in heavy rain from the railway station at Bomaderry on the northern bank of the Shoalhaven River opposite Nowra. These new First Year cadet-midshipmen were the 1915 Entry to the Naval College and were to be joined the following evening by the older cadets of the 1913 and 1914 Entries (the 'Third' and 'Second' Years). All arrivals were met with a supper of hot cocoa and cold meats.

The rough road from Nowra left a big impression on the cadet-midshipmen with them having to get out of the bus and push it through the mud. A cadet-midshipmen in the inaugural Jervis Bay edition of the *RANC Magazine* wrote:

> We do not feel justified in complementing whoever is responsible for the road from Nowra to the Huskisson corner. Personally we passed a good part of the time occupied in traversing it in the air, but thanks to the excellent road which connects it with the College and which was constructed by the Home Affairs Department, we arrived in good spirits.[2]

The need for the New South Wales Government to fund improvements to most of the road to the new College with the Federal Government only funding the section on its Territory, not only affected the uneven quality of the road but would later prove the death knell to the proposed railway link as well.

In daylight, the boys saw that the Naval College was still a partial construction site. The Wardroom was not yet complete and the single officers lived in the Captain's house. The cadet-midshipmen were luckier than the officers with their two pristine double-storey accommodation blocks completed. These buildings overlooked a large grassed Quarterdeck adorned with a mob of grazing kangaroos. To the seaward side of the Quarterdeck was the gymnasium surmounted by an imposing clock tower. The classrooms were on the north and south-side of the gymnasium. Joe Hewitt of the new 1915 Entry recalled:

> My first impression of the Royal Australia Naval College ... was that its whole layout was most picturesque. Situated on Captains Point, well above sea level, new buildings, built of brown oiled timber and white stucco and tiled roofs were sited on a unified architectural concept ... Gum trees had been thinned out in such a way as to reduce the hazards of bush fire and at the same time to create a charm to the whole environment. A group of gum trees was being removed to allow a flagstaff to stand out centrally.[3]

The aptly named Point Perpendicular at the northern entrance to Jervis Bay drew the observers gaze. Ben Howells wrote following a subsequent bush walk with Eddy Nurse:

> The cliff was perfectly perpendicular presenting a flush unyielding mass of hardened stone to the desperate onslaught of the mighty deep. Drawing back it has to receive its share from a power of boundless

'Its whole layout was most picturesque'- The Royal Australian Naval College at Jervis Bay. The clock tower above the gymnasium with class rooms either side look over the grassed Quarterdeck which was used for sport and parade training.
(State Library of Victoria)

reserve behind, then slowly it would rise as though in wrath and with a grand steady sweep roll forward to fling itself with a roar upon its immoveable barrier.[4]

The Naval College had been erected in what had been virgin bushland and 'dangerous snakes were being killed almost daily when we first went to Jervis Bay, but they were gradually exterminated from the precincts of the College'.[5] On one occasion Bill the Bulldog proudly showed Duncan Grant a large black snake he had freshly killed.

The Quarterdeck became the focus for parade training and perhaps more importantly, for all team sports and athletics. Commander Grant was often the referee and recalled in later years:

> I was more than delighted to see in what sporting spirit and with how thorough an understanding for the reason of it all they took this initiation—they were a grand crowd of youngsters.[6]

The Naval College in its new location drew rugby teams from the Sydney private schools with Church of England Grammar, Newington College and King's School among those making the journey in the first year.

The College also played in the local rugby, soccer and Australian Rules competitions. To stiffen the team against these older local competition, Grant had some of the officers and sailors complement the teams. Lieutenant Commander Boddie recalled one Australian Rules match against Huskisson:

> Our opponents were a big and burly, and unskilled crowd, but we were winning, when one of their biggest players caught me by the jersey and hurled me high in the air, to fall on my right shoulder and break the collar bone. When the match ended, Grant who had been the referee, drove me back to the College, over the very bumpy track which I found trying in the extreme. The surgeon strapped my arm tightly to my body, and put the forearm in a sling, and for a week I suffered the miseries of cramp and growing pains. This should have continued for another two weeks, but my patience was exhausted and I persuaded Mrs Wheatley to cut off the bandages. As I had been forewarned by the surgeon, this has meant a permanent kink in my collar bone, which would be a disfigurement in a lady but is no more than an inconvenience to my tailor. Some of the cadets were inclined to make too much fuss if they got injured on the football field, and Grant, who as I said before had refereed the match, had not for some time noticed my disappearance from the field, took this opportunity in a short talk to the Cadets, to quote me as an example of how to leave the field unobserved if one got hurt.[7]

In the hinterland beyond the Naval College buildings, a nine hole golf course was fashioned as was a cross-country course. Cyril Sadleir won the inaugural race closely followed by Alfred Conder and Dick Cunningham. In the nearby lagoon, rowing and other boat-work were able to be undertaken.

The pristine surrounds were embraced by many of the College staff and their families. The new houses conformed to the College's architectural theme and were spacious for their time. However, for a number of years some of the non-teaching staff, such as study corporal James Condor and his family had to live in rude canvas sided huts left by the construction workers.[8] Gardens sprouted, the ground and bushland were a paradise for the growing brood of young children. Fish were abundant in the bay and angling and oyster collecting were favoured pastimes. A correspondent called 'Cousin Kate' wrote of a visit to the Naval College for *The Mail* of Adelaide:

Another fascinating sight is to watch the cadets seining - which, being interpreted, is fishing with nets. This is a picture for the brush of an artist. A big cutter puts out to sea with the nets, and on her return a score or so of perfectly built lads, their bronzed, beautifully moulded limbs suggesting young Greek gods, stand on every available part of the boat helping to haul in the nets. At intervals a figure will dive over the side and come up smiling to clamber into the boat. The nets are drawn up on to the beach, and the haul eagerly scanned.[9]

Cadet Midshipmen inspecting the net after seining in Jervis Bay.
(W L Reilly Collection)

The new Home Affairs Department physician Dr Rabinovitch was a talented artist and he was frequently joined in the bushland and foreshore by Senior Naval Instructor Charles Franklin who was a keen photographer. Dr Wheatley had left his work at Navy Office and returned to the College with his wife and two daughters. His son Ross was already at Jervis Bay as a Second Year cadet-midshipman. The Wheatley's home soon had officers regularly visiting for 9 pm tea. Because of their remoteness from Nowra, Mrs Wheatley took on the task of giving dancing lessons to groups of cadet-midshipmen.[10]

The isolation of the Naval College was not welcomed by all and it encouraged the reemergence of some of the earlier inter-family tensions. A perceptive Eric Feldt recalled the new Naval College was:

... all that could be desired. And there we were in a beautiful college, miles and miles away from everywhere. That was what was wrong with it. It was too isolated, and everybody, including the senior officers, eventually got a Jervis Bay mentality – rather feeling that the world revolved around it, which it doesn't.[11]

The National Census was conducted in May 1915 and reported that the Naval College's population consisted of 17 officers, 87 cadet-midshipmen, 78 ship's company, 12 civilian workers, 44 women and 52 children. A total of 287 inhabitants in all.[12]

II

Because of the Naval College's remoteness many staff acquired some means of transport for travel to Nowra. A new officer, Lieutenant Campbell Cotton-Stapleton RNR, acquired a motorbike and sidecar. This added to his colourful image in the eyes of the cadet-midshipmen who had given him the nickname of 'raked-aft' because of his habit of walking with a backwards lean. Unknown to the cadet-midshipmen was that Cotton-Stapleton 'had a weakness for the other sex, and suffered from a series of embarrassing entanglements'.[13] Perhaps unwisely, these were to include the daughter of the Reverend Hall.

A more common means of transport was horse and sulky and at a newly established nearby farm some of the officers agisted their horses. The farm was owned by a son of the wealthy Beale family who manufactured pianos in Sydney of that name. All went well with these arrangements until one day Naval Instructor Moyes' horse was found prostrate. The former racehorse had evidently digested too much sand from the tufts of grass. Despite some rudimentary treatment, the horse died. With the 'unwilling co-operation' of the cadet-midshipmen the corpse of the horse was dragged about half a mile to a clearing and brushwood applied for a cremation. Boddie wrote:

> For several days there was a great blaze, and we thought the cremation had been satisfactory, but soon a dreadful stench of decaying horseflesh

polluted the atmosphere of the entire College buildings, and we were obliged to rekindle the fire on the remains, and keep it stoked for a further week. It was a surprise to me that a cremation was such a formidable undertaking.[14]

On 17 June 1915 Captain Charles Morgan arrived to take command of the Naval College. Like Bertram Chambers he was a navigation specialist and so accustomed to instructing junior officers at sea. They also shared the distinction of having been court martialed for hazarding their ships. In late 1913 Charles Morgan had been reprimanded for the stranding of the cruiser HMS *Ariadne* with the Lords of Admiralty noting they thought the sentence at his court martial too lenient. Morgan had been due to sail for Australia in August 1914 but in the aftermath of the *Ariadne* incident suffered a nervous breakdown and was briefly admitted to the Royal Naval Hospital Haslar. In the New Year he was found unfit for sea service and transferred to the Retired List, but still deemed suitable for the Naval College.[15] Morgan was not new to Australia, having served on the Australian Station as a young officer. In 1889 he had married Constance Von Der Hey, daughter of the Sydney representative of the German-Australian Steamship Company. He returned again in 1894 to navigate HMS *Orlando*, the flagship of the Australia Station.[16]

Morgan was a competent but stern officer who soon made himself unpopular with his sailors by his well-intentioned but unwanted visits to their houses while they were at work. On one occasion Chief Fairfield's wife 'gave the Captain a bit of her tongue, about his interfering habits, to which he took great exception, and thought seriously about sending Fairfield back to sea.' Morgan was placated by Grant and Boddie and 'a gross injustice avoided'.[17]

Constance Morgan, in contrast to her husband, was well regarded by most and she tried to avoid being entangled in the still brooding feuds among some married couples. The disharmony did reach the ears of the Fifth Estate and it was reported:

Officialdom and its wife at our Naval College, which shifted up from Vic. to N.S.Wales during the year, sighed loud relief as it relaxed training and decamped on annual Christmas leave. Things have not been sliding on greased runners at Jervis Bay lately, and Kipling's theory *re* the Colonel's lady and Judy O'Grady being sisters under their skins doesn't apply at the college. Social difficulties, my dear! Chaplain Hall and his wife, who couldn't abear it, go back to England without tea or presentations; and Mrs (Captain) Morgan reigns in Arctic aloofness. Talk of writs and libels flies around, while everyone wonders just how peace may be kept.[18]

Despite these strains Constance Morgan regularly entertained visitors to the Naval College while officers and their wives as well as cadet midshipmen were regularly hosted to events at the Captain's House. Constance also helped form the Naval College Band which was financially assisted by Frank Albert.[19] Her efforts were greatly appreciated by the cadet-midshipmen. Constance Morgan struck a particular rapport with Chief Cadet-Captain Frank Larkins with whom she would correspond and encourage when he later joined the Grand Fleet.

The demands of the war were such that officers and sailors were often drawn back to the Fleet and the College was left short-staffed. Mr Dix, by this time universally known to the cadet-midshipmen as 'Daddy' Dix, became the term officer of the Pioneer Class.

The remoteness of the Naval College was in part to be eased by the provision of a training vessel. In preparation for her arrival, Captain Morgan surveyed the approaches to the Naval College in a skiff to ensure sufficient depth of water. In October 1915 the 145-foot steam yacht HMAS *Franklin* finally arrived. In 1906 the former *Adele* was built in Scotland for wealthy South Australian pastoralist Henry Dutton. She was acquired by the Navy for seamanship training and to undertake a fortnightly voyage to Sydney for supplies. She was crewed on alternate voyages by the two senior classes of cadet-midshipmen. The portents were not good. John Armstrong, one of delivery crew wrote home, 'we arrived here safely but the trip was horrible. Everybody except five or six were sea sick and I was not one of the six'.[20] *Franklin* was to leave an indelible impression on the cadets. Peyton Kimlin captured the prevailing view of their training vessel:

At sea, most of the Cadets either lay down and weltered in their agony, or hung over the side and made peculiar noises with their necks. They began to ask one another if they had been 'over the side?' This would appear to mean in ordinary language, 'Has the supreme moment arrived'? Personally I was continually kept in suspense, waiting for the supreme moment, while on the other hand there were several Cadets who had twenty or even thirty 'supreme moments'. I lay near a bucket of sea water wondering whether I should kick it or merely use it as a receptacle. I decided on the latter course. Cadets lying about the decks with pallid faces, would suddenly rise, and dash with fearful energy to the side. There, amidst sundry gurgles of satisfaction, a present would be laid at the feet of Neptune. It is not particularly pleasing if the Cadet concerned mistakes your feet for those of Neptune. In conclusion I may say that I did not (emphatically) enjoy my first trip in the *Franklin*.[21]

Reputedly only Frank Larkins was never sea-sick in *Franklin*.[22] Indeed her corkscrew motion was even a test for the hard-bitten sailor. John Collins recalled:

Once when on stokehold training, I had a shovel of coal poised to throw into the furnace when the Chief Stoker Instructor, also shore based, stopped me. Without ceremony he vomited heartily into the shovel, and remarking, 'Bile, Sir, only bile', he motioned me to continue firing the boiler. It was good training for the future.[23]

In addition to her awkward motion, *Franklin* had cramped quarters. Instead of the regulation 18 inches between hammocks, there was only 15 inches. Eric Feldt said that as a result when the ship rolled:

... every hammock piled up on top of the one on the down side then swung across and piled up against the one on the other side. We were too sick to eat, and we were pretty tired from the work we had done, and when we came back, we were generally just about all in.[24]

While Chambers and Grant had a common approach to Naval college discipline, this was not so with Morgan and Grant. This was brought into stark relief with an incident involving *Franklin*. At the end of 1916's first term the cadets embarked in *Franklin* for leave. Only those cadet-midshipmen who had to get the Melbourne express were to disembark in Port Kembla to make connections, the remainder were to complete the passage to Sydney. It was an extremely rough passage and some seasick

The Naval College tender HMAS Franklin.
Among the Pioneer Class only Frank Larkins was not sea sick in her. In later years two of the class commanded Franklin. (State Library of Victoria)

cadets also disembarked at Port Kembla to make their own way by train. Morgan was furious. Cadet Captain Joseph Burnett was disrated and those other cadets involved were given six cuts with a cane in a mass flogging parade. Joe Hewitt in the junior class later wrote:

> Those who were flogged had the utter sympathy of those of us who would have been so punished. We would have disembarked, too, had we been in their circumstances. Resentment of Captain Morgan's attitude to us flared. When it was known that Commander Grant, who carried out the floggings, had all the cadets he had flogged assemble outside the messroom on the Quarterdeck and apologised to them, there was a brighter light in our disciplinary code ... Morgan (was) a sadist of the worst kind and a discredit to the Royal Navy.[25]

Eldridge summed up Grant's approach to discipline as, 'the tone he aimed at was one of straightforward manliness, and this, too, the cadets absorbed with great facility.'[26] Grant later wrote, 'Owning up to any misdemeanour came easily. They always told the truth even when they knew punishment would follow, and I also stressed the necessity of good manners'.[27]

III

As the Naval College grew in size the internal structure and hierarchy of cadets further developed. Frank Larkins and Jack Newman remained Chief Cadet-Captains and were joined by eight Cadet-Captains. Eric Feldt, Joseph Burnett, Rupert Long and Win Reilly were among the number. Like prefects in a school, they had both authority and responsibilities. Paul and Frances McGuire wrote in the *Price of Admiralty*:

> Cadet Captains lived lordly but somewhat lonely lives. The junior, in his Second Year, ranked senior to a Fourth-Year man: although tradition and discretion suggested tact in dealings with his elders. The Cadet-Captains presided at table. They served out the food. They also served unofficially but on accepted occasions corporal penalties. They could enter dormitories in their boots. They sat at higher desks in class and cast a disciplinary eye on the herd. A Cadet-Captain had an extra shilling on the weekly pay or pocket money of one shilling a week for First Year, one shilling and threepence for Second Year, one shilling and sixpence for Third and Fourth. He could stay up until 10 pm, though even the Fourth-Year Cadets had to turn in at 9.30 pm. He was exempt from fagging. Others fagged for the Cadet-Captain: cleaned his boots and fetched and carried. He wore a thin gold band on his left sleeve. He handled (dinner) Gongs. He also handled a gym shoe in the interests of public order. But he suffered something of the loneliness that attends the great.[28]

Fagging was a practice inherited from the English public school system where young pupils would have to act as personal servants to older pupils. If the standard of work such as cleaning was not up to standard a 'fag' may receive some form of punishment. The Naval College combined a boarding school punishment system with the Naval Discipline Act. The most serious punishment was expulsion, which was awarded by the Captain but had to be confirmed by the Commonwealth Naval Board. Lesser punishments were caning, stoppage of pocket money, loss of leave or extra drill. The most common offences were being late, talking in studies, untidy quarters, wearing boots in the dormitories or smoking.[29]

For many the discipline meted out by the Cadet Captain was preferable. Harold Farncomb reflected that, 'In my four years at the College I had only about four beatings and I'd have fared much worse if I'd been paraded before the Captain'.[30] But in a system where physical punishment was routinely administered by fellow cadets there was great potential for it to become a brutalised environment. Oswald Frewen, an earlier graduate of Britannia Naval College wrote:

> I think the fundamental mistake lay in putting certain ones, or in many cases uncertain ones, of the same seniority as their fellows, in authority over them. In the last analysis discipline depends on personality and character. Throughout the Navy, from earliest days to now, there have been happy ships and slack ones, depending on the character of their executive officer. By and large, the system of confidential reports and selective promotions weeds out the technically unfit and advances the efficient. But this is a process extending over several years at least. To choose a boy after six month's experience is a hazardous gamble.[31]

The familiar figure of Commander Duncan Grant on the Quarterdeck. (Grant Collection).

Fortunately, in large measure due to the vigilance of Duncan Grant the imperfect system worked. To their credit the Pioneer Class proved to be principled leaders. It would however not always be the case at the Naval College. A decade later beating became so prevalent that the junior cadets would revel in the two weeks interlude prior to the swimming carnival because they knew they would not be beaten less they showed bruising in public.[32]

The daily routines developed at Geelong were largely retained. The larger numbers of cadet-midshipmen necessitated cold showers in the morning for all except the Cadet-Captains who could enjoy hot water. All cadet-midshipmen placed their names on bath lists for a twice a week evening hot bath.

One of the highlights of the day was the 11 am morning tea or 'Stand Easy'. Cadet-Midshipmen could run across the Quarterdeck from the Studies block to the Mess Hall for a bun and milk. This was a departure from having to double around the Quarterdeck on all other occasions. On mornings when rumour reported rock-cakes in place of buns or biscuits, competition was severe. Rock-cakes for reasons buried in the hearts of cadet-midshipmen were considered delicacies. Senior Years were sometimes troublesome on rock-cake days, until Commander Grant ordered that each Year's just ration should be set out in its own gunroom instead of in the General Mess.[33]

The routines, discipline and punishment as practiced at the Royal Military College, Duntroon at the time are worthy of note. The daily and weekly routines were very similar between the two institutions with the cadets being fully occupied until completion of compulsory Divine Service on a Sunday. The Commandant at Duntroon enforced a similarly strict discipline for infringements of College routines and regulations. This included smoking cigarettes, although smoking a pipe was considered gentlemanly and encouraged.[34] The difference was in the punishment. At Duntroon cadets were subjected to extra drill or being confined to barracks. Fagging was 'strictly prohibited' at Duntroon and its regulations stated, 'No cadet is allowed to perform any menial service for another cadet'.[35] Another difference was that as early as 1912 Duntroon cadets had, with official sanction, commenced 'initiation ceremonies' of junior cadets. The ceremonies of this period involved naked cadets having to have a cold bath with treacle and axle grease.[36] This Duntroon 'rite of passage' only became more harsh over time.

IV

On 26 April 1915 the newspapers reported the Allied landings at Gallipoli in the Dardanelles on the previous day. George Armitage's older brother, Captain Harold Armitage was in the first wave of Australian troops ashore.[37] Also present was Frank Larkins' twin brother Brian

Chief Cadet Captain Frank Larkins and his twin brother Brian who saw action at Gallipoli. (Larkins Family)

who by virtue of his size had as a fifteen year old been able to pass for an eighteen year old on enlistment.[38] The casualty list was also keenly read by the staff at the College and Instructor Hannay learnt his brother had been wounded in the head.[39] Over successive weeks the cadets read of growing Australian casualties in the newspapers. The news from the Dardanelles had spurred many young men to join the Army. They included four brothers of Ben Howells and the oldest brothers of Joseph Burnett and Harry Vallentine.[40]

Nine months after leaving the Naval College Harry Vallentine signed up to go to sea once more, but this time with the merchant navy. Harry's first ship was the Commonwealth Line troopship *Miltiades*[41] transporting the AIF troops to England. Mr Dix's seamanship training soon shone through and at 15 years old Harry was promoted from Deck Hand to Ordinary Seaman. This involved his pay being increased from £1 to £5 per week. Harry's ships were invariably involved in troop convoy work.

Adrian Watts on leaving the Naval College had returned to school at Frankston, but on 14 July 1915 Adrian enlisted in the Army. He reported his age as 18½ years, but after two weeks undergoing initial training at Seymour the 16-year-old was discharged for being found to be underage.[42]

Considerable efforts were made by the College staff to maintain strong links between the College and the Fleet. The cadet-midshipmen visited warships when they anchored in the broad expanses of Jervis Bay. The three torpedo boat destroyers *Warrego*, *Parramatta* and *Yarra* anchored off the College on 28 April 1915 to embark the cadet-midshipmen for a sea day. Norman Calder wrote, *A Certain Day in April* which began:

> T'was on a day in April, The 28th we'll say;
> The sky was at its bluest and so was Jervis Bay.
> When lo ! Around the island three T.B.D's appeared,
> Led by the Flagship *Warrego*,
> Straight for the College they steered.[43]

Less poetically, outside the Heads there was a high sea running and the cadets struggled to maintain their footing as they toured their assigned ships. Boddie accompanied them, 'I had already disposed the Cadets about the Engine and Boiler Rooms, and on the Bridge, when I felt it advisable to adjoin to (Chief Engineer) Doyle's cabin for a gin'.[44] *A Certain Day in April* concluded with:

> T'was on a night in April,
> The 28th I'm told,
> When 28 Cadets were seen
> All shivering in the cold.[45]

In August Captain Morgan and the Board of Studies reviewed the progress of all cadet midshipmen. Jack Lecky was viewed with concern and warranted a formal warning on account of his academic progress, general slow physical development and general demeanour. Jack had indeed some problems with his feet which may have contributed to his comparative lower fitness.[46] The Naval Board wrote to Jack's sister Frances, informing her that without a dramatic improvement Jack would have to leave the Navy at the end of the year. Frances in reply wrote to Captain Morgan stating:

> I beg that before taking this very definitive step you will consider the fact that the boy is an orphan without any means at all. Prior to his entering the Naval College he was entirely dependent on me for support and my exertions as a shorthand writer. I have telegraphed and written to my brother urging him the absolute necessity for greater efforts, of which I am sure he is capable, and I beg that you will delay making a final decision until after the examinations at the end of the term.[47]

In late September 1915 the cadet-midshipmen embarked in *Franklin* for a typically rough voyage to Sydney to witness the launch of the cruiser *Brisbane* at Cockatoo Island dockyard. *Brisbane* was a sister-ship of the now famous *Sydney*. She was the largest warship to be built in the

British Empire outside of Great Britain. Once *Franklin* docked and the cadet-midshipmen were on dry land they 'replenished their empty holds'[48] with a corresponding improvement in morale.

The cadet-midshipmen joined over 8,000 spectators crammed into every vantage point to witness the ceremony. The official party included the Governor-General Sir Ronald Munro-Ferguson, Prime Minister Andrew Fisher, the Minister for Defence Senator Pearce and the Minister for the Navy, Mr. Jensen. On his arrival the Governor-General inspected a guard of honour and the cadet-midshipmen.

In one of the many speeches to the assembled gathering, Mr Jenson said that another cruiser the *Adelaide* would shortly be laid down on the slipway soon to be vacated by *Brisbane*. It was also the Government's hope that she would be followed by two super-dreadnought battleships *Perth* and *Hobart*.[49] The spectators welcomed the news and it was readily reported in the newspapers, especially the Hobart *Mercury*.[50]

To rousing cheers, the Prime Minister's wife, Mrs Jane Fisher, launched the *Brisbane* with a bottle of Australian wine and the words 'I name you *Brisbane*, I wish you success and opportunities to win new honours for Australia and the King's Navy'.[51]

The launching was described by the Adelaide *Advertiser* as 'a feat of shipbuilding by a young Commonwealth where the industry is still in an infant stage'. It went on to say that 'the launch of the *Brisbane* in the middle of a great world-war is especially worthy of note as another reminder of the splendid part taken by the Australian Navy in the defence of the Commonwealth and the Empire'.[52] Not to be outdone *The Argus* patriotically printed a poem to mark the occasion.

> Another link in the steel-strong chain which holds us heart to heart,
> Another pledge to the old, old vow which swears we'll never part;
> While life doth last and love doth last we'll give thee of our own -
> Dear Motherland, accept this gift we lay before thy throne.
> Forged in the heat of a southern sun, framed neath an Austral sky,
> Worthy indeed this ship shall be to float they flay on high,
> Fanned by the breath of a south-sea breeze,

kissed by the foam-flecked spray,
Did ever a child of War awake as this one wakes to-day?
We bargain not in windy words, and not in idle boast,
We speed her sliding down the slip, and make her name a toast.
Remember ye that gaunt grey wreck on Cocos' barren rocks,
Where seagulls pick the whitened bones around the old sea-fox!
Another link in the steel-strong chain which holds us heart to heart,
Another hound slipped from the leash to play a winning part;
Her flag is broken to the wind, her steel had met the sea -
Dear Motherland, accept this gift we give you this day.[53]

At the conclusion of this memorable day the cadet-midshipmen proceeded on a week's mid-term leave. On return they had to prepare for both the annual Regatta Day on 10 November 1915 and the week-long end of year examinations in the second week of December.

The first Regatta Day at Jervis Bay was held in ideal conditions. The College workboat *Tender* took officers, families and cadet-midshipmen to the finish line of the course half-way between Captain's Point and Huskisson. The course was marked with buoys from its start near the bayside town. The afternoon was filled with a succession of rowing races for both cadet-midshipmen and sailors with the College's collection of gigs, cutters, skiffs and sculls. In the much anticipated third year's race the boat with the crew of John Collins (stroke),

Many of the Pioneer Class had a professional photographer take their photograph in their uniforms for the family. This is Cadet-Midshipman Cyril Sadleir. (Sadleir family)

Horace Thompson, Harold Farncomb, James Esdaile, Eric Feldt, Eddy Nurse and Dick Cunningham (the cox) easily won by five lengths. In the premier race, the Champion sculls, Frank Getting came second in an excellent race to the outstanding rower in the College, Gordon Gould (1914 Entry). It had been an enjoyable afternoon with the cadet-midshipmen enjoying the afternoon tea in *Tender* as much as the boat races.

Following end of year examinations, the first year at Jervis Bay drew to a close. The cadet-midshipmen proceeded on leave on 16 December. Leaving for the last time however was Jack Lecky who was to be formally discharged from the Navy four days later.[54] Indeed the Naval Board notification to Frances Lecky was only signed on the day of discharge.[55] This letter was the first communication since August. In a letter Captain Morgan had written earlier in the month to the Naval Secretary to justify his recommendation:

> Cadet Midshipman Lecky is not without intelligence by any means, but it is of a certain order. He is of a complex nature and surprises by knowledge of things, which he is not required to know. It is not, however, particularly in regard to his studies, that his withdrawal has been advised. His physique is very poor, being distinctly below that of the other Cadet Midshipmen, although organically sound. He is very much behind his colleagues in this respect. His personality is such that it is considered he is not at all the type of boy required as an Executive Naval Officer, and it is the unanimous opinion of the Board of Studies, an opinion with which I entirely concur, that there is no prospect that he will develop in this respect. I would venture to submit to the Naval Board that it is possible he might prove satisfactory in the Accountant Branch, should they consider him worthy of trial.[56]

In January, Jack Lecky's grandfather wrote to Captain Morgan seeking an explanation for the decision, stating 'If such a decision is final, I think in the boy's interest it is better that we should have an explanation. His character is at stake and we are entirely in the dark, which is most unsatisfactory'.[57] In reply Captain Morgan somewhat evasively wrote that:

> The final decision does rest with me. It is entirely in the hands of the Naval Board. I am charged with the duty of submitting to them

the names of any Cadet-Midshipmen it is considered, for one reason of the other, should receive a warning on intimation of withdrawal. Before any such step is taken, each case receives the most earnest consideration, firstly by all concerned and secondly by the Board of Studies. The final opinion (the word decision had been crossed out) is then communicated by me to the Naval Board. My report to the Naval Board being entirely confidential, I regret I cannot give further official information, but, I think, I am entitled to tell you that the withdrawal of your grandson is no reflection whatever upon his personal character or his good conduct while here.[58]

Jack journeyed home to the West facing an uncertain future. He went to live with his married sister Frances Canning. Returning to school was out of the question and in the new year Jack secured a position as a clerk.

In another significant departure at the end of the academic year, the Reverend William Hall and his family prepared to return to England. His posting at an end the Halls were booked on the February sailing of the RMS *Medina*. To many of the cadet-midshipmen Hall was, after Duncan Grant, the most influential figure at the Naval College. A commanding presence both at the pulpit and in the classroom, Hall was, unknown to the cadet-midshipmen, also a troubled and divisive figure.

In recent months the Halls' behaviour had unsettled Captain Morgan. Hall had suggested to the Captain they both establish some 'recognition signals' to enable Hall to pass important information. Hall had also told the Captain that he had recently seen a man on a Sydney street who he remembered had worked for the British secret service when he was posted to the British Embassy in Constantinople. Hall thought there might be other agents who were employed for surveillance, particularly of vital installations such as Naval College waterworks. He thought the latter was at risk of being contaminated with cholera.[59] Morgan wrote that the departure of the Hall family was 'not a matter of universal regret'.[60] Hall's nature came more fully to light on his departure in spectacular but closely guarded terms. In an incident shortly before they left the Naval College, Mrs and Miss Hall had warned the nursing sisters, Carrie Saunders and Evelyn Slade that there would be 'dreadful happenings' including a shooting that might soon take place at the College.[61] Similar forebodings were told to Lieutenant Commander Boddie by Reverend Hall. He had earlier told Boddie he had engaged private detectives 'in connection with his private affairs and they had stumbled across some vast conspiracy which would prove a menace to the safety of the Empire.'[62]

On 20 February 1916 an agitated Morgan wrote to the Naval Secretary seeking the urgent assistance from the Naval Board in a matter that 'gravely affects the welfare of this Establishment and the honour and integrity of a certain officer, or officers, and myself and a member of the Naval Board.'[63] He reported that for a considerable time he believed that Hall and his family had exerted a prejudicial influence on the Naval College and spread malicious rumours about members of its staff. Morgan had tried to have Hall leave on civil terms and had obtained undertakings by all staff that on the Halls' departure they or their families would 'never discuss them in any way'.[64]

What shifted Morgan's stance had occurred on 18 February 1916. He learnt that Hall's daughter did not sail in *Medina*, rather she had travelled to Kiama to compel Lieutenant Cotton-Stapleton to marry her. Morgan sent Grant, Reverend Frederick Riley and his wife to Kiama to persuade Miss Hall to rejoin her parents and prevent a public scandal and 'if possible save the girl's good name'.[65] Morgan wrote:

> I fear the success hoped for is not being attained. Lieutenant Cotton-Stapleton I believe to be an honourable gentlemen and I will be no party to his being made the victim of what, as far as I can judge, savours of a conspiracy to enmesh him. It is all very sordid.[66]

During the conversation Grant had with Miss Hall she stated that Morgan or someone in his household was 'guilty of German tendencies or in some manner dealing improperly with the enemy'.[67] Concerned that the Halls would repeat this accusation in England,

Morgan sought assistance from the Naval Board. Action was swift. The Naval Board convened a secret Court of Inquiry on 22 February at Navy Office under the leadership of the Second Naval Member, Captain Gordon Smith, RN. Hall was directed to leave *Medina* and he would be able to rejoin her by train when the ship embarked passengers in Adelaide. Grant, Wheatley and Riley also travelled to Melbourne for the Court of Inquiry while others gave hurriedly written dispositions for consideration.

Most revealing in the Court of Inquiry was the testimony of Reverend Hall. He related to Captain Smith that his suspicion of German interest in him and the Naval College dated back pre-war to his passage to Australia in RMS *Otranto*. Onboard a young German had sought a position with him as his Secretary. Hall thought he saw the man again in Geelong. Also in North Geelong, Hall suspected the Post Master was of German origin and suspected the mail to the Naval College was being tampered with. Hall then produced one of the 'tampered' letters for Smith to inspect. Turning to the Jervis Bay period, Hall stated:

> I have seen a Chinaman pass a large envelope to another Chinaman who passed it to a third, who appeared to be Chinese and who rode away on horseback and had the seat of an officer. I walked around our house on several occasions in the last two or three months and have seen people who looked ordinary folk but their walk and straight backs and the rest of their appearance struck me as being of distinctly military bearing. They were also in Chinese dress. These are the general reasons for my very firm personal impression that the College is watched and marked by German agents.[68]

Hall did not explain the connection between the Chinamen and Germany. When asked about his questioning the loyalty of Morgan, Hall disingenuously replied:

> I am as positive as I can be that I would not be so indiscreet, but words may have been twisted. I have certainly said openly that I would not trust my own brother if he married a German or my own sister if she married a German. I have been told - I do not know whether it is true or otherwise - that there is German ancestry on either Captain Morgan or

Mrs Morgan's side. If anyone twisted these words of mine and suggested they applied to the Captain that would be quite sufficient to raise the question.[69]

When pressed on the matter, Hall went on to say 'I have no reason for doubting Morgan's loyalty or integrity, but if there was German ancestry anywhere I would indeed need very strong proof to make me believe in a person absolutely'.[70] The Court then turned to Wheatley's loyalty. Hall stated:

> I have absolutely no proof which would hold good in a Court of Law. That I say distinctly. I personally do doubt his loyalty to this extent and I would never communicate anything to him, that was of a confidential nature. I must go back a little bit however. I trace the whole of the present unhappiness at the College to events which happened since Dr. Wheatley's arrival. Year 1913. The point I am trying to prove is that I trace the first signs of any lack of discipline, signs of unhappiness, to dates following on the arrival of Dr. Wheatley. I must say that I consider his appearance to be German. His mother's maiden name was Wilhelmina Basedow, of Kapunda, South Australia.[71]

After stating he was suspicious of Wheatley asking for books of wireless telegraphy, Hall was more revealing when he said:

> But what I am trying to prove is that unhappiness and disorder in the College dated from Dr Wheatley's appointment. The first indication was this. Dr. Wheately assumed an attitude of absolute independence with Mr Brown. He refused to consult with him in the ordinary way. He said he was an independent authority. This information was given me by the Director of Studies as his second. The next indication which is not evidence, because I did not hear it first hand, is that in Geelong where Mrs Wheatley was then living it was said that Dr. Wheately was going to take his rightful position as head of the institution and that the Director of Studies and myself would have to go, and the attitude of Dr. Wheatley confirmed this. I trace the unhappiness at the College and the lack of discipline in the teaching staff to the presence of Dr. Wheatley and to no other cause. Dr. Wheatley being of German parentage, it does not appear right to have a man of German parentage at the College. I would say that he has succeeded in his presumed object and that he is at present in the highest position in his branch, and that is quite wrong as he is a man of German origin.[72]

Hall's carefully qualified response did not appear to reflect his and his family's true suspicions. In Cotton-Stapleton's disposition he stated that Miss Hall said that 'Dr. Wheatley is also in the Secret Service of the German Government and was acting as such when on the Navy Board, Melbourne'.[73]

At the end of the Court of Inquiry, Captain Smith reported to the Naval Secretary, that 'There is not the slightest reason to doubt the loyalty or integrity of any officer at the College.'[74] Smith went on to find that the allegations against Wheatley had no foundation based on his German heritage. Smith noted however:

> That this action on the part of the Rev. Hall and his family was taken primarily on account of the ill feeling which existed between the families of the Rev. Hall and Dr. Wheatley, and with a view to rendering Dr. Wheatley's position in the College untenable. That as the statements made were mainly in the form of insinuation the Court do not consider that there are sufficient grounds for taking action against the Rev. Hall.[75]

A copy of the report was forwarded to the Admiralty and Morgan was at pains to ensure it would be available when their Lordships considered Hall's future employment.[76] The Halls rejoined *Medina* for passage home.

Captain Morgan's fears about his good name in the hands of Reverend Hall were not realised. Within a year of his return to England Hall would be dead from blood poisoning.[77] On news of his death Norman Calder wrote:

> ...he took the Church services and religious instruction and was quite broadminded in his approach to Holy Writ. He taught us lots of old English songs round the piano. We all thought of him as a God. He endeavoured to instill into us all the old English customs, taught us sea shanties, naval customs, religion, conduct. His teaching was Gospel. Personally he is the one man who was the greatest influence for good in my life.[78]

Reverend Hall also helped instill the notion that the unofficial religion of the Navy was Church of England. It was perhaps appropriate that during the week that news of Hall's death was received at

Jervis Bay, the Most Reverend John Wright, Archbishop of Sydney arrived at the Naval College. The Archbishop, a leading Evangelical had been an outspoken supporter of conscription and who made pre-dawn walks to the Sydney wharves to farewell every troopship.[79] Wright travelled to the Naval College to confirm 35 cadet-midshipmen into the Anglican faith. There were some conversions which included Norman Calder from Presbyterianism and John Collins from the Roman Catholic faith. John's conversion had little to do with Hall for although John's father was Roman Catholic and he had a Christian Brothers schooling, his mother was strongly of the Church of England faith and his maternal grandfather was an Anglican minister.

VI

The 'Hall Affair' coincided with the return of the cadet-midshipmen. For the Pioneer Class it was for their final year at Jervis Bay. The College now boasted a corps of cadet-midshipmen 120-strong. Admiral William Creswell's vision of a first-class Naval College was nearing realisation. The *College Magazine* reported:

> Both officers and Cadets from the beginning of the year had been seized of the importance that lay behind the words 'Fourth Year,' now used for the first time, and as the year slowly ran out its appointed course anticipation sharpened into definite expectation of great doings.[80]

As part of the planning for graduation of the Pioneer Class, Duncan Grant had conceived that just as at Dartmouth Naval College a gold King's Medal be presented to the midshipman who had best demonstrated gentlemanly bearing, officer-like qualities, character and good influence on his fellows. As with the Royal Navy the King's Medalist would have that honour recorded next to his name on the Navy List with the letters KM. In mid-1914 to obtain King George's consent, Grant had Admiral Creswell write to the Admiralty via the High Commissioner in London, who in turn would consult the Colonial Office, and finally write to the King. Not unsurprisingly other wartime matters had taken priority and by June 1916 the correspondence was reported lost in Whitehall.[81] Grant restarted the process, but this time he had the Governor General write direct to the Secretary of State for Colonies on 20 September 1916.[82] The delay would mean that one of the highlights of a Naval College Graduation would not take place for the Pioneer Class.

Grant had more success in his specialist field of physical training. As at Osborne where great store was placed in military gymnastics, the gym was fitted not only with wooden bars along the walls but climbing ropes hung from the high ceiling. On one occasion however Grant's son Seafield recalls:

> Father, on one of his walks round the College, went into the Gym, where he found three cadets, Bill (his bulldog) with his jaws clamped round the knot of the climbing rope, which had been hoisted to the top of the Gym, some twenty-five feet from the floor. He knew that if he called out, Bill would let go and that would have been the end of him. One of the Cadets spotted Father and without a word being spoken, lowered Bill to ground level. They then apologised for their prank, and no further action was taken.[83]

On 1 April the College staged a gymnastic display in a crowded and flag-bedecked gymnasium. Music was rendered on the piano by

Some of the Pioneer Class relaxing in their Gunroom. (WL Reilly Collection)

Frank Getting in the Naval College working uniform (RAN).

Peyton Kimlin and Naval Instructor Riley. The event opened incongruously with a bayonet fighting display between Eddy Nurse and Petty Officer Price. John Collins was to be Eric's opponent in a second match but had been injured in practice. This was followed by an exhibition on the horizontal bars by Grant, Chief Petty Officer Dyer, Jack Newman, Eric Feldt and Ben Howells. Petty Officer Price then gave an impressive display of rope climbing that ended 'with his head-first descent most thrilling'.[84] Not to be outdone Jack Newman, Frank Larkins and Dick Cunningham gave a display of chair tricks. Grant and Eric Feldt had a close fought bout with sabres. The Second Year cadets then gave a Swedish drill display which included jumping over 'living' vaulting horse that 'gradually grew from a pony to a draught'[85] with more cadets being added to the horse. This was followed in short order by blind-fold boxing, illuminated club swinging and wrestling. The occasion culminated in a vaulting horse display tableaux with three pyramids, the largest having a uniformed Dick Cunningham atop the structure. At the climax he magically produced an Australian flag. 'The spectators testified in no uncertain way to the excellence of the display'.[86] A *Sydney Morning Herald* reporter on a tour of the College witnessed the cadet's gymnastic prowess and wrote:

> If arrangements could be made for a gymnastic display by our cadet-midshipmen in the Sydney Town Hall the public would be able to form an estimate of the magnificent work that is being done.[87]

The reputation and facilities of the Naval College at Jervis Bay began to appear in the press and following a record number of applicants for the next entry a correspondent wrote:

No wonder there are 429 applicants for the 30 vacancies at the Australian Naval College at Jervis Bay. Apart from the fascination of the future that lies ahead of the cadet, the college itself is a far more luxurious place than the most fashionable of English public schools. Dormitories and studies are the last word in modernity and comfort; there is a gymnasium with every device to enthrall the heart of youth; and there is the bay. There can be nothing lovelier than Jervis Bay in fine weather, viewed from the 'quarterdeck' of the college. The only sign of civilization is the distant lighthouse on the North Head. All else is amethyst blue water, shining white beach and sage green bush. On the waters of the bay the boys learn to swim, surf, sail boats and manoeuvre steam launches. Ashore, picked naval officers teach them the rudiments of every branch of their profession, and the discipline, ethics and conventions which the British navy has taken about 900 years to amass. The cadets are as carefully selected as their instructors. Each of them has to be a sort of physical, moral and mental super-boy. As recently as two years ago Australian parents were sending their youngsters to the other side of the earth to enter the British navy. The idea was that the Australian navy was a fleeting folly that would die with the downfall of the Labor Government, and that, in any case, no Naval or military College of worth could be instituted in Australia. Since then the Australian navy has won fame, and the local Service Colleges have become almost embarrassingly popular. Never in history has a great idea been justified so quickly.[88]

In March 1916 two tragedies befell the Naval College in quick succession. *Franklin's* Chief Engineer was the 27-year old Sub-Lieutenant James Macleod[89] who had 'a rather forbidding countenance.'[90] He fell madly in love with Dr. Wheatley's 17-year old daughter Vivian but she could not tolerate his attentions. On the afternoon of 9 March, while the rest of the Wheatley family were at a picnic, Vivian shot herself in the temple with a small pistol.[91] On hearing the sound Dr. Wheatley rushed home. Vivian died in his arms. A suicide note was afterwards found by her distraught parents. Vivian's death 'cast a gloom over the whole College'.[92]

Vivian's suicide, which was reported in newspapers as an accidental shooting, had another consequence for Dr. Wheatley. Frederick Brown had become aware through former colleagues at the Naval College

'The spectators testified in no uncertain way to the excellence of the display' The tableaux was an exhibition Duncan Grant had used in the Royal Navy Colleges and brought to Jervis Bay to stretch the athleticism and teamwork of his cadet midshipmen. (Grant Collection)

that Wheatley had been the source of the allegations that led to his dismissal. Brown had subsequently launched legal proceedings to sue Wheatley for slander. However, on learning of Vivian's death Brown 'dropped the case, a foolishly chivalrous action which was dictated by common decency'.[93] Brown remained bitter and thirty years later wrote to Eldridge:

> Meanwhile Wheatley had achieved his ambition, and the withdrawal of legal action has resulted in the truth never being brought to light. Even after all these years I shall take swift action against any attempt, even by implication, to attach any stigma to my departure from the College.[94]

The following week five of *Franklin's* sailors were returning to the Naval College from nearby Huskisson in a sailing gig. They were not paying sufficient attention to the conditions as the wind was light. A sudden squall hit the gig and before the sailors could adjust the sails they capsized. William Flowers and Alexander Carter managed to swim clear of the sails, ropes and fishing tackle and clung to the gig. Able Seaman Erle Boyd rescued John Hennigan and Dominick Healy both non-swimming Irish-born 26-year olds and brought them to the skiff.[95] Boyd then swam over five kilometres to shore then ran a couple of kilometres along the beach to the Naval College to raise the alarm. A rescue boat was dispatched to pick up the others. The Naval College also telephoned to Huskisson and a motor boat was sent to the scene. This boat picked up the hypothermic William Flowers and Alexander Carter, who were still clinging to the boat. After nearly five hours John Hennigan and Dominick Healy had succumbed to the elements with Hennigan being lost only fifteen minutes before the arrival of the Huskisson boat.[96] *The Advertiser* reported that Erle Boyd's 'plucky action aroused great admiration throughout the district. He is none the worse for his long and heroic action'.[97]

VII

On 1 September 1916 Major-General John Parnell, the Commandant of the Royal Military College, Duntroon motored to the College. He was accompanied by the Duntroon rugby team to play their first match at Jervis Bay. Because of the war Duntroon training had been cut to two years which helped reduced the age difference between the players. It still meant the youngest Duntroon players were of the same age as the oldest cadet-midshipmen. On seeing the size of the Duntroon players there was a 'severe slump in the Naval Rugby shares reported from Wall Street'.[98] Eric Feldt who was normally Captain of the College team was sidelined with an injured leg and Frank Larkins would take his stead. Despite all this, Grant and Naval Instructor Hannay were quietly confident in their team which had been unbeaten in their lead-up matches against the Sydney school teams.

The following morning Captain Morgan received a telegram from the President and officials of the New South Wales Rugby Union wishing both teams well for the match.[99] That afternoon there was tremendous excitement among the cadets. Both teams were given a rousing reception by the cadets, the staff and their families as they ran onto the Quarterdeck.

The inaugural Naval College vs Duntroon Rugby Match.
(Grant Collection)

From Duntroon's kick-off, the game was fast and spirited. After ten minutes half-back Jack Newman drew his opposite number then passed the ball to John Collins who scored a try to the loud cheers of the home crowd. A nervous Harry Showers missed the conversion. Duntroon clearly smarted, played with even greater determination and toughness and shortly evened the score with a field goal. Frank Larkins now led the other forwards Frank Getting and Eddy Nurse to answer the Army challenge and moved the game into Duntroon's quarter. The pressure paid off in the form of a penalty and this time Frank Larkins took the kick himself and the Naval College drew ahead by three points. Within minutes of the kick-off Duntroon had regained possession and their speedy winger had scored a try in the corner to level the score six-all. The conversion was missed and both teams were locked together in tough ruck and maul play until Jack Newman once again broke free. Joe Burnett got the ball and raced over the line for a try. Harry Showers neatly potted the conversion. When the referee blew the half time whistle the game's unexpected scoreline was Navy 11; Army 6.

The second half was an equally physical affair but once again Jack Newman was able to set up a try for Kevin Dudley (1914 Entry). The Duntroon players now showed the spirit and determination for which they were well-known and feared. They were able regain possession

The two teams after the inaugural Naval College vs Duntroon Rugby Match. The younger RANC team is in the white jerseys. (RAN)

shortly after resumption of play and in an excellent back-line move had one of their players sprint over the College line to score a try. The conversion was unsuccessful. The game however was sealed with one final forward push led by Frank Larkins with Gordon Gould scoring the final try of the match. Shortly afterwards the final whistle was blown with the final score Navy 20; Army 9.

Eddy Nurse described the match in his diary as a 'titanic struggle'.[100] whilst the *RANC Magazine* reported that Commander Grant was even seen to smile. Major-General Parnell wrote in the *Royal Military College Journal* somewhat disingenuously, 'as the Military College at the time of the match had only the two junior classes in residence, the full strength of the College was not represented'.[101] It was indeed one of the College's finest sporting moments and rarely would it best Duntroon in the future.

VIII

On the evening of Saturday 28 October 1916, Commander Grant motored into the Naval College from Bomaderry. Beside him was a diminutive but quite unmistakable figure. It was Prime Minister Billy

Hughes. On that day had been held the national referendum to decide whether Australia should introduce military conscription. After an arduous campaign to gain support for conscription, Hughes had cast his vote in Wollongong. He had been then due to join the Melbourne express at Moss Vale to take him to the southern Capital for a cabinet meeting. The strain of the referendum campaign however was too much for Hughes. *The Sydney Morning Herald* reported that 'he had been unable to sleep for the past two nights, and was in a highly nervous state'.[102] With the ready assistance of the local Tourist Bureau a couple of days break was organised with the assistance of the Naval College. Hughes had a restorative stay in the Captain's house and took in the natural beauty of the Naval College. During strolls through the grounds Hughes met the cadet-midshipmen who were surprised to suddenly meet their Prime Minister. After this short interlude Billy Hughes was driven to Moss Vale and caught the express to Melbourne. There he rejoined his cabinet colleagues to ponder the now gloomy news of a referendum defeat.

Prime Minister Billy Hughes and Commander Duncan Grant outside the Wardroom.
(Grant Collection)

As the term drew to an end all the cadet-midshipmen sat the final year exams on 5 December 1916. It was the last hurdle before graduation and sailing to join the Royal Navy's Grand Fleet. Although a gifted student in literature and especially poetry, Ben Howells had for four years struggled with the more technical subjects. Nearly a century later his son John wrote:

His long struggle to maintain self respect as a student at studies the value of which he was now starting to question, must have been wearing. And his gentle meditative spirit rebelled against the regimentation of naval life.[103]

Over recent months Ben had written to members of his family about his unhappiness and doubt about the Navy as a career. This culminated in final year examinations where he handed in blank sheets for some subjects. Grant sought to understand the reason for Ben's poor showing and to encourage him to remain in the service. Ben however told Grant that he 'could never become an efficient naval officer and would rather be a private in the AIF with [his] four brothers'.[104] Ben would not join the Grand Fleet.

The academic results of all the cadet-midshipmen are preserved to this day in the Naval College Museum. They show that in the 1913 Entry there was remarkable consistency in individual ranking over the four years of study. The sustained high achievers were Harold Farncomb, John Collins, James Esdaile, Eric Feldt, Eddy Nurse and Dick Cunningham.

IX

Naval College life in the first two weeks of December was dominated by preparing the Pioneer Class for their departure for the Grand Fleet

A relaxed Pioneer Class. (Reilly Collection)

and their Passing-Out Parade. After four years close association there was a strong bond, particularly with those staff who had been with the Naval College since the Geelong years. The class gave Commander Grant and Mr Dix gifts followed by three cheers.[105]

On 7 December a steamer arrived from Sydney with the midshipmen's sea chests, uniforms and kit needed for service in the Grand Fleet. Also onboard was the Reverend Andrew Hardie who would accompany the Pioneer Class to England. Hardie had been posted to replace the Chaplain in *Melbourne*. Captain Morgan had earlier unsuccessfully requested to the Naval Board that Dix also accompany the midshipmen on their voyage to England. A replacement however could not be found to backfill Dix at Jervis Bay.[106] In the same correspondence Morgan sought advice as to which Grand Fleet ships his midshipmen were destined to serve in. He concluded with the observation that:

> I shall also be glad if I may be informed when I can give the Fourth Year Cadet Midshipmen any idea as to where they are likely to go when they leave, and how they will possibly be grouped. They are naturally intensely interested and anxious for information, and their keenness, and their anxiety to prove their worth to the outside world is quite remarkable.[107]

Over the next couple of days midshipman's patches were sewn on monkey jackets, old gear disposed of and the cadets went to a series of afternoon teas at various homes. Norman Calder wrote:

> Sunday 10th December. Had usual church etc. Had last communion at college. In afternoon went to Mr Dix's. All the fourth year. Had bonza time. Good feed and happy time. Governor General (Sir Ronald Munro-Ferguson), Mr Jensen & Co arrived. Came to church. Went for a walk after tea. Commander gave us some more hints about when we get to sea. Took off my buttons & tweed off my coat. Turned in at 10.[108]

The following day the cadet-midshipmen gave the Governor General and his party a demonstration of their now famous gymnastics display. This was concluded with a speech to the cadet-midshipmen by the Minister of Navy Mr Jensen. Afterwards the class received the new mess jackets, tunics and great coats and started packing their sea chests.

The long anticipated Passing-Out Day had finally arrived; Saint Finnian's Day, Tuesday 12 December 1916. The Governor-General would be the Reviewing Officer and in his words 'bid Godspeed to the departing Midshipmen'.[109] He had been joined by Admiral Creswell who had travelled down to Jervis Bay with a correspondent from *The Sydney Morning Herald*. As Creswell negotiated the road from Nowra he reflected on the Navy and this momentous occasion to the reporter:

> The life of the Navy is a life apart. It may be likened to one of the great monastic orders. The political life of the day sees changes. The work of the Navy goes on regardless, to a large extent, of the political issues. The life of the Navy, during the past ten years, does not seem to have been realised by the public. The old idea of a comparatively idle life on foreign stations has disappeared. The past decade has been one of strenuous endeavour, of practical work in the North Sea, and of the maintenance of that efficiency which has served the Empire in such good stead during the past two years.[110]

For the correspondent it was his first visit to the Naval College and he reported:

> As we cross the heights leading down to Captain's Point, with the college buildings visible four miles away, the idea of a life apart appealed to me. Here, indeed, was a miniature monastic order nestling by the waterfront in a pear-shaped bay, with clean white sand marking the foreshore. It seemed a sylvan retreat, this spot where the personnel for Australia's Navy were being trained. Outside the Heads the sea was running. The wind was a little treacherous. There was even a tendency to squalls. This sea brought the sylvan retreat into relationship with the stern business with which it is concerned. The call of the sea was there. The spirit of the Navy was there.[111]

At 11.15 am a bugle sounded and the cadet-midshipmen were paraded for the Governor-General. The smartly turned out and drilled parade was a credit to Mr Dix. The *Herald* correspondent wrote of the graduating class, 'Fine manly fellows they are for the most part, keen for work, eager regarding their future, and already with a true sense of duty and honour – characteristic of the Navy'.[112]

On completion of the parade the proceedings adjourned into the gymnasium for the prize-giving. The interior had been suitably decorated with signal flags and other nautical adornments. 'By a magic wand in the possession of the Naval Board the old Fourth Year had disappeared, and in their place were seen 25 [sic 23] Midshipmen, who thoroughly looked their part.'[113] Joe Hewitt observed:

> ... we saw our senior contemporaries in midshipman's uniforms – no lanyards now – white tabs on the lapels of their monkey jackets. We felt envious of them going to join the Grand Fleet. They would be on active service.[114]

Before asking the Governor-General to present the prizes Captain Morgan recalled the history of the College from its inception in Geelong, the guiding hand of Admiral Creswell and the achievements of the College since moving to Jervis Bay. Morgan, always the disciplinarian, stated that:

> The discipline and general behaviour of the cadet-midshipmen had been highly satisfactory. He thought that it had been clearly proved that the idea frequently expressed that the Australian would never become amenable to strict discipline was an entire fallacy. He was a little shy at first, but his perception was keen, and directly he appreciated the value of what was being taught, and that the instructors knew their business, he was fully satisfied that there was no better material in the world with which to deal. He responded most readily. The strictest possible discipline prevailed.[115]

During the proceedings the *Herald* correspondent noted Creswell's reflective and proud countenance. This graduation ceremony was the last major milestone of his great Navy-building endeavour. He would retire in 1919 after years of unremitting advocacy for a strong Australian Navy and would become known as the 'Father of the Royal Australian Navy'.[116] Fittingly, the Naval College would later be commissioned as HMAS *Creswell*.

Following Captain Morgan's speech, Sir Ronald then congratulated each of the prize winners. The audience 'were not behind with their applause'[117] in the tightly crammed gymnasium. Harold Farncomb excelled academically winning prizes in French, History, English as well as being runner-up in Seamanship and Navigation. John Collins won the Otto Albert Prizes for both Seamanship and Engineering Theory whilst James Esdaile won the Navigation, Mathematics, Physics and Chemistry prizes. Harry Showers won the prize for Practical Engineering. The prize for the best aggregate performance was deservedly won by Harold Farncomb followed by James Esdaile and John Collins. Naval Instructor Eldridge later opined to his daughters that both Collins and Farncomb would have stellar careers but that one would inevitably break the other's heart.[118]

The Pioneer Class Graduation. (RAN)

The ceremony closed with a moving and eloquent speech by Munro-Ferguson. He told the Midshipmen, 'You who inherit the blood, have been trained here in the traditions of a race which for 300 years and moreover never lost its hold on the sea'. After painting the challenges that await them in the Grand Fleet he concluded by saying:

> Providence has showered its choicest gifts on Australia to enable her to defend her freedom. And now your country which has done so much for you in sending you across the seas to learn through experience, that

art of naval defence which is seen at its best in the British Navy, so that you may aid in achieving the end that Australia shall be 'truly master in her own seas.

I wish you all honour and glory under the White Ensign. I know you'll look back with gratitude and affection to Jervis Bay, where you've beat Duntroon and whence you go forth to play the noblest game of all. I am sending the following cable to the King:

> Sir Ronald Ferguson, with humble duty, begs to inform your Majesty that he has to-day said good-bye to the first contingent of Cadets who have passed out of Jervis Bay Naval College as Midshipman to be posted to your Majesty's Fleet. Sir Ronald is confident that they are fitted by training and character to worthily maintain the traditions of your Majesty's sea service.[119]

In one of the longest entries of his diary for the year, Norman Calder recorded the momentous day as follows:

> Tuesday 12th December. Got up at 7. Dressed in ½ whites, with white shoes & midshipmen's jackets. At 11.15 all fell in. Inspected by Governor General. Then went in for the prizes. Cinematograph & press present. Captain Morgan read his speech. Then prizes were presented by Governor General. Very good prizes... Made a fine speech. Praised us up. Sent telegram to King about us. Meeting ended by three cheers for King & three for GG. After it had photos taken about five times also by cinematograph. After dinner started to pack. Heard I came 9th in exams. Did much better than I thought. Had a parting feed & then concert. Very good. We gave some final choruses. Sang Auld Lang Syne. Said goodbye. Turned in. Did not get to sleep till 1.30 am. Plenty of noise.[120]

The following morning the bleary-eyed Midshipmen were woken at 3.30 am and forty-five minutes later were being driven in the charabanc[121] to Bomaderry railway station. As it had begun for the boys at Jervis Bay, so it finished. It was raining heavily and the charabanc broke down. As a result, they missed the morning train. Instead, they had breakfast at Nowra to await the afternoon train and read what they thought was a good account of the Passing-Out Parade in the newspapers.

In a remarkable and lengthy editorial *The Sydney Morning Herald* linked the graduation of the Pioneer Class with the recent 'No Vote' in the Conscription Referendum. The newspaper, which had supported the Yes campaign, wrote that:

> The Jervis Bay midshipmen may have done their country a service before they leave by shaming the adults who allow so much of the burden of defence to fall upon mere boys. If it is contrary to the Australian tradition to allow one man to profit by another's exertions, it should be abhorrent to any of us to realise that to find the examples of efficiency and discipline remaining in the community we must look to the naval and military colleges.[122]

As his Naval College years drew to an end, John Collins reflected on the experiences of the Pioneer Class:

> Having learnt our lesson in the early days of 1913 we had a wonderful four years at the College. I never ceased to marvel that so many things dear to a boy's heart were included in working hours. Fancy spending a forenoon being taught how to sail a cutter, to send and receive semaphore messages, to operate a lathe, or to work out a sun sight. Up at 7 am for a swim before breakfast, and at the double all day till 'Lights out' we were busy.[123]

On the evening of Wednesday 13 December the midshipmen finally arrived by train from Nowra at Central Railway Station in Sydney. They were met by Frank Albert and his son Alexander who took them for a most welcome dinner at Restaurant Rainaud in Kings Street. Frank's friend and theatrical entrepreneur, Hugh McIntosh then hosted them to a show at his Tivoli Theatre.

The following morning the midshipmen in their best uniforms reassembled at the Albert's residence. They then took the tram to Bronte to visit Otto Albert's grave at the Waverley Cemetery. For most of them it was their first visit and they saw their signatures engraved at the base of the Otto's column. They placed a wreath on his grave and had a group photograph taken next to it. The visit greatly affected both Frank Albert and the midshipmen.

The Pioneer Class at Otto Albert's Grave. (George Kimlin)

Afterwards the Albert family took the midshipmen to Farmers Department Store for luncheon. In the afternoon most of the class returned to Central Station where they waited to take their respective trains home for leave. For some it would be their last Australian Christmas.

Chapter 4
Midshipmen At War

Remember that your vocation deliberately chosen is War. War as a means of Peace, but still War, and in the singleness of purpose for the Empire's fame prepare the time when honour and welfare of that Empire may come to be in your keeping, that by your skill and valour, when the time arrives and fortune comes your way, you may revive the spirit and perpetuate the glory of days that tingle in our hearts and fill our memories.

An extract from Alston's Seamanship hung in each Naval College Gunroom[1]

I

As a result of his final year results Ben Howells was discharged from the Navy. Under the conditions of his entry, Ben's father John had to repay £250 for his son's tuition. For a retired man of 79 years of age after having to provide for ten children in his working life, it was too much money. He wrote to the Navy that he could not afford the amount. His son's service was terminated in any case.[2] For Ben the decision was received with mixed feelings.

Ben was of very strong and admired character.[3] During his College years Ben had excelled in rugby and rowing, earning colours for both sports.

Such was the bond of their shared experiences Ben and Eddy Nurse were to remain life-long friends. On hearing of the Navy's decision, Frank Larkins wrote to Ben:

> We will miss you very much, we will miss your silence and clever repartee in the gunroom, but most of all in the football team. It will be very hard to find an adequate substitute. But I suppose it will be for the best.[4]

In searching for direction Ben sought the counsel from Reverend Arthur Burnaby, formerly of All Saints' Church near his home town of Yandoit. True to his religious and philosophical interests Ben considered missionary work and Burnaby suggested a calling to the Ministry. To prepare himself Ben established a gruelling six days a week home studies regime which including teaching himself Latin and Greek. On Sundays he would attend the local church twice in the day.

On 13 January 1917 the Reverend Andrew Hardie and eight of the Pioneer Class joined the Orient-Pacific Line passenger ship RMS *Omrah* in Sydney for the long passage to Plymouth. Of the remainder of the class, all but George Armitage would embark in the planned port calls to Melbourne, Adelaide and Fremantle.[5] Due to an injury to his eye George would have to sail the following month from Melbourne in the troopship SS *Ballarat*.[6] Among *Omrah's* 700 strong military contingent were 168 Army tunnellers bound for the Western Front. These men were drawn from the coal mines and would be employed to dig tunnels under German lines where massive explosive charges could be placed. Also onboard were reinforcements for machine gun and artillery companies and a Flying Wing.[7] The aviators included Lieutenant Arthur Cobby who was to become Australia's greatest ace by shooting down 29 aircraft[8] over the Western Front.

At the appointed time *Omrah* cast off to the cheers and tears of hundreds of family and friends that waved from the wharf and held on to streamers till the last. The ship threaded her way through the various Saturday sailing races being held on Sydney Harbour. Once clear of

The Pioneer Class sailed in RMS Omrah *to UK to join the Grand Fleet.*
(Green Collection/State Library of Victoria)

the Heads *Omrah* steamed down the coast for the three-day passage to Melbourne. *Omrah* had been commissioned in the same year that the Pioneer Class were born and at 8,130 tonnes was a substantial passenger ship for her time. Her triple-expansion engine gave her an above average maximum speed of somewhere between 15 and 17 knots depending on her loaded state. *Omrah* had earlier in the war been requisitioned by the Australian Government as a troopship to take the first Australian Imperial Force to Egypt. While *Omrah* was part of that large first Anzac convoy, she had to embark some of *Emden's* survivors who were transferred from the overcrowded cruiser *Sydney*.

On 16 January 1917 after an uneventful passage to Melbourne, the midshipmen were joined by twelve of their class mates. While in port some of them went to see the popular pantomime 'The House that Jack Built'. Returning to his lodgings at midnight, Norman Calder wrote, 'My last night in Victoria. It is hard to realise that we are leaving home for a great adventure'.[9]

The following afternoon there was a flurry of activity on the dock as more soldiers and equipment joined *Omrah*. Just before 4 pm family and friends disembarked the ship to more tearful farewells. Norman Calder wrote that evening:

The last I saw of them was all of them waving and darling Mother drying her eyes. May all of us meet again the same as we left. Dear old Grandad is a real old hero. The parting must come and the future is in God's hands. I will try and be a credit to the family and lead a clean life as mother wished me to before we left whatever maybe the cost.[10]

For the passage to England the midshipmen had been put into bridge watches. This still left much time for participating in lectures, sporting activities, concerts, card games and reading. After a short port visit to Adelaide *Omrah* made a rough passage across the Great Australian Bight. She berthed in Fremantle on 21 January. Whilst in port the ship embarked James Esdaile and Cyril Sadleir along with her final stores, victuals and coal. A decision was made not to give the troops leave for the two day visit. This unpopular action was short-lived. The soldiers spoke to the coal-loaders who informed the Captain they would go on strike unless the men were given leave. General leave was promptly granted and all the soldiers dutifully returned for the ship's sailing on 24 January 1917.

Norman Calder with his Grandfather William Calder. (Calder Family)

As *Omrah* left Australian waters the Captain ordered various drills to exercise the emergency stations and launching boats. He also directed that items that could float to be untied to increase the amount of flotsam should the ship be torpedoed. Four days into the voyage *Omrah* reversed course. The passengers were told a German raider was possibly loose in the southern

Winn Reilly on deck in RMS Omrah. (WL Reilly Collection)

Indian Ocean. The order to return to Fremantle was based on a cablegram from the Admiralty to the Naval Board reporting that a German submarine was off Capetown.[11] On 1 February *Omrah* was back in the Swan River. With the raider threat proving a false alarm, it was only an overnight port call to top up sufficient coal for the passage to South Africa. The second attempt to sail to South Africa was uneventful with *Omrah* anchoring in Durban's harbour on 16 February. This, the first of countless foreign ports to be visited by the Pioneer Class, was a hive of activity.

In Durban there were troopships with 14,000 soldiers embarked for the Mesopotamian campaign. It was not until the evening that *Omrah* got alongside to coal and store the ship. While this activity was underway the midshipmen took rickshaws or trains into town to see the sights, post letters and look for some amusements. To the midshipmen the large presence of 'natives' and 'coolies' distinguished Durban from Australian cities.

The Omrah *on passage. Lifeboats were swung out because of the ever present U-boat threat. Members of the Pioneer Class in white sun hats can be seen conversing with some of embarked troops.* (WL Reilly Collection)

The following evening *Omrah* sailed on the two-day voyage to Cape Town. The ship waited five days for a convoy to assemble. On the afternoon of 24 February the armed merchant cruiser HMS *Orcoma* led *Miltiades, Walmar Castle, Omrah, Ulimaroa* and *Anchises* past Cape Point into the Atlantic Ocean. A large swell was running and some ships rolled heavily to the discomfort of the troops. The convoy caught up with the slower troopship *Waitamata* that had been sent ahead. The ships formed two columns on either side of the *Orcoma* and slowed down to *Waitamata's* ten knots.

On the passage to Sierre Leone all the ships conducted gunnery practices while sporting competitions, lectures and reading occupied the passengers. The highlight of the leg was the Crossing-the-Line ceremony to mark the crossing of the Equator. Because of large number of novices King Neptune's courtiers took a representative group to pay due homage to the King. Peyton Kimlin and Eddy Nurse were the chosen midshipmen to be 'painted, scraped and dunked'[12] in the good natured ceremony.

On 9 February the convoy formed into a single line formation and proceeded into the large harbour and the port of Freetown. For three days the local port workers coaled the ships of the convoy. Fortunately for the troops and sailors the cool Harmatta wind from the Sahara afforded Freetown its most pleasant weather of the year. Norman Calder wrote:

King Neptune and his court in RMS Omrah. *(WL Reilly Collection)*

We visited the army officers club up on a hill and we had a drink and played billiards and then we had a frugal meal of tinned tongue and dry bread at a hotel. We walked up Kissy Street, the principal street of the native quarter and then we returned to the ship in time for afternoon tea (and we were very thirsty) and after tea and dinner I played bridge right up till about 11.30 pm when I turned in. I couldn't live in Freetown for a pension.[13]

At 8.30 am the convoy weighed anchor and proceeded to sea in calm conditions. The fins of many sharks drew the close attention of the troops lining the guardrails. The escort of the convoy for the next leg was strengthened by the presence of HMS *King Alfred*. This cruiser, while only as old as *Omrah*, was now obsolete, being too slow and vulnerable for fleet actions. The now normal shipboard routine was resumed. Food onboard remained the subject of much attention by the passengers. Peyton Kimlin preserved a menu of luncheon for 17 February as a souvenir. It proclaimed pea soup, Royal Sea pie, soused fresh herring, roast sirloin of beef, semolina pudding and oat cakes.

As the convoy entered the North Atlantic it became colder and the midshipmen delved into their sea chests for warmer clothes, particularly for their watches on the bridge or in the crow's nest. Three days out from Plymouth the convoy escort was further strengthened by four destroyers led by HMS *Goshawk* which patrolled ahead of the merchant ships. The following day a full gale had blown up and the temperature dropped even further. In the early evening the on-watch midshipman in the crow's nest sighted Eddystone Light off the Cornish coast.

At 3 am on 27 February 1917 *Omrah* entered Plymouth Harbour. After the long voyage most midshipmen anti-climatically saw England for the first time out of their cabin portholes. Mid-morning the midshipmen took a steamer up to Devonport dockyard where they were met by Sub-Lieutenant Denis Pelly from *Australia* who would look after them until they joined their ships. Arrangements had been made for the Pioneer Class to take an afternoon train to Portsmouth. The train passed through the rolling countryside of Dorset and Hampshire before reaching Portsmouth about 11 pm. The weather was bitterly cold and for many it was their first sight of snow. Queenslander Eric Feldt wryly remarked that he 'wasn't warm again for another four years'.[14] The Midshipmen were taken to HMS *Excellent*, the famous RN gunnery training school which is located on Whale Island in Portsmouth Harbour. They spent two weeks at 'Whaley' where they undertook gunnery and parade training and induction into the RN ways. Eric Feldt thought:

> ... we were sent there to make us realise what discipline really was. As it happened, we found Whale Island fairly easy. It wasn't as tough as Jervis Bay was as far as discipline was concerned.[15]

Whilst at *Excellent* the midshipmen were taken in groups to the naval tailors, Gieves and Company, to be provided with the necessary uniforms and other kit to complete their outfit. Gieves was synonymous with a well-attired naval officer and any 'proper' officer would have a career-long account with the company. Gieves had a proud history and its founder, James Gieves had worked for 'Old Mel' Meredith who had tailored the tunic that Nelson wore at the Battle of Trafalgar.

On 3 April with their RN induction training drawing to a close, the Pioneer Class were paraded in their new Gieves uniforms before the Commander-in-Chief, Portsmouth, Admiral The Honourable Sir Stanley Colville who wished the class good luck for their time in the Fleet.

The next evening the class dined together for what was to be the last time. The one empty chair was that of Harold Farncomb who was turned in to Haslar Naval Hospital with pneumonia and would have to join his ship when he had recovered. The following day they took the train to Scotland to join their ships. During their initial sea training they would serve in either a battleship or battlecruiser. In each capital ship up to twenty midshipmen were accommodated in the gunroom. Within the little world of the gunroom a sub-lieutenant was in charge and there would be a hierarchy of senior and junior midshipmen.

For the first time the Pioneer Class came into contact with their RN contemporaries. The original plan was for the class to be split in two and embark in *Australia* and HMS *New Zealand*. The ever-concerned Captain Morgan had even tried to get one of their old Naval College officers serving in the Grand Fleet such as Lieutenant Commanders Pope and Boddie to be appointed their 'Sea Daddies'.[16] However, the battlecruisers had insufficient space in their gunrooms and the Pioneer Class were split into four groups. The Australian Naval Representative in London, Captain Francis Haworth-Booth, worked with the Admiralty to select the four ships. Each of the ship's Commanding Officers were friends of Haworth-Booth and he had 'made special representations to them re these Australian midshipmen, and I am sure they will be specially looked after'.[17]

The first group comprising Joe Burnett, Alfred Condor, James Esdaile, Rupert Long, Win Reilly and Cyril Sadleir were posted to the battlecruiser *Australia*. With all German warships cleared from the Pacific and Indian Oceans, their flagship was a part of the Battle Cruiser Force based at Rosyth in Scotland. Flying his flag in the ship was Rear Admiral Arthur Leveson who commanded both the 2nd Battle Cruiser Squadron and His Majesty's Australian Fleet.

The second group comprising George Armitage, John Collins, Eric Feldt, Lloyd Gilling, Peyton Kimlin and John Newman joined the battleship HMS *Canada*. This two-year old super dreadnought was originally ordered for Chile, but because of the outbreak of war was acquired by the RN. As a member of the Grand Fleet she was based in Scapa Flow in the Orkney Islands off the northern Scottish mainland.

The third group of Norman Calder, Harold Farncomb, Paul Hirst, Frank Larkins, Horace Thompson and Leigh Watkins were assigned to join one of the Grand Fleet's newest battleships, HMS *Royal Sovereign*. The 30,000 tonne behemoth had a complement of nearly 1,000 officers and sailors. She was armed with eight 15-inch guns which were then the RN's largest guns.

The final group of Dick Cunningham, Frank Getting, Hugh MacKenzie, Eddy Nurse and Harry Showers joined the battlecruiser HMS *Glorious* in Rosyth. This ship had only commissioned the previous month. *Glorious* and her sister-ship *Courageous* possessed an unmatched speed for a capital ship of 31 knots and a shallow draft for possible operations in the Baltic. The midshipmen had already had a close view of *Courageous* then fitting out in the Portsmouth naval dockyard. The qualities of these ships were achieved by only having half the number of 15-inch guns compared to the *Royal Sovereign* and being very lightly protected with armour. This made them vulnerable in any engagement with the heavy units of the German High Seas Fleet.

On 5 April the midshipmen took the Portsmouth train to Waterloo station. Those of the class with extended family in London spent a couple of hours visiting them before mustering at Euston station. The midshipmen bound for the Grand Fleet took the *Jellicoe Express* to Thurso while those Rosyth-bound caught the *Caledonian*. By chance, while waiting for their trains Eric Feldt, Leigh Watkins and Norman Calder met their first Commanding Officer from Geelong, Captain Chambers, on the platform. Eric recalled that 'it was quite a breath of friendliness to meet him'[18] and the boys proudly told him of their posting to *Canada* and *Royal Sovereign*. Chambers had left the cruiser *Roxborough* and was serving as the Admiralty Port Officer in Scapa responsible for the many small support vessels that succoured the Grand Fleet in its remote anchorage. Following his excellent performance in this post, Chambers would go on to be promoted Rear Admiral later that month. His first appointment as a Flag Officer was to coordinate convoys operating out of Halifax, Nova Scotia. Chambers would play a notable part in the relief efforts immediately after the Halifax Explosion on 6 December 1917.[19]

II

As the Pioneer Class travelled north they took with them one final piece of guidance from their mentor Commander Duncan Grant. He had thoughtfully penned for them 'Hints to Cadets on Passing Out', which was later republished in the *RANC Magazine*. It provided them practical advice for midshipmen on joining their first ships. He wrote:

> Lie low for a fortnight after joining. During this time GET TO KNOW EVERY CORNER OF THE SHIP. Write up your Watch Bill, and Division List carefully and get to know every man in your Division, Gun Crew and Boat. Keep these lists up to date.
> Make your boat's crew take an interest in their boat. Ditto with your gun's crew. If they see that YOU take an interest THEY will. Try to be a REAL HELP to the officer of your Division and your Watch. A GOOD Midshipman of the Watch, a GOOD Midshipman in charge or second in charge of a gun's crew and a GOOD Midshipman of a Division, is worth his weight in gold to the various officers concerned. Don't be too ready to report a man. Talk to him first, or talk to the Petty Officer in charge before you talk to him. Be friendly, but not too friendly, with the Quartermaster of your Watch. He is an old hand at the game, and can teach you much.
> Don't be afraid of the sound of your own voice – after the first fortnight. As Midshipman of the Watch get to know everything that has happened or is likely to happen; what boats are away, what they are doing, when they will return; what officers are out of the ship and when they will return; what the barometer is doing; the direction and force of the wind; which is the Watch on Deck; which is the Duty Sub (Lieutenant) of the Watch; what the hands are doing, and if they are at dinner, the time they turn to again; if guns are covered, etc.
> In addition, at sea, the formation of the Fleet; when they last altered course; the speed; whether you are in station; name of the next ahead and astern; how many revolutions are necessary to get up into station or to drop back; what you would do if a man fell overboard; see what there is handy to take with you if you jump in after him (grating, oar, etc); how many revolutions to a knot; the time you are likely to get into harbour, etc.
> As Midshipman of a boat always take your telescope with you; see that the boat's signal book is in the boat; don't forget to report to the Officer of the Watch before you carry on; see that your crew are properly dressed and have their boots with them; see they do not talk in the boat or loll about; never make fast alongside a gangway, always lie off smartly, and see that your crew do the same.
> As Midshipman of a gun: First of all find out ALL ABOUT IT; worry round it in your spare time with the Petty Officer; find out all about the ammunition supply, etc.

When you have been given a job to do, don't go away when the job is NEARLY finished; wait and see it completely carried out. Get your label 'I can trust him to carry it out'. When you have occasion to give an order, see that it is strictly carried out. If you have been given an order that you do not quite understand, don't be afraid of asking the officer to repeat it; it is better to risk a little invective than to deliver a wrong message.

Don't loaf or loll about, even if you think there is nothing to do. You can always find work if you look for it. Be punctual to the minute when going on Watch and at other times. Punctuality is the ESSENCE OF EFFICIENCY. Be careful with your dress; a smart officer is smartly dressed. If you are told to find anybody or do anything, find HIM or do IT; don't start by asking questions.

Don't be too officious. Don't be an 'aye-server'. Don't nag at the men. Don't get excited in an emergency. Keep your head; sit still and do nothing, rather than rush about and do the wrong thing. Give your orders as if you meant them to be carried out. Don't give them as if you were asking a favour of the men. Become EFFICIENT. Let the men feel you know more about it than they do themselves, and be sure that you DO.

Don't shirk your duty in order to pander to popularity with the men. The men respect a strict and just officer but certainly do not respect one who is too 'chummy' or anxious to please.

Don't be afraid of 'Talking Shop'. It is not taboo in the Navy. Finally, remember that 'There is nothing the Navy cannot do', only some things are more difficult than others.[20]

On Good Friday, after over 24 hours of travel, the Grand Fleet midshipmen reached the terminus of Thurso and were taken by motorbus to Scrabster Harbour to await a tender that was to take the mail round the Grand Fleet. The *Canada* midshipmen disembarked first while *Royal Sovereign* was the last ship in the mail run. The midshipmen found their hammocks in the spacious Gunroom and retired 'terribly hungry and tired'.[21]

The battlecruiser midshipmen for their part arrived in Rosyth only to find their ships at sea and spent the chilly night in an old depot ship. On 8 April the imposing battlecruisers returned to port and the midshipmen joined their ships.

The Pioneer Class had joined the RN's heavy units at a time of some unease. From the outset of the war the Grand Fleet under Admiral Sir John Jellicoe had worked assiduously for the opportunity to have a great and decisive battle against the German High Seas Fleet. For this reason, the British Fleet had been split with the fewer and faster battlecruisers based at Rosyth. The Scottish port was closer to the German bases and gave the battlecruisers the best chance to gain enemy contact. The more numerous battleships of the Grand Fleet along with their supporting cruisers and destroyers, had been redeployed from their southern bases to the safe but isolated anchorage of Scapa Flow. Ships of both forces spent their time either conducting training in-port or at sea, undergoing maintenance or undertaking sorties that usually began with great expectation but invariably ending in disappointment.

Jellicoe's best opportunity to engage the Germans finally came on 30 May 1916 thanks to Professor Ewing's team of code-breakers in Room 40 at the Admiralty who alerted of a possible sortie of the German Fleet into the North Sea. Both the Grand Fleet and the Battle Cruiser Force sailed as soon as steam was available. The next day the British battlecruisers under Vice Admiral Beatty came into contact with their German counterparts off Jutland. Both battlecruiser forces were scouting ahead of their respective battle-fleets. Beatty attempted to lure the German battlecruisers and with them their battleships towards the approaching Grand Fleet. Beatty succeeded in his task but at a terrible cost. Three of his lightly armoured battlecruisers, *Invincible*, *Indefatigable* and *Queen Mary* blew up under accurate German fire during the running engagement. Of the 3,343 officers and men in the three ships only 17 souls survived. The battlecruiser *Australia* was normally part of the 2nd Battlecruiser Squadron with Rear Admiral William Pakenham flying his flag in the ship. But fate stood in the way of *Australia* and this titanic battle. On 22 April off Horns Reef *New Zealand* collided with *Australia* in foggy conditions, the latter requiring dockyard repairs at Devonport. The Admiral shifted his flag to *New Zealand*. While there was great disappointment onboard *Australia*, with three battlecruisers blowing up at Jutland, it was also a case of what might have been.

The Battle of Jutland ended inconclusively. Just when the two opposing fleets joined battle towards the end of the day, where the weight of British numerical superiority would be felt, the German Fleet under Vice Admiral Reinhard Scheer managed to execute a difficult manoeuvre that cleared them from the clutches of the Grand Fleet. At Jutland the British lost more ships and twice as many men as the Germans. The High Seas Fleet never again however contested for dominance at sea. Beatty replaced Jellicoe in the Grand Fleet, with Pakenham assuming command of the Battlecruiser Force. Jutland was a bitter pill for the RN and for the last year the British had desperately sought another opportunity to decisively engage their quarry.

III

In *Glorious* the Australian midshipmen found the Gunroom run by two sub-lieutenants with a total of twenty midshipmen, or snotties, as they were called onboard. Eddy Nurse wrote:

> It was a strange life we had entered. I didn't like it much. The sub-lieutenants and senior snotties made the junior 'snots' fag for them and beat them if necessary. A survival of the public school I suppose. We five were of course junior snotties. But we were so big and strong compared to them that they didn't order us about with much assurance. We did minor fagging duties for a while until for some trifling thing they decided to beat 'Bagger' (Dick Cunningham). He was the smallest of us. Getting organized the revolt. We marched in en bloc, told them we refused any further fagging and demanded the release of 'Bagger'. Though they outnumbered us four to one, they didn't do anything more than argue. We won on points, and they made us senior snotties forthwith.[22]

On the positive side of the ledger, the battlecruiser had a fine Commanding Officer in Captain Charles Miller who had been made a Companion of the Order of the Bath for his gallantry in command of the cruiser HMS *Nottingham*. The ship had been in the thick of the action in the Battle of Jutland, but her luck ran out when she was torpedoed and sunk in August 1916.

In *Royal Sovereign* the midshipmen were more fortunate with their Sub-Lieutenants, but had a particularly difficult Navigation Officer who supervised their training with a jaundiced eye. Eric Feldt in *Canada* described their living quarters:

> The gun room of the *Canada* was a compartment on the portside abreast Y turret. It had one skylight and no other opening except the door forward. It was, I suppose, about 30 feet by 15 in dimensions, and it held about thirty midshipman and three sub-lieutenants who were in charge of them. A table took up one side of it, and there were a few chairs and there was a locker for each individual. We had a messman who was paid by the mess who put our food on the table, which consisted of navy rations, supplemented by whatever we paid for. Two stewards served it, and we were fed not really very well, because a few months later many of us came out in boils.[23]

Like their class-mates in *Glorious*, the Australians in *Canada* rejected the prevailing fag system which did not endear themselves to their RN counterparts. Eric Feldt believed 'as we were Australians, we were expected to misbehave, and the hand of authority was quite ready to descend on us'.[24] This was not helped by some of the Australians having difficulty with understanding the English accents and this was taken as opposition to authority. Invariably they were collectively referred to as 'the bloody Australians'. But workable relations were established and indeed some firm friendships were made that would be maintained through the years. Among the RN midshipmen were some notable officers. They included Robert St Vincent Sherbrooke who in World War II would gain a Victoria Cross for his valour in command of the destroyer HMS *Onslow* in the Battle of the Barents Sea. An age contemporary of the Pioneer Class was Bill Andrewes, who was a son of the Canon of Winchester and had passed through Osborne and Dartmouth naval colleges. He had been in *Canada* for the Battle of Jutland and would rise in his career to Admiral.

Naturally enough, *Canada* always had midshipmen of the Royal Canadian Navy. Among the three Canadian midshipmen onboard were two future admirals Roger Bidwell and Edmund Rollo Mainguy.

The latter became one of the first Canadian officers to be the professional head of their Navy.[25] John Collins wrote of life in *Canada*:

> We had a very happy time owing to the two subs (sub-lieutenants) Barnham and Belfield, and we were lucky to have a wonderful executive officer. HMS *Canada* had Robin Campsie Dalglish, well-known out here; he was later on flag officer out here. Dalglish was the perfect commander for a midshipman. He treated him as a human being but as rather an inferior human being. All midshipmen, you know, are well, the lowest form of marine life but he just went one step above that.[26]

Commander Dalglish, who as Collins indicated would later command the Australian Squadron in the inter-war period, was an Australian in the RN. As a boy he grew up on a sheep station in the Goulburn area of New South Wales. Dalglish was representative of a handful of Australian boys whose parents could afford the substantial annual fees for their sons to attend the Royal Naval Colleges prior to the creation of the Royal Australian Naval College. Other notable Australian-born officers who would influence the careers of the Pioneer Class were John Crace[27] and Philip Bowyer-Smyth.[28]

Canada's commanding officer was Captain 'Jimmy' Ley[29] who was tall, slightly deaf and of nervous disposition. He was suspected by the Gunroom as being a bit mad. In one episode as *Canada* came into port, he rushed up to the Midshipman of the Watch and said, 'Tell him, tell him, 20 minutes, 20 minutes!' and rushed off again. The midshipman concerned was a very philosophic type, and when we asked him what he did about it, he said, 'Oh, I just went and hid for 25 minutes, knowing that whatever happened would have happened by that time'.[30]

Those older hands like Bill Andrewes recounted stories of their previous commanding officer, Captain William 'Maddo' Nicholson [31]who also seemed to be operating on the edge of sanity. It was with this run of Captains that the new Commanding Officer joined the ship. He was the decorated, but somewhat eccentric, Captain Adolphus Williamson, who earlier in the war had seen arduous service in East Africa.[32] John Collins recalled 'he was small and bright-eyed and his trimmed beard looked like a bird's beak'.[33] Indeed Williamson gloried in the nickname of the 'Partridge'.

Even by the accommodating standards of the day for senior officers, Williamson was troubling. Amusing if disconcerting anecdotes quickly began circulating the ship of various incidents involving the 'Partridge'. A treasured Williamson possession was a folding chair given to him by an Admiral in his early career. The 'Partridge' would not be parted with it, to the point that his 'Coxswain carried it after him about the upper deck like a caddy with a golf bag'.[34] He also disconcerted the midshipmen on one occasion by coming into the Gunroom and telling them:

> Dundee was the greatest root-producing area per acre in the United Kingdom and its marmalade was made chiefly from carrots, turnips and the lowest form of Swede. You now understand why Dundee elected Winston Spencer Churchill as its member of Parliament.[35]

In February 1918 during an operation in which the Grand Fleet units provided cover for a convoy bound for Norway, matters came to a head in *Canada*. When John Collins came on watch on the bridge one moonlit evening he found the unusual presence of both Captain Williamson and Commander Dalglish. He was to slowly understand the reason for Dalglish's presence. Williamson spied John and asked whether he was a 'racing man'. Replying uncertainly that he was, Williamson told John that he was retiring to his sea cabin and that he was to be called every three minutes with a racing term. John recalled:

> The first I selected, I remember, was 'Ten to one the field, five to one bar one', which would have surprised any honest bookmaker. Being doubtful of my ground, and not feeling nearly so grown up, I made the report in a small voice. This enraged the Captain, who roared at me to let him hear it. I complied, and the shouting continued every three minutes for what seemed a long time.
>
> At last he decided to change his sea boots for snow boots and return to the bridge. As I started to pull off his sea boots he cautioned me to treat him gently as he had the royal blood of the Abyssinian kings in his veins. By this time I had concluded that the Old Man was more than a little eccentric, and reported the conversation to the Commander. To my surprise he took no action but told me to carry on doing what I was told.[36]

The Quarterdeck of the battleship HMS Canada. *The occasion is the performance by musicians from the US battle squadron in 1918. Visible are John Collins, Eric Feldt and Jack Newman under the 14-inch gun with the ship's bulldog mascot. Peyton Kimlin is behind the piano.* (George Kimlin)

After a few more antics the 'Partridge' sat on his folding chair with a rug around him and ordered John to stand by him and place a cough drop in his mouth whenever he coughed. Before John went off watch at 4 am the 'Partridge' ordered him to bring him some hot cocoa. When he returned with steaming jug on a tray the 'Partridge' immediately drank the contents in one gulp.

Not long after John Collins wearily retired to the Gunroom, the entire formation of ships had to alter course twenty-five degrees to port in accordance with the navigation plan. Shortly after the young Officer-of-the-Watch had settled on the new course the 'Partridge' ordered 'Starboard twenty-five'. Commander Dalglish immediately told the Captain that he had ordered the wrong course and *Canada* was brought back into line. The 'Partridge' then ordered the Yeoman of Signals to send by 10-inch flashing light to the Flagship:

> It was not the fault of the Officer-of-the-Watch that we got out of station. It was my fault. We hope by good manoeuvring soon to regain our proud position in the line.[37]

'Insanity was an occupational hazard of a naval career.' Eric Feldt in HMS Canada where there was a succession of eccentric commanding officers. (Feldt Family)

To send such a signal, particularly in a fully darkened formation in an operational sortie, was demonstrably aberrant behaviour that would be observed by the Flagship. It was what Dalglish had been waiting for. As the signal started to be sent he ordered it to be stopped and then sent by a smaller red flashing light a personal message to the flagship to inform the Admiral that he was taking over command and placing the Captain under restraint below. Captain Williamson left the ship when she returned to Scapa Flow. He received care at Yarmouth but would be dead within a year.[38] Eric Feldt concluded that based on *Canada's* three captains and 'fortified by later experience that insanity was an occupational hazard of a naval career'.[39] Fortunately his confidence in RN senior officers was somewhat restored with the arrival of the experienced battleship captain Hugh Watson whom Eric deemed 'the sanest man you could ever find anywhere'.[40]

IV

In February 1917 George Armitage finally sailed for England in the troopship *Ballarat* which had embarked reinforcements for the 2nd and 4th Brigades. She was a four year old P&O ship which George soon learnt from the troops was on her 13th troop run to England. Such was the misgiving that nine superstitious stokers jumped ship in Fremantle rather than continue the voyage.

Ballarat called into many of the same ports as *Omrah* and from Sierra Leone she was part of a nine ship convoy for the final leg to England.

The escort was strengthened with the arrival of some destroyers for the final hazardous passage up the English Channel. The last day of the voyage was Anzac Day and during the afternoon preparations were underway for a dinner in honour of Gallipoli veterans who were among the troop contingent. The ship would dock in Devonport that evening. However, *Ballarat* had been detected by Oberleutnant zur See Max Viebeg in the small German submarine *UB-32*. Just after 2 pm Viebeg fired a torpedo at close range which struck *Ballarat's* stern. Her starboard propeller and her aft 6-inch gun were destroyed, the main steam pipe fractured and the aft watertight bulkhead blown in. Private Arthur Creswick recalled that the ship 'shook like a leaf'.[41]:

> The first ten minutes were thrilling moments as we were all prepared for the worst as we shook hands with our mates. At the rate she was sinking, it was evident that every man would have to take his chance in the water. I threw off my coat and boots and tied a piece of rope around my waist, so as to be able to tie myself to a raft or anything I could get floating, knowing that I could not possibly hold on long with my hand, as the water was almost freezing. I afterwards found out only two points above freezing point. There was no panic on our deck, every man kept his head, and only one man jumped overboard before the order was given, but at the other end of the boat there were several of the Infantry men jumped overboard, shortly after being hit, others got injured, one or two got their legs broke, but as far as we know, all were saved.[42]

The destroyers closed the scene and dropped depth charges in an unsuccessful attempt to destroy the submarine. *UB-32* managed to evade the counterattacks. On his return to port Viebeg was promoted to Kapitänleutnant with effect the day after the attack. Coincidentally, *Ballarat* was *UB-32's* 13th and largest victim.[43]

Fortunately for *Ballarat* the sea was quite calm. George Armitage along with some other crew and passengers tried to release a lifeboat but found the release mechanism was rusted. Some of the other boat fittings were in a similar state.[44] As these forlorn attempts were made the destroyers *Lookout* and *Phoenix,* as well as some trawlers came alongside the stricken *Ballarat* and took off the 1752 crew and passengers including George. Thanks to regular boat drills and the troops' excellent discipline there was no loss of life.

The troopship Ballarat *sinking after being torpedoed by* UB-32.
(State Library of Victoria)

Ballarat later sank eight miles off the Lizard while being towed inshore. Late that evening the survivors were landed at Devonport. The following morning the somewhat bedraggled survivors marched to the accompaniment of a band to the nearby naval barracks to the great cheers of the townsfolk. *Ballarat's* captain Commander GW Cockman, RNR later received the thanks of the Admiralty and the Australian troops were congratulated by King George V for their feat.[45] After receiving a new uniform outfit from Gieves, George Armitage found himself on the *Jellicoe Express* to join his classmates in *Canada*.

Unbeknown to the Pioneer Class the issue of awarding the first King's Medal to an RAN College graduate had not been forgotten. On 9 December 1916 the King acceded to the proposal[46] in accord with his desire that the award follow as close as possible to the Osborne practice. Among other things this involved the commander, Headmaster, Engineer and Chaplain recommending to the Captain the worthy nominee. The inaugural King's Medalist was Winn Reilly. The King had determined that during the war gold medals would not be awarded and a copper substitute was to be presented and replaced with the gold medal at a later date. In May 1917 the King bestowed Winn Reilly the King's Medal on the deck of *Australia*.

Winn Reilly (in the foreground walking towards a group of officers) was presented with the King's Medal during King George V's visit to HMAS Australia. *In this photograph the ship prepares for the Monarch.* (WR Reilly Collection)

Winn's selection was a surprise to some and Norman Calder confided to his diary:

> I heard that Reilly was awarded the King's Medal for been the most influential cadet at the college. I think he was the most uninfluential chap and he was hated and disliked and was a sucker all round. Larkins, Long or Getting should have got it but not Reilly.[47]

The Australian midshipmen had quickly settled into the Fleet routines. In harbour, the midshipmen were turned out at 6 am and did physical drill on deck for half an hour even in the snow. After breakfast they joined the rest of the ship's company fallen-in by parts-of-ship on the upper deck for prayers and to receive orders for the day. After which there would be training with their parts-of-ship or instruction in gunnery, navigation, engineering, seamanship or torpedo theory. The only variation would be spending long hours in charge of one of the ship's boats around the anchorage.

Generally, their ships would get underway once a week for training or for a sortie. When opportunities arose the midshipmen would attempt to visit each other in different ships for a change of scene. Eddy Nurse wrote:

We had all work of minor duties in the ship. Had a division of men and had a group of guns each; each man a picket boat, and when at sea kept watch in the foretop or submarine lookout. These jobs were quite difficult enough. All our spare time was spent in the Gunroom. There was plenty of drinking and smoking and swearing and filthy stories and bullying and minor cruelties. Before long I began to smoke and later to have a drink now and then.[48]

In gunrooms and wardrooms across the Fleet, officers had a monthly mess account for food and wine. The size of the wine bill was reviewed by a vigilant Captain to ensure his officers were not drinking to excess. A warship, especially in the remote Scapa Flow, became the place where young officers learnt both the socialising element of alcohol and the pain of the hangover. For some the institutionalised role of alcohol within the navy became an extremely difficult aspect of naval life to negotiate. The relative temperance of naval officers was frequently commented upon in their annual performance reports. Indeed, in the RN at this time it warranted a specific section in the report. Peyton Kimlin wrote to his kindred soul Ben Howells of his life in *Canada* in the following terms:

> The hospitality of the RN is remarkable. When you go into a strange mess everybody rises up and falls over himself to give you drinks and cigarettes. This is one of the decent things about the navy and it is about the first thing you notice about it.
>
> Another thing is the absolutely impersonal nature of gunnery instruction. The substitution of the word 'target' for an enemy ship full of human beings like yourself whom you are out to kill is a strange thing; inasmuch as it does not convey or suggest to me any of the feelings which I experienced just before I was going into action. When you come back to port again, everything seems so damned ordinary, in contrast to the tremendous issues at stake (in your own mind) a short time before. You come back to port and you coal ship, you curse the wind, weather, coal dust, and you curse the Hun for lying in his lair and keeping you awake at sea. Then you finish coaling, you wash yourself, and sleep for the next 24 hours and wonder whether the Hun will come back.[49]

About 11.30 pm on 9 July 1917 the majority of the Grand Fleet were at anchor or otherwise in the confines of Scapa Flow. The silence of the

'You finish coaling, you wash yourself, and sleep for the next 24 hours and wonder whether the Hun will come back.' Coaling in HMAS Australia. (RAN)

anchorage was broken by an immense explosion which consumed the battleship HMS *Vanguard*. All ships went to action stations assuming the Fleet was under submarine attack. Unusually for that time there was quite a few boats in the water. They were waiting to take officers from a concert in the battleship HMS *Royal Oak*. These and other boats, invariably coxswained by midshipmen including some from the Pioneer Class were sent to where *Vanguard* had been at anchor minutes before. Both *Canada* and *Sydney* were just half a mile from *Vanguard's* anchorage. In *Canada*, fearing sabotage:

> Jimmy Ley put extra sentries on the magazines and told them to shoot anybody that went there out of hours, but the only one who ever went there out of hours was old Jimmy himself, who used to go round seeing the sentry was there. But they didn't shoot him fortunately.[50]

There were only two survivors who were picked up by *Sydney's* boats. The sea was covered with oil but the violence of the explosion was such that there was very little débris. Among the 842 dead were two of *Sydney's* crew who were onboard the *Vanguard* in the ship's cells at the time.[51] More fortunate was *Vanguard's* gunnery officer and future Rear Admiral Commanding the Australian Squadron, Wilfred Custance who was dining onboard a nearby ship.

A Board of Enquiry was chaired by the now Rear Admiral William Nicholson and on which *Canada's* Captain served. It concluded that the explosion was probably caused by transferred heat from a bunker fire setting off cordite in an adjacent magazine, or abnormal deterioration of the cordite.[52] During the war four other ships blew up due to the spontaneous detonation of cordite.[53]

There was a difference in the experiences of the midshipmen embarked in the remote Scapa Flow-based battleships from that of the midshipmen in the battlecruisers based in Rosyth. There was little diversion for those in Scapa Flow with only the occasional walk or sporting fixture on a bleak island in the anchorage. Eric Feldt wrote home of a dinner onboard one of the visiting battlecruisers where there was talk of 'long forgotten things girls, trees, and things like that'.[54] Eric was also receiving letters and parcels from his girlfriend Gwen back in Nowra. He wrote to sister Pat that:

> She writes very nice letters, I'm beginning to think I've shot my bolt, I look forward to them so much. If my feelings are the same as now, when I get enough 'oof' I shall certainly do the deed. It's a great feeling, isn't it, Pat?[55]

For those based at Scapa Flow leave was particularly welcome and most of the Pioneer Class had relations to visit and stay. Norman Calder wrote reflectively to his mother of one such visit:

> We heard the guns firing so we knew it was an air raid. Really the war isn't realised in Australia. When I heard the guns barking, coming nearer and then receding and knowing that the bombs were being dropped and men and women and children were losing their lives, I think I realised in a small extent the awfulness of the war.[56]

The long periods of fleet inactivity between opportunities for action tested the sailors' morale in both the British and German fleets. In a letter from Eddy Nurse to Ben Howells in which he welcomed Ben's news he would enlist in the AIF, he lamented:

> You will find me lazy and all the rest of it through lack of work and quite different to what I used to be. You say something about being in the 'thick of it'. It's absolutely the reverse. It's rotten, dinkum, same old routine day after day, nothing exciting. Now then we go exercising and that's all. It's funny the letters I get, hoping the North Sea is not using me roughly, etc. etc.—heartbreaking they are, really. So you see how we stand.[57]

In dealing with this morale challenge Admiral Jellicoe and his successor Admiral Beatty were able to sustain generally good morale. They did so by an active sea training regime and a vigorous sporting program. The centrepiece of the latter was the annual boxing championship. In 1917 it was held on 22-23 August onboard the battleship HMS *Ajax* at anchor in Scapa Flow. In the lead up to the event ships conducted preliminary contests in the different weight divisions to decide upon their ship's champions. To the surprise of the Grand Fleet officers the Australian midshipmen figured prominently in the officers' bouts. Thousands of Grand Fleet officers and sailors watched from any upper deck vantage point to view the boxing ring set up on the battleship's deck. In the preliminary fights, Leigh Watkins, Hugh MacKenzie, Harry Showers and Dick Cunningham all won their preliminary bouts. Frank Larkins was then unlucky to lose his match. Perhaps the most memorable match of the first day was Frank Getting's light heavyweight match which had to be stopped in his favour. At the end of the day a Jervis Bay midshipman was left to contest the finals in each weight division. The following afternoon, Admiral Beatty and other flag officers, viewed the hard-fought finals from ringside seats. Dick Cunningham after weeks of sweating down and starving won the bantamweight championship. Frank Getting won his light heavyweight championship bout with a technical knock-out in the first round. Harry Showers and Hugh MacKenzie had to fight each other in the preliminary final. Hugh MacKenzie won on points and then went on to win the middleweight in great style. Beatty presented the cups to the winners and Harry Showers received a good loser prize. Norman Calder wrote that he 'witnessed a great victory for Australia' and wrote to Commander Grant with the stunning results.[58]

Frank Getting's boxing victory was put into perspective when he received a letter from his only brother George, dated 7 October 1917. George, a Private serving in the 5th Field Ambulance, had been wounded by shrapnel in the back during the Battle for Passchendaele while tending wounded at an advanced dressing station on the Menin Road. He had been moved to the Canadian 7th General Hospital at Etaples near the coast where he wrote he was getting 'tip top' treatment. While at Etaples he also wrote to his Parisian relatives saying he was hoping to see them soon. Eleven days later George Getting was dead, likely having succumbed to infection.[59] It was a cruel irony for their father Paul Getting who had emigrated to Australia for a new life away from the Old World.[60]

Another killed in the same battle was Joe Burnett's oldest brother William who was serving as a Sergeant in the 35th Battalion.[61] William had joined the AIF following the Gallipoli landings but was discharged in May 1916, following the death of his mother and sole remaining parent. Once the family situation had stabilised William rejoined in November 1916.

Also destined to serve on the Western Front was Adrian Watts. Shortly after his eighteenth birthday he left his position as a clerk and successfully enlisted in the army for a second time. He became a sapper and sailed from Melbourne on 28 February 1918 in the troopship *Nestor* as one of the reinforcements for the much depleted Signals companies in the AIF. Coincidentally *Nestor* had also taken young George Getting to the war in an earlier voyage. Ben Howells' reading of the German advances on the Russian Front led him to also enlist in the AIF on 12 July 1918. With four other sons in the AIF this was against his parents' wishes. They were saved any further anguish as the war would end before Ben completed his initial training.

VI

During the course of the war both the British and the Germans had laid increasingly sophisticated minefields in the North Sea to constrain and sink some of the opposing naval forces. In the Heligoland Bight there were German minefields silently guarding the approaches to the German naval port of Wilhelmshaven. There were also British minefields laid to sink German submarines departing to attack Allied merchant shipping. In late 1917 the British had become increasingly aware of German minesweeping efforts to remove the British mine threat to their U-boats. These activities were protected by ships of the High Seas Fleet. In early November reports from British agents, Room 40 and RN submarines indicated that some German heavy units were at sea. On 16 November 1917 the Admiralty ordered a battlecruiser and cruiser sortie supported by the First Battle Squadron of the Grand Fleet.[62] *Glorious* was one of the battlecruisers whilst *Royal Sovereign* and *Canada* were among the assigned battleships. It was intended that the cruisers would engage the German minesweepers on the outer edge of the minefield with the battlecruisers ready to engage any German heavy units drawn into the battle. The battleships would lie further offshore to come in and settle the matter if needed. Onboard *Glorious* Eddy Nurse wrote:

> After evening quarters (4 pm) the Captain cleared lower deck and had everyone aft. He then addressed us. We already had steam up and were about to leave for the North Sea. He told us that the Admiralty had fairly definite information of the enemy's movements and that we were going out to surprise them. We could expect to go into action, all being well, about 7 am next day. We steamed out that night and steered towards Heligoland.[63]

In *Royal Sovereign* Norman Calder was in charge of one of her 6-inch guns. In anticipation of a great battle Norman Calder wrote on his eighteenth birthday:

> I hope we go into action but I think the (6-inch) batteries will suffer. I will try and do my duty and if I don't come out of it I suppose we must

take it as it comes. However I don't suppose they will be out when we get there.[64]

The prospect of action at 7 am highlighted the accuracy of information about German movements possessed by the Admiralty. The looming battle however was fraught with the additional dangers from the various minefields in Heligoland Bight. To further complicate matters some sown mines were 'permanent' whilst others were fitted with thirty-eight day sinking plugs to neutralize them when no longer needed for a mission. The RN, in an attempt to keep track of this complicated and changing situation, gave the charting and promulgating responsibility of these minefields to the Hydrographer of the Navy. He would in turn report minefield coordinates to the Admiralty and the Commander-in-Chief, Admiral Beatty. Unfortunately this clear, if complex, picture was not passed in the same form to Beatty's subordinate Admirals. Therefore as the five Admirals and Commodores commanding the battleship, battlecruiser and cruiser squadrons proceeded into the evening gloom towards their assigned stations, they all had differing versions of the minefield charts.

For their part the Germans had embarked on a 'Sticfahren' or 'thrust voyage' to accurately chart a clear passage through the British minefields. In command was Rear Admiral Ludwig von Reuter, a veteran of both the Battles of Dogger Bank and Jutland. He was flying his flag in the battleship *Kaiser* with her sister-ship *Kaiserin* in company. In closer support of the German minesweepers were cruisers and destroyers. The two German battleships, armed with ten 12-inch guns apiece were no match for the larger and more powerful heavy British units closing in on them.

At 6.30 am on 17 November the two battlecruisers *Courageous* and *Glorious* neared the Germans. In support were two light cruiser squadrons and a brace of small destroyers. Acting Vice Admiral Trevylyan Napier flew his flag in *Courageous*. About ten miles to the west were six battlecruisers *Lion* (Vice Admiral Pakenham), *Princess Royal, Tiger, New Zealand* and *Repulse*. The officers and sailors all readied for action. As expected

Battleships and battlecruisers at sea in 1917.
(WL Reilly collection)

multiple sightings of three groups of German ships were made. To the north were a clutch of destroyers and minesweepers, a central group of U-boats and to the south some light cruisers. Eddy Nurse's battle position was in charge of the forward triple 4-inch gun just below the bridge on the starboard-side. It was a relatively exposed position close to the forward 15-inch gun turret. He wrote:

> Anyway, everybody was ready to go to action stations about 6.45 am and sure enough at a couple of minutes to 7 'action stations' sounded off. I rushed up to my S1 group of 4-inch guns, got them loaded and ready. And then I saw two German cruisers on the horizon.[65]

Both *Glorious* and *Courageous* opened fire almost simultaneously. Because the western horizon was still in gloom the arrival of the battlecruisers' 15-inch shell splashes announced their arrival to the Germans. Eddy Nurse, his heart pounding, recalled:

> Our 15-inch guns boomed and all 4-inch guns opened fire as well. The range was but 11,000 yards. Our first shot blew my cap away - I couldn't see it straight away and left it. I watched the German cruisers between shots and then saw flashes from their guns. I said to myself 'Those shells will be here in 20 seconds or so. Will I be blown up? What should I be thinking of in these my last moments?' But I didn't think of anything in particular. It was all very exciting. Of course we

were all used to our own gunfire. I had at times been able to see 3 or 4 feet down the muzzles of our 15-inch guns as they fired. But we were belting along at 30 knots and everyone was excited. I rushed orders about loading and banging of breech blocks and so on. Then their shells commenced landing round us – fountains of water would go up just in front of us. But within a minute, the Germans realising their inferiority in strength had one of their destroyers put up a thick black smoke screen which completely hid them. I think our own 15-inch guns went on for some time after. However that was the last we saw of them. Our four own light cruiser squadrons went in after them at full speed in close formation with rapid spitting of flame from their guns. It was a great sight. Later they got within range of the big German ships and got some 15-inch into them and retired.[66]

Admiral von Reuter undeterred by the enemy strength pushed his cruisers and destroyers forward to protect his small ships. The German destroyers laid smoke to provide a visual cover but it was too late for the armed trawler *Kehdingen* which was struck by a British shell and started to sink. From *Lion's* bridge Vice Admiral Pakenham could hear the battle and see the gun flashes. He ordered his battlecruisers to increase speed and close the enemy. For the British Admirals, uncertainty surrounded the growing battle. Dense smoke from the German destroyers, combined with an incomplete knowledge of the German strength behind the smoke called for some caution. Not so the fearless Commodore Walter Cowan, a contemporary and close friend of Admiral Beatty.[67] He commanded the First Light Cruiser Squadron from the cruiser *Caledon*. Without hesitation he led his three other cruisers *Galatea*, *Royalist* and *Inconstant* through the German smokescreen and immediately entered a hot engagement with German light cruisers *Nürnberg*, *Pillau*, *Königsberg* and *Frankfurt* on the other side. Napier took *Courageous* and *Glorious* supported by the cruisers of Rear Admiral Edwyn Alexander-Sinclair's 6th Light Cruiser Squadron (*Cardiff*, *Ceres*, *Calypso* and *Caradoc*) to the south. This was to skirt the smokescreen and try and re-engage the enemy.

At about 8.10 am Napier found three of the German cruisers which he re-engaged with sustained fire. After ten minutes the German cruisers

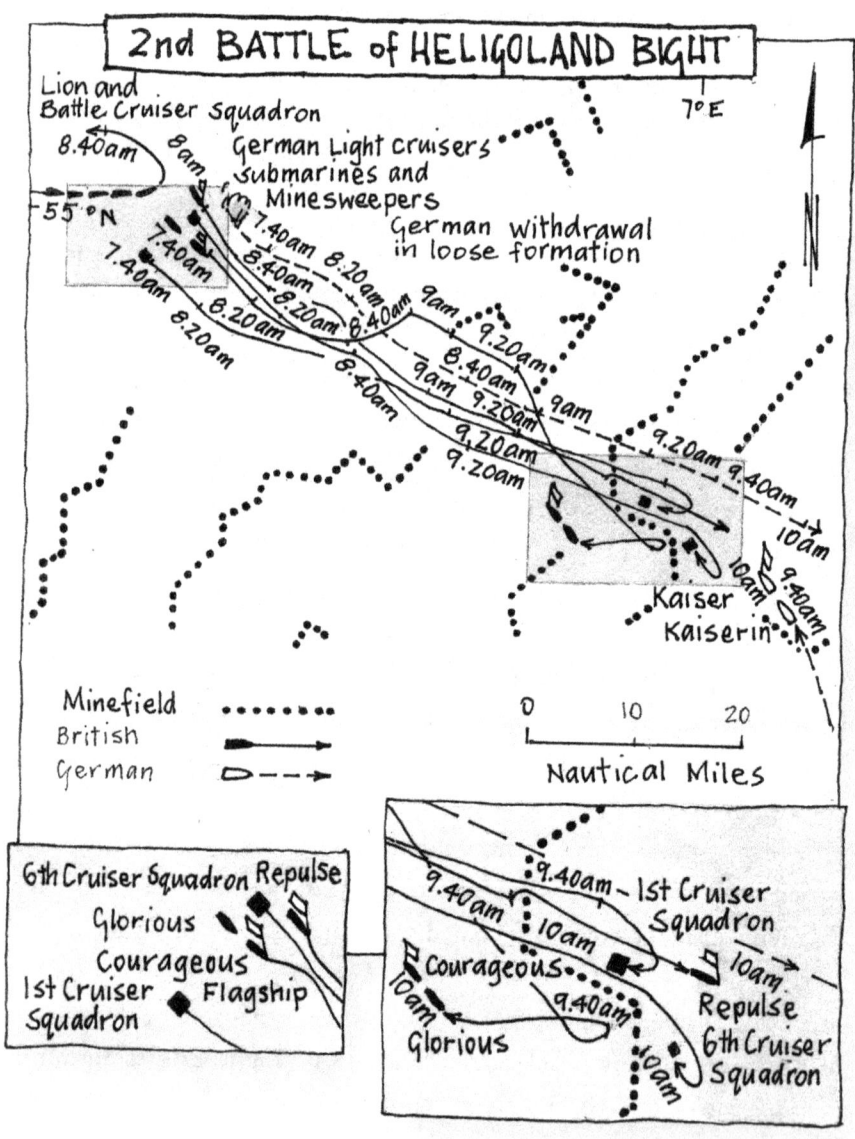

were receiving hits and were in a perilous position. They had succeeded in drawing the British ships in a southeasterly direction whilst the minesweepers had retired north-east to the awaiting German battleships. At 8.20 am the German cruisers laid another smokescreen which caused the obscured British ships to check their fire. Von Reuter ordered his destroyers to add a further smokescreen. Napier, mindful his ships were nearing the minefield, would not follow and bore away to the north-east until the situation became clear. Shortly thereafter the smoke cleared and the 6th Light Cruiser Squadron, the closest to the enemy exchanged telling blows with the German cruisers.

Napier resumed the chase. At 8.58 am Pakenham in *Lion* ordered a general recall. This was based on his assessment that the force was getting too close to the minefield and his reading of Napier's signal reporting lost contact with the enemy as a final report. This was far from the case. Napier sent clarifying signals to buy more time for his force to re-engage the elusive enemy. As the chase to the south-east continued the 6-inch armed cruisers of both British cruiser squadrons continued the action when their quarry became intermittently visible. Von Reuter in an effort to break off the engagement, ordered yet another smokescreen, followed by a torpedo attack. Both *Royalist* and *Cardiff* were narrowly missed by torpedoes which crossed their bows. At 9.30 am another smokescreen was laid and further unsuccessful torpedo attacks were launched from both destroyers and a submarine. At about this time Napier assessed he was once again nearing the limit of the safe water from the minefield. He was receiving reports of damage to the German cruisers in the continuing gunnery exchange. This encouraged him to hang on. At 9.40 am *Calypso* was hit by a shell on the upper conning tower which killed not only its occupants but Captain Herbert Edwards and other officers on the bridge. *Calypso* remained in the fight with her gunnery officer Lieutenant Henry Clarke assuming command. Just as the valiant cruiser was righting herself the squadron had heavy shell splashes fall among them. These were from *Kaiser* and *Kaiserin* who had worked around to the south.

Caledon was hit by a 12-inch shell from one of the battleships.[68] Among the wounded was 21-year old Ordinary Seaman John Carless who continued to man his 6-inch gun. For his actions he was posthumously awarded the Victoria Cross. His citation read:

> For most conspicuous bravery and devotion to duty. Although mortally wounded in the abdomen, he still went on serving the gun at which he was acting as rammer, lifting a projectile and helping to clear away the other casualties. He collapsed once, but got up, tried again, and cheered on the new gun's crew. He then fell and died. He not only set a very inspiring and memorable example, but he also, whilst mortally wounded, continued to do effective work against the King's enemies.[69]

The British cruisers came round to port to open range with the new battlecruiser HMS *Repulse*, which had been sensibly detached by Pakenham to support the engagement, providing much needed cover. The final exchange was from *Repulse* which hit *Königsberg* with two 15-inch shells. The first struck among her funnels and caused a serious fire in her coal bunker and killed nine sailors.[70] The second failed to explode and would eventually adorn Admiral von Reuter's home on a wooden pedestal.

Dense fog now rolled in and effectively lowered the curtain on what would be known as the Second Battle of Heligoland Bight. Eddy Nurse recorded:

> Our Captain 'Dusty' Miller fumed up and down our bridge. Apparently we had direct orders not to follow up and everybody was wanting to rush in. Our Grand Fleet was some distance behind all ready for a big fleet action—another Jutland. But nothing happened.[71]

This fleet action was to be the only one the Pioneer Class would experience and their presence in the battle was proudly reported in Australian newspapers with the banner line *Australian Midshipmen in Action*.[72] For *Royal Sovereign* and *Canada* midshipmen it was a day closed up in their various action stations and only hearing the thud of guns in the fog. Eric Feldt recounted:

> We couldn't even see the next ship ahead until she burnt a search light on us. Later, we heard that the Admiral in the *Emperor of India*, flagship leading our column, had pulled his officers about him on the

bridge and said, in his hoarse voice, 'I don't know where we are. I don't where the enemy is. If I see anything, I'm going to ram. More steam, engineer, commander, more steam'.[73]

For *Australia's* midshipmen the ship was once again in dock when an engagement had taken place. Harry Showers wrote to classmates in other ships of the experiences of the *Glorious* midshipmen. Dick Cunningham related in a letter to his parents, 'This was the first real show the Australian cadets have had. It was jolly fine so far as we were concerned. We were not hit, though shells fell all round'.[74]

VII

At the beginning of January 1918 with *Glorious* in dock, it was arranged for her five Australian midshipmen to have a month's experience in submarines. They received orders to join the large K-Class submarines on Australia Day.

The K-boats were unique, at the technological cutting edge and controversial. They were unique in that they had steam propulsion replete with two retractable funnels for operations on the surface. The steam boilers gave the K-boats a speed of about 24 knots. That was enough to keep station with most of the fleet although the newer capital ships such as *Glorious* could still outpace them. The procedures to prepare for diving underwater and revert to battery propulsion were complicated and fraught with opportunities for both mechanical failures or human error. Already there had been numerous accidents and 'near misses' with the luckless *K13* sinking on her acceptance trials. One submariner said the problem with the K-boats was they had 'too many damned holes'.[75]

The K-boats were at the technological cutting edge because like the earlier but slower J Class, they were designed to operate with the Fleet. Hitherto submarines with their slow speed had operated on lone patrols to sink ships in areas where their prospective targets were likely to pass. The concept for the K-boats was that they would keep pace with and ahead of the Fleet. As the two opposing battle fleets closed for action the K-boats would submerge and hopefully wreak havoc on the German High Seas Fleet.

The concept was ahead of its time and operations with the Fleet by a submarine would not become a practical proposition until the advent of nuclear-powered submarines over forty years later.

The radical nature of the K-Boats and their succession of mishaps led inevitably to controversy within the RN. Indeed this started as soon as their concept was first mooted in 1913. Admiral Jellicoe wrote presciently, 'The most fatal error imaginable would be to put steam engines in a submarine'.[76] Among the submariners they were deeply unpopular because of their complexities, inherent risks and that they tied submariners to the Fleet rather than acting as free agents. The Commanding Officer of *K15*, Commander George Bradshaw reflected the mood:

> I never met anybody who had the least affection for the K class and they were looked on with fear and loathing. After all, they murdered many of their officers and crews.[77]

At Rosyth, there were two K-Boat Flotillas to work with the battlecruisers. The 12th Flotilla was led by Captain Charles 'Tiny' Little in the light cruiser HMS *Fearless*. The five *Glorious* midshipmen joined the 13th Flotilla commanded by the experienced submariner Commander Ernest Leir in the light cruiser HMS *Ithuriel*. Frank Getting joined *K11*, Eddy Nurse *K12*, Hugh MacKenzie *K14*, Dick Cunningham *K17* while Harry Showers joined *K22* (the salvaged and renamed former *K13*).[78] There were other junior officers receiving submarine experience in the Flotillas and these included Midshipman Lord Louis Mountbatten in the 12th Flotilla. Dick Cunningham, like most of the midshipmen was assigned the task of being the Captain's 'doggie' with the loosely defined task of following the Captain and running messages. From this vantage point Dick got a good appreciation of how the submarine organization worked and the crew liked the young Australian. One of their number, George Kimber remembered Dick seventy years later as a 'nice young chap'.[79]

Because of the complexities of the *Kalamity Ks* their commanding officers were all commanding a submarine for at least the second time. Eddy Nurse's commanding officer was Lieutenant Commander John

Bower who had successfully commanded *E42* on patrols out of Harwich. Eddy's reception onboard *K12* differed greatly from his more formal experience on joining *Glorious*:

> The first thing my Captain asked me was 'Can you play bridge?' I said 'not very well Sir.' He threw me a book of the rules and said I would have 48 hours clear to learn. But I played the same night and all went well.[80]

The K-boats had only been shifted from Scapa Flow to Rosyth the previous month. Admiral Beatty hoped this move for them to join the battlecruisers and the 5th Battle Squadron would give the K-boats more chance of seeing action. The standard routine in Rosyth was for departures of the squadrons and flotillas to occur during the evening. The ships would proceed down the channel with only dimmed navigation lights. The ships had to negotiate multiple booms strung across the channel to prevent German incursions. This sailing routine reduced the opportunities for any spies to report movements and increased the targeting difficulties for any German U-boat lying in wait off the Firth of Forth. The evening sailings however increased the navigational difficulty not only from the shoals along the waterway, but also heightened the risks of collision between the warships and small craft that used the Firth of Forth.

On the evening of 31 January 1918, the Rosyth-based fleet proceeded out of harbour for a major exercise, code-named EC1, with the Grand Fleet in the North Sea. The formation of about forty Rosyth ships were under the command of Vice Admiral Hugh Evan-Thomas who transferred his flag from the battleship HMS *Barham* to the battlecruiser *Courageous*.

Harry Showers found that the evening had a special significance to the ship's company of *K22*. It was one year to the day that many of the present crew had been rescued from the bottom of Gareloch when the boat, then unhappily named *K13* had sunk on builder's trials. While 48 men were rescued, 32 were not so lucky. On this evening the overriding sentiment in the boat was just to survive the anniversary.[81]

At 6.30 pm *Courageous* weighed anchor and led nearly forty warships downstream in strict radio silence. Just over half a mile behind the battlecruiser were the cruiser *Ithuriel* and her 13th Flotilla in order *K11*, *K17*, *K14*, *K12* and *K22*.[82] Once at sea these submarines would screen ahead of the battlecruisers *Australia*, *New Zealand*, *Indomitable* and *Inflexible* who followed about 30 minutes behind with their attendant destroyers. This group was strung out over 10 miles. They were followed at an interval of about 15 minutes steaming by a similar formation of the cruiser *Fearless*, the 12th Flotilla (in order *K4*, *K3*, *K6* and *K7*) and finally three battleships of the 5th Battle Squadron and their screening destroyers.

It was an increasingly misty night and the formation was proceeding at 16 knots. In the submarines there were typically five men on the open conning tower, the commanding officer, the officer of the watch, the quartermaster, signalman and a lookout. The remainder of the crew were either manning their leaving-harbour stations down below, having dinner or were in their bunks to rest before their night watches.

At 7.06 pm as *Courageous* passed by May Island and through the opened inner boom she increased speed to 19 knots. She was followed about five minutes later by the cruiser *Ithuriel* and her 13th Submarine Flotilla.

As the 13th Flotilla passed May Island, visibility was anywhere between one half to a mile. The bridge crews in all ships strained to keep sight of the dimmed white stern light of the vessel ahead. At about 7.10 pm Commander Thomas Calvert in *K11* sighted the dimmed white light of a vessel she was both overtaking and converging on a collision course. He altered course and reduced speed. It was one of the minesweeping trawlers *Culblean*, *Strathella* or *North King*. The trawlers on seeing the submarine's looming lights turned on navigation lights to full brilliance. With the submarines only 500 yards apart there was no time for Calvert to indicate his actions. Commander Henry Hearn in *K17*, which was the next boat, conformed to *K11*'s movements.

Commander Tom Harbottle in *K14* initially saw the two submarines go off their assigned navigation track and maintained his course. Then he sighted the red portside lights of two of the trawlers on her starboard bow.

The surprised *K14* came around to port to keep clear of the minesweepers. Critically at this point *K14's* rudder jammed and the boat continue to circle in port back towards the following submarines. At the same time Harbottle switched his navigation lights to full brilliance and thankfully saw the next in line, *K12*, pass safely astern of him.

Harbottle expected the last in line, *K22*, would pass even further clear of his position. Instead of stopping to unjam his rudder, Harbottle noted:

> ... that the two boats astern of me had followed in my wake, I decided not to stop, but went full speed on my port screw and slow ahead starboard endeavouring to check the swing to port and at the same time get out on the port wing of the Fleet's advance.[83]

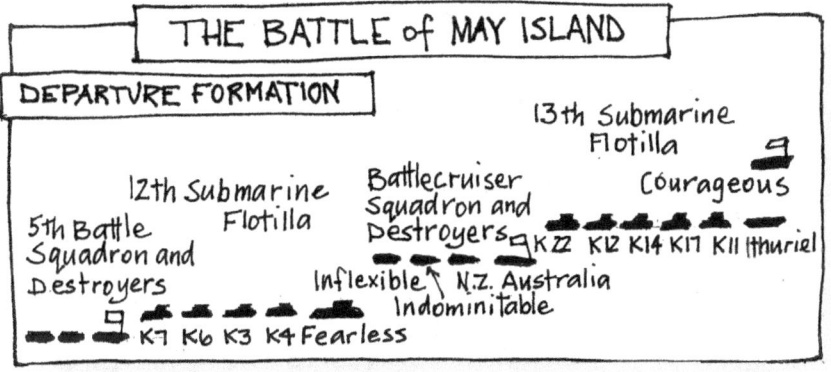

After six minutes the rudder was freed and *K14* increased speed to resume her course. *K22* however, had maintained the navigation track and her officer of the watch was attempting to relocate *K12's* stern light. Instead at 7.16 pm he detected a red portside light of a vessel fine on the starboard bow, crossing ahead of *K22*. He ordered hard a starboard to avoid collision and alerted the crew below to the impending collision.[84] Harbottle in *K14* had not seen *K22* until too late.

At a closing speed of over 20 knots it was impossible for Harbottle to avoid collision and *K22* sliced into *K14* cutting off a part of her bow.[85] The collision occurred before all the watertight doors could be shut. Harry Showers was responsible for the forward door. He ordered it to be closed once all the men who could be seen had clambered aft. Just as the door was being shut a faint call was heard and Harry instinctively plunged into the darkened fore end with the water steadily rising. He found and brought out 20 year old Able Seaman George Knell and then closed the door.[86]

Like Harbottle before him, Commander Charles De Burgh's first reaction was to prevent any of the oncoming warships from ramming the damaged *K22*. A jury rig of lights was tied to the conning tower to illuminate the boat. Meanwhile down below the crew, including Harry Showers, were involved in either assessing the damage or controlling the flood in the forward compartment of the submarine. A particular dread for submariners was the fear that the water ingress would reach the battery compartments where their combination would result in lethal chlorine gas filling the boat's interior. In the course of his work Harry was exposed to leaking chlorine gas and would later say he took up smoking to rid himself of the taste.[87]

For Hugh MacKenzie and the rest of the crew in *K14*, matters were more desperate as they tried to prevent the boat from sinking. *K22*'s bow had sliced deep into the portside crew sleeping quarters behind the torpedo compartment. A part of the bow had broken off and two sailors were drowned. From the central control room efforts were coordinated to close watertight doors. This was hampered by loose gear and wreckage, but the crucial door to the damaged forward compartments was sealed. The situation in *K14* remained perilous. On the bridge, Harbottle had a sailor join him with a signal pistol ready to ward off any oncoming shipping with a flare.

Meanwhile *K22* was able to limp clear of the planned navigation track to avoid being struck by following ships. De Burgh signalled in a coded message to *Ithuriel* that both submarines had been in a collision and were down by the bows. For some time however *Ithuriel* and the lead section of the Flotilla remained unaware of the accident and continued to proceed to sea.

While encoding the message may have prevented any German warships from intercepting the message, it wasted precious time as it was prepared for transmission. More time was consumed at the other end in decoding. It was over an hour before Commander Leir received the report in *Ithuriel*. This was too late to warn the four battlecruisers of the 2nd Battle Cruiser Squadron following the 13th Flotilla.

Australia, with James Esdaile, Joe Burnett, Winn Reilly, Rupert Long, Alfred Conder and Cyril Sadleir manning various leaving harbour stations on the bridge and elsewhere approached the stricken submarines. At 7.38 pm on passing May Island the first three ships altered course and increased speed to 21 knots in accordance with the navigation plan.

Captain Oliver Backhouse and Rear Admiral Arthur Leveson on *Australia's* bridge were first alerted to trouble by one of Harbottle's red flares arcing out of the mist. This drew their attention to an odd array of lights on the water. As they rapidly closed the scene a small light flashed 'HAVE BEEN IN COLLISION REQUIRE ASSISTANCE'. Leveson detached the destroyer HMS *Gabriel* to assist these unknown ships. It was unfortunate more information was not provided which would have resulted in greater assistance.

Australia, *New Zealand* and then *Indomitable* passed clear of the submarines. The last in the line was *Inflexible*. In that ship the officer of the watch was late in receiving the order to alter course in accordance with the navigation plan. So when the ship came onto the new course she was to port of the planned track and on a collision course with the hapless *K22*. *Inflexible* had also lost sight of *Indomitable's* stern light. Alerted by the red light they saw one collection of white lights. When they saw another white light they mistook it for the illusive *Indomitable*. A green starboard sidelight appeared to be associated with it. At a couple of hundred yards distant a collision was inevitable. At 7.40 pm *K22's* bridge staff watched transfixed as one of the battlecruisers' escorting destroyers missed them by about 10 feet. A sailor looking astern for more ships coming out of harbour, shouted a warning but it was too late. *Inflexible* was bearing down on *K22*. Both ships had only seconds to manoeuvre to avoid each other. And their efforts were in vain. *Inflexible* struck *K22*, a glancing blow along about thirty feet of the submarine's bow section. *Inflexible's* bow ripped off the starboard external ballast and fuel tanks. The force of the blow also pushed the boat down and on to its side. Many of the crew between decks sustained injuries against fittings from this unalerted collision. Surprisingly to all onboard *K22*, their luck seemed to have turned and she survived her collision. The crew on the conning tower read INFLEXIBLE on the stern nameplate as the battlecruiser steamed on into the night.[88]

Captain Oliver Backhouse and Rear Admiral Arthur Leveson in HMAS Australia *managed to avoid the damaged* K-22. (RAN)

It was not until about 7.40 pm that Commander Leir in *Ithuriel* finally received a properly decoded signal reporting the collision. What he didn't know was that *Gabriel* was already in attendance. He decided to reverse course and with his remaining submarines render assistance. Navigation lights were switched to full brilliance. In an attempt to keep clear of the Fleet he planned to complete a slow turn to starboard which should have taken his ships to the south of the channel. At 8.10 pm his Flotilla commenced the turn in succession in a long 'conga line'.

This was a fateful decision. While understandable and borne out of a sense of responsibility for his submarines, it involved a hazardous undertaking with the darkened Fleet still proceeding out of harbour at increasing speed. A more prudent course of action would have been to report the accident and have Vice Admiral Evan-Thomas in *Courageous* to allocate rescue coordination duties to a Flag Officer or ship further down the exiting line of ships.

The implications of Leir's decision became apparent soon enough. As he completed his turn he found himself right ahead of *Australia* on a collision course. *Ithuriel* was able to alter course and passed about 600 yards to the south of the battlecruiser. Her submarines were less nimble and the last in the line was *K12*. As Commander Bower saw *Australia* loom out of the mist he ordered 'hard a starboard'. Eddy Nurse wrote:

> We were very lucky in *K12*. It was only by the grace of God and Bowers good judgement that the *Australia* didn't sink us outright. In the darkness he saw her about 240 yards away, ordered the helm hard over and we slid past her huge bulk at a relative speed of about 30 knots.[89]

Rear Admiral Leveson also deserves credit. In quickly sizing up the situation he decided the best chance of avoiding collision was to maintain course. *Australia* missed *K12* by less than five feet and her wash caused the submarine to roll very heavily.

Besides the battlecruisers, *Ithuriel* and the submarines had also to repeatedly dodge the screening destroyers. There were multiple near misses and the 13th Flotilla's formation became increasingly ragged and strung out. *K17* brought up the rear. It was hoped that the rest of the Fleet were clearing the channel further to the north.

Having successfully passed the outgoing battlecruisers and their destroyer screen Commander Leir sent a signal informing Evan-Thomas of the collision and his decision to return to render assistance. Because of the backlog of signals, this report was not read by the Admiral's staff until 9.20 pm, an hour and forty minutes after the decision was taken.

The next group of ships to negotiate past was *Fearless* and the 12th Flotilla. At this stage Captain Little in *Fearless* was still unaware that the 13th Flotilla was returning.

At about 8.30 pm the bridge watch in *Fearless* detected a series of white steaming lights fine on her port bow crossing from left to right ahead of her.

Shortly after another contact was sighted about half a mile astern of the others. In accordance with the Rules of the Road, *Fearless*, as the privileged vessel, held course and Captain Little expected the approaching ships to alter course and pass astern. *Fearless* switched on its navigation lights to full brilliance. At a relative speed of in excess of 30 knots events moved quickly. When a collision seemed inevitable, Little ordered full speed astern and came hard to port.

In *K17* the order was given to close all watertight doors. Down below many of the crew, feeling seasick in the conditions, sprang from their bunks to accomplish the task.[90] The rakish bow of *Fearless* tore into *K17* just forward of the conning tower near the wardroom. As the ships separated *K17* passed down the portside of *Fearless* and started to settle as tons of water entered the ruptured hull.

Inside the submarine it was a scene of havoc. The surge of water was all powerful in the forward end of the boat. The water poured into the battery compartment causing the loss of lighting and the creation of a greenish cloud of chlorine gas. In spite of the hellish conditions below all the crew miraculously managed to escape to the upper deck. Those not already in the water moved progressively aft as *K17* settled by the bows. Commander Hearn and his signalman remained on the bridge to try and ward off any approaching ship. As the submarine gathered momentum in its final dive the crew members slid into the oily and chilly waters. *K17* had remained afloat for only eight minutes following the collision with *Fearless*.

The speed of the unfolding accident was such the Captain Little only had time to order one prolonged and two short blasts (the morse letter D), the signal 'keep clear'. No other orders or information was provided to the submarines behind him. They took individual avoiding action as the picture unfolded in front of each submarine bridge.

The first of the 12th Flotilla boats, *K4*, went astern, *K3* went to port of the line to get clear. *K6* tried to alter course to avoid a submarine in front of her. It was too little too late. *K6* cut deep into *K4* which sank rapidly carrying her entire crew with her to the depths. *K7*, which came astern to avoid a collision, nevertheless lightly touched the masts and conning tower of the sinking *K4*.

What was even more tragic was that the reversing *K7* ploughed into the crew of *K17* still all floundering in the water. Some books dealing with the incident state that following destroyers passed through the survivors.[91] However, the Court of Inquiry and the Court Martial of Commander Leir, which remained closed in the National Archive until 1994, record it was *K7*.[92]

Despite an extensive search, of the 56 *K17* crew members only nine survived the churning and frigid waters, with one of those dying onboard *K7*. Dick Cunningham was not among the survivors and his body was never recovered. Eddy Nurse, himself lucky to survive the night, wrote:

We were ordered back to harbour and when safely anchored in Birkenhead Roads talked over the thing till about 2 am. We didn't want to go to bed. Cunningham was in the *K17* and had been a good pal of mine.[93]

K14 was towed back to port by the destroyer HMS *Venetian* whilst *K22*, after discharging 150 tons of fuel and water, was able to return at 3 knots under her own steam. A Board of Inquiry into the collisions was held in the battleship HMS *Queen Elizabeth* and found that Commander Harbottle of *K14* was partly responsible for the collision with *K22* by not stopping and should have sounded 'Ds' on his siren when his helm jammed. It was also found that Lieutenant Sanford in *K6* and Lieutenant Commander Gravener in *K7* could have done more to avoid their respective collisions.[94] At Commander Leir's subsequent court martial the charge of 'negligently or by default losing HM Submarine *K17*' was not proved and he was acquitted.[95]

The news of Dick Cunningham's death took a week to reach his class mates in the Scapa Flow battleships. It was met with shock and disbelief. Most did not even know their classmates were in the K-boats. Dick had been such a strong and indomitable character in the class. This had been underscored by him winning the Fleet boxing championship for his

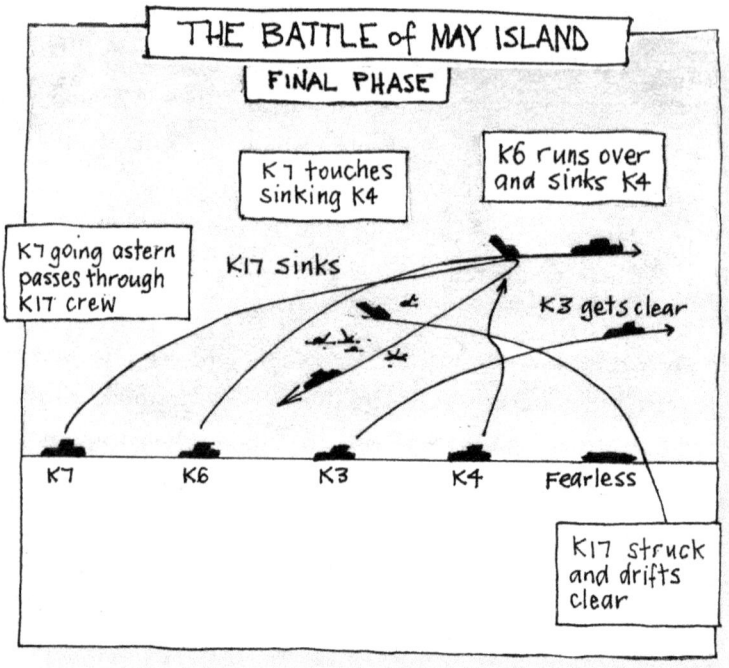

HM Submarine K-6 *showing her two funnels aft of the bridge. She sank her sistership* K-4 *which was lost with all hands.* (RN)

weight division. Norman Calder wrote, 'I never thought he would be the first to go'.⁹⁶ Peyton Kimlin wrote to Ben Howells with the news and, now keenly aware of mortality and Ben's prospective service on the Western Front, requested one of Ben's 'poems as a memento - you understand?'⁹⁷

On 9 February Dick Cunningham's father, Headmaster of Hurstville Public School received an Admiralty telegram that his son 'was drowned in the North Sea on a submarine on active service'.⁹⁸ This news came as a complete shock as his parents thought Dick was still in *Glorious*. Dealing with their son's sudden death was not helped by the sketchy details provided of the incident. In March 1919 Dick's father wrote to the Naval Secretary in Melbourne complaining that 'the information received from the Admiralty has been meagre'. In particular he asked where Dick was buried. The Naval Secretary cabled the Australian Naval Representative in London for more information but was only able to report the depth of water precluded any salvage operation of the submarine. By implication Dick's body could not be recovered.⁹⁹ Dick had actually escaped *K17* and his body had probably been washed out to sea with the tide. Dick's mother was inconsolable at his loss and burned all his letters in her grief.

'I never thought he would be the first to go.' Midshipman Dick Cunningham. The first of the Pioneer Class to be lost at sea.
(RAN)

The *Kalamity Ks* had not finished with the Pioneer Class. A fortnight after the loss of *K17*, Frank Getting and Eddy Nurse proceeded out of the Firth of Forth in *K11* and *K12* led by *Ithuriel*. They were to be part of an escort of a convoy from Scotland to Norway. These convoys had been subjected to attack from German cruisers and destroyers and it was hoped the K-boats would be able to even the score. Instead they ran into the atrocious weather of a North Sea gale. The submarines rolled violently up to 40° each side. Between decks there was considerable damage and disarray from loose items flung around compartments. Eddy recorded that he didn't eat for 36 hours and wrote 'it was the worse thing I've experienced and on we limped into Scapa Flow, feeling like drowned rats'.[100] On 19 February he wrote, 'My term in the *K12* was up. It was a tremendous relief to get away from her'.[101] It was a feeling justifiably shared by virtually all K-boat sailors.

VIII

On 30 March 1918 the *Australia* midshipmen were buoyed by the arrival onboard of Mr Dix as the Chief Gunner. He brought with him news from Jervis Bay and the best wishes of Duncan Grant who was now once more the Acting Captain of the Naval College. Dix made a great impression in the flagship, as he had done at Jervis Bay. A report of his service onboard gives an insight to the influence this former sailor had on the Pioneer Class:

> Mr Dix is a remarkably fine officer in every way. He adds a character of sound common sense and high moral tone. His influence for good on his younger messmates is most pronounced. He is a sportsman and a very good one. He is very deeply read especially in naval history.[102]

In the same vein as the *Glorious* midshipmen's service in submarines was aimed as broadening their experience, so too the junior officers of *Australia* were individually placed into the ships of the 13th Destroyer Flotilla. These destroyers routinely screened the Battle Cruiser Force. So it was that in March 1918 Joe Burnett served in HMS *Vesper*, Rupert Long in HMS *Vega* and Winn Reilly in HMS *Ulster*.

In March 1918 the Battle Cruiser Force once again mounted an operation to refresh and expand the British offensive minefields off the Kattegat, that body of water that lies between Denmark and Sweden. In this way German submarines may fall victim to mines as they commenced their patrols. Operation *AH* involved the minelayers *Princess Margaret* and *Angora* which were protected by four cruisers and eight destroyers with five battlecruisers led by *Lion* remaining offshore in case German heavy units arrived on the scene. The screening destroyers included *Vega*.

On 16 March the force sailed from Rosyth in murky conditions. Key to the operation was the ability of the minelayers to fix their positions with some precision so that the new minefield could be properly charted. Once in the Kattegat approaches it was clear that thick fog was going to make the operation impracticable. The ships duly returned to port to await improved conditions. Another sortie was made later in the month but this operation was similarly frustrated by fog. It was decided to wait until mid April for another attempt.

As the cruisers and destroyers forayed into the Kattegat about 5 am on 16 April, a strong north easterly wind cleared the fog and the operation proceeded. These improving conditions also started to reveal small vessels in the middle distance which the destroyers were dispatched to investigate. The destroyers cleared for action. Rupert Long in *Vega* was in charge of Number 3 4-inch gun. *Vega* and *Vimera* headed towards the first vessel which was the German trawler *Odin*. There were a further nine trawlers operating in the general vicinity. The destroyers removed the fishermen and one by one sank the trawlers by gunfire. *Vega* took part in the sinking of three trawlers.[103]

Over a hundred fishermen were embarked in the destroyers for landing in Leith and internment for the remainder of the war. Rupert Long returned onboard *Australia* with a fine report of his performance and the experience of at least having seen some action.[104]

During 1918 the Midshipmen were ever-alert for opportunities to see more action. One of the first opportunities to surface was a call for volunteers for the Royal Naval Air Service which, among other roles, flew bi-planes off either seaplane carriers or ships of cruiser size or larger to spot for gunfire and provide reconnaissance. James Esdaile, Harold Farncomb, Peyton Kimlin, Hugh MacKenzie, Eddy Nurse, Horace Thompson and Leigh Watkins all volunteered. Such were the hazards of the specialisation that letters were sent to their parents seeking consent. In the end none of the midshipmen were successful applicants. Hugh MacKenzie and Eddy Nurse also applied for service in RN gunboats on the Tigris River in present-day Iraq. Whilst the Admiralty acknowledged their applications they heard no more.

The rite of passage for all midshipmen was the written and oral examinations they undertook at the end of their Fleet time. Somewhat misleadingly called the Seamanship examination, it also covered navigation, gunnery, torpedo and some engineering. The Pioneer Class and other midshipmen serving at sea in the second half of the war had been spared having to meticulously complete a Midshipman's Journal, which would also have been critically assessed at this time. An examination board chaired by a captain would quiz the midshipmen on any range of evolutions, tactics or naval particulars. In the weeks leading up to the examination, the midshipmen studied whenever time and their inclination allowed. Ship's officers would generally provide ready assistance to their midshipmen, as the performance of the midshipmen reflected well on their captain and ship.

A challenge for the Pioneer Class was that their fortnight of examinations coincided with the Fleet boxing tournament. Preparations for both posed a dilemma, especially as there was a desire to repeat the previous year's great success. Hugh MacKenzie had remembered that in the 1917 championships there were few entries in the heavyweight division. He convinced Eddy Nurse that there was a fair chance they could end up in the final and 'pat each other around the ring and end up, one of them the Champion and the other the Runner up'.[105] As it transpired a couple of heavy set rugby playing officers entered and Hugh was beaten in an early bout. The tall and lanky Eddy fared better and managed points decision wins to reach the final, which was the climax of the championship. It was a brutal affair and Eddy ended up outside the ropes and when presented the runners up-cup could only see through one eye. Earlier, Peyton Kimlin was runner-up in his weight division.

The Australia *midshipmen with other members of the Gunroom stretching their legs on one of Scapa Flow's islands in 1918.* (WL Reilly Collection)
Back L to R: *Cyril Sadleir and Alfred Condor. Front is Winn Reilly on extreme left and Rupert Long on extreme right.*

When the results of their seamanship examinations were announced, all of the Pioneer Class had passed. This outcome was proudly announced by the Minister for the Navy and duly reported in the national press[106]. Now cleared for promotion, on 1 September members of the Pioneer Class became Acting Sub-Lieutenants with a single gold stripe on their sleeves.

Over the coming weeks the majority of the Pioneer Class left their ships and did so with mixed feelings. Peyton Kimlin stayed in *Canada* to consolidate his training whilst Winn Reilly was slated to become one of *Australia's* Officers of the Watch. Such was the performance of the Australian midshipmen that Commander Dalglish sought members of the next Australian batch for *Canada*. He wrote at the time:

> Personally, I have a very high opinion of all the Australian Midshipmen I have yet met. They are far above our own in intelligence and much better educated. I am afraid we are suffering from the cramming our own lads get at Osborne and Dartmouth, where they are certainly not taught to reason and I think have never had their brains properly exercised.[107]

The Pioneer Class results were a vindication of the egalitarian approach of the Naval College championed by Creswell, Pearce,

Chambers and Grant. They were to be further validated by the results of the 1914 Entry. Captain Henry Mawbey, RN, Commanding Officer of the battleship HMS *Agincourt* wrote:

> The success generally speaking of the scheme of education and training at the RAN College, is I think, accentuated, when the fact is taken into consideration that the selection of candidates is made on a <u>far</u> wider basis than is the case in the Imperial service, although the actual conditions of entry are similar. In manners, general conduct and appearance there is no noticeable difference between any of the Midshipman RAN and of these characteristics I can speak highly. The system of practically open competition which obtains, I understand in Australia, seems to me to have thoroughly justified itself, and the competition being extremely severe (about 17 to 1) the boys entered should be the pick of the community. The advantage of such a system i.e. of selection <u>from the very first</u> on a wide basis are here exemplified.[108]

On leaving the ships the Pioneer Class members all received a S-206 Officers Report from their Commanding Officers. The RN's '206' as it was commonly known, assessed an officer's general conduct, ability, temperance and special attainments. An RAN variant of the S-206 would evolve with more specific assessments on character, energy, tact, initiative, power of command as well as intelligence, physic, temperament, administration, seamanship and general officer-like qualities. These reports were vitally important for officers and their contents affected both their promotion and future postings in the Navy. Crucially, the 206 was a 'closed' report which meant an officer rarely saw its contents. The result was at times a brutally candid assessment of officers. In a typical example of the 206, Captain Charles Miller of *Glorious* reported that Frank Getting was, 'Inclined to chafe under authority, but takes advice to heart. Keen and good at athletic games. Should do well'.[109] The sporting prowess of an officer was invariably remarked upon in these reports and seen as an important attribute for a naval officer.

In lieu of the 206, the officer only received a small certificate known as a 'flimsy' which was supposed to be a summary of the 206's main contents. It was not uncommon however for the 'flimsy' to be silent on any criticism of an officer's performance contained in the 206.[110] In a typical flimsy Eddy Nurse was reported by his Captain to have ' ... conducted himself entirely to my satisfaction, a capable and promising officer'.[111] A clue to a poor 206 was if an officer's flimsy only said 'to my satisfaction'.

For most there was the opportunity to have some time in London. The now more mature young men were seeing a different side to the city. They found the Australian Officers Club was a home away from home. The Club was the place to meet up, read Australian newspapers, hear accounts of the Western Front from Army officers and obtain lodging, food and drink at moderate prices. Norman Calder's diary entry of 26 October 1918 captures the mood:

> Not a bad day but a big mist over London. I got up at 9 am and had breakfast at 10 am and met Nurse and Showers who were also going to do a gunnery course. Larkins and I went round to the Bank where I drew out £5. We had lunch at the Club and then played more billiards and Burnett and Esdaile strolled in about 3 pm. They are also going to do the course. Watkins also strolled in. Then six of us took a taxi and all got in and went to the Strand Palace where we booked a box at 'Yes Aunt'. We also ordered a table at the Trocadero. We went back to the Club and left again about six and had a good dinner at the Troc. We went up to the bar and Burnett and I managed to coax the others away and we went to the show. It was very good and they made up a verse about us much to the delight of the audience. I went back to the Club and the others turned up later.[112]

By the end of October most of the Pioneer Class had proceeded back to *Excellent* for the Destroyer Gunnery course. This prepared them for their year's service in these much smaller ships where they would obtain their bridge watchkeeping certificates. This qualification was the foundation of their service as seaman officers. There were some noteworthy exceptions. The King's Medallist Winn Reilly remained in *Australia* to become one of the bridge watchkeeping officers. Lloyd Gilling and Frank Getting were appointed to the battleships *Barham* and *Benbow* respectively.

The majority of the Pioneer Class were at *Excellent* when the Armistice ending the fighting was signed on 11 November 1918. At noon of that day innumerable sirens and whistles were sounded in the city and the port. All *Excellent* personnel were fallen-in on the parade ground and Captain Back announced the fighting had ceased. Everyone sang 'God Save the King' and gave the Monarch three cheers followed by a prayer of thanksgiving by the chaplain. *Excellent* then secured for the day. Norman Calder recorded, 'Portsmouth was crowded and full of joy. Everybody singing and dancing ... We had fizz [champagne] for dinner and met a lot of Yanks. Afterwards we went down to Southsea and met three topping girls. Mine was very pretty and we had a real good time. I managed to catch the last train home'.[113] For other class members such as Eric Feldt and John Collins serving in destroyers, the news was received in similar manner. Eric recorded:

> Armistice Day came as a great surprise to us, as it did to most people. I confess, I got tight twice that day–once before lunch, slept it off in the afternoon, then got tight again that night.[114]

On 21 November Winn Reilly, Lloyd Gilling and Frank Getting were able to witness the surrender of the German High Seas Fleet from their respective capital ships. In a remarkable meeting the two massive fleets rendezvoused in the North Sea. In a closely choreographed event the German fleet, commanded by Rear Admiral von Reuter of Heligoland Bight fame, was escorted into the Firth of Forth. *Australia* was given the honour with leading the British port column and escorted the battlecruiser *Hindenburg* into port.[115]

Rupert Long and George Armitage missed these historic events because in October they left England to join the RAN torpedo boat destroyers *Huon* and *Torrens* in the Adriatic. They travelled on a troop train from France and George was given the unenviable job of being the senior officer responsible for the troops onboard. On arrival at the home port of Brindisi Rupert found because an influenza epidemic had swept through *Huon* he would have to spend some time in *Parramatta* before joining his ship.

The six Australian ships[116] had been operating against the Austro-Hungarian Navy since October 1917. The destroyers' primary mission was to prevent the Austrian submarines from entering into the Mediterranean.

They also found themselves escorting merchantmen from the Mediterranean and into the Adriatic. The ships had been hard-worked and sailors from *Australia, Sydney* and *Melbourne* were sent out to relieve or backfill the crews.

To help detect Austrian submarines a layered defence across the entrance to the Adriatic was established comprising submarines, the torpedo boat destroyers, armed trawlers, barrage nets and then American submarine-chasers. *Huon, Parramatta* and *Yarra* were each provided a kite balloon which had a basket slung underneath for a junior officer to act as submarine lookout. The balloon in turn was secured to the stern of the destroyer by a winch. When the ship manoeuvred at speed the effect on the balloon was dramatic with the young officer having to hang on for dear life as his basket almost touched the sea in the turn. Prior to leaving England George Armitage, along with John Collins, who later joined the destroyer HMS *Spencer,* gained their Free Balloon licenses for this duty. The training included a dozen parachute jumps from a stationary balloon followed by a solo balloon flight in case the tether had to be cut. George's solo flight ended eventfully when he threw out the anchor which, instead of arresting his progress, caught and then up-rooted a fair section of a hedge. The now air-borne hedge cut a swathe through a nearby cabbage crop. George 'found it strange that the farmer took some persuading to help pack up the balloon'.[117]

By the time George Armitage and Rupert Long joined the torpedo boat destroyers the Austrians had already attempted what was to be their last offensive sortie with the loss of their battleship *Svent Istfan*. Instead of encountering Austrians, the two sub-lieutenants found themselves involved in machinations with Russia. On 3 March 1918 Russia and Germany signed the Treaty of Brest-Litovsk which ended their hostilities. Among other concessions to Germany, the Russian Bolshevik Government had ceded some of their Black Sea Fleet to the Germans in the now notionally new independent state of Ukraine.

In late October *Yarra, Torrens* and *Parramatta* left the Adriatic for the Ottoman capital of Constantinople to join the Allied ships in a show of strength following the Turkish surrender.[118] En-route on 12 November 1917, as the ships steamed passed Anzac Cove on the Dardanelles, the ships hoisted Australian flags from their port yard-arms 'in honour of Australia's glorious dead.' For George Armitage it was an opportunity for seeing the shore where his older brother Harold first saw action. Harold survived Gallipoli but in 1917, at the age of 22, and an Acting Major, was killed by a sniper's bullet at Noreuil on the Western Front.

During November and December all six Australian torpedo boat destroyers would be engaged in a variety of tasks in the Black Sea. This often consisted of ascertaining the political situation in ports and if necessary evacuating British nationals. They found part of the Ukraine under control of the Don and Kuban Cossacks who were strongly anti-Bolshevik and were seeking British support. On one occasion *Swan* proceeded up into the Sea of Azov to Marioupol and Taganrog with the French destroyer *Bisson* to engage the Cossack leadership. After discussions with General Pyotr Krasnoff, the Cossack Ataman and the presentation of the Order of Saint Vladimir 4th Class to Commander Bond, *Swan* returned to Sevastopol. The destroyers shortly departed with some British nationals and minor Russian aristocracy who sought passage out of Russia. George Armitage recalled that such was the wretched condition of their passengers that 'the flees and lice, bugs etc., were a terrible problem after these people were transported in the ship'.[119]

Enduring much more hardship at this time was Harry Vallentine. After service as crew in troopships he like some of the other members of the Pioneer Class wanted to see more action. Harry therefore joined the British Army and was now part of the British Army of the Black Sea[120]. He was a Rifleman in the 4th Battalion of the Rifle Brigade and was camped 300 km inland from the Bulgarian Black Sea coast near the capital Sofia. Since November 1915 a French, British and Serbian force including the 4th Battalion had pushed the Bulgarian Army along the Macedonian front. Malaria was endemic and both opposing forces were weakened by the disease. By July 1918 nearly two hundred of the 4th Battalion were hospitalised. Despite this and limited resources the Allied force attacked the Bulgars in difficult terrain. By September 1918 the Bulgarian Army crumbled and revolted with an armistice signed at the end of the month. For Harry and his comrades their duties became one of occupation and providing some form of law and order. As the weather cooled, influenza raged through the Army and in Harry's battalion a further 350 soldiers were hospitalised. Harry's commander, Major Kennett wrote tersely, 'Move up country continued. Considerable hardship. Rations short. Only one blanket per man'.[121]

For the other members of the Pioneer Class their time in their RN destroyers and sloops varied greatly. For some, like John Collins in *Spencer*, their ships visited European ports still in a euphoric mood following the end of the war. The biggest challenge was to survive the hospitality. For others their ships were being prepared to pay off into the Reserve Fleet and they had to move from ship to ship to get sufficient sea service to obtain their bridge watch-keeping certificates. Eddy Nurse was placed in the unusual position of standing by a brand-new destroyer *Spear* which would shortly commission in Scotland. Fortunately for him he was posted in February 1919 to *Warrego* before *Spear* joined the Mediterranean Fleet. For Eddy joining the *Warrego* 'was like getting home'.[122]

At the same time Adrian Watts, having spent time in training at Biggleswade in Bedfordshire, had crossed the English Channel. He finally marched into the Australian Staging Camp at Abancourt on 29 January 1919. Two days later Adrian joined the 4th Division Signal Company at Rouan. The Division had fought at Gallipoli, Bullecourt, Messines, Polygon Wood, Hebuterne, Dernancourt, Villers-Bretonneux, Hamel and Amiens. By the Armistice the division was much depleted. The newly arrived Adrian soon found himself an Honorary Sergeant.

IX

'Getting home' became the focus for tens of thousands of Australians in Europe. In the larger picture there was a severe shortage of merchant ships to return troops to Australia. General Sir John Monash established a scheme to provide training to soldiers in England whilst they waited. The Pioneer Class returned to Australia in three groups. The first batch to reach home shores were George Armitage, Rupert Long and Eddy Nurse in the torpedo boat destroyers. On 6 March 1919 the six small destroyers, accompanied by *Melbourne*, sailed from Devonport bound for Australia via the Mediterranean and the Suez Canal. With the almost magnetic pull of their families the flotilla made a fast passage reaching Darwin in twenty days. Indeed Rupert Long's *Parramatta* and the *Yarra* both ran out of fuel off Darwin and had to be ingloriously towed into port by *Warrego*. After an equally quick passage down the east coast the ships arrived in Sydney and leave was taken.

The remainder of the Pioneer Class were caught up in two initiatives to rebuild the war-worn RAN Fleet. The British government responded to an Australian request with an offer of surplus warships to meet their future naval requirements. This was a welcome development. The Australian Fleet had lost its two submarines in the war, and many ships, even the flagship *Australia*, had become obsolescent, caught by the accelerated technological development spurred by the war. Some ships were just worn-out. The outcome for the RAN was that it was gifted six submarines and six destroyers.

Therefore the next batch of the Pioneer Class to begin their voyage home were its 'submariners' in the gifted submarines and the accompanying surface ships. The new RAN submarine flotilla consisted of the large ocean-going J-Class submarines – the *J1, J2, J3, J4, J5* and *J7*.[123] These boats were the largest submarines when built and had served with some success in the RN since 1916. For their own reasons the RN had elected to retain the infamous K-Class as their ocean-going submarine type rather than the diesel-electric J-Class.

Once it was announced that Australia would accept these submarines, officers and sailors of the RN submarine arm were asked to volunteer to transfer to the RAN or to be loaned until such time that the RAN could fully man the squadron. Thirty-one sailors from the RAN Fleet volunteered for submarine service and this group was strengthened by some of the survivors of HMAS *AE2* released from Turkish captivity.[124]

The new Australian submarine flotilla was commanded by the legendary Commander Edward Boyle, VC RN, who gained his Victoria Cross for taking his submarine *E14* through the minefields in the Dardanelles and breaking out into the Sea of Marmora on 27 April, 1915. *E14* went on to sink two Turkish gunboats and the large troopship *Gul Djemal*. Boyle commanded the submarine depot ship HMAS *Platypus* while the J-boats themselves were all commanded by experienced RN submariners.[125] The only RAN officers to join the J-boats were six members of the Pioneer Class.[126] They were Frank Getting in *J1*, Frank Larkins in *J2*, Harry Showers in *J3*, Leigh Watkins in *J4*, Jack Newman in *J5* and Norman Calder in *J7*. In addition, Alfred Conder and Cyril Sadleir sailed in the depot ship *Platypus* for the squadron's voyage to Australia.[127] Perhaps surprisingly there was a strong representation of *Glorious* midshipmen who had not been deterred by their service in the K-boats.

After many weeks of preparation on 9 April 1919 *Sydney*, *Platypus* and the six J-boats sailed from Portsmouth for Australia. The ships had an inauspicious start to their long voyage. Weather conditions were far from ideal and maintaining any formation proved problematic. The submarines were steaming on the surface and rolled heavily.

During the first night *J1* lost her wireless aerial in the rough weather. Worse was to come. Jack Newman was the officer-of-the-watch in *J5* and in very poor visibility he sighted a barquentine sailing vessel without navigation lights burning about half a mile on the port bow. It was the French *Terreneuvien Yolande* who was on a parallel course and being overtaken by *J5*. Jack calculated he would pass clear of *Terreneuvien Yolande* but he under-estimated how much the barquentine was moving about in the following sea. *Terreneuvien Yolande* yawed one final time as *J5* was about to overtake her and the submarine 'touched' the barquentine.[128] Jack stopped engines and called his Captain, Lieutenant J.R. Peirson who later wrote in his Collision Report:

> We both watched through glasses and she appeared perfectly seaworthy and normal. I watched till out of sight. No lights were shown and no distress signals made.[129]

The situation in *Terreneuvien Yolande* was in fact more desperate than may have been obvious from *J5*. She sank within thirty minutes of the collision, fortunately with no loss of life. In the subsequent Board of Inquiry Lieutenant Peirson received the 'severe displeasure' of the Lords of the Admiralty for leaving the barquentine without ensuring that she was in a safe condition.[130] For his part Jack received a letter stating the:

> Naval Board desire that an expression of their displeasure may be communicated to Sub-Lieutenant Newman with reference to the Court of Inquiry as to circumstances of collision between French Sailing Vessel and HMA Submarine *J5*.[131]

The Australian Government later paid £4,922 in compensation to the French owners of the stricken vessel.[132]

On 13 April the submarine flotilla limped into Gibraltar with various engine defects. Leading Seaman T.M. 'Taffy' Jones, a sailor in *J2* later wrote 'owing to the sea conditions, none, except the few on watch, could venture on deck as, in anything but a calm sea, the hull was awash most times'.[133] At Gibraltar 'the crews saw all they could: some of us tried to drink all we could'.[134]

The following day back in Portsmouth, the flagship *Australia* was honoured with a visit by the Prince of Wales to thank the Australian Fleet for their contribution to the war. The Prince met the officers who included Winn Reilly and Joe Burnett who were both watchkeeping officers. *Australia* flew the broad pennant of Commodore John Dumaresq, RN who previously commanded *Sydney*. He was the first Australian-born officer to command the Australian Fleet. In addition to the Prince of Wales, Dumaresq hosted onboard the Australian dignitaries Prime Minister Billy Hughes, Sir Joseph Cook, Senator Pearce and General

HMA Submarine J-1 in which Frank Getting served and was damaged in the transit across the Bay of Biscay.
(Green Collection/State Library of Victoria)

Sir William Birdwood.[135] The battlecruiser sailed the following day for Australia in company with the cruiser *Brisbane*. Among the officers in the cruiser was Lloyd Gilling who had joined after four months service in the battleship HMS *Barham*.

A message from the King was received which highlighted the RAN's contribution to the war and concluded with:

> I heartily thank the Government and the People of Australia for their generous provision of so valuable a Naval Force, and I wish to express my gratitude to all ranks and ratings for faithful and devoted service during the War.... May they carry with them and hand down to their descendants the same spirit of kinship and unity that has animated them throughout the arduous trials from which the Empire has emerged victorious.[136]

Both *Australia* and *Brisbane* soon arrived in Gibraltar to join the submarine flotilla. On the next leg to Malta the luckless *J5*, who had broken an intermediate propeller shaft, was taken in tow by the flagship. *Sydney* for her part, had *J2* in tow which had the same defect. Indeed the intermediate shafts were problematic for all boats and this was due to their frequent clutching and de-clutching for the formation-keeping for which they were not designed.[137] For these members of the Pioneer Class it was their first visit to the historic naval base at Valetta Harbour.

The Prince of Wales with the officers and sailors of HMAS Australia.
(WL Reilly Collection)

On Anzac Day 1919 the ships sailed once more and four days later reached Port Said and the entrance to the Suez Canal. As conditions grew hotter awnings were rigged over the decks of the submarines. Such was the heat inside the boats that many of the crew took bedding to the upper deck to sleep under the awning. After a short fueling stop in Aden the flotilla reached Colombo on 16 May 1919. *Australia*, keen to finally return to home shores, left *Sydney* and *Platypus* to escort the submarines.

Prior to *Australia's* arrival in Fremantle on 28 May Commodore Dumaresq received the following message from the Acting Minister for the Navy, Mr. Poynton:

> On behalf of the Federal Government I wish you a hearty welcome back to Australia after your perilous duties in other parts of the world. The Royal Australian Navy has received its baptism of fire and officers and men have upheld the great traditions of their forefathers, and have proved that our race has in no way deteriorated. The world owes its liberty today to the Allied navies' decisive actions at sea, making it possible for the land forces to be reinforced with troops and all requisites for their operations.[138]

The officers and sailors received a tremendous welcome after over four years absence from Australia. Approximately 60% of the ship's company were Australians and those from the west took leave from the ship after the parade through the city. The hospitality accorded to the flagship was extensive and it became clear that the duration of the four day port visit was ill-judged in its length. At the appointed time of departure about eighty sailors had mustered on the quarterdeck and requested the port visit be extended. Commodore Dumaresq would not countenance this request. Besides the manner in which it was tendered, the arrangements for similar port visits with their extensive ceremonial commitments and hospitality had been made for Adelaide, Melbourne and Sydney. There was however further trouble when some stokers left the engine room which delayed the ship's sailing. This incident, later known as the '*Australia* Mutiny' soured the visit and eventually led to the court martial and imprisonment of five sailors.[139]

On 15 June the memorable visits to the southern capitals by *Australia* and *Brisbane* culminated in their return to the 'cradle of the Australian Navy'[140] as Dumaresq described Sydney Harbour. The old cruiser *Encounter* in which Joe Burnett, Winn Reilly and Lloyd Gilling had undertaken their interviews in 1912 boomed out an eleven gun salute which *Australia* reciprocated. *The Queenslander* recorded, 'The ferry boats welcomed the flagship with shrill noises, and thousands of people gathered on the shore, waving flags and cheering'. The first aboard the flagship to welcome Commodore Dumaresq was the hero of the *Sydney-Emden* engagement Commodore John Glossop.

Meanwhile the submarine flotilla was still making its slow passage to Australia. By 18 June it had completed a most welcome port visit to Singapore where some of the engineering defects could be attended to by the dockyard. The next leg would take the flotilla through the calmer waters of the Dutch East Indies to Thursday Island and the entrance to the Great Barrier Reef. The weather leaving Singapore was calm and in the tropical heat many of submarines' crew resumed their practice of sleeping on the upper deck. On the morning of 20 June the submarines were sailing through the Karimata Strait that separates Sumatra from Borneo. At 6.30 am a sailor onboard *J2* noticed Frank Larkins was missing. After a search of the boat and careful inquiry it was assessed that he had been probably washed overboard around 3.30 am when a small wave came inboard. Frank had been seen just twenty minutes before in his bedding. 'Taffy' Jones wrote:

> The mishap was signalled to our parent ship. All the submarines turned back to search. In line abreast they kept a keen lookout but saw no sign of the lost officer. At dusk the search was given up and submarines turned back and joined the *Platypus*. The whole of *J2's* crew were mustered in the control room. Our captain held a burial service for the unfortunate officer. They were a band of downcast men who stood there bareheaded.[141]

One of Frank Larkins' fellow officers onboard later recorded 'As an officer he showed quite exceptional capabilities and keenness, and his unfailing cheerfulness and good humour made him charming as a friend'.[142] Chaplain Alexander Tulloh in *Platypus* later wrote to Frank's parents:

> He was a splendid young man, courteous, cheerful and capable. Everybody liked him and thought well of him. My own feelings towards him were of deep attachment and regard.[143]

Duncan Grant eulogised Frank Larkins in the Naval College magazine:

> Sub-Lieutenant Larkins was a member of the 'Pioneer' Year and was the first Cadet-Captain and Chief Cadet-Captain elected at the College. He possessed in a marked degree those qualities which make for leadership, and in no way did he abuse his powers. In games he was particularly prominent. In Rugby he was captain of the team, and was one of the best forwards the college has had.[144]

Frank Larkins was the undisputed leader of the Pioneer Class. His close friend Frank Getting wrote to Larkins' parents:

> Your son was our leader in everything. At college, as you know, he was our games leader and our senior captain, and one we always looked for wherever we were. I knew him probably better than anyone else in our term, and I cannot say I have met a finer and fairer fellow.[145]

Frank Larkins onboard the submarine J-2. He was photographed by Jack Newman who came over for a visit on passage. Frank and other members of the crew slept on the upper deck during tropical nights. (Newman Collection)

The remainder of the squadron's passage for the squadron was uneventful. Despite Frank Larkins' death, the arrival in Sydney on 10 July 1919 was joyous and generous with the Governor General in attendance. 'Taffy' Jones recalled:

> We gave three cheers. We received a great welcome: hundreds of boats met us; the ferry steamers cock-a-doodle-dooed themselves hoarse. We were home.[146]

This reception was but a prelude to the largest parade to be yet held in Sydney. On Sunday 20 July 1919 a spectacular Peace Procession was staged through the city streets. The parade, over 10,000 strong, was headed by the officers and sailors of *Australia*, then followed contingents from the other Fleet units and the visiting battlecruiser *New Zealand*. The bulk of the three and a quarter mile procession comprised the soldiers who had fought on the Western Front and in the Middle East. The latter included nearly 450 members of the famous Light Horse. The 'Men of Anzac'[147] were followed by the Peace Pageant that included munition workers, YMCA and Red Cross volunteers. To accompany the parade over thirty bands, supplemented by musical societies, were situated along the route. *The Sydney Morning Herald* reported, 'All the city thoroughfares were densely crowded. The main streets seen from a height, were an extraordinary spectacle'.[148] In the afternoon vast crowds descended on the Harbour foreshore to witness a regatta and aquatic events. In the evening the two battlecruisers and other warships provided a spectacular light display of lights outlining their silhouettes. In addition search lights and rockets lit the sky. The Governor General, Sir Ronald Munro Ferguson remarked in a speech that day:

> Today we close a great war era. The peace we celebrate has a special significance for our Commonwealth, which commemorates the achievements of the first Australian Imperial Force ever put in the field by a united Australian people. And today, the victory won, we enter on days of peace. Let us grapple with equal unity and courage with its problems, and, remembering great sacrifices and triumph, set ourselves to secure the progress and prosperity of our country.[149]

While the parade may have closed the Great War there was still eight of the Pioneer Class to reach home. Adrian Watts and his unit returned to Australia in the troopship *Raranga* on 27 October 1919. He was discharged to civilian life, for the third time, the following month. Harry Vallentine would be discharged from the British Army and return to Australia in 1920.

The remaining six class members had joined the new destroyer squadron which consisted of the destroyer leader *Anzac* and *Stalwart, Success, Swordsman, Tasmania* and *Tattoo*. John Collins joined *Stalwart*, James Esdaile *Success*, Harold Farncomb *Anzac*, Eric Feldt *Swordsman*, Paul Hirst *Tattoo* and Horace Thompson *Tasmania*. Although new ships they were in varying states of repair and some were still running trials which delayed their departure for Australia. The biggest delay was the difficulty in mustering sufficient men back in Australia to return to England for the commissioning crews. The numbers of sailors who wanted to return to civilian life had surprised Navy Office. As such the ships did not all commission into the RAN until 1920. The patience of those who had not got home was sorely tested.

While waiting for ships to leave for home Harold Farncomb learnt of an Intelligence Officer's course being held at Greenwich Naval College. He convinced Eric Feldt that both of them should attend the course for something to do and to be closer to the bright lights of London. For both officers it was an eye-opener to the role of Intelligence in shaping the requirements of future ships but more particularly in ensuring naval forces are deployed in the right strength and in the right time and place.

Eventually the new destroyer squadron sailed from Plymouth on 26 February 1920. In contrast to the submarine squadron, they had a largely uneventful passage to Australia via the Mediterranean, the Suez Canal and Singapore. However Eddy Nurse did record that he earned his commanding officer's ire by losing a classified publication overboard whilst in Gibraltar. The ships, in another remarkably quick passage, arrived in Sydney Harbour on 29 April 1920. John Collins later wrote when he told people he had 'just returned from the war, people were inclined to ask 'What war?''.[150]

Horace Thompson served in HMAS Tasmania *for her delivery voyage to Australia.*
(Green Collection/State Library of Victoria)

X

The Pioneer Class had finally returned to Australia. They had taken part in the last Fleet action of World War I and experienced life in one of the largest fleets ever assembled. The war had accelerated the development of new technologies, especially submarines. It was in these imperfect craft that they had lost Dick Cunningham and then Frank Larkins. They were two talented young men with still so much to accomplish in their lives. Neither family would have a grave to tend nor a place to mourn. The sea that had exerted such a fascination to both Dick and Frank was their final resting place.

For the remainder of the Pioneer Class, who had left Australia as boys, they had returned to its shores as mature young men. They were ready to launch into the next phase of their careers. The Navy had changed markedly as a result of its war experience. It would rapidly reshape once more in the post-war years in ways that these Argonauts would find both challenging as well as rewarding.

Chapter 5
The Inter War Years

No grim invader lurks without,
With a strange devised banner,
No malcontents within to rout,
In thorough naval manner;
No civil strife, no threat to life,
No sudden call to action.

Anon (circa 1936)[1]

I

In the aftermath of the Great War, Australia had to come to terms with a grievous toll of over 61,500 dead and more than 155,000 wounded.[2] In a nation with a population of five million this translated into bereavement on an unimagined scale. Like most Australians, few members of the Pioneer Class were untouched in their immediate or extended families.

Whilst the navy in the pre-war years had symbolised in a tangible way, the aspirations of the young nation, it was the Anzacs, often represented as a stone soldier atop one of these innumerable memorials erected in towns and cities across the continent that now represented the united Commonwealth. This was hardly surprising, if for no other reason than the degree of collective experience. During the Great War about 9,000 men joined the RAN. In contrast over 330,000 men served in the Australian Imperial Force.[3] The deeds and sacrifices of the diggers at Gallipoli and on the Western Front were seared into the national consciousness. The RAN for its part, while it helped keep the sea lines of communication open, only the taking of German New Guinea and the sinking of Emden gained widespread public attention.

The nation's losses were also financial. The heavy fiscal burden on the Commonwealth would greatly hamper nation building. The parlous state of national coffers was soon to have an impact on its defence forces. After the 'war to end all wars' there was a great desire to return to a more modest navy and army.

II

In 1919 a sea change took place at the Naval College with the abrupt end of the Duncan Grant era. On the evening of the Armistice Cadet-Midshipmen Charles Childers and Charles Willes[4] became drunk at celebrations involving both sailors and other cadet-midshipmen. They were charged and Grant recommended to the Naval Board that they be expelled. The Naval Board telegraphed Grant seeking further information on the matter. Following Grant's reply, the Naval Board sought the Minster's approval for dismissal as:

> ... these Cadets are Senior Cadets and were guilty of an offence practically in the presence of about 100 juniors at a time when these Junior Cadets are receiving their first impressions of the Service and when it is most important that there should be no lack of discipline.[5]

However the Acting-Minister of the Navy, Alexander Poynton—perhaps not unreasonably, did not want to dismiss Childers and Willes given the occasion was the Armistice celebrations and that the beer had been given to the cadet-midshipmen by some of the sailors. The Naval Board suggested in a compromise that if the two young officers passed their end of year examinations that they could be appointed as Paymaster

Clerks.⁶ Willes failed his examinations and left the Navy, but Childers passed and Poynton would not dismiss him.⁷ Duncan Grant, feeling his position was untenable, resigned on principle so ending his association with the Naval College dating back to 1912. The matter drew national attention. The *Queensland Courier* in reporting the matter wrote:

> By taking the step he has taken Mr. Poynton has imperiled the whole system of naval training, and, therefore the whole future of the Australian Navy. He declared that he will not allow the careers of these two boys to be blighted, but he shows himself prepared not only to blight Captain Grant's career, but to destroy the Naval College as an officers school. If the head of the College has no power to expel boys for bad behaviour, he has no power to enforce discipline at all; he has no power to prevent two young scamps from corrupting all the other boys in the college; he has no power to give Australia such naval officers as will be a credit to their country. Captain Grant was compelled to resign. There is no naval officer in the world, unless he is already a rotter, that would willingly accept the position on Mr Poynton's terms. And if the Ministers of the Commonwealth Government do not promptly reverse the Poynton policy, the people should determine that the matter shall be carried much further. The navy is far too important to be the plaything of a Poynton.⁸

Letters of protest were published in newspapers about the affair, an 'ordinary parent' wrote:

> To many parents, whose sons are in training at Jervis Bay, it seems that it should be more rightly have been termed the Naval College catastrophe, for the silent, unobtrusive work of Captain Grant has gone on for six years, with little publicity, but nevertheless with splendid efficiency. First as commander [second in command], and then as captain, he has been in close personal touch with every midshipman who has left the RANC for the Grand Fleet, and with every cadet who was selected for training at Jervis Bay. Those parents whose sons have shared in the results of this work, or who have through their sons been privileged to gain glimpses of it, know that the work of moulding the Australian cadet-midshipmen into naval gentlemen and officers has been largely the impress of Captain Grant ... .

Those who have met the captain know him to be a British Naval gentlemen, of fearless integrity and large-hearted courage. In studies, sport, and recreation he was a comrade as well as commander – alert in every sense of the word, as keen on the football field as he was devoted to the conduct of their lives, to regard for their fitness, to the progress of their education. He had the allegiance of his officers, and the reverence of his boys; 120 boys, aged 13 to 17 years, to whom he stood 'in loco parentis'. Reverence in the best sense of the word is not an easy thing to hold, but Captain Grant had it. We are just building up a new nation. Some of us are trying to learn the best ways of doing it. The loss of this born leader of boys is a loss to our nation-building. But, whatever the outcome, Australian naval history will one day place faithfully in its log-book the six years service at Geelong, and at Jervis Bay, of Captain Duncan Grant, RN.[9]

This view was also shared by the Governor General, Sir Ronald Munro Ferguson, who wrote to the Admiralty to state that Grant had served with marked distinction and success and regarded Captain Grant's loss as irreparable.[10]

On 1 August 1919 the Australian Fleet formally reverted to the control of the Commonwealth Government. This provided the opportunity for the Government to review and reduce the sentences of the *Australia* mutineers. Commodore Dumaresq and the First Naval Member Rear Admiral Sir Percy Grant had offered to resign. The newly arrived Rear Admiral Grant was Duncan Grant's uncle. In the following week's sitting of Parliament the *Australia* mutiny, Grant's resignation and Poynton's role in both affairs were raised by members of the Opposition.[11] Poynton maintained expulsion was too severe a punishment and that a reprimand would have sufficed. In the press Poynton was castigated for attempting to overturn Commodore Glossop's court martial sentencing of the *Australia* mutineers. *The Queenslander* editorialised that it was Glossop who 'imparted inspiration to our young navy, and if he is to be driven out of the service because of a false public sentiment in regard to a lot of mutineers it will be a disgrace to Australia'.[12] It went on to conclude:

Captain Grant the officer responsible, very properly resigned, and so a very capable officer is lost to the service because a few cadets are not inclined to accept discipline, and wanted to indulge improperly in drinking. The Australian Navy, under such conditions, is likely to become a useless and expensive machine, for without a very strict discipline its value in war will be slight. Mr. Poynton by means of the political machine happens to be Minister for Defence, and yet in impairing the efficiency of the navy as shown in the above instances, is doing the greatest harm to Australia which it is possible for any one man to do.[13]

Captain Duncan Grant and Frank Albert onboard Boomerang. (Grant Collection)

The week before these matters were raised in Parliament Duncan Grant sailed from Port Melbourne for England in RMS *Osterley*.[14] On 5 December 1919 Frank Albert and his family, as had become the tradition, hosted the newly graduated Naval College Class to luncheon at Farmers Department Store before they would join the Fleet. There were three toasts, the first to the King, then a silent toast to the memory of Otto Albert and the third 'accompanied by musical honours' to Captain Grant for his service to the Naval College.[15]

In 1923 Duncan Grant renewed his naval friendships when he returned to Australia as the Official Secretary to the new Governor of New South Wales Admiral Sir Dudley de Chair. Grant, a long time bachelor, had married the widow Mrs Beatrice Paine just before returning to Australia. They were to have two Australian-born sons; both would follow their father into the RN.[16] The older son, Seafield, would be awarded the prized King's Medal at Dartmouth.[17]

III

One of the biggest challenges for any fledgling navy was to adequately train its officers and sailors in the wide array of duties required to operate a warship at sea. In order to both train in a cost-effective manner and ensure that standards were maintained, the RAN would continue to be dependent on the RN. From an operational perspective this arrangement meant that officers, sailors and warships of the two navies were seamlessly inter-changeable. This approach was unlikely to change when Vice Admiral Sir William Creswell finally retired as the First Naval Member on 9 June 1919. He was replaced by a series of RN admirals whose tenure would stretch until 1948. The only exception was Admiral Sir Francis Hyde a former RNR and RN officer who had transferred to the RAN in 1912 and was in office from 1931-1937.

As a result of this 'parent-child' naval relationship, Australian naval officers would regularly return to the RN for training or exchange service throughout their careers. For many young officers, including the Pioneer Class, the close and repeated contact with Britain and the RN could lead some of them to adopt the speech and social mores of an RN officer. It was not what Chambers and Grant had necessarily envisaged. This cultural osmosis could create a distance between some Australian naval officers and their sailors.[18] This was even though the same RAN officers were still seen as distinctly Australian to men in the RN. The adoption of some of the British speech and values was not unique to the Navy, as attested to by British accented Australian Broadcasting Corporation announcers for many decades in the twentieth century. The difference in outlook and the 'Britishness' of the RAN officers was arguably in contrast to their Australian Army counterparts who had less contact with the British Army through their careers. This closer contact was in part due to a RAN requirement for most of the inter-war period for RAN officers to be reported on at least once in their present rank by an RN reporting officer to be eligible for promotion. This practice was to help ensure that RAN standards did not slip, a risk in any small navy.

Under this construct, the Pioneer Class as Sub-Lieutenants were required to return to England for Lieutenants' courses at Greenwich Naval College. They would go on to attend associated specialist courses at other training establishments. For some, they would also consolidate their training with postings to RN ships before returning to Australia. After a period of consolidation at sea as Lieutenants the Pioneer Class would then negotiate with Navy Office as to what specialisation they would embark upon. These streams at the time were gunnery, navigation, torpedoes, anti-submarine warfare, war staff, communications, submarines, engineering and hydrography. Gunnery had been traditionally pre-eminent, but the technological advances during the Great War had challenged the elitism that was associated with this specialisation. Over the next couple of years the Class would progressively select their individual specialisation, or have it selected for them. They would then return to UK for specialist training and possibly exchange service in a RN ship.

Not surprisingly John Collins and Joe Burnett selected the specialisation of gunnery. Harold Farncomb specialised as a War Staff Officer who would typically serve on the small staff of a flag officer afloat. Among the rest of the class Norman Calder, Rupert Long and Winn Reilly undertook the technically demanding Torpedo specialisation, Lloyd Gilling and Harry Showers navigation, Jack Newman communications, Frank Getting submarines while Alfred Conder and Cyril Sadleir opted for hydrography. James Esdaile was one of the first two RAN officers to specialise in the new anti-submarine field.

Eddy Nurse was the only one of the Class to opt to transfer from the Executive Branch which could command a ship to become an Engineer in the Engine Room Branch. This came about when in 1919 Eddy was discontented and seriously contemplating leaving the Navy. His commanding officer in *Swan*, Commander William Burrows encouraged Eddy to stay in the service and during his counseling found that Eddy found most fulfillment when working in the engine room.[19]

Requisite to becoming a specialist, officers except engineers had to obtain a bridge watch keeping certificate which attested to the competency of an officer to take charge of the ship and her men at sea. This certificate was obtained from the ship's commanding officer after demonstrating such competency for some months. For Peyton Kimlin this proved a challenge. Peyton was the first of his class to return to Australia. On 1 July he joined HMAS *Suva* to obtain his certificate. The ship was a former Australasian United Steam Navigation Company steamer that plied the Brisbane-Suva route until being requisitioned by the British Admiralty for naval service in 1914. A week before Peyton joined *Suva* she was commissioned into the RAN as a Special Service Vessel to be used by Admiral of the Fleet Viscount Jellicoe to enable him to tour Australian and south-west Pacific waters as part of his review of naval defence requirements.

Serving on Jellicoe's staff was the then Captain Francis Hyde who also commanded *Suva* for the short commission. Hyde watched with increasing concern Peyton's practical seamanship and leadership abilities. For Peyton, the close scrutiny of a senior officer in a small vessel with an eminent naval passenger, where each port visit demanded attention to every detail of seamanship and ceremonial must have been a nightmare. In contrast, for someone such as Winn Reilly or Harold Farncomb, it would have been a golden opportunity to impress and gain potential future support for advancement. However, as soon as 4 August Captain Hyde wrote a Special Report on Peyton which said:

> I regret to report that Sub-Lieutenant Peyton J. Kimlin, RAN appears to possess none of the attributes which go to the making of a Naval Officer. He cannot be trusted as a watchkeeper, either at sea or in harbour; he appears to be incapable of correctly interpreting or of carrying out an order given either verbally or in writing, and has no command of men. He has been logged for neglect of duty whilst in HMAS *Suva*, and to the end showed no sign of improvement.[20]

On the return of *Suva* to Sydney, Peyton left the ship. He joined the flagship *Sydney* and here his fate rested with Commodore Dumaresq.

HMAS Suva *in which Peyton Kimlin served as a trainee Officer of the Watch.*
(RAN)

The Commodore was asked by the Naval Board to render another report in six months. The only problem with this plan was that in the normal course of events the Pioneer Class were due to commence courses at Greenwich in the new year. It was decided, somewhat generously, that Peyton would attend the course as a Provisional Lieutenant. On 18 October 1919 he and ten others of the Class sailed in the Aberdeen and Commonwealth Line steamer *Demonsthenes* to England.[21]

In some respects the training at Greenwich was a return to the old peacetime routine. It was the last time that the Pioneer Class would be together in any numbers and this brought out their competitive sporting spirit. They played dominant roles in the various teams while Leigh Watkins won the officer's middleweight boxing competition. Eddy Nurse and some others in the class played rugby for Greenwich including a match in Cologne against the British Army of Occupation. The team's hazardous flight in three aeroplanes was the first for many players. Harry Showers went on to play rugby for the RN, as did Joe Burnett and Winn Reilly with both also representing the United Services. In addition Joe also played tennis for the Navy at Wimbledon.[22]

At the end of the course there were examinations in mathematics, physics, mechanics and navigation. Winn Reilly topped the course of both RN and RAN officers with a score of 799 out of 1000. He was awarded the gold Goodenough Medal, which suggested he had deserved the earlier King's Medal. James Esdaile was a close second (782) followed by John Collins (755), Joe Burnett (754) and Lloyd Gilling (754). At the bottom of the Class was Peyton Kimlin with a score of 462.[23] The President of the Royal Naval College was Admiral Sir William Pakenham who had flown his flag in *Australia* during the war. He wrote to the Navy Secretary to report on Peyton:

Joe Burnett played rugby for the the Royal Navy and the United Services. (Burnett Family)

> This officer has just completed his course of instruction at this College, during which his conduct both in study and out, has been entirely satisfactory. His instructors report him 'very zealous' ability, fairly good but rather below the average of his Class; takes an interest in his work, but not very accurate.[24]

Unlike most of the class who would remain for further training or exchange service with the RN, Peyton would have to return to Australia to obtain his watchkeeping certificates. Captain Hugh Thring at Australia House wrote, 'I would add that during the last month whilst he (Kimlin) has been waiting passage to Australia he has been under my personal observation and I cannot speak too highly of his conduct on all occasions'.[25]

On return to Australia Peyton joined *Brisbane*. She was commanded by none other than Captain Hyde. On 11 June 1921 Hyde wrote a report to Commodore Dumaresq on Peyton's performance, which stated he:

Some of the Pioneer Class and their RN contemporaries at Whale Island in 1920.
(JB Newman Collection)
Front row on left is Winn Reilly who was awarded the Goodenough Medal for topping the entire Lieutenant's Course. Jack Newman is second from the left in the third row.

> Possesses no Officer-like qualities, has no power of command and is looked upon by the Lower Deck[26] as a joke. It is difficult to understand how any person who has spent so long in the Service has remained so completely ignorant of an officer's ordinary duties and of the ordinary routine, customs and phraseology of the Service.[27]

After citing various examples of poor performance in evolutions and ship activities to substantiate his assessment, Hyde did state in support of Peyton, 'I am informed that he is a good musician and a boxer above the average. The Executive Officer reports he appears well-meaning'.[28] Four days later however, Commodore Dumaresq wrote to the Naval Secretary that:

> I deeply regret that I have formed the opinion that this Officer is not only of no value in any Ship or Establishment as an Officer, but that his presence is actually detrimental to the progress of efficiency, morale and discipline in the RAN. I therefore feel it is my duty to submit

that Lieutenant Kimlin may be placed on half pay in accordance with Statutory Rule No. 156/1920, which will give him an opportunity of finding an occupation ashore. I make this submission on plain facts and without prejudice to his good intentions.[29]

Commodore Dumaresq's recommendations were duly accepted and Peyton was placed on half pay on 1 July 1921 and left the Service on New Year's Eve. Peyton returned initially home to the Wimmera District. Unsure of his future direction he had a short stint at his Uncle George's cane farm in Queensland before deciding to take up the vocation of his father and grandfather and become a teacher. This would also better allow him to indulge in his great passion – music. While onboard *Brisbane* and with his career in the balance, Peyton was completing the musical *The Mystic Nile* which he lodged for copyright on 25 July 1921. He went to Melbourne to complete teacher training where he found Ben Howells also enrolled.

Since the end of the war Ben had received motivational and financial support from his older brother Lyn. This included obtaining a tutor to help him matriculate. In 1920 he gained admission to Melbourne University. His enthusiasm and prowess in rugby were undiminished and he played in the university's First XV. Ben's abiding interest remained English literature and in particular poetry, graduating with a Bachelor of Arts with Honours.[30] He thus became the first of the Pioneer Class to receive a tertiary qualification. Ben intended to gain a Diploma of Education and also be ordained as a Church of England clergyman. He still hoped to become a missionary.

Adrian Watts also entered university and followed his father's path and studied architecture. During the 1923 Victorian Police Strike a public spirited Adrian was one of 5,000 volunteer 'Special Constables' organized under the leadership of Sir John Monash to re-establish order after looting had taken place in parts of Melbourne. Adrian was issued with a baton and armband and retained the former as a souvenir.

Adrian however, found architecture studies 'rather a dry sort of subject' and changed tack. From his earliest days at the Naval College Adrian had been a talented artist and it was to this he turned as a vocation.

He studied at Leyshon White Commercial Art School on Little Collins Street, Melbourne. The School's motto was *Art That Pays* and for £25 taught a comprehensive course in pen and ink artwork to allow its students to gain work providing newspaper advertisements, magazine and catalogue illustrations, caricatures, book covers, show cards and tickets. Adrian was to prove a talented illustrator in most of these forms of work and was fortunate to work in a period that was the golden age for commercial artists. He soon undertook advertising artwork for movies shown at Hoyts cinemas and regularly provided cover artwork and illustrations as well as cartoons to the

One of Adrian Watts' 'If oft used saying came true' cartoons from Punch Magazine. (NLA)

Australian *Punch, Pals* and *Smith's Weekly* magazines.[31]

In 1922 Adrian first had a cartoon accepted for *Punch* and in the following year began a popular cartoon series entitled *If oft used sayings come true* which ran until May 1924. He also did a number of covers which are among his best work. Adrian was also commissioned to draw cartoons on naval themes such as when the British Special Service Squadron visited Australia.

Adrian had a particular affinity for publications that promoted the values and interests of the returned soldier. He contributed cartoons for *Smith's Weekly* which labelled itself as the Diggers' Paper'.[32] By the end

Adrian's Watts' poster for the 1922 American silent movie
Down to the Sea in Ships. (Hoyts)

of 1921 the newspaper had a weekly circulation of over 150,000. The artwork in *Smith's Weekly* was one of its greatest strengths and attracted some of nation's leading cartoonists. One of the finest was Stan Cross. He spawned two famous cartoons - *Mr & Mrs Potts* and *Dad & Dave*. He passed the former on to Jim Russell to pen to lasting fame while Adrian took over *Dad & Dave* for a short period.

Another publication that commissioned Adrian's illustrations was the *Aussie* magazine. This publication, which was created by Phillip Harris from a 'diggers' magazine on the Western Front and from 1921 published in Sydney. *Aussie* remained hugely popular with former diggers and attained a circulation of 100,000 copies. It often featured Adrian's artwork on its monthly cover, including its special fifth birthday edition.[33] Adrian's success was held up by Leyshon White in his school prospectus as indeed a graduate who had made art pay.[34]

IV

After their eventful voyage to Australia, the six J-Class boats of the Submarine Flotilla needed extensive refits at Garden Island and Cockatoo Island dockyards. This provided an opportunity for the seven members of the Pioneer Class to take war service leave and be reunited with their families. The realities of supporting these complex submarines so far from their country of origin were soon apparent. Although some thought had gone into the problem there were insufficient spares and expertise for the task. Work proceeded slowly but this provided time for the location of their new base to be finalised. Once again the Naval Board turned to the Geelong Harbour Trust and Osborne House.

On 18 February 1920 *Platypus* led *J1* and *J4* out of Sydney Harbour for passage to their new home in Geelong. Two months later they were joined by *J5* with Jack Newman aboard. But Harry Showers and Norman Calder remained in Sydney with *J3* and *J7* for many months as their boats awaited new batteries from England.

Although Geelong was not the most sheltered of locations, Port Phillip Bay provided a broad expanse of water well suited for Captain Boyle's task of honing the Flotilla's skills. The destroyer *Swordsman* was soon attached as a target vessel to the Flotilla with the submarines firing practice torpedoes at her or any other warship visiting Melbourne. This included the prize 'target' of *Australia*. The Flotilla ventured to Hobart and Sydney for port visits which drew much public interest and subsequent exercises with the Fleet further enhanced the submarines' capabilities.

While having commendable speed and endurance, the J-boats were expensive to maintain and this cost was exacerbated by the boats being worn by war service, the cost of shipping spares from England and the inexperienced local workforce. As such the recent refit of *J7* had cost £110,861, well in excess of the budgeted RN estimate of £28,300[35]. In order for the Navy to live within its means, on 4 October 1921 the Naval Board ordered *J1*, *J2* and *J5* to be paid off into reserve. They would remain alongside the extended wharf at Geelong.

This cutback was but a reprieve. In early 1922 the Naval Board were told their budget was to be cut next financial year by a further £500,000. *Australia* had already been paid off and it was reluctantly decided to disband the entire Flotilla in order to keep the more versatile cruisers in commission. This decision was approved by the Minister for Defence on 22 November 1922.

The disbandment was not only tragic news for the submariners but also for the citizens of Geelong where the Flotilla had become a part of the community. An example of this integration was Norman Calder joining the local United Grand Lodge of Free Masons in January 1922.[36] It is unknown if any of his classmates also became members. As he moved around during his service with the RN, Norman would join a local lodge. When in London it was one near Hampton Court. Membership of the Free Masons had assisted RN officers in their advancement for decades and in 1927 Admiral of the Fleet Earl Jellicoe became a Senior Grand Warden. The significance and influence of Freemasonry was on the wane from its peak in the Victorian era Navy when the Prince of Wales was Grand Master of England. Andrew Gordon in *The Rules of the Game: Jutland and British Naval Command* wrote that Freemasonry, 'generally benign, in many ways laudable, occasionally pernicious and, to some, risible was part of the Navy's social scenery'.[37] The role of the Free Masons in mentoring more junior members or in any preferment and promotion of members in the RAN is less clear.

V

Between 1920 and 1923 the Pioneer Class progressively returned from their British training. The Fleet they returned to as Lieutenants was reduced in size and stature to a Squadron of ships. By the end of 1921 in addition to the five submarines there were only the three cruisers *Brisbane* (James Esdaile and John Collins for a short period), *Sydney* (Paul Hirst), *Melbourne* (Eric Feldt and later John Collins) and four destroyers *Anzac*, *Stalwart* (Harold Farncomb), *Swordsman* and *Huon* (George Armitage) and one sloop *Geranium*. The ships were often under-manned and in *Melbourne* for example, John Collins and Eric Feldt were the only bridge watchkeeping officers.

The return of the Pioneer Class made a noticeable impression, for this was the first time Jervis Bay graduates were widely seen in the RAN as trained officers. None made a greater mark than John Collins. Reporting on him as the Gunnery Officer, Captain John Stevenson in *Brisbane* marked him as an officer of exceptional ability and wrote that he was 'the best product of Jervis Bay I have met so far'.[38] Chief Petty Officer Edward Hammond, then an Assistant Gunner's Mate recalled:

> I had already served under the strictest and most efficient Gunnery Officers in the RN and in my opinion, Lieutenant Collins was equal to the best and wholly loved by his gun's crew. In the year 1921 Fleet field gun competitions were held in the Sydney Domain with honour as the only prize, when the *Brisbane* gun-crew won two out of three runs. Lieutenant Collins was the inspirer of the victory. It was a great privilege to serve under him.[39]

As his class mates embarked on their next stage of their naval careers, Hugh MacKenzie decided to leave the Navy. For Hugh the experience of waiting in the UK onboard *Anzac* to return to Australia 'was enough to drive anybody up the wall'.[40] He had concluded that if this was the peacetime Navy then it was too dull for him. Hugh had an eye condition that he had prior to entry to the Naval College which he now drew to a doctor's attention, saying it was caused, 'by gazing into a telescope looking for submarines'.[41] He was found to have amblyopia or 'lazy eye' in the left eye.[42] On this basis he was invalided out of the service before he had to return to Greenwich for further training. More of the Pioneer Class were to shortly leave the Navy but in much different circumstances.

In March 1921 Rear Admiral Grant embarked in *Brisbane* to attend a meeting in Penang with the RN Commanders-in-Chief of the China and East Indies Stations. They discussed how their ships would cooperate in Imperial defence in the new strategic environment following the Great War. The focus of their attention was the emerging naval might of Japan and the comparative stretch of the RN in these straitened financial times. The Anglo-Japanese Alliance was due to expire in 1923 and there was uncertainty as to the naval dynamic between these two powers into the future.

At the Penang meeting the Admirals agreed that Japan was the most likely naval threat and that their three naval squadrons would have to operate in a coordinated fashion with Singapore as their centre of gravity. This view reflected the emerging strategy originally conceived in Admiral Jellicoe's 1919 tour in *New Zealand* that Singapore should become the premier naval base east of Suez and that the naval squadrons, including the Australian Fleet should hold out against any aggression until the British main fleet would arrive from European waters. This strategic assessment was endorsed in June at the 1921 Imperial Conference which was held in London attended by Prime Minister Billy Hughes. Indeed, the Conference agreed to the building of a fortified base at Singapore with Britain providing most of the funding for its construction. The Main Fleet strategy was to have far-reaching consequences in years to come, not only for nations but for the lives of sailors and soldiers.

In November of that year the Washington Naval Conference took place under the auspices of the new League of Nations. In the wake of the 'war to end all wars' it was a bold attempt to limit the size of the major navies. For Britain and the US, the Conference was seen as a means to constrain Japanese naval expansion. The Conference led to a range of limits to the numbers and size of various warship classes. Among the casualties of the subsequent Treaties[43] would be the once imposing *Australia* which was scuttled off Sydney Heads on 12 April 1924 as part of the British capital ship reductions. Her plunge was watched by Lloyd Gilling, navigating officer of the cruiser *Adelaide*. Many lamented the demise of the just 11-year old flagship. But such was the advance in naval technology during the war that the battlecruiser was outclassed by ships just a few years younger. In addition the RN had stopped producing ammunition for her now obsolete 12-inch guns.

The impact of the desire to reduce both defence forces and their attendant fiscal demands were much more immediately felt. The Commonwealth Government decided to reduce naval expenditure by 20% from 1923. Ships were to be paid off and the personnel strength of the Navy substantially reduced. Officers and sailors were invited to apply for redundancy. On 10 July 1922 letters were sent from the Naval Representative in Australia House to naval officers then serving in Britain. After explaining the plan to reduce the size of the RAN he wrote:

> The Commonwealth Naval Board therefore invite RAN Officers serving in H.M. Ships and Establishments in Home Waters to make application to resign voluntarily under the conditions set out below, observing that acceptance of such resignation is not guaranteed.[44]

Compensation terms included one month's pay for each completed year of Service, for members of the Pioneer Class it would amount to a total of £532. Officers were invited to respond by 15 July. Winn Reilly, then topping his specialist Torpedo course, wrote back to Australia House accepting the offer to resign. Winn's reason for wishing to leave was predominantly financial. When he saw the gathering affluence of his former Geelong College friends outside the Navy he concluded his best opportunity to secure his future was in civilian life.[45] The application from the inaugural King's Medalist surprised the Naval Board who refused his application. Winn challenged their decision and his father 'arranged to have some political pressure applied'.[46] The Naval Board reconsidered its position and subsequently wrote that 'it would be distinctly unfair to penalise Mr Reilly because of his greater efficiency'.[47] The other members of the Pioneer Class to take up the Naval Board's offer were Eric Feldt and Leigh Watkins.

The naval redundancy had been particularly timely for Eric Feldt. In 1922 he had a short holiday on Norfolk Island and recalled:

> It broke me. The freedom of life ashore and being able to do what you felt like doing, not having to think of what a senior officer would think of something of all the time, just to put the cap on it with me, and I decided to leave the Navy as soon as I could. When I got back to Sydney I found that there was a retiring scheme.[48]

On his resignation Eric was sent to the Naval College to fill in as a Year Officer for a couple of weeks. It brought Eric back to his naval roots, but all the same he thought it was an odd thing to do. At the end he recalled:

> I packed up, travelled back to Sydney and the sun was still shining, the breeze was blowing, the trees were green, and the world was just the same, although I wasn't any longer in the Navy.[49]

Eric on combining his savings, severance pay and war gratuity had about £700 to secure his future. He decided to buy a schooner to trade between New Zealand and Norfolk Island. His search for a suitable vessel led him to Hobart where he bought a ketch. After some inquiries with his contacts in Norfolk Island Eric concluded the trade with the island would not be profitable. He therefore converted the ketch for cray fishing in Victorian waters where it was legal to use pots. Eric's crew consisted of a former destroyer sailor and an old RN chum, Charles Simons, who had migrated to Australia. With Westernport Bay as their base, they had initial success in their venture. However one night at anchor in the bay the weather came up and the ketch was being blown onshore. The normally reliable engine would not start and they attempted to clear the anchorage under sail. It was to no avail and, hit by an extra large wave, the ketch was forced ashore. Without the funds to repair the boat, the now near destitute Eric sold the wreck.

Eric's life was about to take an even more decisive turn. He took the train to Melbourne and called on John Collins' mother Esther, who had been so hospitable to a young country Queensland boy during his Geelong years. He found her at her flat suffering from malaria which she had contracted following a recent trip to Papua. Eric took Esther to her daughter-in-law to be looked after. Despite her malarial condition, Esther administered parental advice and suggested to Eric that he seek his fortune in New Guinea.

Eric had become intrigued by New Guinea when *Melbourne* had visited Samarai Island, Rabaul and Madang. So with 'nothing else in mind or anything I could think of and no capital,'⁵⁰ he applied for a position in the Colonial administration on 1 August 1923. Unbeknown to Eric, Esther had commended his name for preferment to Senator Sir George Pearce, now the Minister of Home Affairs and Territories. For his part Eric also wrote to Senator Pearce to apply for 'any subordinate position offering'.⁵¹ In his letter Eric contained excerpts of his flimsies and also highlighted how as a boy in a Swedish household that he spoke Pidgin with Kanakas before he spoke English. Senator Pearce directed Feldt's application be placed before fellow Western Australian Brigadier General Evan Wisdom the Administrator of New Guinea.⁵² Wisdom agreed that Eric would fill the last of ten vacancies for clerks in Rabaul. Eric's application was processed in Rabaul by the senior accountant, Reginald Halligan⁵³ who remembered him from *Melbourne's* port visit. Halligan perceptively noted in his brief to the Administrator that Eric was 'a good type of man' whose credentials to be a clerk were not strong, but in time may have the makings for a patrol officer.⁵⁴ On 1 November 1923 Eric was advised of his appointment and just eight days later he sailed from Brisbane in the Burns Philp island trader *Melusia*.

Up to 1914 New Guinea had been administered by three colonial powers. From 1828 the Dutch controlled the western half of the island known as West New Guinea as part of the much larger Dutch East Indies. From 1885 the Germans ruled the north east segment of the island as well as later day New Britain and New Ireland collectively known as German New Guinea. It was administered on the Imperial Government's behalf by the German New Guinea Company. The southern sector of the island was the Australian possession of Papua which had been handed over from Britain in 1902.

Following the Australian invasion of German New Guinea this territory came under Australian military administration. The proclamation following the capture of Rabaul ended with 'now you give three goodfeller cheers belonga new feller master. No more um Kaiser ... God Save Um King'.⁵⁵ The Australian control of German New Guinea became legitimized under a League of Nations Mandate. The military administrators of the territory were colloquially known as the 'Coconut Lancers'. Among other things they oversaw through the Expropriation Board the seizing of all German property be it government, company or personal. The monetary value would be credited against the Treaty of Versailles reparations to Australia. One of the most shameful outcomes was that the personal possessions of German settlers were seized and sold at auction. They were given receipts for credit by the German Government on their return to their homeland. Due to hyper-inflation in Weimar Germany these receipts were virtually worthless.

The transitional military control came to an end through the 1920 New Guinea Act. The civil administration remained centered at Rabaul on New Britain Island. Papua and New Guinea would remain separate entities for the foreseeable future. The New Guinea colonial administration was small with only 206 government employees located around the islands and settlements.[56]

Eric commenced work in November 1923 as a Clerk 2nd Division Class K. Rabaul was a picturesque town on the eastern arm of the deep water horseshoe shaped Simpson Harbour. The bay was actually part of a large volcanic caldera with two of its vents being the volcanos Vulcan and Tavurvur. The latter volcano had last erupted in 1878. The town itself was a typical well-ordered German style settlement with mango trees lining some of the streets.

As predicted by Halligan, Eric found the allure of this wild country outside his small office too much.[57] He soon became a patrol officer. Eric was embarking on a dangerous and ill-rewarded career. The Australian Government had from the outset wanted New Guinea to be self-funded. Eric's annual salary of £342,[58] while comparable to the £365 of a Lieutenant Commander, was without the medical coverage and other benefits of the Navy. However, he would be entitled to three months furlough after 21 months service. Furthermore, the 'stool polishing' administrators at Rabaul were renowned for skimping on any 'discretionary' outlay. For example, ten shillings was deducted from his pay for each day in *Melusia* and rent was charged for his spartan unfurnished quarters.[59] To add to this, knowledge of dealing with tropical disease was in its infancy and many white settlers either had to eventually leave the climate due to health reasons or were buried in forlorn graves on the outskirts of European settlements.

In his capacity of Patrol Officer Eric Feldt joined the very experienced Lieutenant Colonel John Wolstab[60] and his deputy GWL 'Kaasa' Townsend[61] who were charged with mounting a patrol to prevent further incidents of head-hunting along the Sepik River in 1924. Because of Eric's naval experience he commanded the ketch *Aloha* which supported the expedition. The experienced District Officer and later Administrator, John McCarthy[62] wrote more generally about headhunting that:

> ... unless a head was taken by a middle-river Sepik man he was forbidden to wear the genital covering of the tanned skin of flying fox and so was forced to walk naked and listen to the smirking of women. No parent would permit their daughter to marry a man whose lack of attire proclaimed him unworthy to be thought a warrior.[63]

In the most recent outbreak members of the Japondai tribe were killed while still in their sleeping baskets[64] when tribesmen from three neighbouring villages of Yambon, Malu and Awatip descended upon them early one morning. 'Kaasa' Townsend wrote:

> In all, 28 Japondai people lost their heads, which were boiled and scraped, then moulded with clay into which the original hair of the victim was set, to be triumphantly displayed in the House Tambarans of the victors.[65]

Wolstab and Townsend established a protected camp near the now deserted village of Malu to base their operations. They visited Yambon and Eric later recalled the interchange with the elders:

> ... we had an interpreter, and the natives asked us why we had come to kill them. It was a fair question from their point of view. A few years before, some men, whom they didn't know, in a place, Versailles, that they'd never heard of, had placed them under the trusteeship of Australia, which they'd also never heard of, and Australia had applied its laws, which they didn't know and wouldn't have approved of if they did, and here we were enforcing them. The answer to this basic question, which

we couldn't make them understand, of course, was that if we didn't come there, somebody else, the Japanese, in those days, first guess, would. The natives wouldn't have believed that anyway and couldn't have understood it. They had their own little life in their own villages and didn't know anything beyond that. The idea of bringing them under control and that enforcing peace would be to their benefit was a state of affairs they couldn't imagine. It is a very awkward point, that.[66]

Eric's task was to provide logistic support and extraction when required. Passage along the Sepik called for watchfulness particularly when *Aloha* came within spear-throwing distance of the bank. After several ill-directed spears Eric rigged some walled screens which gave him, his Chinese engineer and native crew much needed protection but became a haven for equally hostile mosquitoes.

During one supply trip the strong current compelled Eric to tie up on the bank near the village of Togowie. He set up hurricane lamps in the surrounding bushes and police sentries for the night. All was well until as they prepared for their evening meal, the Chinese engineer realised the ship's cat had taken shore leave. Fearing for the fate of the cat the engineer wanted to go into the village to rescue their mascot. The police told him the village was 'no good and he would surely be killed in the darkness'.[67] Undeterred, the engineer marched into Togowie shouting

Eric Feldt and his crew of Aloha *during the 1924 Sepik Expedition.* (NAA)

THE INTER WAR YEARS 187

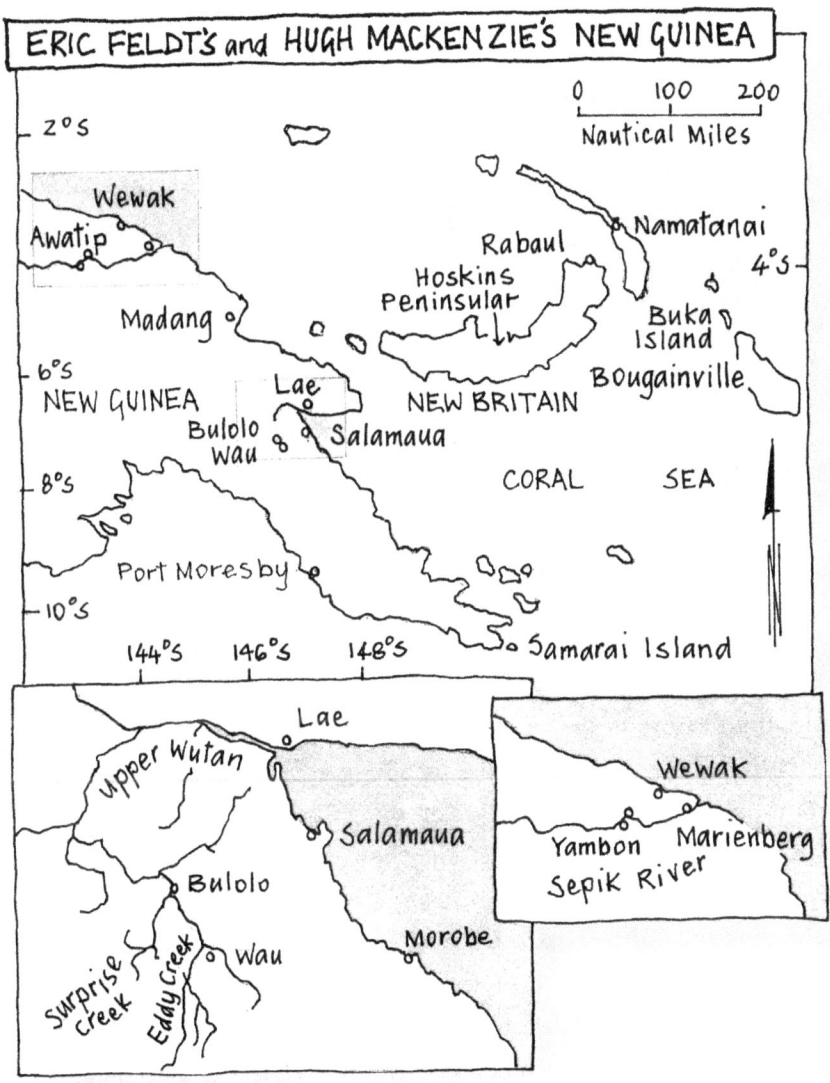

'Kanaka he steal pussy belong me'.[68] From *Aloha* Eric could hear much commotion from the village and ordered his police mustered for action. As they spread in a line and moved towards the village they saw the figure of their engineer marching back with his hurricane lamp and the cat under his arm followed by protesting villagers.

Shortly after this incident the expedition withdrew having been unable to find any natives definitely involved in the recent head-hunting. But the abrupt intrusion of the patrol intimidated the tribesmen sufficiently for them to stop further head-hunting raids. The remarkable Father Kerschbaum who had been in New Guinea since 1912 formed the view, which Eric eventually came to share:

> If they won't stop headhunting, shoot them. That will save lives in the long run. You may kill a few, but that will save the lives of many more who will be killed in the headhunting.[69]

The expedition was a valuable experience for Eric and helped establish his reputation for reliability and having the makings of a future District Officer. Shortly after Christmas in 1924 Eric acted as pilot for the newly acquired Administrator's vessel *Franklin* which was to take the Administrator Brigadier General Evan Wisdom[70] and his senior staff on a tour of settlements. Eric surprised many by his detailed knowledge of the ship because it was the same old *Franklin* from Naval College days. Because of his childhood exposure to Pidgin, Eric was soon fluent in the closely related New Guinea variant Tok Pisin. Eric was disappointed to find that that only Wolstab among the General's staff could speak Tok Pisin. Eric became an early and strong advocate of teaching Tok Pisin to administration officers to make them more effective in the field. The tour gave Eric a great feel for the diversity of the territory and on his return he was assigned to Buka Island off Bougainville. It was an ideal location for Eric whose health had been failing. Eric vividly described his new post:

> Buka Passage is a beauty spot. There is the deep water in the Passage itself tailing off to green where it gets shallower, then the coral reefs looking brown, the white sand of the beaches themselves and the

luxuriant green of the trees of those tropical islands. It's a lovely spot and at night, particularly with the moonlight on it, when you've got a canoe coming up with all the natives chanting in time to the paddling, it really did have some of the romance of the tropical islands.[71]

Accompanying Eric Feldt was Eric Robinson who was one of the more engaging and colourful characters then in New Guinea. Robinson could not pronounce his 'Rs' and would introduce himself as 'Ewic Wobinson'. He was therefore known universally as 'Wobby'. Like Eric, he developed a great interest in the people and culture of New Guinea and they became firm friends. Robinson was an avid photographer and chronicled his service through that medium.[72] He later became famous for his extended service in the malarious Sepik area, earning the nickname of 'Sepik Robby'. He said his secret to his long tenure was a philosophical approach to life and regular intake of gin.

Despite Buka's better environment Eric Feldt's health further deteriorated and he was given leave in Australia. Eric regularly suffered from malaria and recalled that, 'with a really bad attack of malaria, you have the feeling that you are going to die, but you are afraid that you won't'.[73]

After a short break and with finances at a low ebb Eric returned in late 1925 to relieve 'Kaasa' Townsend as Acting District Officer at Wewak on the north coast of mainland New Guinea and 950 km from Rabaul. The district was under control and Eric's duties included ensuring that the census and taxation were done, acting as Magistrate and ensuring the regulations relating to engaging and employing native workers were adhered to. Eric saw the district as one full of promise and developed plans to put in roads to the larger villages that were on the grass plains beyond the range. It was an isolated life with few whites in the district and for most of his tenure he was the only government official in Wewak.

While Eric began to make his way in colonial administration, Hugh MacKenzie also sought his future in New Guinea. Newly married, Hugh obtained his merchant navy certificates and in 1921 first visited Rabaul on a trader. He then worked on various ships between Queensland, Papua and New Guinea. He and Eric would later cross paths.

VI

For the Pioneer Class members who remained in the Navy the early 1920s was a period of gaining professional development predominantly through specialist training with the RN and consolidation either with the RN or the much reduced Australian Squadron. Norman Calder after the disbandment of the submarine arm returned to UK for the demanding torpedo course. He found Eddy Nurse there attending the Long Engineering Course. During the summer break in 1925 both of them spent a couple of weeks in Southern France. Norman, who was fascinated by the odds associated with gambling, had 'a system' he wanted them both to try at the casinos. Eddy later wrote:

> We tried this system out with a capital of £4. With 28 losses in succession we had gone through our £4 in not quite 20 minutes and decided to abandon the 'system'! When not using the system we had quite a bit of moderate luck.[74]

John Collins' star continued to rise as he entered this career phase. He was demonstrating the promise remarked upon by the staff at Jervis Bay. His Captain at HMS *Excellent* had written following his specialist Long Gunnery Course:

> A very keen officer who should do extraordinarily well. Came out top of (the) Long (Gunnery) Course but being RAN was not eligible for the Egerton Prize. Plays all games. Very pleasant personality.[75]

John upon reconsideration was awarded the Egerton Prize. This period was rewarding in other ways for John. His older brother Dale had established himself in London as a successful writer with a best-selling account of his time as a crewman in a global circumnavigation in *Sea-Tracks of the Speejacks Round the World* and two novels. In 1925 his second novel, *Ordeal* became a play and then was made into a movie called *The Ship from Shanghai*.[76]

It was exciting for Dale and John who both enjoyed the attractions of London and ventured to the continent when John's training allowed. Arguably Dale's literary circle expanded John's more limited naval horizons.

Harold Farncomb had also excelled as a non-specialist gunnery officer in *Stalwart*. He may well have specialised in gunnery were it not for his 1922 appointment to the Squadron Commander's staff of Commodore Albert Addison then embarked in *Melbourne*. Onboard he found James Esdaile serving as a bridge watchkeeping officer. On a deployment to the south west Pacific islands, Harold rekindled his interest in intelligence and operational staff work. He also gained an appreciation for the broader strategic context within which the Squadron operated. His excellent intelligence reports drew praise from the Naval Board.[77] It was from this interest that in 1924 Harold undertook the War Staff Officers' course at Greenwich followed by three months consolidation as Staff Officer Operations and Intelligence to Rear Admiral, First Battle Squadron in the battleship HMS *Malaya*.

On 9 February 1923 the idiosyncratic Billy Hughes resigned for the last time as Prime Minister to be replaced by the urbane and capable Stanley Bruce. Senator Sir George Pearce was a firm supporter of Stanley Bruce and became a close confidant. From a national security perspective, Bruce was an outstanding choice. A wounded veteran of the Gallipoli campaign where he gained a Military Cross, he was well-travelled with extensive business and political contacts in the United Kingdom. In 1921 he had been part of the Australian delegation to the League of Nations. Prime Minister Bruce attended the 1923 Imperial Conference where his broader views that linked trade, defence and national security were in accord with the spirit of the meeting. The Conference reinforced the 1921 Conference view that the RAN should be able to protect the sea lines of communication on the Australia Station and harass any enemy until the British Main Fleet arrived from the Mediterranean to operate out of the yet to be fully developed base at Singapore. Following the conference, Bruce's government authorised special appropriations of

£8 million to acquire two County Class heavy cruisers, two large 'O' Class submarines and the construction of naval fuel installations in Sydney and Darwin.[78] It was the genesis of a reinvigorated Australian Navy.

The Government decision to acquire new submarines was a recognition of their importance for both national and imperial defence. It was hoped as finances allowed that the flotilla could grow to six boats. For Frank Getting, these developments were of great personal and professional significance. In 1923 he married Emma Forsayth in Sydney and sailed in September 1924 for England. For officers in the interwar period all service in the UK was unaccompanied but one could convert the First Class ticket for two of Second Class.[79] The young couple crossed the United States by train and spent time in vibrant and exciting New York. Frank Getting and Norman Shaw (1914 Entry), undertook additional training before joining RN submarines as the First Lieutenants (or second-in-command). Frank spent seven months in the 500 tonne *R4* and then moved to the larger 1,000 tonne *L21* for another five months. After the initial excitement and glamour of an overseas appointment, Emma found the lot of a naval officer's wife in bleak British sea ports in poorly heated lodging, with little contact with her husband and few friends, a draining experience. For Frank the demands only increased when he and Norman commenced their 'Perisher' course in March 1924 with two RN officers. The legendary Perisher course was an intensive mix of classroom and sea training to assess the suitability of an officer to command a submarine. In 1924 the course had at its disposal a flotilla of 'H' Class submarines as well as sundry surface ships to act as targets. Both Australian Lieutenants were very competitive with each other but Norman received slightly better marks in the sea assessment. Both passed and Frank's report from his 'Teacher', Commander Colin Cantile RN, read:

> A keen and capable officer who has taken great interest in the course and has carried out good attacks. He has plenty of self-confidence and initiative and has a good power of command. He should make a good and reliable Commanding Officer of a submarine.[80]

Frank Getting in commanding HM Submarine H47 *was the first of the Pioneer Class to command a warship.* (RAN)

On completion of the course Frank was appointed to command *H47* while Norman was given *H27*. Both boats were based at Portland on the English Channel. The 'H' Class were cramped but popular among submariners. The *H47* was five years old with a crew of 22 within its 52 metres length and 510 tonnes displacement. For Frank taking his first command was a momentous occasion. To have achieved command of a warship within eleven years of joining the Navy was an impressive achievement. He was the first of the Pioneer Class to reach this important milestone.

Unlike Frank Getting, Harry Showers decided to pursue a specialisation in Navigation following his service in the 'J' boats. After obtaining his 'N' qualification with the RN in 1923 he joined HMS *Badminton* to consolidate his training. The ship was a Hunt Class minesweeper, one of a class known affectionately as *Smokey Joes* if they were burning anything other than the best Welsh coal. *Badminton* was an ideal ship for Harry to hone his skills. As well as obtaining a qualification in minesweeping Harry was recommended for the First Class Ship Course in navigation.

The centerpiece of Prime Minister Bruce's naval plans were not the 'O' Class submarines in which Frank Getting was destined to serve, but the two County Class heavy cruisers. These handsome 10,000 ton ships were spacious and seaworthy and were graced with three distinctive tall raked funnels. They were to become iconic symbols of the Australian interwar navy. However, these ships were in the future, and the early 1920s were difficult for the Navy. The Squadron was war-worn and not all of it could be funded to go to sea. Until the Great Depression and its widespread unemployment, the Navy's pay and conditions made it unattractive to an increasing number of officers and sailors. This was particularly true for those with families to support. For officers with talent there was at least the prospect of promotion and its increased pay, as well as the professional opportunities afforded by specialist courses in Britain and exchange service with the RN.

It was within this difficult environment that the Navy established a routine of exchanging cruisers with the RN to give an entire ship's company the experience of operating in a larger naval context. In 1924 an early opportunity was presented with the world cruise of the British Special Service Squadron. The squadron was commanded by Vice-Admiral Sir Frederick Field who flew his flag in the largest warship then afloat, the battlecruiser HMS *Hood*. She was accompanied by *Repulse* and five D Class ships of the 1st Light Cruiser Squadron. While very much a 'show the flag' exercise in which over a million people would visit the squadron, it presented a wonderful training opportunity. Therefore, when the Squadron ended its seven port visit of Australia, *Adelaide* left with them on 20 April 1924. Among the officers were Lloyd Gilling serving as Navigating Officer and Joe Burnett as Gunnery Officer. *Adelaide* visited New Zealand, Fiji, Hawaii, Canada and the United States and was the first Australian ship to pass through the Panama Canal. For Lloyd it was professionally tremendously rewarding. There was also an opportunity to renew acquaintances in *Hood* where he had served as the Assistant Navigator for two years immediately following his 1920 navigation course. Onboard the battlecruiser Lloyd demonstrated to Captain John Wilfred Tomkinson, RN[81] that he was a zealous and reliable officer who showed considerable promise as a navigator.[82] When *Adelaide's* Captain John Stevenson left the ship in UK he wrote of Lloyd that he was 'one of the best Jervis Bay officers I have met. Considerable powers of discipline. Ambitious, rather quick

The battlecruiser HMS Hood, *flagship of the British Special Service Squadron alongside in Melbourne in April 1924. Lloyd Gilling served for two years onboard as the Assistant Navigating Officer*
(Green Collection/State Library of Victoria)

tempered and impatient. Highly skilled navigator.'[83]

Adelaide and the Squadron finally arrived in Portsmouth on 28 September 1924. After maintenance, *Adelaide* visited various ports and then enjoyed Christmas leave in Portsmouth. It was during this time that Joe Burnett met Enid Ward, the youngest daughter of a local Councilor. They married in what the local newspaper described as a 'picturesque wedding', with Lloyd Gilling serving as best man with his new Captain, George Massey, RN and the other *Adelaide* officers forming a guard of honour after the church service.

Adelaide finally sailed for home on 10 January 1925. After his service in *Malaya,* Harold Farncomb joined the cruiser for the return voyage. *Adelaide* reached Sydney on 7 April after nearly a year away. Joe Burnett left *Adelaide* soon after her return to be Officer-in-Charge of the Gunnery School at *Cerberus*. This was a most welcome shore posting with Enid. Lloyd Gilling left the ship the following year with a glowing report from Captain Massey and the prospect of advanced navigation training in UK. Massey's report however did warn Lloyd that he 'should guard against over-confidence'.[84] Harold Farncomb, meanwhile, became Staff Officer (Operations and Intelligence) to the Commodore Commanding the Australian Squadron and would remain in that post for three years, in the course of which he came under the approving eye of Commodore Hyde.

Eddy Nurse also returned to Australia 'at long last' in 1925 in the Aberdeen Line steamship *Euripides*.[85] He had been away from Australia for over five years. In that time he had completed his specialist training, consolidated this in the cruiser HMS *Dauntless* and then obtained his First Class Certificate on the Long Engineering Course.

VII

While charting of the world's oceans and coastlines is fundamental to the safe navigation of navies and the merchant marine alike, it was not considered a specialisation that would necessarily lead to command of major warships or flag rank. Despite this the appeal of hydrography was strong for Alfred Condor and Cyril Sadleir. They immersed themselves in the charting of Australia's coastline and offshore waters. In the 1920s the Australian chart folio still had charts with soundings made by Matthew Flinders, Phillip Parker King, John Lort Stokes and even James Cook. The charts of northern Australia were particularly patchy and there was still the opportunity for hydrographers to fill in dotted coastline within bays and inlets and to name prominent points.

Surveying was exacting. Sir William Wharton in his definitive text of the period, *Hydrographic Surveying*, declared that:

> It is difficult to say that any one step in the construction of a chart is more important than another, as each is necessary for the completion of the whole, and an error anywhere may cause a disaster.[86]

Hydrography was both time consuming and labour intensive. Hydrographic ships would typically embark two or three survey motor boats which would be used to put ashore parties to establish triangulation points on the coast. These structures would then have their latitude and longitude determined with as much exactitude as possible. The shore parties would work with the ship or in the case of inshore work, the survey motor boats, to establish the position of the coastline, prominent points in the hinterland, the depth of water, the nature of the sea bottom and the tides. This work was achieved through the use of sextants, lead-lines, station pointers for plotting fix positions of recorded depths, theodolites with compass attachments for observing magnetic variation, beam compasses, a plotting table and associated instruments. A typical detached shore party comprised two officers, three survey recorders, two boats crew and, two leadsman. The measurement of tides required a three-man tide party to observe half-hour readings over a minimum of 29 days. The demands of the work were counter-balanced by the informality of camp-life, pristine and remote landscape and an over-riding sense of accomplishment.

The hydrographic specialisation had four grades. Alfred achieved his initial H4 qualification in August 1922 and joined the survey vessel HMS *Fantome*, then operating on the Australia Station as an assistant Surveyor. *Fantome* conducted surveys of the approaches to Torres Strait as well as sections of the Great Barrier Reef. Alfred's Commanding Officer, Commander Patrick Maxwell, RN reported that he was:

> A very hardworking and keen young officer, has a clever brain and a considerable aptitude for practical work with instruments, delicate machinery etc. Inclined to be a little casual about his personal appearance, but his fault is improving and he should do well in the special line he has taken up, namely Hydrographic Surveying.[87]

When the ship paid off in 1924 Alfred undertook further study in England and attained his H3 qualification. He then joined HMS *Ormode* to consolidate his training. The ship was on the North America and West Indies Station and Alfred performed well in the surveys in the Caribbean. His report from the ship described him as:

An officer who is very popular with both officers and men. Always cheerful and ever ready to make the best of things. He has an even temper and is not easily put out. He is keen on games and social functions generally.[88]

More professionally important he was assessed as 'a good all-round surveyor with an ideal temperament'.[89] After his successful period with the RN, Alfred returned to Australia in 1925. He joined the survey ship HMAS *Geranium* in 1925 where he found classmates Horace Thompson serving as First Lieutenant and Cyril Sadleir an Assistant Surveyor, now with a H4 qualification.

During that year *Geranium* and HMAS *Moresby* worked together to survey large areas of northern Australia and the Great Barrier Reef. Harry Showers was in *Moresby* serving as the Navigator and had also obtained his H4 certificate. It was welcome happenstance to have four of the Class at sea together again. The following year Alfred achieved his H2 qualification and then transferred to *Moresby*. The ship was under the command of Captain John Edgell, RN a gifted surveyor who would later become one of the longest serving Hydrographers of the

In 1925 Horace Thompson, Cyril Sadleir and Alfred Conder served together in HMAS Geranium *conducting hydrographic surveys in northern Australian waters.* (NLA)

RN⁹⁰. Harry benefited from Edgell's guidance and by the time he left the ship to navigate *Melbourne* was a meticulous and confident navigator. Under Edgell's and then Captain Denys Henderson's exacting tutelage, Alfred similarly prospered and attained the coveted H1 certificate which qualified him to be in charge of a survey. He was the first RAN officer to achieve this qualification.

Cyril's career took an unexpected turn. Whilst serving in *Geranium* his hands started to shake and he was found difficulty completing his chartwork. His condition, while not accurately diagnosed, was in fact relapsing-remitting multiple sclerosis. In October 1926 Cyril's hopes of emulating Alfred's career in hydrography were finally dashed when he was invalided out from the Navy. Like many suffers of multiple sclerosis, Cyril would have interludes when his symptoms would largely disappear allowing him to lead a normal life.[91]

VIII

In 1923 James Esdaile along with another RAN officer Lieutenant Harry Melville (1914 Entry), attended the RN's fourth Anti-Submarine (A/S) specialist course. It was conducted at HMS *Osprey*, the Anti-Submarine School at Portland. Much was expected of these two officers as the RAN developed plans, concepts, training and equipment to counter the submarine menace. On his specialist course James did exceedingly well and the Captain of *Osprey* reported that:

> Lieutenant Esdaile is a very talented officer. He is of a good natured, quiet, even tempered disposition. He has marked powers of discernment and great sagacity. He carried out his duties with thoroughness and ability. When qualifying as Lieutenant A/S he obtained a very high standard and a first Class certificate. He is an officer of considerable promise.[92]

By virtue of his competence and the part he needed to play on his return to Australia, James was attached to *Osprey* on completion of this course until November 1925. He further excelled in his involvement in experimental anti-submarine work as well as instruction. On return to Australia, he did not go to sea, but instead went to Navy Office in Melbourne to help flesh out the RAN plans for its anti-submarine capabilities.

As it developed these anti-submarine plans the RAN was in regular correspondence with the RN. Conceptually, the anti-submarine capabilities would have to protect shipping inside ports and their approaches, as well as taking a more offensive stance at sea. This would be to protect both naval and merchant shipping. The key technologies were a magnetic loop detection device that would passively detect submarines when laid on a harbour bottom; passive hydrophones fitted to small vessels and the more elaborate active sound ranging Asdic sets (later called sonar) to be fitted to warships and converted auxiliary vessels. Asdic generated a sound signal and then calculated the bearing and range of the submerged object through the echo of this signal. The technology and Asdic sets were evolving at a significant rate and James Esdaile had trial experience with the new Type 115. The RN hoped this set would provide greater detection ranges and ships being able to operate them at higher speed.

James Esdaile on passage from England. As one of the first anti-submarine officers in the RAN he played an important role in planning Australia's anti-submarine defences. (Esdaile family)

In 1925 the British Committee for Imperial Defence, which acted as a defence planning agency for the Empire, completed a paper on the *Requirements for Minesweeping and Auxiliary anti-submarine vessels at various Empire ports in the event of war in the East.*[93] James Esdaile's first task in Navy Office was make an assessment of the report. He was highly critical of the proposed placement of the systems. His trials experience had showed him how system performance could vary greatly depending on location. He proposed that the RAN undertake a series of trials to better understand system performance in the different conditions around Australia. This was aligned with the Admiralty proposal to develop global Asdic charts to give ships an indication of local conditions and the presence of natural underwater features that could be mistaken for submarines (known as non-subs). After some deliberation the Naval Board initially allocated £21,000 for a loop cable and an Asdic for local experiments, pending the results of further RN trials. But there was still uncertainty about the best way forward and Commodore Hyde favoured a greater emphasis on anti-submarine capabilities for the Australian Squadron rather than around the ports.

In November 1926 a conference was held in Navy Office to bring together the differing views on anti-submarine measures. James Esdaile, by now the inaugural Squadron A/S Officer in *Sydney* was in attendance. The conference validated James' and others' position that the priority was to obtain an Asdic set in preference to acquiring loops or hydrophones. It was proposed to fit the first Asdic in *Platypus* for training purposes. The subsequent complication was that the early RN Asdics, such as the latest Type 117, were failing to live up to expectations. It would be some years yet before a RAN warship would be fitted with Asdic.

Like their contemporaries, the young men of the Pioneer Class found their twenties and early thirties a period of immense change in their lives as they completed their transformation to adulthood. Almost all found their life partners in marriage. There were some notable unions. In keeping with the social mores of the time, naval officers not infrequently married into wealthy families. This belied the mens' humbler origins.

Depending on the circumstances, this misalignment of social status with the modest naval officer's pay could create tension. For some this would become a reason to leave the service for a second career that would offer greater remuneration and the maintenance of a certain lifestyle.

The first to marry was twenty-one year old Harry Vallentine, who since returning from service in the British Army was a farm hand at Yenda in the Riverina. He married Irene Marshall in Sydney and the following year they had a daughter, Margaret. Also marrying as a twenty-one year old was Horace Thompson. He and his young wife Louise spent much of 1921 at Jervis Bay where Horace was given command of *Franklin,* then still the College tender. Fittingly, one of the other early marriages was at the Naval College. On 22 October 1924, Cyril Sadleir married Dr Wheatley's surviving daughter Phyllis. Cyril was serving in *Brisbane* and fellow officers from the ship and Naval College formed an arch of swords outside the chapel. His best man was shipmate Emile Dechaineaux (1916 Entry). On completion of the wedding ceremony the cadet-midshipmen pulled the bridal car down to the wardroom for the reception.

The following year Adrian Watts married journalist and poet Lilias Grieve. Perhaps driven by considerations of having a more stable income Adrian briefly tried service in the Fire Brigade but soon returned to his more satisfying, if financially precarious life as an illustrator.

Among the other Pioneer Class who had left the Navy, most were establishing themselves. After receiving his degree from Melbourne University, Ben Howells decided upon a teaching career rather than that of a missionary. His first school was Traralgon Higher Elementary School. He was well reported upon by the District Inspector and in 1926 secured a position at Swinburne Technical College where he was to remain for a decade.

After a short period in his father's stockbroking firm Winn Reilly also decided to go to university. As he demonstrated on his torpedo course, Winn had an outstanding technical mind and gained entry to the University of Melbourne where he obtained a Bachelor of Electrical Engineering. Winn worked diligently in his studies and completed the last three years of his degree in two years. In 1925 Winn returned to the UK and worked for two years in a variety of firms to gain practical consolidation of his degree. While there he played rugby once more, this time for the Wasps Club. On return to Australia he co-founded the consultation practice of Reilly Page Engineering. After two years Winn moved to Sydney to set up a new firm with another engineer. This new venture did not succeed and in 1929 Winn joined the innovative Hume Pipe Company in Sydney.[94]

Peyton Kimlin followed the path of many a young teacher by being sent to small rural schools to learn the fundamentals of his profession and fill positions in more remote locations. One such school was at Woodend, which at the time was but a tiny settlement for timber workers and their families. His brother George visited Peyton at the rough old local pub where Peyton was billeted. It had few rooms:

> ... one of which had a huge smokey fireplace, in front of which sat an old bearded bushie, complete with hat and pipe, his dog, an Airedale lay stretched across the hearth. Occasionally, the bearded one would take his pipe out of his mouth and spit accurately on to the dog's back. He would then lift his foot and with a large muddy boot rub the spittle in. From this position neither moved during my stay.[95]

While teaching in northern Victoria, Peyton learned that teachers in New South Wales earned a better salary. The difference was significant enough for Peyton to cross the Murray River in June 1927. His first appointment was as an assistant teacher at Hay Public School. Both in rural Victoria and New South Wales Peyton continued to compose. In 1928 he completed another musical entitled *Carnival* in collaboration with Sax Paige who also ran the Paige Publishing Company on Flinders Lane in Melbourne.[96] At the beginning of the 1929 school year Peyton moved once more, still as an Assistant Teacher, to Coolamon Central School in the Riverina. He was a welcome addition as the Coolamon school had grown to over two hundred children with the closure of smaller schools in the district. Peyton taught a combined fourth and fifth class. In the winter of 1929 he caught scarlet fever as part of an epidemic that swept the district. It resulted in two deaths and the temporary closure of the school. There was however a silver lining for Peyton, which was a month's convalescence in Melbourne and an uninterrupted period to compose once he felt fit enough to do so.[97] *A Foxtrot* is a product of his Coolamon period.[98] After his initial tenure in country New South Wales, Peyton successfully applied for a teaching position in the northern beaches area of Sydney. It was within this new environment that he would further extend his musical talents.

During the remainder of the 1920s Harry and Irene Vallentine lived in rural Victoria where Harry tried to support his growing family of three children with a variety of work. Harry had a serious addiction to gambling. Whether it had developed in his merchant navy or British Army service is unclear. His gambling grew to the point that he told Irene to return to Sydney with the family otherwise he would spend all their money. On 3 July 1929 Harry appeared before a magistrate in Parramatta for disobeying an earlier order to support his wife and children. He was fined £15 11s 6d with the prospect of prison should he default. The *New South Wales Police Gazette* dispassionately described Harry in the following terms:

> He is 30 years of age, 5 feet 8 or 9 inches [1.7m] high, medium build, about 11 stone weight [70kg], dark complexion, dark-brown curly hair, dark-brown eyes, sharp features; usually dressed in navy-blue clothes, black shoes, and a grey felt hat; a labourer or a linesman.[99]

Harry, separated from Irene and his family, returned to Victoria and undertook jobs ranging from fruit seller to barman. The responsibility of raising the family would rest solely with Irene.

Another of the Class to face personal challenges was George Armitage. In January 1925 he was appointed to the destroyer *Stalwart* as the First Lieutenant and second in command. On the paying off of the ship he and many of the ship's company commissioned her sister ship *Success*. George initially proved to be a 'very capable First Lieutenant'[100] who demonstrated a particularly good knowledge of destroyer gunnery. No doubt this was from his time in *Torrens* at the end of the war. George was however starting to drink excessively. In the Navy during the period of the Pioneer Class' service a nip of spirits was about a third of the price of a beer and so drinking was often based on spirits.[101] So it was the case with George. His growing dependence on alcohol was not helped by him having responsibility for the wine accounts. Irregularities in these accounts in both *Stalwart* and *Success* led to a Board of Inquiry. This found George had behaved with gross negligence and had an excessive wine bill. The Board ordered special quarterly reports to be made of his performance.

George's problems with alcohol became even more serious. At 9 am on 27 January 1926 the Captain of *Success*, Lieutenant Commander Cyril Hill, RN returned onboard his ship which lay at a buoy in Farm Cove in Sydney Harbour. He was told that George, who was the Officer of the Day had left the ship at 8.40 am without handing over to his relief, the Gunner, who had yet to arrive onboard. George had told the gangway staff he had to pay some wine accounts ashore before the ship sailed at 6 pm that day. He went to pay the accounts at Penfolds Wines and then at the Tooth's Brewery both on George Street. He was offered drinks at both establishments and then met a friend with whom he shared another drink at a hotel near the Central Railway Station. His next recollection at about 7.30 pm was waking up in the park near the station. By the time he returned to Man-O-War Steps, *Success* had sailed and George joined HMAS *Platypus* at about 9 pm where he was placed under arrest. He subsequently rejoined his ship in Jervis Bay under escort.

On 12 February 1926 with the Australian Squadron in Hobart, a court martial was held for George Armitage onboard *Platypus*. The President of the Court Martial was Captain Hector Boyce RN, Commanding Officer of *Sydney*. The prosecutor was *Sydney's* Commander and former Naval College officer Cuthbert Pope. George was charged with improperly leaving his ship and absence without leave. George pleaded guilty but maintained that 'the liquor I had drunk contained some deleterious ingredient, for the quantity I consumed was quite insufficient to account for the condition into which I fell'.[102]

George was found guilty on both counts. His punishment was dismissal from *Success*, forfeiture of a year's seniority and a severe reprimand. The court martial must have been a melancholy experience for his College instructors Morton Moyes and Thomas Dix who were serving in *Platypus* at the time.

While in *Platypus* George was initially restricted in his alcohol allowance which was later relaxed. During the 1926 Spring Cruise he started to consume large amounts once more and was subsequently discharged to Flinders Naval Depot when he had to be admitted to Adelaide Hospital on *Platypus'* sailing. His final prophetic report from the ship encapsulated his situation:

> A capable and experienced officer, but handicapped by his apparent inability to refrain from excessive drinking which must in time affect both his professional ability and his health.

As is usual for an officer struggling professionally, George Armitage was posted to a ship with a senior captain in command. This was *Melbourne,* commanded by Captain Julian Patterson, OBE, RN. Here George's professional performance declined and he led an 'abnormal and secluded life and seldom goes ashore'.[103]

While the Squadron's 1926 Spring Cruise had been an unhappy experience for George, it presented, like other cruises, social opportunities for officers and sailors alike to meet a likely spouse. This was just the case for Norman Calder who met Nancie Dixon at a Melbourne Cup eve dance. They 'noticed each other across the room' but, it would be nearly four years before they would be able to marry.[104]

Far from the social whirl of the Melbourne Cup, Eric Feldt was being once again relocated to another colonial outpost. In March 1927 he sailed to Namatanai on New Ireland which he found a 'different kettle of fish altogether' to Wewak. Namatanai, like Rabaul was a well laid out traditional German style settlement. Eric as Acting District Officer had a very large house to himself, a separate office and barracks for his native police as well as a small schooner to visit the nearby islands. Importantly the settlement had a very good climate and the natives were all on the coast. This meant:

There were mountains in the district, but there were no natives in them, so you didn't have to go. And you didn't have to sweat over mountains in the hot sun, as I had had to in Wewak.[105]

The district itself was law-abiding. The good price for copra generated both employment and a satisfactory living standard. Eric got on well with the native population as well as with the planters and the Chinese merchant families who operated small trading stations dotted along the coast. Eric recalled:

> Now it was good, flat country and I had a horse so as to ride down the coast, stop at every plantation to inspect labour, then I would go on and stop at the Chinese trading store. Well, the Chinese were a hospitable race and they believe in keeping in with the Kiap[106] and on every store veranda there would be two bottles of beer and a glass put out ready for me. Well, I couldn't keep up with that. Not every two miles. However, it was very nice to have an occasional beer while you were on patrol, riding a horse rather than sweating your skin off in the hot sun, as it had been in Aitape and Wewak.[107]

Such were the attractions of this idyllic part of New Britain that when the Expropriation Board offered a group of plantations for sale, Eric and his friend Jack Melville put in a bid for one. Unfortunately, their bid was too low and Eric remained in Government service. In September, 1927 Eric returned south to Brisbane for well-earned restorative leave. Like those before, this spell was a very social one and on 17 December while driving along Kedron Park Road Eric was detained by police for driving under the influence of alcohol and taken to the Watchhouse. He was subsequently released on bail

Eric Feldt on restorative leave at Yeronga.
(Feldt Family)

and paid a fine.[108] A chastened man, he returned to New Guinea with more money in his pocket than usual and armed with a collection of gramophone records, including that of his beloved Caruso.

After the success of *Adelaide's* deployment with the Special Service Service squadron *Brisbane* deployed to the RN's China Station in 1925 and in the following year *Melbourne* spent several months on exchange in the Mediterranean Fleet.[109] Serving in *Melbourne* as her Gunnery Officer was John Collins. Also onboard were Commander Moyes from his Naval College days and Chaplain Hardie who had accompanied him in *Omrah*. *Melbourne* was the only coal-burner in the First Cruiser Squadron. On arrival in port *Melbourne's* officers would join her sailors in the filthy and back-breaking task of coaling ship whilst their contemporaries in the more modern oil-fuelled D Class cruisers relaxed in their wardrooms. John later reminisced:

> With all officers and men hard at it for many hours, always against time and each hold competing against others, it worked wonders in getting the ship's company together. Like many coal-burning ships, our cruiser became infested with rats and our solitary ship's cat could not compete with them. We had an air rifle in the Wardroom and used to take pot-shots at them as they ran along the top of the ventilation shafts but we seldom did them much damage.
> Eventually a professional rat-catcher was hired in Malta and results were awaited. We were not impressed by his antiquated gear or by the fact that he never displayed his catch. However, we paid him off after three days on his assurance that the ship was now free from rats. It soon became evident that the rat-catcher had been a fraud; the rats were as bad as ever. [Ernest] 'Dusty' Rhodes the First Lieutenant, then took matters in hand. He bought a dozen modern rat-traps and that night set them round the ship. Next morning in the grey light of dawn he went round the traps, having dug out from somewhere a trapper's fur cap. We gathered in the Wardroom for early tea after 6 am. 'Hands fall in' when 'Dusty' appeared at the Wardroom door, looking very much more professional than the Maltese rat-catcher. Without comment he held up the morning's catch, the ship's cat![110]

Like the RAN ships attached to the Grand Fleet during the Great War and her successors assigned to the Mediterranean Fleet, *Melbourne* was extremely competitive in any evolution or sporting contest against RN ships. This ranged from beating the record time it took the ship's company to march the twelve miles from Malta's Ghain Tuffieha rifle range back to the ship in the Grand Harbour (2 hours and 44 minutes) to winning the Fleet swimming championship. On her final departure the dynamic Commander-in-Chief Mediterranean Fleet Admiral Sir Roger Keyes, who himself had done so much to energise his Fleet, signalled 'If the Australian Navy had any more ships as efficient as HMAS *Melbourne* there is no doubt of the part that Navy will play in any future emergency'.[111]

On *Melbourne's* return passage to Australia Rhodes and John Collins had their fortunes read near the pyramids by an old soothsayer called 'The Limit'. John recalled:

> He demanded two English pounds to tell our fortunes, which we thought over the limit, so we arranged to be told only one thing each for five shillings. After the usual drawing in the sand and so on he told us we were not ordinary tourists but were travelling on some sort of duty. He said to 'Dusty', 'You will marry that girl within six months'. He had been wooing Ula for a long time and they were married as forecast. He turned to me and said 'You will be told to change your job—not be sacked but do something different—the day before you arrive at your destination'. The evening before the ships arrived in Melbourne a signal was received from the Navy Office directing me to leave the ship there and take up the unexpected appointment as Naval Liaison Officer for the 1927 Royal Visit of the Duke and Duchess of York. I am in no way psychic and never dabble in such things. However, in view of the success of the five shilling investment, I regretted having quibbled over the pound, for it would have been interesting to know the rest of the story.[112]

The purpose of the Royal Visit was to open the new Parliament House in Canberra on 9 May 1927. The Duke and Duchess of York had taken passage in the battlecruiser HMS *Renown*. One of the features of the opening would be a ceremonial arrival of the Duke and Duchess with a mounted escort which would include the Admiral and John Collins. There is a truism that naval officers and horses do not mix. On that premise both naval officers prudently practised their horsemanship in Melbourne with soldiers waving flags to try to upset the horses. All went well until John's compliant mount was given to Brigadier General Charles Brand at late notice. The new horse was a doubtful 'light horse hairy' from the Duntroon stable with number '13' stamped on his hoof. John recalled the Parliament House opening as:

> ... a trying experience. The wretched animal was terrified of the noise and people, and even more unhappy than I was. I just managed to prevent it bolting but, by the end of proceedings, I could not have been more covered in foam had I been on the bridge of a destroyer in a gale.[113]

In contrast to John's view of the event, the newspapers reported on a 'brilliant pageant' with over three thousand servicemen drawn from the three services in attendance. This included cadet-midshipmen from Jervis Bay and a contingent from *Renown*. In addition to speeches by the Duke of York and Prime Minister Bruce, Dame Nellie Melba sang the national anthem before the assembled gathering of about 15,000 people.[114] Tragically one of the air force aircraft crashed during the flying display and 28-year old Flying Officer Francis Ewen died of his injuries.

After the opening John Collins remained in *Renown* with the Royal Party. This provided a privileged view of the rapturous reception the Duke and Duchess received at the various Australian and imperial ports for the return passage to the UK.

XI

In 1927 Harry Showers married his late friend Dick Cunningham's sister, Jean. They had met on his return from the Grand Fleet when Harry came to express his condolences and explain the circumstances of Dick's death to his mother. At the time of their marriage Harry was serving once more in *Sydney*. Chaplain Hardie who had joined *Sydney* from *Melbourne* officiated at the wedding held at nearby St Stephens Church.[115] Eddy Nurse who had been a close friend of both Harry and Dick was the best man. The Captain and officers of *Sydney* gave the bridal couple an engraved silver tea set which was to become a treasured possession.[116]

As was to be expected class mates often served as the best man if they were not at sea. Such was the case for Harold Farncomb's marriage to Jean Nott in 1927. John Collins, before taking on his Royal escort duties was best man and James Esdaile was groomsman. Harold had met Jean when both were on passage to Europe with Jean enroute to study in Paris. Jean came from the wealthy family that owned the David Jones department store chain. This would assist Jean to follow Harold and set up house in different ports as his career required.

During 1927 a small cadre of Australian officers and sailors were standing by the two cruisers *Australia* and *Canberra* being built on the Clyde. After leaving *Renown* John Collins joined the group. He was to be the gunnery officer of the new flagship. As such he was also to be responsible for the gunnery proficiency of the Squadron. It was a coveted and well deserved appointment.

Also joining *Australia* was Rupert Long. As a torpedo specialist he had also to be the expert on chemical warfare as it affected the ship and the squadron. Rupert had recently undertaken chemical warfare training. Increasingly however, it was not these fields that excited Rupert's fertile mind, rather it was naval intelligence work. Within a year of completing his 1922 torpedo specialisation course he had applied to attend a short course on intelligence. His timing was not good with the Navy still smarting at losing their first King's Medalist, Winn Reilly from the same course. Intelligence was not considered a specialization and in refusing Rupert's request the Naval Board noted that there was 'no special advantage likely to be obtained in a Lieutenant(T) undergoing the Intelligence Course'.[117] Rupert was undeterred by this rejection and bided his time. In 1925, while serving in *Anzac,* he also acted as the Flotilla Intelligence Officer in addition to his torpedo duties. In that capacity he wrote a detailed intelligence report on the visiting US Fleet that gained the

The new heavy cruisers Australia *and* Canberra *fitting out after their launch at John Brown shipyard, Clydebank where the battlecruiser HMAS* Australia *had also been built.* (JA Collins Collection)

written appreciation of the Naval Board.[118]

Just three months behind *Australia's* building schedule was her sister ship *Canberra*. As both ships neared completion their ship's companies were assembled. *Melbourne* had sailed to the UK to provide the nucleus of *Australia's* crew and was then to be scrapped. In the case of *Canberra* the bulk of her ship's company came from *Sydney* and took passage to Glasgow in the liner *Beltana*.[119] *Canberra's* commanding officer would be Captain Massey formerly of *Sydney* and before that *Adelaide*. The commonly accepted practice was for the captain to have a say in the selection of his officers. It was therefore not surprising that Lloyd Gilling rejoined Massey as his navigating officer. This is a critically important position in any new ship in which comprehensive trials are undertaken to document her operating characteristics. Also assigned to *Canberra* was Joe Burnett as her gunnery officer and Norman Calder as the torpedo specialist. All these Pioneer Class members while standing by their new cruisers shipped a half stripe to become Lieutenant Commanders.

The Sydney Morning Herald proudly reported that the graduates from the Naval College, who were gunnery, torpedo and navigation officers in the ships:

> ...has attracted attention in British naval circles, where the opinion has been expressed that such appointments give a healthy stimulus to Australian sentiment in regard to the Royal Australian Navy, and a truer Imperial significance to that Navy's character.[120]

Australia was launched on 17 March 1927. It was an unusually beautiful spring day for the Clyde. The correspondent for the Adelaide *Advertiser* wrote:

> The new *Australia* is waspish and rakish, 600 feet long, and seems to be all forecastle and quarterdeck, each of which mounts four eight inch guns in twin turrets. Every line connotes speed. It will not be surprising if she exceeds 33 knots. The streamline from the razor bow to the sharp cut stern is only broken by the anti-torpedo bulge amidships. Nevertheless, she looks a veritable speed machine. This whippet literally strained at the leash when the main chocks were removed at ten this morning. She cribbed an inch or two, and then when Dame Mary Cook on the stroke of twelve dashed a bottle of Australian burgundy against her side as a christening, and pressed the button operating the electric rams, the cruiser quivered and shot down the ways to the accompaniment of shrill cheers from hundreds of school children. Altogether it was one of the most perfect launchings seen on the Clyde.[121]

Canberra was launched two months later by Princess Mary. With much less fanfare the rebirth of the Australian submarine arm was also taking shape. In February 1927 both Frank Getting and Norman Shaw travelled up to Barrow-in-Furness in Scotland to stand by the new 'O' Class boats. With a crew of 54 and a displacement of 1,800 tonnes, they were much larger than the 'H' Class. They were also more sophisticated and embodied all the experience of submarine operations in the Great War. Importantly they were the first submarines to incorporate a sonar for underwater detection and ranging.[122] It was decided that Getting and Shaw would initially be the First Lieutenants rather than commanding the new boats. This was to conform to the British practice of having very experienced submarine captains in command of large submarines. This was accepted with as good graces as Getting and Shaw could muster. Commander Hugh Marrack, DSC, RN was senior officer and well-known to both Australians. After a year fitting out and trials both *Oxley* and *Otway* sailed from Fort Blockhouse for Australia on 8 February 1928. To send them off a band played 'Waltzing Matilda' and the wives and families accompanied the submarines down the harbour in a small ferry.

Although the British government desired the new submarines to take passage to Australia via South America to show these modern boats to potential buyers, the Australian Government wanted them home by the most expeditious route which was the now familiar passage through the Mediterranean and the Suez Canal. It would prove to be a delivery voyage unlike any other in Australian naval history.

The first leg to Gibraltar was uneventful, but when alongside in that port, small cracks were detected in the engines of first *Otway* and then *Oxley*. Although these new design engines were still operating smoothly, more cracks appeared in both boats on the passage to Malta where authorities in England and Australia were informed. After initially blaming the RAN submarine engineers for excessively high revolutions, investigations were initiated in the lead boat of the class HMS *Oberon* where cracks were also found. It was then accepted that there was a design and manufacturing flaw. New components needed to be designed, produced and sent to Malta. This was not a quick fix and it was clear the crews of the two boats would be in Malta for at least six months. In May 1928 it was decided to place both boats into Immediate Reserve and remove fuel, stores and ammunition. The crew were accommodated in an old minesweeper HMS *Stoke*. As Commander Marrack would serve more than his allotted two years with the RAN due to these delays, it was decided he would return to England and the newly promoted Lieutenant Commander Frank Getting assume command of *Oxley*. In addition to the work to replace the faulty engine components, Frank and Commander Gordon Hine, DSO, RN in *Otway* organised sport and other training to maintain morale. For a lucky few, their wives following

The submarines Oxley *and* Ovens *alongside in Malta on their delivery voyage to Australia.* (The Argus/State Library of Victoria)

from the UK had broken their passage home and stayed with their husbands in Malta. Another welcome visitor was *Melbourne* on passage to UK with part of *Australia's* commissioning crew.

In contrast to the 'O' Class boats, *Australia* commissioned in Portsmouth on 24 April 1928 with as much pomp and circumstance as could be mustered. She immediately hoisted the flag of the newly promoted Rear Admiral George Hyde, Flag Officer Commanding HM Australian Squadron. The Admiral's much trusted Flag Lieutenant and Squadron Communications Officer was Jack Newman who had already served with him for two years.

Admiral Hyde was an impressive officer and was to go on to have a most significant influence on the Navy for the next decade. As Peyton Kimlin had found to his detriment in *Suva*, Hyde was an outstanding seaman and this stemmed from his unusual career. Hyde wanted to join the RN from an early age but his parents could not afford the fees. Instead he first went to sea in the merchant marine in 1894 and had sailed around Cape Horn in the clipper *Mount Stewart*. In 1896 Hyde joined the RN as a reserve officer and was eventually transferred to the permanent navy. In 1910 he was lent to the Commonwealth Naval Force, the precursor to the RAN, and seeing greater opportunity in

Australia—and lesser class conscious—transferred to it in 1912. Hyde too had stood by a ship at the John Brown shipyard, in his case as the commissioning Commander of the battlecruiser *Australia*. During the war Hyde had commanded the British cruiser HMS *Adventure* in Irish waters where he was also Flag Captain to the formidable Admiral Sir Lewis Bayly. He joined Admiral Jellicoe's staff for his 1919 review of Australia's naval defences. In 1926 Hyde had been promoted to Commodore in command of the much reduced Australian Squadron. This Portsmouth day was therefore a momentous day, not only for the Navy but for Hyde.[123]

As the two cruisers prepared to leave for Australia their men were feted in London and Portsmouth. Contingents attended the Derby, the Trooping of the Colour and Buckingham Palace. A memorable banquet was hosted by the Lord Mayor of Portsmouth who said, 'Although we have entertained many potentates, no body of guests has given the Corporation greater delight.' When 'he referred to the *Emden* episode there was vociferous applause'. Lord Lovatt in the spirit of the occasion, and to a storm of applause said 'the Australians were the finest individual fighters in the world'. In response and to great ovation Admiral Hyde said that the cruisers 'were visible proof that Australia had not neglected the teachings of history. The Australian Navy was dispatched under the wing of the Royal Navy, and must continue thus for many years'.[124]

On 17 July 1928 King George V visited both *Australia* and *Canberra* in Portsmouth before the flagship left on her homeward voyage. On arrival in each ship the King was received with a piping party, the Captain, his officers, a Royal Guard and band. John Collins and Joe Burnett were both responsible for their respective ship's guards and much effort had gone into their preparation. The King had high standards and had been known to be withering in his criticism of a poorly turned out guard. John scored a success by having the front rank of the guard composed of bearded sailors with some very credible specimens. The bearded King was clearly delighted and the subsequent inspection of the ship proceeded smoothly.[125]

Rupert Long being introduced to King George V onboard HMAS Australia.
(Long Family)

On 3 August *Australia* sailed home via Montreal, Quebec, Halifax, Boston, New York, Annapolis, Jamaica, the Panama Canal and Wellington. It was the opportunity for Australia as a nation to show the flag in ports rarely visited. From his years in Irish waters Admiral Hyde had established very cordial links with many US naval officers operating under Admiral Bayly's command and some of these acquaintances were renewed in these visits. The powerful *Australia* caused considerable interest wherever she went as being the first example of a modern cruiser to visit. The hospitality received by *Australia's* crew rivalled that of the Great White Fleet in Australia. A correspondent from *The West Australian* reported that Admiral Hyde told of the reception at Boston that:

> the only uncomfortable feature of the entertainment was the resultant loss of sleep. Everyone had a splendid time, and the desire of the Bostonians to show the Australians courtesy seemed limited only by the capacity of the officers and men to accept so much hospitality.[126]

In the New Zealand capital, Prime Minister Joseph Coates hosted the officers and spoke of the importance of 'Australia's new instrument of safety'[127] to the protection of trade in local waters. After a fast passage across the Tasman, the Flagship triumphantly arrived in Brisbane on 15 October. She was met by Prime Minister Bruce who had been instrumental in acquiring the new heavy cruisers. The Prime Minister made a stirring and widely reported speech to *Australia's* ship's company on her quarterdeck in which he said:

> You belong to a service which has been intimately associated with the destinies of our race. No nation in the world can boast the record and traditions which you possess. We are naturally proud to have an independent Australian Navy, but we are even prouder still to be joint heirs to all the great traditions of the British Navy. We have been tried and tested in the smoke of battle and destiny may unhappily decree that we be tried again. If any enemy decided to come against us he must come across the sea. You men of this young and growing Australian Navy have the great responsibility of setting the standard by which our country in its hour of peril shall rise or fall. Let your justifiable pride in this new and wonderful cruiser be the basis of your pride in the whole Australian Navy. Let the enthusiasm with which you have contributed towards its magnificent cruise be maintained in all that you do in the future. If you do that we can look to you with confidence, knowing that in your keeping our nation's safety and honour shall not suffer.[128]

On 23 October *Australia* finally arrived in Sydney and on her day of public inspection at Circular Quay over 25,000 people toured their new flagship.[129] For her part *Canberra* had an equally successful but much lower key voyage via South Africa.

Three weeks after *Australia's* triumphant arrival in Australia the two 'O' Class submarines finally left Malta. Ten years after the loss of Frank Larkins on the delivery voyage of the 'J' Class, the new 'O' Class sailed through the same waters enroute to Thursday Island. They arrived on 23 January 1929 to be met by the faithful *Platypus* or the *'Old Bus'* as the sailors now called her. The new flotilla port-hopped down the coast visiting Townsville and Brisbane. They finally arrived in Sydney on 14 February, a year and a week since the submarines had set sail from England. *Canberra* arrived in Sydney two days later.

The submariners went on well deserved foreign service leave after their unexpectedly prolonged separation from families. For some, however,

The newly commissioned HMAS Canberra *still awaiting its aircraft catapult. Among the commissioning officers were Joe Burnett, Norman Calder and Lloyd Gilling.* (RAN)

it had been too much. On 22 May 1929 Frank and Emma Getting filed for dissolution of their marriage.[130] Emma remarried in the following year.

After leave and maintenance Commander Hine and Frank Getting set about re-introducing the Navy to submarines. This included both boats visiting the Naval College. Frank gave a 'lantern lecture' to the cadets on submarines. As a Naval College graduate and now a submarine captain, the physically imposing Frank made a great impression on the cadets. His lecture 'increased still further our desires to see the 'real thing''.[131] The next morning cadets were ferrying out to both submarines at anchor in Jervis Bay. Both boats got underway in the bay and submerged to the wonder of the cadets. The accompanying officer Lieutenant Eric Mayo wrote that:

> The visit, besides being of great interest, also served to give some more definite shape to our view with regard to the part which submarines can play in modern warfare.[132]

However, the submarines were not to play a role in the RAN. By the end of the year, the cost and complexity of the boats, in the increasingly straitened times, led to them being placed in Reserve. Every couple of weeks the submarines would go to sea to dive and then return alongside. On 10 May 1930 Frank Getting had the forlorn duty of decommissioning *O In* the following year both submarines were transferred to the RN who were reducing the size of their fleet and paying off older submarines. The two modern Australian boats were a useful addition to their 'O' Class boats.

Frank Getting had proved to be an exceptionally good submariner and was reported to be 'always cheerful and showing a fine spirit at all times'.[133] But even to Frank it must have been a depressing time. He had given his all to submarines and it had arguably cost him his marriage. He was now at a turning point in his career as he returned to general service. Sensibly he was sent to the RN to re-establish his career and he became a watchkeeping officer in the old battleship HMS *Marlborough*. The ship was Flagship of the Third Battle Squadron under none other than Rear Admiral Hyde who was attached to the RN for a year before returning to Australia to become First Naval Member in 1931.

XII

The new cruisers were much needed additions to the Squadron whose calendar was a mix of training and showing the flag activities around the country. The year began with the Hobart Regatta and associated naval exercises followed by return to Sydney then a winter cruise to Queensland with some ships involved in a circumnavigation of the continent.

James Esdaile, now a Lieutenant Commander, returned to Britain for additional service with the RN. In September 1928 he once more joined *Osprey* and thence the battleship HMS *Resolution* of the 1st Battle Squadron as a watchkeeping officer and anti-submarine specialist. Before returning to Australia at the end of 1930, James spent five months at *Osprey* working with new anti-submarine equipment. He received an excellent report from *Osprey* which rated his professional ability as exceptional and recommended him for early promotion.[134]

Also serving in the RN at this time was Harry Showers. He had left *Melbourne* in October 1927 and sailed with his new bride Jean to Britain to obtain his First Class Navigation Certificate at HMS *Dryad* at Portsmouth. Then in March 1928 Harry joined the destroyer leader HMS *Douglas* which served as the sea-going command ship for the Captain, 1ˢᵗ Submarine Flotilla. It was a demanding position for Harry who had to work closely with the commanding officers of the submarines in the Flotilla. In 1930 another round of reduction of officer numbers was undertaken. His Captain reported to Australia House that based on his performance in *Douglas* it was in the best interests of the RAN to retain Harry.[135]

In April 1928 Harold Farncomb joined the battlecruiser *Repulse* as an officer of the watch and turret officer. He performed well but not exceptionally so. Towards the end of 1929 he had a stroke of good fortune. The Navy had a position for a captain to attend the 1930 course at the Imperial Defence College. At the height of the Depression, Treasury officials in Australia baulked at the cost of the passage for another officer and insisted one already in UK fill the position.[136] Harold, due to leave *Repulse,* was selected even though he was two ranks junior. Harold was not over-awed and excelled in this stimulating environment. His final report from the Commandant, General Bartholomew said Harold:

> Has mental ability considerably above the average even of students here. Broad-minded, well read, shrewd and clear and incisive in debate. He has character and good judgement and his good work has been not only valuable to himself but to everyone else here.
>
> I regard Lieutenant-Commander Farncomb, who is still young, as very promising and likely to develop into an extremely valuable Officer who, as he gains experience, will be fit for the most important work on the staff.[137]

XIII

At the beginning of 1928 Eric Feldt had returned to New Guinea from a break in Australia. His new assignment was once again filling a gap in the District Officer ranks, this time the senior post in Madang. The former German settlement, 300 km along the coast from Wewak was a plum appointment. Eric had not been in post long before, in May 1928, he was reassigned once more at short notice to Salamaua as an Assistant

District Officer 2nd Division. The small settlement is 250 km further east from Madang in Morobe Province but only 30 km by sea from the Morobe provincial capital of Lae.

At first Eric thought he had the incurred the wrath of a 'stool polisher' to be sent to this lower rated district. The settlement stood on a low-lying isthmus between a headland and the mountainous interior. But Salamaua with its rudimentary waterfront was a now a bustling settlement, being used as a staging point for gold prospectors in the Wau goldfields 50 km inland. The trading companies Burns Philp and Carpenters had established stores to equip the eager prospectors. Salamaua was also a place where the prospectors could have a break from the goldfields and, naturally, there was a pub. The Administration had been slow in providing infrastructure and sufficient police presence. On his arrival Eric was met by his predecessor who said 'there's a vacant house there, but no furniture in it. That's all I can do for you'.[138] He promptly left Salamaua and Eric soon found the post to be in complete disarray. This assignment was to be his most challenging and the one in which he arguably made his greatest professional contribution.

When Eric arrived in Salamaua it had been two years since gold had been discovered by an old time prospector Bill Royal. He discovered his strike at 2,000 metres on mist-clad Mount Kaindi in the crystal clear waters of the upper Eddy Creek.[139] There were immense challenges in extracting and selling the gold. While the location did not appear remote on the map it was an arduous six day trek from Salamaua up and over the Black Cat Gap to the settlement of Wau at 1,100 metres altitude. It was from Wau that over 200 prospectors fanned out on their search for further deposits.

To support goldmining Salamaua became a centre for recruiting native labour with attendant tensions. The changeable and at times bitterly cold weather in the mountains led to deaths among the ill-clad coastal New Guineans. The local tribesmen were not averse to attacking prospectors or stealing their supplies. It was within this milieu that Eric set about putting right the administration of the district.

Eric's approach was first to regain the confidence of the local native population who had been pressed into labour by both the prospectors and the administration itself. He did this by paying for short periods of labour in and around Salamaua such as rebuilding administration buildings and providing individual huts for the native staff. These short stints meant that the labourers would not be sent up into the mountains. The other key element was undertaking regular patrols through the district to quell intertribal conflicts and reestablish government authority.

Fortunately, Eric had an excellent group of patrol officers who just required leadership and support. Some were involved in extending rudimentary roads from Salamaua as well as hacking emergency airstrips out of the jungle for the Junkers planes that had started to fly around the province. Eric soon flew to Wau and then walked to Eddy Creek to meet the Warden of the Goldfields and generally understand the mining operation in progress in the mountains. He was pleased to see that the native workers were well cared for and treated in accordance with the Native Labour Ordinance. What surprised him was that the prospectors were not the stereotypical collection of seasoned old timers, criminals, adventurers, misfits and probably worst of all, naïve hopefuls straight from the city. The conditions in the early days meant that only the well-equipped prospector was working these fields. For these men two years on the fields probably earned them on average £5000, although some would earn much more money.[140]

The introduction of the airstrip at Wau and aircraft with sufficient carrying capacity meant that most cargo could be flown direct to Wau with only a day's trek into the goldfields. This removed the arduous six day trek which was an immense burden lifted from the native carriers. When Guinea Airways were setting up flights to Wau, Eric was asked for a recommendation of someone to run the Wau office. He suggested a 20-year old Errol Flynn then working at Gizerum Plantation. Flynn did not stay long and left with unpaid bills for the lures of acting and eventual Hollywood stardom.[141]

A blight on the Salamaua area was the prevalence of Blackwater fever. Eric roughly calculated that the toll to the disease among the coastal population was equivalent to casualty rate on the Western Front in the Great War. Such was the mortality that mourners at funerals, in which Eric often had to officiate, had their regular seats and duties. He recollected that the funerals had 'perhaps more precision than we should have'.[142] Ironically, Blackwater fever, which is a complication from malaria and results in kidney failure, could be caused by an autoimmune reaction between the malaria parasite and quinine.[143]

In contrast Eric was also called on to assist newborn arrivals in Salamaua. On one occasion he had to make a crib for the newborn son of the Guinea Airways local manager. He constructed it from a piece of tarpaulin made into a navy-like hammock and secured inside a wooden VB beer case. The quickly finished crib was escorted up the main street by a proud crowd to the anxious mother.[144]

An important duty of Eric's was to be the local magistrate. By the nature of Salamaua, he had to hear cases involving more Europeans than was usual. In matters involving both races, Eric was at pains to provide due weight to the testimony of natives. The conviction of whites by this evidence caused some initial resentment, but the corrosive effect on law and order of not doing so was unacceptable to him. His cases ranged from murder and theft to transgressions of the Native Labour Ordinance. Those appearing before him included Hugh MacKenzie who was now the owner and master of the small schooner *Lady Betty*, Hugh was bringing native recruits to Salamaua. The boat was overloaded and there had been a complaint. Eric fined Hugh £30 which he calculated to be the cost of another trip to Salamaua. On finishing the case they both went to the pub for a beer.

In July 1929 Salamaua was graced with a visit by the Governor General of Australia and his wife, Lord and Lady Stonehaven.[145] They had embarked in the seaplane carrier HMAS *Albatross* for a tour of New Guinea. Eric mustered all the local Luluais or headmen[146] to greet the vice-regal couple. This was followed by drinks with the white community in Eric's modest residence. The Stonehavens then went up country to Wau where they viewed the gold mining operation.

At the end of 1929 Eric went on nine months extended leave. He left Salamaua in the experienced hands of 'Kaasa' Townsend. After a visit to family and friends in Brisbane he travelled through South East Asia visiting Angkor Wat and Saigon in Indo-China, as well as Hong Kong, Manila and Singapore. Besides a curiosity about the region, Eric wanted to see the working conditions of the native labour compared to New Guinea. He concluded that the economic situation for unskilled labour was comparable. In contrast however, the poorer education system in New Guinea meant skilled Chinese and Australian labour had to be imported at much higher rates of pay.

Returning broke but rejuvenated to Salamaua, Eric saw that fundamental changes had occurred in the goldfields. He wrote in his annual report:

> The field may now be said to have evolved definitely from an alluvial field, worked in a desultory manner with primitive appliances, to one in which the huge lode formations and alluvial deposits require to be worked by organizations having the capital, up-to-date machinery, and skilled labour necessary for their exploitation on scientific lines.[147]

Aerodromes were now in place at Salamaua and Bululo. Lae was reportedly one of the busiest aerodromes in the world moving heavy mining equipment and stores to Bululo. The key equipment, moved in small sections by three Junkers aircraft, were two large 1,100 tonne dredges. These machines mechanically extracted the alluvial gold. The days of the independent prospector were numbered, steadily displaced by large mining companies.

Between 1928 and 1930 more of the Pioneer Class married. Jack Lecky, after some years as a clerk in the Midlands area of Western Australia, secured jobs as a farm hand and then a construction worker with the West Australian Railways. It was farming that Jack found most satisfying and he cleared 2,000 acres of arable land near Southern Cross with his older brother Kenneth. Shortly thereafter in 1928 he married Ida Carter whom he met during his earlier years in the district.

On the unusually late date of 30 December 1929 Paul Hirst, who had only been in command of the destroyer *Success* for a couple of months, married Eve the second daughter of Sir Joseph and Lady Carruthers at Saint Mark's Church, Darling Point. Sir Joseph had served as Premier of New South Wales from 1902 to 1908. In his prime, the free-trading and out-spoken Carruthers had been one of the most dominant state politicians of his day. To Eve, Paul was the dashing captain of a destroyer. To the canny politician he would have also been the son-in-law of a long established Tasmanian family and therefore not necessarily the typical naval officer with limited financial means. As is the tradition, a garland flew on the masthead of *Success* to mark her Captain's memorable day. The honeymoon in Paul's home state of Tasmania involved Eve making her own way to Tasmania to join Paul, whose ship was with the rest of the Squadron for exercises and the all important Hobart Regatta.

It was also during this period Ben Howells met Dorothy Huhs, who was a gifted music teacher. On 23 December 1930 they were married at All Saints Church in Kooyong. They shared a great interest in both education and children. Dorothy was an exceptional woman who grew in confidence and stature to become the long-serving President of the Victorian Federation of Mothers' Clubs. At its height the Federation had 500 clubs and a membership of 45,000. Frequently campaigning for various causes that related to the education of children and the rights of the mother, Dorothy was an influential opinion maker in Victoria for a generation. Ben was Dorothy's most stalwart supporter. He helped with her speeches, with behind the scenes administrative assistance and as a sounding board for her ideas.

For three years in *Moresby*, Alfred Conder undertook surveys of the waters around Gladstone, Hervey Bay, Mackay, the Whitsunday Islands and Brisbane. By the nature of her work *Moresby* made numerous port

'I hear that your engagement is broken off. Did you have a row?
Oh, no ! I broke it gently. I just told her what my pay is.'
This Adrian Watts' cartoon that appeared in a 1922 edition of the Australian Punch magazine captures the misalignment between a naval officer's social standing in the inter-war period and his modest salary. (NLA)

visits to Brisbane and Alfred managed to maintain a courtship with Eleanor Kerwin, daughter of the influential Queensland politician Dr P.E. Kerwin. On 28 August 1929 in 'the first naval wedding solemnised in Brisbane for some years'[148] Eleanor and Alfred were married at Saint Stephen's Cathedral, Brisbane.[149] The service was officiated by the Catholic Archbishop of Brisbane assisted by the Chaplain of the visiting flagship *Canberra*.[150] Eleanor was reported in the social pages as being resplendent in a Paris gown of ivory chiffon and silver sequins. Alfred in his dress naval uniform was supported by his captain who was his best man. The large congregation included the Governor of Queensland, Sir John Goodwin, the Queensland Premier, Mr Arthur Moore and, the Flag Officer Commanding His Majesty's Australian Squadron, the illustrious Antarctic explorer Rear Admiral Edward Evans[151] (also known as 'Evans of

The wedding of Ben Howells to Dorothy Huhs on 23 December 1930 at All Saints Church in Kooyong. Both teachers they shared a great interest in both education and children. (Howells Family)

the *Broke*' due to a hard fought battle whilst commanding that destroyer). Other members of the Pioneer Class present were Joe Burnett, Norman Calder, Lloyd Gilling and Eddy Nurse who were all serving in *Canberra*.

XV

Following the port visit to Brisbane, *Canberra* left Moreton Bay and sailed north. The still new heavy cruiser was undertaking a circumnavigation of the continent to show off one of the centre-pieces of the new Navy and to be present for Western Australia's Centenary celebrations. Following the navigationally demanding passage up the inner Great Barrier Reef, *Canberra* called into Thursday Island. The ship was due to leave on the evening of Friday the 13th. It was an old sailors' superstition that sailing on this date is an ill-omen for the remainder of a voyage and a request was made to the Captain to delay sailing until after midnight. Lloyd Gilling had judged the 10 pm departure on the tide and Captain Massey dismissed the request. *Canberra* sailed for uneventful port visits to Darwin and then Broome.[152]

On 20 September 1929 after an enjoyable visit in Broome, *Canberra* cleared the anchorage at dusk for passage to her next port of call of Geraldton. The cruiser would follow in reverse the tracks she had entered port. Lloyd Gilling as the Navigating Officer was both conning the ship and in charge of the navigation. Eleven minutes after weighing anchor on the bridge 'a vibration was felt and it was realised that the ship had touched some obstruction'.[153] Down below it was a different sensation. Petty Officer Claude Choules recalled, 'I heard a tremendous clatter along the ship's hull. It sounded like machine-gun fire, but louder'.[154] Astern power was ordered by Captain Massey and then *Canberra* was stopped in the water. In the engine room Engineer Commander Arthur Mears received a report that Number 1 dynamo 'had failed owing to loss of vacuum, which was due to sand being drawn into it by suction'.[155]

The ship was stuck fast to a sandbank. Commander James Boyd ordered all available sailors to the after end of the ship. With the band playing the sailors jumped in unison with the engines running full astern. Unsuccessful, the sailors and band were ordered to the bow and repeated the performance. After they jumped down aft for a second time, *Canberra* freed herself from the sandbank.[156] An inspection of the hull found buckling of plating on the port side but it was not sufficient to prevent the continuation of the circumnavigation. *Canberra* would have to be docked in the new year at Cockatoo Island to replace the damaged section of the hull.

There is no more sickening feeling for a navigating officer than to realise he had been responsible for a navigational error that has hazarded his ship. The inevitable consequence of the grounding was that Lloyd Gilling would be the second of the Pioneer Class to face a court martial.

On 25 November two successive courts martial were held in the Wardroom of *Canberra* whilst the ship was at anchor in Jervis Bay. The first was for Captain Massey who was accused of hazarding his ship.

The President of the Court was Captain John Stevenson, the Captain Superintendent—Sydney. The evidence presented that *Canberra* ran aground on a charted sandbank with a 20 foot sounding. Allowing for the tide, this depth would have been insufficient for *Canberra* to safely pass over. This sandbank had not been marked as a hazard by Lloyd Gilling or noticed by Massey when he approved the departure plan.

Captain Stevenson and his fellow members of the Court Martial board then considered whether the charge had been proven. In time honoured practice each officer presented his view with the most junior speaking first. Massey was found guilty. Rear Admiral Evans gave a statement of mitigation in which he said, Massey:

> ... appears to have some private means which he uses very generously and discreetly in the Empire's service ... he is modest, conscientious and thoroughly efficient Captain, and a great gentleman who commands the respect of his superiors throughout the squadron.[157]

Massey received a reprimand but remained in command. In the afternoon Captain William Chalmers, RN, the Commanding Officer of *Australia* convened the court martial for Lloyd Gilling. The second court martial covered much of the same ground as the first. In preparing the navigational track for the departing ship, Lloyd Gilling admitted that:

> I did not observe the 20 foot sounding near which the ship touched. It is surrounded by much deeper soundings and is not properly distinguished on the chart. It was, in addition, partially obscured by the first preliminary line which I had laid.[158]

While accepting his error Lloyd noted that his Captain had viewed and approved his navigation plan. He also said in mitigation that in the accompanying Admiralty *Australia Pilot* which provided guidance to mariners for the area that other shoal depths of the same or lesser depths are noted in the text but this depth, which is closer to the fairway is not mentioned. This view was supported by navigating officer Lieutenant Commander Arthur Tate who was called in support of the defence. Lloyd went further in his evidence by saying:

> I submit for the consideration of the court the need to distinguish

this serious danger is a piece of serious neglect by the officers carrying out the survey. It is neglect also that the sailing directions should be defective in this regard.[159]

The prosecution while accepting that the *Australia Pilot* was deficient contended that this did not absolve the Navigating Officer from careful examination of the chart. Finally, the court martial was presented with abstracts from Lloyd's S.206 reports. They included an assessment from Massey when both officers had served in *Adelaide* in the same positions and they did in the *Canberra*. It read:

> To my entire satisfaction. A very capable and efficient officer and a conscientious, trustworthy and reliable Navigator with plenty of confidence in handling the ship.[160]

By mid-afternoon all evidence had been presented and after just 20 minutes deliberation:

> The Court finds that the charge against the accused of negligently or by default hazarding HMAS *Canberra* is proved in that the said hazarding was due to the accused having omitted to scrutinize Chart No. 858 sufficiently carefully to notice that a sounding of twenty feet lay in the track of the said ship.

In respect to Lloyd Gilling's Sentence, the Court:

> ... having taken into consideration his previous very good character and ability as shown in evidence and also the mitigating circumstances in that attention was not drawn to the 20-foot shoal in the sailing directions, adjudges him the said Lieutenant Commander Lloyd Falconer Gilling, Royal Australian Navy to be reprimanded.[161]

The following day Lloyd Gilling was posted from *Canberra*, a sad end to his tenure as commissioning navigating officer of one of the Navy's two new heavy cruisers. Lloyd had up to the grounding demonstrated more than the usual talents as a navigating officer and had gained the appreciation of the Naval Board for his development of Harmonic Prediction Tidal diagram, while Admiral Evans had earlier assessed Lloyd would 'undoubtedly do well in higher rank'.[162] Massey afterwards wrote that Lloyd was 'Undoubtedly an officer of personality and it would be a great pity if one error of judgement should adversely affect his career'.[163]

Many Admirals had a grounding early in their career. Indeed, it was said that over time a court martial allows your name to be known but the grounds for its recognition become forgotten. It would be well within Lloyd's powers to get his career back on track. He was appointed to attend staff course at Greenwich and took passage to the UK in *Moldavia* on 10 January 1930.[164] On completion he joined the staff of Flag Officer Commanding 1st Battle Squadron in the Mediterranean Fleet, first in the battleship *Revenge* and then *Resolution*. By happenstance also serving in *Resolution* was James Esdaile. Lloyd's admiral was one of the most influential and respected admirals in the RN during the inter-war period, Vice Admiral Sir William Fisher. Lloyd prospered as part of Fisher's staff and the Admiral recommended Lloyd for accelerated promotion and wrote of him, 'Exceptional. Very valuable addition to staff. Never speaks without thinking. Very good social qualities'.[165] Lloyd's career was back on track.

Alfred and Eleanor Conder sailed for England three months after Lloyd Gilling in *Port Alma*. The Port Line ships which took passengers and frozen meat to Britain were popular one-class ships for the Pioneer Class as they stretched their single First Class tickets to two of a lesser class. Alfred had been selected for a two year exchange position as a Naval Assistant to the Hydrographer of the Royal Navy. It was a tremendous opportunity for Alfred and would prepare him to eventually lead his navy's hydrographic service. Also taking passage to England was Joe and Enid Burnett with their two small boys in *Port Bowen*. Joe was to serve on the instructing staff of the Gunnery School at Whale Island until the end of 1930. He then joined the destroyer leader of the 5th Destroyer Flotilla, HMS *Wallace* as the Flotilla Gunnery Officer.

Norman Calder on the eve of his departure from *Canberra* married Nancie Dixon after their prolonged courtship. Norman had to attend advanced torpedo courses in UK prior to becoming the Squadron Torpedo Officer. The newlyweds sailed in *Port Dunedin* and their 'honeymoon cruise' included a port visit to Wyndham on the north west coast to embark frozen meat.

In contrast Harry and Jean Showers were returning to Australia after nearly three years away. Harry was appointed the Master Attendant in Sydney. This high profile appointment for a navigator entailed organizing the berthing of warships at the base at Garden Island as well as undertaking movements of warships with tugs. Now a Lieutenant Commander, Harry had become known while on service with the RN as 'an able navigator, careful and methodical, gets through his work with a minimum of fuss'.[166]

In 1930 Cyril Sadleir took up oyster farming on the Hawkesbury River north of Sydney. This was not a lucrative venture and put considerable pressure on Cyril and Phyllis's marriage. Phyllis left Cyril and they divorced in 1931. Phyllis would remarry in the following year and settle for a period in Fiji where her new husband was a policeman.

XVI

1930 was also a momentous year for John Collins. He met Phyllis McLachlan through mutual friends at a beach party the previous year, and they were married on 3 June 1930. Rear Admiral Evans and other officers from *Australia* attended the wedding. The event was enhanced by it coinciding with the King's Birthday. The Flagship secured to No.1 Buoy in Sydney Harbour was dressed overall with signal flags and fired a 21-gun salute at noon.

The charismatic Evans was an important influence on John Collins at this period of his career. John described him as a 'human dynamo',[167] and had reveled in his position as the squadron's and *Australia's* gunnery officer under Evans' leadership. There was mutual respect for each other's capabilities and Evans rated John as an exceptional officer worthy of early promotion.[168] Evans, however felt that John needed to be broadened in outlook if he were to be a success in higher command. He therefore recommended John for a destroyer command. This was not surprising for Evans was arguably the most daring destroyer Captain of his generation. In the month following his wedding John was appointed in command of the destroyer leader *Anzac*.

John of course joined Paul Hirst in the destroyer flotilla. Paul had proved to be a popular Commanding Officer and *Success* was a happy and efficient ship. During his tenure the destroyer won the Otranto Shield for Squadron gunnery. On leaving *Success* in April 1930 Paul received his flimsy from Commander John Durnford which said, 'to my entire satisfaction. A keen and capable Destroyer Commanding Officer who has maintained his ship in an excellent state of cleanliness and efficiency'.[169] What he did not see was Rear Admiral Evans' comments on the AS.206 penned by Durnford which said 'I concur generally except that Lieutenant Commander Hirst is <u>not</u> gifted with average Commanding Officer's initiative and he lacks imagination'.[170] Evan's remarks would hinder Paul's chances when he became eligible for promotion.

John Collins' time in *Anzac* was more successful. The ship performed well and his tenure also provided challenging situations for her Captain when things did not go according to plan. An example was when he brought *Anzac* alongside the flagship only to have an engine order not correctly repeated and his ship badly damaged *Australia's* pristine accommodation ladder.[171] At the end of his tenure in command John received a glowing report from Evans who once again recommended his early promotion.[172] At year's end, he and Phyllis moved to Flinders Naval Depot near Westernport where John was appointed as First Lieutenant of the training establishment.

On 6 January 1931 John handed over *Anzac* to James Esdaile. For James command of *Anzac* also represented an opportunity to break from the confines of his specialisation. After six months in command, Evans considered James 'a zealous and promising officer who should do well in higher rank'.[173] He recommended that he serve in a large ship before his promotion to Commander. Accordingly, James first joined *Platypus* as Executive Officer where he excelled and then as First Lieutenant Commander in *Australia*.

By 1932 Rear Admiral Evans had been replaced by Rear Admiral Robin Dalglish who since his time as Commander in *Canada* had found time to twice represent Britain in Fencing at the Olympics. Dalglish had a particular focus on raising the operational efficiency of the Squadron and was similarly impressed with James Esdaile. Accordingly, he also endorsed the recommendation for early promotion.[174]

At the end of 1931 John and Phyllis Collins sailed to Britain in *Port Hobart*, so that John could attend Staff Course at Greenwich. This was the final preparation he would need for promotion to Commander. He would be joined on the course by Joe Burnett who had completed a successful posting to *Wallace*. Captain Geoffrey Watkins, DSO, RN, his flotilla commander wrote of Joe:[175]

Paul Hirst was 'a capable, keen and zealous' Commanding Officer of HMAS Success. *(RAN)*

A fine type of colonial officer. He is tremendously keen on his job (gunnery in particular) ... He promises to do well in the higher ranks of the Service.[176]

Not surprisingly both Joe and John excelled on their Staff Course and the Director said of them both:

They are zealous, efficient and thorough and should do extremely well as Commanders. I have been impressed with their personality.[177]

Also on service with the RN was Rupert Long. After undertaking advanced torpedo training at HMS *Vernon* he joined the cruiser HMS *Sussex* in the Mediterranean from which he gained fine reports.[178]

While John Collins, Joe Burnett and Rupert Long were taking their next steps in their promising careers, George Armitage took a different course. By 1929 his performance was such that he was no longer on quarterly reports and had finally been promoted to Lieutenant Commander. His promotion was in accordance with the automatic promotion rule that promoted an officer after achieving eight years seniority as a lieutenant. In June 1931 however, George elected to be discharged from the service under the Reduction Scheme. As part of that Scheme he was assisted in securing a position as a Clerk Division III in the Taxation Department.[179] By this stage his marriage was failing and Madge would move to South Australia with the children.

In 1931 Paul Hirst also decided to resign from the Navy. The previous year he had the satisfaction of taking *Success* to his native state Tasmania for a most memorable visit. But like many in the Navy he had just missed the birth of his first child and there was a strong pull to return to the land. His family had farmed in the Launceston district for generations. Paul and Eve acquired *The Marshes* near Saint Helens. After a couple of good years of farming, in 1934 they sold the property and acquired *Ashbourne* of 13,200 acres near Carrick to raise sheep and mixed crops.[180]

XVII

In March 1931 Eric Feldt was tasked with tracking down the murderers of the well-known German prospector Helmuth Baum and eight of his carriers. Baum had been prospecting in the lands of the Kukukuku people, who were the most warlike and feared head-hunting tribal group in New Guinea. A Kukukuku warrior would typically be about five foot tall with a cassowary bone through his nose and be armed with a short blackpalm bow, cane-shafted arrows with sharp blackwood points, a large oblong wooden shield and a lethal stone club. The latter would be out of sight under a bark cloak. It was one such club that had done in Helmuth Baum. Such was the terror the Kukukuku could engender that the native coastal people viewed them as 'the terrible ones in the bark cloaks who come down from the mountains and kill us'.[181]

Once word had been received of the deaths, Eric chartered three Junkers aircraft to take him with a dozen native police and three weeks supply from Salamaua to Surprise Creek near where the attack had occurred. After interviewing some of Baum's surviving carriers Eric trekked inland. After eight days walk he arrived at the nearest Kukukuku village to the scene of the attack and later wrote:

> Natives fled on our approach, going up and down the slopes at speed we couldn't hope to equal, their bark cloaks flowing out behind them. They slapped their sterns at us in the age-old gesture that is the New Guinea version of the 'raspberry'.[182]

Eric was in a challenging position. It was clear from accounts of the assault, that Kukukukus from a number of villages had been involved in the brutal assault. Besides the possibility of an attack on his small party, the task of finding the perpetrators and then bringing them out of Kukukuku lands for trial would be difficult. He likened it to being 'as easy as catching a muruk (cassowary)'.[183] Yet his approach to the matter was clear:

> A District Officer has a further duty than the punishment of a single crime, however serious that crime may be. The country has to be brought under a rule of law, so that men may go about peacefully in the future. To walk away and do nothing would not bring that condition nearer.[184]

Knowing full well that the villagers would be prepared to wait in the bush indefinitely for the police to leave their village, Eric directed his police to eat not from their own supplies but from the village garden. After ten days, with the garden being stripped bare, it became too much. Seven tribesmen entered the village and after a short scuffle they were quickly handcuffed. Eric recounted:

> Next morning, we took them to the site of Baum's camp and re-enacted the killing, pointing accusingly at them. In sign language they denied any part of it, but there was guilt in their eyes. We set off then on our journey home, the prisoners hand-cuffed, with a length of kunda (cane)

through their arms, held by a policeman ahead and astern of them.

When we had been on our way for an hour or two I heard a sound like a cassowary crashing through the bush. One of the prisoners had been working his hands during the night, wearing away the steel of the handcuffs. He snapped the link, swung over the edge of the razorback ridge we were on, and got clear away.

At one camp on the way we bought a bunch of bananas from a Kukukuku for a small knife. Then we searched the prisoners after he was gone and found the knife on one of them. It would have been very useful for cutting the kunda. We left the knife sticking in a tree.

The long days of walking, the night watches and the stand-to at dawn, the climate and constant strain, told on us. Our feet were giving out and we were all thin. After we reached the Upper Watut and discharged the carriers and borrowed rice to get them to their homes. I went to Bulolo and, with the beard I had, I was not recognized.

One prisoner signalled that his handcuff was too tight, and so it was eased, and he slipped it that night, but an alert police boy bowled him over and held him. I flew out with six prisoners next morning.[185]

The matter did not end with the arrival of the six Kukukukus at Salamaua. While on remand, one died shortly thereafter of mouth cancer and the remaining five managed to escape custody.[186] Of these, two got back to Kukukuku lands, two were quickly recovered and one Eric had named 'Joe' had the misfortune to be caught by the Buang people. They brought Joe in trussed up like a pig, with small wounds on his back and chest as a payback for brothers who had been killed with Baum. Eric did nothing about that as in his view the Buangs had shown considerable forbearance. Joe went to hospital for treatment.

In a subsequent patrol by Assistant District Officer Nick Penglase, two Kukukukus who took part in the attack on Baum and his carriers were apprehended. They were subsequently imprisoned for less than a year and returned home. While two of the Kukukuku also returned to their village, Eric wrote:

> Joe remained and learned some pidgin. In the process he learned far too much to implicate himself in the murder of Baum. Some months later he was taken back and released, and disappeared. Then, one day

Two of the Kukukuku tribesmen apprehended by Eric Feldt for the murder of Helmuth Baum and eight of his porters. (Source unknown)

at Wau, a line of bark capes came out of the bush, there was the sound of clucking speech, and a crowd of Kukukukus arrived at the District Office, peacefully to trade sweet potatoes for knives and beads and salt. Their leader was Joe, come good at last.[187]

Hugh MacKenzie continued life as a trader and met Betty Brown in 1930, who had been previously married to a barrister in Rabaul. Hugh and Betty were married two years later in the German mission town of Marienburg on the Sepik. Both loved the islander life but knew Sepik was not the place to settle. In 1933 they sold *Lady Betty* and bought a larger ketch they named *Pato*, the local word for duck. In fitting out the vessel Betty did the carpentry to save the 18 shillings a day for the services of a carpenter.[188]

Eric also found a woman who would face the challenges of life in New Guinea. Nancy Echlin was a journalist and niece of General Sir Brudenell White. They met in Brisbane and were married in January 1933. Nancy approached life in New Guinea positively and expatriate Sarah Chinnery wrote in her diary on 27 January 1933 that Eric had 'just returned from South with his bride, a very nice girl who is intensely interested in the new life she is seeing for the first time. They are going to Madang'.[189]

An account of Nancy's Madang experiences appeared in Narrabri's *North West Courier*. She extolled the charms of the town and the domestic support of the natives and said that 'anyone can be happy in New Guinea provided they are interested in their home surroundings and can cultivate a sense of humour where housekeeping is concerned'.[190]

Betty MacKenzie landing in Rabaul Harbour in 1933 with the MacKenzie's Pato *in the background.* (Sarah Chinnery-NLA)

After his divorce in 1931 from Lilias, Adrian Watts also married in 1933. His new wife was Galie Honey whom he met in the course of his growing career as an illustrator when she was Secretary to the promoter JC Williamson. Professionally, Adrian's portfolio of work had expanded. In addition to illustrations in magazines such as *The Australian Journal*, he drew for the Myer catalogue and completed film artwork for cinemas. Adrian was an active member of his local Returned Service League branch at Caulfield. His artwork adorned both the local branch's magazine *Furfs* as well as more substantially the songbook *With the Diggers 1914-18*.[191]

XVIII

By the end of 1931 Alfred Conder had made his mark at the Hydrographic Office. He had designed a True Wind Indicator that the Meteorological Office was considering for production and fitting to all RN ships. He also represented Australia at the 1931 Conference of Empire Survey Officers held in London by the Colonial Office. The Hydrographer Vice Admiral Percy Douglas, his old Captain from *Ormonde*, recommended Alfred to be assigned command a survey ship.

Alfred had, however, contracted testicular cancer and he was treated at the highly regarded Lister Private Hospital in London. Eleanor's mother sailed to England to join the couple to provide support. In early 1932 the three returned to Sydney in *Orsova* where Alfred came under the care of the respected surgeon Archie Aspinall. The treatment, however, was to no avail and on 8 June 1932 he died in a private hospital on the North Shore. His body was solemnly taken across the harbour in a naval launch to Man-of-War steps and thence taken in the funeral train to Rookwood cemetery. He was accompanied by Eleanor, the family, some of the Pioneer Class and other naval colleagues, six of whom would act as pall bearers. At the internment there was a naval funeral guard and over two hundred officers and sailors to farewell an officer of warmth and brilliant promise. Eleanor remarried two years later to a former British Army officer and moved to Ceylon.

Alfred Conder's professional legacy, which should have been as the first RAN College graduate to be Hydrographer of the Navy, remains his well-crafted hydrographic surveys particularly of the Great Barrier Reef where a shoal, reef and hill bears his name as does Condor Point on Melville Island. His classmate, shipmate, hydrographic colleague and friend Cyril Sadleir would later christen his daughter Denise, derived from Alfred's middle name of Denis.

Health issues struck another member of the Pioneer Class whilst on service with the RN. In 1932 Lloyd Gilling, while serving in the battleship *Resolution*, suffered a perforation of his right ear drum during a 15-inch gun firing. The injury became infected and failed to heal. In February 1933 when Lloyd joined the cruiser HMS *Curlew* as the navigating officer his treatment continued. This culminated in an operation at the naval hospital in Malta but he remained deaf in his right ear. The following month after a strenuous walk in the hills around Valetta, Lloyd reported to sickbay with symptoms that were diagnosed as a 'slightly strained heart'.[192] He was given bed rest in *Curlew* and placed on a simple diet. A couple of days later Lloyd was found in a weakened state in the bathroom with a high heart rate. The following day he was sent to the hospital ship

RFA *Maine* and given an x-ray. Lloyd was found to be suffering from extensive tuberculosis of both lungs with one of them having a cavity.[193]

Tuberculosis had long been the scourge of the Navy. Damp, humid, confined and crowded compartments had for generations allowed the transmission of this disease. In the 1930s the incidence of tuberculosis in the RN was still higher than in the civilian population and double that of the Army and Air Force. In 1941 Surgeon Rear Admiral Sheldon Dudley wrote:

> The decisive factor left untouched which determines the high incidence of tuberculosis in the Navy is density of population. The work for which a warship is designed prohibits any increase in the number of square fleet of deck space per man, and the density of population must increase as more space is taken up by machinery, which requires additional men to work it. All measures that have been introduced in the last thirty five years, namely the drive to get earlier diagnosis by periodical medical examinations and weighings of the men, elimination of dampness and dust between decks, the great improvement in the protective qualities of naval rations, and increase and perfection of the air supply, have not been accompanied by any decrease in the morbidity of pulmonary tuberculosis.[194]

It would not be reduced until the advent of more comprehensive x-ray screening as well as the introduction of air-conditioning into ships. For Lloyd Gilling this was all in the future. Lloyd's efforts to successfully restore his naval fortunes had come to an unexpected and abrupt end. In June 1932 he was invalided from the Navy. Clearly Lloyd in the normal course of events would have gone on to sea command and his naval future had great promise. With his parents and all his siblings already dead and with friends in southern England and cousins in Yorkshire, Lloyd decided to live modestly in Hampshire. This would also allow him to be in close proximity to the hospitals and sanatoriums well versed in tuberculosis treatment.

XIX

From the early 1930s the dogs of war were once again getting restless in the Pacific and then in Europe. With the *raison d'etre* of the Navy to fight and win at sea, preparations began for the potential conflict. These years were ones in which the Pioneer Class made some of their most significant contributions to the Navy.

There was growing concern about the rising Japanese military and its designs in Asia. This was highlighted by the Japanese occupation of southern Manchuria in September 1931 and the occupation of Shanghai four months later. Discussions between the RAN and RN took place on Japanese naval capabilities and how they could threaten British and Australian security interests in the Pacific. The Imperial defence strategy still centered on building Singapore into a fortified naval base, which when combined with modest British and Australian naval forces in the Pacific would hold out until the main British Fleet arrived in force.

The Singapore strategy was undermined by two factors. The first was that the global economic situation delayed substantial work in Singapore while funding a rejuvenation of the RN. The other was whether Singapore should be the site for such a base. Admiral Henderson for example in 1923 wrote from retirement that he considered Sydney a much more secure location for a RN naval base in the Pacific.[195] For their part the Admiralty, through analysis and exercises, became keenly aware of Singapore's possible vulnerability from Japanese attack. In 1933 the Admiralty assessed 'the principal air menace to which that base will be exposed will be attack by seaborne aircraft'.[196] It was a realistic assessment and the exercises by the US Navy during the period demonstrated the potency of long range attack by aircraft carriers with large air wings.[197] The Japanese possessed such ships in growing numbers. The British pinned their defensive hopes on two elements. The first was maintaining a substantial British submarine force on the China Station that could significantly constrain the Imperial Japanese Navy (IJN).[198] The second was building up land based torpedo bombers of the British Air Striking Force in Singapore to be able to attack the carriers at a distance from the island.[199] This strategy would depend of course on providing the necessary forces to the Far East in whatever conflict ensued.

As part of the rejuvenation of the Australian Squadron in the early 1930s it was agreed that *Anzac* and the S Class destroyers would be replaced by the larger *Stuart, Vampire, Vendetta, Voyager* and *Waterhen* all of Great War vintage. There was also recognition that modern light cruisers were needed to augment *Australia* and *Canberra*.

One particular threat that the IJN posed was interdiction of shipping by its large and modern submarine fleet. In 1932 the Admiralty wrote to the Naval Board suggesting the Australian Squadron would have an important role 'in countering or reporting any steps the Japanese might be taking to contest the passage of the Strait of Malacca by the British Main Fleet'.[200] Implicit in this proposed tasking was an anti-submarine capability. On 15 October 1932 another meeting in Navy Office was convened chaired by the Assistant Chief of Naval Staff, Commander Angus Nicholl and attended by Harold Farncomb, now a Staff Officer to the First Naval Member, Vice Admiral Hyde, and James Esdaile from the Squadron to review the state of anti-submarine capabilities.[201] Once more the limitations of loops were discussed, as was the slow but still promising progress of Asdic. It was estimated that an Asdic set for an auxiliary vessel would cost about £700 and could be relatively quickly fitted. The Navy however considered that the submarine threat did not warrant additional expenditure when 'there are so many arms of the service with prior claims.'[202]

The meeting recommended that while an Asdic could not be acquired at present 'an up-to-date A/S defence scheme for Australian ports should be prepared for submission to the Admiralty'.[203] The Rear Admiral Commanding the Australian Squadron was asked to supply two anti-submarine specialists to prepare the scheme. James Esdaile and Lieutenant Commander Stanley Spurgeon (1916 Entry) were nominated. Their report, *Seaward Defence of Australian Ports,*[204] was completed on 7 February 1933. This was a watershed document as it was the first Australian report on anti-submarine defences for Australian ports. It took as guidance the Admiralty's assessment of which Australian ports were vulnerable, by virtue of their geography, to submarine attack. The report examined port defences as well as the defence of port approaches. It then provided in some detail the vessels, fixed defences and personnel to secure against the submarine threat. The report became the blueprint for anti-submarine defences that would be implemented to varying degrees in World War II. After consideration by the Naval Board the report was forwarded to the Committee of Imperial Defence at Whitehall.

Harold Farncomb's potential as a staff officer was fully realized in his tenure in Navy Office. Admiral Hyde rated him an 'excellent staff officer in every respect'.[205] On 30 June 1932, Harold was the first of the Pioneer Class to be promoted to commander. He left Navy Office to become Executive Officer of the flagship *Australia,* the most prestigious appointment for a commander in the RAN. The position was exceptionally demanding with a ship's company of about 700; it required an officer with professional competence, a strong personality and leadership, a consistent approach to discipline, well-honed organizational skills and unremitting attention to detail. One of the officers onboard, Lieutenant Arthur Storey, recalled that Harold:

> ... succeeded one of those despotic domineering RN commanders of the 'old brigade'. He made an immediate impression with his fair mindedness, justice and efficiency. He was always slightly aloof but earned the respect and admiration of the officers and ship's company.[206]

Unsurprisingly, Harold was reported on by the Commanding Officer of *Australia*, Captain William MacLeod, RN as an 'exceptionally able executive officer'.[207] Among his wardroom officers was Instructor Commander Morton Moyes.

Harold was joined in *Australia* by Harry Showers who was appointed Navigating Officer of the Flagship and hence also the Squadron Navigating Officer. In the assessment of Rear Admiral Dalglish, Harry was a 'first Class Squadron Navigating Officer, efficient and hardworking'.[208] He was also an excellent instructor of the young officers on the bridge in all aspects of his beloved navigation, pilotage in confined waters and ship-handling. One of the junior officers, Sub-Lieutenant Leslie Brooks, who had first joined the Navy as a sailor and had been a Navigator's Yeomen before 'changing over' to be an officer, later wrote 'Harry Showers was perhaps the most delightful officer I ever served with ... I cribbed many a trick of his in pilotage'.[209]

Harold Farncomb was not to have the company and support of his class mate for very long. On 30 June 1933 Harry Showers was promoted to Commander and sent to take command of the Naval College. It was not to Jervis Bay he travelled, but to Flinders Naval Depot. By 1930 the effects of the Great Depression had taken hold in the Navy. In that year the Naval College moved to Flinders, because with reductions to the intakes of officers, the College at Jervis Bay was viewed as too expensive to maintain. Up to 1930 there were still staff at Jervis Bay from the Grant years. Little assistance was given to those who chose to move with the Naval College to Victoria. To rub salt into the wounds they were subjected to a 12% pay cut. The relocation prompted Dr. Wheatley to finally retire. To Eldridge and others who helped found the Naval College the relocation was a 'national disaster'.[210] The old college buildings were leased and became guest houses and hotels. At Flinders, the Warrant Officers Mess was cleared out and made into the Naval College. The considerable college impedimenta was once again subjected to the rigors and losses of a sea voyage. It was into this environment that Harry Showers joined once more the Naval College.

In any other circumstances the return of one of the Pioneer Class to command the Naval College would have been a great moment to celebrate. In many respects it still was and Harry, more than any of his predecessors, could relate to his cadet midshipmen. Their numbers were much reduced from the College he left in 1916. There had been no intake in 1931 and the 1932 Entry of 22 cadet midshipmen was the smallest on record. Harry directed considerable energy on 'protecting' and fostering the Naval College ethos within the larger Flinders Naval Depot. His main focus was the training and welfare of the cadet midshipmen. He was highly regarded by the boys and the then Flag Officer Commanding the Australian Squadron, Rear Admiral Wilbraham Ford wrote of Harry that, 'No officer could have exhibited more thought and attention to the training of Cadet-Midshipmen. The high rate of retention of the young officers reflect much credit upon him'.[211]

In January 1934 Harry was joined at Flinders by Norman Calder when the latter assumed command of the Torpedo School. Norman, with a heavily pregnant Nancie and three-year old Michael, had the prospect for the first time of extended time ashore and a normal family life. Life on a 'married patch' in a naval establishment was a welcome alternative to the uncertainties and expense of finding rented accommodation. It was also an immersive experience for both adults and the children with the latter, as in the case of Michael, often gravitating to a naval career in later life. It was also one where childhood incidents can gain greater, if unwanted prominence, such as the occasion Michael lit some pine needles to create a small fire. Unfortunately, it was high summer and soon there was soon a substantial blaze among adjacent pine trees requiring the Depot fire brigade and press-ganged sailors to extinguish the blaze. 'The culprit watched in horror' but fortunately for Michael, and no doubt Norman, he was never identified.[212]

Unfortunately the command of the Naval College at Flinders Naval Depot was for only one year. Harry was therefore not accompanied by Jean and his family.[213] In September 1934 he handed over to his good friend Commander Hector 'Hec' Waller (1914 Entry). Harry and Jean left Australia in *Orsova* so he could receive further training and then undertake sea service with the RN. After completing a senior tactical course at Portsmouth, he joined the new light cruiser HMS *Arethusa* as Squadron Navigating Officer and Staff Officer (Operations) of the 3rd Cruiser Squadron in the Mediterranean Fleet. In 1936 an Arab revolt commenced against British rule and the increased Jewish immigration into Palestine. *Arethusa* became part of the Haifa Naval Force which patrolled off the coast to prevent the importation of arms. In addition, the Force landed naval platoons to protect installations and promote law and order. Harry excelled in the planning and execution of these irregular operations.[214]

Harold Farncomb's tenure in *Australia* proved to be a memorable one. The ship embarked the Duke of Gloucester from Melbourne where the Duke had officiated at Victoria's centenary celebrations. The passage to Britain involved Royal visits to various ports en-route, with all the attendant ceremonial. It resulted in Harold being made a Member of the Victorian Order for his services. While in British waters *Australia* also participated in King George V's Silver Jubilee Naval Review. In August 1935, before the ship departed Britain for an exchange deployment in the Mediterranean Fleet, Harold left to take up a position in the Intelligence Division at the Admiralty.

In similar fashion Joe Burnett and John Collins were promoted to Commander at the end of 1932 on completion of their Staff Course. Joe returned to Australia to join his old ship *Canberra* as Executive Officer. He exhibited a strong, but quieter and more reserved style than that of Harold Farncomb, but he was clearly marked as an officer of considerable potential.[215]

For his part John Collins was appointed to the Plans Division of the Admiralty where his section was responsible for developing plans for the port defences not only of the UK but also key ports of the Empire. This position was to provide invaluable experience when he eventually served in Navy Office.

On 31 December 1933 James Esdaile was promoted to Commander and returned to Navy Office. Interestingly, the now Vice Admiral Hyde, noted that James was 'up to the standard of RAN Commanders ex Jervis Bay, [of] which I regard the standard as high'.[216]

James attended the Greenwich Staff Course in 1935, but had returned by 3 December to marry Desiree Ursula Finch at St John's Anglican Church in Toorak. Desiree was the daughter of the wealthy Melbourne businessman Cecil Finch. It was one of the society weddings of the year with *The Argus*

'Up to the standard of RAN Commanders ex Jervis Bay, which I regard the standard as high' - Commander James Esdaile. (NAA)

reporting 'Naval uniforms, with all the splendour of gold braid, which was worn by the groom and his attendants and the guard of honour added to the picturesque scene.'[217] Among the large bridal party were the six and seven year-old sons of Joe Burnett, Patrick and Rory who served as page boys in white sailor suits. Both would join the Naval College in turn.

While the anti-submarine capabilities were receiving attention, if not adequate resources, another area in dire need of overhaul was naval intelligence. Fortunately for the Navy in 1934 the persistence of Rupert Long paid off and he was finally appointed to a naval intelligence post as District Intelligence Officer and Staff Officer to the Captain Superintendent, Sydney. Rupert came to the job after completing the Greenwich staff course. For him there were two highlights of the course. The first was a lecture by the First Sea Lord Admiral Sir Ernle Chatfield who emphasised the importance of monitoring merchant shipping movements to glean any march to war.[218] The second was a study tour to Germany which included a visit to some of their warships. The resurgent Germany impressed Rupert in many ways and his family nickname of 'Von' came from this period.

At first glance the District Intelligence Officer position was an unremarkable one. Some of his predecessors, including classmate George Armitage had not been well supported by superiors and made little progress. From a personal perspective the position ashore was both desired and welcomed by Rupert as his wife Heather was suffering from liver disease and benefited from the medical facilities only a city could provide.[219]

From a career perspective, Rupert's posting was very unfortunate in its timing. The promotion system of the day involved Lieutenant Commanders from three years seniority receiving a report every six months on their suitability for promotion. This reporting cycle would continue until reaching five years seniority when an officer went out of the 'promotion zone' and was 'passed over'. The officer could not then be promoted except by special direction of the Naval Board. Rupert had been very well reported upon in *Sussex* prior to his current posting and had been recommended by the Commander-in-Chief Mediterranean for accelerated promotion.[220] His report from Greenwich however was lackluster with Rupert surprisingly described as being 'rather quiet and retiring and with no marked personality'.[221] It was therefore just at the end of his promotion zone that he went into a low profile position out of specialisation.

Rupert found the naval intelligence centre poorly organised and resourced. It resided in cramped quarters within the headquarters which hampered its papers being properly filed. To Rupert the situation gave him a clean slate not only to fashion the position to his own liking but to effectively rebuild the naval intelligence structure from its foundations. He was championed in his efforts by the incumbent Captain Superintendent Cuthbert Pope, who Rupert well knew from the Geelong years at the Naval College. Indeed, Pope continued six monthly reports even after Rupert was out of the zone, in an ardent attempt to get Rupert promoted. In May 1935 he wrote:

> I cannot speak too highly of this officer whom I assess to be one of the most efficient, capable and hardworking officers in the RAN, and to be lacking in no quality or attribute of a good officer ... Although now passed out of the promotion zone I feel I should be remiss in my duty if I did not continue to recommend his promotion.[222]

Six months later Pope wrote:

> I strongly recommend his promotion as a special case for the benefit of the service, honestly believing that there is not a better officer in the whole of the RAN.[223]

Rupert's approach to establishing a viable naval intelligence organization was multi-faceted. Naval intelligence during the period involved both the collection and analysis of information. This intelligence then had to be proactively disseminated to the benefit of the Australian Squadron and the Naval Board. In respect to collection, he fostered links with police, port authorities, ship's masters and businessmen. Following Admiral Chatfield's advice, Rupert commenced monitoring the movement of German, Italian and Japanese merchant shipping.[224] He also recognized the need to greatly reinvigorate and expand the old coastwatcher network which dated back to 1913. While Rupert was prescient about the growing German threat, he saw the increasingly belligerent Japan as the greatest danger to Australia's security. To that end he foresaw the need to refocus the approach to coastwatching from one of having coastwatchers dotted around the Australian coast, to developing an advanced network in the islands to Australia's north. This, however, remained in the future.

Among the many contacts Rupert made in his post was a young and patriotic businessman Harold Nobbs. The Canadian born Nobbs[225] was a keen yachtsman and discussed with Rupert the idea of bring together the fledgling volunteer yachtsmen organisations into a more coordinated body that in time of war could help provide harbour security at ports around Australia. Rupert was immediately attracted to the idea but could not obtain a similar interest from Navy Office. It remained an idea whose time had not yet arrived.

On 10 October 1935, Rupert had recently returned from visiting coastwatchers along the New South Wales south coast. He arrived in his office only to be informed that his wife Heather had died suddenly in their home. A grief stricken Rupert took his young wife's ashes back to her family's property at Tamrookum where they were buried alongside her father's grave. The period following Heather's death were the darkest days of Rupert's life. He contemplated leaving the Navy to start afresh with a career in medicine a possibility. In the end, as is so often the case for those at a crossroads, the Navy provided a new challenge. In April 1936 Rupert was appointed as the Assistant Director of Naval Intelligence and Staff Torpedo Officer in Navy Office in Melbourne. In Captain Pope's final report he wrote:

Vide previous eulogistic reports which already contain everything which I can think of to say, except of course that his splendid service was continued up to the moment of departure.[226]

Remarkably Captain Pope's efforts for Rupert Long's promotion were in vain and Rupert's next annual S.206 performance report would not be written until 1941! While Rupert was at the top of the seniority list for Lieutenant Commanders, promotion during this period was intensely competitive. For the 47 Lieutenant Commanders on the Executive List there were only 15 Commander positions.[227] With a still sluggish economy there was a very high retention rate and less than a handful of officers promoted each list. Already five officers with less seniority who had joined the Naval College after Rupert, had been promoted to Commander.[228]

Rupert, despite having to come to terms with being a 'passed over' Lieutenant Commander, had a position of some responsibility. From Melbourne, he oversaw the work of the seven District Intelligence Centres at Brisbane, Sydney, Hobart, Port Melbourne, Port Adelaide, Fremantle and Darwin. He effectively was responsible for the Navy's intelligence organization as he reported directly to the Assistant Chief of Naval Staff. The organization also fed and was informed by the wider British Admiralty naval intelligence network.

Rupert met an outstanding public servant in the Melbourne office named Walter Brooksbank. Walter was a Gallipoli veteran who had also served on the Western Front earning a Military Medal and a commission. His corporate knowledge of Australian Naval Intelligence was without parallel. He first worked as a public servant in the Sydney Naval Intelligence Centre in 1922, just one year after its establishment and compiled the *Monthly Australia Station Intelligence Reports*. Both Rupert and Walter had a passion for intelligence work and their individual strengths complemented one another. They would become life-long friends.

Not content to rely just on the intelligence gathered from the regional centres, Rupert greatly expanded his network of information gatherers. In 1936 he was joined for a period by Commander Philip Walter, RN, who proved to be a kindred spirit to Rupert. Walter had spent four years on the China Station and had seen first hand the Japanese policy in China. He had then worked in the Naval Intelligence Branch in the Admiralty. Another support to Rupert in Navy Office both professionally and personally was Jack Newman, who assisted him through his knowledge of both communications and the workings of the headquarters. In August 1936 Hitler assumed absolute power in Germany on the death of President Paul Hindenburg and the Naval Intelligence effort had to be split between Germany and Japan.

From his position in Navy Office, Rupert was able to more effectively champion the idea of a Volunteer Coastal Patrol. On 27 March 1937 it was founded by Harold Nobbs, William Giles and Captain Maurice Blackwood, DSO, RN retired. The latter was to provide the technical expertise to train the yachtsmen in navigation, signaling and reporting. Over time the links with the Navy would grow as its value became more evident.

The Navy Office Rupert had joined had grown only modestly from the days of William Creswell. The Naval Board consisted of the Minister for the Navy, the First Naval Member (the Chief of Naval Staff), the Second Naval Member who was responsible for personnel matters and a Finance and Civil Member. The Board was supported by a Secretary, who from 1914 until 1946 was the impressive George Macandie.[229] He had helped Creswell establish Navy Office in 1903 and possessed a peerless corporate knowledge that benefited both the Navy and the many naval officers who arrived in Melbourne for their first shore posting. It has been said 'if Creswell was the father of the RAN, Macandie was its benign and watchful uncle'.[230] The total Navy Office staff, including accountants and typists was about 100. The naval staff officers only numbered five.

For those in the Pioneer Class who were to serve periodically in Navy Office, it was a challenge to find a suitable home for their families on their modest means near Navy Office. This would often involve families moving into houses being vacated by other naval families moving up to Sydney. Similarly in Sydney there were clusters of rented houses and apartments in suburbs near Garden Island. During the inter-war period

The Royal Sydney Golf Club offered honorary membership to the officers and the Club became a social hub for the families. Winn Reilly, who had a natural aptitude for golf, served on the club committees for many years.

In late August 1934 John and Phyllis Collins were enjoying a few days away from London in the Cornish fishing village of Portwinkle. It was a beautiful seaside village but the tides could be strong making swimming dangerous at times. Returning to their village lodging after a round of golf, the couple heard shouts of alarm from some locals. Two girls had been swept out to sea at the eastern end of Whitesand Bay. The Looe Coastguard seven miles to the west had been alerted, but their arrival would be too late to save the girls. John and Phyllis struck out for the eastern end of the bay collecting and connecting clotheslines from homes as they went. Reaching the closest point to the girls, they found one girl had already been rescued by a boy also attached to a line. The other girl was further out and clinging to a rock in the tidal rip. John stripped to his underwear and with a line knotted around his waist, supported by Phyllis acting as 'reel man' in the fashion of an Australian lifesaver, swam out to rescue the girl. His efforts were successful in recovering the now unconscious and badly cut girl and he returned to the accolades of villagers who had assembled to watch the rescue. He was subsequently awarded a Royal Humane Society Testimonial on Parchment.[231] The following year it was presented to him before a large crowd, prior to the launch of the Melbourne Steamship Company's passenger ship *Duntroon* at Newcastle on Tyne.[232]

In January 1935 John Collins left the Admiralty after being assessed as an 'exceptional staff officer'.[233] He was rewarded with the plum appointment as the commissioning Executive Officer of one of the new light cruisers. The ship, to be named *Sydney*, was part of a three year program approved by the Government in April 1934.[234] She would be eventually joined by two sisterships transferred from the RN and to be renamed *Perth* and

Hobart. Their symmetric lines with two tall well spaced funnels made them among the most graceful cruiser designs ever produced. In service they were immensely popular, with improved crew accommodation and an excellent weapons layout. Importantly, *Sydney* was fitted with Asdic and as such was the first RAN surface ship so fitted.[235] Of note among the many newspapers articles about the weapons fit of the 'splendid new cruiser' no mention was made of the Asdic.[236]

John Collins joined *Sydney* at Swan Hunter yard on the Tyneside. Like so many ships, *Sydney's* life-long happy and efficient 'personality' and reputation were forged in her first commission. The overriding influences were her commissioning commanding officer, Captain JUP Fitzgerald, RN[237] and well selected officers and sailors in key positions. The new Captain, known to John when both were at Greenwich, had just returned from Paris where he served at Naval Attaché. Fluent in both French and Spanish, Fitzgerald was an eccentric of a competent type that often found a home in the British military officer class. John summed him up as follows:

> Fitz was a fire-eater. A wild Irishman, he feared no man and delighted in doing those unconventional things we all want to do but haven't quite got the courage. He was beloved by the ship's company, who would have followed him anywhere, and he was always thoughtful about their welfare. I suspect he must have been somewhat of a trial to his senior officers for, despite a lifetime in the Service, he still regarded authority and convention as rather a joke.[238]

For some Executive Officers, Fitzgerald would have been a nightmare to serve under, but John thoroughly enjoyed the stimulation and the work of implementing the latest direction from his unconventional Captain. Importantly, John would always stand up to his captain if his ideas could have adverse unintended consequences or were inherently unsafe. An early such test was on passage in the cold Bay of Biscay when the Captain ordered 'hands to bathe', that is stopping the ship for the crew to have an ocean swim. John remonstrated and later Captain Fitzgerald said that, 'We are going to get along all right. I wanted to see whether you were a

HMAS Sydney *fitting out at Swan Hunter.*
(The Argus/State Library of Victoria)

'yes' man. If you had piped the 'hands to bathe' I would have got a new Commander in Gibraltar'.²³⁹

Fitzgerald and John Collins, with their contrasting characters but equally high professional standards, made for a very good team. Ordinary Seaman Robert Moore, a 17-year-old bosun on the bridge, wrote of the two men that Fitzgerald or 'Jup' as he was soon called, endeared himself to the sailors. He made great efforts to better understand the Australian way of everyday life, such as the need for a daily bath or shower. In contrast to his Captain, Moore later wrote:

> John Collins was a different type, neat, quiet, direct and always moved smartly and with a purpose. He inspired confidence.²⁴⁰

On 29 October 1935 *Sydney* sailed from Portsmouth. Instead of the usual delivery voyage through the Mediterranean and Suez to Australia, the Abyssinian Crisis intervened and the Commonwealth Government offered *Sydney* to the UK Government for service until the international

Before HMAS Sydney *left the Tyne, Captain JUP Fitzgerald and Commander John Collins hosted the Lord Mayor of Newcastle and other dignitaries onboard.* (State Library of Victoria)

situation had stabilised. Initially *Sydney* served with the 2nd Cruiser Squadron based out of Gibraltar. The other ships were the Leander Class cruisers *Orion, Neptune* and *Leander* with whom *Sydney* would work closely in the future.

Not long after arriving in Gibraltar some of *Sydney's* sailors contracted measles and then mumps. The cruiser was put into quarantine. Captain Fitzgerald, in his inimitable style obtained approval for an independent cruise away from the fleet. *Sydney's* first Christmas away from families was spent in Lisbon where the Portuguese proved delightful hosts to the entire ship's company. In February 1936 *Sydney* left Gibraltar for a refit in Malta and then attachment to the 1st Cruiser Squadron based in Alexandria. Already with the squadron was *Australia* as part of the RAN-RN cruiser-exchange program. As expected there were many reunions as officers and sailors rekindled friendships after their long separation.

The Commander-in-Chief Mediterranean was now Admiral Sir

William Fisher with whom Lloyd Gilling had previously served. Fisher was known fondly by sailors as the 'Great Agrippa'. He was famous for making unannounced visits to his ships to inspect their material state and talk to the crew. On one occasion he visited *Sydney* and was found by John Collins engaging in conversation with some sailors lined up outside the sickbay. The subject of the conversation was in which port the sailors may have contracted their venereal 'condition'.[241]

Fisher relentlessly drove his fleet to maximise its operational efficiency. Both Australian cruisers relished the demanding exercises and the competition with RN ships in any sporting event in port. This training gained added impetuous with the German occupation of the Rhineland on 7 March.

In a much appreciated gesture Fisher detached both ships to visit Gallipoli. To enable all Australians to attend, those RAN officers on individual exchange service in other Mediterranean Fleet ships were rounded up by the destroyer HMS *Basilisk* who rendezvoused with *Australia* and transferred them for the pilgrimage.

In the early morning of 30 April 1936, the two cruisers anchored off the village of Khelia Liman and a Turkish delegation, accompanied by Lieutenant Colonel Cyril Hughes of the Commonwealth War Graves Commission, came onboard *Australia* and extended a gracious welcome and outlined the extensive arrangements for the four day visit. For Commanders Collins and Arthur Spurgeon (1914 Entry) the smooth running of the visit was to be their chief responsibility. Soon afterwards boat loads of around 700 men from both ships made the journey to shore. At Anzac Cove two ships' chaplains officiated at a commemoration service. Also attending were the Turkish hosts and more significantly Turkish veterans of that terrible campaign. One of the *Sydney's* older sailors had participated in the campaign as a soldier while more than a few had their own family ties to the place. The service left a profound effect on all those who attended.[242]

As has since become the time-honoured custom, after the

service the men were left to their own devices. They wandered the battlefield and visited the graves. Some sailors were looking to pay their family's respects to a relative buried so far from home. Colonel Hughes, himself a veteran of the campaign, took John Collins and other officers on a walk of the battlefield. What surprised them was the many remnants such as water bottles, rifles, boots, cartridge cases and even some human bones still strewn about the battlefield. John later remarked he could now start to appreciate the stories his older brother Reg told of his service at Gallipoli. On reflection he wrote:

> The cemeteries, perfectly kept in lovely settings, were a credit to the commission and the Turkish gardeners who tended them. In fact, it may seem a strange thing to say, to me they were of great beauty, unlike any cemeteries elsewhere. They were not depressing and I personally left with a feeling of contentment, satisfied that the Anzacs on Gallipoli rest in peace.[243]

On return from Gallipoli, the cases of mumps increased in *Sydney* and the new C-in-C Admiral Sir Dudley Pound put the ship once more into quarantine. Yet again Captain Fitzgerald had a scheme. This time *Sydney* sailed for Cyprus where he knew of a perfect bay on the south east coast where a fresh water stream ran into the sea. After some difficulty they found the bay, or one very much like the one in the Captain's memory. Sailors were put ashore for recuperation.

Not long after the second quarantine *Sydney* and *Australia* detached from the Mediterranean Fleet. After a rough passage both cruisers arrived in Fremantle on Sunday 2 August 1936. Over ten thousand people lined the wharves to greet them.[244] On 11 August *Sydney* finally sailed into Sydney Harbour and passed at Bradley's Head the mast of her Great War namesake which had been erected as a memorial whilst the new cruiser was under construction.[245]

Another arrival in Sydney was Peyton Kimlin. After many years teaching in small country towns he was drawn to the city for its musical opportunities. Soon after Peyton met Myra Bullock who was an art teacher in the school in Manly where he taught. Her artistic flair would encourage

The graceful HMAS Sydney on completion.
(*The Argus*/State Library of Victoria)

and complement his musical skills. Myra and Peyton were married in 1936 and immersed themselves in the Sydney artistic milieu.

In September 1936 Harry and Jean Showers returned to Australia from the Mediterranean Station in the Orient Lines' *Ormonde*. It proved an eventful passage with the ship nearly running aground in Fremantle when a tug rope parted at the port entrance. Then when coming up the New South Wales Coast a fire broke out in a cargo hold. The fire among coir rope caused considerable smoke and heat which buckled the bulkhead to the neighbouring dining saloon. Harry assisted Captain Thorne, Master of *Ormonde* in the pilotage into Twofold Bay as well as providing advice in damage control. Fireman with breathing apparatus were sent from Sydney to help extinguish the blaze. The Naval Board received a letter of appreciation for Harry's assistance.[246] On return to Sydney, he once again became Squadron Navigating Officer, this time in *Canberra*.

Cyril Sadleir, who had tried to make a go of oyster farming for another two years had since moved from Sydney to Victoria. He returned to the sea in 1936 this time in the merchant marine. He would, however, have to spend considerable time in hospital whenever multiple sclerosis began to take greater hold of his life.[247]

By this time Hugh MacKenzie, after fifteen years sailing the waters of

New Guinea, had earned enough and had seen enough to acquire virgin land on the Hoskins Peninsula of New Britain. It was lush country with panoramic views of volcanic peaks. He and Betty established the Megigi and Matavulu Plantations and grew coconuts and cocoa.

On 1 July 1937 Harold Farncomb became the first Royal Australian Naval College graduate to be promoted to Captain. The significance of this naval milestone was such that his promotion was reported in the national press.[248] Harold had excelled in the Admiralty's Intelligence Division and had added an ability to speak German to his French fluency. In September 1937 he returned to Australia. The one element missing in his otherwise stellar career was sea command. The Naval Board appointed Harold to the two-year old sloop HMAS *Yarra*. A small ship for a Captain, it nevertheless provided him not only with the experience of sea command but also exposed him to the challenges of integrating a mix of permanent and reserve sailors into a close knit team. The Flag Officer commanding the Australian Squadron, Rear Admiral Wilfred Custance assessed at the end of Harold's period in command that he 'should make an excellent Cruiser Captain'.[249]

In 1937 Rupert Long once again found personal happiness. He had met Vera Cliff on a double blind date. The daughter of Sir Walter and Lady Carpenter, she was a divorcee with two young boys and possessed a strong and engaging personality. In August Rupert married Vera at her parent's large house in the well-to-do suburb of Killara in Sydney. Winn Reilly served as Rupert's best man.[250] Sir Walter had extensive business interests in Papua and New Guinea including copra plantations and processing plants, a shipping line and Carpenter Airlines, whose services Eric Feldt had often used in the course of his duties.

In November 1937 Jack Newman left *Canberra* where he had been the Squadron Signals Officer and joined the Director of Naval Signals Communications, Commander Neville Harvey, RN in Navy Office as his assistant. On leaving *Canberra* the Flag Captain, Captain Alexander Wilson, RN stated in Jack's report that, 'he undoubtedly has brains, and is nimble witted'.[251] Indeed in a succession of reports since attaining his specialisation Jack had become highly regarded for his outstanding technical knowledge of communications. But the view had developed in his performance reports that this expertise had come at the expense of knowledge of other aspects of a ship's operation. Jack therefore would not be highly competitive for a sea command. In any case he was the ideal choice to help Harvey revitalise naval communications. To this work Jack applied exceptional drive and energy.

By 1937 the Naval Board had agreed to expand the network of communications stations and Jack helped finalise the successive submissions for Naval Board consideration, these including recommendations on appropriate names for the facilities. Jack later wrote:

> First were the Darwin stations for which we suggested *Coonawarra*. ACNB [Naval Board] wanted to know why and we said it was an appropriate Aboriginal word meaning a loud voice (the fact that it was in the language of an extinct tribe which once inhabited part of Victoria was not mentioned). After a surprising amount of correspondence the Board finally agreed.
> Next came a Direction Finding (DF) station in Western Australia for which we suggested *Jandakot*. More quizzing—to which we gave the reason that it was the name of the locality, which was true.
> Next came *Belconnen* which was approved with only a perfunctory 'what for'—the board seemed to be losing interest. This was too good to miss so we proposed *Harman*, as a contraction of Harvey and Newman, which was OK'd without questions.[252]

While naval communications began its much needed expansion, further steps were underway to develop the Navy's anti-submarine capabilities. By 1937 the Admiralty had provided technical specifications for the manufacture and deployment of harbour loop systems and offered training for the fitting of anti-submarine booms across ports. The Navy was also finally provided with funds to acquire five Type 123 Asdic sets for its destroyers, ten sets for smaller vessels, three indicator loops (for Sydney, Darwin and Fremantle) and associated training sets.[253] James Esdaile, now back at Navy Office, worked on the details of installing the loops and booms in the major ports.

In 1938 John Collins with his planning experience in the Admiralty to the fore, joined Navy Office as the Assistant Chief of Naval Staff and Director of Naval Intelligence. The Chief of Naval Staff was by now Vice Admiral Sir Ragnar Colvin, an able administrator who had been encouraging the Government to increase war preparations.

One element of that effort was the rewriting of the *War Book* which distilled the actions to be taken across Government departments on the outbreak of war. John Collins would be responsible for the work of the staff officers in preparing the Navy's contribution to the book. In this task John forged strong professional relationships with Thomas Hawkins[254] who had served in Navy Office since the days of Creswell and by 1939 headed the Naval Branch and so was responsible for the main signal office and its cyphering work. Some naval officers had been dismissive of this tall and slimly built career public servant. One of John's finest gifts was his keen judge of character and Hawkins would repay this respect many times over. Another important figure assisting in this work was the Secretary to the First Naval Member, Paymaster Captain James Foley. In later years this diarist would shed a fascinating light on the Navy of his time. An associated piece of work to the *War Book* was the updating of the *Special Telegrams*. At face value these were simply code words for ships with associated actions in periods of tension and in time of war. Nevertheless, the development of the underlying disposition of ships and their employment required careful thought.

On joining Navy Office John was briefed by Rupert Long on the state of naval intelligence and James Esdaile on anti-submarine preparations and what they had achieved in overhauling these increasingly important aspects of naval operations. In Rupert, John had a staff officer who 'bore a hand were it seemed to be needed',[255] as such he wrote a useful paper on the need to locally manufacture sea mines.

In respect to anti-submarine capabilities, John Collins himself made an important contribution. He correctly assessed that there was a gap in anti-submarine defences between the ports and the open ocean where sophisticated sloops (such as the *Yarra*) and destroyers would operate with the cruisers. In February 1938 he wrote a minute entitled *A Plea for Smaller Sloops in Larger Numbers* to Vice Admiral Colvin. The minute called for a small but robust escort of simple design and modest armament in some numbers needed to be produced. John suggested a variant of the British Halycon Class minesweepers with which he was familiar. About 18 such vessels would be needed. James Esdaile undertook more analysis and in March 1938 produced a more realistic, if daunting figure of 42 anti-submarine escorts. James wrote:

> This calculation gives the number which, at present, it is quite impossible even to consider ... the conclusion to be drawn is that for any money expended on new vessels, the aim should be to obtain the greatest number of vessels that are capable of performing efficiently the A/S duties required of them. An elaborate gun and torpedo armament is not required by A/S vessels working in Australian waters.[256]

The response to the increasingly urgent need for escorts was three lines of development. In the first instance two additional sloops *Parramatta* and *Warrego* would follow-on from *Yarra* and *Swan*. While small but sophisticated warships, they were of a proven design. In addition, local production of the latest RN destroyer type, the large Tribal Class, could help address the need for ocean going escorts. An examination of RN coastal escorts offered nothing suitable for local conditions and so the Naval Board asked the Director of Engineering, Rear Admiral Percival McNeil to come up with a design. His team came back within a fortnight with the general outline of a 500 tonne escort with Asdic, depth charges, a modest gun armament and an ability to be fitted for minesweeping. It was estimated the little ship with its simple construction requirements and reciprocating engine could be produced for about £100,000. It was the design James Esdaile and John Collins had so dearly wanted and would eventually become famous as the Bathurst Class corvette. In the

John Collins and James Esdaile played pivotal roles in the development of the indigenous Bathurst Class corvettes. This is HMAS Warrnambool *in her wartime configuration.* (Green Collection/State Library of Victoria)

end sixty corvettes were built, of which twenty were ordered for the Admiralty and four for the Royal Indian Navy.

In regard to his intelligence responsibilities, John Collins quickly came to appreciate Rupert Long's much greater expertise in this field than his own and the improvements Rupert had instituted in Navy Office. He saw his job as providing top cover to allow Rupert to get on with his reforms. Rupert had by the beginning of 1939 cultivated contacts in business, the police, port authorities and the merchant marine. A particular focus was the South West Pacific and his family connections with the Carpenter business empire in New Guinea and the Solomons proved particularly fruitful.

By this time Rupert's merchant shipping plots were showing a gradual withdrawal of German shipping from global routes and it was clear to him war would not be far away.[257] Concerned about the provision of essential supplies in the face of submarine and raider attacks, Rupert considered tea, tobacco and phosphate fertilizer were particularly vulnerable and reserves should be stockpiled. Rupert urged Admiral Colvin to raise the matter of phosphates with government. Not convinced the Admiral was sufficiently seized by the matter, Rupert on his own cognizance, called on Mr Harold Gaze at the British Phosphate Commission head offices in Melbourne. Here he found in Gaze a like minded individual and additional imports of the precious fertilizer soon commenced. By the time that supplies were cut off there was over a year's supply in country.[258]

XXII

Many naval officers who had reached the stage in their careers where they had been passed over for promotion, unlikely to have sea command, or were of a specialization in which they were too senior for a sea-going billet, joined the Auxiliary Service. This organisation embraced a range of shore based duties that allowed warships to be effective at sea. These included port defence, communications, logistics and munitions.

In 1936 Eddy Nurse was the first of the Pioneer Class to transfer to the Auxiliary Service when he entered the Naval Inspection Branch. Eddy joined at a critical time for this small but growing organization which was responsible for inspecting ammunition magazines both ashore and in ships as well as ensuring that guns and torpedo tubes were within safe tolerance. Admiral Jellicoe in 1919 proposed that the Naval Inspection Branch expand its inspection responsibilities to also oversee Australian production of ammunition to strict Admiralty specifications.[259] Such production would be strategically important to both Australia and Britain as an alternate source of supply.

To prepare Eddy Nurse for his duties he was sent for specialist training with the RN and returned to Australia to become the Assistant Inspector of Naval Ordnance. As such he became responsible for the inspection of all armament stores manufactured in Australia and joined the staff at Maribyrnong Munitions Factory.

In 1937 Norman Calder was appointed Aide-de-Camp to the Governor General, Lord Gowrie[260] who was a fellow Free Mason. Following this short appointment Norman joined Eddy Nurse in the Auxiliary Service to command the Naval Reserve Depot in Port

Melbourne. His work was overseeing the growing tide of men joining the Naval Reserve and providing them initial and weekly training. On a personal note the appointment gave Norman the opportunity to renew his love of the track and the Calders moved to a house within a kilometre of Caulfield Racecourse. The final transferee to the Auxiliary Service during this period was Jack Newman who was placed in charge of the RAN Shore Wireless Service.

From late 1938 like a returning tide, at first a few and then most of the eight Pioneer Class who had left the Service in the inter-war period rejoined or were called up on the Emergency List. As young veterans of the Great War some would still be able to go to sea but most would serve ashore.

The first to return was Eric Feldt in April 1939. Eric who was now Warden of Wau goldfields had been on leave in Brisbane when Rupert Long floated the idea of him heading a new Naval Intelligence Centre in Port Moresby. From there Eric could greatly expand the Coastwatcher network in both New Guinea and the Solomons. Eric was the logical but nonetheless an inspired choice for this pressing task. He knew not only the islands, but the diverse and individualistic Islander community who could fill the ranks of the Coastwatchers. In this initiative Rupert had the enthusiastic support of John Collins who was still nominally responsible for Naval Intelligence. In obtaining Naval Board approval for the Port Moresby naval intelligence centre both men drafted a persuasive minute which gave a sense of their shared strategic view of the Japanese threat:

> Evidence is becoming increasingly available to support the belief that Japan has adopted a 'Southwards Advance' policy and she is developing increased attention to New Guinea and other island territories.[261]

On 1 July 1939 Paul Hirst became First Lieutenant at Flinders Naval Depot. With some sense that this would be his duty for the duration of the war, he moved the family with him from *Ashbourne*. Also leaving the land was Jack Lecky. He sold his property at Southern Cross and moved into Merredin where he started a fruit and vegetable store.[262]

Winn Reilly who earlier in 1939 had been appointed Pipe Sales Manager for Australian Iron and Steel took leave from the company to return to uniform. As a Lieutenant Commander, Winn joined the Engineering and Construction Branch in Navy Office. But 1939 was a notable year for Winn for another other reason. In June he had won the Royal Sydney Cup by three strokes, holding off professional golfers for the memorable win.[263]

Cyril Sadleir lived in a boarding house in South Yarra near Navy Office and had also been contemplating returning to naval service. Although walking with a cane, Cyril's health had improved and his spirits had no doubt been lifted by his courtship of Lauris Parker. They met at Cyril's lodging where she was the housekeeper and companion to her aunt.

In September he joined the Naval Reserve Depot in Melbourne to assist with the intake of Reserve officers and sailors.

XXIII

On Australia Day 1939 Harry Showers, after navigating thirteen ships in his career to that date, finally joined a ship to command. It was the sloop HMAS *Swan* and he soon gained a reputation for having a clean, smart and efficient ship.[264] The sailors' recollections in *Swan* and future ships under his command was consistently that Harry was 'always a gentleman and a good skipper'.[265]

In May 1939 Harold and Jean Farncomb sailed once more for Britain. Harold was to commission the cruiser *Perth*. This was the first time a Royal Australian Naval College graduate had assumed command of a cruiser. It led the Minister for Defence, Geoffrey Street, to say that the appointment was an indication of the 'growing up' of the RAN.[266]

The majority of the officers and ship's company sailed to Britain in the tramp steamer *Autolycus*[267] on 15 May. The ship was a former sheep carrier and retained that distinctive odor. Berthing had been built in the holds to accommodate about 500 sailors. A large proportion of these sailors came from the old *Adelaide* which had been placed in reserve.[268] There were also many fresh from recruit school at Flinders Naval Depot. The sea routine revolved around keeping the cramped quarters clean, lectures, training for the Royal Guard that would be paraded at commissioning and physical training. The crew were fortunate that their physical training instructor was champion athlete Petty Officer Julius Patching. Known universally as 'Judy' he would in later life become Secretary General of the Australian Olympic Committee.[269]

As the old *Autolycus* approached the Isle of Wight for passage into Portsmouth the crew rushed to the upper deck to catch a glimpse of the majestic three-year old passenger liner *Queen Mary* as she slid past to commence a trans-Atlantic voyage. As they entered port most of them received their first view of a modern naval fleet contrasting with the masts of Nelson's historic flagship HMS *Victory*. Once alongside the dockyard they went onboard their new ship and joined a sprinkling of RN personnel including the Executive Officer, Commander William Adams, RN[270] already onboard. They did not warm to Adams or apparently Harold Farncomb. Ordinary Seaman Basil Hayler recalled that:

> Later in the day lower deck was cleared. This is when the whole ship's ships company is mustered on the upper deck for some particular purpose, in this case for an address by our Commanding Officer, Captain HB Farncomb. Although he was disliked by most, being a strict disciplinarian and very severe on those brought before him on report, I found him to be very fair and a good Australian naval officer, probably because I was young and conditioned to strict discipline, and expected that of our officers, most of whom were held in awe by most young sailors. After introducing himself he outlined the programme for the ship's renaming ceremony and our return trip to Australia which I am sure he suspected, but would not say, would be interrupted by the declaration of war with Germany sometime soon.[271]

Perth had briefly been commissioned in the RN as the HMS *Amphion* and was renamed in Portsmouth on 10 July 1939 to considerable fanfare in the presence of the Princess Marina, Duchess of Kent. Also present was that champion of the RAN, Stanley Bruce, now High Commissioner in London who welcomed the Duchess to 'Australian soil' for the first time.[272]

Unusually for a RAN ship commissioning in British waters, *Perth* did not undergo an extensive work up, rather there was a desire for *Perth* to represent Australia at the World Fair in New York. It was therefore with high morale that *Perth* crossed the Atlantic arriving in the mesmerising metropolis of New York on 4 August. The ship fired a 21-gun salute as she steamed past the Statue of Liberty. Once alongside at Pier 53 at the foot of West 13th Street, Harold Farncomb paid a formal call on the office of the charismatic Mayor of New York, Fiorello La Guardia.

Like many high profile visits of its type, *Perth's* visit to the World Fair was replete with social engagements and attractions for the officers and sailors by day and night. These included free tickets to Radio City and baseball games. Broadway and other attractions also beckoned. There would be ample opportunity to both enhance and put at risk the Navy's reputation during the visit. Having commissioned only five weeks before and so still settling in as a cohesive unit, *Perth's* crew was particularly vulnerable. The New Yorkers' hospitality was legendary in the RAN following *Australia's* 1928 visit. It knew no bounds in the festive World Fair atmosphere.

The tramp steamer Autolycus *was converted to take the bulk of HMAS* Perth's *commissioning crew to the UK.* (Green Collection-State Library of Victoria)

The centerpiece of *Perth's* contribution to the World Fair was her support for the opening of the Australian Pavilion on 11 August—'Australia Day'. *Perth's* band and a large contingent of officers and sailors gave the opening a distinctly naval flavour.

In what appeared a routine administrative matter, Commander Adams had made a poorly considered decision. In accordance with RN instructions for the America and West Indies Station, sailors had to wear during the day summer white uniform and in the evening the blue winter uniform. This would involve for those already ashore a return onboard to change before proceeding ashore once more. This decision by 'Flip the Frog', as Adams was now known by the sailors, was immensely unpopular. It was made in the context of a sterner British approach to 'good order and discipline' that certainly the more junior members of the ship's company had bristled at since commissioning. After a day or so of this dress routine some sailors objected to the requirement and gathered on the forecastle to discuss the matter. When he confronted the sailors Adams ill-advisedly mentioned the word 'mutiny'. The sailors were initially placated by the already popular gunnery officer, Lieutenant Warwick 'Braces' Bracegirdle[273] who told

Harold Farncomb leading three cheers at the opening of the Australian Pavilion at the 1939 World Fair in New York. (HB Farncomb Collection)

them their grievance would be brought to the attention of the Captain. Harold Farncomb returned onboard 'showing the effects of the generous hospitality'[274] from one of the many World Fair functions. He was told of the situation and quickly defused it. The following day, while the summer uniform remained the dress for the day, sailors could request to wear the winter uniform if they would be out in the evening. Unfortunately, the incident was reported in the New York Press with headlines such as 'Aussies mutiny—officers too British' with a sailor quoted improbably saying that 'Our officers are being too blanky limey'.[275] These reports found their way to the front pages of the Australian newspapers. The incident was generally reported in more humorous terms and the 'mutiny' led 'Oriel' in *The Argus* to pen the following poem:

> A life on the ocean wave is not what it used to be,
> When a shipload of the brave have crossed the stormy wave,
> They've got to act like wowsers, which they never did before,
> And put on creamy trousers, if they want to go ashore!
> What a bore!
> For to-day it's not enough to be hardy, bold and strong,
> You have to be more than tough.
> Or something is sure to be wrong,
> if your colour scheme should clash,
> You may lose a fortnight's pay,
> And be careful that your sash is tied the proper way.
> Well a day!
> The sailor who is naughty,
> When sailing on the sea,
> Will find his captain haughty and forfeit morning tea,
> And when he gets his shore leave,
> The captain makes it clear,
> That he will get no more leave,
> If he drinks that horrid beer,
> Dear, oh dear![276]

On 16 August *Perth* finally and perhaps gratefully sailed from New York. Her planned passage was to take her to Kingston, Jamaica and then through the Panama Canal to Australia via San Francisco and Honolulu.[277] *Perth* arrived in Kingston in the company of her near-sister ship HMS *Orion*. They would be destined to operate together for some months. The deteriorating international situation led the Admiralty to request that *Perth* remain in the Caribbean to seize German merchantmen should war be declared.

XXIV

By August 1939 the years of German aggression, as well as France and Britain's responsive policy of appeasement, came to their inevitable denouement. On 22 August the Admiralty sent the first of its warning telegrams to the Fleet and also to the RAN. The following day the German-Soviet Union non-aggression pact was signed. The RN mobilised its Reserve in response. As the international situation continued to deteriorate the small Navy Office staff was deluged with Admiralty signals that had to be decoded and actioned where appropriate. Navy Office was much depleted with Admiral Colvin in London and the Second Naval Member, Commodore Maitland Boucher on sick leave. This left John Collins as a junior Captain, the senior officer in Navy Office, and effectively in command of the Navy.

As war loomed, John Collins needed to clarify whether receipt of an Admiralty telegram commencing hostilities with Germany would automatically involve the RAN. He was without the counsel of the only other flag officer in the Navy, the Rear Admiral Commanding the Australian Squadron, based in Sydney. Rear Admiral Wilfred Custance was on sick leave with what would prove to be a terminal illness.[278] John resolved the question in the most direct manner and rang the Prime Minister. John later recalled:

> So, I rang on the secret phone Menzies who was of course in Canberra - I was in Melbourne at the Navy Office - put the problem to him. He said, 'Well, that means the Navy's going to declare war before the Commonwealth of Australia, doesn't it?'

I said, 'Well, it does if I send "Australia Total"'. He says, 'What do you want to do?' I said, 'I would like to say 'Australia Total Germany' when we get 'Total Germany' from the Admiralty'. He says, 'Oh, well', thought a moment. He didn't refer to anybody; I could almost hear him thinking. He said, 'All right. When 'Total Germany' comes you can say 'Australia Total Germany' at the same time.' And so the Navy really declared war before the Parliament had agreed. It was a very great step forward, I think, a very great act by a big man; Menzies really took his life in both hands by doing that.[279]

After his call with the Prime Minister, John informed the Admiralty of Menzies' decision to assist in their war planning. Looking back, this telephone conversation also marked the beginning of a relationship between naval officer and politician that would mature from one of growing mutual professional respect to friendship. It would span four decades.

During this frenetic period John made an important organizational change. On 25 August he divested himself of the role of Director of Naval Intelligence that he had held in addition to that of being Assistant Chief of Naval Staff. Rupert Long now formally assumed the role that he in practice was undertaking. Importantly this change gave Rupert the authority that he needed to engage with the other services and further improve naval intelligence capabilities.

On 27 August the Navy commenced requisitioning merchant vessels for use by either the RAN or the Admiralty. They would be converted to auxiliary merchant cruisers, store ships and port examination vessels. Requisitions would later extend to privately owned craft for harbour and inshore patrol duties. Among the first batch was the coastal passenger liner *Westralia* and Horace Thompson was appointed her Executive Officer after four months back in the Navy. On the same day naval control of shipping was established whereby the Navy would monitor and control the movement of merchant ships on the Australia Station. The following day Navy Office followed the Admiralty lead, and with Australian Government approval, the RAN was placed on a war footing. Next day all reservists were mobilised.

Captain Harry Showers recommissioned HMAS Adelaide *just hours before the German invasion of Poland. Here one of the cruiser's 6-inch guns conducts gunnery practice.* (RAN)

Despite all the challenges it had faced in recent months, the overworked Navy Office under John Collins' leadership had overseen the personnel strength of the Navy swell through recruitment and reservists. This enabled the Navy to once again recommission *Adelaide*. Harry Showers, after just nine months in *Swan* was made an Acting Captain and placed in command. *Adelaide's* commissioning on 1 September took place just hours before the German invasion of Poland. General mobilisation of British forces was ordered that evening.

In her 1938 refit *Adelaide* had been converted to burn oil rather than coal, her gun armament modernised, she had been provided with depth charges and her range extended. This enabled her to be employed escorting merchant convoys or countering German surface raiders. However she would not be a match for a modern enemy cruiser. Harry's complement of permanent and reserve officers and sailors ranged from his very experienced engineer Commander Walter Armitage, who had stood by the ship while she was in Reserve, to youngsters for whom *Adelaide* was their first ship. Harry had the ideal temperament to bring this disparate group together and form a happy and efficient ship's company.

During 1939 as threat of war grew ever more likely, there was an increasing rate of Australians sealing their courtships in marriage.

The wedding portrait of Cyril Sadleir and Lauris Parker
(Deni McKenzie)

On 2 September, Cyril Sadleir and Lauris Parker were married at Scots Church. He soon thereafter joined the Naval Reserve Depot in Melbourne to assist with the intake of Reserve officers and sailors.

On day of the wedding—the very eve of war—members of the Pioneer Class were either at Navy Office in key positions, in the case of Harold Farncomb at sea in command, or were helping to expand the Navy to a size hitherto unknown. The inevitable conflict would see the Pioneer Class make their greatest contribution to the Navy and the nation. As with the mythical Argonauts there would be deeds of valor as well as tragedies on a personal and grander scale.

Chapter 6
Captains at War

It is difficult—but not necessarily impossible—in peacetime, when the stresses and unpredictabilities of war are hard to imagine (and still harder to simulate), to identify who would be good at it.
Admiral Sir John 'Sandy' Woodward GBE, KCB, RN[1]

I

At 9.15 pm on 3 September 1939, Prime Minister Menzies having met with his cabinet, made a radio broadcast in which he announced:

> It is my melancholy duty to inform you officially that in consequence of a persistence by Germany in her invasion of Poland, Great Britain has declared war upon her, and that, as a result, Australia is at war. No harder task can fall to the lot of a democratic leader than to make such an announcement.[2]

At sea at the time of the broadcast the Australian Squadron was far flung. *Perth* remained in the Caribbean to help intercept German merchant shipping that plied their trade between Germany and South America. Harold Farncomb told the ship's company that if they came across a German pocket battleship that 'he would head straight for it, firing his guns and ram it.' From that point on he was known onboard as 'Fearless Frank'.[3]

The Australian Squadron was temporarily commanded by Captain Wilfred Patterson, CVO, RN in *Canberra* until the arrival of Rear Admiral Jack Crace RN from the UK. Frank Getting was still *Canberra's* Commander. The cruiser had sailed the previous evening from Sydney and proceeded down the coast. The Squadron would grow in strength as warships came out of reserve as men, stores and dockyard capacity allowed. The priority was to deploy ships to war stations off Fremantle and off the Sydney-Melbourne trade route. To that end *Sydney* supported by *Voyager* and *Vampire* took station in the west, while *Hobart* joined *Canberra* and remained off the New South Wales coast. They would be joined by *Australia* as soon as she completed her refit.

As in the Great War, the port of Sydney was of vital importance for the Navy as a base to generate and sustain its expanded fleet and when necessary repair its battle-scarred warships. In September Horace Thompson joined the base staff at *Penguin* whilst Leigh Watkins also briefly joined but was soon released. As a refrigeration engineer his skills were still needed in industry. In November 1939 James Esdaile left Navy Office to be Senior Staff Officer to the Commodore in Charge, Sydney. James had had a difficult time working with the demanding Admiral Colvin in Navy Office[4] and no doubt welcomed a return to Sydney and the fleet. Chief among the challenges he faced in was the strengthening of the Sydney port defences against submarine attack along the lines he had proposed in 1933.

Also returning to Sydney in November 1939 was Norman Calder who became District Naval Officer and oversaw the considerable expansion of the naval reserve depot at Rushcutter Bay to an establishment that also took on anti-submarine, gunnery and radar training. It also became a busy base for harbour defence motor launches and auxiliary patrol vessels. Norman and the family took up residence in 'the cottage' next to the depot and in August the following year the depot was commissioned and he became the first Commanding Officer of HMAS *Rushcutter*.

II

The sea war for Britain and her Dominions against Germany had as its essence protecting the free use of the sea for trade and movement of the Army as the strategic situation dictated. For the German Naval High Command the commencement of World War II was at least four to five years earlier than they would have wished. German naval plans included an ambitious building program that would have seen a much larger fleet including two aircraft carriers and around a dozen battleships, twenty cruisers and over 170 submarines. With such a fleet Germany could have posed a much greater threat to Britain and her sea lines of communication. Clearly such possibilities did not rate high in Hitler's calculus in September 1939. The Kriegsmarine therefore had to fight a different sea war with a more modest fleet. The only modern battleships *Bismarck* and *Tirpitz* were still completing and there were less than sixty submarines in service.

The German naval strategy was one often chosen by the weaker naval power, a trade war or to the Germans—*Handelskrieg*. To effect this strategy the Kriegsmarine's submarines would conduct a campaign against merchant shipping in the North Sea and Atlantic. Its surface fleet of battlecruisers, pocket battleships and cruisers would attempt to evade the RN and range individually on trade routes.

The Kriegsmarine augmented its fleet with ten merchant ships converted to auxiliary cruisers, or raiders as they were more commonly known. The most modern of these raiders was Ship 41 which was converted in 1940 during her construction. Ship 41 was subsequently named *Kormoran* by her Captain and her armament was typical. It consisted of six 5.9-inch guns, a powerful anti-aircraft armament, torpedoes, mines and two Arado 196 floatplanes. This was comparable to a light cruiser but without the armour and speed of a warship. In the case of *Kormoran* one of her 5.9-inch guns came from the World War I battlecruiser *Seydlitz* made famous from her exploits at the Battle of Jutland.[5] Her armament was concealed with drop-down panels that facilitated rapid engagement. In addition, the raiders had additional bunkers, storerooms and accommodation to allow them to operate for many months without rendezvous with supply ships. The hoped for consequence of *Handelskrieg* was to cause havoc and consume a significant number of Allied warships to counter raiders.

In May 1939 Hitler directed the Kreigsmarine to 'make its own preparations for the war against British and French merchant shipping'.[6] As early as August submarines and warships with their attendant supply ships were steaming to their war stations. To deal with the German threat, the Admiralty required a global and coordinated response. The British Government sought from the dominions control of significant portions of their small navies to be part of this global effort to secure the seas. To that end, the Australian Government received a request for ships to be transferred to Admiralty control. The response was conditional with the Commonwealth Government authorising which ships could leave the Australia Station.[7]

III

In order to prepare and position the scarce units of the Australian Squadron to where they would be required and to judge how many could be allocated to the RN for the global conflict, the Naval Board and the Government became more reliant on naval intelligence. As such the workload on Rupert Long was considerable. Besides the provision of daily naval intelligence assessments he had to develop and foster a range of links with the Admiralty, the Army, Air Force and the various police forces. Rupert was keen to coordinate intelligence efforts, but at the same time was wary of attempts by the other two services to combine into a single entity lest naval interests were lost in a predominately Army enterprise.

Undertaking the duties of Director Naval Intelligence (DNI) as a Lieutenant Commander made the task more difficult for Rupert. His Army counterpart, for instance, was a Colonel. It was in the Navy's interest to promote Rupert and finally on 6 April 1940 he was made an

HMAS Perth *passing through the Panama Canal enroute to Australia on her delivery voyage.* (RAN)

Acting Commander. In his work Rupert was assisted most ably by Walter Brooksbank who progressively took on more of the workload. Walter would become known as 'B1' as a differentiator to his younger brother Lieutenant Gilbert Brooksbank—'B2', who also joined Rupert's team.

Central to his view of the role as DNI, Rupert believed his organization must gather intelligence and not just rely on Admiralty reports. His efforts were to take a number of forms, but perhaps the most mysterious and least documented was his cultivation of contacts in Australia and overseas to provide reports to him or to carry sensitive information. Rupert's biographer Barbara Poniewierski[8] assessed he had between 150 to 160 'agents' by the beginning of the war. Although the details remain sketchy, it appears his contacts provided, among other things, information on German and Japanese commercial activities in Australia and the neighboring islands and well as any noteworthy shipping movements. Rupert was clearly in his element as more strands were brought together in his intelligence web. 'B1' later wrote of Rupert's style:

> The picture of Commander Long which I retain strongest in my mind after the passage of these far-from-uneventful years is that of him seated at his desk, with his jacket removed even on a Melbourne winter's day. Alongside him would be his inevitable glass of milk and his cigarette-box, which frequently required refilling, not only for his

own needs but for those of the constant stream of callers who drifted in from places far and wide. He would make available even to the most junior subordinate officers the capacious leather armchair close by, and his greeting invariably took this form: 'Sit down old boy! Help yourself to a cigarette ... Shoot'.

This attitude was not contrived: it was natural. And it certainly produced results, for each of his callers felt that he could speak to the DNI with absolute freedom, and, if he happened to have a chip on his shoulder, that he would be given a patient hearing - even if a glance at the DNI's 'INWARDS' basket showed that it was filled to overflowing. For Commander Long set great store on the human factor, and it was because of this that he was able to get the best out of his officers - both naval and civil.

When he found himself confronted with a particular 'sticky' problem, it was his habit to rise from his desk, walk around in front of it (the secraphone being in his way) and look out through the window, which overlooked St. Kilda Road. There, with his hands thrust deep in his trouser pockets, gently he would rock to and fro on his heels, ostensibly watching the traffic or gazing out at the Shrine of Remembrance lying directly opposite - and which, through the loss of so many of his former shipmates, meant a great deal more to him than it did to the average passerby. A sudden lift of his right shoulder and a sharp left-about-turn would indicate that he had found the solution to the problem.[9]

As a practitioner in the intelligence field for many years Rupert saw a particular national vulnerability in the lack of an organization focused on internal security against foreign espionage. Rupert was one of the main advocates to form an organization along the same lines as the British MI6. It would, however, take some time before such an entity was formed.[10]

In Rupert's assessment the invigoration and expansion of the coastwatcher network was of paramount importance. While work was needed to improve upon the network around Australia through the District Intelligence Offices, priority had to be establishing the network in the islands to the north of the continent. In this endeavour he needed Eric Feldt. In late August 1939 Rupert was finally able to get the Naval Board to approve the funds and on 8 September 1939 Eric was appointed Staff Officer Intelligence Port Moresby. This innocuous title belied the importance of the position.

Rupert had charged Eric to develop an organisation by which intelligence could be obtained in an area consisting of Papua, Mandated New Guinea, the Solomon Islands and the New Hebrides and the surrounding waters. This daunting task was to be achieved with virtually no staff or equipment. A sum of £200 was allocated to travel through the territories to enlist the services of civilian volunteers. Rupert had every confidence that Eric with all his extensive and first hand knowledge of both the islands and the resourceful breed of men and women that lived along the coasts, could establish such an organisation. Indeed, Eric with his naval appreciation of the required product and practical technical bent was uniquely placed to do so.

Commander Rupert Long as Director of Naval Intelligence in his St. Kilda Road office. (RAN)

Eric immediately set about an exhausting tour of the New Guinea coastline and the islands using a mix of Carpenter Airways and RAAF flights, coasters, launches and schooners. He identified key strategic locations, sized up prospective coastwatchers and gave them the pitch - warts and all. Many of the men he had known for a decade. They were district officers, patrol officers, planters and missionaries. All were resourceful and independently minded islanders. Eric's selection of candidate coastwatchers was critical. He later wrote:

> The essential conditions for a coastwatcher to operate behind the enemy lines were a sufficient area to hide himself in, rugged country to deter pursuit and friendly natives. If an observation post could be established on high land at a distance from the enemy base, as at Buka Passage or Buin, that was an advantage, particularly if inaccessible

country lay between the post and the base. Jungle was the best cover but it did not provide food, while a clearing was necessary for dropping supplies.

The ability to handle natives was the principal factor in the survival of coastwatchers. This can only be obtained by experience and many qualities and facets of personality go towards it. No single virtue, or even experience alone, makes this ability – it is a conglomerate of many qualities, all leavened by experience. However, it can safely be said that no one without experience of natives could survive, whatever other qualities he had. This meant that coastwatchers were men who had lived in the Territories and they had the virtues and vices of those people. In general, they had all enjoyed life on a high economic level and were, in consequence very independent. Their association with a native race had given them the habit of command and these two qualities, added to a considerable clannishness among them, made them highly individualistic, so that the best results could only be obtained from them by making full use of their high degree of intelligence and by trusting each man completely —a trust which was never misplaced.[11]

Eric's engagement of the Lutheran missionary Reverend Harold Freund on Rooke Island off the New Guinea coast was in many ways typical. Eric wrote to Rupert Long of his conversation with Freund after arriving in the small ketch *Siassi*:

There Reverend APH Freund was interviewed and he undertook to act as a Coast Watching agent. Mr Freund made clear his attitude to me as an Australian, he had every instinct to help, as a Missionary he had some misgivings, but felt that as he was accepting the protection of British Forces, he could not let any misgivings stand in his way. He impressed me as a very sincere man and I personally have no doubts as to his loyalty. I supplied him with a copy of the *Coast Watching Guide*... At the moment his teleradio is out of action but I arranged with the district Officer, Salamaua, for assistance to be given him in repairing it.[12]

For his part Harold Freund recognized why Eric had made the trek to enlist him:

Having been far and wide in New Guinea for years Eric Feldt knew all the strategic spots where it would be valuable to have someone with a radio to report movements of ships, and, naturally, any aircraft also. He knew that Awelkon, 1,700 feet above sea level had a complete view of

Vitiaz Strait through which ships from South-east Asia had to pass if they wanted to get to the eastern end of New Guinea and Port Moresby and Australia. In fine weather we could see right over to the New Guinea mainland. When Feldt put the proposition to me, I told him normally clergymen do not take part in such activities, but that, since there were special circumstances, and since I was the only white man living at Awelkon, I was willing to do what he wanted.[13]

Another new coastwatcher Paul Mason believed Eric's easy personal rapport and genuine concern for his men entrenched confidence in Eric's leadership. This was to be increasingly important for coastwatchers as they endured their individual hardships and dangers.[14]

The Teleradio 3B was critical to Eric's vision for the coastwatching organisation. Amalgamated Wireless of Australasia (AWA) had produced the Teleradio and the Government of Papua established a network through their territory. A more limited network existed in New Guinea. In all thirty three sets had potential to be used for coastwatchers. Critically for Eric the Teleradio 3B was robust, its component parts could be carried to a new location with the help of about a dozen native carriers and it could have a discrete frequency crystal for coastwatcher transmissions. In addition, a code system that was within the ability of the coastwatchers to use could be provided. The Navy had devised a code called the Playfair system based on key words and Eric had further modified it largely based on suggestions from Jack Newman into the 'Feldt' method to make it more suitable.[15]

Eric requested an additional eighteen radios to extend the network into New Guinea, the Solomons and New Hebrides. The need for more radios had been anticipated by Navy Office as had a teleradio crystal with the unique coastwatcher frequency (X frequency). Because of the range of the Teleradio 3B a hub and spoke network was established by Eric. The hubs being at Port Moresby, Rabaul, Tulagi and Thursday Island where listening watch was kept on X Frequency. Eric's civilian radio expert David Laws would then visit the new coastwatchers to provide the radios and instructions on it and the Playfair system. It was not lost on the new coastwatchers that the recognition book contained more Japanese than German silhouettes.[16]

The contribution of Walter Brooksbank in revitalising the coastwatcher cannot be underestimated. He had done much towards reconstituting the coastwatchers in Australia and had written the original *Coastwatching Guide*. In Eric's words, 'B1' had 'borne the long struggle to build up the coast watching organization [and] provided me with all the information—a considerable amount—which would be of use to me'.[17]

An important aspect in Eric's view was the military and legal standing of the coastwatchers. The Australian based coastwatchers were all civilians. Eric successfully advocated that those located overseas should be made members of the naval reserve, or if they had previously been in the military, then that of their former service. The intent was to give them and their families some financial benefit. Eric was realistic enough to assume that there would probably be widows in need of future assistance. He also reasoned if captured they would as military personnel, be treated as prisoners of war and not spies. Rupert and his staff set the administrative wheels in motion which included sending uniforms to these remote localities. Due to the requirement for men joining as officers in the naval reserve to have some previous sea experience, Rupert organized for those who did not to join another service but still be part of the coastwatch organization.[18]

In a remarkable effort, by December 1939 Eric had written a comprehensive report to Rupert that detailed the structure, location and the coastwatchers for the organisation. It was a network that would extend over half a million square miles. Where there was a location that did not have a suitable islander, Eric recommended a small naval team to be dispatched. In his report to Rupert, he stated he had an organisation that 'would really work'. With that letter began an unremitting flow of correspondence that lasted over the five years of war between these two classmates. Invariably letters from Eric to Rupert began with his old College nickname of 'Dear Cocky ...' In these letters, besides covering operational matters, Eric would seek Rupert's assistance to acquire meagre funds, mundane articles such as attaché cases, intercession on the part of a coastwatcher for allowances or a naval rank. This assistance also extended to the rudimentary office in the leaky and dilapidated Port Moresby hut that served as the naval headquarters. Initially Eric was assisted by a young reservist Ordinary Seaman Telegraphist James Gill whom Eric and Rupert managed to get promoted to Sub-Lieutenant. This helped him in running the office when Eric was off visiting coastwatchers. Eric wrote to Rupert early on that, 'I assure you I push back stuff to you only when it is completely defeats me. I herewith now proceed to brown you off'.[19]

After a series of letters seeking intercession Eric wrote, 'Hope I am not driving you mad with my numerous personal letters—say the word if I am'.[20] In dealing with Eric's issues Rupert was invariably responsive, even in the face of other competing demands. In working the bureaucratic levers and in his encouraging responses to Eric, Rupert was keenly aware of Eric's intense character and at times his strong emotions. Eric had maintained his lack of patience for 'stool polishers' from his Rabaul days. This shortcoming was more than offset by his peerless talents and knowledge for his most vital work. Tensions between the men did exist as Rupert tried to keep up with Eric's demands, but humour and goodwill were manifest. In one interchange Rupert wrote:

Dear Eric,

Thank you for keeping me so well in the picture of happenings in Port Moresby, and your territory. You are, in fact, so good at this that I am finding it difficult to keep pace with your questions, or at least to find satisfactory answers to them. For the moment I do not propose to deal with them, but merely to pump back a few questions at you.[21]

In reply Eric wrote:

Dear Cocky,

Thanks for your letter—the suavity with which you put me off and push stuff back at us is a revelation to one who has known you for twenty-seven years. However, as you have sent us a writer and are sending Hugh MacKenzie, I'll take it gladly.[22]

While Rupert and his staff were impressive in their ability to support the growing coastwatch organization, there were times when even they struggled. It led Rupert to end one missive with 'I am afraid however that the old sleeve is singularly devoid of aces'.[23] Their correspondence, though official, includes many personal references and allusions to their warm friendship. One letter from Rupert, after Eric's relocation to Townsville in May 1941 where air operations were then controlled, ended with:

> Cheerio old man. I hope you have your wife with you by now. They can be curses sometimes but they do stop us going off our rocker. Please give her my kindest regards. All the best from the bunch of thugs down here and from me. Look after yourself.[24]

What also shines through this correspondence is that both men were together engaged in a great endeavour. They appreciated, perhaps more than others, its strategic value to the war effort and from a personal perspective they probably knew that this would be the crowning achievement of their lives. Finally, it is clear from their letters that while the intelligence they gained from their courageous coastwatchers was keenly appreciated, they never lost sight of the perils of each and every coastwatcher. Eric wrote in a report to the Naval Board that, 'Only men of the highest type with supreme courage and the highest sense of duty, were of use'.[25]

During 1940 as the war clouds gathered in the Pacific, more Teleradios were manufactured, coastwatchers conducted training with the Playford code and new coastwatching sites established. By November, with the help of RAAF flying boats the coastwatcher network was in place and suitably equipped. Rupert was mindful of the growing workload and the need not to ask too much of Eric's health that had been diminished after years battling bouts of malaria. So in the same month Eric was joined in Port Moresby by his classmate Hugh MacKenzie, who left his plantation at Megigi on the north coast of New Britain and had rejoined the Navy as a Lieutenant. Hugh was an ideal choice because he would also be able to go out and help expand the coastwatching network. Indeed, Hugh was soon sent to survey the Solomons and Eric was able to conclude a report to Rupert with:

Well all the very best old son. MacKenzie is now visiting Talasea, Garun, and Fondo and will return here next week. He has had a good look at the Solomons and now is au fait with the whole area should I be shifted, drop dead, or get DTs. Cheers Eric.[26]

Their time together in Port Moresby however, was short-lived for by December Rabaul's defences were strengthened with an AIF battalion and a small RAAF base with some aircraft. Rupert had decided that a Navy Intelligence Officer was required in Rabaul to manage that hub. By virtue of Hugh's many years as a planter on the island, he was the natural choice.

Perhaps the final piece in the broader intelligence puzzle for Rupert was cryptanalysis, the intelligence drawn from code breaking. While Australia had played an important part in cryptanalysis in World War I under Dr Wheatley, it was a lost local capability. Rupert was one of the few officers to receive the product of British decryption of German signals known as Ultra for provision to Admiral Colvin. He therefore knew that such a capability must be reborn in Australia. Rupert encouraged Colvin to champion the establishment of such a capability, but Prime Minister Menzies was unconvinced and preferred to rely on the British, concerned that an Australian capability would be expensive and take too long to establish.[27] This view was supported by the British themselves, who did however think that a small cryptographic cell under the DNI with a focus of intercepting Japanese signals was warranted.[28] For their part the British had established in 1934 the Far East Combined Bureau (FECB) in Hong Kong to intercept and break Japanese traffic. By September 1939 the FECB had moved to Singapore.

From an Australian perspective Menzies' views were unfortunate on a number of grounds. Firstly, if there was concern about the Singapore holding out as a bastion, what would happen to the FECB capability if it fell? As Menzies himself stated, cryptanalysis capabilities took time to establish. Arguably therefore the sooner it was established, the better. Finally the cost of maintaining such a capability would pale into insignificance compared to the loss of even one ship. This is not to mention the lives saved through the gleaned intelligence. In this matter, like so many, Rupert would have to progress in small steps.

Working in the FECB was a brilliant former RAN officer who had transferred to the RN in 1930 because of his talent in cryptography. He was Commander Eric Nave and was the same age as the Pioneer Class. Rupert Long spoke to Nave when he was on sick leave in Australia from Singapore. Nave would prove to be the key in establishing an Australian cryptographic capability. Rupert had Nave and Jack Newman, now the Director of Signal Communications, develop a modest plan for the small intercept and cryptanalysis cell in Melbourne. The proposal for both a radio direction finding and cryptanalysis capability was presented to the Defence Conference in Singapore in October 1940. Now with the support of Britain and the prospect of New Zealand and Dutch cooperation Menzies gave approval for the cell. Joe Burnett, who had taken over from John Collins as Assistant to CNS, wrote to Admiral Colvin:

> This is a matter of the greatest importance for the Australian Station. The organisation and cost of putting into operation is very small, and is strongly recommended.[29]

While Nave built the team, Jack Newman set about expanding the facilities and equipment in Darwin, *Harman* and the new Special Intelligence Bureau in Melbourne as well as helping to facilitate the exchange of information with the Dutch facility in Batavia. By mid-1941, with the help of the RAAF, there would be an ability to intercept some Japanese naval and merchant shipping communications. Of Rupert at the end of this critical period Eric Feldt wrote:

> On him had fallen much of the burden of building up the Naval Intelligence Division, and it had been a thankless task, calling for patience and equanimity. Lack of funds had prevented him from carrying out his ideas in full, and now he had to work against time to fill in the blanks. He was a leader rather than a driver, and, if anything, over-indulgent of the faults of his juniors. Years of secretive work had developed in him an indirect, oblique approach

to problems, a habit which he sometimes carried to extremes. Experience had given him a wide knowledge, and he combined a capacity for working long hours with an unfailing good humour. Above all his other virtues was his ability to let anything alone if it functioned properly.[30]

Perhaps the most pressing issue for Rupert was providing to the Naval Board and to the fleet, timely intelligence on German raiders. He had been seized by this German threat for some time and wrote:

> ... the position known from espionage and Intelligence and as known by us in Melbourne, and from our own contributions to the general pool in London, made it quite clear, before Germany started things, that her raider effort would be something for the world to wonder at. It was clear, in London, at least, that German raiders could not be bottled up and that they would appear in forms and of individual power (as in the case of the *Kormoran*) not thought of in the '14/18 war.[31]

For the foreseeable future they would be the main naval threat in the Pacific and Indian Oceans. In addition to the Admiralty reports, the DNI team collated any reports from merchant ships or coastwatchers of suspicious sightings as well as direction finding and signal intercepts. The very real threat of raiders was to be brought home on 18 June 1940 when the liner *Niagara* struck a mine off Auckland. It transpired that the mine had been laid by the German raider *Orion*. Rupert primarily drew the fleet's attention to information on raiders through Weekly Intelligence Summaries. Inevitably though, it was a fragmented picture with information on where raiders had been rather than where they were. Vigilance was essential.

IV

While Eric Feldt, Hugh MacKenzie and Jack Newman were working with Rupert Long and Joe Burnett to establish adequate intelligence capabilities, others in the Pioneer Class were returning to uniform or from shore to sea. On 4 October 1939 Harry Vallentine left his work as a rigger but forsook the Navy and instead enlisted in the Australian Army for service

Niagara *alongside in Melbourne. She was the first victim of German raiders and sank with 8 tonnes of Bank of England bullion bound for the USA. Remarkably most of the gold was recovered the following year.* (State Library of Victoria)

in the 12th Garrison Battalion, quickly advancing to the rank of Sergeant.

On that same day Acting Captain Frank Getting joined *Kanimbla* then fitting out at Cockatoo Island as an armed merchant cruiser for the RN but with an RAN complement. The ship had seven 6-inch guns of Great War vintage fitted to her decks with other modifications of a modest nature. As was the practice in the RN, many of the existing merchant marine crew were retained onboard as naval reservists and were augmented with naval personnel to undertake such tasks as gunnery and communications. Of the naval personnel some were permanent service like Frank, others were long time reservists[32] and still others had joined the reserve for the war. Inevitably there was a clash of cultures. Frank, coming fresh from *Canberra,* insisted on naval discipline and routines which proved unpopular. To some onboard his style was seen as aloof and unapproachable, especially by the merchant mariners and reservists. It was important to gain the support of these merchant marine officers and sailors as they had much to offer. Compared to a cruiser, *Kanimbla* was underpowered and slow to respond to changes to her engine settings. She was also much more influenced by the wind when coming alongside a berth at slow speed. After a few indifferent berthing episodes Frank left the task to his very experienced merchant marine navigator Lieutenant Gerhard Heyen. While some of the junior officers and sailors were highly critical of their Captain, the situation in *Kanimbla* was far more complex than they appreciated.

On 15 November John Collins handed his Navy Office duties over to Joe Burnett. John was to command his old ship *Sydney*. Admiral Colvin perceptively wrote in John's confidential report:

> One of the most able staff officers I have met. Keen, enthusiastic and fertile of ideas. Has a most orderly mind and is at the same time a rapid worker. Sometimes apt to be over keen and to tread on toes but this I feel will be corrected by experience.[33]

One of the first visitors to Joe Burnett's office was Frank Getting. With his experience in the 1920s of training in the Geelong based J boats, Frank had brought the newly commissioned *Kanimbla* to Port Phillip Bay for work up training. It also allowed him to call in at Navy Office to better understand his ship's future duties as an armed merchant cruiser. Both Joe and Jack Newman came and visited the ship, the latter to check over the communications department. The week of training was slow but effective. Frank wrote that 'I have every reason to believe that I can produce an efficient Armed Merchant Cruiser in quite a short time'.[34]

John Collins' experience in joining his cruiser was a complete contrast. *Sydney* was in Fremantle after completing patrol work and gunnery training. John found his former ship to be a happy and efficient one with still the same 'feel' as in her first commission. Early on he told the ship's company:

> Work hard, play hard, keep steaming and don't drift. Enjoy what you are doing. No one gets far if they don't and keep smiling.[35]

There were still many 'old hands' onboard who welcomed their former Commander back. Another familiar face was the Executive Officer, Commander Thomas Hilken, RN who John knew from his exchange service. Hilken wrote in his diary 'We had lived at Mayo Court together in 1933 after Edith and I got married, and all four were very good friends'.[36]

The ship was however suffering a seasonal epidemic of mumps and *Sydney* had a dozen cases including the navigating officer Lieutenant Commander Clive Montgomery, RN who John Collins had discharged to Subiaco Infectious Hospital. For the next month *Sydney* continued to escort merchantmen and conduct general training operating out of Fremantle. In an incident not unknown to new Captains, John lightly damaged his ship when coming alongside. Among the ships *Sydney* escorted through her patrol area included the old *Waitamata,* which had been part of *Omrah's* convoy to England in 1917, and *Duntroon,* which John had seen launched in 1927. On 13 December Harry Showers called on John in Fremantle and *Adelaide* took over duties in Force ZZ and *Sydney* steamed east to her home for a welcome Christmas break and dockyard maintenance. During this passage the news of the British victory at the Battle of the River Plate was announced. Hilken wrote 'We are all beginning to feel very much out of the war, and our daily dawn stand to seemed like playing at war'.[37]

After Christmas *Sydney* operated off the east coast and on 13 January she anchored in Jervis Bay. Also at anchor was *Leander*. Officers and sailors exchanged visits. Most notably, *Leander's* Commander showed Hilken how he had all the ship's boats fully provisioned in case the cruiser was torpedoed. Hilken resolved to implement the same regime in *Sydney*.[38]

On the same day Horace Thompson returned to the Squadron. Horace was appointed to the Huddart Parker passenger liner *Westralia* which was also being converted to an armed merchant cruiser[39] along the same lines as *Kanimbla*. The duties of the Executive Officer during the hurried modifications and commissioning were many. It was a role for which Horace, after just three months back in naval uniform performing censorship duties, and with a decade away from the Navy, was ill-equipped. By end of March his Captain, Commander Alvord Rosenthal (1915 Entry) determined a more current sea going officer should be appointed and Horace was reassigned to the shore base *Rushcutter* as Extended Defence Officer and Chief Examining Officer Sydney. Thereafter, a note was placed on his personal file stating 'Not to be employed at sea except in emergency'.[40] In these new duties Horace was responsible for the operation of the indicator loops and boom defences across Sydney Harbour.

On 25 January 1940 John Collins took the Governor General Lord Gowrie, Prime Minister Menzies and three other members of the war cabinet for a day at sea in *Sydney*. John was keen both to impress and to educate his guests. He therefore organized for the armed merchant cruiser HMAS *Manoora* to act as an enemy target. The cruiser closed *Manoora* at speed and conducted an impressive 6-inch gunnery throw-off firing and 4-inch and machine gun anti-aircraft firings before returning to port. At the end of the month John confided in Hilken that *Sydney* was under orders to sail west again, and then, after five or six weeks patrol work, she would join the British East Indies Squadron.[41]

Before *Sydney* sailed to the west John and Phyllis Collins hosted the officers and their wives or girlfriends to a cocktail party at the Royal Sydney Golf Club. Underlying the perceived benign threat of raiders on the Australian coastline at the time, Phyllis and a number of the wives and their children sailed in *Manunda* to Fremantle a couple of days after *Sydney*. This was to enable them to see more of their husbands when the ship returned to port.[42]

Unlike *Sydney*, Frank Getting and *Kanimbla* were to have their first Christmas away from home. They sailed on 8 December for Hong Kong for fuel and stores before patrolling off the neutral Japanese coast to prevent the movement of German shipping. As *Kanimbla* passed through New Guinea waters Rupert Long had Frank examine anchorages that could be used by enemy raiders. Frank reported the large number of bays suitable for hiding and in a validation of Rupert's strategy he remarked that 'the most economical way of keeping the whole area under observation is by flying boat or sea-plane supported by coastwatching using the portable W/T sets.' Frank also validated Jack Newman's work by noting how High Frequency long range communications had much improved with Australia in the area since the powerful transmitting station at Belconnen had entered service.[43]

On the passage north the complexities within *Kanimbla's* ship's company became more apparent. Some of the long term reservists

Frank Getting as Commanding Officer of HMS Kanimbla. *(RAN)*

objected to being sent off the Australia Station. Of these Frank Getting thought some had business interests and other work that would be affected by overseas service. Frank was keenly aware he had an unhappy ship on sailing from Sydney. Once at sea some of the former merchant navy officers and senior sailors 'expressed disappointment at the strenuousness' of the normal naval three watch system and having to do drills and adopt the naval divisional system of caring for the well being of sailors.[44] Matters came to a head when some of the old hands complained about the rotten potatoes being served. Frank tasted the potatoes and found them to be 'excellent' and told the Leading Hands of Messes that if 'the hands did not wish to eat the food it was to be "ditched" and no issue in lieu would be made'.[45]

Frank held firm on the passage and drilled the ship for its future boarding duties. He also had officers and petty officers use the Divisional system to run to ground any issue that was affecting morale. On arrival in Hong Kong he asked the Commander-in-Chief of the China Station, Admiral Sir Percy Noble[46] to address the ship's company on the strategic situation and the role to be played by *Kanimbla*. Equally effective in building morale and ship identity were 'runs ashore' in port where sailors saw themselves as '*Kanimbla* sailors' in the milieu of a larger fleet. Frank wrote to Navy Office that, 'Since arriving in Hong Kong the whole atmosphere has changed and the young ratings especially seem extremely happy'.[47]

Shortly after *Kanimbla's* first patrol began the cruiser HMS *Liverpool* intercepted the Japanese passenger ship *Asama Maru* within sight of Mount Fuji.[48] Twenty one Germans who were suspected of trying to return to Germany via Siberia were removed from the ship and subsequently interned in Hong Kong. This action led to a formal protest from the Japanese Government and inflamed popular feeling in the still neutral Japan against Britain. In part to assuage this feeling the Chamberlain Government agreed to return nine Germans who were unsuitable for military service to Japan. *Kanimbla* was assigned this delicate task because she still wore her peacetime paint scheme and looked like a merchant ship. On the six day passage Frank learnt more of the prisoners' background. They were all mariners, led by a Captain Groth who had plied the South American run to Germany for the Standard Oil Company. In the early morning of 29 February *Kanimbla* entered the busy port of Yokohama to be met by Japanese naval and Foreign Office officials as well as the British Naval Attaché. For those not involved in the prisoner handover there was ample opportunity to view the 'strange' but modern appearance of Japanese warships in port.[49] Frank had a number of his officers deployed in various vantage points around the ship to surreptitiously sketch and detail the Japanese warships.[50]

After the prisoner supply, and receipt notes were signed, the handover was effected. Well treated and fed in *Kanimbla* they bid a friendly farewell in front of a battery of Japanese press cameras. Before leaving port the British Naval Attaché informed Frank that the German ships in Japanese ports were unlikely to try their hand with the British patrols so prominent but there were still about 1,000 Germans who might try to take passage on foreign shipping.

The subsequent patrols were generally about three weeks in duration and involved surveying the shipping in the area and approaching any suspicious vessel. In an effort to disguise *Kanimbla's* presence and encourage movement from German shipping, Frank had two white stripes painted on her funnel and flew the Dutch merchant ensign when in visual range of Japanese sampans.[51] In any lull in activity Frank maintained drills and initiated a 6-inch gun loading and .22 rifle competitions between

Getting Busy - This cartoon produced in Kanimbla *highlights the success of the ship's patrols off Japan.* (Geelong Maritime Museum)

the different parts of the ship. The latter became very popular and helped maintain morale.

The most notable incident in *Kanimbla's* deployment occurred on 15 March 1940. The ship had been ordered to patrol east of the Tsurugu Strait to try and intercept the Russian merchantman *Vladimir Mayakovsky*.[52.] The Russian ship was bound for Vladivostok from America with a cargo of wolfram ore that was thought to be bound for Germany. The ore was the main source of the metal tungsten used in such applications as armour piercing ammunition.

Mayakovsky was sighted in the afternoon with her name painted on her side in large letters and *Kanimbla* closed to about 500 metres on her starboard beam passing an instruction to 'Heave To'. *Mayakovsky* tried to communicate a report to Russia which *Kanimbla's* wireless office attempted to jam. As *Mayakovsky* was refusing to obey any signalled instructions Frank ordered a warning shot from the portside 3-inch gun to be fired. This had no effect, but two rounds from the after 6-inch gun finally did the trick. By the time the Soviet ship came under Frank's control the weather conditions had deteriorated to the point that a boarding party could not be sent across. By the evening both ships were riding out a gale and it was not until the following afternoon that a boarding party was sent to *Mayakovsky* for an inspection. Even then the evolution was undertaken with some difficulty with *Kanimbla* and the newly joined HMS *Moreton Bay* releasing oil into the water to dampen the wave motion.

The difficulties facing Frank in completing the inspection multiplied. His boarding party reported that *Mayakovsky's* cargo was suspicious but she was short of fuel, water and food. Frank decided to take *Mayakovsky* to Hong Kong for a thorough inspection. In respect to the resupply of food this could be easily managed, but the transfer of the first two commodities would likely require *Kanimbla* coming alongside *Mayakovsky*. While preparations were being made a further weather front swept the area and the three ships rode out another gale. With an open ocean transfer problematic, Frank could either effect the transfer in the shelter of Saddle Island off the Chinese coast or in the lee of the nearby Japanese island of Hachijo Jima. The Boarding Party Officer estimated there was insufficient fuel to reach Saddle Island and so Frank opted for Hachijo Jima even though it would breach Japanese sovereignty. The Commanding Officer of *Moreton Bay* Commander Edmund Mount Haes, RN 'cleared his yardarm' when he signalled to *Kanimbla* that 'I must register my official protest about Hachijo Jima. The matter is now in your hands'.[53] As the ships closed the island there was negligible shelter and Frank elected for both ships to shape course for Hong Kong and trust in improving conditions to effect a transfer. This was achieved on 20 March with much effort made to protect the sides of *Kanimbla* with coconut and gymnasium matting. During the transfer *Mayakovsky's* steering gear was repaired. After a slow but largely uneventful passage on the morning of 27 March *Kanimbla* transferred control of *Mayakovsky* to the French cruiser *La Motte Picquet* at the entrance to Hong Kong Harbour. Frank viewed this protracted, but in the end successful operation, as one that demonstrated the abilities of his ship and the teamwork and ingenuity that underpinned the outcome.

In June 1940 *Kanimbla* was finally released from the blockade patrols and sailed to Singapore and thence to East Africa for convoy escort work as well as patrols to locate and destroy German raiders. The ports of Durban and Aden became familiar to the ship's company. During July the ship conducted a sweep through the Chagos Archipelago looking for signs of raiders.

Sightings of merchant ships were less frequent than off Japan and all ships were challenged by flashing light or signal flags with Allied merchant signals replying with a coded response. Any suspicious ship was closed to resolve its identity. The ideal was getting close enough to effect this work while not closing into the possible gun or torpedo range of a disguised raider. Frank alarmed some of his bridge team on one occasion by closing to less than a mile from a merchant ship that was having difficulty responding to *Kanimbla's* challenges.[54]

Although the new tasking for *Kanimbla* was a welcome break from blockade work, the exploits of John Collins in *Sydney* an ocean away were keenly followed and particular pride was felt by the half dozen men who had previously served in the cruiser.[55]

V

At the end of February 1940 *Perth* finally arrived in Australia and the ship's company marched through Sydney's streets before the Governor General, Lord Gowrie. In an echo from their New York visit, *The Sydney Morning Herald* focused on their uniforms reporting, 'They wore white uniforms of tropical service and struck the coolest day Sydney has had for weeks'.[56]

Harold Farncomb found nearly all the Pioneer Class far-flung, however Harry Showers in *Adelaide* was at least in port. The latter ship sailed on 10 April with the British battleship HMS *Ramillies* to escort the first elements of the AIF convoy, codenamed US.2, from Melbourne to Fremantle. The convoy consisted of *Dunera, Ettrick, Neuralia* and *Strathaird*. While US.2 with 7,000 troops, was not so grand as the initial convoy of what now became remembered as the 1st AIF convoy, there remained strong echoes to 1914. The convoy commodore was Commander Rupert Garsia, RAN[57] who had served in the first *Sydney* when that ship detached from the first convoy to intercept *Emden*. The historic links were further strengthened in Fremantle when *Adelaide* handed her duties over to the later *Sydney*. The convoy with *Nevasa* joining the group in Fremantle sailed for an uneventful passage to Columbo.

Adelaide remained in the west to escort merchantmen and to respond to any reports of enemy sightings. It proved mundane work with *Adelaide* occasionally joined by other cruisers escorting merchantmen to Fremantle. In June this included *Canberra* now under the command of Harold Farncomb; he was first RAN officer to command one of the heavy cruisers. *Canberra* escorted the recently requisitioned troopship *Strathmore* from Fremantle to Capetown and then for the next month patrolled the South Atlantic and Indian Oceans to counter the German raider threat.

Harold's transfer from *Perth* to *Canberra* came at his behest. On 1 June the Naval Board discussed new fleet dispositions following an approach from the Admiralty. The eventual plan was for *Australia* to be deployed for service with the RN in Atlantic, *Canberra* would serve in the East Indies Station, initially sailing to Capetown. Meanwhile *Adelaide* and *Perth* would remain on the Australia Station with Rear Admiral Crace's flag transferring to *Perth*.[58] The following day Crace was approached by Patterson with Harold's request to transfer to *Canberra* 'as a possible chance of seeing foreign service'.[59] The timing for a transfer was propitious as Patterson's relief Captain Sir Philip Bowyer-Smyth, RN was arriving from the UK that week. Admiral Colvin approved the change on 3 June and Bowyer-Smyth was told on his arrival in Adelaide that he would command *Perth*. On 6 June the handovers took place and Crace noted in his diary the 'tremendous business' of all the command changes occurring at once.[60]

At first glance Harold's request was unexpected. *Perth* had not been in commission a year and normally commanding officers would be in command for at least two years. From a personal perspective it would be expected that commissioning captains would form a particular attachment to their ship. Yet this did not appear to be so. Harold's intellect, quick brain and professional competence gained the respect but not affection of *Perth's* company. One of his officers, Lieutenant Commander Charles Reid wrote that Harold was:

> ... a very strict disciplinarian without being harsh. ... It goes without saying he had the welfare of personnel and the Service as a whole at heart'.[61]

Harold's gunnery officer Lieutenant Commander 'Braces' Bracegirdle reflected that in *Perth*, Harold was very reserved and quiet and did not routinely joke with either his officers or men. He cleared lower deck to address his ship's company on only four occasions.[62] Harold's stated rationale of transferring to *Canberra* to obtain overseas service was questionable. Both *Sydney* and *Hobart* were deployed and it would have been a reasonable assumption to expect *Perth* to be next. Indeed as it panned out *Perth* saw more action, such as the Battle of Matapan, than *Canberra* during the period of Harold's tenure. More likely Harold wanted to command the bigger heavy cruiser and as a specialist War Staff officer he was arguably better placed than any other RAN captain to act as Flag Captain to Rear Admiral Crace.

VI

In contrast to the trade protection duties undertaken by *Adelaide* and *Canberra*, *Sydney* after leaving convoy US.2 was ordered to Columbo for fuel and to receive further orders. The Commander-in-Chief East Indies, Admiral Ralph Leatham inspected the ship and was impressed by both her material state and her men. However he was not to have her under his command for very long.

For some months Italy threatened to enter the war as a German ally and Anglo-Italian relations had greatly deteriorated. The British Government commenced bolstering the Mediterranean Fleet and sought an Australian contribution. Admiral Colvin had strongly advocated the employment of the RAN in the Mediterranean, not only for the contribution the ships could make, but also to give the ships battle experience.[63] The Australian War Cabinet agreed to the deployment of a cruiser and the destroyer flotilla.

By virtue of her disposition in the Indian Ocean *Sydney* assumed the first rotation despite not having the opportunity for her sailors to bid farewell to their families.

The Mediterranean Fleet was under the command of the resolute Admiral Sir Andrew Browne Cunningham. Best known by his initials—ABC, Cunningham would come to be regarded as one of Britain's greatest fighting Admirals. Importantly, for John Collins and Hec Waller, who was commanding the elderly 10th Destroyer Flotilla,[64] Cunningham was an old destroyer man who sought out action wherever possible. He had commanded the destroyer HMS *Scorpion* for an incredible seven years including most of the Great War. On the first Anzac Day *Scorpion* took part in the minesweeping effort ahead of the landing and then engaged the Turks close inshore. At the end of the campaign Cunningham covered the Anzacs withdrawal from Gallipoli. As such he had a high regard for Australians. Both Australian Captains were to prosper under ABC's inspiring leadership. When Prime Minister Menzies later met Cunningham he wrote that 'he had a degree of personal magnetism which I have known to be surpassed only by Lloyd George and Winston Churchill'.[65]

Cunningham's aggressive leadership style was based on giving broad direction with the expectation that subordinates would use common sense and initiative to achieve the strategic aim. In Cunningham's words—'Let intelligent anticipation be your watchword'.[66] John Collins later wrote, 'Admiral Cunningham's orders were brief, and it was not unusual to proceed to sea with only verbal instructions from the C-in-C'.[67]

Sydney arrived in Alexandria on 26 May 1940 and John Collins soon called on Cunningham. He was told he was to come under the command of Vice Admiral (Destroyers) and join the 7th Cruiser Squadron which was comprised of four British cruisers *Orion*, *Gloucester*, *Leander* and *Neptune*. The Vice Admiral was the very experienced destroyer commander John Tovey, who like Collins was a veteran of the Second Battle of Heligoland Bight. Both officers, along with the other cruiser captains worked well together.

Two weeks after *Sydney* arrived in Alexandria Italy entered the war. The Italian Fleet was larger and more modern than the British Mediterranean Fleet. It also included a large submarine force. Despite this Cunningham was determined from the outset to assert a psychological superiority through aggressive sweeps and an eagerness to engage the enemy irrespective of the odds on the day.

To *Sydney* sailors, Cunningham soon became an admired leader and postcard photographs of Cunningham, available in souvenir shops in Malta and Alexandria, would eventually find their way into personal photograph albums. Rather than the monicker 'ABC' many *Sydney* sailors referred to Cunningham as 'Grandpa'.[68]

Operating in the Mediterranean was a very different experience for John Collins. Besides operating as part of a large fleet the threat was no longer German raiders. Besides the Italian Fleet there was the threat posed by the Regia Aeronautica Italiana (RAI) with over 2,000 combat aircraft. As such, at any given moment, there could be an attack from below, on or above the sea.

On 19 June John Collins and a number of commanding officers were called onboard *Warspite*. He returned to *Sydney* with the news that they would likely see their first action in the form of the bombardment of the Italian held seaport of Bardia. On the morning of 21 June *Sydney*, in company with the old French battleship *Lorraine* and the cruisers *Orion* and *Neptune* closed Bardia. The targets were two batteries of 8-inch guns placed on opposite points of the harbour, a military camp further inland and an oil depot. Just before dawn *Sydney* launched her Seagull aircraft to spot the fall of shot for the ships. *Lorraine* and *Orion* took on the 8-inch batteries which after a short duel were destroyed. *Sydney* had equal success with the military camp while *Neptune* set fire to the fuel depot. *Sydney* expended nearly 150 rounds from her 6-inch guns. The Italian response was to launch three CR42 biplane fighters which attacked the slow and ungainly Seagull. Her pilot Flight Lieutenant Tom Price wrote:

... the first burst from the Italians had shot away our aileron controls. Bursts from the second plane, right on our tail, riddled the rudder and the after section of the hull until it looked like a sieve. It seemed dollars to doughnuts that the old Seagull would be blown into pieces within a few seconds.[69]

Price managed to nurse the battered Seagull to Mersa Matruh—120 miles distant where it broke up on landing. Price and his observer Lieutenant Commander Jack Bacon both survived unhurt. For John Collins 'It was a very gentle baptism of fire for *Sydney*'.[70] On 22 June the French Government signed an Armistice with Germany and hence the Bardia bombardment was the last operation undertaken by Vice Admiral René-Émile Godfroy's French squadron. Cunningham was able to negotiate with Godfroy for the peaceful disarming of his warships in Alexandria. The combined entry of Italy and loss of the French tipped the scales in the Mediterranean heavily in the Axis favour. Characteristically, Cunningham was undeterred and at the end of the month his Fleet sailed to escort two vital convoys in the Eastern Mediterranean. The 7th Cruiser Squadron provided cover for the Malta originated convoy.

Early in the afternoon of 26 June a Sunderland flying boat detected three Italian destroyers about 35 miles distant potentially aiming to intercept the convoy that evening in the Antikythera Strait between Greece and Crete. Vice Admiral Tovey closed the Italian destroyers with his Squadron at 29 knots, leaving the convoy to the close escort of British destroyers. At around 6 pm and in failing light the Squadron sighted the three destroyers *Espero, Zeffiro* and *Ostro* on the horizon and just before 7 pm the cruisers opened fire at 20,900 yards.[71] The destroyers commanded by Captain Enrico Baroni in *Espero* had been unaware of the British presence and were actually ferrying supplies to Bardia. Heavily outmatched the destroyers increased speed and made smoke to cover their escape. They also fired a brace of torpedoes to further deter their superior foe. Despite the range *Espero* sustained at least one hit and fell out of line. With the other two Italians making good their escape, Tovey detached *Sydney* to 'Deal with the straggler'.[72]

A Seagull V seaplane on the catapult of one of the Perth Class cruisers
(State Library of Victoria).

Sydney closed to 14,000 yards and fired a broadside into the *Espero*. Captain Baroni was determined to fight to the end and *Espero* returned fire with her four 4.7-inch guns. It remained an unequal fight and soon *Sydney* had landed salvoes with her 6-inch and 4-inch guns into the stricken destroyer that knocked out most of her guns and hit the bridge. There was fire along most of *Espero's* length and she was sinking steadily by the bows. *Sydney* closed *Espero* while John Collins and Hilken discussed the best way to save as many lives as possible. Both cutters were lowered to recover the Italians. As Hilken wrote later that day:

> Suddenly to my astonishment I saw two shells burst in the water a few hundred yards away, one abreast the bridge and one of our quarter. At about the same time someone else saw her fire a torpedo. It was a gallant but foolish action, as it compelled us to open fire. We gave her four broadsides, and it seemed to me that nearly half the shells hit. I could see them bursting inside her and throwing bits of her into the air.[73]

The last salvo by *Sydney* had a devastating effect and *Espero* rolled over in flames. *Sydney* closed once more to rescue the Italians. Everyone not on watch came on deck to help with jumping ladders and the succor of survivors. Stoker Eric Evans, who was one of the Navy's most meticulous and observant diarists of the war, wrote:

> My shell room crew were allowed up at this stage to have a look around, but it was an awful sight every survivor was covered in oil fuel, the wounded ones being in a pityful [sic] state, all were wearing the old type kapok lifebelt clothes that had to be cut off. Many of the wounded were taken to our bathrooms, given a good hot bath, given dry clothing donated by our men followed by coffee, cocoa, food, and cigarettes, they were afterwards quartered in the Recreation Room under Guard, the wounded in the Sick Bay and Passages were attended by our two Doctors, who with their staff worked hard all night.[74]

The impact of witnessing the agonies of the survivors was also mixed with a reflection on what could have been if *Espero's* torpedo had found its mark. *Sydney* rescued 47 sailors from the water and remained recovering survivors for as long as John Collins thought safe from Italian air or submarine attack. He then ordered a cutter left with a light burning for other survivors. Because of Hilken's preparations the cutter was fully provisioned. The sailors thought this was 'a very generous and typically British gesture on the part of our Captain'.[75] John later wrote of the action:

> My only hope was that some of the poor devils still swimming would be able to find the cutter. They had fought very bravely against hopeless odds, and they deserved a better fate.[76]

As *Sydney* cleared the scene cries could still be heard in the darkness on both sides of the ship. Seven of the *Espero* sailors reached *Sydney's* cutter and survived their ordeal.[77] One of them, Luigi Cantanni would eventually emigrate to Australia after the war and establish his own electrical business.[78]

On the return passage there was a burial at sea for some of *Espero* sailors who had succumbed to their wounds. After the ceremony John Collins addressed the Italians. As he spoke his words were translated into French by Hilken and *Espero's* doctor in turn translated them into Italian. John told them their names would be given to authorities for their next of kin and they would be made as comfortable as possible. Interspersed in his address was 'Grazie' from the *Espero* sailors.[79]

Espero was Italy's first destroyer loss of the war. Her courageous Captain Baroni went down with his ship and was fittingly posthumously awarded Italy's highest bravery medal, the Gold Medal of Military Valour. For John Collins the battle demonstrated the fighting resolve of the men of the Italian Navy and the care he needed to take to preserve whatever tactical advantages he and *Sydney* would possess in any future engagement.

There was little time to reflect on what would become known as the Battle of the *Espero* Convoy. For Cunningham the successful battle was a mixed blessing. Nearly 5,000 6-inch rounds had been expended by the 7th Cruiser Squadron in the largely long range engagement. *Sydney* had fired 686 6-inch and 4-inch rounds herself. This engagement so depleted the fleet supplies that the next Malta convoy had to be delayed a fortnight until ammunition stocks could be replenished.

The convoy operations, besides their logistical necessity, provided the means to draw the Italians out to sea and thereby provide the opportunity for Cunningham to even the balance of power. On 7 July his forces sailed from Alexandria in three groups to independently rendezvous 150 miles from Malta. The first group consisted of the 7th Cruiser Squadron and *Stuart*; the second group Cunningham's flagship HMS *Warspite* and a destroyer screen while the third group had the slow battleships *Royal Sovereign* and *Malaya* as well as the aircraft carrier *Eagle* and a destroyer screen. The following day while the British ships were subjected to high level bombing from the RAI, an Italian force of two battleships and a destroyer screen was sighted by the British submarine HMS *Phoenix* about 180 miles east of Malta. From that time Sunderland flying boats tracked the Italians. Cunningham correctly suspected that the Italians were at sea to escort a convoy. He now altered the course of his ships to place them between the Italians and their homeport of Taranto. During the evening of 8 July John Collins closed *Sydney* up to Action Stations at the Second Degree of Readiness in case they encountered the Italians through the night.

'An excellent cruiser Captain, bold, tenacious and determined' John Collins in command of HMAS Sydney (RAN)

By the morning of 9 July the British Fleet had consolidated and the 7th Cruiser Squadron was eight miles ahead of *Warspite* with the other battleships a further eight miles astern. There was a blue sky, a fresh breeze and the Mediterranean was a deep blue. By breakfast the Sunderlands, supported by aircraft from *Eagle* had provided Cunningham with a more complete picture of the enemy. There were two battleships, ten cruisers and eighteen destroyers in two groups approximately 90 miles distant. By 2 pm the Italian commander Vice Admiral Inigo Campioni also had consolidated his battle fleet into one force and was steaming to the north towards the British.

Campioni's great strength was his 8-inch gunned heavy cruisers which outnumbered and clearly out-classed Cunningham's 6-inch light cruisers. He also had, if well employed, more effective battleships. His modernized *Giulio Cesare* and *Conti di Cavour* were capable of 26 knots and were each armed with ten 12.6-inch guns with a range of 31,280 yards.[80] In contrast only the modernized *Warspite* with a speed of 24 knots and eight 15-inch guns could match the Italian's range.[81] The partially modernized *Royal Sovereign* and *Malaya* were a couple of knots slower and had not had their 15-inch guns modified to fire at a greater angle and therefore were at a range disadvantage of nearly 8,000 yards compared to the Italians.[82] Cunningham did possess the obsolescent *Eagle*, but with only 17 Swordfish torpedo bombers it was more valuable for reconnaissance and had only a marginal strike capability.

Characteristically Cunningham was undeterred by the numerical superiority of the Italians and keenly awaited the action. Just after 2.35 pm *Stuart* was ordered to join the destroyer screen around *Royal Sovereign*. Ten minutes later *Sydney* reported seeing smoke on the western horizon and a further seven minutes later *Neptune* reported the Italian battleships. For the first time in the Mediterranean since the Napoleonic wars two battle fleets were to engage one another.

The employment of the cruisers screening ahead of battleships was a classic, but rarely executed role. The sense of anticipation in both battle fleets was intense. John Collins, who in the Second Battle of Heligoland Bight 23 years earlier, had forlornly heard the distant thuds of the cruiser engagement from *Canada*, was now to be at the centre of the action.

At 3.20 pm the 7th Cruiser Squadron altered course to the north to roughly parallel the Italians and increased speed to 27 knots. Soon thereafter they returned fire on the leading Italian light cruisers *Abruzzi* and *Garibaldi* who were soon joined in the exchange by *Barbiano*, *Guissano*, *Aosta*, *Attendolo*, *Montecuccoli* and *Savoia*. *Sydney* hoisted the Australian flag on the foremast just as an Italian salvo fell astern of the ship. Despite the range the Italian fire was accurate with *Neptune* receiving a hit. Shells also fell close to *Sydney* with the concussion felt by those between decks while shell fragments shot away signal halyards.[83] The hard-pressed Tovey opened the range between the cruisers. It was at this critical moment in the battle that Campioni could have pressed home his advantage and overwhelmed the 7th Cruiser Squadron.

At 3.26 pm Cunningham provided much needed relief with *Warspite* firing ten rapid salvoes at the Italian cruisers. This caused them to lay smoke. *Warspite* then came under fire from *Giulio Cesare* at 3.48 pm. Then a wave of Swordfish torpedo bombers from *Eagle* passed by the starboard side of *Sydney* enroute to an ultimately unsuccessful attack on the Italian battle fleet. The aircrew from the newly joined *Eagle* had had little practice with high speed targets and had hitherto been involved in protecting trade routes.[84]

Admiral Campioni in an effort to simplify matters ordered that *Conti di Cavour* direct her fire on the other two still out of range battleships. This actually negated his tactical superiority, but it is unlikely Campioni appreciated the significant differences between the three British battleships.

In contrast, Cunningham had his flagship engage *Giulio Cesare* with her forward turrets and *Conti di Cavour* with her after turrets. For the next ten minutes the battleships exchanged salvoes with even the out of range *Malaya* opening fire. The Italian heavy cruisers also closed *Warspite* to add their fire against the veteran battleship. Tovey closed the heavy cruisers which turned their attention to his four light cruisers.

In a turning point of the battle, as range opened between the battleships, *Warspite's* last salvo hit *Guilio Cesare* knocking four boilers out of action and reducing her speed to 18 knots. At 26,000 yards it was one of the longest range hits by a gun in naval history. With the scales now tipped and the prospect of the two distant British battleships entering the battle proper, Campioni turned his battle fleet away and had his cruisers cover the withdrawal. Once again a smokescreen lay between the forces.

For the cruisers the battle remained intense. *Bolzano* received three hits from *Neptune*. The *Stuart* and other destroyers were unleashed into the fray to try and obtain a torpedo hit on the Italians. As *Stuart* passed close by *Sydney,* sailors on the cruiser's upper deck 'cheered them on in good old Australian language'.[85]

As the range with the enemy ships opened the threat would now come from the air. At 4.40 pm 126 RAI aircraft finally appeared and conducted a high altitude bombing on both the Italian and British Fleets, fortunately to no effect. For the next couple of hours and then again into the next morning the Fleet was subjected to repeated air attacks. Stoker Evans wrote:

> All hands had a hurried meal in relays, during this period. Enemy aircraft continued heavy bombing attacks but for all that, the appetites were excellent, Jack gets hungry when fighting ... Here they

come again wave after wave this time. Bombs dropping all round us, splinters and fragments falling on the upper deck and clattering against the ship's side, no hit, no one hurt, its a marvel - lucky '*Sydney*' ... the bombs can be seen falling and the noise is much like a fast moving train, the ship is zigzaged at high speed to dodge them, good eye sight and quick thinking on the part of the Captain is the saviour of the ship.[86]

The poor performance of the RAI caused considerable acrimony in Rome, but Benito Mussolini was happy to accept the RAI propaganda that the Italian forces had 'annihilated 50 per cent of the British naval potential in the Mediterranean'.[87]

To John Collins it was a memorable battle with excellent visibility such that 'the whole exciting picture was clear before us'.[88] Once again he was struck by an outstanding example of Italian courage when a small destroyer laid smoke between the dueling cruisers at considerable hazard to herself. *Sydney* had fired 411 6-inch rounds in the battle and by the time the Fleet returned to Alexandria, after enduring numerous air attacks, she had expended all her 4-inch ammunition.

The Battle of Calabria, or the Battle of Punto Stilo as the Italians named it, gave confidence to both sides and importantly their respective convoys reached their destinations. Cunningham believed *Warspite*'s hit on *Guilio Cesare* had an important effect on the Italian mentality.[89] The engagement had further strengthened the confidence his ship's company had in John Collins. For *Sydney* however, the battle was but a prelude to her greatest action.

Cunningham was keen to maintain pressure on the Italian Navy and in particular their ability to utilise the waters of the central Mediterranean. On the afternoon of 17 July, Vice Admiral Tovey ordered John Collins to take *Sydney* and the destroyer HMS *Havock* on an east to west sweep north of Crete to intercept any Italian shipping in the Gulf of Athens. The cruiser had just completed a much needed hull clean in the Alexandria dock, but still awaiting a replacement aircraft after losing her Seagull at Mersa Matruh. In the operation *Sydney* was also to support another group of ships Tovey had ordered to sea, the 2nd Destroyer Flotilla - *Hyperion, Ilex, Hero* and *Hasty*. Both groups, having completed their respective sweeps, would exit through the Antikythera Strait between Crete and mainland Greece and the return to Alexandria.

Commander Hugh Nicolson RN in *Hyperion* led the 2nd Destroyer Flotilla. His mission was to sweep for Italian submarines north of Crete. Nicolson was also born in 1899 and his term at Dartmouth was the British contemporary to the Pioneer Class.

At about the same time as Tovey issued his orders, the Italian Naval High Command known as the *Supermarina*, issued a directive to Rear Admiral Ferdinando Casardi to intercept any British merchant shipping in the Aegean with his 2nd Cruiser Division. Casardi was flying his flag in the light cruiser *Giovanni delle Bande Nere,* which was in Tripoli in company with the other cruiser of the Division *Bartolomeo Colleoni*. Casardi intended to first search in the vicinity of the Dodecanese Islands. His Division also had to pass through the Antikythera Strait but from the south. The *Supermarina's* selection of the 2nd Division while making sense in terms of their geographic disposition, did not play to the Italian's strength, namely their preponderance of heavy cruisers. The latter would have over-matched anything they encountered but for the British Battle Fleet.

By midnight on 18 July the three groups of ships were converging on the waters to the north west of Crete with the presence of the opposing forces unknown to each other. Admiral Casardi was promised aerial cover for his sortie but it had yet to materialise. He did not utilise any of his four Ro.43 seaplanes because the swell precluded use of the catapults on the exposed forecastles of his ships. At 5 am on the morning of 19 July Casardi ordered *Bartolomeo Colleoni* to launch a Ro.43 for a sweep ahead, but the aircraft had a defect and did not launch, and in any case the weather remained marginal for flight operations. If an aircraft had been flown off it would have likely reported the 2nd Destroyer Flotilla no more than 20 miles distant, close to the Cretan coast and approaching Cape Spada. The two forces were now on a roughly opposite courses.

As Casardi entered the Antikythera Strait he was cognisant of the potential for a British submarine to be lying in wait and he increased the speed of his cruisers to 25 knots.[90]

At 7.19 am lookouts in Casardi's flagship sighted British destroyers to the east. It was about an hour after sunrise and the ships were difficult to discern in the dazzling light. The destroyers had just fallen out from dawn action stations with the appetising prospect of breakfast. Three minutes after the Italians, the lookouts in *Hyperion* reported to Nicolson two Italian cruisers to the west. He immediately ordered action stations once more and battle ensigns hoisted. Nicolson brought the flotilla around to starboard to parallel and then close the enemy. Importantly, he also sent out an enemy contact report. *Hyperion* and *Ilex* opened fire despite being out of range.

In *Bande Nere* Casardi reasonably assumed the enemy flotilla was the screen for a large formation. At 7.27 am he opened fire on the destroyers and at the same time opened the range and increased speed to 30 knots. Casardi was concerned about a torpedo attack on his ships which was confirmed by an erroneous report of torpedo tracks fifteen minutes into the engagement.

Sydney and *Havock* were forty miles to the north west. John Collins was using the latitude Cunningham gave his Captains by delaying his move into the Gulf of Athens to execute his primary task in order to provide support to the 2nd Destroyer Flotilla until they were clear of the Antikythera Strait. While not knowing their exact position he had given himself until 8 am before steaming north. His initiative and judgment were to be rewarded.

On receipt of Nicolson's enemy contact report, John Collins gathered his Commander, Navigating Officer and Gunnery Officer to the bridge. He told them he assessed the Italians cruisers were 6-inch rather than 8-inch cruisers. He feared 'scaring the cruisers away'[91] and so resolved to maintain radio silence and when in contact to close the range as soon as possible to obtain hits. After the discussion John ordered ordered his ships to increase speed and to close the battle.

Up to this point John Collins had maintained radio silence to mitigate the risk of Italian air attack spawned by the radio emissions. As he had learnt from the *Espero* action, it was important to carefully husband what advantages he possessed. His radio silence of course was a source of uncertainty to both Admiral Cunningham at sea in *Warspite* and to Nicolson. John explained in his report:

> I realised that I was placing Commander Hugh St. L Nicolson, DSO, RN in an awkward position, and running a certain degree of risk on non contact, by not informing him of my position, course and speed by W/T (wireless telegraphy) on getting his enemy report. I was however determined to make full use of surprise, as we had not been sighted by aircraft since leaving Alexandria. I appreciated that, if I made a wireless signal, the enemy would learn that other forces were in the vicinity and make away through the Straits.[92]

John's decision was in accord with accepted naval tactics. Surprise was specifically discussed in the Royal Navy tactics manual - *The Fighting Instructions* which advised:

> Surprise should be the aim in planning an operation, and Captains of ships should try to achieve it in executing the particular plan.[93]

The northern group, like Nicolson's destroyers, had also fallen out from dawn action stations and breakfast was the main focus. John Collins informed the ship's company on the broadcast that:

> ... one of our four destroyers scouting to the south of us, have reported two enemy cruisers, we are now proceeding to back them up, all hands are to complete breakfast as quickly as possible and be in battledress at 0815h.[94]

There was cheering through the ship. All sailors who had not had breakfast were relieved by the watch below, while others did the myriad of checks to prepare for the battle.[95] As *Sydney* and *Havock* steamed south at 29 knots the Italian cruisers and Nicolson's destroyers were engaged in a battle frustrated by shifting visibility and smoke. The destroyers outranged by the cruisers were hard-pressed and dodging the fall on shot. Meanwhile Casardi also requested an air strike on the destroyers from the nearby Egomil airfield on Rhodes. Then at 8.30 am Casardi reported:

... several salvoes fell near the *Bande Nere* coming from our port side where a thick bank of low fog could be seen. It was only possible to distinguish the flashes of guns and the hulls of ships, not their numbers.

In *Hyperion* these gun flashes provided an answer to the question of *Sydney's* whereabouts. To those on the destroyer's bridge the:

... orange flashes of the *Sydney's* opening salvo, the most welcome sight in the world. She came rushing to the southward, on the port beam of the Italians, guns flashing, battle ensigns streaming, and such a smother of foam at bow and stern that from the destroyers one seemed to hear the high-tensioned scream of the machinery driving her across the water.[96]

On *Sydney's* bridge the recognition of the distinctive silhouette of two Condottieri Class cruisers was received with relief as indicating they were up against 6-inch cruisers as predicted by John Collins. From the outset *Sydney* had the advantage of better visibility and always having a target to engage should one become shrouded by haze or smoke. The recent experience of long range engagements had led John and his Gunnery Officer Lieutenant Commander Michael Singer, RN to engage the targets in text book 'ladder' and 'zig-zag' groupings of salvoes. Essentially, these groupings were ways to ascertain through observed shell splashes the bearing and range of the targets in a systematic way. Once the bearing and range was found, they then followed with broadsides. In contrast to the worked-up *Sydney*, the war for the Italian cruisers had revolved around escort work and both ships had missed the Battle of Calabria. This was their baptism of fire.

The absence of *Sydney's* aircraft for spotting was keenly felt. But despite this *Sydney* started to record hits, the first on *Bande Nere* where a round went through the forward funnel and killed four sailors. At this point the Italians were hampered in their range finding by not being able to clearly see their new adversary. Casardi turned his ship 90° to starboard.

Finally, at about 8.45 am, Italian lookouts identified their two new foes through the mist as a *Sydney* class cruiser and a *Gloucester* class cruiser. *Havock's* two raked funnels could reasonably have been mistaken for a *Gloucester*. It was however a critical mistake which shaped Italian thinking.

To his credit Casardi however initially resolved, 'From the moment of meeting the enemy I considered that my task must be to engage him'.[97]

For the next 15 minutes Casardi adjusted his course to open the range and provide an opportunity for all of his guns to be brought to bear on the 'British cruisers'. For the Italians the modest swell was adversely affecting their rate of increasingly accurate fire. The engagement now took the form of a chase, with at times only *Sydney's* forward guns being able to be brought to bear on the Italians. Firing was further hampered by Casardi laying smoke which led John Collins to shift target to *Bartolomeo Colleoni*. This ship, under the command of Captain Umberto Novaro, had been closely following behind her flagship and was straddling *Sydney* with effective fire. *Bartolomeo Colleoni* was the first to receive a telling blow with a *Sydney* shell exploding in her after boiler room which dramatically slowed her as well as causing damage on her upper deck. At 9.21 am *Sydney* herself received a hit from *Bande Nere* through the forward funnel. It did not however, have any effect on her fighting ability.

In *Bartolomeo Colleoni* the resultant loss of power put the ammunition hoists of all 6-inch guns out of action. Only the six 4.7-inch guns were able to be fired with what ammunition was on deck. As the range now quickly closed *Sydney's* 6-inch guns were firing up to 15 rounds a minute. Further hits were now scored. One of the design weaknesses of the Condottieri class was that their aircraft hangars, with highly combustible aviation fuel were right beneath the bridge. Soon a large fire raged through the forward superstructure of the ship. *Bartolomeo Colleoni* was done for and Casardi left the cruiser to her fate. He later wrote in his report:

> I witnessed the last glorious moments of the cruiser. For a few seconds she seemed to be surrounded by columns of water from the enemy's salvoes. No one appeared on deck, all onboard showed their extremely heroic will to fight by their calm, implacable behaviour, The inequality of the fight was, however, sadly evident; an explosion occurred in the bows due, probably, to the blowing up of the forward magazine. Immediately after, two very high columns of water alongside the dying ship showed that torpedoes from the enemy destroyers, now at last near

CAPTAINS AT WAR 319

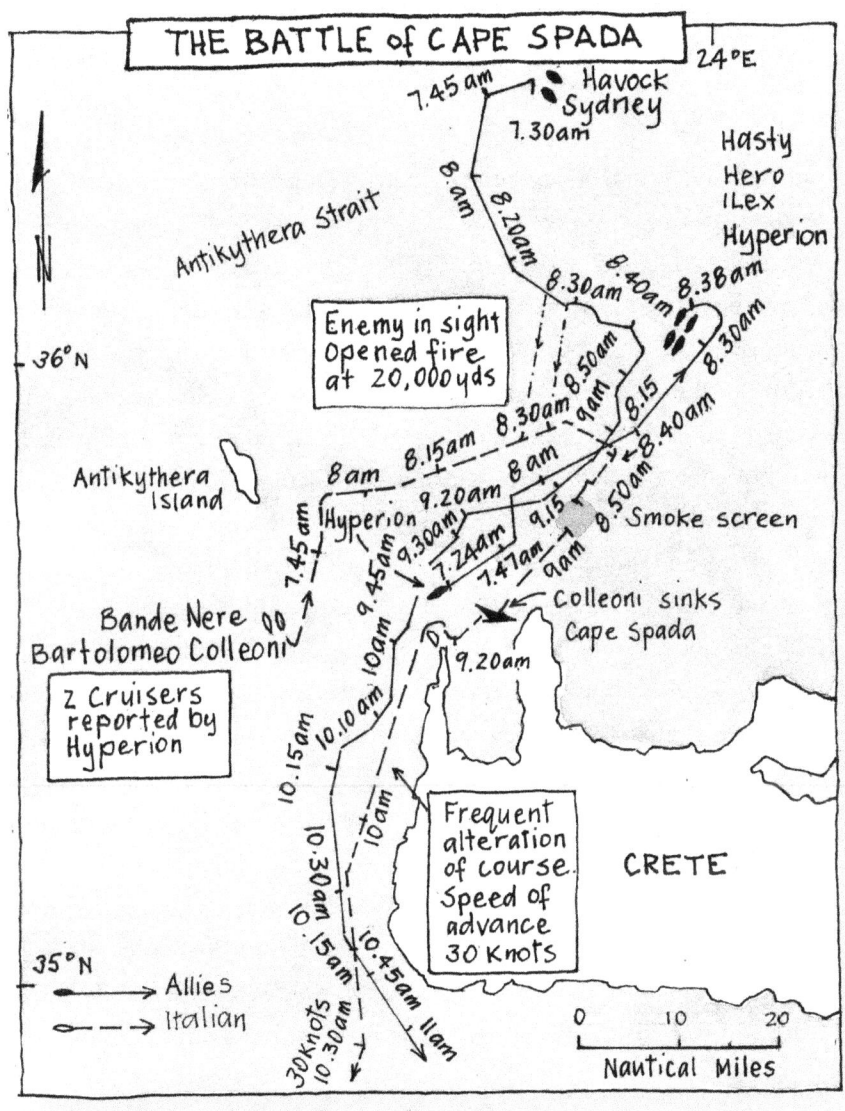

their prey, had struck. A huge cloud of mixed black and white smoke, then the glorious warship—her upper deck almost level with the water - heeled over to port and sank. Such was the epic end of the Royal cruiser *Bartolomeo Colleoni*. It does not suffer by comparison with the most heroic episodes of sea warfare. The name of Captain Umberto Novaro, who commanded her, and all the rest of his comrades ought to be written in letters of steel so as to preserve their memory.

In reality the situation onboard *Bartolomeo Colleoni* was more confused and brutal. Engineering sailors, scalded from burst team pipes were being brought up from the machinery spaces to dimly lit, chaotic, congested and damaged passage ways. Signalman Artemio Torselli nearly fell overboard when he went through a forward watertight door to find open ocean and clear sky rather than the next compartment in the bow section. In the absence of a working broadcast, the order to abandon ship was being passed by word of mouth. Sailors gravitated to the stern of the ship and then jumped clear. Midshipman Launaro lowered the ensign and wrapped it around himself as he entered the water. Meanwhile, the seriously wounded Captain Novaro was carefully assisted by four sailors into a raft and was paddled clear of his stricken ship.[98]

Critically Nicholson had *Hyperion, Ilex* and *Havock* stop to pick up survivors. John Collins soon ordered him to leave only one ship and to rejoin the action. In the ensuing chase another hit was scored on *Bande Nere* and her speed was reduced to 29 knots for about twenty minutes. This gave John some hope of landing a further telling blow with his fast dwindling ammunition. If *Bande Nere's* speed could be cut, then the destroyers could deliver a torpedo attack. Reluctantly, with the range opening once more and with only four rounds left per gun, John broke off the battle.

Sydney steamed close past *Bartolomeo Colleoni* and John ordered Nicholson to finish her off with torpedoes. Stoker Evans captured this moment:

> As we are now flat out, she (*Bande Nere*) is certainly damaged if only we could get up to her what a day for Australia it would be, but we cannot get another ounce of speed, and she has got out of our range.[99]

The Bartolomeo Colleoni *stopped and done for.* (State Library of Victoria)

The intensity of *Sydney's* 6-inch gun firing was such that the shells left in the guns in case of another attack, heated to the point that explosive started to ooze like treacle out of the nose fuzes. Sailors had to gingerly remove the shells and lower them overboard. Even 24 hours after the battle some shells that did not leak were still too hot to touch.[100]

Throughout the action Cunningham in *Warspite* had been trying to follow the battle through the wireless traffic from John Collins and Nicholson. He later wrote:

> All I knew was that the destroyers were being chased, and that Collins, regardless of any odds, was closing them at full speed. After that dead silence. It must have been quite two hours later that our feelings of anxiety were changed to triumph when the *Sydney* reported she had hit and stopped one of the cruisers.[101]

As had now become their trademark, the RAI bombers arrived late on the scene and conducted high level bombing which curtailed the rescue of Italian survivors. One bomb hit *Havock* which then sought assistance from *Sydney*. John Collins turned back, with the ship's company keenly aware of the further danger that *Sydney* would be exposed to by possible air or submarine attack.

The entry into Alexandria was a memorable one. As *Sydney* approached the port HMS *Liverpool* flying the flag of Flag Officer Commanding 7th Cruiser Squadron, Tovey signalled 'Well Done Australia'. *Liverpool's* ship's company lined the deck and cheered *Sydney*.[102] Lieutenant John Ross wrote of the scene:

> Our berth was near the inner end of the harbour, a distance of close to two miles from the boom, and as we moved down between the lines of ships we were given a wonderful ovation—in fact a 'royal welcome' in every respect. Each ship had cleared lower deck and as we passed they each gave us three terrific cheers, followed by a loud burst of clapping, whooping and whistling. It could not have been louder or more sincere had it been in response to an announcement that the war was over. We were so filled with pride by this kind gesture that we would not have changed places with anyone in the world.[103]

Thousands of Egyptians and soldiers also crowded the quay to cheer the cruiser. On reaching their assigned berth Stoker Evans wrote, 'and so closes a chapter that will go down in naval history as unparalleled in naval warfare where a cruiser fought two, sinking one and badly damaging the second'.[104]

Cunningham soon came onboard to congratulate John Collins and the ship's company. When asked about what guided him to loiter before proceeding into the Gulf of Athens, John said 'Providence guided me, Sir,' to which Cunningham replied 'Well, in future you can continue to take your orders from Providence'.[105]

That evening Commander Hilken wrote that, 'We had never dreamed of such a reception - our feelings being rather a blend of disappointment that one enemy ship had escaped and thankfulness that we had done the same'.[106]

On the following day John Collins astutely invited all senior officers and commanding officers of ships in port onboard to a reception where they gained a first hand account of the action. He then made himself available to press representatives. In his report to the Admiralty on the Battle of Cape Spada, Cunningham wrote:

> The credit for this successful and gallant action belongs mainly to Captain JA Collins, CB, RAN, who by his quick appreciation of the situation, offensive spirit, and resolute handling of HMAS *Sydney*, achieved a victory over a superior force which has had important strategical effects. It is significant that, so far as is known, no Italian surface forces have returned into or near the Aegean since the action was fought.[107]

Cunningham also rightly observed the accuracy of *Sydney's* gunnery, in part attributed to the 2,200 rounds she had fired in the last six weeks. Behind that statistic was also a crack team lead by John Collins who had retained his passion for his specialisation and drove excellence down through his gunnery officer and senior sailors.

The Battle of Cape Spada was the first in which the Italians lost a major warship. The Italian Foreign Minister and Mussolini's son-in-law Count Ciano wrote in his diary that Mussolini, 'today was depressed on account of the loss of the *Colleoni*, not so much because of the sinking itself as because he feels the Italians did not fight very brilliantly'.[108]

The engagement gained headlines in newspapers around the world. *The Times* in London called the battle 'An Australian Triumph' and stated that the achievement of the second *Sydney* eclipsed that of her namesake when she sank the SMS *Emden* in the Great War.[109] In a similar vein, Winston Churchill, as he did as First Lord of the Admiralty twenty-six years earlier, congratulated the current *Sydney* on her 'brilliant action' sinking an enemy cruiser.[110] King George VI promptly made John Collins a Companion of the Order of the Bath. Nicolson, Hilken and *Sydney's* Engineering Officer Commander Lionel Dalton received Distinguished Service Orders. John was at great pains to ensure other men were recognized for their service and twenty officers and sailors also received awards.[111]

In Australia the news of the 'Stirring Exploit of HMAS *Sydney*' made the front pages across the nation.[112] In Sydney the New South Wales Premier Alexander Mair ordered flags to be flown from all Government and commercial buildings in the city and schoolchildren to be given a half day holiday. Sydney's equally patriotic Lord Mayor Stanley Crick promptly established a HMAS *Sydney* Fund to enable public donations for individual medallions for the ship's company and plaques for the ship and Town Hall.

From all parts of Australia newspapers drew on hometown born *Sydney* sailors for a local angle. Pride of place was the Hobart *Mercury* who proudly wrote about the '*Sydney's* achievement under a Tasmanian commander'.[113] John Collins' mother was interviewed by *The Age* and said that, 'I feel that in Australian homes today the families of every member of the crew from the youngest seaman up, will be sharing my happiness'.[114] One of John's teachers from the Christian Brother's College was interviewed and recalled, perhaps not unexpectedly, that the 12-year old was 'an extremely quiet, gentlemanly little fellow, with no interest in more violent forms of life'.[115] The Principal, Reverend Brother Thomas Garvey more robustly said that the 450 boys gave three cheers to John Collins at Assembly and that 'such courageous actions were expected of Old Boys of the College'.[116]

Admiral Sir Edward Evans, who played such an influential part in John Collins' earlier career, was interviewed in London and said that the Australian was 'one of the most brilliant gunnery officers who served under him' and that the victory 'will thrill the civilised world'.[117]

His smart appearance, ready smile and quick mind all contributed to John Collins being lionised by the press. He had all the attributes of a naval hero. For his part, and possibly through his exposure to wider society through his brother Dale, John was unusually adept in his dealing with the media. This was construed by some in the Navy as John being self-promoting and he earned the nickname of the 'Kolynos Kid' after the popular toothpaste, for his regular appearances in the media.[118] Whatever the motivations, John from this point had entered the pantheon of Australian heroes. His active engagement with the media helped the war effort and raised the public profile of the Navy.

In a postscript to the battle, Captain Novaro, who was surprised to learn of the identity of *Sydney* because Italian propaganda had earlier

Captain John Collins with Commander Thomas Hilken and other HMAS Sydney *officers and sailors who were awarded medals for their service in the Battle of Cape Spada. (The Argus/State Library of Victoria)*

reported her sinking, succumbed to his wounds. John Collins and the destroyer Captains from the action acted as pall bearers at his funeral while *Sydney* also provided the funeral parties for *Bartolomeo Colleoni* sailors who had died in hospital.[119] On a positive note seven exhausted *Bartolomeo Colleoni* survivors swam up to 42 hours to reach the Cretean shore and subsequent internment in India.[120]

After repairs, maintenance, embarkation of a new aircraft and the application of a camouflage paint scheme, *Sydney* rejoined the varied work of the 7th Cruiser Squadron. On 27 July at sea with the battle fleet, *Sydney* was once again straddled by RAI high level bombing. Late the following month the battle fleet, now strengthened by the modern aircraft carrier HMS *Illustrious* and the battleship HMS *Valiant*, was again at sea escorting a Malta bound convoy from Alexandria while the Gibraltar based Force H escorted another convoy from Gibraltar. Although the Italian battle fleet was also at sea this time Cunningham concentrated on protecting the vital convoys and did not seek battle.

As part of this operation however *Orion*, *Sydney* and *Ilex* were detached to bombard Italian shore installations on Scarpanto (Karpathos) Island. During the early morning of 5 September the *Orion* closed the port of Pigadio, whilst *Sydney* and *Ilex* closed Makri Yalo. John Collins had *Sydney* disguised with her forward funnel painted to resemble the slimmer funnel of the Condottieri Class. *Sydney's* primary target was the Makri Yalo airfield and as the ship closed the coast she launched her aircraft for spotting at 5.59 am. The bombardment was timed for 6.20 am and on the final run in a motor boat was observed 3,000 yards distant in Castello Bay. John thought it a civilian craft but it soon increased speed and was identified as a motor torpedo boat. Soon another torpedo boat was sighted. Assessing *Sydney's* disguise and the poor light would buy time John did not open fire on the torpedo boats, rather he had his team concentrate on the imminent shore bombardment. Lieutenant Commander Philip Saumarez DSC, RN in *Ilex* did not hesitate. Stationed 1,000 yards astern of *Sydney* he immediately opened fire on the first torpedo boat and increased speed to put the destroyer between the torpedo boats and the *Sydney*. Soon *Ilex* had scored a hit on the first boat and shifted target. *Sydney's* 4-inch guns joined the surface action while the 6-inch main armament opened up on the airfield. *Sydney's* aircraft usefully identified and reported a further three torpedo boats which were soon deterred from launching an attack by the sight of two stopped and burning torpedo boats. After expending 135 rounds *Sydney* had severely damaged the airfield and both ships retired.

The following month a similar convoy operation occurred. Once more Cunningham detached *Sydney* and *Orion* towards the end of the operation, this time to bombard the port of Maltezana on Stampalia (Astypalaia) in the Dodecanese islands. According to Count Ciano on 12 October Mussolini decided to invade Greece in response to the entry of German troops into Romania. This was to restore the Axis balance in the Balkans and maintain Mussolini's standing with the Italian public.[121] Soon after that decision there began a build-up of Italian forces in already occupied Albania.

Due to the time of year with its heavy rains, the roads were problematic. Great reliance would be placed on shipping, particularly from the port of Brindisi where the *Supermarina* established a Headquarters[122] —the *Maritrafalba*, to coordinate convoys across the Adriatic.[123]

At 2 am on 28 October the Italian Ambassador presented an ultimatum to Greek Prime Minister Ioannis Metaxas to open the Greek borders to Italian troops. Metaxas replied, 'Then it is war.' As a former Greek General, Metaxas had paid attention to national defences and the Greeks soon had the Italians on the back foot.

While the invasion further complicated the strategic situation it did offer Cunningham the prospect of greater port access in the Mediterranean. In particular Crete, half way between Malta and Alexandria, was of great importance to him. As such he soon had his ships heavily committed to running convoys of troops and their impedimenta into Crete and mainland Greece. In Piraeus *Sydney*, with her distinctive two funnels and graceful lines became a familiar sight to the locals and John Collins reported they called out the ship's name and cheered every time she entered port. In the first week of November *Sydney* took nearly 500 troops, two trucks and a pair of Bofors guns to Suda Bay which was to become an advanced base for the Navy. Once in port the entire ship's company helped unload the stores. *Sydney* also disembarked her Walrus aircraft to conduct regular reconnaissance flights from the port.[124]

In addition to supporting the army in Greece, Cunningham set in motion an operation aimed at altering the naval balance with an air attack on the main Italian Fleet base at Taranto using Swordfish torpedo bombers from *Illustrious*. It was an audacious plan as carrier borne aircraft had not previously executed such an attack. As a diversion, and to further disrupt Italian shipping between Italy and Albania, he directed the 7th Cruiser Squadron to conduct a simultaneous sweep into the Aegean. This was a shrewd if calculated move, for the *Maritrafalba* in Brindisi had only been assigned three armed merchant cruisers, two destroyers and ten torpedo boats to escort these strategically important convoys.

The *Supermarina* had no doubt reasoned the close proximity of the Italian Battle Fleet at Taranto would deter an incursion by major British surface forces.

During the afternoon of 11 November Vice Admiral Pridham-Whippell flying his flag in *Orion* detached from the Battle Fleet and led *Ajax*, *Sydney*, *Nubian* and *Mohawk* towards the Strait of Otranto. The two destroyers were deployed on either wing as pickets for any sighting. If there was to be an encounter it would be a night engagement and ships prepared for action. This included laying towing gear out on deck in case they or another ship was disabled.

At 11 pm *Illustrious'* Swordfish commenced their attack on the anchored Italian battle fleet. At the same time Pridham-Whippell's cruisers passed through the Otranto Strait. Earlier in the evening John Collins had told the ship's company that the force was 'looking for trouble that night' and then closed the ship up for action.

With the Strait empty of ships, Pridham-Whippell altered course towards the 140 km stretch of the Aegean between Brindisi and the Albanian port of Vlorë. Ahead of Pridham-Whippell was an Italian westbound convoy returning to Brindisi having discharged troops and vehicles at Vlorë. The two fully darkened formations were steadily closing one another, but their presence was unknown to each other.

Leading the convoy was the World War I vintage, three funnelled torpedo boat destroyer *Nicola Fabrizi* commanded by Lieutenant Giovanni Barbini. Astern of *Nicola Fabrizi* were the merchantmen *Antonio Locatelli*, *Premuda*, *Capo Vado* and *Catalani*.[125] Bringing up the rear was the 4.7-inch gun armed merchant cruiser *Ramb III* commanded by Commander Francesco De Angelis, who was also convoy commander.

The sea was calm, visibility excellent and the full moon was rising. Because of these conditions at 2 am De Angelis ordered his ships into their day formation. He brought *Ramb III* to the head and deployed *Nicola Fabrizi* to the up-threat southern side of the convoy. The slow merchantmen steamed a steady course at 8 knots while the faster ships commenced a zigzag course.

At 1.15 am *Mohawk* made the first sighting of the convoy. Three minutes later Barbini in *Nicola Fabrizi* sighted the approaching warships and ordered Action Stations, to prepare the torpedoes and bring all boilers on line. Soon thereafter *Nubian* only 4,000 yards distant opened fire on *Nicola Fabrizi* which received hits, one of which destroyed her communications compartment. Near misses also sprayed her upper deck with shrapnel. In return the plucky torpedo boat opened fire with her four 4-inch and two 3-inch guns as well as firing torpedoes at the enemy. From the bridge Barbini could see his gun crews trying to maintain fire despite mounting casualties. He ordered smoke and tried to manoeuvre to screen the convoy but *Nicola Fabrizi's* machinery plant was seriously damaged. In contrast to *Nicola Fabrizi*, *Ramb III* did not close to engage the cruisers and only fired 19 rounds in the battle, mainly from her rear mountings.

Pridham-Whippell ordered starshell to be fired to further illuminate the scene. Soon all his cruisers were engaging the convoy. *Sydney* opened fire on *Antonio Locatelli*, scoring multiple hits and setting her on fire. After ten salvoes *Sydney* shifted target to *Premuda* which was also set ablaze after eleven salvoes. *Sydney* now turned her attention to the embattled *Nicola Fabrizi* and fired five salvoes at her before returning her attention once more to *Antonio Locatelli* and *Permuda*. These were left stopped and ablaze. *Sydney* then shifted target to *Capo Vado*. This ship and *Catalini* were also being engaged by the other cruisers. In addition to gunfire the three cruisers each fired two torpedoes apiece into the convoy. In response at 1.40 am *Nicola Fabrizi* fired a torpedo which passed close astern of *Sydney*.

HMAS Sydney *engaging the convoy in the Battle of Otranto Strait.*
(*The Argus*-State Library of Victoria)

Ten minutes later, with the convoy aflame and sinking, Pridham-Whippell ordered his force to retire at 28 knots before heavy cruisers from Taranto inevitably arrived on the scene. John Collins later wrote that the battle was:

> ... not without its element of excitement as three six inch cruisers found themselves well to the north of the Narrows with Italian bases containing vastly superior forces in their rear. The possibility of a hit from aircraft, E or U-boat, was in mind. It was fortunate that the torpedo fired by a convoy escort missed astern of *Sydney*.[126]

While *Ramb III* continued on her westward course, Barbini, nursing a serious leg wound, had *Nicola Fabrizi* close the merchantmen to rescue survivors. The rear ship of the convoy, *Catalani* had hoped to escape as the rest of the ships were engaged. She altered course back to the Albanian coast but two cruisers spotted her and quickly set her ablaze. Although the last to be hit, she was the first to sink at 2 am. *Antonio Locatelli*, the first merchantman to be hit, had uncontrollable fires forward and aft. At 3.35 am with her crew in lifeboats and rafts she heeled over and sank. Both *Premuda* and *Capo Vado* suffered damage to their machinery and extensive fires took hold. Within an hour of *Antonio Locatelli* they were also at the bottom of the Aegean.

With eleven dead, the battered *Nicola Fabrizi* slowly made passage for nearby Sazan Island where the Italian hospital ship *California* was fortuitously in port. The faltering Barbini remained on the bridge refusing medical attention until the survivors had been transferred to *California*. Meanwhile the torpedo boats *Curtatone* and *Solferino* arrived on the scene and rescued a further 140 sailors.

As Pridham-Whippell predicted, the Italian response was swift. The *Supermarina* sailed five cruisers[127] and three destroyer squadrons from Taranto and Brindisi. It was, however, too late. To rub salt into the Italian wounds, the CANT reconnaissance plane sent out to locate the cruisers, found them back with Cunningham's Battle Fleet and was duly shot down by a Fulmar fighter in full view of the fleet.

In the wake of the Battle of Otranto Strait, the *Supermarina* strengthened the escort force for convoys and only undertook daytime sailings. Commander De Angelis of *Ramb III* was censured for his feeble defence of the convoy. In contrast, Lieutenant Commander Barbini was awarded the Gold Medal of Military Valour. In his nomination the Commander of *Maritrafalba*, Captain Romulus Polacchini wrote of Barbini's:

> ... truly exceptional qualities of calm courage, of contempt of danger, daring unparalleled. All of his officers and the entire crew have spoken of him with expressions of the highest admiration; survivors of steamships have told me that his action had been that of a hero.[128]

For the next month the hard-worked *Sydney* operated with the Fleet in supporting both the Greek operations and maintaining supplies to Malta. After first collecting her Walrus amphibian aircraft in Suda Bay, it was to this island fortress that John Collins took his cruiser on 23 December for a well earned refit. Also in port was the worn-out *Stuart* having her machinery plant attended to. The following day and for the first time in months, sailors were able to take 48 hours leave. On Christmas Day sailors placed greenery on the masts and yardarms and the officers served their men the traditional Christmas lunch. John gratefully accepted the hospitality of Malta's Governor Lieutenant General William Dobbie,[129] and his wife at the 17th century San Anton Palace for two days. The Palace was a welcome break from the ship with its beautiful walled gardens, tennis court and library.

At the end of *Sydney's* stay John entertained the Governor and other senior officers to dinner onboard. On 8 January the two Australian ships left Malta. For *Sydney* it was for the last time. She was to be replaced in the Mediterranean by *Perth* who she met in a fleeting port call to Alexandria. Cunningham signalled to *Sydney*:

> Much regret that there will be no opportunity for me to come onboard and personally say goodbye to you all. *Sydney* has been with us from the beginning of the Italian war and has borne with us the rough when things were difficult and the better times which we have had lately. We have all

admired her efficiency and the fiery spirit which animated all on board. She was first to show the enemy that whatever the odds he ran great risk of destruction if he encountered our ships. We part with you with great regret and the best wishes of the whole Mediterranean Fleet go with you. I hope you will have a happy home-coming and that your countrymen will give you the reception you deserve.[130]

Among the many other valedictory signals was one from Hec Waller which said, '*Au revoir* and best of luck. We shall feel lonely without our glamour girl'.[131] This well captured the impact of *Sydney's* exploits on the national imagination. In *Sydney's* Wardroom fragments from *Bartolomeo Colleoni's* shell that hit the funnel were framed and displayed proudly next to an *Emden* relic. Among the latest litter of kittens from the ship's cat were 'Bardia', 'Espero', 'Colleoni' and 'Scarpanto'.[132]

As *Sydney* cleared the southern entrance of the Suez Canal and proceeded down the Red Sea escorting convoy SW.4B as far as Somaliland, John Collins could reflect on a brilliant operational deployment. Arguably it was the most successful in the RAN's history. While he had inherited a very efficient and happy ship, John had taken *Sydney* to a new level of war fighting efficiency. In particular *Sydney* had become a crack gunnery ship. Fate had also played its part. The large number of rounds fired in successive actions of increasing complexity meant *Sydney* exuded an aggressive confidence in battle. John had demonstrated a coolness under fire and an ability to think carefully through issues in the fog of war. He ably assessed risks and opportunities and then seized the chance to engage the enemy. Admiral Pridham-Whippell assessed John Collins in a performance report as 'an excellent cruiser Captain, bold, tenacious and determined'[133] whilst Cunningham wrote:

> I have the highest opinion of this officer and much regretted losing him and his most efficient ship from the Mediterranean Command.[134]

John Collins and Cunningham had established a fine rapport based on mutual respect. Cunningham also recognized John's position as the senior RAN representative in the Mediterranean. The admiral for example increased the meat ration for RAN sailors at John's request to double that of their RN counterparts.[135] John's leadership would be sorely missed by the RAN units remaining in theatre.

Sydney's passage home across the Indian Ocean was via the idyllic Seychelles. Her return to Australia was keenly anticipated by many and for different reasons. On 22 November the Opposition Leader John Curtin raised in Parliament the issue of mounting losses of merchantmen in Australian waters. He went further to say, 'There is worse. If an enemy can mine our waters, the next step which we must contemplate is that it can raid our ports'.[136] Curtin said 'it seems imperative that the Government must soon consider the allocation of the units of the Australian Navy'.[137] He went on to call for better equipping of the RAAF and improved coordination between the two services.

Curtin followed up the matter on 2 December at the Advisory War Council where he expressed his concern about dispositions of the Australian Squadron in the face of repeated German raider attacks. Admiral Colvin tried to placate the unease and stated that while the Squadron was understrength with *Perth* enroute to the Mediterranean, *Sydney* and *Westralia* would soon return.[138] What does not appear to have been discussed is why *Perth* had been allowed to leave the Australia Station before *Sydney's* return. The Mediterranean Fleet was clearly in a better position to absorb the dip in numbers while the cruiser swap took place. For the Government, under increasing pressure, *Sydney* could not get back soon enough.

Sydney herself was soon reminded of the German threat when on 24 January she received a Raider Distress Message from the British merchantman *Mandasor*. John Collins cut short *Sydney's* Seychelles port visit to conduct a sweep of the nearby area. Neither *Mandasor* nor a raider was found. The merchantman had been intercepted and sunk by the raider *Atlantis* which then cleared the area and headed back into the South Atlantic.

The rest of *Sydney's* passage home via Fremantle was uneventful and near midnight on 9 February the cruiser stole into Port Jackson and anchored in Watson's Bay near the mouth of the harbour. Soon launches with reporters embarked, lay off the stern seeking interviews. Despite the late hour and mindful of newspaper deadlines, they were welcomed onboard and John Collins patiently went through *Sydney's* Mediterranean exploits. Sailors also gave the reporters the view from the lower deck including their admiration for their Captain and 'Grandpa' Cunningham.

Early the following morning Crace came onboard for the passage in the cruiser up the harbour. From nearby Darling Point Phyllis Collins and an excited 4-year old Gillian looked out from a friend's home to see the camouflaged cruiser looking imposing in the bright Sydney sunshine. As *Sydney* got underway throngs of small boats followed her in procession, not to the Garden Island naval base, but to the port's premier berth at Circular Quay adjacent the city. At the Quay were hundreds of families who had not seen their loved ones for at least ten months. They were officially welcomed by the Governor General Lord Gowrie, the First Naval Member, Admiral Colvin and the Navy Minister Billy Hughes. The latter gave an overly long speech and received catcalls from the impatient crowd.[139]

The following morning the Premier and the Mayor came onboard to present the ship's victory plaque as well as a silver rose bowl for the Wardroom. At 11.45 am John Collins led the ship's band and 400 of his men in a triumphant march from his ship up George Street to the Sydney Town Hall.[140] Over 200,000 people cheered *Sydney* in what *The Mercury* described as 'the most extraordinary mass demonstration seen in any city in Australia since the war began'.[141] Confetti and streamers were thrown from buildings. At times John had to stop to untangle his legs from the streamers. *The Mercury* reported of their fellow Tasmanian:

> Captain Collins marching at the head of his men with his white cap at a jaunty angle, certainly looked the proudest man in the world.[142]

The triumphant arrival of HMAS Sydney *into Sydney Harbour 10 February 1941. (The Argus/State Archives of Victoria)*

At the Town Hall John Collins thanked the large mass of Sydneysiders for their 'overwhelming welcome'.[143] Inside the Town Hall the Mayor unveiled the victory plaque to which John remarked that while the cruiser would pass, the plaque would go on. At the evening reception John gave an excellent narrative of the cruiser's Mediterranean exploits in a 'breezy' but captivating style.[144] He was at pains to highlight not only the achievements of his men but also their opponents. In particular, he singled out the bravery of Captain Baroni and *Espero*. In part he said:

> The Italian High Command seems to be obsessed with the idea of preserving ships but, at the same time, we saw instances of great bravery by the Italians.[145]

The welcome home for *Sydney* was without parallel and would have no doubt exceeded Cunningham's expectations. In a postscript of the day an Inverell schoolboy sent John Collins a note which said 'Congratulations. Bonzer holiday. Please sink another ship'.[146]

VII

In contrast to the exploits of John Collins, Harold Farncomb in *Canberra* and Harry Showers in *Adelaide* were involved in the lower public profile but strategically vital work of convoy protection from the threat of German raiders in the Pacific and Indian Oceans. From June 1940 a system was in operation whereby *Adelaide* and *Perth* would escort ships on the east coast, with *Perth* handing them over to *Canberra* in the Indian Ocean. The convoys often included the large liners *Queen Mary*, *Aquitania* and *Mauretania* containing Australian and New Zealand troops bound for the Middle East.

During this period the Kreigsmarine's intent was to deploy as many as six auxiliary cruisers as well as either a pocket battleship or cruiser to attack Allied shipping in the South Atlantic, Pacific and Indian Oceans. To support the force an array of merchantmen were requisitioned or captured to act as supply ships, with some operating from Japan. The first raider to enter the Pacific was *Orion*. Because the names of these ships were unknown to the RN, *Orion* was given the designation of 'Raider A'. She rounded Cape Horn in May 1940 and steamed into New Zealand waters to lay mines with *Niagara* sinking the following month. *Orion* was later joined by *Komet* (Raider B) which, with the assistance of the Soviet Union, had entered the Pacific via the Arctic Ocean. The South Atlantic and Indian Oceans however had better prospects for raiders and that was where the main German effort was concentrated. *Atlantis* (Raider C) captured her first South Atlantic ship in May 1940 and would later enter the Indian Ocean. She was followed by *Thor* (Raider E) which never went beyond the South Atlantic. In July *Pinguin* (Raider F) sank her first ship in the South Atlantic and entered the Indian Ocean in August. In February 1941 the pocket battleship *Admiral Scheer* had entered the Indian Ocean and rendezvoused with *Atlantis*. The battleship had the previous month sunk the armed merchant cruiser HMS *Jervis Bay* in the South Atlantic.

Alderman Crick, The Lord Mayor of Sydney presenting commemorative medallions to the men of HMAS Sydney *with Captain John Collins proudly watching on.* (*The Argus*/State Library of Victoria)

Finally, the modern *Kormoran* (Raider G) entered the Indian Ocean in April 1941 having sunk eight merchantmen on her South Atlantic passage. *Kormoran* was commanded by the 38-year old Korvettenkapitän Theodor Detmers who was the youngest auxiliary cruiser captain in the Kriegsmarine. Detmers had previously commanded destroyers and was well trained in combined torpedo and gun engagements. He used this technique when sinking his merchant ship quarry.

The German raiders, while coordinated from German Naval High Command, would generally operate independently and deploy for differing periods depending on success and resupply. To counter this significant and changing raider threat the British had been able to maintain a force in the South Atlantic and Indian Ocean of one or two older aircraft carriers and half a dozen cruisers. Inevitably, this force had to be reactive to reports of suspicious sightings that invariably came from merchant ships about to be captured or sunk. The vital collation of these reports along with intercepted signals and coastwatcher reports to recommend deployment of scarce warships was the work of Rupert Long's team in close consultation with their colleagues in the Admiralty. However luck or chance would still prove a major factor in the war against the raiders and their attendant supply ships.

The raider *Orion* after her foray in New Zealand waters cruised the waters of Fiji and then New Caledonia in search of trade. For two days from 14 August 1940 *Orion* loitered off Noumea. In that time she intercepted and sank the French cargo-passenger ship *Notou* which had a regular run from Newcastle. Before leaving the area Korvettenkapitän Kurt Weyher launched his Arado seaplane on a flight over Noumea harbour. The aircrew reported large public gatherings in the squares and streets of the New Caledonian capital.

After her New Caledonian sweep *Orion* steamed into the Tasman Sea to intercept shipping between Australia and New Zealand. At dusk on 20 August she sighted through rain squalls the Wellington bound British steamer *Turakina,* 400 miles from her destination. *Orion* closed to about 5,000 yards but Captain James Laird in *Turakina* elected to fight, as he vowed he would, if ever attacked. *Turakina* opened fire with her single 4.7-inch gun on the stern. *Orion* returned fire and her third salvo hit *Turakina's* bridge. Weyher later wrote:

> Shots from the enemy's 105 mm gun were far from inaccurate. The first ten fell short, the next whined over the forecastle and bridge, then came hits astern.[147]

The first sea fight in the Tasman Sea was a brave, but one-sided one with *Turakina* soon a blazing wreck. As *Orion* closed to 300 yards to recover survivors, *Turakina* opened fire again narrowing missing the German. Weyher thought the *Turakina's* gun crew 'quite crazy',[148] but they had nearly inflicted a mortal blow. *Orion* fired further broadsides and two torpedoes to finally finish off the blazing *Turakina*. After *Turakina* sank, *Orion* spent five hours searching for survivors. The last survivor, a 17-year old, attracted attention with a cry just as *Orion* was

The German auxiliary cruiser Kormoran *fuelling a U-boat in the Atlantic enroute to the Indian Ocean.* (Source unknown)

going to clear the scene. Captain Laird and thirty six of his sailors lost their lives that evening. On receipt of *Turakina's* distress message Trans-Tasman trade was suspended and HMS *Achilles* and *Perth* carried out a sweep of the Tasman Sea.

Orion had, however, shaped course for south of Tasmania and on 3 September was briefly sighted but not identified by a RAAF aircraft in the Great Australian Bight in poor visibility. Unknown to *Orion* she was steaming astern of the major troop convoy US.4[149] under the charge of Harold Farncomb in *Canberra*. The near detection by the RAAF and the indication of clear surveillance coordination from listening to local radio traffic was enough for Weyher to head further into the Southern Ocean and thence pass through the Tasman Ocean and then north into the western Pacific.

Pinguin after operating with modest success off Madagascar headed towards north west Australia sinking *Benavon* and capturing *Nordvard* enroute and then the Norwegian tanker *Storstad*. The latter was converted at sea to a minelayer and 110 mines transferred. *Pinguin* and *Storstad*, now renamed *Passat*, headed for the Great Australian Bight and Bass Strait to lay mines. During November and December three ships, *Cambridge*, *City of Rayville* and *Nimbin* were subsequently mined and sunk.

From the earliest days of the war the Admiralty had been concerned about the sophistication of German mines. In particular, their development of a magnetic mine that did not require physical contact with the target ship. Rather the mine only needed to detect the ship's proximate magnetic signature to detonate its charge. To counter this threat scientists at the Admiralty Research Laboratory devised a magnetic device that could be towed by minesweepers to explode the mines. They also discovered that each ship's magnetic signature could be considerably reduced if wire coils were placed along her hull and an adjustable electrical current passed through the coils. This was called degaussing. However, to complicate matters each ship was different and its signature varied over time and, to a lesser extent, where in the world she was steaming.

Fortunately for Australia, in 1940 Dr David Myers who headed the Electrotechnology Section of the National Standards Laboratory at the University of Sydney was in Britain. He was asked by the Admiralty to assist in degaussing research. He brought back to Australia valuable expertise that would enable the RAN to protect both naval and merchant shipping. Importantly, Professor Sir John Madsen, Chairman of the National Standards Laboratory placed the facilities of the Electrical Engineering Department at the Navy's disposal for this vital task.[150] Winn Reilly was selected and promoted to Acting Commander to bring these latent capabilities together into a viable capability. With his electrical engineering skills combined with his industrial experience, intellectual facility and an ability 'to get to the bottom of any problem' he proved an excellent choice.[151]

From early 1941 Winn Reilly built up a core of eleven naval and civilian engineers in Sydney. He worked closely with Madsen, his team and the Sydney County Council to design and build equipment resulting in a degaussing range on the bottom of Sydney Harbour and sets of degaussing coils to be fitted to ships. A network of such sites were also established in Melbourne, Fremantle, Brisbane and Adelaide with Winn supervising their establishment and operation.

Some ships, such as the mammoth *Queen Mary*, were too big to run over the range and so Winn organized for divers to go under her and measure her signature for subsequent degaussing adjustment.

The Australian degaussing capability worked collaboratively first with the RN and then also with the USN to ensure that their ships' degaussing systems could be tuned for effective operation in the southern hemisphere. It was complex and in many respects experimental work which required close engagement between Winn's team, the University and the Admiralty. By the end of 1942 his organization reached a mature state with hundreds of ships receiving this invaluable but hidden defence.[152] Such was the scale of the RAN's degaussing operations that a search of the National Archives of Australia reveals over 2,000 files related to the wartime degaussing of ships.[153]

VIII

The Noumea public gatherings observed from on high by *Orion's* aircrew were part of a much larger drama being played out across the French colonial empire. The fall of France and the creation of the Vichy regime under Marshal Pétain on 16 June 1940 created a quandary about allegiance in these outposts. As a counterpoint, within days of the creation of the Vichy State, General Charles de Gaulle had formed a Free French government in exile in London. The geographic location, political disposition, loyalties of colonial elites and their respective populations would independently determine the allegiance question within the various colonies.

Strategically, New Caledonia was important for its globally significant mineral reserves of nickel and chrome that had been the subject of increasing German and Japanese investment over recent years.

Both metals had application in arms production where their corrosion and wear resistance were highly prized. In addition, New Caledonia was proximate to important trans-Pacific shipping routes and could provide an invaluable base for German raiders.

From British and Australian perspectives, it was highly desirable for Governor Georges Pélicier in Noumea to rally to the Free-French cause, as had been the case with the French Resident Commissioner Henri Sautot in the New Hebrides condominium. Sautot had 'fanned the flame and led them and turned out to be a natural leader.'[154] The majority of New Caledonia's population was equally so disposed and on 26 June the local assembly—the Conseil Général—passed a resolution in favour of the Free-French cause. Governor Pélicier however was more cautious. While making public statements aligned to the general mood, he still followed the edicts of the new Vichy government. For example, on 29 July Pélicier informed Sautot of the Vichy requirement to send names of officials supporting de Gaulle. His perceived timidity and inability to engage with the people on local issues made him an increasingly isolated and unpopular figure.[155]

In viewing this unfolding situation the Australian and British Governments, while wanting the same outcome, had different views on the way forward. The Menzies Government tempered their approach with concerns about how whatever action taken would be viewed by Japan. The tack taken was to offer prospects of trade and food security to New Caledonia as a means to achieve a declaration of allegiance. To effect this Australia needed official representation on the island.

In late July the Department of External Affairs sent a telegram to the French speaking Bertram Ballard, who was the Australian Government Solicitor in the New Hebrides to wind up his affairs and report to Canberra.[156] He was to become the inaugural Australian diplomatic representative in Noumea. Ballard was an ideal choice as he knew well both the trade issues and the politics of the region. After hurried briefings and preparations, which included the provision of a large box with stationery and a typewriter, Ballard travelled to Newcastle to await the next nickel carrying cargo ship from Noumea. Fate was to take a benevolent hand in his enterprise. He was to embark on *Notou*, but his essential stationary box had not yet arrived and so he was instructed to await the next ship. *Notou* was, as earlier described, captured by *Orion* on her passage to Noumea. Had Ballard taken that ship not only would he have been captured, but also potentially the diplomatic code book in his coat pocket.[157]

In contrast to Australia, the British position, which was informed by their High Commissioner for the Western Pacific, Sir Harry Luke, called for more audacity in the matter.[158] The British thought that de Gaulle needed to swing waverers to his side by a naval presence in the region. While de Gaulle may have agreed to this recommendation he did not possess a warship in the western Pacific. The Vichy Government did, however, have warships and it dispatched the sloop *Dumont D'Urville* from Tahiti to New Caledonia to help quell any Free French ferment.

Alarmed by these developments Britain suggested to Australia that more determined steps were needed to achieve a Free French New Caledonia. De Gaulle had helpfully proposed that Henri Sautot be installed as Governor in Noumea with the assistance of a British warship. The Admiralty suggested the only viable warship in the region, with the presence and firepower to outclass *Dumont D'Urville*, was the cruiser *Adelaide*. While the Australian Department of External Affairs viewed such a plan with disquiet, Menzies was now convinced the time had come for action.

On 1 September Harry Showers received orders that *Adelaide* might be required to embark Monsieur Sautot in Vila for passage to Noumea. If ordered to proceed he was to consult with both British Resident Mr HR Blandy and Sautot and to stand by for further direction.[159] Having quickly made preparations, on 2 September *Adelaide* sailed from Sydney to initially proceed to Brisbane for a top-up fueling and thence steam with all dispatch to Vila.

Reminiscent of Bertram Ballard, Harry Showers' start to the enterprise was inauspicious and indeed could have resulted in an abandoned mission. On the first night out of Sydney *Adelaide* collided with the southbound 8,300 tonne freighter *Coptic*. Both ships were fully darkened and the first Harry knew of the collision was being jolted by the impact in his bunk. His bridge team only saw the looming shape of *Coptic* one mile distant and no effective avoidance action had yet taken hold. In *Coptic*, the cruiser was not even seen until impact. Miraculously, the near head-on collision was but a glancing blow. Damage was minor and both ships after checking each other's well being, continued their voyages unimpeded. Just a few degrees difference in the angle of impact could have resulted in a catastrophic collision and heavy loss of life.

Coptic had been steaming along the promulgated southbound path for merchantmen. Because ships steamed without navigation lights in wartime this was set 24 miles inshore of the northbound route. In the interests of time *Adelaide's* passage plan from Sydney to Brisbane more closely followed the inshore route and in hindsight this decision courted such an incident.[160] In a post-war legal settlement the Commonwealth paid £35,000 in damages.[161]

What was clear in this developing affair was that the character of each protagonist would play an important part in the outcome. The other key figure was the Commanding Officer of *Dumont D'Urville*. He was Capitaine de Frégate Pierre Toussaint de Quievrecourt. Although the rank equivalent of a Commander, he was four years older than Harry Showers, having joined the French Navy in 1912. He came from an established French naval family with his father having served as the Comptroller General of the Navy in Lorient. De Quievrecourt was a known quantity to Navy Office with Rupert Long having called on him when *Dumont D'Urville* visited Sydney at the beginning of the year.[162] The Frenchman was a man of strong conviction who saw the Vichy regime as the legitimate French government. He had been alarmed that Pélicier had not annulled the Assembly resolution and going beyond his brief he recommended to the Vichy regime they install a new Governor and for New Caledonia to develop stronger trading ties with Japan and the United States.

On arrival in Vila Harry Showers called on Blandy and Sautot. His consultation with the former 'had however convinced me that the time for action was by no means propitious.'[163] Blandy had recently been to Noumea and considered the majority of the population positively disposed towards de Gaulle. On another positive note, the next day de Gaulle formally instructed Sautot to assume the Governorship. It was also learnt that Governor Pélicier had been replaced by the garrison commander Lieutenant Colonel Maurice Denis.

During the Vila port visit Harry Showers' instructions were also modified. It was decided that it would be better for Sautot to arrive in Noumea in the Norwegian tanker *Norden* rather than a foreign warship. *Adelaide* would therefore act as escort. Troubling intelligence was also received that the Vichy sloop *Admiral Charnier* with a hundred troops embarked, would arrive in Noumea in about a week. Harry was concerned that *Adelaide* would be less than omnipotent if facing the

'Just a few degrees difference in the angle of impact could have resulted in a catastrophic collision and heavy loss of life.' MV Coptic *which collided with HMAS* Adelaide *on the evening of 2 September 1941.* (Green Collection/State Library of Victoria)

two albeit smaller warships. He was also unsure in the ability of the de Gaullists to organize themselves ashore.[164]

There was therefore no time to delay matters until more propitious timing. The plan was for the de Gaulle committee in Noumea, under the leadership of Monsieur Raymond Pognon, to carry out a 'coup de force' at 1 am on 19 September, just prior to the arrival of Sautot. The de Gaullist Committee's ambitious plan was to kidnap the Governor, de Quievrecourt, the Officers Commanding Troops and Artillery along with the Chief Censor. This plan was soon the talk of the streets and was sensibly replaced by the modest one of sending a delegation to request the Governor's resignation.

Adelaide and *Norden* sailed from Vila on the morning of 16 September with Harry Showers allowing ample time for the passage. This was just as well with *Norden* not even able to reach 10 knots. Enroute *Adelaide* conducted gunnery practices with her main armament.

Communications and co-ordination of intent between the Department of External Affairs, the Navy and the British Government would be vitally important. Arrangements were far from ideal. The Department of External Affairs had less than a handful of overseas missions and Ballard had in his words:

> ... a heavy telegraphic job; I myself drafted the telegram, I coded them, I typed them and got the carbon in the wrong way and typed them again and went down and handed them into the Post Office; and then when cables came in I had to do the reverse process, it was a very very long job.[165]

A man of 'whose personal bravery I have the highest admiration'. Monsieur Henri Sautot (R) who Harry Showers helped install in Noumea and the British Resident, Mr HR Blandy (AWM)

The British Consul, Mr WA Johnston, who was also the Admiralty Reporting Officer, had a similar arrangement except that unlike the unmarried Ballard, his wife did the coding and typing. Harry Showers was best placed with a secretarial staff and communications centre. The RAN had not caught up with the fact that cables should be going direct to Ballard and instead were being sent to the Admiralty Reporting Officer. This was not conducive to a coordinated Australian position and quite rightly annoyed Ballard. Fortunately he and Johnston worked closely together.[166]

On the afternoon before *Adelaide's* arrival, *Dumont D'Urville* berthed alongside in Noumea and later Governor Denis signed a proclamation declaring a 'State of Siege' in Noumea with an associated evening curfew from 9 pm. Soldiers and sailors duly took post around the town. Soon thereafter Raymond Pognon called on the Governor and informed him of the next day's arrival of Sautot accompanied by a 'British' cruiser. Reputedly, the Governor was so astounded that he forgot to have Pognon arrested.[167]

At 6.15 am on 19 September *Adelaide* and *Norden* approached the entrance to Noumea harbour. It was expected that a boat flying the Free-French flag bearing the Cross of Lorraine and throwing kerosene tins over the side to glisten in the sun, would come out to invite Sautot to enter Noumea.[168] No such boat was visible. Undeterred, *Norden* entered the port flying a large Norwegian ensign. Harry Showers decided to slowly follow, but at 7.30 am a guard-boat from *Dumont D'Urville* closed *Adelaide* and questioned her intentions. Harry became concerned that her embarked guard could board and take control of *Norden*. He therefore had *Adelaide* close the tanker to prevent any interference.

Ashore the British Consul called on the Governor at 8 am and requested permission to visit the 'British' cruiser. The Governor refused and stated he was waiting on information from the guard boat as to the cruiser's intention. In the meantime he considered the cruiser to be hostile to himself if not to France. He added that he had given orders for the forts to open fire on the cruiser. Fortunately the garrison refused to obey the order.[169]

The de Gaullist Committee supported by several hundred armed Civil Guard were the next to call on the Governor. He gave the Committee permission to go out to meet their 'self appointed' Governor. In the face of the delegation the Governor did not cut an inspiring figure and appeared pale, indecisive and clearly stressed by the developing crisis.[170]

Meanwhile in the harbour, as both ships came further into the port, Harry Showers could see the French sloop more clearly. She was moored with her stern to the wharf and her bow facing into the harbour in a Mediterranean moor. This restricted her arcs of fire and in any case her guns were unmanned. Ashore Free French flags could be seen among the gathering crowd and flying from the mast of the Pilot Station. Disconcertingly a signal was then run up from the same station 'You Must Not Enter Harbour'. Harry elected to continue the entry into the port. He was finally rewarded with the sight of a boat closing *Norden*. The delay in its arrival had been caused by it twice breaking down. The news for Harry when the boat subsequently arrived alongside *Adelaide* was not promising. Following the declaration by the de Gaullist Committee one of its members was arrested and the Vichy forces, mainly *Dumont D'Urville* sailors controlled the port, the town and approaching roads. The de-briefing was finished with a warning that *Adelaide* could still be attacked by the forts.

Harry elected to remain in port until 6 pm and await events. Among other things time was needed for the presence of the cruiser to be felt. Indeed from shore *Adelaide* cut an impressive sight and in Ballard's words 'prowled up and down in Noumea harbour like a caged lion, stripped for action'.[171]

By 11 am it was clear events had indeed started to turn. The Pilot Station hoisted a signal to enter port. On the strength of this Harry embarked Sautot and allowed *Norden* to leave port. Harry had Sautot replace his distinctive pith helmet with one of the ship's steel helmets. Both men waited impatiently on the bridge for developments. Harry reminded Sautot if no boat arrived by noon he would return him to the New Hebrides. It was an agonising time for Sautot who feared a Free

French failure as in Dakar. But just after 11 am one of the officers on the bridge spotted a boat flying the Free French flag heading for *Adelaide* to the great relief of Sautot and all those on the bridge.[172]

The boat bore the news that the Governor had given way to public opinion and that Free French elements were in control of the town. The armed sailors from *Dumont D'Urville* had been jeered by the crowds and returned onboard their ship. Monsieur Sautot buoyed by the news, proceeded into Noumea in the boat and landed to the rapture of about 2,000 people.[173] The thick-set former soldier then marched ahead of a procession to Government House where he called on the Governor. Denis said 'You traitor—I should arrest you.' When Sautot dared him to do it, Denis replied 'How can I, with all these people present and that foreign 8 inch [sic] warship outside?'[174] Denis then arranged for Sautot to formally assume the Governorship at 3.30 pm that day. *Adelaide* in Harry's words:

> ... continued throughout the remainder of the day and night to patrol off the harbour entrance with the object of inspiring confidence ashore, exercising restraint on *Dumont D'Urville* and maintaining my mobility if *Admiral Charnier* arrives.[175]

After lunch Ballard and the British Consul came onboard with little news except that the forts had indeed been ordered to open fire on *Adelaide* but the garrison had elected to remain neutral. Both men returned later in the afternoon with the news that while the majority of the people and the 800 strong Civil Guards supported Sautot, there were still Vichy supporters who might try and overthrow him. Johnson and Ballard both feared 'the possibility of an unfortunate incident during the night was therefore very great'.[176] Sautot wisely spent the evening outside in the capital.

Harry Showers maintained *Adelaide*'s harbour patrol throughout the night. It proved to be an uneventful evening ashore and the cruiser went to anchor in the morning. At 11 am a request was received from Sautot to extend *Adelaide*'s stay a further two days to act as a counter to *Dumont D'Urville*. Harry readily agreed.

Sautot's concerns were fully justified as in the course of this time two attempts were made to reinstall the former Governor. These were forestalled with the assistance of farmers and police who continued to gather from the hinterland.

For his part de Quievrecourt tried to pressure Harry Showers through letters to leave Noumea. In reply Harry merely responded that *Adelaide* was in Noumea at the request of the Government of Noumea. Time was on the side of the Free French and it was soon learnt by de Quievrecourt that *Admiral Charnier* was returning to Saigon. Reportedly the ship had damaged a propeller and needed docking.[177]

On 22 September Harry Showers, Johnston and Ballard called on Sautot. Among other things the presence of *Dumont D'Urville* was discussed. Harry informed Sautot that de Quievrecourt in accordance with naval custom was calling on him later that morning and he offered to act as intermediary to resolve the presence of the sloop. Harry had drafted a letter to de Quievrecourt for Sautot's consideration. It gave him, de Quievrecourt, the option of *Dumont D'Urville* changing allegiance to Free France or having safe passage to sail to Indo-China. The letter was duly signed.

Over coming days through meetings between the two captains and correspondence affirming discussed positions, Harry Showers was able to gain the confidence of de Quievrecourt and provide his ship with a dignified exit strategy. De Quievrecourt, realising New Caledonia was lost to the de Gaullists, was at pains to ensure his ship was sufficiently provisioned for passage to Indo-China and that those loyal to the Vichy regime would be well treated in his absence and able to take subsequent passage in the steamship *Pierre Lotti*. Harry was able to gain agreement from the Governor, and encouraged actions in accordance with this agreement. Harry was assiduous in recording agreements and ensuring there was no deviation.

On 24 September Ballard was able to report to Canberra that 'the situation has very much improved during the last 36 hours'.[178] Importantly, Sautot led the commemorations of the colony's anniversary in the town square which was also attended by Ballard, Harry Showers and a contingent of *Adelaide* sailors.

Another potential player in the power struggle was the Japanese Government. On 25 September Harry Showers, Johnston and Ballard had lunch with Japan's new Consul Tokitaro Kuroki to explain developments and assuage any concerns. Later that day *Dumont D'Urville* duly sailed 'in a most seamanlike manner'.[179]

The following day it came to light that small incidents of retribution by de Gaullists were starting to occur and that there was a risk that the undertakings given to de Quievrecourt would not be honoured. Harry Showers thought it essential that the de Gaullist Committee be formally made aware of these undertakings. Johnston and Ballard agreed and thought Harry was the best person to deliver this speech. On 27 September, after consultation with the Governor, it was agreed that he would address the Committee in Sautot's presence later that afternoon.

Harry read from a carefully crafted two-page speech that affirmed the role of *Adelaide* in providing 'contingent support' to the Governor and then outlined the undertakings given to Captain de Quievrecourt with the agreement of the Governor. These undertaking revolved around

HMAS Adelaide's *Guard marching through the streets of Noumea to a wreath laying ceremony at the cenotaph.* (RAN)

the safe conduct of *Dumont D'Urville* and repatriation to Indo-China of those Vichy adherents who so wished to avail themselves of passage in *Pierre Lotti*. Towards the end of the speech Harry Showers said:

> ... you can be of great assistance by using your best endeavours towards restoring harmony among all sections of the community, and especially by dissuading your followers from all provocative or retaliatory speech or action.[180]

The Committee listened intently. Then in an impassioned oration Raymond Pognon said:

> It is not necessary nor right for me to give Captain Showers or the British authorities any assurances as they have already received these from the Governor, but I do assure the Governor on behalf of every member of the de Gaulle Committee of our complete and absolute loyal assistance—even unto death if necessary—in the observance and carrying out of the assurances he has given.[181]

The meeting ended with Harry Showers assuring the Committee that no Vichy warships were enroute to New Caledonia. From this point Harry decided to withdraw from the political discourse and remained clear of Government House. The only significant contribution still being made by *Adelaide* was providing a guard on the gangway of *Pierre Lotti* to keep good order until she sailed. During this denouement the Gunnery Officer of *Adelaide* inspected the forts to find the batteries in a useless state.

As a result of the successful Free French transition in Noumea the Australian Government resolved on 28 September that should *Dumont D'Urville* or *Admiral Charnier* approach New Caledonia 'naval and air action will be undertaken to intercept and immobilise these ships, using force if necessary'.[182]

For his part de Gaulle 'badgered' other Governors in the Pacific to emulate Sautot's exemplary example.[183] On 2 October General de Gaulle sent a congratulatory telegram to Henri Sautot which said:

> Thanks to your adroit and speedy handling, the operation has been effected without bloodshed. Please convey my congratulations to supporters of Free French Movement for their courage. Those four days will stand out in the history of Free French and New Caledonia.[184]

Three days latter *Adelaide* sailed out of Noumea harbour. Just prior to his departure Harry Showers received a letter from Monsieur Sautot which read:

> I have the pleasant task of expressing to you, your staff and your crew, the heartfelt gratitude of New Caledonia and that of her Chief, for the very effective support which you lent us towards consolidating the rallying of the colony to Free France.
>
> It is thanks to the presence of HMAS *Adelaide* that the political events of last September have taken place without any bloodshed, in accordance with the express recommendations which I received from General de Gaulle.
>
> Further I shall never be able to forget your fortunate intervention with regard to Capitaine de Frégate Toussaint de Quievrecourt, commanding the French sloop *Dumont D'Urville*, an intervention thanks to which this ship left Noumea without causing any trouble.
>
> As I said to you yesterday evening at Government House, the memory of your cooperation of HMAS *Adelaide* towards the rallying of New Caledonia to Free-France will remain in the history of this colony and will earn for you the gratitude of its population.[185]

At Sautot's request *Adelaide* left behind her 15-man guard in *Pierre Lotti* and the ship eventually sailed for Brisbane on 11 October.[186] Because of German raider action she was the sole remaining New Caledonian supply ship and so the passengers were transferred to *Tanda* for passage to Saigon. Fortuitously *Tanda*'s master was Captain MB Skinner who had long been a source of useful information for Rupert Long.[187]

The successful conclusion to the Noumea episode reflected well on both Harry Showers and the Navy. In his report, that was considered by the Australian Cabinet, Harry was fulsome in his praise for Blandy, Johnston, Ballard and his ship's company. He concluded by saying of Henri Sautot that he was a man for 'whose personal bravery I have the highest admiration'.[188]

For their part the Naval Board wrote of Harry Showers that they 'have noted with pleasure that he successfully carried out a difficult task with excellent judgement, tact and ability'.[189] The appreciation was also shared by the Department of External Affairs where the Secretary, Mr WR Hodgson wrote to his Navy Department counterpart that:

I was greatly struck with evidence of initiative, clear thinking, and decision of the Commanding Officer in most difficult and confusing circumstances.[190]

The events in Noumea harked back to gunboat diplomacy in the halcyon days of the British Empire when British Prime Minister Lord Palmerston reputedly said 'If I had a difficult bit of diplomacy on hand, I'd send for a naval officer'.[191]

IX

The next German raiders to pose a threat to Australian trade were *Atlantis* and *Pinguin*. On 20 September 1940 the French cargo-passenger ship *Commissaire Ramel* in mid-ocean reported being shelled. She was a victim of *Atlantis* and on 10 November the Norwegian tanker *Ole Jacob* suffered a similar fate after also sending a distress message. *Canberra* was a week out of Bombay having escorted another large troop convoy to that port[192] and was directed to join the search for the raider. The following day *Automedon* also reported being attacked. Although Harold Farncomb extensively used his embarked Walrus its air search proved fruitless. This was unfortunate because *Atlantis* had captured among *Automedon's* mail a pessimistic British classified report on Singapore defences that was to find its way to Tokyo.

In the wake of the unsuccessful *Automedon* search *Canberra* arrived at the entrance to Fremantle harbour at 6 am on 20 November. Harold Farncomb had his Walrus catapulted off to the nearby Maylands aerodrome as the ship entered port. At 5 pm the ship received a Raider Distress Message from the British refrigerated cargo ship *Maimoa*, 808 nautical miles to seaward of Fremantle. While awaiting orders, Harold recalled the ship's company from shore leave and raised steam. By 10.30 pm the cruiser sailed out of Fremantle leaving 80 sailors still ashore. As the ship closed *Maimoa's* last reported position *Canberra* received a further Raider Distress Message, this time from *Port Brisbane*. Her position was 285 nautical miles to the north west of *Maimoa*. Harold altered course towards the latest victim and passed to the south of *Maimoa's* position to account for any drift by lifeboats. At 7.30 am on 22 November lookouts sighted an empty lifeboat from *Maimoa*. She had been a victim not of *Atlantis* but *Pinguin* who had recovered all the crew. At dusk that day *Canberra* closed three lifeboats under sail with 27 crew including Second Officer EW Dingle of *Port Brisbane* onboard. The survivors were soon given food and *Canberra* sailors provided some of their clothes.

The attack on *Port Brisbane* was atypical. She had been initially sighted by *Storstad* who reported her presence to *Pinguin*. The raider closed *Port Brisbane* in the darkness and then in short order shone a searchlight on her and fired a warning shot. When Captain Ernst-Felix Krűder saw *Port Brisbane's* two 6-inch guns were being manned he opened fire on her at short range. The bridge, radio room and funnel were soon hit, killing the radio operator. Captain Steele in *Port Brisbane* ordered his men away from the guns to prevent further losses. Krűder embarked 61 of the crew including her sole woman passenger and then torpedoed the burning ship. *Pinguin* earlier in the day had picked up an Australian Broadcasting Commission (ABC) evening news report that the Minister for the Navy, Billy Hughes had stated in Parliament that *Canberra* was searching for the raider that sank *Maimoa*. On this basis Krűder elected not to loiter to look for the other lifeboats.[193]

The German raider attack on Port Brisbane *was atypical. Here is the ship in Victorian waters in happier times.*
(Green Collection/State Library of Victoria)

Second Officer Dingle said that *Pinguin* had steamed north west and for the next three days *Canberra* fruitlessly combed the area looking for the raider before returning to Fremantle. In a letter of thanks for *Canberra's* care for *Port Brisbane* survivors, Dingle told Harold Farncomb of his premonition that *Canberra* will have changed fortunes against the raiders and enjoy 'the success desired by all'.[194]

Meanwhile *Komet*, having replenished in Japan commenced her first foray in the South West Pacific. In October *Komet* rendezvoused with *Orion* and supply ship *Kulmerland* and the three captains decided to work together and concentrate on southern Pacific waters. They opted initially to attack the strategically important phosphate trade running out of Nauru. The main destinations for this phosphate were Australia and Japan.

Nauru was well-known to the Germans having been part of the German Marshall Islands Protectorate up to 1914. It was now a League of Nations mandate of Australia with Britain and New Zealand as co-trustees. The three Governments established the British Phosphate Commission which operated four ships for the phosphate trade as well as resupply to the island. The ships were *Triadic, Trisaster, Triona* and *Trienza*. There was no harbour and ships in suitable weather had to secure to buoys and load from cantilever jetties. Because of the absence of a large sheltered anchorage ships awaiting cargo would lie off the island.

By 6 December the three German ships were passing the Solomon Islands enroute to Nauru. The *Triona* was sighted and after a chase she was shelled and torpedoed with the loss of three of her crew. Critically, no distress signal had been sent. This sinking was just four days after John Curtin's urging for action against raiders at the War Advisory Council.

The following day the German ships closed Nauru. The plan was for the raiders to bombard the island's infrastructure but the unfavourable weather forced them to search for any ships off the island. They soon sighted *Triaster, Triadic* and the British steamer *Komata*. In addition, the Norwegian *Vinni* was just underway bound for New Zealand. One strange ship was sighted by the Harbour Master and Administrator but after discussion it was assumed to be a Japanese phosphate ship and no alarm given. It is likely they had sighted *Komet* which was still in her disguise as the *Manyo Maru*. It was a fateful decision and later that night *Vinni* became the first victim, sunk by *Komet*. The next day *Triadic* and *Triaster* were sunk in turn by *Orion*. *Triadic* had passengers embarked and one child was wounded in the action.[195] The escaping *Komata* met the same fate at the hands of *Komet*. From ashore smoke from *Triadic* and then *Komata* became visible.

At 10.48 am the Administrator signaled to the Naval Board of strange Japanese vessels and the fires seen in *Triadic*. The Naval Board quickly appreciated the situation and issued warnings to all shipping in the vicinity. There was however no warship to dispatch. *Canberra* was in the Indian Ocean, *Manoora* in Darwin and *Adelaide* in refit in Sydney. *Perth*'s absence was now keenly felt.

The fate of the other ships remained a mystery. Had they been sunk, captured or escaped the raiders? The answer came two weeks later. On the morning of 21 December the three German ships anchored off Emirau Island in the Bismarck Archipelago. They disembarked 496 of the crew and passengers from ten ships they had sunk.[196] Although Kapitän Eyssen was comfortable to land all prisoners, Kapitän Weyher in *Orion* was concerned about the information the European and Australian crews could provide to the Allies. He therefore retained these men onboard for eventual internment in Germany. Unknown to the Germans there was a coastwatcher on Emirau but fortunately for them he was still awaiting a teleradio.[197]

On offloading the sailors the three ships went their separate ways - *Orion* to the Caroline Islands for maintenance, *Komet* to Rabaul where she was to mine its approaches and *Kulmerland* to Japan for resupply. Before leaving Emirau, Eyssen left a sailing boat for the survivors so that a call for help could be sent to Kavieng—70 miles distant. Eyssen did not want news of the landing to get out before his ship had a chance to mine off Rabaul. He demanded a promise from the survivors to wait 24 hours before setting off. Eyssen's plans were soon to go awry. The Emirau plantation manager organised local men to canoe to nearby Mussau Island where Pastor Arthur

Atkins had a motor boat. Four men led by the Chief Officer of *Rangitane* reached John Merrylees, the District Officer at Kavieng, in the early hours of 24 December. By noon the news had reached Port Moresby and thence relayed to Melbourne. Eyssen had been hoping to have completed his mining operation by that time, but unfortunately for him the operation had to be aborted when *Komet's* minelaying boat became unserviceable.

In Navy Office the report of the landing of survivors energised a staff otherwise hopeful of a quiet Christmas Day on the morrow. Rupert Long directed Hugh MacKenzie in Port Moresby to Emirau to glean vital intelligence and decide who should be sent to Melbourne for further interview. Hugh took the journey by seaplane along with a doctor and essential supplies. Another aircraft was sent to Rabaul to fetch another doctor and the Administrator. The 7,000 tonne cargo/passenger ship *Nellore* in port at Rabaul was ordered to sail for Emirau. Hugh hoped to be able to delay *Nellore's* sailing until an aerial sweep had ensured the raiders had cleared the area. This was prudent as *Nellore's* sailing order had been read by Eyssen courtesy of captured merchant codes.[198] After an overnight stop in Rabaul, Hugh was able to intercept *Nellore* and divert her to Kavieng. Unfortunately, the seaplane was damaged when landing and he was delayed while repairs were effected.

The sinking of phosphate carrier Triona *was a prelude to a coordinated attack by German raiders off Nauru which resulted in four other sinkings.*
(Green Collection/State Library of Victoria)

An air sweep of the area revealed an empty ocean and by the afternoon of Christmas Day the seaplane arrived to find the steamships *Shamrock* and *Leander* had already reached Emirau. Among those marooned was Chief Officer Hopkins of *Rangitane* who warned of a possible attack on Nauru. Indeed *Komet* did return on 27 December to bombard the island's infrastructure.

Hugh MacKenzie began a series of interviews to piece together which ships had been sunk, the identity of the raiders, their characteristics and possible plans. There was a large amount of conflicting information and Hugh used his professional experience to try to synthesise a coherent picture of the raider operations. He was acutely conscious that time was of the essence. The following evening he sent six mariners to Port Moresby by flying boat for eventual interview by Rupert Long in Melbourne. Along with these men were two rolls of film which contained pictures of the three German ships at anchor. A sailor also had a postcard of *Kulmerland* which confirmed her identity. On 30 December the mariners reached Melbourne for their interview with Rupert and his staff. The following day Hugh had finished his final interviews at Emirau. This combined set of interviews revealed the fates of *Notou*, *Holmwood*, *Ringwood* and *Turakina*. It also confirmed that the Germans had captured two Mercantile codes. This information was passed on to an Admiralty eager for news.

The sinkings off Nauru were unprecedented in the history of raider operations in both world wars and demonstrated the threat from coordinated operations. The German raiders had by Christmas 1940 sunk or captured 34 merchantmen in the Pacific and Indian Oceans with the loss of nearly 100 men, women and children. Strategically, it had resulted in periodic disruptions to shipping routes, not to mention the loss of valuable materiel for the war effort. While John Curtin in Parliament and officers such as Rupert Long in Navy Office were alive to the magnitude of the threat, there appeared an unwillingness to change strategy or allocate more warships to the task.

The raider campaign escalated as Germany's most potent raider, the pocket battleship *Admiral Scheer*, entered the Indian Ocean on

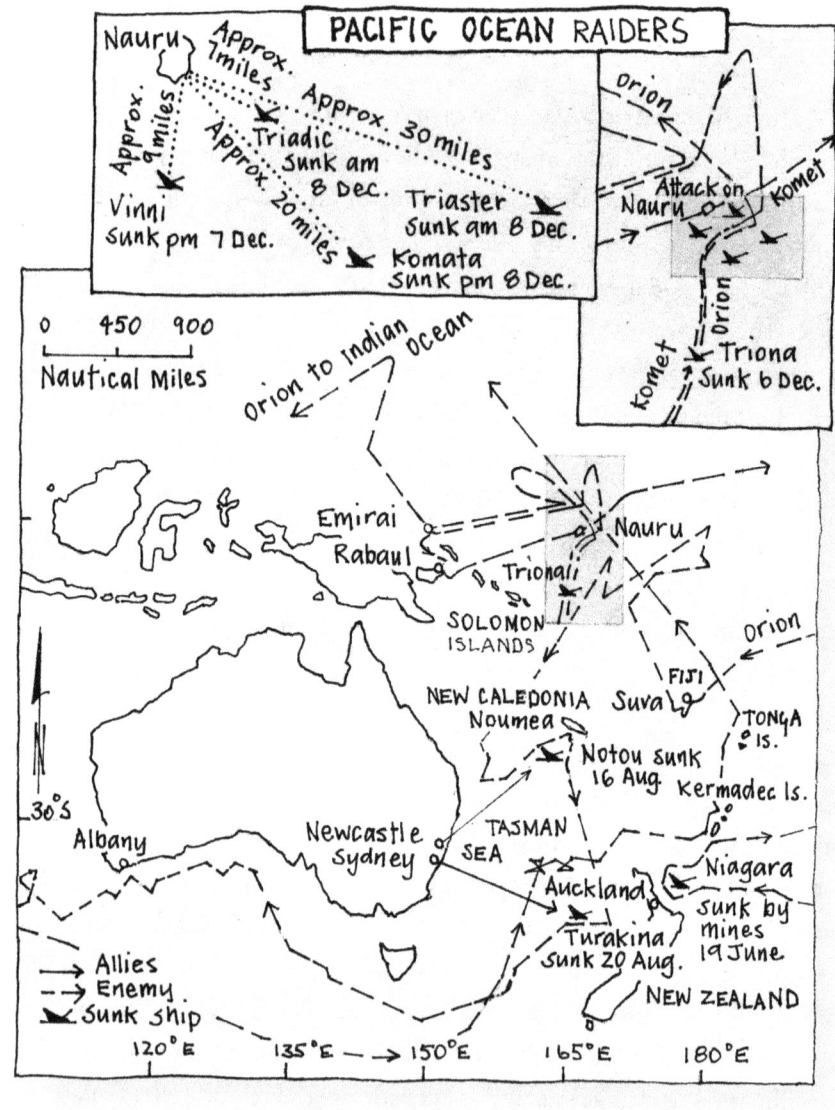

14 February. 1,000 miles east of Madagascar she rendezvoused with *Atlantis* and the captured vessels *Speybank, Ketty Brøvig* and the supply ship *Tennenfels*. *Ketty Brøvig* was a Norwegian tanker that had been taken by *Atlantis* only a fortnight earlier. She was quickly brought alongside the battleship to top up the latter's bunkers.

On the 21 February the steamship *Canadian Cruiser* reported being attacked by a German warship and the Commander-in-Chief East Indies, Admiral Leatham directed the cruisers *Emerald, Hawkins, Capetown* and *Glasgow* to join the hunt. On 22 February a Walrus from *Glasgow* located *Admiral Scheer* 300 miles to the south east of *Canadian Cruiser's* last position. At this point *Canberra*, who had just handed a convoy over to HMS *Leander* off Colombo, was directed to join the operation. The search, now also involving *Australia* which had been escorting a South Atlantic convoy, lasted for four days. After this time it was clear that *Admiral Scheer* had escaped the dragnet.

But luck was about to turn. On 27 February *Leander*, steaming west of the Maldives, closed and challenged a merchant vessel. At a range of just 3,000 yards the vessel hoisted the Italian naval ensign and opened fire with her two 4.7-inch guns on *Leander*. Fortunately for the cruiser the opening salvo missed and *Leander* replied with five devastating salvoes that caused extensive fires and her foe to sink. The ship was the newly converted Italian raider *Ramb I* which was about to commence a foray off the Dutch East Indies.

Canberra now joined *Leander* and they conducted a dispersed but coordinated search of the ocean between the Seychelles and the Chagos Archipelago for any other raiders. On the morning of 4 March *Canberra's* Walrus was catapulted off to search the sea near Saha De Malha Bank. At 11.28 am the lookout from the masthead sighted smoke on the horizon and then two masts and a funnel. *Canberra* closed the mystery ship at 25 knots. Soon Lieutenant Claud Malleson in the Walrus was reporting that there were in fact two ships. At 11.50 am the aircrew reported the ships were an armed raider and a tanker in company. About this time the two ships separated with the tanker steaming south and the 'raider' to the north. Harold Farncomb ordered the tanker to alter course to the north and the 'raider' to stop. These signals were ignored and at 12.05 pm *Canberra* fired a warning shot across the bows of the 'raider' who was then about 21,000 yards distant. With no sign of heeding the warning, Harold ordered his gunnery officer Lieutenant Commander Donald Hole to engage the 'raider'. He elected to keep outside the range of the possible 5.9-inch guns, the standard fit of a German raider. The absence of any reply from the 'raider' did not surprise Harold who later wrote:

> I considered that this was due to the fact that we were outside his maximum range, I also thought it possible that he would withhold his fire in the hope that HMAS *Canberra* would close and present a favourable torpedo target. HMAS *Canberra* was therefore manoeuvred to keep the range over 19,000 yards.[199]

As John Collins found in the Mediterranean, the down-side of this tactic was the small number of hits on a target at this range. By 12.16 pm however the 'raider' was on fire. Five minutes later the Walrus, which had dropped bombs in the wake of the tanker, reported an explosion from her and she was now slowly sinking. Harold kept his distance from the 'raider' lest *Canberra* be torpedoed and instead closed the sinking tanker. An enterprising Malleson had the pilot land the Walrus near the stricken ship. Malleson stripped and swam to the ship to assess its condition. He later wrote:

> I regret that the sensible course of using the rubber dinghy did not occur to me, and for my own peace of mind I did not see the several sharks that were cruising round until I was safely back in the aircraft.[200]

On the basis of Malleson's report that the tanker might be able to be saved a boarding party was put onboard and set to work. The boarding party however, found the engine room flooded with scalding water from the boilers and the ship increasingly taking water. It was just a matter of time before both ships sank with the tanker assisted by some 4-inch rounds from *Canberra*.

Meanwhile as dusk settled *Leander* arrived on the scene and attended to the sinking 'raider'. The cruisers recovered German, Norwegian and Chinese sailors as well as an array of documents from both ships.

The sinking of Ketty Brøvig.
(*The Argus*/State Library of Victoria)

The true identity of both ships were soon revealed. The 'raider' was the German supply ship *Coburg* and the tanker was *Ketty Brøvig*. They had been ordered by German Naval High Command to rendezvous with the raider *Pinguin* and support her in mining operations off Australia. The interception was a major blow to the German raider campaign.

During the brief action *Canberra* had fired 215 rounds of 8-inch ammunition. This expenditure earned the admonition of Admiral Leatham who wrote critically of Harold's tactics:

> It was correct that *Canberra* should have taken precautions against the possibility of the supposed raider firing torpedoes, but I think it was being over cautious to avoid approaching nearer than 19,000 yards on this account. Had a more effective range been attained quickly the enemy might have been identified sooner and much ammunition saved.[201]

This letter was sent to Navy Office and the Flag Officer Commanding the Australian Squadron. This criticism from the vantage point of both hindsight and a desk ashore was unfair. It failed to acknowledge that the Walrus had identified *Coburg* as a raider. More significantly the high expenditure of ammunition was a worthwhile cost compared to the risk to a warship getting too close. Leatham underestimated the lethality of German raiders. They were superior for instance to the British Armed

Merchant Cruisers as the three defeats of British AMCs by the German *Thor* attested. The last of which resulted in the sinking of HMS *Voltaire* and had occurred only the previous month.[202] In contrast Leatham praised *Leander* 'for ridding the seas of a potential menace to shipping before it had time to do any harm'.[203] It is unclear whether Leatham knew how close *Leander* came to disaster in the battle with the less formidable *Ramb I*. Importantly, the letter regarding *Canberra's* actions sent the wrong message to cruiser captains in any such future meeting at sea.

The dangers of the German raider were further reinforced in the western Indian Ocean on 8 May when the heavy cruiser HMS *Cornwall* closed a suspect ship detected by her aircraft. The ship identified herself as the Norwegian *Tamerlane*. The cruiser ordered the ship to heave to or she would fire. When they were 19,000 yards apart *Cornwall* fired a warning shot. The distance closed however to 12,000 yards and the suspect ship, which was the raider *Pinguin* opened fire on *Cornwall*. In the initial minutes of the engagement the cruiser had a power failure and then suffered two hits which disabled her primary steering gear and started a small fire. Fortunately for *Cornwall* she was able to use her speed to open the range and rectify deficiencies before resuming the battle. In the ensuing engagement, which lasted 30 minutes and with nearly 350 rounds expended, the raider received a catastrophic hit in her sea mine magazine. This led to a massive explosion and heavy loss of life of both the Germans and their prisoners. While Harold Farncomb was criticised by Leatham for not getting close enough, Captain PCW Mainwaring, RN in *Cornwall* was chided by the Admiralty for getting too close. Specifically, in their analysis of the engagement the Admiralty highlighted Mainwaring's lack of attention to the changing situation and 'for holding on to the idea that the suspect might still prove a friendly neutral although in view of her suspicious behaviour all the evidence was very much against it'.[204]

Pinguin and *Ramb I* had shown that Axis raiders were a dangerous adversary that if cornered were well prepared to trade blows with cruisers.

X

Cyril Sadleir served at the Flinders Naval Depot from the outbreak of the war as a divisional officer for initial trainees. A very popular and smartly presented officer, Cyril continued to struggle in his duties due to his still undiagnosed multiple sclerosis. By July 1941 it was considered that his 'defective memory' was such that he was no longer suitable for training.[205] Cyril was posted as Officer-in-Charge of the War Signal Station first to Cape Otway and then at Wilson's Promontory.

Another of the Pioneer Class to rejoin the Navy was George Armitage who left his position at the Taxation Office in July 1941. After a short period at Flinders Naval Depot he became the Extended Defence Officer and Chief Examining Officer at Port Phillip responsible for the challenging of all shipping coming into the Port of Melbourne. Based at Queenscliff and somewhat removed from the other naval facilities in the area, George once again struggled in his duties with there being a 'suspicion of intemperance'.[206] After an inspection by the District Naval Officer he was posted to the naval operations staff in Brisbane but now under a three monthly reporting regime.[207]

In contrast to the exploits of the serving members of the Pioneer Class, those four not in uniform contributed in other ways to society. Jack Lecky ran his store in Merredin while Leigh Watkins had resumed his work as a refrigeration engineer after his early call-up to the Navy.

Ben Howells had progressed in the teaching profession and was now Senior English Instructor at the Footscray Technical School. He found that the institution, founded in 1916, was still under the leadership of its inaugural Principal Charles Hoadley. This charismatic figure had, like Ben's instructor at the Naval College, Morton Moyes, particpated in Mawson's Australasian Antarctic Expedition. Under Hoadley's leadership Footscray became the largest diploma teaching school in the Victorian education system. The school was an environment where Ben was allowed to innovate, such as his course on report-writing to better prepare students

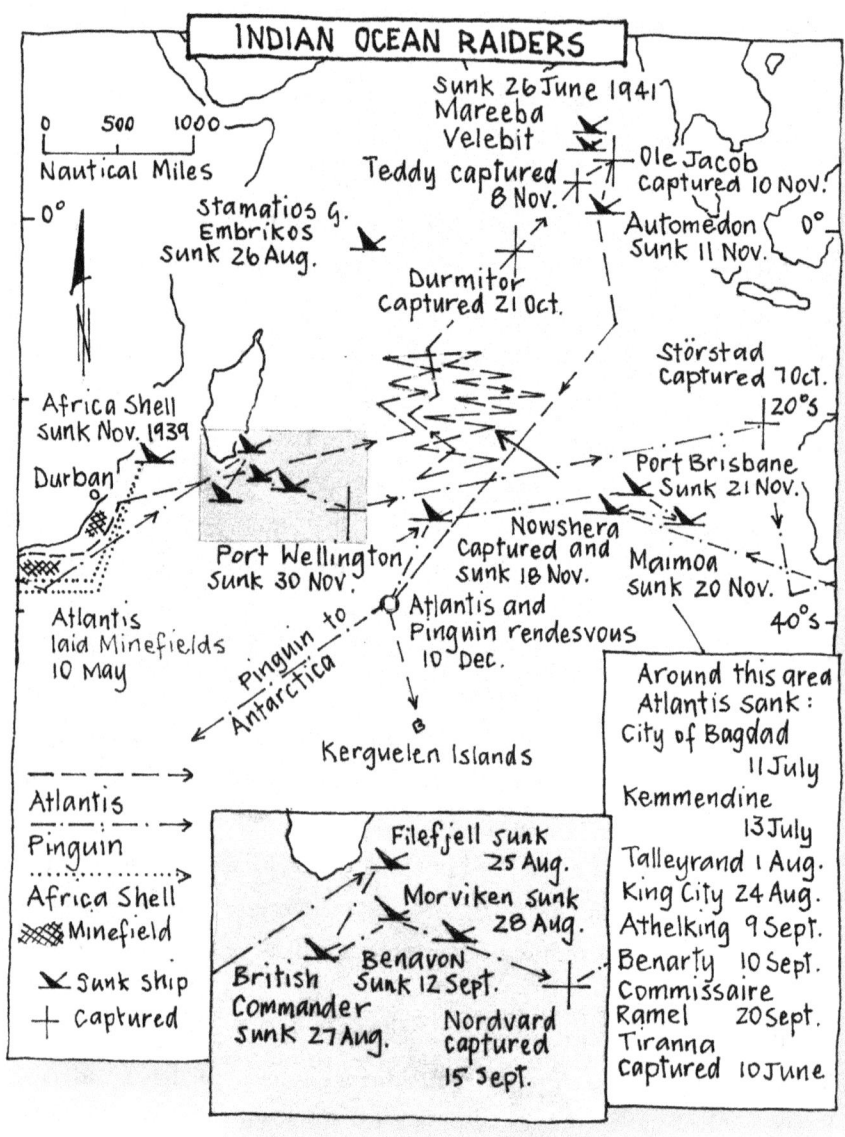

for industry. During the war he also taught at night school and gave words of encouragement to those wishing to join the Services.

Three innovations Ben introduced were a Tramping Club, the school's first concerts and, following the example of Duncan Grant, he founded and edited the school magazine - *Blue and Gold*. In his 1941 editorial he explained the rationale for founding the magazine in war time and wrote:

> We live in stirring times which for future generations will be fraught with the same deep interest which the days of Drake and the Armada, for instance, hold for us. Therefore, any new venture launched by us now must possess for future students of this school, a special value and must materially contribute to the building up of a worthy school tradition. For when our nation emerges victorious from this war and the school achieves stability there will be preserved successive issues of this magazine, a record of the war activities of our school and its old boys and of our reactions to these momentous times which should be a source of pride and inspiration for those who follow after.[208]

Ben also promoted rugby at Footscray and in 1941 his school team played the Naval College at Flinders Naval Depot with the cadet midshipmen narrowly winning 17 to 16.

Like his friend Ben Howells, Peyton Kimlin continued teaching. He also maintained his involvement in the Sydney music scene. The latter extended to ballet and an association with what is now called the First Australian Ballet. The company was established in 1931 by Louise Lightfoot and the remarkable Ukrainian-born Mischa Burlakov who was once a soldier in the Tsarist Army. On 5 June 1940 the ballet company performed at Burlakov's studio near Circular Quay a performance of one Australia's early ballets—*Billabong*[209]. Peyton Kimlin wrote *Billabong's* score while his wife Myra wrote the scenario and designed the costumes and staging. The choreography was by Burlakov.[210] Peyton then worked on an 'Egyptian' ballet with excerpts first performed at a First Australian Ballet performance at the East Sydney Technical College in September. A fuller version was performed as *Pharon Son of Egypt* by the Ballet at the NSW Conservatorium of Music on 15 December 1941.[211] This was to mark the beginning of Peyton's long association with the Conservatorium.[212]

XI

Among the array of defensive measures that could be employed by the Navy, there was one that had yet to be embarked upon. That was to lay defensive minefields. These could either be laid in the approaches to strategic ports or further afield at the entrance to straits and passages that ships must transit such as in the Great Barrier Reef or the South West Pacific. Each mine could be laid in position with a 'sinker' which would anchor it to the bottom. Inside the sinker a mooring wire would unwind to a length as determined by the depth mechanism. The desired depth could be calculated taking into account the depth of water and the desired target for the mine be it a submerged submarine, a large ship sitting lower in the water or a smaller vessel drawing less water. For Allied ships to navigate in a mined area, mines had to be sown in a precise pattern and classified safe routes through the minefield promulgated.

In September 1940 the War Cabinet approved a strategy to manufacture sea mines for the first time in Australia, convert a merchant ship into a minelayer and lay a series of defensive minefields in Australian and South West Pacific waters.[213] The mines would be produced to an Admiralty design at the Ford Motor Plant in Geelong with an initial batch of 500 units. The ship selected for minelaying was the three-year old 3,000 tonne coastal freighter *Bungaree*. Her commissioning Commanding Officer was Norman Calder who joined her at Garden Island on 3 November 1940 where she was still fitting out. There were six months of modification work before commissioning. Earlier in the year Norman had been made an Acting Commander and he was to prove an ideal choice for command of HMAS *Bungaree* for a number of reasons, including his abiding interest in betting.

Norman found that *Bungaree* was a spacious 'shelter deck' ship well suited to her new role. The shelter deck, which was one deck below the main deck, ran unobstructed for the length of the ship. It was here that 250 mines on wheels could be accommodated on four sets of mine rails that were being welded in place. Like a railway there were junction points to allow the combined mine and its sinker go out one of two mine chutes being cut into the stern of the ship. An additional 173 mines could be stored in the holds. *Bungaree* did have her limitations, chief among them was a slow coal fired reciprocating engine with only one propeller. Norman's memories of coaling in the Grand Fleet came to the fore, but more significantly *Bungaree* would not be a particularly manoeuvrable ship when minelaying.

The ship's name recalled the nineteenth century intrepid Aboriginal elder 'King' Bungaree who among other exploits accompanied and aided Matthew Flinders on his explorations around Australia. Norman quickly realised that precise navigation was to be critical in laying the defensive minefields. As the Navy's hydrographic service had suspended much of its activities, Norman was able to acquire some survey motor launches to augment his ship's boats. His commissioning navigating officer was Lieutenant Commander D'Arcy 'Tommy' Gale, a H2 surveyor who had come from *Adelaide* where he had been a most valued navigating officer to Harry Showers.[214]

Bungaree's complement of 13 officers and 250 sailors was a mix of permanent service and reservists. Fortunately, they included men who had served in the ship when she was operated by the Adelaide Steamship Company. Prime among them was Engineer Lieutenant Commander Bernard Brodie who had stood by the ship building in Scotland. At 53-years old he was the oldest man onboard. Equally important to Norman was the mine laying team on the shelter deck. They had a core of permanent navy torpedo specialist sailors for this was demanding and dangerous work to both sailor and ship. They were ably led by the conscientious and hardworking Commissioned Gunner (T) Henry Jeffries on loan from the RN. Norman was well pleased with his ship's company, but like Frank Getting in *Kanimbla*, he approached sea command with a detached manner from his men. This was Norman's natural style and he later wrote 'my nature does not permit close familiarity with really anyone'.[215] As in *Kanimbla*, naval discipline rankled with some new to the Navy and for a time they gave *Bungaree* the monicker '*Altmark*' after the recently intercepted German prison ship.

While *Bungaree* was fitting out Norman sought expertise on where and how to lay minefields. His initial port of call was Navy Office where he learnt the first field had to be laid off Port Moresby but the precise planning would be left to him. While Norman had received some mining training in his Long Torpedo Course, he thought his practical understanding of the odds at the racetrack might be more useful. He wrote:

> To ascertain whether a minefield was worthwhile from the physical deterrent angle (quite separate from the strategic value) involved primarily that of probabilities. I had a bit of a reputation as a bit of a gambler (inclined to bet on anything) and hence had some practical knowledge of the meaning of the word probability.[216]

Also finding the Admiralty *Mining Manual* thin in its guidance, Norman called on the mathematicians at the University of Sydney. In particular, Norman was seeking guidance on how to develop the ideal mining patterns. He recalled:

> I had hoped to be given an equation or formula, a child's guide where one just had to substitute accepted figures for symbols, and presto, we had the best pattern to use and the probability of success. What I got back was a tome, about half an inch thick, which after reading made my confusion... A grand effort on the part of the university, and much appreciated, but a mass of equations and figures too abstruse for the simple sailor. I tried it out on other people but received no enlightenment, so I knew it had to be me to go about it to the best of my ability. I used up lots of squared paper drawing rows of mines at various depths and spacing. I must have reached some answers but in many cases it was hit or miss.[217]

On 9 June 1941 *Bungaree* commissioned at Garden Island and sailed for Port Phillip Bay for the purpose of training and embarking the first outfit of mines. After production of each batch of mines at the Ford plant they were shipped by rail 32 kilometres to the old ammunition depot on Swan Island. There the Naval Ordnance and Inspection Branch would complete a final inspection and store the mines awaiting *Bungaree's* arrival. The mines would then be shipped once more by rail to Geelong where they were loaded in an exacting and measured manner onboard *Bungaree*, not by wharfies but by the ship's sailors. Such was the quality of production and the stringent inspection regime Eddy Nurse had instituted that Norman Calder rated the mines as 'almost perfect specimens' that were superior to the UK produced mines.[218]

Norman Calder was well familiar with Port Phillip Bay from his time in the J class submarines. Its relatively sheltered confines were ideal for practicing mining and other drills. After embarking a practice load out Norman commenced the minelaying training and general drills. Once the ship's company was up to Norman's standard *Bungaree* took on her first outfit.

Although Japan had yet to enter the war a defensive minefield off Port Moresby was to be *Bungaree's* first assignment to be followed by Torres Strait and then a series off the various passages in and out of the Great Barrier Reef. *Bungaree* arrived in Port Moresby on 13 August 1941. Whilst *Bungaree* had been fitting out prior to commissioning Norman flew to Port Moresby to help plan the minefield. On arrival in Port Moresby Norman was flown over the prospective minefield in a RAAF Catalina aircraft.

Norman Calder was the first Commanding Officer of HMAS Bungaree. Here the ship is in Sydney Harbour. (RAN)

The reconnaissance proved worthwhile and *Bungaree's* first minelay was undertaken without incident. An observer's view of *Bungaree* at her deadly work belied what was going on in the mining deck. Norman later wrote:

> Once minelaying began, the noise on the mining deck was shattering and awe inspiring with the wires singing under the strain and although the rails had been greased the sinkers with their four rollers prevented anyone hearing anybody else except by shouting into the ear itself. The crew of the mining deck had to be so well trained that each man knew exactly what to do without being told and be on the alert for possible 'foul-ups'.[219]

After each field was laid *Bungaree* would return to Sydney for maintenance and short leave and then sail down to Geelong for another mineload. *Bungaree's* slow speed gave the Ford factory and Swan Island time to manufacture and assemble the next batch of mines.

After the success of the New Guinea minelay, *Bungaree* was ordered to mine various passages along the Great Barrier Reef that allowed ships to pass through the reef from the Coral Sea. As always precision in navigation was required and Norman's acquisition of the survey boat proved useful as the charts still bore the surveys of Captain Matthew Flinders from 1802.

The work in the Great Barrier Reef was interrupted by an order to lay two fields in New Caledonian waters. Prior to sailing from Sydney the ship's company had to be inoculated against plague and when Norman informed his medical officer of the task, which required to be commenced that day for it to be effective, he found him 'rather 'full' which I was later to find out was the rule rather than the exception'.[220] Norman therefore tasked the inoculation to the senior Sick Berth attendant and confined the medical officer to his cabin for the voyage rationing him to two whiskies a day. At the first opportunity Norman replaced his doctor.

Such was the importance of this minelaying task that *Bungaree* was escorted by the armed merchant cruiser *Manoora*. On arrival in Noumea Norman Calder called on the Governor Henri Sautot who after Harry Showers' efforts in *Adelaide* was very welcoming. The ship arrived during mardi gras. After months of mundane sea time, the warmth of the day, the local hospitality combined with the powerfully unfamiliar spirit absinthe available in the many cafes resulted in a memorable if chaotic run ashore for *Bungaree* sailors. Their raucous return up the gangway which was located just outside the Captain's cabin coincided with the Governor's visit onboard to sample Australian champagne. Prior to *Bungaree's* departure for the minelay Norman once again took a RAAF Catalina flight to survey the prospective minelay area. This was in the northern approaches to the islands with the target for the minefields being any submarines wanting to attack shipping entering Noumea.

Bungaree's New Caledonian minefield would be followed by further fields in the Great Barrier Reef and in New Zealand. All the time the production in Geelong was gathering pace and the output, under the watchful eye of Eddy Nurse and his team, eventually reached 3,000 mines a year. *Bungaree* and Eddy's Branch formed a strong bond as the minelayer returned time again for another load of this sinister and lethal weapon.

XII

By early 1941 it was clear that the war would be protracted and in the Pacific the outlook was bleak as tensions grew with an increasingly bellicose Japan. The sinews of Australia's modest war production were growing and the Australian Squadron was steadily expanding.

In April 1941, after ten years ashore, Paul Hirst was to once again to command at sea, this time one of the new corvettes that John Collins and James Esdaile had been so instrumental in developing. Before doing so he returned the family to *Ashbourne*. Their return was reported in the front page of the *Launceston Examiner*.[221] Eve would go on to run the property with the help of Italian prisoners-of-war. Paul initially joined the sloop *Warrego* to get back his sea legs. He had arranged this with her captain, his old friend from the Naval College and son of Dr. Wheatley, Commander Ross Wheatley. Paul was to command the new corvette HMAS *Toowoomba* then building at Walkers shipyard at Maryborough, Queensland. After a couple of weeks of anti-submarine training at HMAS *Rushcutter* on Sydney Harbour, Paul stood by the ship at the shipyard with his growing crew.

The sixty *Bathurst* class corvettes were without doubt the Navy's most successful and significant local shipbuilding program. At just 56 metres in length and 965 tonnes, the designers were mindful of the modest industrial base upon which the ships were to be built and maintained. The simple and reliable reciprocating engines for example could be built by engineering firms with little marine experience. With a crew of 70 sailors, mostly new to the sea, the corvettes were to prove themselves as extremely versatile. They could escort merchant ships, conduct hydrographic surveys, sweep for mines and even support the army with shore bombardment from their single 4-inch gun. Beloved by their crews, the corvettes were invariably tight knit and ready for whatever duty would come their way. Paul Hirst was only one of a handful of commissioning commanding officers of the corvettes who had permanent navy experience. Initial concerns by his crew that he would be a martinet were quickly dispelled and his personable demeanour combined with his professional competence quickly instilled confidence and pride.

XIII

One of the most important aspects of Jack Newman's work in establishing robust naval communications was to create a pool of skilled officers and sailors for the much expanded network. In this he had the great good fortune to meet the formidable Mrs Florence Violet McKenzie who founded and led the Electrical Association for Women. Australia's first female electrical engineer, 'Mrs Mac' as she was universally known, had in 1939 established the Women's Emergency Signalling Corps (WESC). At her classrooms at 10 Clarence Street, Sydney Mrs Mac provided free training in telegraphic and visual signalling to women and by the start of the war had 120 graduates.

In 1940 Mrs Mac had written to Billy Hughes, who was then the Minister for the Navy, offering the 'services of our Signalling Corps, if not acceptable as telegraphists then at least as instructors.'[222] She followed the letter with a visit to Navy Office and the Naval Board agreed to send an officer to test the skills of WESC members. In January 1941 Jack Newman visited WESC and found the women in their smart green WESC uniforms 'almost as good as the men, in fact'.[223] He recommended that they join the Navy. Over the next three months Jack waged a paper war within the Navy to have the Women's Royal Australian Naval Service (WRANS) established. This was realised on 21 April 1941 and the following week twelve WESC telegraphists and two other WESC telegraphists to serve as cooks arrived at HMAS *Harman*. They were accompanied by the protective Mrs Mac and attired in their WESC uniforms. It would be four months before the RAN could provide a naval uniform. This notable event in the Navy's history went unreported on Hughes' direction that no publicity be accorded this break with tradition.

In June the first two WRANS sailors arrived in Melbourne. Their growing numbers would bolster and expand not only Navy Office but also the fledgling communications interception capabilities. As at *Harman* the welcome on the ground was less than helpful and once again Mrs Mac was on hand to right matters. In this case the designated accommodation was unsuitable and on a typical cold and wet winter Melbourne night she found accommodation at the Travellers' Aid Society. It became a most welcoming home for two months. For his part Jack Newman lent money to the young women sailors who had yet to be paid and organised proper accommodation to be provided. He and Lieutenant Commander John Brame created a roster for officers and their wives to entertain the young women. One young WRANS sailor reminisced:

> We hiked all over Melbourne with 'The Boss' viewing beautiful parks and various other places of interest. Lieutenant Commander and Mrs Brame used to entertain us at dinner in their flat—some wonderful times were spent with them.[224]

In addition to the growing numbers of female officers and sailors in Melbourne their male counterparts also became more numerous. Although the women were always welcome in leading Melbourne hotels and dance halls some refused male sailors admittance on the grounds because their uniform did not have a tie. This incensed Rupert Long who took it upon himself to intervene. He sent some of his men to investigate and then wrote in protest.[225] On a more positive note, a Royal Australian Naval Patriotic Committee was established under the chairmanship of ship owner Mr David York Syme[226] with John Collins' brother Reg, as Honorary Secretary.[227] Through their efforts a Navy House was opened in October 1940 where sailors could obtain bed and breakfast for one shilling and sixpence and dinner for ninepence.[228]

The WRANS made a tremendous contribution to the war effort and by 1945 they represented 10% of the Navy's personnel strength. Jack Newman remained their champion. A young WRAN 'Billie' Donoghue later recalled:

> Commander Newman's shrewd perspicacity, practical open-mindedness and immense zeal, in his capacity of Director of Naval Communications, spawned the 'enfant terrible' of the old salts—the WRANS.[229]

To many members of the WRANS, Jack Newman was intimidating. Jo Miller wrote of Jack as being 'awesome, a stern disciplinarian, with a keen intelligence, sharp wit, and a reluctance to suffer fools gladly—none-the-less having a deep concern for the welfare of his WRANS and pride in them'.[230] Jack, in a wartime interview, told a journalist:

> I have the honour of having persuaded the Naval Board that the WRANS would help us to a great extent. My conviction has been more than justified. They have proved themselves reliable, zealous, intelligent and well-behaved. In fact, their work is beyond all praise, I don't know how we would get along without them.[231]

Jack was to become known to that first generation of WRANS as the 'father of the WRANS'. The 'mother' was no doubt Mrs Mac. Once the WRANS were established she continued to train and mentor her young charges who would fill its ranks. In later years she became the much loved Patron of the Ex-WRANS Association and would remain so until her passing in 1982 at the age of 92.

XIV

By early 1940 the Japanese Government, after nearly three years of war in China, was calculating whether to chance its arm on military operations a much grander scale. The immediate objective would be to secure vital resources for the nation's economy. In April 1940 the Japanese Navy received increased readiness orders for a possible attack on the Dutch East Indies.[232] On 22 September 1940 Japanese forces invaded the weakened Vichy French Indo-China. This now put Malaya and Singapore within range of Japanese land-based bombers.

As previously described the British strategy in the Pacific was for Singapore to be a forward bastion and for British and Commonwealth forces to hold the line until superior forces arrived to win the campaign. While in the early 1930s the vulnerability to carrier based air attack was keenly appreciated, as was the need for strong submarine and land-based air forces, the competing demands of other theatres and an underestimation of Japanese military capabilities led to totally inadequate defences. The only area where there was some British strength was land forces but these alone could not stem any Japanese onslaught.

At the time of the fall of France Winston Churchill attempted to assure the Australian and New Zealand governments that Singapore, while under strength, could be defended. The concept was that a small battleship or battlecruiser force along with a fast aircraft carrier would be the kernel around which Dominion and British cruisers and destroyer would concentrate. Even if this force did materialise it would likely be outclassed by the Japanese Fleet which included by 1940 ten battleships, eight aircraft carriers, a dozen heavy cruisers and over seventy submarines.[233]

Since 1939 there had been a series of conferences in Singapore, London and in Washington on Pacific security involving Australia, Britain, the Netherlands and the US. In August 1940 the hard-pressed British even floated the idea with the Americans of basing the US Asiatic

Fleet in Singapore. The prospect of defending a bastion of the British Empire was not appealing to the US.[234]

At a number of the Singapore conferences members of the Pioneer Class attended or led the delegations. Joe Burnett attended as the naval representative at the Singapore Conference in October 1940 in which he gained support for an Australian cryptanalysis capability. It was at this conference that Australia was requested to provide an army brigade for Singapore's defence.[235] Joe later observed to Admiral Colvin that the British were 'interested in any suggestion for making good their own local deficiencies but rather uninterested in Australian and New Zealand naval activities'.[236] Joe also detected a resentment on the part of civil authorities in Singapore towards the military efforts to make Singapore a fortress. In addition, the officials in Malaya were fixated on tin and rubber production at the expense of defence preparations. In summary, he thought that 'it is most disquieting to find a state of affairs this far removed from what was expected at the Empire's main naval base in the Far East'.[237]

Prime Minister Menzies was alarmed by the report from the Singapore Conference and so briefed the Advisory War Council on 25 November. It was agreed at this meeting that Menzies should fly to London to talk to Churchill. Menzies later wrote:

> The whole reason why I went to England was to discuss the Japanese menace and to urge the strengthening of the defences of Singapore!
>
> Our own military advice was that while Singapore was a well-equipped British naval base, it had no capital ships or carriers, and grossly inadequate air defence. Figuratively, and perhaps literally, its guns pointed in the wrong direction. The whole establishment was unfitted to repel a Japanese attack, either amphibiously or by land.[238]

Menzies' concern about the Japanese threat was well placed but the latter were yet to commit themselves. In March 1941 Hitler was briefed by Grand Admiral Eric Raeder that the Japanese were unlikely to strike at Singapore until Germany had invaded Britain.

This hesitation frustrated the Germans, who like Britain attached an over-inflated sense of importance to Singapore. Raeder's brief continued:

> If Japan holds Singapore, all other Far Eastern questions in connection with the USA and Britain will be solved, including Guam, the Philippines, Borneo and the Dutch East Indies. Japan wants to avoid war with the USA if possible, and she could do this if she could take Singapore by a decisive attack as soon as possible.[239]

In December Menzies wrote to Churchill seeking naval reinforcements for Singapore. In reply Churchill explained this was not possible due to increased German naval strength and without ruining the situation in the Mediterranean. Part of Churchill's calculus was the likelihood of further Japanese aggression had not increased.[240] Menzies was not comforted by this assurance and on 24 January 1941 left for London by flying boat. The aircraft stopped in Batavia and Singapore where Menzies had discussions with key officials. While impressed with the 'clear-headed' Dutch Governor General Jonkheer Alidius van Starkenborgh Stackouwer, he was less so with the British Commander-in-Chief Far East, Air Chief Marshal Sir Alan Brooke-Popham.[241] In his other discussions with the military leadership in Singapore, Menzies wrote, 'I got no impression that they were aware of the realities of their position'.[242] Following his talks, Menzies directed that senior level talks must take place as soon as practicable.[243] That night he wrote:

> We must as soon as possible tell Japan 'where she gets off'. Appeasement is no good. The peg must be driven somewhere. I must make a great effort in London to clarify this position. Why cannot *one* squadron of fighters be sent out from North Africa? Why cannot some positive commitment be entered into regarding naval reinforcement of Singapore? At this stage, misty generalizations will please and sustain the Japanese, and nobody else.[244]

In London, while the Japanese threat was recognised, to Menzies' disappointment the approach seemed to be to let matters 'drift' until the

US position became clear.[245] Meanwhile, the Australian War Cabinet met on 14 February to discuss Singapore. Also present were the three Australian Chiefs of Staff and Brooke-Popham who had flown from Singapore. The latter assessed that Hong Kong could hold out against against a Japanese attack for four months, while Singapore had the ability to withstand the Japanese for six to nine months until British reinforcements arrived. Not all were convinced. The lack of capital ships and sufficient land-based aircraft combined with the uncertainty of the US position made for a bleak situation. There was little the Cabinet could do in the broad, but they did decide to further bolster the defences of Darwin, Port Moresby and Rabaul.[246]

For their part, during 1941 the US position on countering the Japanese was inconsistent. Indeed on such key strategic issues like the defence of the Philippines it changed more than once. Critically, while the war plans were produced by the US Joint Army Navy Board the flow-on force disposition and lower level planning lacked cohesion and constancy. For example, the version of the war plan, known as *Rainbow 3*, envisaged a modest strengthening of the Asiatic Fleet including deployment of an aircraft carrier.[247] It also contemplated a US, British and Dutch alliance. Unfortunately, the plan would be superseded and the naval reinforcements in later versions of the plan would be assigned to the Atlantic. In the Philippines there was not the unified command structure with a national commander-in-chief that there was in Singapore.

At the end of February Brooke-Popham chaired an Anglo-Dutch-Australian conference in Singapore. The US also sent the Chief of Staff to the Commander-in-Chief Asiatic Fleet, Captain William Purnell as an observer. Admiral Crace supported by Jack Newman was the RAN representative. The overriding principle, subject to respective government approval, was one of mutual defence. The defence strategy had to assume that the US might not enter the conflict. It was assessed that a Japanese attack on Australia and New Zealand was unlikely but that Singapore would come under threat from a Japanese advance down the Malay Peninsula from occupied Indo-China. An attack on key oil producing areas of the Dutch East Indies was also possible. There was recognition that the sea lines of communication would come under attack and that Australian, British, Dutch and New Zealand cruisers would be needed for convoy protection. The conference, while progressing co-ordinated defence preparations, underestimated the Japanese offensive capacity.

On 22 March 1941 the War Cabinet met with Acting Prime Minister Arthur Fadden chairing the meeting. Cabinet was briefed on the Singapore Conference and they affirmed 'that an essential part of our strategy must be to hold Port Moresby, Rabaul, New Caledonia and the Fiji-Tonga area.'[248] Of most concern to the Cabinet and the Service Chiefs was that there was not arising from the Conference a 'co-ordinated naval plan for the Far East'[249] and this was 'a serious handicap in the organization of our Far Eastern defence measures'.[250] As a result of the Cabinet meeting the Commonwealth wrote to the UK Government asking for a meeting at the Commander-in-Chief level to progress this matter. This lack of progress was viewed with similar misgiving by the Commander-in-Chief of the US Asiatic Fleet, Admiral Thomas Hart. He also thought that Australia and New Zealand were too defensively minded and needed to contemplate 'an offensive against the other fellow's [Japan's] trade routes'.[251]

Importantly, before this next conference was held the British and the American had talks in Washington. An outcome of the Washington discussions was that the April 1941 Commander-in-Chief level conference in Singapore could proceed 'on the basis of Anglo-United States-Dutch co-operation'.[252] Admiral Colvin led the delegation with a Colonel and a Group Captain representing the other two services. He took passage in *Sydney* while John Collins was still in command of the ship.[253] On the passage from Sydney the ship refuelled in Townsville where John caught up with Eric Feldt over 'a few pots'.[254]

At the conference, chaired by Admiral Sir Geoffrey Layton, the Commander-in-Chief, China Station, the planning assumption was that war would eventually involve Germany, Italy and Japan against the British Empire, its Allies and the United States. The Conference reaffirmed the assessment that invasion of Australia was unlikely.

Of particular interest at the Conference was for the first time the expounding of the US strategic analysis as it stood at that time. This included a statement that 'Singapore while very important, was not in the United States view, absolutely vital'.[255] The US approach in any conflict with Japan would be to rely on its naval superiority in the Hawaiian based Pacific Fleet. This Fleet would protect the US western seaboard and sea lines of communication. Offensively, this Fleet would attack Japanese mandated islands and Japanese sea lines of communication. The US did not plan to reinforce its Philippines' based Asiatic Fleet and pessimistically stated it 'did not expect to be able to hold the Philippines against determined attack and be forced to withdraw'.[256] This view would change. When Douglas MacArthur was recalled from being the Field Marshal of the Philippines Army to be Commander of the US Army Forces in the Far East he persuasively argued that the Philippines could be defended and a build-up of both aircraft and men followed. Hart did not share this optimism[257] and wrote in his diary 'Douglas knows a lot of things which are not so; he is a very able and convincing talker—combination which spells danger'.[258]

In his diary after the Conference Hart wrote of Brooke-Popham 'Well he certainly is not impressive'.[259] Hart later said he 'was a flier, with all the RAF characteristics which I never liked'.[260] In Hart's view Brooke-Popham's staff were not 'world beaters' and had become unduly cocky based on the recent British successes in the Mediterranean.[261] Hart would later suggest to Washington that they mention to the British that Brooke-Popham was not up to the task.[262]

In contrast Admiral Layton impressed the US delegation and was seen as 'a fine example of the blue-water school of the Royal Navy'.[263] It was agreed that Layton would command the combined forces which would include some assigned units of the Asiatic Fleet. This was in accord with Hart's long held view that a unified approach would be essential in the face of such an adversary.[264] Layton alluded to the possibility that a new senior Admiral might come out to replace him. This was a puzzling development to the Americans at this critical time.[265]

At the conference Layton highlighted the shortage of senior staff in his headquarters in the face of the work ahead, such as the development of the co-ordinated naval plan. Mindful of Cabinet's impatience for this plan, Admiral Colvin offered Layton his best Captain—John Collins. It was agreed he would become an Assistant Chief of Staff when he turned over his command of *Sydney* to Joe Burnett.[266] The visit gave John an invaluable insight into his next appointment as well providing ample opportunity to gain guidance from Colvin on the return passage to Australia.

Another visitor to Singapore, but this time at the working level was Rupert Long. He was a keen observer of the scene. He had been sent to Singapore by the three Chiefs of Service because of:

> ... a hunch that I had that we were not getting all the Intelligence and therefore what we were getting was of little or no value, and also because we were getting no 'information' of a reliable nature of conditions existing in that area. I know that I was horrified at what I saw and heard and at the tremendous amount of invaluable intelligence that we in Australia had failed to receive. I was horrified at the laissez faire attitude of everybody I met there, with the sole exception of Brooke-Popham, and yet the system and other major personalities in the area, had him beaten.[267]

Rupert sought during his visit to encourage greater coordination between the different services and headquarters in Singapore. This bore fruit within the umbrella of FECB now under the Commander-in-Chief Far East. To help ensure the flow of intelligence Rupert put RAN liaison officers into Layton's headquarters.

On 17 June John Collins arrived in Singapore to assume duties on Admiral Layton's staff. In a move that demonstrated some confidence in Singapore's defences, he was joined shortly after by his wife and daughter. John found Layton a personable and experienced flag officer. Layton had been a submariner in the Great War and had commanded *K6* in the 'Battle of May Island' when it sank *K4*. However he had spent little time in the Pacific during his career and had only been appointed to the China Station in September 1940. In Rupert Long's view John had a difficult challenge and wrote that:

> Layton the charming host, but uninspired to say the least, was in fact the ostrich [about the Japanese threat] and Collins possibly spent his time frustratingly trying to dig him out of the sand.[268]

One of John Collins' first tasks was the development of the urgently needed co-ordinated naval plan. Its title was Plans for the Employment of Naval and Air Forces of the Associated Powers or PLENAPS. In developing PLENAPS John had to establish productive working relationships with the Admirals commanding the Dutch and US naval forces in the region.

In Batavia, John met Lieutenant Admiral[269] Conrad Helfrich who was in command of all forces in the Dutch East Indies. Javanese-born, he was like John the son of a ship's doctor. Helfrich was aggressive by nature and determined to defend the colonial possession which he saw as an inseparable part of the Netherlands. Importantly, Helfrich already had a good rapport with Layton.

John called on Admiral Hart in Manila in November 1941. By this time Hart hosted or met a series of 'visiting firemen' as he termed them to discuss the deteriorating strategic situation. Hart was notified by his staff he had another British officer to dinner who was in Manila to discuss PLENAPS. In his diary Hart wrote:

> The Britisher is Captain Collins, of the Australian Navy, a very attractive man, and also, able. Is the Planner man of the Singapore Staff - was Captain of *Sidney* [sic] where she sank my Italian harbor mate out there *Colleoni*. Dinner went off very well, after we found out who was really coming.[270]

Hart also made a strong impression on John Collins who said of the admiral that, 'He was a man after my own heart'.[271] Hart and Layton had some similarities. Both admirals were Great War submariners. Hart had commanded a submarine flotilla operating with the RN and had got on well with his British counterparts.[272]

However in contrast to Layton, Hart had considerable experience operating in the Pacific. He had first visited Japan in 1922 and formed the view that 'Mr Jap' would be a formidable adversary.[273] Hart also visited Australia in 1925 when in command of the battleship USS *Mississippi*. Since assuming command of the Asiatic Fleet in 1939 Hart had seen first hand the Japanese activities in China. He like Layton, had withdrawn ships from China while at the same time trying to build up submarines and patrol aircraft forces in the Philippines.

In the subsequent discussions with Collins, Hart and his staff outlined that with the new found resolve to defend the Philippines the US naval forces would be more independent than previously advised.[274] From a US perspective PLENAPS was problematic and it was felt that it was too defensive.[275] In fairness to John Collins and his staff, PLENAPS was based on making best use of the available forces. It was difficult to advance offensive operations when there were scarce assets. In addition, as Hart well knew, it was hard to throw stones at the plan when the Asiatic Fleet was itself not being reinforced.

From a broader perspective the British did envisage a scenario where they would move land forces into southern Siam prior to a Japanese invasion of Malaya under Plan *Matador*.[276] The Japanese High Command for their part, in September 1941, after months of covert intelligence gathering, authorised detailed planning and preparations for the invasion of Malaya and Singapore.[277]

John Collins' talents and performance had also come to the attention of the Admiralty and on 6 October the Naval Board and Admiral Layton were asked whether he was recommended for the position of Deputy Director of Naval Intelligence in London. If selected he would have to be in place in the Admiralty from 1 January 1942 for up to three years.[278] This placed Layton in a difficult position as his carefully worded reply indicated:

> Captain Collins is an officer of outstanding ability and I would recommend him without hesitation. I must point out however that he

has only recently joined my staff where he is doing most valuable work on Far East war plans. I would strongly deprecate his removal at present juncture and with developments in prospect in next few months his work is likely to increase in importance.[279]

The prospect of losing John Collins to the Admiralty, potentially for the rest of the war, would hardly have pleased the Naval Board. Their response has not been found. Whatever the case, clearly the Admiralty had second thoughts and sent a signal on 8 October stating the obvious:

> Captain Collins was specially selected for appointment at Singapore to increase naval liaison between Australia and Far East. Consider it undesirable to remove him for this appointment at present.[280]

On 25 October 1941 the battleship HMS *Prince of Wales* and the old battlecruiser *Repulse* sailed from UK for Singapore. Absent was an aircraft carrier. It was planned for HMS *Indomitable* to be part of the force but she was completed too late to sail with the task group.

On return to Australia after his four months sojourn to UK and Middle East, Menzies found he had lost both popular and party support. His offer of forming an all-party national Government along British lines did not find sufficient favour. A week later on 28 August Menzies resigned from the Prime Ministership in favour of the Country Party Arthur Fadden. The latter's Government lasted but five weeks when it lost support from two independent members of Parliament. John Curtin was in turn asked to form a Government. He would bring even greater attention to defence preparedness in the Pacific.

In Navy Office the focus on Japan was also reflected in the selection of the new Chief of Naval Staff. After four years and in poor health Admiral Colvin left office. Although there was a thought by Curtin for him to remain in Australia to chair meetings of the service chiefs, he instead became Naval Adviser to the Australian High Commissioner in London.[281] Colvin saw that his greatest contribution to the RAN was to prepare the ships for the future rigours of global conflict. He told the War Cabinet at his final appearance:

Australia now had a 'made' Navy which had proved itself in the sternest of all tests. Every ship of size in the RAN had used its guns in action ... Man for man and ship for ship Australia has a Navy second to none in the world.²⁸²

The new Chief was Vice Admiral Sir Guy Royle who had been the British Naval Attaché in Tokyo in the twenties and had commanded the aircraft carrier HMS *Glorious* in the thirties. He was well suited to the next phase of the war and under him in Navy Office Frank Getting and Rupert Long would work constructively. Rupert for his part continued to monitor Japanese merchant ship movements. Towards the end of 1941, just like the receding of the ocean before a tsunami, these ships virtually disappeared from the seas. Only the tankers running the San-Diego-Japan oil trade continued to maintain their peacetime pattern. Navy Office awaited the inevitable.²⁸³

The campaign against the German raiders clearly demonstrated the vital importance of a well co-ordinated intelligence effort between the Services and their conduct of operations be similarly orchestrated. Up to the middle of 1940 there had only been established two Area Combined Headquarters, one in Melbourne and the other in Port Moresby. These were focused on operations. Rupert Long and Joe Burnett believed the next logical step was the creation of a combined intelligence centre. Accordingly, Joe wrote to his Army counterpart on 11 July 1940 outlining the proposal and requesting a meeting to discuss better coordination between the three Services.²⁸⁴ Within the week the Chiefs of Staff had met and a Joint Planning Committee established which recommended the establishment of the Combined Operational Intelligence Centre or the 'COIC' as it was called.

On 16 October 1940 the COIC met for the first time with Rupert acting as its inaugural Director. His appointment reflected his leading role in its conception and the maritime focus of the COIC.²⁸⁵ The COIC soon provided the Chiefs of Staff with twice daily situation reports of 'hot' intelligence matters as well as providing specific reports and bulletins. Importantly the COIC became a key source of accurate data. Rupert was in his element and one of his staff latter recalled:

> The other Directors of Intelligence would get up and expound on the situation. Director of Air Force Intelligence particularly giving a most impressive description of sorties—numbers and types of planes—numbers and types of bombs dropped, damage done etc. etc. etc. At the end of it one felt most impressed at the Air Force effort but had only a vague idea of what had actually been achieved. Cocky would then get up and would splash the canvas with a broad sweep— he'd speak for only a few minutes—but when he sat down you had a mental picture of the strategic position, uncluttered with petty-fogging detail. In other words DAFI's briefing would have been fine in a carrier, but Von's was of the calibre required for Chiefs of Staff and left the others for cold.[286]

On 12 May 1941 the position of Assistant Chief of Naval Staff passed once more to a member of the Pioneer Class when Joe Burnett handed over to Frank Getting. Joe's hard work in Navy Office was reflected in his exceptionally high scored report in which Admiral Colvin wrote:

> As Deputy Chief of the Naval Staff his work has been outstanding and he has a grasp as wide as I have known in any officer. He is full of initiative, most loyal and tactful and extremely hard working. One of the most promising and exceptional officers I have met.[287]

Joe Burnett had been in a unique position in Navy Office where as the senior Executive Branch Captain, he read and commented upon for the First Naval Member all reports from the ships at sea as well as the array of intelligence reports. Joe had an unrivalled view that should have ideally prepared him for a cruiser command. John Collins' reports from *Sydney* were the stand-out from the Squadron, not only in reporting upon her exceptional service in the Mediterranean, but also for the wealth of insight provided in his reports. Joe was delighted therefore to be rewarded with the prize appointment to command the famous *Sydney*.

On 15 May 1941 *Sydney* was alongside in Fremantle having completed a series of patrols and training. For the second time in successive appointments, John Collins handed over his duties to Joe Burnett. *Sydney* had been a central part of John's life for nearly five years over two appointments and he had deep bonds both with the ship and with some of the ship's company who had been with the cruiser since her commissioning in England. He and his wife were presented with a beautiful model of the ship which had been made onboard. It was a difficult wrench, but navies have long recognized that there is generally a limit to how long a Captain can maintain his physical and mental powers in the face of the demands of sea command. Joe Burnett found a happy ship with a very experienced team, the vast bulk of the officers and sailors having been onboard since even before the commencement of war. Joe made a positive impression as a well tempered and prudent captain who took advice.[288]

Sydney resumed her patrols and escorting of merchant shipping. The main threat remained German raiders which the Admiralty assessed were likely to be still at large in unknown numbers in the South Atlantic and the Indian Oceans. In the middle of June *Kormoran* after a fruitless sweep near the Maldives steamed east into the Bay of Bengal in search of prey. She was rewarded on 26 June with first the Yugoslav *Velebit* and then the Australia sugar carrier *Mareeba*. Both transmitted distress signals before being sunk. Their fate would remain a mystery for some time and initially it was thought they had both succumbed to bad weather. After his success, Detmers decided to clear the area. *Mareeba's* log indicated she had sighted a British cruiser less than a day ago. This was HMS *Durban*.[289] *Kormoran* steamed towards the Dutch East Indies with a view to cruising south of Sumatra and Java. After sinking the Greek *Stamatios G. Embricos* on 23 September, *Kormoran* steamed deep into the southern Indian Ocean and rendezvoused with the supply ship *Kulmerland* on 16 October, 600 miles west of Cape Leeuwin. The merchant seamen were transferred and much needed supplies from Japan were taken onboard. Detmers learnt his ship would be relieved in December by *Thor*. He determined that *Kormoran*, in one of her final sweeps, would close the south-west coast of Western Australia and then steam north and mine the approaches to Fremantle on passage. As *Kormoran* closed the coast these plans were abruptly altered when signal traffic from *Canberra* was picked up. The cruiser was clearly escorting a convoy and Detmers decided instead to keep off shore and then head to Shark Bay further to the north to mine its approaches.

Between her patrols off the west coast *Sydney* was sent to Williamstown Naval Dockyard for much needed maintenance and leave. This allowed cadet-midshipmen and recruits to tour the famous cruiser. Joe Burnett took the opportunity to have his two sons Patrick and Rory, both destined to be cadet-midshipmen, onboard for a night at sea.

Sydney's next duty was to take over the escort of the Malaya-bound troopship *Zealandia* from *Adelaide*. *Sydney* and *Zealandia* sailed from Fremantle on 11 November bound for the Sunda Strait whence *Zealandia* was handed over to *Durban*. *Sydney* then reversed course to return to Fremantle. By 3 pm on the afternoon of 19 November *Sydney* was to the west of Shark Bay steaming south and her lookouts sighted the smoke and masts of a lone merchantman heading north east. It was a beautiful day with a medium sized southerly swell and a moderate breeze to cool the ship. Joe Burnett had the Officer of the Watch close the merchant ship which,

The first Australian ship to encounter the German raider Kormoran *was the freighter SS* Mareeba. *She was sunk on 26 June 1941.*
(Green Collection/State Library of Victoria)

on sighting *Sydney*, altered course to the west and had slowly increased speed. At about 15,000 yards range Joe had the Officer of the Watch alter course so that *Sydney* came round to the west to come up the stern of the merchant ship on her starboard quarter. This approach was the textbook tactic when closing a suspicious vessel, as it presented the smallest target, while also not allowing the potential enemy to bring any more than a stern gun to bear on one's own ship. In that approach Joe should have had a pre-determined distance that at which point, if he was not happy with the identity of the merchantman, he would cease closing. This should have been driven by the lethality of the German 5.9-inch gun, which was 19,000 yards.[290]

Yet, on this occasion, *Sydney* continued to close. Joe ordered a repeated signal to the merchantman by light and flags of the coded message 'NNJ', but to no avail. Eventually he ordered the plain language signal 'What ship'. The slow and sloppy reply by flags was 'STRAAT MALAKKA'. In recent months this Dutch merchantman had plied the trade from east African ports to the Dutch East Indies and had recently been in Singapore. The flag hoist was hoisted half way up the mast to indicate difficulty in reading *Sydney's* flags. The cruiser closed still further to continue the interrogation.

Sydney however was not closing *Straat Malakka*, rather it was *Kormoran* which was heading towards Shark Bay to lay some of her 420 mines. Although the shipyard provided *Kormoran* with elaborate means to adjust her appearance when at sea, Detmers approach was more simple and pragmatic. He later wrote:

> It is much more important to know all about ships of a similar tonnage and structure, and to know their approximate routes; and that you can choose yourself a likely disguise which has a good chance of proving impenetrable.[291]

Detmers on sighting a Perth Class[292] cruiser decided to play for time and see if he could lure *Sydney* even closer. Hence the decision to reply by flags rather than the quicker light. In the meantime his crew silently manned their action stations.

A particular concern for Detmers was the preparations *Sydney* appeared to be making to launch her aircraft. The aircraft's engine was started and then shut down. If launched, the aircrew may have been able to notice some of the disguises and armament of the raider from their aerial vantage point. Whether because of a mechanical defect or change of mind the aircraft was not launched.

Sydney then asked 'where bound' to which Detmers replied 'Batavia'. All the time the range was slowly closing and by this time the ships were only three thousand yards apart. Detmers had expected to be ordered to heave to. This would have made it difficult to manoeuvre and for at least half his weapons to be able to bear on *Sydney*. It would probably have force him to immediately open fire on *Sydney*. But he was not so ordered, which gave him the feeling that *Sydney* did not believe his ship to be suspicious. The fact that the aircraft was not launched also supported this view.[293]

Detmers however, wanted to play for more time. Although *Sydney* was well inside the range of his 5.9-inch guns he wanted the cruiser to be within range of his 37 mm and 20 mm anti-aircraft guns so that they could be used against *Sydney's* crew. Detmers slowed *Kormoran's* speed and *Sydney* came up to 1,000 yards on her beam. Detmers was further reassured when he saw a *Sydney* cook on the deck getting some fresh air. At exactly 5.30 pm Detmers ordered the German naval ensign hoisted and then once flying, 'de-camouflage'.

Six seconds later *Kormoran's* gun crews opened fire on the unsuspecting *Sydney*. At such close range it was a case of who fires first wins. It was an intense close quarters engagement more reminiscent of the Battle of Trafalgar than World War II. The destructive power of their guns however, were far greater than in the days of Horatio Nelson and the carnage was appalling.

Sydney's opening salvo went over *Kormoran*. In contrast *Kormoran's* crew were well drilled in this close-quarters style of sea fight. Each of *Kormoran's* guns were assigned a different target along *Sydney's* superstructure. *Kormoran's* opening salvoes of her forward 5.9-inch gun hit *Sydney's* bridge, almost certainly killing Joe Burnett and the rest of the bridge crew and disabling the forward gun direction system. As a result eight *Kormoran* salvoes were fired into *Sydney* before the next reply from the cruiser.

Kormoran next discharged three torpedoes, two sped harmlessly ahead of *Sydney* but the third struck abreast the forward 6-inch gun sending a large column of water in the air and the cruiser visibly shook along her length. This hit and a direct shell hit on the next turret put the forward armament out of action. *Sydney* was able to fire two torpedoes herself but they failed to hit her foe.

Sydney was the only one of her class to have single 4-inch guns without protective shields. Following service in the Mediterranean John Collins, as an interim measure, had vertical steel plating fitted in lieu of the guardrails on the 4-inch gun deck. Joe Burnett in his short time onboard wrote a request to have protective shields fitted to each gun added during the ship's next refit.[294] As a result, her exposed gun crews were struck down by a barrage of 20 mm rounds from *Kormoran's* bridge. In addition, 37 mm shells poured into *Sydney's* bridge 'like a stream of water'.[295] *Kormoran's* midship 5.9-inch gun then hit the Walrus aircraft, starting a major blaze amidships in *Sydney*.

The stricken *Sydney* was not done for just yet and the steeliness that made her famous in the Mediterranean, came through as she traded deadly blows with *Kormoran* with her after 6-inch gun crews firing over open sights. There were twenty men in each gun and magazine. The Petty Officer in charge of the third or X turret was particularly accurate in firing his guns which won the admiration of Detmers.[296] After one round into *Kormoran's* funnel he hit the engine room setting off a major fire that would spell the end of *Kormoran*.

Sydney now turned towards *Kormoran* and slowly passed across her stern. *Kormoran's* anti-aircraft guns crews mercilessly devastated the now exposed starboardside of *Sydney*. More 5.9-inch gun shells were fired into the now silent cruiser that was slowly opening range and increasingly shrouded in smoke. The engagement had lasted only thirty minutes.

Detmers still intended to close *Sydney* once more, but the engine room fire was now out of control. For a further twenty-five minutes the stationary *Kormoran* poured gunfire into *Sydney* until distance and growing darkness caused him to cease fire.

In *Sydney* intense fires raged from the bow to the stern and there was major flooding in the forward part of the ship from the torpedo hit. Sailors were fighting fires and using wooden shoring to stem the flow of the sea into the ship and prevent the bow from falling off. The intense fire on the bridge spread aft to join the intense blaze around the aircraft. The damage control effort must have been overwhelming to *Sydney's* survivors who were likely without many of their officers and senior sailors, killed in the initial engagement. Detmers later wrote:

> Up until 2100 hours [9 pm] we could see the glow, and then we saw the flames suddenly dart up even higher as though from an explosion, and after that the battered hulk of our enemy disappeared into the night.[297]

Detmers turned his attention to abandoning ship before the fire reached some of the ship's ammunition and mines. His engineers set scuttling charges to hasten *Kormoran's* end before a massive explosion took place. By 11.30 pm the survivors had got clear of *Kormoran* in an assortment of lifeboats. At 00.35 am the raider was rent by a large explosion and the large flames only died down when she sank stern first to the depths.

Detmers and about 300 of his crew had taken to a motley collection of two rafts and five lifeboats. The latter including boats from *Kulmerland* and one of her victims *Nicholas D.L.* While on the first morning the craft kept together, over time their differing characteristics would cause them to separate.

The first indication ashore that something was amiss was on the 21 November when *Sydney* did not arrive in Fremantle. The District Naval Officer in Fremantle, Captain Charles Farquhar-Smith sent a signal to Navy Office alerting them. Initially there was little concern because she could have been delayed in her escort work and *Sydney* would have been maintaining radio silence.

HMAS Sydney's *4-inch gun crews were particularly exposed. John Collins had steel plating fitted in lieu of guard rails abreast the guns. Joe Burnett went further and submitted a proposal to have protective shields fitted to the gun mounts.*
(*The Argus*/State Library of Victoria)

On the morning of 23 November the troopship *Aquitania* picked up 26 survivors from one of *Kormoran's* rafts. It was unclear whether they were victims or from a German raider and the ship maintained radio silence for fear of drawing attention to herself. Detmers saw *Aquitania* but did not fire a flare hoping that a neutral vessel might pass by. By the end of the day Navy Office twice sent signals to *Sydney* to establish contact.

On the morning of 24 November RAAF aircraft commenced an unsuccessful search for the ship. Navy Office also spoke to Admiral Crace that morning about *Sydney* and opined that she may have fallen victim to a Vichy submarine.[298] The mystery however started to be revealed that afternoon when a signal was received from the Shell tanker *Trocas* reporting that she had rescued 25 German sailors about 120 nautical miles north-west of Carnarvon. A subsequent *Trocas* signal stated the sailors were from *Kormoran* and they had been in a sea battle. The Naval Board now deduced that *Sydney* had been in a battle with *Kormoran* and on the morning of 25 November seven Hudson and five Wirraway aircraft took off in a coordinated search. The search bore fruit with the five lifeboats being detected. The boats either made it shore by themselves or their occupants were rescued by the steamships, *Koolinda, Centaur* and *Wyrallah*.

On 26 November the newly appointed First Naval Member Vice Admiral Sir Guy Royle and the Navy Minister Norman Makin briefed the Advisory War Council on the facts then known and the likelihood that *Sydney* had been sunk.

The Germans were subjected to a series of interrogations. Detmers was first interviewed on 28 November at Carnarvon by Lieutenant Commander James Rycroft, the Staff Officer (Intelligence) at Fremantle. It was from this interrogation that Detmers first learnt the identity of his foe. He later wrote of his conversation with his First Officer Lieutenant Commander Kurt Förster:

> 'The *Sydney* Förster' I exclaimed. 'We must have sunk her. What a coincidence! And almost at the spot where the first *Sydney* destroyed the *Emden* in the 1914/18 war. That's poetic justice if you like.'[299]

For Detmers the engagement was more than the historic coincidence of the *Sydney* name. It was a single ship engagement without parallel whereby an auxiliary cruiser had sunk a warship, let alone a cruiser. Of the engagement Detmers wrote in his memoirs:

> Of course our trump card in the whole affair had been our effective camouflage; but for that the result would have been very different. However, we utilised our advantage to the full and we took the trick. Without that the *Sydney* would never have sailed into the trap. I had managed to obtain the most favourable position possible for the opening the engagement and I exploited it to the full. And I was proud beyond expression of the magnificent conduct and bearing of the men who served under me.[300]

The subsequent interrogations of the survivors picked up by *Aquitania* were conducted by the German speaking Harold Farncomb. While there were variations in detail, some dissembling and embellishment, the circumstances of the battle were clear enough.

The coastal steamer Koolinda *was one of four ships that picked up survivors of the German auxliary cruiser* Kormoran. (State Library of Victoria)

While further fruitless searches for *Sydney* continued, rumours started to circulate outside official circles of her loss or that of *Australia*. A public announcement had to be made. The first task was to inform loved ones and this was done by telegram on 26 November 1941. Rear Admiral Crace also hand wrote a condolence letter to each family. The duty of informing the nation was that of the now Prime Minister John Curtin who on the evening of 30 November issued the following statement:

> HMAS *Sydney* has been in action with a heavily armed enemy merchant raider which she sank by gunfire. The intimation was received from survivors from the enemy vessel who were picked up some time after the action. No subsequent communication has been received from HMAS *Sydney*, and the Government regrets that she must be presumed lost.[301]

He went on to say that,

> While regretting the loss of a fine ship and her gallant complement the people of Australia will be proud that she and they upheld the traditions of the Royal Australian Navy and completed a glorious career in action against the enemy.[302]

The following day newspaper front page headlines across the country carried news to the nation. *The Canberra Times* typified the coverage and devoted two pages to the tragedy including listing the 645 names of those missing, presumed dead.[303] The newspaper said 'No name in Australian naval history is dearer to Australian hearts than that of HMAS *Sydney*.'[304] Its editorial mourned the loss and concluded with the warning:

> The war is coming closer to Australia. The loss of the *Sydney* is a call for Australia to be fully aware of how close the war is.[305]

In her home port of Sydney the news had special poignancy. The Lord Mayor Alderman Crick vowed to establish a HMAS *Sydney* Replacement Fund. There was a later submission considered by the Naval Board for the Tribal class destroyer *Warramunga* then under construction to be renamed *Sydney* with the other Tribals to be named *Melbourne* and *Brisbane*. The decision was deferred and not reconsidered.[306]

Back in Western Australia Detmers was concerned he would be subject to a court martial but he and his crew were sent to prisoner of war camps in rural Victoria to join former members of German Afrika Korps captured in Africa. One of his sailors died in Perth of an illness contracted prior to the battle. He was buried with naval honours and the family of one of *Sydney*'s sailors generously offered to tend the grave.[307]

At least one unknown sailor survived *Sydney*'s plunge to the ocean depths. He was able to reach a carley float but did not survive to reach land. Two months after the battle the float with his body was seen drifting off Flying Fish Cove, Christmas Island. He rests in a grave at Geraldton where an evocative HMAS *Sydney* Memorial now stands.

In the absence of any *Sydney* survivors conspiracy theories about the cruiser's loss abounded. Indeed the fate of *Sydney* would not become clear until she and *Kormoran* were located and photographed in March 2008 by shipwreck hunter David Mearns and his team in *Geosounder*. The Defence Science and Technology Organization (DSTO) led the detailed analysis and complex computer modelling based on Mearns' exceptional photographs. Tellingly, this analysis concluded that *Sydney* received at least 87 5.9-inch and 400 37 mm shell hits. This generated over 200,000 steel fragments throughout the ship.[308] It was fearful punishment with few parallels in naval history. The DSTO analysis concluded that:

As *Sydney* sustained hit after hit, the damage to both equipment and crew multiplied along with the loss of numerous capabilities. Figures presented propose that at least 70% of the crew were incapacitated or trapped in spaces due to fires and escape passages blocked.[309]

The computer modelling indicated that *Sydney's* end probably came between 2 to 4.5 hours after the battle.[310] Exhausted sailors would have laboured through the night to bring fires under control. The ingress of water would have eventually caused the stricken cruiser to sink with the weakened bow coming off the rest of the ship in her death plunge. The remainder of that proud and famous ship followed the bow to the depths of the Indian Ocean. At least her adversary had also gone, and could do no further harm to merchant shipping.

Surprisingly, in the face of the compelling evidence resident in the two wrecks, new conspiracy theories have still been spawned. They are perhaps in response to the difficulty many Australians have in accepting that their most famous warship could have been bettered by an inferior foe. Yet naval history, like the annals of other human endeavour, is replete with such examples. Of note John Collins always accepted Detmers' account[311] and the official Naval historian Hermon Gill's judgement, which has stood the test of time was that:

> It is easy to be wise after the event but having said that, it remains difficult to escape the conclusion that *Sydney* was lost because she failed to observe prudent tactics in the situation that arose on the afternoon of 19th November, 1941.[312]

One of the features of war at sea is that the fate of hundreds of officers and sailors rests on the, at times, split second decisions of their captain. It has been suggested by Gill and by other historians that the criticism of Harold Farncomb in wasting ammunition in her long range engagement of *Ketty Brøvig* caused Joe Burnett to get too close to *Kormoran*.[313] This seems doubtful. While the rationale for Joe Burnett's decision to close *Kormoran* will remain a mystery, clearly by getting so near he demonstrated that he did not suspect *Kormoran's* true identity.

It is known from one of the last letters to leave *Sydney* that Joe Burnett had taken his ship to action stations when closing a suspicious merchantman just three weeks before her final battle. Of that incident, Leading Aircraftman Keith Homard wrote:

> In 3 minutes every man was at his post with all guns loaded and ready and in 10 minutes we had the plane ready to take off. We clapped on speed and raced to where the look out had sighted a ship but to our disappointment it was one of our own.[314]

It is also known from a sailor who briefly served in *Sydney* that during another occasion when investigating an unidentified ship that *Sydney's* Walrus was launched to examine it.[315]

The decision to get so close to *Kormoran* was inexplicable, noting the carnage the German raiders had wreaked so far in the war. Joe Burnett was not however the only captain to make that error, and *Leander's* close quarters engagement of *Ramb I* is a case in point. *Sydney's* last battle involved Australia's greatest loss of life in a single day since the heaviest fighting on the Western Front during World War I.

For its part the Admiralty, after the disastrous battle which had followed a series of encounters with German raiders, issued a *Battle Summary* on these engagements. It contained the following warning:

> There is a possibility that commanding officers under-estimate the offensive power of raiders. They should be warned that enemy raiders are often powerfully armed with guns and torpedoes and if fitted with modern RDF [radar] may be able to open fire even at long range with great accuracy.[316]

Joe Burnett's decisions on that fateful afternoon immeasurably coloured later assessments of his otherwise stellar career. His old chief Admiral Colvin however wrote in *The Times*:

> When the time came for him to go to sea – a time to which he eagerly looked forward – I had no doubt he would acquit himself successfully as he had at the Navy Office. He did, and whatever mischance that befell that gallant and illustrious ship, Burnett I know went with honour. The Royal Australian Navy will have cause to miss him sorely in the future and those of us who knew him will honour his memory.[317]

For John Collins the loss of *Sydney* was a deeply personal one and he said he felt that bereavement every Anzac Day with the absence of his many comrades from the march.[318] He later wrote:

> To me there has never been before nor will there ever be again a ship quite to compare with the cruiser *Sydney* of World War II.[319]

Following the release of Gill's official history, John Collins wrote to Gill about the historian's criticism of Joe Burnett. He wrote:

Captain Joe Burnett on the bridge of HMAS Sydney. *(RAN)*

You make the comment, 'Why Burnett did not use his superior speed and armament, did not confirm his suspicions by asking Navy Office, etc.?'. It must be remembered that it was late in the afternoon and *Sydney* had no radar.[to maintain contact with the unidentified ship during the night] A reply from Navy Office to a 'check mate' signal would not have been received before dark and it would therefore have been too late. Whatever advantage in speed you have, you cannot get close to a ship that alters away without eventually getting into a position of torpedo disadvantage. Work it out yourself with two matchsticks.

The real question to me is why he did not fire a broadside across the raider's bows? I have read elsewhere that the Captain of the raider decided to abandon ship if *Sydney* opened fire. I agree that it might have been a good thing to fly off the aircraft but I do not know, (a) whether it was serviceable, (b) whether the state of sea was suitable for recovery. In any event it is mighty hard to pick a disguised raider from the air. I repeat, in my view, the only question is why did he not fire across the bows.[320]

What is clear is that if *Sydney* had fired warning shots Detmers would have opened fire and not abandoned ship. The outcome is unlikely to have been as dire for *Sydney* as was her actual fate. John Collins hoped that his letter would find its way to the archives for posterity. It did, but it also remained undisturbed for nearly 60 years among Gill's papers in the Australian War Memorial.[321]

But perhaps the last word on this national tragedy should go to one of *Sydney's* lost sailors. On the cruiser's return from the Mediterranean he prophetically told a journalist:

> You know we were so lucky that sometimes it scared me. I used to wonder when our luck would leave us, because I knew that when it did, it would leave us just when we most wanted it.[322]

Chapter 7
Sad Songs of the Death of Sailors

We sit on the half-tide rocks
Where the moonlit waters glisten,
On the sea-wet rocks, and sing
Sad songs of the death of sailors
and the end of their journeying;

Allan McNicoll, Sea Voices, 1932[1]

I

On 2 December 1941 *Prince of Wales*, together with *Repulse* and their escorting destroyers, berthed in Singapore. Despite the absence of an aircraft carrier their arrival was a great morale boost for everyone. Embarked in the battleship was the new Commander-in-Chief Eastern Fleet, Admiral Sir Tom Phillips. John Collins called on the Commanding Officer of *Prince of Wales*, Captain John Leach, who was an old friend. He found that *Prince of Wales* had not had an opportunity to properly work-up before sailing for the Far East and was seeking a month's training before embarking on operations. Disconcertingly, John Collins also found within the leadership of the task group, now designated Force Z, very little useful experience in the Pacific. There was also a reluctance by the staff to read PLENAPS.[2] They regarded the document as 'old regime'.[3]

Known as 'Tom Thumb' by the sailors because of his five-feet two-inch height, Admiral Phillips was a controversial selection. Unusually, he had not commanded a battleship in his career and had not been to sea since being a Commodore before the war. Instead he had been in the Admiralty and had the confidence of the First Sea Lord, Admiral Sir Dudley Pound. On a positive note, on 5 December Phillips flew to the Philippines to see Admiral Hart. Unlike some of his staff, Phillips had read PLENAPS and sought two US destroyer divisions as envisaged in the plan. The two Admirals spent the next day in candid discussions. Importantly, Phillips got a strong sense from Hart of the imminent Japanese threat. Hart wrote in his diary:

> Well I acquired considerable respect for Phillips—looks like as good an Englishman to work with as I have had for some time. Upon the whole they have not much changed their ideas—still are disposed to disperse forces, guard everything, and be so thin that nothing is really guarded. At least they now know what we think about it.[4]

By the end of the day the two Admirals had struck up a good rapport. Hart told Phillips that Destroyer Division 57 he had dispersed to Borneo would be able to join his force when hostilities commenced.[5] They bid farewell and did not to see each other again.

Some months earlier the FECB in Singapore had shared information with the Asiatic Fleet's cryptanalysis unit based at Corregidor in the Philippines (known as Station C or CAST). They were a crack organization which had had most success at that time in traffic analysis. The British assistance allowed CAST to have more success in breaking some of the Japanese coded signals. Unlike MacArthur, Hart had made it his business to sit down with his code-breakers and regularly read the Japanese signal traffic about naval movements in Indo-China. He understood that important information could be gleaned from signal traffic analysis even if the coded signal was not broken down. On the strength of this work Hart deployed Catalina reconnaissance aircraft to track Japanese warships and transports as well as to deploy forces in case of a looming attack.

The month that Admiral Phillips and his staff had hoped to prepare for Force Z did not materialize. Five days after their arrival the Japanese struck. On the north east coast of Malaya, just after midnight on 8 December Japanese cruisers and destroyers of the Kota Bharu Invasion Force[6] commenced a bombardment prior to an amphibious landing of troops from the 18th Division. This was about 50 minutes before the attack on Pearl Harbor at just before 8 am on 7 December (Hawaiian local time). Less than nine hours later the Japanese attacked Hong Kong.

Not long after the landing in Malaya, in Melbourne Walter Brooksbank was at home in bed and received a telephone call. It was Rupert Long 'That you, B1? Japan!' B1 replied, 'OK, I will be right in.'[7] Brooksbank later reflected that:

> That little incident serves to remind me that, of all the senior officers, attaches, etc. with who, from time to time, I discussed the question of the possibility of Japan entering the war and of the likely extent of her offensive operations, no one, as events were later to prove, had a more realistic and accurate appreciation of the situation than Commander Long. It was his conviction that it was well within the capabilities of Japan to carry out an offensive of truly major proportions that caused him to give priority to the extension of our coast-watching network in New Guinea and the Solomon Islands. And for the task he could, of course, have chosen no one better than Lieutenant Commander Eric Feldt.[8]

On the same day in the Philippines at 5.30 am (Philippines local time), three hours after the Pearl Harbor attack, orders were received from Washington to execute Plan Rainbow 5 which included the bombing of Japanese airfields in Formosa. It was not until 11 am that Major General Lewis Brereton finally gained approval from MacArthur to launch a strike with his bombers. It was too late. At 12.30 pm Japanese aircraft bombed the two main US airfields—Clark and Iba Fields. They destroyed 18 of the 35 B-17 Flying Fortress bombers and 53 of the 107 P-40 Warhawk fighters as well as 28 other aircraft. The Philippines was effectively lost on that afternoon. The other US trump card was the Asiatic Fleet's 23 submarines. In the course of the Japanese invasion nine submarines conducted ten attacks on both warships and transports. None was successful and it was not until 1943 that it was discovered that the magnetic exploder and the associated contact fuze in the Mark.14 torpedo were defective and then rectified. These defects had a profound impact on the war.[9]

This Japanese version of a 'blitzkreig' was to leave the United States and Britain reeling. The near simultaneous attacks on Malaya, Pearl Harbor, Hong Kong and then the Philippines was without parallel in terms of sweep and destruction. For Australia the Japanese threat, so long feared, had became a reality. On news of the attacks, Prime Minister John Curtin in a national radio address announcing the war with Japan, said that, 'This is the gravest hour in our history.'[10]

It was to be the sternest test for the RAN and it heralded its darkest days. The British Imperial strategy unsustained by sufficient forces, crumbled with unexpected suddenness. Hong Kong, which was to be able to hold out for four months, instead surrendered in eighteen days.

In Malaya initial opposition to the Japanese landing at Kota Bharu by British and Indian troops supported by Hudson bombers of the tenacious RAAF Number 1 Squadron, was spirited and led to the heaviest Japanese casualties of the campaign.

On the evening of 8 December Phillips sailed in *Prince of Wales* with *Repulse* and four destroyers —*Electra, Express, Tenedos* and HMAS *Vampire*, to attack the Japanese invasion forces. It was initially planned that the ships would be provided air cover by some of the fighters based in Singapore and along the Malay Peninsula. However, the losses both on the ground and in the air of these aircraft, particularly the outclassed Buffalo fighters, meant that Phillips was informed there would be no air support for his operation. For this sweep to have any success John Collins believed surprise was essential.[11] This view was shared by Phillips and he sailed just before dusk on 8 December. While Phillips had decided to abandon his operation if detected by reconnaissance aircraft, he was an admiral who still had yet to grasp the full lethality of air attack. For if Force Z was detected so close inshore it would be only a couple of hours before a strike could be launched. Captain Stephen Roskill recalled that when Phillips was in the Admiralty:

> I had a stormy interview with Phillips on this matter when I brought back to the Admiralty first-hand reports of the effect of [aerial] bombing off Norway in April 1940. Phillips would not accept that it was suicidal to send warships to operate off an enemy-held coast without air cover.[12]

In the instance of the Norwegian campaign, Phillips thought 'greater courage and resolution' was needed to counter dive-bombers.[13] On the night of 9 December reports of a Japanese landing near Kuantan were passed to Phillips who altered course towards that port. Unknown to Phillips, during the afternoon his ships had been tracked by the Japanese submarine *I-65* which reported their presence. It was only a matter of time before the Japanese launched an attack by land-based aircraft. If that did not prove effective the Japanese fleet consisting of two battleships, eight cruisers and twelve destroyers would intercept Force Z.[14] Three seaplanes from the cruisers shadowed Force Z at dusk.

The following morning at about 11 am the first of four waves of land based Japanese aircraft attacked Force Z. When the first reports of damage to Force Z came into the War Room in Singapore, John Collins set about organising tugs and Destroyer Division 57 to join the understrength Force Z. Before he had got too far in this work Phillips' deputy Rear Admiral Arthur Palliser came over with a signal and said to John, 'You need not worry about the tugs. They are both sunk'.[15] Belatedly a handful of fighters arrived in time to chase the final wave of Japanese bombers away. The destroyers, having rescued the survivors, made good their withdrawal to Singapore.

It had been less than 48 hours since *Prince of Wales* and *Repulse* had sailed and now they lay at the bottom of the South China Sea. Among the 830 dead were Admiral Phillips and Captain Leach. Churchill, who had hopes Force Z would prove a sufficient deterrent to Japanese aggression, later wrote:

As I turned over and twisted in bed the full horror of the news sank in upon me. There were no British or American capital ships in the Indian Ocean or the Pacific except the American survivors of Pearl Harbour, who were hastening back to California. Over all this vast expanse of water Japan was supreme, and we everywhere were weak and naked.[16]

In Singapore the news of the sinkings had more immediate implications. The first was the loss of the Commander-in-Chief, Eastern Fleet. John Collins had the presence of mind to rush down to *Dominion Monarch* which was about to sail with Admiral Layton embarked. Layton returned to the Headquarters and said to the shaken staff, 'I'll take over. What is the situation?'[17]

In Melbourne, unaware of the fate of the two British capital ships, Rupert Long as Director of COIC completed on 9 December an appreciation of the 'Japanese situation' which was presented to the Service Chiefs and then onto Government. In his remarkably accurate assessment Rupert noted the Japanese attacks to date and suggested that they would:

1. Push through to Burma to cut the Burma Road.
2. In the Philippines attempt to suppress American naval and air strength in the area.
3. Attack the Dutch East Indies and North Borneo with its oil supplies from Indo-China, Hainan and/or Palau.
4. Launch an attack on New Ireland/New Britain, but specifically on Rabaul from Truk.
5. Conduct subsequent attacks on New Hebrides, New Caledonia and Fiji.

Rupert reasoned that a direct attack on Australia and New Zealand was unlikely at this stage, but that there could be raids by submarines or air attack from aircraft carriers or even shelling by Japanese warships against strategically important coastal centres.[18]

In the wake of the loss of *Prince of Wales* and *Repulse,* John Collins concluded that it was just a matter of time before Singapore fell and he arranged for his family to take passage in *Nellore*. They disembarked in Batavia staying at Admiral Doorman's residence while waiting for a flight to Australia. John managed to join them for Christmas with the

Doormans. The plane which would take Phyllis and Gillian south was shot down by the Japanese enroute to Batavia. They instead embarked on another aircraft and got through to Darwin. To underscore their luck the next scheduled flight was also lost.[19]

Luck was also a subject in discussion in Sydney. On Friday the 13th December the newly commissioned *Toowoomba* sailed in company with the equally new HMAS *Wollongong*. The sailors thought it an ominous omen and those looking for bad luck pointed out that the *Toowoomba* pennant number J157 added up to 13.[20] The corvettes, built on the Admiralty account, were purportedly sailing for Britain via Singapore. Paul Hirst knew with the developments as they were it was unlikely *Toowoomba* and the other corvettes would go beyond Singapore.

In the Singapore War Room the news was bleak. The movement of the Japanese Army down the Malaya Peninsula seemed unstoppable. Despite being numerically inferior, the enemy had superior jungle fighting skills as well as greater firepower with their light tanks and manoeuvrability with bicycle equipped infantry. They were also greatly assisted by control of the air and the sea. From the day of the invasion Penang was subjected to daily bombing raids and it fell on 17 December.

The inexperienced defending troops often compared unfavourably to the battle-hardened Japanese. This was the case of the 11th Indian Division and on 23 December its commander Major General David Murray-Lyon was somewhat unjustly relieved of his command. Four days later, after months of considerable strain Brooke-Popham was finally replaced by Lieutenant General Sir Henry Pownall. John Collins was more charitable than most towards Brooke-Popham, particularly about the Air Marshal's public utterances about the ability to defend Singapore. From Churchill down there was a high degree of bluff to deter the Japanese with forces assigned to the theatre. John later wrote Brooke-Popham, 'knew very well that it would have been folly to tell the world we lacked many of the requirements of defence'.[21] What remains clear, however, was that these forces were not used to their fullest effect.

In contrast to the strained festivities John Collins experienced in Batavia, Paul Hirst enjoyed a peaceful Christmas Day as *Toowoomba* and *Wollongong* lay at anchor off Thursday Island at the entrance to the Torres Strait. Both ships then spent the next five days sweeping the channels for any mines. The reason for this concentrated work became apparent to the corvette crews when on New Year's Eve the US heavy cruiser USS *Houston*, five destroyers[22] and the tanker *Harry Ludenbach* passed through the swept channel. Three days later the US and Australian ships under the command of Captain Albert Rooks in *Houston* escorted the US troopships *Clairmont*, *Willard A. Holbrook* and *Bloemfontein* to Darwin.

In the face of the unfolding crisis the long awaited unified command was established. On 4 January General Archibald Wavell was made Supreme Commander of the American-British-Dutch-Australian Command (ABDACOM). He established a headquarters at Bandung near Batavia. This was 120 kilometres from the naval headquarters at Surabaya. The Commander, Ground Forces was the Dutch Lieutenant General Hein ter Poorten while the Commander, Air Forces was the British Air Chief Marshal Sir Richard Peirse.

With Singapore's prospects looking increasingly bleak and the need for the naval forces to carry on the fight against the Japanese, Admiral Layton moved his headquarters. On 5 January he sailed from Singapore in the cruiser HMS *Dragon* for Batavia. Layton's relocation was but a stopgap as he was to become the inaugural Commander-in-Chief, Ceylon. It was planned from Ceylon that the Eastern Fleet under Admiral Sir James Somerville would be regenerated.

The ships of the US Asiatic Fleet were progressively withdrawn from the Philippines, particularly after the effective destruction of the Cavite naval base on 10 December. A large proportion sailed to the Dutch East Indies and Admiral Hart arrived in Surabaya via the submarine USS *Shark* on Boxing Day. He was 'absolutely aghast' to learn from the Dutch Governor General that he had been appointed the Commander Naval Forces, under Wavell. He immediately sensed that the Dutch had lost confidence in the US Navy after the Philippines debacle, and he didn't blame them for this view. Hart was initially 'in very much of a daze, as to what to do next' but was pleased his name was clearly not sufficiently blackened in Washington for the Philippines defeat. However, at 65 years old and approaching three years into his Asiatic Fleet command, Hart told Admiral King he thought they should have picked another officer because of his 'doubtful endurance'.[23]

The other key naval appointments were Rear Admiral Palliser who was appointed Hart's Chief of Staff, while the Dutch Rear Admiral Karel Doorman became the Commander Combined Striking Force. John Collins was promoted to Commodore 2nd Class which was a temporary rank. Initially his position was Commodore Far East Squadron but on 20 January it was changed to Commodore Commanding the China Force. The one officer without a combined command position was Admiral Helfrich. This remained an awkward situation for both Hart and Helfrich.[24]

Importantly, part of Hart's headquarters was a strong naval intelligence component. This included a detachment from Station CAST and one of Rupert Long's liaison officers, Paymaster Commander John Proud. For Hart it was vital to quickly develop a shared view of the strategic situation and agreement on how to stop 'losing this damned war, as rapidly, as has been the case these four weeks'.[25] On 27 January he met with Helfrich and John Collins. He later wrote:

> Find that I see eye to eye with Collins—who is now a Commodore—rather better than with anyone else. So when I found that he agreed with some ideas, and decisions of mine which had just about jelled I went into action on them forthwith. We are accepting, as fact the very great probability that the Japs will succeed in driving through to the Malay Barrier, and I am beginning to move indispensable auxiliaries westward from Port Darwin.[26]

John Collins flew his Commodore's broad pennant from HMS *Anking*, a small requisitioned passenger-cargo ship used as both a stores and communications ship. His squadron comprised the heavy cruiser *Exeter* of the Battle of the River Plate fame, *Hobart* under the irrepressible Captain Harry Howden; the obsolescent cruisers *Danae*, *Dragon* and *Durban*, the destroyers *Jupiter, Encounter, Express, Electra, Stronghold, Scout, Tenedos* and *Vampire*; the sloops *Yarra* and Indian *Jumna* and the corvettes *Bendigo, Burnie, Goulburn* and *Maryborough*. This was the largest squadron yet commanded by a member of the Pioneer Class.

The cruisers and destroyers of the China Force would in time have to join the Dutch and US warships to counter the inevitable Japanese naval assault on the Dutch East Indies. The Dutch naval force consisted of two light cruisers *De Ruyter* and *Java*, the destroyers *Witt de With, Kortenaer* and *Banckert* and 16 submarines. The US Navy had assembled the cruisers *Houston* and *Marblehead* along with the destroyers *Alden, Edwards, Ford, Paul Jones* and *Pope*.

The most pressing task of the modest China Force was to evacuate civilians and military forces from Singapore to the Dutch East Indies or beyond. On 11 January Paul Hirst as Senior Officer sailed *Toowoomba, Wollongong* and *Ballarat* from Darwin for an uneventful passage through the Lombok Strait to Tanjung Priok arriving on 18 January. They found the port a 'second Singapore' with various ABDA ships including *Yarra* in harbour. The corvettes now joined John Collins' squadron. On the same day Kuala Lumpur fell.

On their advance south down the Malay peninsula the Japanese encountered the Australian 8th Division under Major General Gordon Bennett. At this point their advance dramatically slowed. Yet by 27 January without any defensive positions in the south the British Empire forces had to withdraw across to Singapore Island. Even defences that might have protected the water supply and the city from artillery fire had been viewed by General Percival as being bad for morale.

As the Japanese closed in on Singapore the urgency of convoy work increased as did Japanese air attacks. By the first week of February the combination of growing ship numbers from Singapore and air raids made Batavia's port of Tanjong Priok the scene of increasing congestion. This was a major concern for John Collins who was keenly aware the ships anchored off the port were also vulnerable to submarine attack.[27]

During the Dutch East Indies campaign HMAS Toowoomba *led a charmed life which many of her sailors attributed to Paul Hirst.* (RAN)

At this time the corvettes found Singapore an almost surreal port. While waiting for the next convoy shore leave was granted and sailors dodged air raids to visit bars and the New World Cabaret.[28] It was during one of these port visits that Paul Hirst addressed his greatest shortfall—air defence. As the corvettes were completed in Australia they were yet to be fitted with modern anti-aircraft guns such as the 40 mm Bofors and the 20 mm Oerlikon. *Toowoomba* was only armed with a low angle 4-inch gun, a 2-pounder and a couple of ineffective Vickers machine guns. One night alongside in Singapore Paul Hirst had his senior sailors 'acquire' an Army Bofors which was duly man-handled onboard in pieces and made 'ready and able in a short space of time'.[29] In subsequent convoy work Signalman James Carpenter wrote:

> We felt immensely happy with such a weapon to help ward off attack from low level. Our Bofors must have been the only one on a corvette in the area and gave other ships with us more confidence. Again 'Digger' Hirst showed his popularity with all onboard and with kindred ships.[30]

The new found firepower arrived onboard just in time. On 5 February *Toowoomba* was subjected to the first air attack specifically directed at her. Five bombers made a succession of runs on the corvette. In the first approach bombs fell less than fifty yards astern, while bombs in the second attack straddled the starboard quarter. Paul Hirst manoeuvred the badly shaken ship and awaited the next determined approach. The third and final run was even closer with the exploding bombs narrowly missing, but leaving smoke marks on the ship's side. Following the attack Stoker Tom King, who was born a fortnight before his captain and in 1924 had served under him in the old *Anzac*, wrote a song based on the popular hit *You Say the Cutest Things Baby* about 'Digger' Hirst's bomb dodging skills. The following day Paul wrote to his wife about the raid:

> Five Japanese bombers took to us yesterday and attacked us three times—anyway they all missed by a few yards and then crossed us with another and another attempt, don't know now how they missed us. Tell you it is just like a rat with a trap because as you know we can't do much to help ourselves.[31]

The manner in which the Japanese used their aircraft greatly impressed Admiral Hart. In particular the way they were able to concentrate their air assets to support their land and sea forces at the right time. This made it difficult for his naval forces to get to grips with the Japanese. Another difficulty was just dealing with the different national demands and sensitivities. He confided in his diary that:

> The British are quite square ... I must say have been fair and open during this last two or three weeks ... Helfrich, is a different cup of tea, however, for he seems to eternally plot to let or make, the Americans do it. At times he is subtle, and at other times his efforts, are so patent that he is imprudent. He does his best to keep his own ships in port.[32]

Hart was also concerned about the other Dutch Admiral. While accepting the challenges Doorman had he was worried about his subordinate's state of mind based on 'some surprising signals'. He met with him on 8 February onboard Doorman's flagship. Hart later wrote in his diary that:

> I'm afraid Doorman has not the dash and drive for it; he is more of the cloistered, war-college type of officer. All in all, I doubt that it will make much difference in the end, and—politically speaking—it's well to put the Dutchman in the saddle. The Dutch are inclined to be critical of anything the Americans do, and their command set-up will stop a lot of their asking why the American Fleet does not win the war.[33]

During the weeks that *Toowoomba* operated in the China Force, Paul Hirst became an almost permanent fixture on the bridge, ready to respond at a moment's notice to a Japanese air attack. In coping with the stress Paul wrote home that:

I am still quite well and am thankful I have no imagination. In fact five minutes after everything was over I could hardly believe it happened.[34]

The corvettes were ideally suited to the escort role to and from the strategically important Palembang with its nearby oil refineries. Located up the Musi River in southern Sumatra, on several occasions *Toowoomba* steamed upriver while aerial dogfights took place overhead between British and Japanese fighters. Their familiarity with the river port was such that Paul Hirst was known among the corvette sailors as the 'Senior Officer of Palembang River Patrol'. Fittingly they would be one of the last ships to leave the port.

On Friday the 13th *Toowoomba*, *Ballarat*, *Wollongong* and *Bendigo* escorted a slow convoy from Palembang through Banka Strait to Tanjong Priok. Hugging the coast they escaped most of the air attacks that were directed at nearby ships transiting from Singapore. However *Toowoomba* was attacked by eight bombers. Despite the ill omens of the day she remained unscathed. Later that day the corvette was detached to pick up survivors from the Dutch tanker *Merula* which was ablaze. *Toowoomba* recovered 42 sailors in a piteous state and landed them at the crowded Tanjong Priok. Of the constant air attacks another of Paul Hirst's sailors, Ordinary Seaman Norm Smith wrote the poem *Last Stop Tjilatjap* which captured the mood:

Out of the sun they came, white flashes, red dots a hazy blur,
Mast high with guns ablaze, staccato roars the air did stir;
Bombs dropped in crowded harbour, ships vanished in walls of flame,
The sons of Nippon had arrived with little opposition to stop their game.[35]

The following day Admiral Hart was replaced as Commander Naval Forces by Admiral Helfrich. The reasons for the change were complex. Wavell had formed the view, valid or not, that Hart was too old and pessimistic, while the Dutch had gone direct to Washington advocating the switch to Helfrich. After some behind the scenes manoeuvering the

US Chief of Naval Operations, Admiral Ernest King suggested to Hart that he ask to be relieved on health grounds. Hart, although making the point there were no health grounds, gracefully acceded.[36] On 16 February Hart arrived in Tanjong Priok to take passage to Ceylon in the cruiser HMS *Durban*. Before departing he went to John Collins' office to bid him farewell. Hart wrote in his diary that night that, 'the Australian ... is one of the best of the British that I've seen out here.'[37]

As anticipated Helfrich demanded stouter defence and was prepared to sacrifice ships and men for that aim. Helfrich was to earn the nickname 'Ship-a-day Helfrich' in the US press over coming weeks.[38]

Although Helfrich had a very different personality to Hart, John Collins forged a good working relationship with him. The Dutchman respected John's battle-seasoned reputation. They did not however, always see eye to eye, such as when John remonstrated with Helfrich after he relieved a Dutch submarine commander for being 'unlucky' following several unsuccessful torpedo attacks on Japanese warships.[39]

On 15 February Singapore finally surrendered. It was Britain's greatest military defeat and consigned a most terrible internment to over 80,000 men. Some men on their own initiative effected an escape. Three Australian soldiers who got away by boat were subsequently found by *Toowoomba* sailors wandering the Tanjong Priok waterfront looking for succour. Paul Hirst agreed to take them onboard where they readily worked as seamen.[40] After experiencing a few air raids onboard, one of their number later landed himself reasoning his chances of survival were better in Batavia than in *Toowoomba*.

The Japanese military now turned all available forces on Dutch East Indies and the Allied naval forces that stood in their way. The Japanese strategy was to take the archipelago through three broad thrusts. In the centre the Japanese had already landed in Borneo. On 10 January they had taken Tarakan and within seven days had land-based aircraft operating from the airfield. Amphibious assaults followed at Macassar in the western Celebes on 9 February and Bali on the 18th. The primary goal

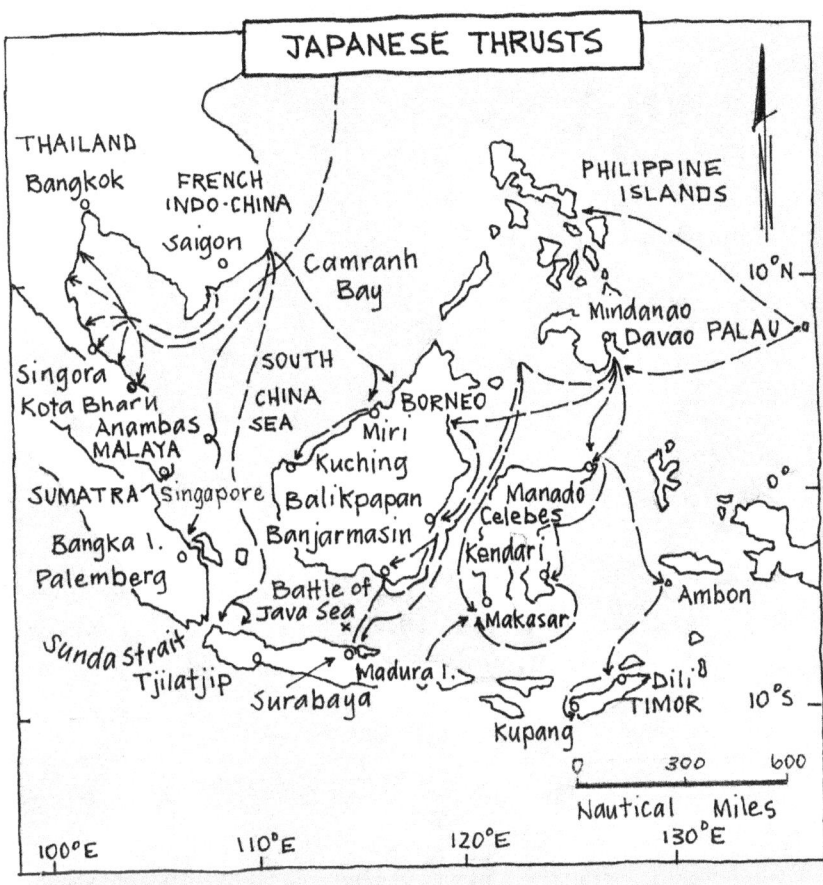

of the central force was East Java with the key naval port of Surabaya. To the east a force landed in eastern Celebes and then on 31 January in Ambon. The final objective of this force was to take Timor. In the west, the Japanese first inserted forces into eastern Sumatra to secure the oil refinery facilities at Palembang and then western Java with the capital of Batavia. The small Allied forces attempting to defend these areas could not deal with the simultaneous and overwhelming thrusts.

Into this cauldron came a third member of the Pioneer Class—Leigh Watkins. He embarked in *Perth* to join John Collins' staff in Batavia. Also onboard were four officers and senior sailors, including Chaplain James Mathieson, who was to transfer to HMAS *Hobart*. Originally *Perth* was to arrive in Batavia escorting a convoy of five empty tankers from Fremantle to bring on fuel from the Palembang oil refinery. As the ships neared Sunda Strait it became clear they were unlikely to obtain their loads. All but the Dutch tanker *'sJacob* were ordered to return to Australia with *Adelaide* directed to escort the convoy. John Collins instructed *Perth* to continue north to bolster the Allied naval force, as previously directed by the War Cabinet, escorting to Tanjong Priok *'sJacob* and two more Dutch ships she picked up along the way.[41]

The transfer of four personnel from *Perth* to *Hobart* was to occur ideally when both cruisers were in port. The opportunity presented itself in Tanjung Priok on 25 February. *Perth* was already in port replenishing and *Hobart* steamed up the harbour and went alongside the oiler *War Sirdar*. A boat was soon organised for the transfer. Also onboard the boat was *Perth's* gunnery officer who was going to visit his counterpart. Across the harbour a formation of 27 Japanese bombers could be seen. Their targets were both shipping and the oil tanks in the port precinct. Soon all ships were engaging with 8-inch, 6-inch and 4-inch guns as well as small calibre anti-aircraft guns. Because of the presence of *Perth's* gunnery officer in the boat it was decided to turn back rather than complete the trip to *Hobart*. As Chaplain Mathieson later wrote 'a fateful day it was to prove'.[42]

Also in port during the raid was *Toowoomba* which added her weight to the defence of the port. For her troubles she received a burst of machine gun fire from a Japanese dive bomber that left a trail of bullet holes on her sweep deck. After the air raid Hec Waller went ashore to a conference. He returned with the news that the force would sail later that day to intercept a Japanese invasion convoy. Waller then sent for his '*Hobart*' officers and Leigh Watkins. Chaplain Mathieson later wrote:

> Captain Waller sent for Owen[43] and myself and Lieutenant Commander Watkins, who was to have joined the Batavia staff. We went up to the Bridge and Captain Waller told us that the Japanese were expected very shortly to attack Java and that undoubtedly the seaboard towns would be occupied. He suggested that rather than go ashore and await the problematic return of *Hobart* we should stay in *Perth*. We agreed,

as none of us was keen on being taken as prisoner. Had we only gone ashore we would have been alright, as *Hobart* came in again later. She passed through the breakwater as we went out, so close to us that the proverbial biscuit might have been tossed on to her deck.[44]

For Leigh Watkins the staff position to which he had been assigned effectively no longer existed and as an engineer he could contribute more in *Perth*. Late that afternoon *Perth* sailed in company with *Exeter*, *Jupiter*, *Electra* and *Encounter*. The following day they briefly entered Surabaya for another planning conference, this time with Rear Admiral Karel Doorman and the other captains. Doorman outlined his plans for intercepting the Java-bound Japanese amphibious force approaching from the Makassar Strait.

The Allied force that left port that night, in addition to those that came from Batavia, now included the cruisers *De Ruyter*, *Java* and *Houston* and the destroyers *Kortenaer*, *Witt de With*, *Alden*, *John D Edwards*, *John D Ford* and *Paul Jones*. Doorman flew his flag in *De Ruyter*. This Combined Striking Force was less formidable than it first appeared. Many of the ships were short of ammunition and carried battle damage or other defects. Few had operated together and so their tactics, procedures and communications were not well established. Only *Exeter* had radar. *Hobart*, which was delayed by difficulties getting fuel, joined *Dragon*, *Danae*, *Scout* and *Tenedos* to block any invasion forces to the western end of Java.

At about 2.30 pm on 27 February after nearly two days of fruitless search in the Java Sea, Doorman decided to return to Surabaya. At about the same time *Hobart* and the Western Striking Force were returning to Tanjong Priok. As Doorman's force was entering port an aircraft had finally detected an approaching Japanese invasion force. The Allied force reversed course and prepared for action.

The enemy invasion fleet was escorted by a task force commanded by Rear Admiral Takeo Takagi. He was a highly regarded flag officer who had commanded both submarines and a battleship in his long sea career. His force comprised the two heavy cruisers *Nachi* and *Haguro*, two light cruisers *Naka* and *Jintsu* and 14 destroyers.[45] The two heavy cruisers were the largest of their type in the world each with ten 8-inch guns. In contrast *Exeter* represented the smallest type of heavy cruiser with only six 8-inch guns. *Houston* was also reduced to six 8-inch guns due to earlier battle damage knocking out her after turret.

At 4.12 pm on 27 February *Electra* sighted *Jintsu* leading one of the Japanese formations. Four minutes later the Japanese heavy cruisers opened fire. The Battle of the Java Sea had begun. Within minutes *Exeter* and *Houston* returned fire but the range was too great for the Australian and Dutch light cruisers. Admiral Takagi had three advantages, the first was his heavy cruisers, the second was a homogeneous force and the third was the large number of lethal and fast 24-inch Long Lance torpedoes. His destroyers launched one long range torpedo attack on Doorman's force without result. Frustratingly due to the range the Allied light cruisers were still struggling to get into action. Hec Waller in particular chafed at not being able to return fire.[46] His experience from the Mediterranean theatre was that the range had to be brought in much closer.

The battle was progressing to the west and the warships were getting closer to the invasion convoy. At 5 pm Admiral Takagi resolved to press home his advantage and released another destroyer attack. His destroyers fired 68 Long Lance torpedoes but only *Kortenaer* was hit. The ship blew up leaving her bow and stern bobbing vertically a few feet above the surface. Miraculously *Encounter* rescued 113 of her 153 crew. About this time *Exeter* was struck by an 8-inch shell knocking out six of her eight boilers. Her speed rapidly reduced to 11 knots and she hauled out of line. The three cruisers astern of her followed, leaving *De Ruyter* exposed ahead. *Perth* and the destroyers laid a smoke screen to protect the vulnerable *Exeter*. Doorman reformed his line and steamed south east between *Exeter* and the Japanese. He then ordered the British destroyers to attack with torpedoes through the smokescreen. The three destroyers were widely separated and attacked independently. As *Electra* came through the other side of the smokescreen she soon found herself in a hot engagement with the destroyers *Jintsu* and *Asagumo*. Four hits were observed on *Asagumo* before *Electra* was hit in the boiler room and went dead in the water. The ship was doomed. After taking further punishment she rolled over and sank about 6 pm.[47] The other two British destroyers survived their foray beyond the smoke screen.

In the gathering darkness Doorman led his force to the north east hoping to work his way around the Japanese cruisers to attack the amphibious ships. At 7.30 pm the force briefly encountered four Japanese ships and Doorman altered his plan and altered course to the south to get between the Javanese coastline and the enemy. At about 9 pm *Jupiter* struck a mine and remained dead in the water slowly sinking. After about an hour Doorman's force was shadowed by Japanese aircraft who dropped flares to illuminate them. The two opposing forces again came into contact at 11.30 pm. *Perth* hit one of the Japanese heavy cruisers but *De Ruyter* was struck down aft and Doorman turned his force away. *Nachi* and *Haguro* then launched a devastating torpedo attack. First *Java* was hit and the whole stern section exploded, then *De Ruyter* blew up in Hec Waller's words 'with an appalling explosion and settled aft heavily on fire'.[48] In that moment the battle was lost. Waller, mindful that Doorman had earlier said that any disabled ship should be left 'to the mercy of the enemy,'[49] took charge of the remainder of the force and cleared the area. Over 850 Dutch sailors had been lost in the two cruisers including Admiral Doorman.

Hec Waller was now senior officer of the Striking Force. With no prospect of getting at the invasion force and with probably six Japanese cruisers against his two, Waller elected to withdraw to Tanjong Priok. Helfrich later unfairly criticised him for doing so. The Dutch Admiral seemed incapable of taking a broader perspective of the war beyond defence of the Dutch East Indies.

Perth and *Houston* returned to Tanjong Priok arriving about 1.30 pm. John Collins ordered them to sail that evening for Australia via the Sunda Strait.[50] Hec Waller had in Captain Albert Rooks a kindred spirit. Rooks had a tenacious fighting spirit which he had imbued into his ship. Admiral Hart said he was 'a splendid officer of the intellectual type'.[51] Both cruisers were ordered to pass through the Sunda Strait and make for the southern Javanese port of Tjilatjap where they could fuel and pick up any Allied servicemen before sailing for Australia. The Dutch destroyer *Evertsen* was to catch up with them when fuelled. The only warships they expected to encounter were the corvettes *Toowoomba, Bendigo, Ballarat* and *Goulburn* which were carrying out an anti-infiltration patrol at the southern end of Sunda Strait.

There were reports of a Japanese convoy to the north east of Batavia but Hec Waller reasoned that the coast should be clear on their westward passage to Sunda Strait. The two cruisers however crossed paths with the Western Java Invasion Convoy. Fifty transports including the headquarters ship *Ryujo Maru* with the Army Commander Lieutenant General Hitoshi Imamura embarked, were in Bantam Bay at Sunda Strait's northern entrance. At the mouth of the bay and between Waller and the Sunda Strait was a strong force of escorting warships. These were Vice Admiral Takeo Kurita's 7th Cruiser Division (*Mogami* and *Mikuma*) and Rear Admiral Kenzaburo Hara's nine ships of the 5th Destroyer Flotilla.[52]

At around 11 pm *Perth*'s lookouts sighted a ship near the entrance to the Strait and sent a challenge by flashing light. It was thought to be one of the corvettes, it was however, a Japanese destroyer—probably *Harukaze*.

Hec Waller ordered *Perth* to close up for Action Stations. The men purposefully went to their assigned stations as they had done so many times before. All doors and hatches were dogged down to maximise the watertight integrity of the ship and prevent the spread of any fire or water ingress. Leigh Watkins' post was in main machinery below the waterline.

At the same time Waller sent an enemy contact report and *Perth* opened fire on the destroyer. Both sides were surprised by the chance encounter. Soon other Japanese ships were observed and *Perth* and *Houston* were each engaging multiple targets. *Perth* received three initial shell hits that caused only superficial damage. In turn the cruisers were wreaking some havoc as was 'friendly' fire from the Japanese warships which missed their intended targets and hit transports. In the mêlée a minesweeper and the transport *Sakura Maru* were sunk and the headquarters ship *Ryojo Maru* and two other transports badly damaged. Imamura and his staff had to jump into the sea and the General spent some time sitting on some flotsam awaiting rescue.

About midnight both *Perth* and *Houston* were rapidly running out of ammunition and Waller decided to attempt an escape through the Strait. They increased to full speed and down below in *Perth* the engineers worked to give all the power they could produce. Five minutes later however one of the dreaded Long Lance torpedoes struck the starboard side of *Perth* and she rapidly started to lose speed. A second torpedo hit the starboard side below the bridge. *Perth's* fate was sealed. Hec Waller said, 'Christ! That's torn it ... Abandon ship'.[53]

As the crew came up from below to take to the water, two more torpedoes hit *Perth*. In the fierce engagement Leigh Watkins and other engineering personnel were injured by fire, steam, acid or shrapnel. They were brought up to the sick bay which had quickly become a scene of carnage and misery. With the order to abandon ship, stretcher bearers took the wounded to the ship's waist where some carley rafts had been cut from their mountings. Leigh was among the wounded who was assisted into the water. He drifted away from the stricken cruiser and into what Ben Howells had once written of as, 'the awful stillness of the listening night'.[54] Leigh was never seen again and was the third of the Pioneer Class to be lost at sea.[55] He joined his friend Frank Larkins in the same archipelagic waters.

In all, about 353 men did not survive the sinking of their proud ship. Among them was the charismatic Hec Waller who had seemed pre-destined to lead the Navy in later years.

Houston battled on alone but she too, was soon torpedoed. The Japanese destroyers closed in repeatedly hitting her with gunfire. Captain Rooks was killed on his bridge and was later posthumously awarded America's highest award for valour, the Congressional Medal of Honor. Just after 00.30 am *Houston* rolled over and sank with the loss of nearly 700 men.

While this action was taking place at the northern entrance to Sunda Strait, the five corvettes to the south could hear the distant thuds of battle.[56] The next morning, realising that the invasion had taken place to the north, Paul Hirst and the other captains decided the best option was to proceed to Tjilatjap. Hopefully there would be sufficient fuel there to allow the corvettes to make it to Australia.

Back at Tanjong Priok the port lay in ruins and was virtually deserted of any shipping that could get underway. *Anking* had already sailed for Tjilatjap where it was initially hoped to establish an operating base. On the morning of 1 March news of the Japanese landing to the east of Batavia came through. Admiral Helfrich informed his British, US and Australian subordinates that he formally renounced control over their forces. John Collins was ordered to relocate to Tjilatjap. He and his staff left later that day over land. Both the road and rail links were chaotic. A signal was also sent to *Perth* and *Houston* directing them to avoid Tjilatjap and proceed to Fremantle. Both ships were of course already at the bottom of Sunda Strait.

On the evening of 1 March John Collins arrived at Tjilatjap. He found in the harbour *Burnie, Bendigo, Stronghold* and a handful of Dutch, British and American merchant ships. Arriving over land in dribs and drabs were servicemen and civilians seeking escape to Australia. They included 75 survivors of the destroyer *Jupiter* who were soon embarked in *Bendigo*. She sailed that evening with most of John Collins' staff also embarked. The following morning more personnel arrived at the port including more survivors from *Jupiter* and *Electra*. John sought the cooperation of the Dutch senior officer to ensure as many people as possible could be evacuated.

Keeping close inshore Paul Hirst's corvettes steamed towards Tjilatjap. In the early hours of 2 March they sighted *Yarra, Jumna* and a small convoy offshore also heading to the same port. At 11.30 am as John Collins was still trying to find space for personnel when *Toowoomba* and the other corvettes unexpectedly arrived. They were a god-send and allowed all British and Australian personnel that John had responsibility for to be evacuated. He instructed the other ships not to enter port. *Jumna* was ordered to try and make Colombo while *Yarra* and her convoy of *Anking, Francol* and minesweeper *MMS.51* were to sail to Australia.

To 'spread the risk of interception' John Collins ordered the ships to leave Tjilatjap in staggered groups and by different routes.[57] *Toowoomba* and *Goulburn* sailed at 6 pm hugging the coast to the east. John sailed from Tjilatjap four hours later in *Burnie*. Both she and *Ballarat* hugged the coast to the west then headed for Australia.

Not all ships made it through. The first to be lost were the tanker USS *Pecos* and the destroyer USS *Edsall*. They were overwhelmed by a force including two battleships and three aircraft carriers[58] on 1 March. Despite the odds, *Edsall* went on the attack with one of her torpedoes narrowly missing the cruiser *Chikuma*. These Japanese ships under the command of Vice Admiral Chuichi Nagumo were part of the force that had so devastatingly bombed Darwin on 19 February.

On 2 March the British destroyer *Stronghold* succumbed to the cruiser *Maya* and destroyers *Arashi* and *Nowaki*. These ships, joined by the cruisers *Takao* and *Atago*, intercepted *Yarra* and her convoy on the morning of 4 March. Lieutenant Commander Robert Rankin, in command of *Yarra* for just three weeks, ordered the convoy to scatter, and like *Edsall* heroically attacked her superior foe. One by one the convoy ships were sunk. The last was *Yarra* herself. *Stronghold* survivors onboard *Maya* were brought up on deck to witness the might of the Japanese Navy. What they saw was the bravery of *Yarra*. One *Stronghold* sailor wrote:

> The destroyers were circling *Yarra* which appeared stationary, and were pouring fire into her. She was still firing back as we could see odd gun flashes. The three cruisers then formed line ahead and steamed away from the scene. The last we saw of *Yarra* was a high column of smoke, but we were vividly impressed by her fight.[59]

The other ships from Tjilatjap survived the gauntlet and John Collins arrived in Fremantle on 8 March. So ended one of the most demanding periods of his career. During an intense nine months, first in Singapore and then in the Dutch East Indies he had demonstrated an acute strategic awareness and an ability to work in complex multinational headquarters. Importantly, he worked constructively to achieve the common aim while

John Collins leaving Tjilatjap in HMAS Burnie *along with his Chief Staff Officer Captain LH Bell, RN.* (JA Collins' Collection)

at the same time ensuring Australian interests were protected. Admiral Layton wrote of John that he was:

> An outstanding Staff Officer with an exceptionally clear brain which he makes full use of. Very thorough, does not form an opinion until he has well considered the subject matter and then he abides by it. He is very loyal and devoted to his service in which he should rise to the highest ranks.
> He has subsequently held the appointment of Commodore Commanding China Force at a very difficult time with success. His executive (military command) capabilities are as high as his Staff qualities.[60]

John Collins' service was recognized by being Mentioned in Despatches for 'gallantry and devotion to duty in Singapore'.[61] It was arguably deserving of greater recognition such as a Distinguished Service Order, but there was doubtless little appetite for too many awards arising from the debacle of Singapore. The appreciative Dutch would in 1943 make John a Commander of the Order of Orange-Nassau. Rupert Long said of his classmate, 'Collins at least kept his head where others didn't and saw in his limited command the right thing to do continuously'.[62]

Since the defeat in the Dutch East Indies, there have been differing judgments on the strategies employed and the sacrifices made by so many. Certainly Admiral Hart remained critical of Helfrich's 'fight at any cost' approach and later wrote of the Dutch Admiral, 'In the Java campaign, he lost a thousand officers and men of the Asiatic Fleet, all killed, I felt quite useless'.[63] Rupert Long who had been unimpressed with Helfrich, was equally critical of his 'suicide was the only course approach' and wrote:

> The Helfrich idea of dying for the sake of dying has been applied in history but never, as far as I can remember—except in Thermopylae—to bring about successful conclusion to a war.[64]

Whatever the validity of the strategies employed, the campaign pitted inadequate forces against the Japanese onslaught. For the RAN it remains a chapter characterised by dedication to the task against great odds. There were demonstrations of great valour and much personal sacrifice. Members of the Pioneer Class played a leading part in the campaign and were among those to lay down their lives.

The day after his arrival in Fremantle, John Collins was made Commodore Commanding Fremantle and Senior Naval Officer, Western Australia. Although physically and mentally spent John had to push himself in this new role. The contrast between the war at Australia's doorstep and the defence preparedness in Fremantle was most marked and he knew greater efforts were needed to prepare for the Japanese.

Among the other arrivals from the Dutch East Indies was Rupert Long's liaison officer, Commander Proud, as well as other Australian and British officers from the intelligence staff. Although having reached the safety of Fremantle they were now 'marooned' with no priority for transport to the eastern seaboard. In desperation Proud rang Rupert who gave 'the expectant warm welcome and better still, priority air passage across for myself and members of the team'.[65]

On 10 March *Toowoomba* and *Goulburn* finally arrived in Fremantle having stopped in Exmouth for sufficient fuel to complete the passage. On arrival Paul Hirst interceded with the Army authorities to ensure that his two 'soldier-sailors' were not charged with desertion. For the next two months the corvettes were able to rest their battle-fatigued crews when not patrolling in the local area. This work was varied in June when the corvettes were sent on rotation to provide an anti-submarine screen for the US Navy's submarine squadron operating out of Albany.

It was during *Toowoomba's* turn in this duty that on 16 July 1942 Paul Hirst received an unexpected signal that he was to be promoted to Commander. Signalman James Carpenter recorded, 'All crew members were delighted and very proud of our old man'.[66] Paul's promotion was the result of the decision to deploy four corvettes to the British Eastern Fleet. He would be senior officer of the group.[67]

Celebrations were short-lived. On the return passage to Fremantle *Toowoomba* struck very heavy seas which tore off the asdic dome as well as damaging some upper deck fittings. The battered corvette arrived in Fremantle on Saturday 18 July. John Collins came onboard *Toowoomba* on the Monday to inspect the damage. Although additional anti-aircraft armament and other equipment were that week to be fitted in preparation for the deployment, Paul Hirst believed that the ship should go into refit to repair the storm damage. There was a different view ashore. For the next week there was uneasiness onboard as Paul confronted shore authorities. On Saturday 25 July—later known onboard as 'Black Saturday', a clear lower deck of all the ship's company was ordered and the sailors mustered on the forecastle. Paul announced he had resigned his command over the issue of the refit.[68] The news stunned the men. In addition, to his highly regarded professional capabilities, his sailors greatly appreciated that Paul was 'not stuffy' and genuinely cared about their welfare. Signalman Donald Fraser described his Captain as 'a bonza bloke'.[69] After the clear lower deck Paul returned to his cabin to pack. A gift was hurriedly produced by his sailors to present to him before he left *Toowoomba* later that day. On Paul's departure 'a gloom settled over the ship'.[70]

Subsequent events vindicated Paul Hirst's position as *Toowoomba* had to be sent to Adelaide to receive the refit he sought. Unusually, her entire ship's company was posted from the ship and dispersed throughout the squadron. It was as if all traces of the incident were to be removed. The full details of this unfortunate incident, involving as it does two members of the Pioneer Class, remains opaque. Neither John Collins nor Paul Hirst recorded their version of events and a concerted search by the author through the National Archives of operational, personnel and technical files did not shed any further light on the matter. Paul's service with the Navy was terminated on 3 August 1942. He returned to his farm to grow flax for the war effort.[71]

II

As one Japanese force surged down the Malay Peninsula and then the Dutch East Indies, another descended on the islands of New Guinea. It was as Rupert Long had so long feared. Yet he in the face of this series of defeats retained his optimism. When Commander Proud finally arrived in Melbourne he reported to Rupert. Proud later wrote of the meeting:

> Most of us remember the rather defeatist atmosphere pervading Australia at that time, there didn't seem to be any check on the Japanese drive south, but I found in Melbourne that Long, far from subscribing to the general defeatism was already planning counter attacks. AIB [Allied Intelligence Bureau] was already working, with men in the field, but Long felt this was only part of the operation and he immediately started planning with large scale Special Operations and propaganda covering not only the Pacific islands but extending into Java and so back to Malaya.[72]

Most importantly at this time however Rupert and his team had in place their coast watcher network to report on Japanese movements. There were now 65 teleradios deployed in the 'hub and spoke' networks. Eric Feldt coordinated the coastwatchers from his headquarters in Townsville.

The two most strategically important ports in the region were Rabaul at the northern tip on New Britain and Port Moresby on the southern coast of Papua. Rabaul was of course the old colonial capital of New Guinea. Although damaged by the 1937 eruption of Vulcan, it still possessed a sheltered deep water harbour with an all-important large airstrip at Vunakanau on the outskirts of the town. It was therefore a potential springboard for operations against mainland New Guinea and the Solomons. A base there might also allow Japanese forces to directly threaten shipping between Australia and the US. Rabaul's strategic importance was also appreciated in Canberra. By April 1941 a garrison, known as Lark Force, of about 1,400 Australian troops was deployed under the command of Lieutenant Colonel John Scanlan. Harry Showers and *Adelaide* escorted the troopship *Zealandia* in this task. The RAAF also stationed ten Wirraways and four Hudson light bombers at Vunakanau. The naval presence consisted solely of Hugh MacKenzie and his staff of ten officers and sailors. Usefully the east-west orientation of New Ireland to the north of Rabaul meant that the coastwatchers on the land were ideally placed to give warning to the Australian forces of Japanese air or naval attacks on Rabaul. However, in sum the combined Australian force was woefully inadequate to counter any determined Japanese attack.

In December 1941 Australian authorities first moved expatriates from outlying islands to Rabaul. As part of this movement the coastwatcher at Maron deserted his post and left his teleradio and the all-important 'X' crystal on the island. On 15 December Hugh MacKenzie, with the assistance of a RAAF Catalina and its crew was able to retrieve the intact teleradio.

By the end of December ships and aircraft had evacuated expatriate women and children from Rabaul. Shamefully this did not include those from the sizeable Chinese community, noting the well documented Japanese atrocities in China. By the time of the first Japanese air reconnaissance over New Britain, Rabaul had the feel of a garrison town.

In early January 1942 elements of the Japanese 4th Fleet under Vice Admiral Shigeyoshi Inoue gathered in Guam and Truk to prepare for a co-ordinated invasion of New Britain and New Ireland. The forces included the aircraft carriers *Kaga* and *Akagi* which had taken part in the Pearl Harbor attack. These operations were in turn to be a springboard to the capture of Papua and New Guinea.

Yet, the first offensive action was actually conducted by the RAAF Hudson bombers which attacked a Japanese floatplane staging point at Kapingamarangi atoll on New Year's Day. Although this raid did little damage, two days later they destroyed a floatplane. On the morning of 4 January the first Japanese bomber attacks on Vunakanau airfield occurred. Later that day coastwatcher Cornelius (Con) Page on Tabor Island proved the worth of the network by giving forty minutes early warning of another raid. This set the pattern for the next week in the prelude to the inevitable invasion. The imminent danger was clearly felt in Canberra for on 6 January the Burns Philp ship *Malaita* arrived with boom defences for the harbour, but orders were received not to discharge the load and instead return to Sydney.

On the morning of 20 January there was an inordinate amount of Japanese reconnaissance activity over New Ireland, Buka, the Admiralties and Salamaua. Hugh MacKenzie and his staff as the hub of the local coastwatchers took down and sifted their many reports and passed a distilled picture to Lieutenant Colonel Scanlan and authorities in Port Moresby and Australia. Coastwatchers at Tabar, Namatanai and then Miole reported around 100 aircraft bound for Rabaul. These aircraft were a strike package from *Kaga* and *Akagi*. On the first report six Wirraways were sent airborne to gain altitude before the arrival of the raid. Among the attackers were Zero fighters which quickly shot down two Wirraways. The remaining Wirraways did their best to attack the 72 bombers and, combined with ground fire, shot down three Japanese bombers. Just as the bombers withdrew a wave of dive bombers appeared and destroyed a Wirraway which had just landed to re-arm and refuel. The raid wrought significant damage on Rabaul but it had shown to Hugh and his staff the potential of coastwatchers to provide early warning and help defend against Japanese air attacks. If there had been modern fighters rather than Wirraways, the story may have been quite different. As Sub Lieutenant John Gill of Hugh's staff later wrote, 'It remained for growing Allied strength to give the idea its practical application'.[73]

The following day a Hudson bomber sighted four Japanese cruisers steaming towards Rabaul. The rest of the invasion force was unlocated. On receiving this report Hugh MacKenzie decided to burn his substantial holding of confidential books and codes in trenches he already had dug. In a testament to the once grander plans for Rabaul, this holding reflected those required for a much larger naval headquarters. It took seven hours of concerted burning to finish the task. In keeping with Hugh's sense of humour and a strong desire to irritate the Japanese, he had the now empty safes filled to the brim with unused paper and other material. They were locked and the keys flung in the harbour.[74]

At 2 am on 22 January Hugh set in train his plans for when the Japanese arrived. He 'procured' three cars and sent five sailors to set up a teleradio at Raluana 25 kilometres south of Rabaul. Gill and three sailors were sent to collect another teleradio Hugh had hidden in the jungle and make for Mount Tuangi. Hugh and Signal Yeoman George Knight went to the Military Headquarters to provide support to Lieutenant Colonel Scanlan who stood to his forces to await the invader.

In lieu of the landing however, was another substantial raid by 70 aircraft that destroyed the gun battery at Praed Point. Not until the evening of 22 January did advance elements of the Japanese 55th Division land at Rabaul supported by cruisers providing shore bombardment. From the invasion fleet in the harbour the Japanese troops fanned out and landed at different points. There was some heavy fighting but Lark Force could not be in all potential landing areas. At dawn the scale of the invasion was evident to the defenders and by the afternoon the port and airfield were in Japanese hands.

Lieutenant Colonel Scanlon had given the order 'every man for himself'. Men streamed south in small groups. Some surrendered or were quickly captured. Unfortunately during their time at Rabaul, the troops had neither been taught jungle survival skills nor guerilla tactics.

At around the same time the Japanese were also landing on New Ireland. In some areas the island is narrow with little jungle in which to hide.

Eric Feldt's men had mixed fortunes. Ken Chambers on Emirau Island managed to escape by boat, narrowly evading a Japanese destroyer. Cecil Jervis on Nissan Island managed to get one signal out reporting a Japanese ship in the lagoon and was not heard from again. Murray Edwards was killed at Kavieng.

At Namatanai, where Eric had been Acting District Officer in 1927, the incumbent was Bill Kyle. Eric regarded Bill as his best friend in New Guinea. Naturally Bill and his assistant Greg Benham were both recruited by Eric as coastwatchers. When both men sighted from their vantage point the invasion force steaming towards Rabaul, they headed eastward collecting ten planters and missionaries along the way. When they reached a cove with a boat Bill sought instructions from Port Moresby. He was told to send the boat but to remain behind. If Eric in Townsville had received that message he would have told both coastwatchers to make their escape. Eric reasoned that on such a small island hiding was difficult and survival would depend on the continued loyalty of the native population. Eric believed, 'natives in general would be sympathetic to us, but not to a degree to endanger themselves'.[75] So it was to prove. Both men located themselves on a ridge near Cape St George and resumed reporting Japanese movements.

It was into this catastrophic situation that the coastwatching organization stepped to save as many of Lark Force as possible. Two days after the invasion Eric ordered Keith McCarthy, who was District Officer and coastwatcher at Talasea, to take his teleradio and head towards Rabaul. Over 300 kilometres of jungle lay before him. McCarthy, like so many in Eric's band, took this daunting challenge in his stride. McCarthy gained the assistance of some Talasea locals and while he went ahead in a launch with two planters, others followed in a schooner to be ready to rescue any soldiers.

In another development the Army had Eric's old boss and friend 'Kaasa' Townsend establish the Australian New Guinea Administrative Unit or ANGAU which would run the civil administration of Papua and New Guinea. 'Kaasa' selected the patrol officer and now Army Captain,

Gwynne 'Blue' Harris to command a collection of boats from Finschafen to sail to New Britain to aid in the rescue. Among the flotilla were three missionaries, including coastwatcher Reverend Freud. 'Harris' Navy' was joined by two more launches from Madang.

When McCarthy reached Pondo Plantation, about 80 kilometres from Rabaul, he found the first group of soldiers. The plantation's launch was damaged and McCarthy had some men work to get it seaworthy. He then moved forward while one of the locals searched to the south looking for soldiers. McCarthy found one group of starving soldiers lying dispirited in a large field. Unbeknown to them, the field they were in was a crop of edible tapioca. McCarthy had to use all his powers of encouragement and cajoling to get the exhausted soldiers to move towards safety.

Closer to Rabaul Hugh MacKenzie met up with Gill's party and realized that the priority had to be the evacuation of the naval and army personnel. He destroyed the teleradio and prepared the personnel for the rigours that lay ahead. On 1 February his motley party reached the Catholic mission at Lamingi. After a couple of days rest he sent the main party along the coast towards Waterfall Bay. He and three others trekked over mountains to reach the Waterfall Bay teleradio by the more direct route. Hugh's party twice narrowly missed Japanese patrols. At Tol Plantation Hugh saw the evidence of a massacre of 150 Lark Force soldiers.

Hugh retraced his steps and reunited with the larger party then pressed on through Tol once more and further along the coast. On 1 March Hugh received a message by runner advising of McCarthy's rescue efforts with an invitation to strike across the island to Open Bay on the north coast. Conscious of the deteriorating condition of the men he considered the best option was to replicate McCarthy's effort on the south coast near Gasmata. Hugh sent a naval party under Sub-Lieutenant Gill over the mountains to inform McCarthy and authorities of his intentions.

Lieutenant Peter Figgis and Hugh continued along the coast to Palmalmal where they found about 100 men at a plantation under the leadership of Major Bill Owen and medical officer Major Edward Palmer.

These officers with the help of the local missionaries and expatriates had constructed a well-ordered rest area which included a native garden for food. Hugh informed them of the rescue plans. Hugh and Figgis then returned to Waterfall Bay to work on an old lifeboat which might prove useful if the rescue did not readily eventuate. On 5 April their efforts were interrupted with word that the launch *Mascot* had arrived from Papua and that everyone was to assemble at Palmalmal for evacuation in the motor yacht *Laurabada*. On the late afternoon on 9 April she sailed with 153 soldiers, sailors and 19 expatriates for an uneventful passage to Port Moresby. Left behind was teleradio technician Dave Laws and 13 troops who were away and could not be contacted. Laws established contact the following week.

On the northern coast McCarthy's efforts also met with success and in the end about 460 soldiers, sailors and civilians were evacuated in Harris' Navy as well as the motor ship *Lakatoi*. The latter reached Cairns with 212 people onboard.

Hugh MacKenzie rendered a thorough report on the work of the naval team on New Britain. Importantly Hugh and Peter Figgis had carefully interviewed five survivors of the Tol and Waitavulu Plantation massacres and recorded for the first time a clear account of the war crime.[76] Rupert Long recommended Hugh receive a Mentioned in Despatches for his service, but this award did not eventuate.

Eric Feldt remained most concerned about his coastwatchers remaining in the New Ireland group. Con Page on the smaller Tabar Island was the most vulnerable. Only his native partner Ansin Bula and a World War I veteran and planter Jack Talmage, offered support. His situation was not helped by the presence of an old German planter who was malevolent and untrustworthy. Eric instructed Page to reduce his transmissions to a minimum and he sustained him through an air drop of supplies. Eric was determined to evacuate Page and organized a US submarine to rendezvous with him. For three nights Page kept vigil in a canoe off the beach but the submarine never came. It had suffered a mechanical breakdown enroute and had to return to port.

Page reported in subsequent messages increased Japanese activity and then when Eric organized a Catalina, the aircraft crew could not find the lone coastwatcher. As feared in June, Page was betrayed and he and Talmage were taken to Kavieng jail where they were executed. A note to Eric from Page was received two years later seeking help to support Ansin Bula who had stuck by the man she loved.

On New Ireland the situation for Kyle and Benham remained equally perilous. They also found themselves responsible for ten soldiers from the Kavieng garrison and a handful of expatriates ably led by the Kavieng coastwatcher and District Officer John McDonald. He had been a Major in the 1st AIF where he had earned a DSO and MC on the Western Front. Eric once more called upon the excellent support he received from the RAAF to drop supplies to the party. Eventually Kyle obtained a plantation boat which could accommodate everyone onboard and sought direction from Eric as to whether he and Benham should evacuate. The pair were actually well placed in the east of the island to report on Japanese movements and Eric was aware of the potential for a naval encounter in the Coral Sea. He therefore told to them to come out if they considered their position untenable. Bravely they elected to stay and bid farewell to their colleagues who made a successful passage to safety.

By the end of May however, the Japanese became more established and set up a civil administration at Namatani. Japanese patrols increased and Kyle and Benham had several narrow escapes. Their capture seemed inevitable. Eric obtained a US submarine to extract them. The submarine kept the rendezvous for two nights but there was no contact. Eric wanted one more attempt, this time involving one of his experienced men, Pilot Officer Cecil Mason who would go ashore to find if the pair were alive. US submarines were heavily tasked with other duties so Eric and Lieutenant Commander Ira Pryce-Jones journeyed to Brisbane and called on Rear Admiral Francis Rockwell at the submarine base on Brisbane River. After initially denying the request Eric showed Rockwell a copy of a message from Kyle which included the following:

Don't worry about us. With extra food and medicine we can last for some months unless there is more patrol activity than there has been up to date. However, I hope you can eventually get us out or we counter-attack, as they seem to murder anyone they find with teleradios.[77]

The Admiral relented and Mason embarked in the submarine USS *S43* to find Kyle and Benham, as well as Leading Seaman John Woodroffe, on Amir Island. On 3 July Mason stole ashore at night in a collapsible canoe and scouted an area he knew Kyle and Benham had once kept post. Mason encountered a villager who was evasive in his answers. Too late Mason saw that he wore an armband with a rising sun. The next night Mason landed at Anir to find Woodroffe. This time a villager told him Mason was alive and a note was provided for Woodroffe. Mason returned onboard. The next night he paddled inshore to hopefully collect Woodroffe. Two hours later as the submarine closed for the pick-up it had to dive with the appearance of a Japanese patrol boat. After a further two hours the submarine was able to surface and closed the shore. There was no sign of Mason or Woodroffe. For the next four nights the submarine surfaced and waited and then reluctantly returned to Brisbane. Cecil Mason and John Woodroffe had both been captured and were later executed. Equally, tragically Kyle and Benham had been captured 18 hours before the first planned submarine extraction and subsequently executed. At war's end both men were awarded the Distinguished Service Cross.

The rapid Japanese advance caused Rupert Long and Eric Feldt to step back and assess coastwatcher operations. For those in unoccupied territory the model could remain the same however, there was tremendous benefit in being able to keep a presence in strategically important areas where there was a reasonable chance to remain covert. This required a greater level of support with two to four coastwatchers at each location. These men were invariably drawn from the three armed services but Rupert wrote to Eric that:

> I consider it essential that the Number One man of each post should be naval. The Americans have learnt to respect Australian Naval Intelligence, but I am doubtful of their reception of posts with RAAF

or Army in charge. Consequently we must ensure that the men are ours, either by transfer from the other Services, or by direct enlistment.[78]

The existence of the coastwatcher network had to remain secret if its covert operations were to be successful. It was at this time, with the change in its focus that Eric Feldt gave the network the code name *Ferdinand* after the bull of that name in the children's book *The Story of Ferdinand* by American writer Munro Leaf.[79] In that story the bull would rather smell flowers than fight in bullfights. Published in 1936, the book was seen as pacifist propaganda and Hitler had it added to the book burning pyres. To Eric *Ferdinand* was not a frivolous code name:

> Besides serving as one of its cloaks of secrecy, this name was an order to the coastwatchers, a definition of the job. It was a reminder to them that it was not their duty to fight, and thus draw attention to themselves; it was their duty to sit, circumspectly and unobtrusively, and gather information. Of course, like Ferdinand, they could fight if they were stung.[80]

As part of the coastwatcher expansion it was important to try and bring the Solomons and the New Hebrides more fully into the coastwatcher network. In June 1942 Hugh Mackenzie was sent to Vila. He quickly recruited three British District officers Harry Josselyn, Dick Horton and Nick Waddel who all were to prove to be outstanding coastwatchers. Eric Feldt called on the British Resident in the Solomons who did not seem to appreciate the immediacy of the Japanese threat. Eric reported back to Rupert Long that:

> The silly old cow doesn't know yet that the war is on and the Jap is dinkum. If the chance arises, I will hang the British Resident of His Britannic Majesty's Protectorate of the Solomon Islands with his Old School Tie.[81]

Despite Eric's difficulties with the British Resident, the Solomons coastwatch organization was, for the most part, able to make the transition to one operating in occupied territory. During the early Japanese forays on Bougainville the courageous work of Jack Read, Paul Mason and Lieutenant James Mackie supported by Sergeant Yuawike and Corporal

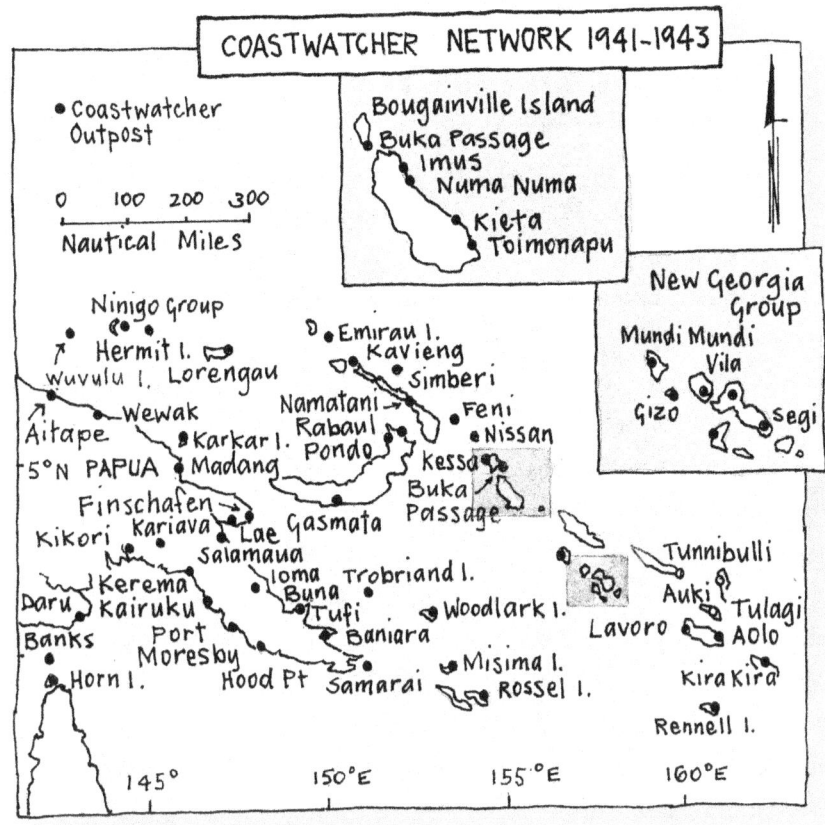

Sali were able to secure covert reporting positions, husband precious supplies, report movements and move some of the expatriates to safety. The small Army detachment based at Kieta also joined Mason.

Tragically, Eric's oldest coastwatcher on the island, Percy Good, whom he hoped to evacuate was caught by the Japanese and executed. The questionable loyalty of the Bougainvilleans in the face of the brutal Japanese occupation meant that the coastwatchers' position was precarious and the coastwatchers had to be ready to shift location at short notice. Percy Good's death emphasized the importance of providing coastwatchers with military status. While this would not protect them from execution then at least they had some comfort in better recompense for their families. Jack Read later wrote:

In our isolated circumstances these appointments meant far more to us than will be generally realised, as we could not authorise financial provision for our dependents back in Australia; but unfortunately a long period elapsed before those authorities were acted upon.[82]

On nearby Guadalcanal, Eric had two coastwatchers. They were the newly arrived Martin Clemens in the east and Ashton 'Snowy' Rhoades on the western side. At Tulagi there was the British Resident William Marchant and a small Australian Army and RAAF detachment along with the Navy Intelligence Officer, Lieutenant Don MacFarlan. In the event of a Japanese occupation Marchant had decided to relocate inland with his radio operator and a missionary. If Tulagi was to be evacuated, Eric Feldt's plan was for MacFarlan to move across to Guadalcanal, which gave him a better chance of remaining unlocated. They awaited the inevitable Japanese forays.

Beyond these major islands in the Solomons group Eric had the elderly Norwegian Lafe Schroader on Savo Island and the New Zealander Major Donald Kennedy on Santa Isabel. On Vanikoro Eric had his only woman coastwatcher, the imposing and resourceful Mrs Ruby Boye. She and her husband, Skov had been in the Solomons since 1928 and both had elected to remain behind.

It was also at this time that Rupert Long supported other more offensive clandestine operations. One was the Far Eastern Liaison Office or FELO, which was led by Commander Proud. The objective of FELO was to reduce the morale of the occupying Japanese and encourage non-cooperation of the local occupied population through propaganda activities. Proud wrote of Rupert's role:

> It was largely because of his enthusiasm that I was able to start the organization of FELO ... Long, I found had arranged for the Navy to allow me to be posted for this service and then set to work to get backing from the Australian Government. This was more than difficult at the time and for months to come all of us went through periods of great depression when we felt we could never achieve anything. Long never gave up in this fight and eventually by the middle of the year he

had the satisfaction of seeing four organisations established to carry out the first phase of the counter attack against the Japanese. I have always felt that if it had not been for Long none of us would ever have been able to get going.

For the rest of the War it was always to Long that the Heads of the Special Services Organisations went for advice and encouragement. Although he had no official coordinating role yet it was he who sorted out the many difficulties that cropped up from time to time regarding spheres of influence and type of operations to be conducted. It was he also, with his wide knowledge of the whole theatre who suggested special operations which were best suited to each of the organisations. And it was he who helped to fight our battles, which were many, with the High Command. No one person contributed more to this aspect of the war against Japan than did Cocky Long.[83]

Later in the year a 28-year old British officer, Captain Ivan Lyon was staying with the Governor of Victoria Sir Winston Duggan after his escape from Singapore. Lyon had a plan to attack Japanese shipping in Singapore in the former Japanese fishing vessel *Kofuku Maru* in which he had reached Australia. After initially getting a cool reaction in Army Headquarters, Sir Winston suggested he talk to Rupert Long. As with John Proud, Rupert was highly enthusiastic about Lyon's ideas and helped gain the support of Admiral Royle. This at least gave it some initial momentum. Lyon's proposal successfully bore fruit as The Allied Intelligence Bureau sponsored Operation JAYWICK the following year with his vessel famously renamed *Krait*.[84]

The Japanese occupation of New Ireland and New Britain had placed New Guinea, the Solomons and northern Australia under direct threat. This was underscored by subsequent air raids on Port Moresby and Darwin. In both instances coastwatchers gave warning of the attacks but their reports were not fully used to advantage.

With the fall of Singapore and the Philippines, Australia and New Zealand became springboards for operations against Japan in the south-west Pacific. On 17 March General Macarthur and his key staff arrived in Australia to much fanfare. A month later he became the Supreme

Commander of Allied Forces in the Southwest Pacific Area. Importantly, the eastern boundary of his command passed vertically though the Tasman Sea and so New Zealand and the Solomons were in the Pacific Ocean Area under the newly appointed Admiral Chester Nimitz. This meant that the RAN would contribute to two different commands for the remainder of the war. Of the Pioneer Class, Rupert Long was most affected by these command changes.

The two key members on MacArthur's staff were his Chief of Staff, Major General Richard Sutherland and his Intelligence Officer, Colonel Charles Willoughby. Both men were complex and to many who dealt with them, unappealing characters. On their arrival in Melbourne, the Australian intelligence resources such as the COIC, were placed under the command of MacArthur's headquarters. Despite the assistance and support Rupert provided Willoughby and his staff he was rewarded with less access to intelligence material.[85] However, Rupert was far too experienced in the game to be thwarted. He used his contacts, including those in Britain and New Zealand to obtain the information he needed for naval intelligence to function.

The arrangements for the critical cryptanalysis capabilities were more complex. The US Navy cryptanalysis unit at Corregidor (Station CAST) was much prized by Admiral Hart and he ensured they escaped to Australia in submarines. The CAST sailors spent a week in Fremantle while Lieutenant Commander Redfield 'Rosie' Mason and Lieutenant Commander Rudolph Fabian flew to Melbourne to visit Navy Office. Mason was Admiral Hart's former intelligence officer and had been responsible for the CAST team in the Philippines and then gone with the Admiral to the Dutch East Indies. He was a fine Japanese linguist while Fabian was a talented cryptologist and had a keen grasp of the trade. Rupert Long and Jack Newman hit it off with their counterparts straight away and they agreed to merge the units. Mason and Fabian immediately moved desks into Jack's office while facilities were secured for the organization.[86] The CAST sailors then took the three day train across the continent.

The Australian contribution which initially had only three linguists was significantly bolstered predominantly by WRANS and notably a gifted group of academics from the University of Sydney that had been recruited by Commander Nave.[87] The Americans found the WRANS to be an intelligent group and willing to learn CAST's advanced methods which included the use of machines and rudimentary punch card computers. The new entity was known as the Fleet Radio Unit, Melbourne or FRUMEL and was established on 12 March 1942. It was located in the new Monterey Apartments in Queens Street, Melbourne. The cryptanalysis elements occupied the top two floors whilst Jack Newman's Directorate of Naval Communications took up the ground floor.

FRUMEL was a naval entity and was subordinate to the Commander of the US 7th Fleet. Both General MacArthur, Admiral Chester Nimitz in Pearl Harbor (who also had the larger Station H or 'Hypo' in Hawaii) and Admiral Somerville in Columbo (with his FECB) were all beneficiaries of FRUMEL's output. Another organization, the Central Bureau, was established under Macarthur's command drawing on the resources of all the Services of both countries and whose focus was less on naval operations.

Lieutenant Commander 'Rosie' Mason became the officer-in-charge of FRUMEL. The bedding down of FRUMEL's disparate groups would take time. There were other elements beyond the Monterey Apartments, such as the intercept stations at Moorabbin, also in Melbourne, the more remote report station south of Darwin, and linking to existing RAN sites. Nave, who Lieutenant Gilbert Brooksbank ('B2') described as 'undoubtedly a genius in his field'[88] was like many gifted men not always easy to work with. He had a difficult relationship at times with both Rupert Long and Jack Newman. This soon extended to the Americans in FRUMEL who believed him to be too lax in protecting the security of their operation.[89] It was at Mason and Fabian's behest that Nave left FRUMEL.[90] By mid-1942 Nave moved to the Central Bureau in Brisbane where he made a very significant contribution to its important work.

Jack Newman's role as the deputy officer-in-charge was to monitor FRUMEL output for the Australians, help obtain resources and assist FRUMEL with the maintenance of good relationships with other sectors of the Australian Government, as well as being responsible for RAN naval long haul communications.

Jack was an archetypal naval communications officer in demeanour and manner and some Americans thought he was British. His image was bolstered by the rumour that he had been whipped with a 'cat of nine tails' as a midshipman. Ensign Duane Whitlock hailing from a small college town in the US mid-west recalled:

> He was a staid individual if ever you've seen one. Carried his kerchief in his cuff. It was really amazing; amusing really, because you could set your watch by that man and he demanded absolute quiet while he was working. He had two WRAN officers working in his office. No typewriters in there. And he would sit at his desk. At Attention. Everything neat, in its place. Anytime between 8:30 and 10 o'clock the door would fly open, in came 'Rosie' Mason. He'd mostly plop his backside down in a chair and put his feet up on Newman's desk, toss his hat over and said, 'Good morning, Jack. What's cooking?' It finally wore the old bugger down. He finally got to be a human being.[91]

Jack in his turn had the capacity to shock some of the more abstemious Americans. Every Christmas he would pour pink gins for the office staff. More substantially, Jack fostered excellent relations with the American officers and worked to ensure that the sailors from the two nations worked harmoniously together. At a practical level he, like Rupert, knew how to work the local bureaucracy to obtain material and other support for FRUMEL's critical work.

The output of FRUMEL and its predecessors was not always appreciated nor used to full advantage. In particular making judgments about the enemy's intent, based on analysis of their signal traffic and in the absence of the decoded message was too radical for some commanders. As previously described Admiral Hart was a convert. So too was Admiral Nimitz. When MacArthur learnt of FRUMEL's existence he asked the newly appointed naval Commander of the ANZAC Area, Vice Admiral

Herbert Leary, USN for briefings from FRUMEL. These were readily given but only to MacArthur with his Chief of Staff sometimes present, but always with his Chief of Intelligence Colonel Willoughby excluded.

At one of the earliest FRUMEL briefings Fabian told MacArthur of Japanese traffic about their plans to invade Port Moresby. MacArthur did not think this could be right and thought the Japanese would take New Caledonia and then threaten the shipping and air routes to Australia. Fabian then went into some detail on the provenance of the FRUMEL assessment. MacArthur was sufficiently convinced. A planning team was due to fly to Noumea later that day and their destination was changed to Port Moresby.[92] This was to be the first significant contribution by FRUMEL to the war effort and did much for their credibility.

By June 1942 the Allied Intelligence Bureau (AIB) brought together all the Allied and single service guerilla and propaganda organizations, including FELO and the coastwatch organization, under MacArthur's command. This was a sensible reform. In this arrangement Eric Feldt commanded the field intelligence 'C' section and Proud the propaganda 'D' section. As the war moved north AIB further matured its field intelligence activities and they were further divided into three geographic areas—the North-Eastern area (Feldt), the Dutch East Indies under a Dutch Commander, whilst a US Lieutenant Colonel was responsible for the Philippines. Rupert Long continued to play a major role in the coastwatch effort, working with Eric Feldt to provide direction, required personnel and the handling of the gleaned intelligence. Indeed the expanded organization needed greater logistical support and as such tested Rupert and his team's creativity in working both the national and Allied logistic systems.

III

On 12 December 1941 Rear Admiral Crace embarked in *Canberra* which became his flagship. As such Harold Farncomb became, in addition to the ship's commanding officer, the Flag Captain and Chief Staff Officer to the Admiral. Crace had a personal staff of just three officers, which in coming operations proved too few. The admiral had had an unhappy time since returning to Australia. He repeatedly felt his authority usurped by Navy Office and complained first to Admiral Colvin and then to the newly arrived Vice Admiral Royle. Crace went as so far as to suggest he should resign from his post.[93] He did have some legitimate complaints. In some respects it was unfair to place a newly promoted Rear Admiral into his position, quite distant from his superior and without the guidance he would have received in a larger fleet formation. A more experienced Admiral might have seized the opportunity to make much needed improvements in the operational effectiveness of the entire Australia Squadron and not be fixated on how many cruisers he had under his command. Irrespective of all this Crace and Harold Farncomb got on very well together. To underscore this point when *Australia* returned to the Australia Station and *Canberra* entered refit, Crace transferred his flag to *Australia* and took Harold with him.

In early February 1942 Vice Admiral Leary directed Crace to command the Anzac Squadron comprising *Australia*, the heavy cruiser USS *Chicago*, the New Zealand cruisers *Achilles* and *Leander*, along with the US destroyers *Perkins* and *Lamson*. On 16 February the Squadron rendezvoused with US Task Force 11 which included the world's largest aircraft carrier the USS *Lexington*, four cruisers and ten destroyers[94] under the command of Vice Admiral Wilson Brown, who was the oldest Admiral at sea at the age of 60. Since the beginning of the war against Japan, Task Force 11 was been the first appearance of a viable force to take on the rampant Japanese navy in the southwest Pacific. Admiral Leary planned to use this force to attack Rabaul. Crace was tasked by Brown to escort the all-important oiler USS *Platte* which would be kept south but would be needed to sustain the task force. Crace rankled at this mundane but vital tasking. On 20 February Japanese reconnaissance aircraft spotted *Lexington* and some hours later she was attacked by bombers from Rabaul. Brown's carrier based fighters shot down 16 Japanese planes for the loss of only two and no ships were damaged. With surprise lost he aborted the planned Rabaul raid. At the beginning of March the two Allied forces

'Everything neat, in its place'. Jack Newman working in his FRUMEL office. Taking notes is Second Officer Joan Cowrie who was a communications sailor and one of the first group of WRANS to arrive in Melbourne. She would complete the first WRANS officers course and served overseas in the Headquarters of the Supreme Allied Commander South East Asia in Ceylon. (RAN)

were joined by Rear Admiral Frank Fletcher's Task Force 17 centred around *Yorktown*. Brown resolved to try another raid on Rabaul and nearby Gasmata while Crace tried to get his force a leading role in any shore bombardment. As these plans were being finalised the initiative was lost by the Japanese invasion of Lae and Salamaua. Brown decided to launch attacks on these towns rather than Rabaul in the hope of disrupting the enemy. They achieved modest success but this did not involve Crace's ships.

With uncertainty surrounding Japanese intentions, Crace was ordered to deploy his force off the Louisiade Archipelago to the east of the New Guinea mainland. Their mission was to counter any Japanese forces sailing towards New Caledonia.

IV

The commanding officer of a warship has an unusually wide array of duties and responsibilities. These primarily include the safety of the ship and crew as well as her effectiveness in battle. He may also be called upon to command a group of ships, or in the case of Harry Showers, play a leading role in geo-politics. Intrinsic to the Captain's responsibilities is the administration of naval discipline onboard his ship which includes acting as the equivalent of a magistrate at sea for matters that fall within his jurisdiction. In the most serious matters involving a court martial he may have to act as Prosecutor to the proceedings held before another Captain.[95]

On the evening of 12 March 1942 a grave offence occurred onboard *Australia* that was to bring these disciplinary responsibilities to the fore and become one of the major events in Harold Farncomb's career. *Australia* with Crace embarked was operating off the Louisiades in company with other ships of the task group. At about 7.40 pm screams were heard on the port side of the forecastle.[96] Sailors rushed to the scene to find nineteen-year old Stoker John Riley in a pool of blood.

Next to him were Leading Stoker Albert Gordon and Stoker Edward Elias, both covered in blood. The stricken sailor was rushed below to the sickbay where the medical staff tended Riley's 14 stab wounds to the back, chest, stomach, side, arms and wrist. Transfusions were administered to counter the massive loss of blood. On learning of the incident Harold went to Crace's cabin and informed him of the attack, then appointed his Commander, John Armstrong assisted by the Master-at-Arms to conduct an investigation.[97]

For the next day Riley fought for his life. He did manage to tell the two doctors something of the attack and that Gordon and Elias were the perpetrators, with Gordon wielding the knife. When asked why they attacked him Riley said, 'Because I found out he (Gordon) was a poofter'.[98] Through Riley's conversations, Armstrong was able to glean that there were probably three other stokers involved in 'practices of unnatural vice'[99] and that threats of blackmail were involved. The identity of some of these sailors was hearsay. Further interviews with some of the sailors mentioned by Riley involved a 'certain amount of third degree conditions'[100] and therefore this pressuring of the witnesses meant some of their information could not be brought forward in any disciplinary proceedings.

Harold Farncomb with Prime Minister Robert Menzies and Rear Admiral Jack Crace. (RAN)

On the evening of the following day, Friday the 13th, Riley died of his wounds.[101] Armstrong continued his investigations as a murder invstigation and found, unbeknownst to Gordon and Elias, that there were three witnesses to the murder. They were Stoker Kenneth Holt who was on the deck above, Steward George Gough further up near the bows of the ship and Leading Signalman John Hagan who had been on watch above the bridge on the port High Angle Director platform. From his vantage point Hagan had the best view. On hearing a scuffle and a desperate man calling out below, he leaned over and saw two men pushing another to the deck and then punching him.

On reading Armstrong's promptly rendered report, Harold Farncomb had Gordon and Elias charged with murder and warned in accordance with the King's Regulations and Admiralty Instructions (KR&AI). Both sailors pleaded not guilty. Harold wrote to Crace seeking a court martial.[102] In preparation for the court martial and conscious that murder was a capital offence, both Crace and Harold agreed that the sailors should have professional legal representation. Crace therefore sought the services of a legal officer to join the ship to defend the sailors. As prescribed by KR&AI, Harold would conduct the prosecution.[103]

On the morning of 14 March the ship's company were mustered on deck and Riley's body was committed to the deep in one of the time honoured ceremonies of the sea.

From a war perspective it was imperative for the court martial to be held as soon as possible and on 15 April it was convened onboard *Australia* in Noumea whilst the ship was in port to replenish. The presiding officer was Captain Robert Bevan, RN, the Commanding Officer of HMNZS *Leander* which was also in port. There were two other *Leander* officers and two from *Australia* on the panel.[104] The Officiating Judge Advocate, who would provide legal advice was Paymaster Commander Patrick Perry. The defence counsel was 32-year old Paymaster Lieutenant Trevor Rapke who before the war had been a criminal lawyer in Melbourne. Rapke had caught a steamer from Sydney and joined the ship in Noumea.

At the beginning of the proceedings Rapke objected to the possible bias of *Australia's* officers on the court martial noting that Harold Farncomb was the prosecutor. The composition was changed so that *Leander* officers were in the majority. The court martial proceedings went for two and a half days in which time Harold brought forward sailors to testify what they had seen and/or heard. In defence Rapke emphasised the burden of proof required of such a crime and asked Captain Bevan, in the absence of such evidence, to acquit the prisoners of murder. Harold noted that Rapke's defence was made with 'forensic eloquence'.[105] He countered, in respect to the issue of identification that Hagan had kept his eyes on the unfolding scene and so, while he could not identify Elias and Gordon his continuous sighting, combined with their subsequent identification by the other sailors, was sufficient to establish identity. Bevan cleared the court to discuss the issue with the empaneled officers and the Officiating Deputy Judge Advocate. After fifteen minutes they elected to continue with the proceedings. In their evidence Gordon and Elias stated they had earlier been talking to Riley between decks and he then had left to go on watch. Minutes later they heard a cry, just like the other sailors, and saw two unknown assailants run away after the attack.

The evidence and concluding statements completed by 11.10 am on 18 April. The court was cleared and the officers of the court martial considered their judgment. After about four hours deliberation Gordon and Elias were found guilty of Riley's murder. Captain Bevan passed the sentence that both sailors were, 'to be hanged by the neck till they be dead onboard one of His Majesty's Australian Ships and at such time as the Board of Administration for the Naval Forces shall direct'.[106] Fortuitously, *Australia* had to sail to Sydney from Noumea to rectify a defect on a propeller shaft bracket and the two sailors could be landed there.

Rapke was unhappy with the verdict and wrote to Harold Farncomb on the day after arrival in Sydney. His letter emphasised that, 'the conviction should be warranted on the evidence before the Court, and that no inferences not warranted by the proved facts should be drawn'.[107] Rapke was dissatisfied that while Riley's statements to the doctors were not admitted, they were common knowledge onboard and therefore known to the two *Australia* officers on the court martial. Rapke believed there was a miscarriage of justice because Harold had made known his personal view of the guilt of the accused. This statement was contrary to legal convention and a potential defect in the proceedings. Rapke also objected that the accused's statements made after the attack were not produced, neither were the accused's version of conversations between them and with Riley. He also believed the conviction wrong in law, the Court misdirected itself and the evidence of identification was insufficient.[108]

On the same day as Rapke's letter, Harold wrote to Crace a statement of mitigation of the sentence. The sequence of the letters and whether Rapke assisted Harold is unknown. Harold wrote that:

> My object is to stress the abnormality of the present times and to draw attention to the probability that this abnormality is likely to produce a warped state of mind in certain men, who in more happy times would be ordinary decent, well-balanced individuals.

The conditions under which ratings on the lower deck, especially Engine Room ratings, are at present living and working are sufficiently well known to need no long description ... The softening influence of the opposite sex is accordingly absent ... Finally, the circumstances of the war, in which life seems to be held so cheap, is an especially evil influence. I am certain that the effect of 2½ years of these conditions in wartime is such as to produce an abnormal, unnatural and perhaps perverse state of mind in some men so that they require a peculiar outlook which warps the reason and judgement.[109]

Harold Farncomb was a devout Christian and when in Sydney he was a regular parishioner at Saint Andrew's Cathedral. Although he viewed homosexuality as abnormal, he was not punitive in any way. Rather he tried to understand the men's desires and to show compassion. A review of the service records of the other men allegedly involved in the homosexual circle shows that Harold did not subject them to any disciplinary action and that they remained onboard to serve their nation.

On 22 April Gordon and Elias were transferred to Sydney's Long Bay Gaol. It was clear to Crace and Harold Farncomb that while they could return their attention to the Japanese there would be more developments arising from the court martial. In particular, they thought and hoped that their sentences would be commuted.

The first appeal came soon enough. The Full Bench of the High Court met in Sydney on 4 May to consider a petition for a writ of *habeas corpus*. This appeal was based on the argument that the court martial as constituted did not have jurisdiction and that the death penalty could not be applied to RAN sailors. On 8 July in individual judgments, the four judges each found that the court martial had jurisdiction and was properly constituted. They also found that while ships and men in RAN ships under the Commonwealth Naval Forces Act 1910-19 could not be sentenced to death for murder, as these ships, including *Australia*, had been placed by the Governor General under Admiralty control and then the Imperial Naval Discipline Act 1866 (as amended) was applicable and a death sentence could be applied.

This unintended legal consequence of transferring RAN units to Admiralty control alarmed the Government. Representations against the punishment also came from across the community and the families of the accused. The Government sought the assistance of Whitehall to commute the sentences. Two approaches were suggested. The first was an approach to the King, and second, for the Australian Government to adopt the 1931 Statute of Westminster which would allow Australia to regain, to all intents and purposes, legal control over its Navy. The Government pursued both measures. On 10 August the King consented to commute both men's sentences to life imprisonment and after eleven years of inaction, the Government adopted the Statute of Westminster.

One would have thought that Harold Farncomb would have found Rapke's continued advocacy for Gordon and Elias troublesome. It is clear from the court martial proceedings, however, that Harold much respected Rapke's professional skills and eloquence. It was on this basis that Harold asked him to remain in *Australia* as the Captain's Secretary. Rapke agreed and it was the beginning of a lifelong friendship.

V

Unknown to the Allies on 15 March 1942 Emperor Hirohito approved Operation *FS* which would extend the Japanese reach to Papua, Fiji and Samoa with a view to isolating Australia from the US. As part of this campaign Admiral Inoue, fresh from his conquest of New Britain, would execute the subordinate Plan *MO* to take Port Moresby from the sea, together with separate assaults on Tulagi in the Solomons as well as Nauru and Ocean Islands. With a sizeable US and Australian naval force in the Coral Sea and FRUMEL beginning to glean the Japanese intent, the stage was set for the first major naval battle of the Pacific War where the Japanese faced equivalent forces.

The Allied units could not remain in the Coral Sea indefinitely awaiting the Japanese invasion fleet. The ships were allowed to return in small groups to Sydney, Pearl Harbor or nearer ports for maintenance and replenishment. FRUMEL would play its part in cueing the Allies both on when the invasion would occur and on the Japanese disposition. As signals were progressively interpreted it was clear that Japanese naval forces were steaming toward various assembly points. The best estimate for the invasion was from the first week of May.[110] In the lead up to this critical time Admirals Nimitz and King decided that Vice Admiral Brown was not sufficiently offensive minded for the impending battle. Put in his place was the aviator Rear Admiral Aubrey Fitch in *Lexington*. The gunnery specialist, Rear Admiral Frank 'Black Jack' Fletcher in the carrier *Yorktown* was senior and would command the force. Nevertheless, King and Nimitz wanted the aggressive aviator Vice Admiral 'Bull' Halsey in command and they dispatched his Task Force (TF) 16 towards the Coral Sea. With a possible arrival in the area of about 15 May it was doubtful Halsey would join in time.

Admiral Inoue's plan was for the Port Moresby Invasion Group of eleven transports, escorted by a small force comprising the cruiser *Yubari*, six destroyers and four minesweepers to proceed on a direct route from Rabaul. The Tulagi Invasion Group was more modest, consisting of only two transports and 10 small warships. To protect the invasion forces were three other Groups. The first was a Support Group with the Seaplane tender *Kamikawa Maru* and two light cruisers to initially protect the Tulagi Group, then once that force was inserted they would help protect the Port Moresby group. The second, a Covering Group

HMAS Australia *leaving Sydney Harbour in her 1942 camouflage.* (RAN)

of the light carrier *Shōhō* and four heavy cruisers under Rear Admiral Aritomo Gotō was to provide close support to both the invasion of Tulagi and then Port Moresby. The third was a Striking Force based around two new fast fleet carriers *Shōkaku* and *Zuikaku* and two heavy cruisers. This force, under Vice Admiral Takeo Takagi, who was the victor of the Battle of the Java Sea, would be the means to counter any Allied interference with the Port Moresby invasion. Finally, Inoue had a Submarine Force of five large I-Class submarines to act as pickets in the Coral Sea and two smaller Ro-Class which would operate near the invasion points. Unfortunately for the Japanese, the I-Class submarines were deployed in their picket line after Fletcher's ships had already passed through their planned patrol line.

By the end of April the opposing sides were in, or closing on, the Coral Sea. Besides the benefit of knowing much of the Japanese plans, some of Fletcher's ships were fitted with the first generation of naval radars to go to sea. Within Crace's force *Chicago* and *Hobart* were so fitted. Typically radar would detect an inbound high flying raid at about 60 miles. The Japanese, although having the initiative as the invading force, lacked both accurate intelligence on the opposing force and radar. Luck and weather would still be important factors in the battle for both sides.

On 1 May coastwatcher Donald Kennedy on Santa Isabel gave warning of the Japanese invasion force heading to Tulagi. This gave sufficient notice for the Army and RAAF detachments to evacuate the island. As pre-arranged with Eric Feldt, MacFarlan relocated to Guadalcanal. There he was surprised to find two old-time island planters Ken Dalrymple-Hay and Andy Andresen who had no intention of leaving their island. They were busy squirrelling away stores inland. The trio formed an unlikely team. There was more to the rotund Dalrymple-Hay than met the eye. A school friend of 'Snowy' Rhoades he was a Gallipoli veteran and had risen to the rank of Lieutenant in the Great War.[111] He would prove to be courageous and resourceful.

On the morning of 3 May the Japanese landed at Tulagi. This invasion was reported by the coastwatchers. Since the 1930s the US Navy had developed and practiced large scale strikes from their large carriers against opposing land and naval forces. Fletcher now unleashed such an attack using 60 *Yorktown* aircraft against the Japanese in Tulagi. While they were too late for the larger warships which had already moved onto Nauru and Ocean Island, they sank a destroyer, three minesweepers and perhaps more importantly four reconnaissance seaplanes. Coastwatchers Kennedy, Schroeder and MacFarlan provided accurate reports to Fletcher on the results of his raid. These were the first of many coastwatcher reports that were to play such a critical part in future US operations.

In the Coral Sea the three Task Forces under Fletcher, Finch and Crace rendezvoused on the morning of 4 May. Fletcher assumed the Japanese carriers would be to the north, possibly still in the Solomon Sea. They were between him and the invasion fleet which would slowly steam towards Port Moresby. Fletcher would have to rely on aircraft flying from Queensland bases and his own search aircraft to locate the enemy. Later on 4 May one of the shore-based aircraft sighted *Shōhō* still in the Solomon Sea but possibly steaming for the Jomard Passage, the entrance to the Coral Sea. Unfortunately when that aircraft went off-task contact was lost. For both Fletcher and Takagi the forthcoming battle was to be characterised by having to make decisions based on fleeting and fragmentary information. The stakes could not have been higher for both Admirals.

On 5 May four *Yorktown* Wildcats intercepted a Japanese reconnaissance flying boat whose disappearance the Japanese correctly surmised indicated the presence of an aircraft carrier in the Coral Sea. Later that day Fletcher was provided cryptanalysis information from FRUMEL and Station HYPO that indicated the Japanese were planning for the invasion fleet to arrive off Port Moresby on 10 May. Working back from that date Fletcher deployed his forces such that he could intercept the Japanese on 7 May.

For most of 6 May both naval forces tried to locate the other. At one point the two carrier forces were only about 160 nm apart. The shore based US B-17 bombers had some success in locating the invasion force, identifying a carrier among the group and conducting an ultimately unsuccessful attack. At 10 am a Japanese flying boat located Fletcher's ships. By the time Takagi received the report his quarry was over 500 km distant. He therefore decided his carriers would close the enemy carriers and launch a strike at first light the next day. Fletcher assumed where there was one Japanese carrier there would be others. He also decided to launch a dawn raid.

Just after 6 am Fletcher launched ten dive bombers to search to the north where he thought he would find the Japanese carriers. Soon after that he ordered Crace to take his ships to the northwest to block the southern entrance of the Jomard Passage. Although this would place these ships outside carrier air cover, Fletcher wanted to ensure no Japanese passed through the Passage. At about this time Takagi launched a dozen torpedo bombers on a southerly vector which was where he judged Fletcher's Task Force lay.

At about 7.30 am Takagi received reports from two scout planes that a carrier, a cruiser and three destroyers were 300 km to the south of him. This aligned with his earlier assessment and he ordered a strike of 78 aircraft drawn from both his carriers. By 8.15 am they were airborne. Just five minutes later a floatplane reported a sighting of Fletcher's group in its correct location to the west of Takagi. This was confirmed ten minutes later by another floatplane report. In a dilemma, Takagi decided not to change his mind. As commonly is the case, ships can be misidentified both in numbers and type by reconnaissance aircraft. Takagi's aircraft found not a carrier group to the south but the US oiler *Neosho* and her escorting destroyer *Sims*.

At the same time Takagi was launching his strike, Fletcher received a sighting of the invasion force which was also incorrectly reported as containing two carriers and four cruisers. He ordered a strike and Finch dispatched 93 aircraft.

The results of these strikes was unexpected by the two Admirals. Japanese aircraft soon realized the identification error. The fighters and torpedo bombers returned to their carriers leaving 36 dive bombers to sink the unlucky *Neosho* and *Sims*. In contrast the American aircraft were more fortunate. They found *Shōhō* at 10.40 am with eight fighter airborne and escorting cruisers to provide air defence. These defences proved ineffective against such a strong strike package. Within 55 minutes and after sustaining 7 torpedo and 13 bomb hits *Shōhō* was at the bottom of the Solomon Sea. She was Japan's first aircraft carrier loss of the war. Admiral Inoue in Rabaul ordered the invasion fleet to reverse course until Takagi had destroyed the American carriers.

At around midday Crace's Task Force was detected by a Japanese floatplane which reported it as containing two aircraft carriers. Too far for Takagi to reach that day, 31 bombers and torpedo bombers from Rabaul that were already airborne were directed to attack. *Chicago* had detected the surveillance aircraft on her radar during the morning and Crace's ships awaited the inevitable attack. The Japanese aircraft arrived at 2.24 pm and executed a most determined attack. The low flying torpedo bombers dropped their torpedoes at about 1000 to 1500 yards from the ships. Crace later wrote of the raid:

> How those torpedoes were avoided beats me ... two on the starboard side ... can only have missed by a matter of feet. Farncomb handled the ship extremely well and it was entirely due to him and a great deal of luck that *Australia* was not hit.[112]

There was also no doubt in the minds of *Australia's* sailors that Harold Farncomb saved their ship that day. The word quickly filtered through the cruiser that their Captain 'was an absolute inspiration on the bridge'.[113] Harold later told his wife that his work during that raid had repaid the years of training the Navy had given him.[114] Howden in *Hobart* also won plaudits from his men following the attack for having evaded one torpedo. He would use his binoculars to watch the aircraft's bomb bay doors open from his reclining captain's chair and violently manoeuvre the ship watching the bombs in flight all the way.[115]

SAD SONGS OF THE DEATH OF SAILORS 459

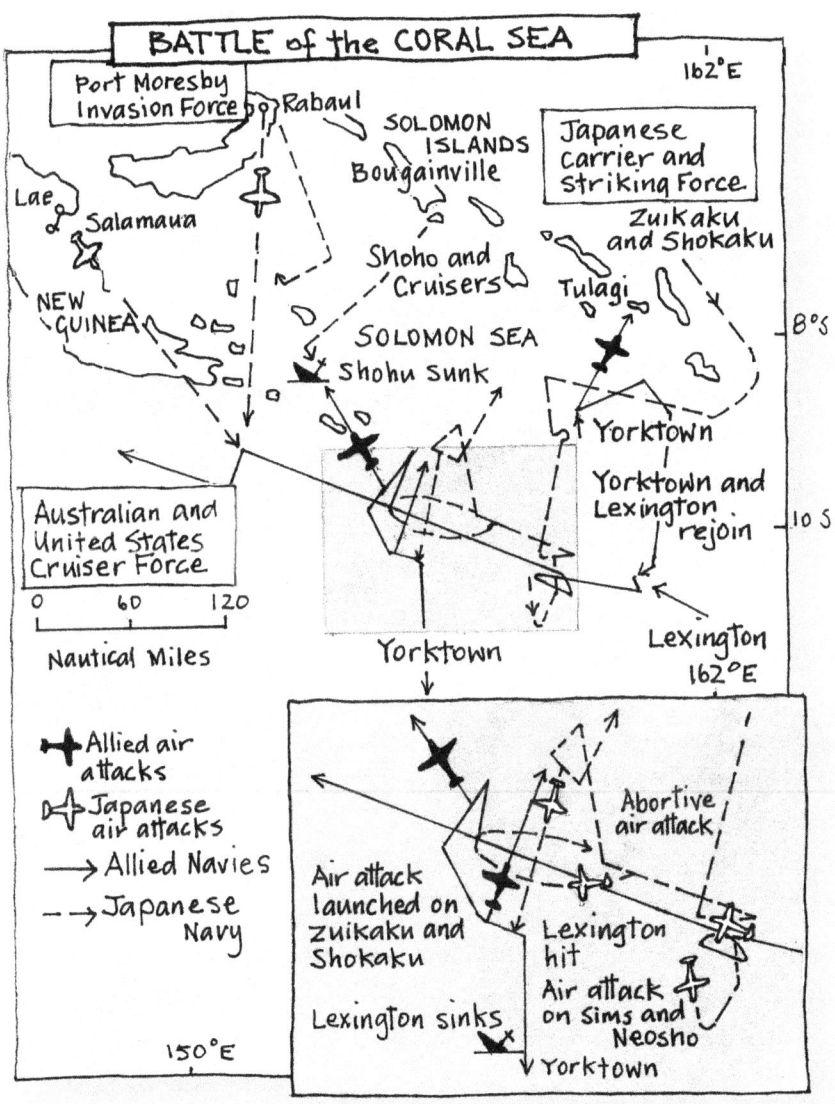

Chicago had also dodged three torpedoes. The defence by the ships was spirited and five aircraft were shot down. To add to the confused picture for Japanese admirals the returning bombers reported they had sunk the British battleship *Warspite* (which was actually in the Indian Ocean).[116] The action for the day was not over for Crace's ships, which were soon subjected to a fortuitously inaccurate bombing attack by US B-17 bombers from Townsville. For the rest of the day the ships were shadowed by a Japanese flying boat. Concerned about his exposed position, Crace sensibly steamed further west to be at greater range from enemy aircraft yet still be able to intercept any Japanese force.

Takagi decided to relaunch some of the aircraft from his morning's strike westward to locate the American carriers. By 4.15 pm he had eight scouting aircraft and 27 torpedo and dive bombers flying west. The scouts saw nothing in cloudy conditions but Fletcher's ships detected the 27 aircraft raid on radar. Eleven Wildcats were vectored to intercept them. Eight enemy were shot down for the loss of three Wildcats and the attack broken up.

The first day in a new era of naval warfare, where fleets attacked one another at great distances with aircraft, proved frustrating for both sides. Quick decisions had to made on fragments, of at times erroneous information. At sunrise the next day both sides launched sweeps to find the other's carriers. The cloud cover which had helped the Americans on the previous day was now over the Japanese forces while the Allied forces were under a clear blue sky. At about 8.20am both the American and Japanese scouting aircraft had near simultaneously located the enemy aircraft carriers. Strikes were hurriedly prepared on all the aircraft carriers. About an hour later 69 Japanese and 75 American aircraft had formed up to attack the enemy. At the same time fighters were launched to fly overhead to protect the carriers. The American dive bombers inflicted three bomb hits on *Shōkaku* which caused substantial damage whilst *Zuikaku* escaped unscathed. Further operations were impossible for *Shōkaku* and she withdrew towards Truk. To the west the Japanese strike was detected about 60 miles from the carriers but was flying higher than the intercepting Wildcats and got through to the American carriers intact. In the resulting attack *Lexington* was hit by two torpedoes and two bombs whilst *Yorktown* suffered a single bomb hit. The most serious situation was in *Lexington* where aviation fuel pipes had been ruptured causing serious fires.

As both Japanese and American strike packages returned home they ran into one another resulting in further aircraft losses on both sides. After determined damage control work both *Lexington* and *Yorktown* were able to recover their aircraft. Fletcher was concerned about his situation with two damaged carriers and the prospect of two undamaged Japanese carriers still lurking to the east. He therefore informed MacArthur he was withdrawing and reported the position of the Japanese ships for B-17 attack.

About an hour after the last Japanese attack *Lexington* was suddenly rent by a massive explosion and fire amidships. An aviation fuel leak had been ignited with disastrous results. This set off further explosions from ammunition and it was clear the mighty ship was doomed. Her end was hastened by five torpedoes from the destroyer USS *Phelps* once the surviving 2,700 men were removed.

By the end of the day the Japanese and Americans had both withdrawn their forces. The operation to invade Port Moresby by sea had ended in failure. The strategic victory for the Allies had come at a heavy cost. *Lexington* and over 650 men had been lost while *Yorktown* had sustained substantial damage.

Left virtually forgotten in the large scale battle were Crace and his ships. While Fletcher and Takagi withdrew, Crace was left standing guard off the Jomard Passage. After two days he took it upon himself to withdraw from the otherwise empty sea.

Of the Battle of the Coral Sea, *The Argus* reported at the time that it was the greatest naval battle since Jutland'.[117] John Curtin in measured tones said:

> Today we can be proud of what has been done, in fact, we can be thankful ... I have no doubt that other battles have yet to be fought as part of the struggle which must continue until the enemy is defeated or we are conquered.[118]

Curtin was indeed right about the battles that lay ahead. But, to paraphrase Winston Churchill, the Battle of the Coral Sea marked the end of the beginning. The Japanese version of the blitzkrieg had been stopped. They would later decide to take Port Moresby overland from the north coast on New Guinea then across a track from the small village of Kokoda. As they had in Malaya, the Japanese intended to employ bicycles for their infantry. It was to prove a major miscalculation.

Strategically, the Japanese still possessed a foothold in the Solomons from which to go back on the offensive. However, they were being covertly watched by Eric Feldt's intrepid coastwatchers and their small band of loyal Solomon Islanders. These coastwatchers were soon to play roles of importance that would have been beyond the imagination of even Rupert Long.

VI

In May 1942 the hard-worked *Adelaide* arrived at Garden Island for a much needed refit. Besides important boiler work the ship would gain 20 mm Oerlikon guns and extra depth charge throwers to improve her effectiveness escorting convoys. The refit provided the crew time to spend with their families and Harry Showers an opportunity to prepare to hand over his command to James Esdaile.

On 26 May *Bungaree* entered port after completing the first part of a minelay off Noumea. This provided an opportunity for Norman Calder and Harry Showers to catch up after much time spent independently at sea. By the end of the month the port became more crowded with the presence of the cruisers *Canberra* and *Chicago* along with the US destroyer *Perkins* and destroyer tender *Dobbin*. These ships, as well as *Bungaree*, were at buoys in the harbour. Also alongside or in dock were the armed merchant cruisers *Kanimbla* and *Westralia* along with the corvettes *Whyalla*, *Geelong* and the Indian *Bombay*. Finally there was the old Dutch submarine *K9* alongside the requisitioned ferry *Kuttabul* which had been converted to an accommodation ship.

Sydney was the most important port in the South Pacific and its significance had grown with the fall of Singapore. As such, attention had been taken to provide adequate anti-submarine defences for the port and its approaches. These were gradually being fitted in accordance with the arrangements conceived by James Esdaile prior to the war as well as some other embellishments. There were eight indicator loops on the bottom to detect ship movements based on a change in the magnetic field. Six of these were outside the heads, one between North and South Heads and the last one between South and Middle Head. There was an Indicator Loop Station adjacent to the Port War Signal Station on South Head. On detecting a potential enemy contact the Indicator Loop staff could report it via a telephone link to the Garden Island operations room.

Horace Thompson, having left *Westralia,* was now Sydney's Extended Defence Officer in charge of these indicator loops and responsible to the Commanding Officer of the shore establishment HMAS *Rushcutter* Acting Commander Harvey Newcomb. This suite of loops was less than it seemed. Due to defects, manning shortages and lack of training only one loop was operational, with even its readings not always believed. In addition to the loops, there was also a partial boom and net arrangement across the middle of the harbour. Only the central section was in place with gaps existing on either side while construction slowly continued.

Horace Thompson was unhappy in his position. Subordinate officers at the Port War Signal Station found Horace to be a heavy drinker with a chip on his shoulder about his career. In his cups Horace would tell these officers that he had enjoyed greater success as a junior officer in the UK than many others in the Pioneer Class. In particular, he resented the promotion of officers who employed their social graces as 'tea cup balancers'[119] to succeed in the Service. He specifically decried the advancement of John Collins and Harold Farncomb.[120]

In addition to the fixed defences, patrols were conducted of Sydney Harbour and approaches by a handful of small converted auxiliary anti-submarine vessels and minesweepers. The most imposing of these were HMAS *Yandra* and HMAS *Bingera,* both about 1,000 tonnes and each armed with a 4-inch gun, asdic and depth charges. These ships were augmented by the harbour defence craft of the Volunteer Defence Patrol. The harbour patrols were coordinated from the Garden Island operations room.

The senior officer responsible for Sydney's defences was the Rear Admiral-in-Charge HMA Naval Establishments Sydney, Acting Rear Admiral Gerard Muirhead-Gould RN. Usefully, Muirhead-Gould, or MG as he was known, had been a member of the Court of Inquiry into the loss of the British battleship HMS *Royal Oak* as a result of a submarine attack in the Scapa Flow anchorage.

Chicago and *Perkins* had of course participated in the Battle of the Coral Sea. Unknown to them some Japanese participants of the battle had also journeyed south. They were five I-Class submarines. Three of them, *I-22, I-24* and *I-27* were each fitted with a 24 metre midget submarine[121] carried in a cradle on their stern casing, while two other submarines, *I-21* and *I-29* each had a hanger with a Glen floatplane.

The first indication of a Japanese presence in New South Wales waters was on the evening of 16 May when the Russian merchantman *Wellen* was shelled by a submarine 30 miles off Newcastle. Three of the crew were injured including the Captain, but *Wellen* replied with machine gun fire into the submarine which was only about 100 yards distant. *I-29* soon submerged. Muirhead-Gould dispatched the Dutch cruiser *Tromp* together with *Arunta* and *Perkins* to the scene and halted shipping for 24 hours. On 23 May *I-29* launched its floatplane which flew a reconnaissance flight over Sydney. Although picked-up by radar its detection was discounted. On return the aircrew reported the harbour contained warships including, erroneously, two battleships.[122] On the basis of this flight it was decided to attack Sydney. A fragment of this traffic was intercepted by FRUMEL.

Before dawn on 29 May *I-21's* floatplane was launched and flew low over the harbour identifying ships and defences. It was sighted by a few observers who thought it was a US Curtiss Seagull with which it had some similarity. This confusion was not the case in *Chicago* which had all its aircraft onboard. Eventually, Wirraways were launched from Richmond air base but neither the Japanese aircraft nor submarine was located. The aircraft was damaged on recovery, but the aircrew was able to provide the required details to the Japanese submarines which had now rendezvoused about 32 miles north east of Sydney.

Remarkably, despite the immediacy of the Battle of the Coral Sea, the *Wellen* attack, the suspicious aircraft sightings—combined with a 29 May New Zealand report of signal traffic potentially emanating from a submarine off Sydney,[123] Muirhead-Gould did not make any changes to the defensive posture of the port. Shipping continued to steam over the indicator loop day and night while shore navigation lights remained fully illuminated. In addition, much of Garden Island remained well lit. Since 1940 work had been underway round the clock on the building of a battleship-size graving dock between Garden Island and the mainland. At night the work area was floodlit from 24 metre towers.

On the afternoon of 31 May the six midget submarine crewmen prepared themselves for their hazardous mission. After a final briefing they had their hair shaved with a lock preserved for their parents. They then were anointed with oil, dressed and prayed. From 4 pm the three midget submarines were released about 7 miles east of Sydney Heads.

With a crew of an officer and petty officer and armed with a pair of 16-inch torpedoes, the midget submarines posed a potent threat to the ships in Sydney Harbour. The craft had a submerged range of about 19 miles and was fitted with net cutters on the bow and at the front of the small conning tower. At around 7.50 pm the cargo vessel *Wyngerie* entered port and passed through the opened boom. Having earlier detected a contact, which would have been *Wyngerie*, at 8.01 pm the indicator loop detected a further contact passing over it. On the trace it was a distinct deviation slightly smaller than that of a ferry. It was Lieutenant Kenshi Chuma's midget submarine *M-27*. As the flotilla leader, *M-27* was in the van of the attack. Unfortunately, due to the normal harbour traffic and unaware what a small submarine's signature would look like, Horace Thompson's team did not report the contact as suspicious. *M-27's* good fortune was short lived. Possibly following the inbound *Wyngerie* she got herself hopelessly fouled in the defence boom on the western side.

The struggling *M-27* was seen by two watchmen on barges used to build the extensions to the boom. One of them, James Cargill, clearly saw the object to be suspicious and rowed towards it and identified it as a small submarine. Cargill hailed the nearby patrol boat HMAS *Yarroma* and alerted it to the threat. Lieutenant Harold Eyers in command of *Yarroma* initially viewed Cargill's report with scepticism and it was not until 9.52 pm that a report of a suspicious object fouled in the net was sent to the Garden Island operations room. Four minutes earlier the second midget submarine Lieutenant Katsuhisa Ban's *M-24* passed unreported over the indicator loop.

Eyers was soon told to close the contact and give a full description. Muirhead-Gould received the first report from *Yarroma* while entertaining at his official residence—*Tresco* at Elizabeth Bay. Among his guests was *Chicago's* Captain Howard Bode. Muirhead-Gould ordered all ships to take anti-submarine precautions and suggested to Bode that he take *Chicago* and *Perkins* to sea. In the meantime Eyers had sent a stoker in a boat to the object. He too confirmed it as a submarine. Eyers also called the patrol boat *Lolita* to close the scene.

Warrant Officer Herbert Anderson in command of *Lolita* soon sized up the situation and informed the Signal station he intended to attack. Because of the depth of water his two depth charge runs failed to detonate. Eyers also sent a second signal at 10.30 pm to report the object was a submarine and requesting permission to open fire. Five minutes later as *Yarroma* was about to open fire and *Lolita* conduct a third depth charge attack, the quiet of the harbour was broken by two large internal explosions in *M-27*, caused by detonation charges set off by Chuma.

Debris from the explosion went 15 metres into the air, fortunately not injuring the watchmen or crews from the patrol boats.

On news of the explosions Muirhead-Gould at 10.36 pm ordered 'ships to take action against attack'. Fifteen minutes later the patrol boat *Lauriana* sighted *M-24's* conning tower proceeding down the eastern channel to seaward of Bradley's Head. *M-24* was heading towards Garden Island and the man-of-war anchorages. On being illuminated by searchlight the conning tower disappeared. As Ban closed his targets he raised his periscope and conning tower once more. At about 10.50 pm *Chicago* sighted *M-24* in her searchlights and fired her anti-aircraft guns at the submarine. Joining the melee, *Geelong* opened fired on *M-24* whilst she was still tied up alongside in refit.

While the cacophony grew in the harbour, at 10.54 pm *Yandra* patrolling at Sydney Heads sighted the conning tower of Lieutenant Keiu Matsuo's *M-22* just 400 yards distant. *Yandra* immediately closed to ram the submarine. *Yandra* struck a glancing blow and then soon gained sonar contact. She then fired six depth charges which Lieutenant James Taplin believed had sunk the submarine.[124]

At midnight Muirhead-Gould boarded *Lolita* and twenty-five minutes later the lights around the graving dock were finally extinguished. During this time and despite the defender's best efforts Ban managed to get into a firing position on *Chicago* from a position near Bradley's Head. At 00.30 am Ban fired both his torpedoes but they missed the cruiser. One of the torpedoes passed under *K9* and exploded under *Kuttabul*. The shock wave lifted the old ship out of the water and broke its back. Brave efforts were soon under way to rescue sailors from the wreck. Fortunately the other torpedo did not explode and could be defused.

Kuttabul had 150 berths. Fortuitously there were only about 40 sailors onboard. Of these, nineteen RAN and two RN sailors were killed. The two British sailors had both survived the sinkings of their respective ships *Repulse* and *Cornwall* and were waiting in Sydney to return to England. Equally tragic, when the pregnant mother of 20-year old Stoker

Kenneth Killeen later learnt of his death in *Kuttabul* she went into deep shock and early labour. Both she and her infant died.

Soon after *Kuttabul's* torpedoing *Perkins* got under way. At the same time more sailors came in from leave to get additional patrol boats and minesweepers into the action. Following his attack Ban slowly made his escape out of the harbour. An indicator loop detection at 1.58 am may have marked his departure. Between 2.43 am and 3.25 am *Perkins* and *Chicago* proceed to sea to relatively safer water. They were joined by *Whyalla* and *Bombay* who conducted anti-submarine sweeps at the approaches to the harbour.

The attack on *M-22* by *Yandra* did not result in her demise. Rather Lieutenant Matsuo elected to lay low and wait for another opportunity to attack the port. *M-22* re-entered the port at 3.01 am which was detected by the indicator loop and managed to pass through the boom defences. At 3.50 am in the vicinity of Bradley's Head, the submarine was sighted by *Kanimbla* which opened fire. *Doomba, Sea Mist, Yarooma* and *Steady Hour* converged on the now cornered quarry and conducted repeated depth charge attacks until 8.27 am. With oil and other debris appearing on the surface it was clear *M-22* had met its fate. When the battered submarine was later raised both Masuo and Petty Officer Takeshi Ourmori were found to have committed suicide.

M-24 made its slow passage towards the rendezvous off Broken Bay. It did not make the distance and its fate remained a mystery until it was located by recreational divers off Sydney's northern beaches in November 2006. In some places the outer casing was riddled by bullet holes, no doubt from *Chicago*.

In the aftermath to the attack there was criticism of *Yarooma* and in respect to the indicator loop personnel, Muirhead-Gould reported to the First Naval Member that 'I must deplore the fact that the human element failed'.[125] There is some evidence that Horace Thompson was held responsible.[126] In his subsequent report Muirhead-Gould suggested some sensible improvements and the Navy avoided the independent inquiry into the attack that was called for from some quarters.

Perhaps because of his report and the particularly cordial relationship he enjoyed with Vice Admiral Sir Guy Royle, Muirhead-Gould escaped any censure himself. Yet as the senior officer in charge of Sydney he clearly had not instilled in his organization a sufficiently vigilant posture, nor provided realistic training, nor insisted on the indicator loops being fully operational, nor acted on intelligence. The US Navy were less charitable and the Commanding Officer of *Perkins* wrote to Admiral Leary that, 'It was good fortune rather than good harbor defence which prevented great damage'.[127] The outcome could have been much worse—the midget attack on Diego Suarez harbour in Madagascar on the same evening damaged the battleship *Ramillies* and sank a tanker.

The action in Sydney Harbour probably involved more RAN vessels than any other in its history, yet there were no medals awarded for individual deeds. For Horace it was effectively the end of his naval career. He was moved from his position three months later and on 1 October 1943 was discharged from the Navy as being physically unfit for further naval service.

More broadly the attack gave much greater awareness of the Japanese submarine threat off Australian waters. *Bungaree* when in convoy found herself providing anti-submarine escort. On 9 June when escorting Convoy CO.1 from Newcastle to Port Phillip, *Bungaree* gained a submarine contact and Norman Calder launched an attack dropping a depth charge pattern on the possible submarine to no result. Over the coming year there would be sporadic losses to Japanese submarines even as far distant as the waters off South Australia.

On 4 June just three days after the Sydney Harbour attack, Harry Showers handed command of *Adelaide* to James Esdaile. For Harry his command of the old cruiser had been a successful one. While not a charismatic Captain, he was highly competent and had an even tempered and paternalist approach which engendered loyalty and respect from his men. When stepping ashore in civilian attire Harry wore a distinctive homburg hat that delighted his gangway staff.[128] James Esdaile would prove

Lieutenant Matsuo's M-22 *being recovered.
The submarine passed three times over the indicator loops but remained
unreported by Horace Thompson's inexperienced team.* (RAN)

to be an equally even tempered and undemonstrative Captain.

Just four days later Harry Showers stood on the quarterdeck of his new command, the cruiser *Hobart* then alongside in Brisbane. He and the ship's company farewelled the former Commanding Officer Captain Harry Howden down the gangway. A more informal farewell would occur at a nearby pub. By custom, Harry Showers as the new Captain would take no part. *Hobart* had returned from the Battle of the Coral Sea largely unscathed under the inspired leadership of Howden. As is so often the case, the personality of *Hobart* was in large measure impregnated by the persona of the Captain. In the case of *Hobart* and Howden it went beyond this. He was the talisman for the ship and after the near miraculous evasive manoeuvres Howden had made in the Java Sea and then in the Coral Sea, sailors felt they owed the safe return of their ship and themselves to him. After the Java Sea Howden wrote that:

> Unsigned notes have been dropped into my sea cabin, expressing in simple language their regard for me, while men either singularly or in groups have frequently approached me, and thanked me for bringing the ship safely through, and have made utterances expressive of their fidelity and loyal following.[129]

There was also a feeling onboard that Howden, through his pre-war contact with the Japanese when on the Yangtse River patrol 'understood the Japanese'.[130] *Hobart's* gunnery officer Lieutenant Commander Richard Peek later wrote of his 'happy warrior captain':

> From him stemmed the spirit which permeated the ship all her life—the spirit of fighting hard, playing hard and being happy in our endeavours.[131]

James Esdaile assumed command of the cruiser HMAS Adelaide *from Harry Showers with the ship further modified for convoy escort work.* (NAA)

Harry Showers was therefore presented with an efficient and happy ship. He had to acknowledge the Howden legacy but at the same time establish his own leadership style. His professional competence and gentlemanly approach to his role soon gained the approval of the ship's company.

On 17 June Frank Getting also took command of a cruiser. It was *Canberra* in which he had served as the Commander. This event marked a moment in time when all the RAN's cruisers were commanded by the Pioneer Class. No other class would hold such a distinction. Nevertheless, the news of Frank Getting's appointment was received with dismay in *Kanimbla's* Wardroom. Her Commanding Officer Captain William Adams, OBE RN[132] heard that officers had said on learning of Frank Getting's posting 'that will be end of *Canberra*'. Adams was sufficiently disturbed to speak to the engineering officer Commander James McGuffog[133] on the matter and was told the Wardroom thought Captain Getting was not up to the task of commanding *Canberra*.[134] Yet, once in *Canberra* Frank was soon regarded as a competent Commanding Officer with a good sense of humour.[135] Sub Lieutenant 'Mac' Gregory recalled an incident where as a young Officer of the Watch he was out of station and being subjected to the ministrations of the Navigator to regain formation. Captain Getting came onto the bridge, quickly assessed the scene and said:

> 'Get back in station Sub, I do not believe the Admiral has invited me on board for dinner.' He grinned and marched off the bridge, of course he knew I needed practice to hone my skills in station keeping.[136]

VII

Whilst FRUMEL could not prevent the attack on Sydney Harbour they played a more significant role in the next major battle in the Pacific at Midway. After the great successes so far in the Pacific war the Japanese high command pondered its next step. In March 1942 Admiral Yamamoto and his Combined Fleet staff pushed for the occupation of the mid-Pacific island of Midway while the US Pacific Fleet was still weakened. Midway would extend the reach of the Japanese fleet and perhaps set the stage for a decisive battle with the US Pacific Fleet aircraft carriers. Admiral Osami Nagano, the chief of the naval staff was not in favour of the plan and foresaw the difficulties of trying to retain Midway after its occupation. As was the case on other occasions Admiral Nagano gave way and the Midway operation was approved. In follow-on operations the Japanese planned to occupy Fiji, Samoa and New Caledonia.[137]

Unknown to Yamamoto both FRUMEL and HYPO were intercepting Japanese signal traffic. While it was clear that a major operation was being prepared, the vital piece of information of where was initially elusive. Crucially FRUMEL and HYPO were able to glean the Japanese intent to occupy Midway Island.[138] The resultant battle which still required skilled command, bravery and determination as well as a fair dose of luck, resulted in the sinking of four Japanese carriers[139] and critically the loss of most of Japan's experienced aviators. The US Navy for its part lost the Coral Sea veteran *Yorktown*. The battle was probably one of the most strategically decisive in naval history. In the short term the Midway defeat caused the Japanese to postpone their invasions of Fiji, Samoa and New Caledonia indefinitely.

In Australia, as the US and Australian ships regrouped from the Battle of the Coral Sea, Rear Admiral Crace was replaced as Commander of the Australian Squadron by Rear Admiral Victor Crutchley, VC, RN. A towering figure, Crutchley had earned his VC at the second Ostend Raid in 1918. In the 1930s he had served on the New Zealand Station and so had previous experience with the RAN and the south-west Pacific waters. Crutchley's reputation had been enhanced by his command of *Warspite* in the Second Battle of Narvik when he took her into the confines of Ofotfjord and sank three German destroyers.

Crutchley hoisted his flag in *Australia* and soon struck a strong rapport with Harold Farncomb and the other captains in the squadron. He also became well liked by the officers and sailors. One anecdote that did the rounds was that when *Australia* once went to action stations and the Admiral was slowly making his way up a ladder to the bridge, an impatient sailor following him gave him a slap on his behind and called out, 'Hurry up you old bastard'. On his arrival at the top of the ladder the sailor was shocked to see it was the Admiral and was very apologetic. Crutchley then said, 'I may be old, young man, but my parentage has never been in question'.[140]

On 24 June 1942 *Bungaree*, this time escorted by *Tromp*, returned to New Caledonia to complete its minefields. Norman Calder found Noumea and its harbour a vastly different place from the sleepy town he had first visited. The US Navy was in port and their presence was significant. Norman later wrote:

> American naval power was awe inspiring. I was in Scapa Flow in 1917/18 and saw British Sea Power at its height. There may have been more ships of the line with attendant cruiser squadrons and destroyer flotillas in Scapa Flow than there were in Noumea, but the 'logistics' provided at Noumea was tremendous, floating docks, landing craft, aircraft carriers, harbour defences and thousands of personnel.[141]

What Norman did not appreciate was that Noumea was now one of the staging points for impending operations in Guadalcanal. While he was not to be a participant in those operations, seven members of the Pioneer

Class would engage in this titanic struggle. The seven—Eric Feldt, Harold Farncomb, Frank Getting, Rupert Long, Hugh MacKenzie, Jack Newman and Harry Showers were either at sea in command of ships, on the islands or contributing to the effort from Australia. Not all survived.

The Solomons represented the furthest edge of Japanese occupied territory and they worked to strengthen their hold on the island group. From this island chain the lines of communication between Australia and America could be interrupted while New Guinea and New Caledonia could also be threatened. After the successful occupation of Tulagi the Japanese occupied Guadalcanal and commenced construction of a strategically important airfield on Lunga Point. These activities were accurately reported by the coastwatchers and it was thought the construction would be completed in August.

Even before intelligence was received about the new airfield, Admiral King in Washington had gained Presidential approval to launch an invasion of key islands in the Solomons. General Marshall was not enthusiastic about the plan, but King said it could be largely done by the Navy and the Marines. The Solomons operation, code-named *Watchtower* was the first American offensive and amphibious operation against Japan. But with the Japanese consolidating their hold of the islands, speed was going to be of the essence.

The overall commander for the operation was Vice Admiral Robert Ghormley, the US Commander of the South West Pacific area who exercised command from Noumea. The senior officer at sea was Vice Admiral Frank Fletcher in *Saratoga*. His Task Force 61 also included the aircraft carriers *Enterprise* and *Wasp* as well as the new battleship *North Carolina*. Rear Admiral Kelly Turner was in command of the amphibious force. The landing was undertaken by the Marines' First Division which had been assembled in New Zealand under the command of Major General Archie Vandegrift. As part of the planning for the operation Vandegrift's assistant operations officer Lieutenant Colonel Merrill Twining visited Eric Feldt in Townsville and obtained a comprehensive intelligence brief on Guadalcanal. A particular concern for Twining was the size of the Japanese forces on Guadacanal and he judged the US estimates were too large. When he asked for Eric's estimate, Twining later wrote 'then he [Feldt] gave me, without comment, a slip of paper on which he had penciled the Ferdinand numbers - numbers about half as large [as the US estimate]'.[142] This provided some reassurance to Twining that the operation had prospects for success.

The invasion forces converged from bases in New Zealand, New Caledonia and Queensland. It was in Brisbane that Rear Admiral Crutchley's supporting Task Force 44 prepared for the operation. It consisted of the cruisers *Australia, Canberra, Hobart, Chicago* and *Salt Lake City* along with the destroyers *Patterson, Ralph, Talbot* and *Jarvis*. Crutchley's mission was to escort the amphibious ships and protect them while they lay off the invasion area.

Prior to sailing for *Watchtower* Crutchley and his staff had made efforts to improve the efficiency and interoperability between the ships. Training inside the confines of Moreton Bay showed that only *Australia* was fully worked up. *Canberra* had just come out of refit and had significant changes to her ship's company. A significant proportion of the American ships had yet to see action.[143]

As Crutchley soon found there were major differences in communications, doctrine and tactics between the two navies. During the Battle of the Coral Sea Admiral Crace had exchanged communications sailors to ensure signals were read and understood among the ships. The US were introducing a line of sight inter-ship radio system called Talk Between Ships or TBS. None of the RAN ships or indeed *Chicago* was TBS fitted.

The second issue was the articulation in one document of how the ships would fight. This was more vexing. Crace had his Staff Officer Operations, Commander Galfrey Gatacre draft a *Cruising and Operating Guide* or COP for the Task Force. This was completed in time for Operation *Watchtower*. The COP essentially explained how RN and RAN ships fought at sea. Philosophically this included much more delegated

HMAS Canberra *leaving Wellington Harbour on 22 July 1942 as part of the Guadalcanal and Tulagi invasion force.* (USN)

authority and use of initiative than was generally the case with the US Navy. While a soundly constructed document it also created problems. Chief among them was that the RAN was contributing just three ships in a large USN operation and they were a minority, even in Task Force 44. While the USN had still not fully standardized their procedures it may have been better for the RAN to adopt those of the US Navy. This latter approach was adopted in the later stages of the war and indeed in future RAN-USN combined operations.

With the Japanese nearing completion of the Lunga Point airfield, the invasion date was set for 7 August. On 14 July Crutchley sailed Task Force 44 for Wellington where it joined Turner's amphibious ships. The following week the combined force sailed and conducted a very thorough amphibious rehearsal in Fiji over a two day period. The passage to the Solomons was also used for planning meetings and the development of detailed orders. The most important meeting involved Fletcher, Turner, Vandegrift and their staffs. In a bombshell Fletcher announced that he considered the operation 'a raid' rather than the permanent seizure of land. He also doubted it would succeed. He said his carriers would leave the Solomons 48 hours after the landing.[144] Vandegrift accepted Fletcher's decision 'with the best grace he could muster'.[145] As the meeting broke up Turner is reputed to have told Fletcher, 'You son of a bitch, if you do that you are yellow'.[146] Ghormley should have been at such a critical meeting and if he had then the early departure of the aircraft carriers would have likely been escalated to Nimitz and King. Fletcher's view of the operation did not coincide with King's, and the former may not have survived long in command. If Crutchley had been present, he would no doubt have been equally aghast at Fletcher's intentions. The potential withdrawal of naval forces from supporting soldiers ashore was an anathema to the RN as their dogged support to the Army at Dunkirk, Greece and Crete had attested.

Crutchley was informed of Fletcher's decision at an otherwise constructive meeting with Turner and Vandegrift in *Australia*. One much needed meeting that was not held would have been between Crutchley and the Captains of the three additional US cruisers, *Astoria, Vincennes* and *Quincy,* that joined Task Force 44.

In Fletcher's defence, the speed of the operation and the uncertainties about the Japanese response created concerns. In particular, he was conscious he had three of the four precious fleet carriers then in the Pacific. Yet, Lady Luck was with Fletcher. In the final two days of the approach there was cloud cover which prevented any Japanese reconnaissance aircraft detecting the Allied invasion fleet.

During the first week of August US B-17 bombers raided Guadalcanal. Reports of these raids were received in the Japanese stronghold of Rabaul. Since 30 July Rabaul had been the headquarters of the Japanese 8th Fleet under the command of Vice Admiral Gunichi Mikawa. A Naval Academy classmate of Rear Admiral Goto, who took part in the Battle of the Coral Sea, Mikawa was a veteran of the Pearl Harbor operation and a rising star in the Imperial Japanese Navy. Mikawa was sufficiently concerned about Rabaul's vulnerability to air attack that he kept his heavy cruisers back at Kavieng. These ships could be called forward when required. With respect to the US bomber raids Mikawa and his staff did not judge them to be a prelude to an impending invasion. Rather Mikawa maintained the view that the Americans would focus their future operations on Papua.[147]

At about 6.20 am on 7 August the peace of Sealark Channel between Guadalcanal and Tulagi was broken by a shore bombardment of cruisers and bombs from carrier aircraft on Japanese positions. The cruisers *San Juan*, *Canberra* and *Chicago* (designated Squadron Y) escorted the amphibious force to land Marines at Tulagi. Meanwhile *Australia*, *Hobart*, *Astoria*, *Vincennes* and *Quincy* (designated Squadron X) were supporting the main group at Guadalcanal.

Surprise was complete. At the Tulagi anchorage carrier aircraft destroyed the 15 Japanese floatplanes at either their moorings or onshore. It led Frank Getting to remark to *Canberra's* bridge staff that he would have thought it impossible in this day and age to achieve such surprise.[148] From his vantage point on Gold Ridge Macfarlan's assistant coastwatcher and old-time islander Ken Dalrymple-Hay could see that the Japanese:

> ... seemed to be taken completely by surprise as here was very little ack-ack to commence with, the ships appeared to have panicked and were going in all directions. Seven or eight ships received direct hits, three of which sank immediately, and others were in crippled condition and were not likely to recover.[149]

By 7 am the first wave of landing craft was heading towards the beach at Tulagi with the Guadalcanal landing craft an hour later. The new coastwatchers Josselyn and Horton were part of that first wave acting as guides and each was later awarded the US Silver Star for his actions. After the considerable anticipation of the invasion, confidence grew in the force and the operation gained momentum.[150]

In Rabaul reports were coming in of the American landings with the Tulagi Garrison reporting that 'the enemy force is overwhelming. We will defend our positions to the death'.[151] In Mikawa, Fletcher and Crutchley had a resolute foe. The Japanese Admiral quickly reassigned aircraft due to launch a raid on Milne Bay to instead attack Guadalcanal and Tulagi. He also ordered a reinforcement troop convoy to be prepared and for his cruisers and submarines to prepare for immediate operations at Guadalcanal.

At about 11.30 am the first coastwatcher air raid warning was given over the teleradio circuit. This report of 24 bombers bound for Guadalcanal was given by Paul Mason. Sensibly Eric Feldt had previously instructed his coastwatchers to report aircraft reports in the clear (without being encoded). This enabled time sensitive information to be acted upon. In the case of this raid Mason's report was received when the bombers were still 320 miles from Guadalcanal. This allowed time for carrier based fighters to be airborne and at height while the ships prepared for the attack. *Australia* was the first to see the raid and opened fire with her 8-inch and 4-inch guns. Little damage was done by the raid and the Japanese lost at least eleven aircraft. Harold Farncomb later wrote, 'we were glad indeed that we had US naval aircraft cooperating directly with us'.[152]

Mikawa was determined to conduct a strike on the invasion fleet with his cruiser force. He sent his broad plan to Tokyo for endorsement. After an initial refusal, Admiral Nagano approved the proposal. Mikawa's flagship the heavy cruiser *Chokai* arrived in Rabaul harbour at 6 pm on the afternoon of the invasion.[153] Mikawa boarded her and sailed within the hour. *Chokai* joined the four other cruisers of the 6th Division *Aoba, Kinugasa, Kako* and *Furutaka* as well as the light cruiser *Yubari* and the destroyer *Yunagi* in the St George Channel. It was a formidable force. The heavy cruisers were larger, more powerfully armed and better protected than *Canberra* and the US cruisers. All the Japanese ships were fitted with 'Long Lance' torpedoes. Although they had not operated as a tactical unit all the Japanese ships had seen some action in the war to date.

Off Cape St George, Mikawa's ships were detected by one of Admiral Hart's old Asiatic Fleet submarines, USS *S38* which was now based out of Brisbane. Her captain, Lieutenant Commander Henry Munson was too close to get *S38* into an attack position but did send a contact report of two destroyers and three larger ships of an unknown type steaming south east. Munson did however enjoy success the next day when he sank *Meiyo Maru* carrying Mikawa's 315 troops to reinforce the Guadalcanal garrison.

At 6 am the next morning Mikawa catapulted no fewer than five seaplanes from his cruisers to search ahead of his force. Mikawa was most concerned about the location of the aircraft carriers. The seaplanes erroneously reported a battleship and a clutch of heavy cruisers off Guadalcanal. Mikawa therefore decided after recovering his aircraft to pass through the Bougainville Strait and proceed at high speed to Guadalcanal to reach there at about 12.30 am that evening.

Meanwhile at 7.39 am Crutchley received Munson's contact report. This report placed these ships about 600 nm away and they might not even have been bound for Guadalcanal. In any case there would likely be subsequent reports if they were to close Guadalcanal. This was a valid assessment because just before Mikawa recovered his seaplanes a Hudson bomber detected the force off the east coast of Bougainville. They were identified as three cruisers and three destroyers. Mikawa temporarily altered course away from his destination to hopefully have his less threatening course reported. His ships were again sighted in the afternoon by another Hudson which identified them as two heavy and two light cruisers still to the north of the Bougainville Strait. Undeterred Mikawa kept closing the Allied force with his planned time for engagement delayed about an hour.

In the late afternoon Mikawa ordered his ships to prepare for battle. Just after sunset he signalled to his ships in Nelsonian fashion, 'In the finest tradition of the Imperial Navy we shall engage the enemy in night battle. Every man is expected to do his best'.[154]

Once the initial landing was completed, Crutchley made changes to his deployments to best provide protection to the amphibious force. These dispositions would change depending on the time of day as the threat from air attack diminished at night. Over the two days Japanese aircraft had bombed the transport USS *George F Elliott* and torpedoed the destroyer USS *Jarvis*, but had lost 36 aircraft thanks to the combination of coastwatcher reports, carrier fighter defence and warship gunfire.

Crutchley deployed two radar-equipped destroyers *Blue* and *Ralph Talbot* to the south west of Savo Island to kept watch and provide early warning of any enemy approach from the north. These destroyers were reputedly the most proficient with radar and a realistic detection range was about six miles. In respect to his heavy cruisers Crutchley deployed them in two groups. *Australia*, *Canberra* and *Chicago* had been trained in night fighting and the tactics of his COP. They would guard the area south east of Savo while the trio he was not familiar with, *Vincennes*, *Astoria* and *Quincy* would patrol to the north east of Savo. The latter group was commanded by *Vincennes*' Captain Frederick Riefkohl. In his *Special Instructions to Screening Group and Vessels Temporarily Assigned*, Crutchley laid out his intent for both groups to be able to act independently or in support of the other depending on the composition of the enemy.[155] The two light cruisers *San Juan* and *Hobart* under the command of Rear Admiral Norman Scott were to patrol the less likely enemy approach of the eastern channel. The other destroyers, were assigned in small groups to either support the cruiser groups or conduct anti-submarine sweeps near the amphibious force. In conception it was a sound plan that would provide defence against air, surface and submarine threats, provided it was well supported by air surveillance from both land based and carrier based aircraft. Without this support the destroyer 'trip-wire' involved too few ships that were too close to both the cruisers and the amphibious force to provide adequate warning.

On 8 August Fletcher, concerned about his growing fighter losses, potential risk to aircraft carriers and low fuel decided to retire his carrier task force on the evening of 8 August. Although foreshadowed by Fletcher before the operation, this placed Turner, Vandegrift and Crutchley and the entire operation in an extremely difficult position. Turner called a conference onboard his flagship, the transport *McCawley*, that evening for the three officers to plan a way forward. It was not until 8.45 pm that Crutchley was advised of the timing of the conference and he decided to steam the 22 miles to *McCawley* in *Australia*. This denuded his force with Captain Bode as next senior assuming command of the the group at 8.55

pm. Crutchley also did not specifically inform Riefkohl of this change although *Vincennes'* communications staff should have been able to follow developments from the signal traffic.

Among the cruisers and destroyers there were both different manning and weapon states as well as different views on possible threats. Since midday on 6 August Crutchley had his ships in the first degree of readiness. This meant that all men were at their action stations and during lulls some personnel were allowed to go for meals. It was a fatiguing routine and unless personnel had hammocks at their action station (and some did) it was unsustainable for more than one or two days. Frank Getting had for example decided that day to relax to the second degree of readiness with half of the men at their stations to allow others to sleep.[156] This meant that half the 8-inch and 4-inch guns were manned but torpedo tubes were at first degree of readiness.[157] All men had to remain fully dressed and Frank and other key officers slept in the few sea cabins close to the bridge. In *Canberra* the guns were unloaded, but Commander Frank Walker in the destroyer *Patterson* had the guns loaded and torpedoes primed.

More critically there was no Commander's appreciation by Crutchley to his Commanding Officers of the possible threat. Based on the Hudson contact reports, some Captains, such as in *Chicago* and *Patterson*, thought there could be a night action and briefed their bridge staff accordingly, while others did not.[158] Clearly, Crutchley fell into the latter camp, but in any case he did not communicate that to his ships.

At 10.30 pm the meeting between Crutchley, Turner and Vandegrift and their key staff was held. To those assembled, Fletcher's decision to leave the Marines was still difficult to stomach. At the very least with three carriers and a flag officer in each, Fletcher had the ability to leave at least one on station and there were sufficient cruisers and destroyers to screen that ship. The meeting was presented with a fait accompli and the question was whether the transports could remain without carrier air cover. There was unanimous agreement that they could not and the next question was how much of the critical supplies were still to be unloaded, and hence when the ships could depart?[159] While Vandegrift knew the state of the Guadalcanal off-load he would have to go to Tulagi that night to make an assessment there. Crutchley offered to take him part of the way to rendezvous with a destroyer to take him the remainder of the journey.

Also discussed at the meeting was the Hudson contact report of three cruisers, three destroyers and two seaplane tenders reported east of Bougainville Island steaming south east. Turner believed that these ships were bound for Rekata Bay on the west coast of Santa Isabel Island possibly to establish a seaplane base.

At 11.10 pm Mikawa relaunched his aircraft for one final sortie. For most of the pilots it was their first night launch. Half an hour later the presence of enemy cruisers was confirmed and their position was plotted on Mikawa's chart. The Admiral thereafter increased speed to 28 knots and closed his ships up to action stations. Mikawa later wrote:

> I had complete confidence in my ships and knew that the Japanese Navy's emphasis on night battle training and practice would insure our chances of success in such an action, even without air support.[160]

A key to the Japanese approach to night engagements was to have a simple plan. Mikawa's was to steam at speed in line ahead passing between Savo Island and Guadalcanal engaging ships as he encountered them and sweep in a counter-clockwise direction around to Tulagi.

At 12.40 am Savo Island appeared on the port bow of Mikawa's flagship. Soon thereafter a destroyer was seen 6 miles ahead crossing right to left. Mikawa assessed that he remained undetected and reduced speed to 22 knots so that large wakes would not be visible. A second destroyer was sighted which again appeared on routine patrol and not to have detected the Japanese. Mikawa's ships passed between the destroyer pickets and closed Crutchley's ships. Now clear of the destroyers, Mikawa became more confident of eventual success. He increased speed to 30 knots and instructed his rear ship the destroyer *Yunagi* to attack the US destroyers.

Chokai's lookouts reported a cruiser fine on the port bow. This was *Canberra* with *Chicago* astern of her. At the same time the seaplanes dropped flares to illuminate the scene. The flares showed three cruisers at about 4 miles distant. Ashore Vandegrift's air operations officer, Major Kenny Weir correctly recognized the distinctive sound of the Japanese seaplane engines. He told Colonel Twining, 'cruiser float planes and not ours. Where there are cruiser planes, there are cruisers'.[161]

At 01.37 am *Chokai* sent Long Lance torpedoes speeding towards *Canberra* and *Chicago*. A couple of minutes later a lookout in *Canberra* sighted a darkened warship and reported this to the officer of the watch, Sub-Lieutenant MacKenzie Gregory, and the principal control officer Lieutenant Commander Ewan Wight (who controlled the armament). At the same time *Patterson* signalled by light to *Canberra* that it had passed on TBS - 'Warning! Warning! Warning! Strange Ships Entering Harbour'.[162]

Gregory ordered Action Stations. While the rest of *Canberra's* bridge tried to see the ship there was an explosion 6,000 yards distant on the starboard side. Frank Getting and other officers rushed to the bridge from their nearby sea cabins. Three darkened warships could be now seen and the order was given to load the guns and train on the targets. The Navigator Lieutenant Commander Jack Mesley took control of the bridge and Gregory moved to his action stations position in the forward control station. Meanwhile Frank ordered Full Speed Ahead and 'Port 35' to open the arc of all 8-inch guns on the enemy. As the ship accelerated there was a report of a torpedo on the starboard bow and Frank ordered 'Starboard 35' to present the minimum target.

When Gregory got to his station he looked through the more powerful binoculars and 'saw a Mogami Class cruiser with her large trunked funnel, only about 3,000 yards away, blasting away at us with her 8-inch armament, I recall saying: "My God! this is bloody awful!" and it was'.[163]

As *Canberra* swung to starboard and her guns attempted to track the targets, *Chokai's* shells hit. The first burst in the plotting office and also wrecked the port torpedo space, damaged the 4-inch gun deck and

The imposing superstructure of Vice Admiral Gunichi Mikawa's flagship Chokai. *The cruiser closed to 600 yards from HMAS* Canberra *and hit Frank Getting's ship with torpedoes and gunfire. The Japanese heavy cruisers were larger and more powerful than both the American and Australian cruisers at Guadalcanal.* (USN)

set the midships aircraft ablaze. The second salvo struck near the bridge. Frank Getting was looking through one of the enemy bearing indicators at the time and was thrown to the deck by the force of the blast. Shrapnel flew through the bridge area and took a fearful toll. The gunnery officer, Lieutenant Commander Donald Hole was killed instantly when his head was taken off. The torpedo officer Lieutenant Commander John Plunkett-Cole, Midshipman Bruce Loxton and Midshipman Noel Sanderson all suffered shrapnel wounds. Only the Navigator escaped injury.

Surgeon Commander Charles Downward was soon on the bridge. He found Frank Getting slumped against a bulkhead. His right leg was shattered and he had suffered multiple other shrapnel wounds. Frank told the doctor to see to the other men and refused to be moved. The second salvo had also knocked out both boiler rooms and the ship soon lost power. All this occurred within three minutes of Action Stations. The ship continued to sustain punishment. According to the Executive Officer Commander John Walsh who assumed command, *Canberra* sustained at least one torpedo hit and 22 hits from gunfire.[164] The stricken ship soon took on a ten degree list to starboard.

Chicago was struck by two torpedoes and slowly cleared to the west away from the action. Most critically Bode did not send an enemy contact report that may have warned Captain Riefkohl and his ships. As Mikawa's ships steamed on their counter-clockwise course they illuminated ships with their searchlights and opened fire in turn. At about 1.50 am Mikawa's cruisers engaged the *Astoria, Vincennes* and *Quincy* group while his rear ship *Kinugasa* still poured fire into *Canberra*. As the range closed more hits were scored on the hapless cruisers. Commander Toshikazu Ohmae later wrote:

> For incredible minutes the turrets of enemy ships remained in their trained-in, secured positions, and we stood amazed, yet thankful while they did not bear on us. Strings of machine-gun tracers wafted back and forth between the enemy and ourselves, but such minor counter efforts merely made a colourful spectacle, and gave us no concern.[165]

Among the US cruisers *Quincy,* although heavily damaged and on fire aft, managed to return fire. One of her shells struck *Chokai* which sprayed shrapnel through the operations room and narrowly missed Mikawa. Having swept through Crutchley's force Mikawa consulted the chart with his staff. The question was whether to continue onto the amphibious force or to withdraw. Ever concerned about the threat posed by the aircraft carriers, Mikawa chose to withdraw. He calculated that his ships would not be able to regain formation after the melee and reach the amphibious force until just before sunrise. Mikawa's cruisers would then be extremely vulnerable to air attack.

On *Australia* Crutchley, in the absence of a clear report from Captain Bode of the battle, decided to keep *Australia* between the cruisers and the transports. If Mikawa had decided on his other course of action, he would have encountered *Australia*. While it would have been a battle against unfavourable odds *Australia* may have finally deterred Mikawa from proceeding any further.

To the east *San Juan* and *Hobart* first saw flares which they took to be deployed by aircraft and then heard and saw an obvious battle on the horizon.[166] Without TBS and with little intelligence passed to *Hobart* as a

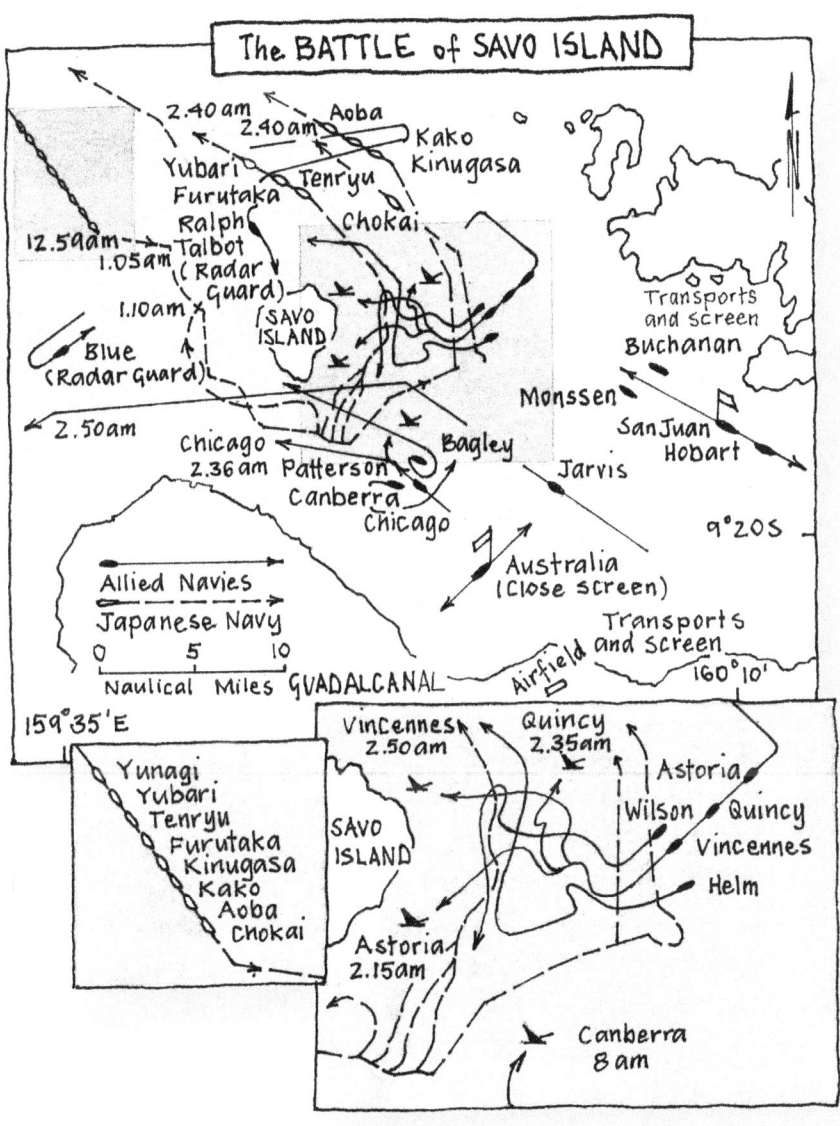

'private' ship they could only speculate. On watch in *Hobart* was her gunnery officer, Lieutenant Commander Richard Peek who immediately called Harry Showers. Peek asked whether *Hobart* should close the action. Harry refused as they were under the command of Rear Admiral Scott and with an uncertain situation still had the role of protecting the eastern approaches.[167]

The impressive *Patterson,* which had engaged *Yubari* and *Tenyru,* returned to assist *Canberra.* The destroyer came alongside at about 3.30 am to assist fighting the fires which were taking hold as without power *Canberra* had no water pressure for fire fighting. *Patterson* also took onboard the badly wounded including Frank Getting. As *Patterson* cast off, the remaining survivors were heartened by Commander Walker's cheery words of, 'Don't worry, we will be back'.[168] Walker was true to his word and he was impressed with the orderly demeanor of *Canberra's* men.

Frank Getting and the other injured were transferred to the troopship USS *Barnett.* Surgeon Commander Downward was ably supported by Able Seaman Henry 'Nobby' Hall, a signalman with only first aid training, who continued to tend to Frank and the others. Frank finally succumbed to his wounds and the faithful 'Nobby' Hall later wrote of his Captain:

> To me he was God! I assisted Surgeon Commander Downward operate on him in an American tin can [destroyer] following Savo Island. He was wounded in many places. What we did was not enough for him. He was kind to his men.[169]

As the Japanese cleared to the north-west they left a scene of carnage. The toll on the force was devastating. *Quincy* and *Vincennes* had been been sunk with the loss of over 600 men. Dawn revealed *Astoria, Chicago* and *Canberra* all fighting to stay afloat. With the prospect of having to withdraw surface forces it was clear *Canberra* could not be saved and she was torpedoed at 8 am by the destroyers *Ellet* and *Selfridge.* While there were initial hopes to save *Astoria* salvage parties lost the fight and she rolled over and sank just after midday.

On news of the engagement Fletcher, despite prompting to launch an air strike on the retiring Japanese, did not send a counter strike.[170] Despite the significant victory Mikawa had achieved, his decision not to go on to attack the amphibious force was later criticised. Mikawa subsequently said if he had known the true disposition of the aircraft carriers he would have attacked the amphibious force. On reflecting on his victory he magnanimously wrote:

> The element of surprise worked to our advantage and enabled us to destroy every target taken under fire. I was greatly impressed, however, by the courageous action of the northern group of US cruisers. They fought back heroically despite heavy damage sustained before they were ready for battle. Had they had even a few minutes' warning of our approach, the results of the action would have been quite different.[171]

On Mikawa's return dash north the decisive victory was soured when the cruiser *Kato* was sunk by *S44*. The First Battle of Savo Island or the First Battle of the Solomon Sea as the Japanese called it was the Japanese Navy's greatest victory against the US Navy after Pearl Harbor.

News of the battle was widely reported in the Australian press with a particular emphasis on Frank Getting's insistence that his men be treated before him.[172] In Sydney, Hazel Getting was interviewed by journalist James Adams and she told him:

> I am proud of Frank. He loved the sea and he was willing if needs be, to give his all for his country. He would not have wanted to go in any other way ... He would have wanted me to be brave now in the loss that I have suffered, but it is not of myself alone that I am thinking. Other brave men too have given their lives, and I wish to express my deepest sympathy to the wives and mothers of those who went down with him. It is up to us to see that the men we loved have not given their lives in vain.[173]

Eric Feldt on learning of Frank's death wrote to Rupert Long, 'Bad luck about 'Hungry'—strewth, no one can say the RAN hasn't done its share'.[174] In Britain Admiral Colvin wrote to *The Times* to say that Frank was, 'A splendid fellow, strong, self-reliant, and so obviously ready for any emergency'.[175]

In the aftermath of the Battle of Savo Island Australia,[176] Britain[177] and the United States[178] conducted separate reviews during and after war to ascertain what had occurred and what had led to the defeat. The post war analysis benefitted from accounts and interviews with some of the Japanese protagonists including Admiral Mikawa himself. These reviews did not comment on the broader strategic setting for the battle. The US Navy's initial review by Vice Admiral Arthur Hepburn, for instance, suggested four factors in the Japanese achieving such complete surprise. They were the ships' inadequate states of readiness, failure to recognize the import of the Japanese seaplane sorties, too much confidence in the destroyer pickets and the failure to communicate the initial action to the other cruisers. This last criticism was specifically levelled at Captain Bode. Relegated to shore duty in Panama, Bode committed suicide on 19 April 1943.

Not surprisingly, Admiral Sir Guy Royle had his preeminent captain, John Collins, comment on the Australian Board of Inquiry findings of the action. John thought the absence of *Australia* in the cruiser formation that night was significant. He wrote that the outcome of the action might have been very different if the more experienced team on the Flagship's bridge had handled the vital first minutes of the encounter. This view was also shared by Crutchley's operations officer Lieutenant Commander Gatacre who thought *Australia's* battle-worthiness and Crutchley's presence would have been decisive and at the very least resulted in the *Vincennes* group being adequately warned.[179]

John Collins was critical of Crutchley's placement of the radar fitted ships which did not optimise the chances for detection and also felt it 'unforgivable' for classmate Frank Getting not having more senior officers, presumably himself or his Executive Officer on the bridge at all times.[180] This later judgment was based on the normal practice in the Mediterranean.

A large number of books have since been written on the battle. Titles such as *Savo: The Incredible Naval Débâcle off Guadalcanal*[181] and *The Shame of Savo: Anatomy of a naval disaster*[182] give a flavour for the historical analysis. The latter work was co-written by *Canberra* survivor Bruce Loxton and makes the plausible claim that the destroyer *Bagley* struck *Canberra* with a torpedo in the heat of the battle. In reviewing the Battle of Savo Island it is worthy to note the words of Captain Stephen Roskill, who in addition to participating in the *Australia* court martial, also served in *Leander* during the later phases of the Solomons Campaign. He cautioned against over-critical analysis:

> It is perhaps endemic in the democratic system of government that we should study and analyse our failures at least as much as our successes. Nor can anyone take exception to such processes—so long as the historian is at pains to understand and to explain, rather than criticise and condemn men who were, as in this case, called on to make extremely difficult decisions in circumstances which, as so often in war, had not been fully foreseen. ... Hindsight is, after all, a very powerful aid to wisdom.[183]

It is with this wise counsel in mind that some cautious analysis is provided. It is clear that up to the Battle of Savo Island the fighting capabilities of the Japanese Navy were not fully appreciated. In particular, its excellence in night fighting and the lethality of the Long-Lance torpedoes. Those who had seen its competence such as Hec Waller had not survived to tell of their experiences. If the Japanese capabilities had been better known then Crutchley may been been more alive to the threat of a night time attack. As was described earlier, some of his captains clearly thought they may have been attacked that night. Crutchley, if similarly concerned, might have ordered stronger night time dispositions, suitably briefed his captains and used a destroyer and not *Australia* to take him to the meeting with Turner. Crutchley did not help matters by not telling Captain Riefkohl of his absence. Riefkohl was senior to Bode and therefore should have been in charge of the entire force. Nor did he inform Rear Admiral Scott.

Radar was very much in its infancy at sea in August 1942. The understanding of its capabilities and limitations were not fully appreciated. Actual performance was also quite variable. Crutchley's disposition had essentially one destroyer patrolling each of the two likely lines of Japanese approach. This effectively meant that each approach had one ship on a patrol line which, depending on where the destroyer was on its patrol beat, allowed for gaps in radar coverage. So leaving aside the poor performance of the destroyer pickets, they were insufficient to provide a high level of detection confidence. A more mathematical approach to deploying radar equipped ships, based on detection probabilities was in the future. In addition, if this limitation was combined with the patchy air patrols, Crutchley may have felt more compelled to launch his own seaplanes to provide routine surveillance during the day. He had four aircraft available that were also not assigned to the equally essential anti-submarine patrols. In contrast, Mikawa had used his seaplanes in an imaginative and unexpected way. Even Harold Farncomb did not fully appreciate the import of the Japanese night seaplane sortie and thought it was associated with an impending air raid.[184] As such he did not report it to Crutchley on his return to *Australia*.

Communications proved a critical weakness between ships with no common satisfactory method available to exchange tactical information. In addition the slowness of passing contact reports from shore based aircraft had an adverse impact on *Watchtower*. Crutchley, not having experience with TBS, could not have been expected to appreciate what a disadvantage not having TBS could be in his flagship. Had he known he may have considered shifting his flag to a US cruiser fitted with TBS.[185] In reviewing Crutchley's actions it needs to be borne in mind that he had an inadequately small staff to support him compared to that of US admirals and of his successors in command of the Australian Squadron.

The Solomons campaign demanded an ability for ships to react to air, surface and submarine attack at very short notice over extended periods. While Admiral Hepburn was subsequently critical of ships' individual readiness, it was clear there was no perfect solution. Days at actions stations had clearly left men overtired. Harold Farncomb later wrote:

> I feel, however, that in operations of this sort, some relief must be given from the continuous state of Alertness required either by providing extra complement to enable Key Officers and Ratings to be in watches during periods of a high degree of readiness, or by relieving ships temporarily after a couple of days. After a certain time the efficiency of personnel

obviously deteriorate due to mental and physical fatigue, and with this deterioration, danger to the ship will ensure if a 'fresh' enemy is met.[186]

Of note, like Frank Getting in *Canberra*, Harry Showers had also put *Hobart* into the same second degree of readiness.[187] From the perspective of contemporary naval operations, this readiness state was perfectly reasonable provided there was a modicum of warning. That warning of course did not come and this was largely due to the fragmented and unsatisfactory coordination of air surveillance provided from both land and sea. What Frank Getting could be criticised for was not having himself or his Executive Officer continuously on the bridge. In fairness to him there was not a culture in the training of the Australian Squadron to standardize best practice based on experiences learnt more broadly in the war. This again lay in the future.

Vice Admiral Fletcher's less than whole-hearted support of the operation has been the subject of much criticism in later years. Although Roskill is alive to the responsibilities Fletcher had to preserve the aircraft carriers, Fletcher was understandably to be loathed by many Solomon campaign veterans.[188] To Admiral King, Fletcher and Ghormley had not demonstrated the resolve he expected. Nimitz eventually became convinced of Fletcher's shortcomings and he was relieved of sea command at the end of the month when the slow steaming *Saratoga* was torpedoed.[189] It was then to King's most trusted and aggressive admiral that he turned, Admiral 'Bull' Halsey. He would have the responsibility to win against an even more emboldened foe.

VIII

The loss of *Canberra*, following the sinkings of *Sydney* and *Perth*, cut the RAN's once six cruiser squadron to three ships. This critically reduced Australia's contribution to the war. Britain, conscious of Australia's plight and with higher priorities for its manpower, offered as a gift HMS *Shropshire*, then just nearing the end of a refit.[190] As near sister to *Australia* she could be readily incorporated into the Squadron and was gratefully accepted. The

Admiral 'Bull' Halsey (L) with Major General Alexander Vandegrift. Halsey provided the determined and aggressive leadership to support the courage of the men ashore and at sea. He soon became a staunch supporter of Eric Feldt's coastwatchers. (USN)

original intent and one strongly supported by Prime Minister Curtin and agreed to by King George VI was for *Shropshire* to be renamed *Canberra*.[191] It was then learnt the US had decided to name one of their Baltimore Class cruisers nearing completion USS *Canberra*. It was therefore decided to retain the name *Shropshire*. The files do not show any thought to rename the ship *Sydney* or *Perth*.

The commissioning Commanding Officer was the now refreshed John Collins. He assumed command on 7 April and the ship was commissioned into the RAN in London. HMAS *Shropshire* came out of her refit particularly well equipped with the latest generation of radars. This made her extremely useful in detecting aircraft and controlling friendly fighters to counter air attacks. After comprehensive refresher courses and a very thorough work-up she was inspected at Scapa Flow by King George VI, Ernest Bevin, the Minister for Labour and Admiral Sir Bruce Fraser on 12 August. They found in *Shropshire* a very experienced ship's company leavened with enthusiastic youngsters. There was a sizeable contingent from the old *Canberra* as well as from the first commission of *Perth*. Impressively, in the Wardroom there were five officers with the Distinguished Service Cross including

John Collins onboard HMAS Shropshire in the UK. (RAN)

Perth's commissioning gunnery officer Lieutenant Commander 'Braces' Bracegirdle.[192] From the outset the *Shropshire* was a happy and well run ship. In no small measure this was due to John's professionalism and respectful demeanor. Bracegirdle later wrote that John was regarded onboard as 'a fighting captain' which gave everyone great confidence.[193] John was also to impress the ship's company with two other attributes, his immaculate ship-handling, particularly when coming into berth and for his peerless skills in deck tennis.[194] *Shropshire* sailed on the inauspicious Friday the 13th but after escorting a troop convoy as far as Gibraltar, she then made an expeditious delivery voyage via South Africa and arrived in Fremantle on 24 September.

IX

It was clear to Rupert Long and Eric Feldt that their coastwatchers would play a pivotal role in the unfolding Guadalcanal campaign. It was important therefore to place in Guadalcanal an officer to both provide the distilled information to the General on the ground as well as coordinate the coastwatchers' sustainment. For this role they needed someone experienced whom they could trust. This was Hugh MacKenzie and he was moved from Vila one week after the landing.

Hugh had strengths and weaknesses in equal measure. In describing him, a contemporary jokingly said, 'He knew no fear, and no organization either'.[195] Like Eric, he had great knowledge of the islands, the local people and the expatriates. He was passionate about looking after the coastwatchers and would occasionally tread on toes in his efforts to support them.

Importantly however, he got on well with the Americans who appreciated his 'islander' unconventionality. Hugh's small team was the impressive 31-year old Lieutenant Gordon Train and a New Ireland native Rayman Martin. Hugh had met Rayman in Vila harbour after he has escaped the Japanese occupation. Rayman was a mechanic, educated in Sydney, and spoke the local dialect of Pidgin. Hugh engaged him straight away, paying his wage out of his own pocket until Rupert Long could sort out how Rayman could join the RAN as an ordinary seaman. Their Lunga Point quarters was an old Japanese dugout shelter by the airstrip with coconut tree logs and sandbags for a roof. When it rained the floor became sodden and sticky. The precious radios were protected by raincoats. Critically, General Vandegrift assigned Marine radio operators to help Hugh maintain continuous teleradio contact with his coastwatchers.

The other coastwatcher to arrive at the base was Martin Clemens whose teleradio had broken and was probably too close to the US Marine positions to be useful. To Vandegrift, having lost most of his intelligence staff on an ill-fated patrol, Clemens was a desperately needed addition to his headquarters. Clemens and Vandegrift's divisional intelligence officer Lieutenant Colonel Edmund Buckley soon struck up a strong rapport and he became a valued member of the headquarters, helping to organize operations beyond the marine perimeter which often included his 60 native police. Clemens was also appointed as the British liaison officer and was no longer part of the coastwatch organization. Buckley, while soon appreciating the value of the coastwatchers and Hugh's role in coordinating efforts, wanted greater control; this placed Hugh in an increasingly difficult position. In October 1942 Hugh also reported to Rupert Long of 'continual nagging friction and petty annoyances from Clemens'.[196] From his perspective, Clemens thought Hugh was too sensitive to any perceived affront.

Following the Battle of Savo Island and the withdrawal of Fletcher's aircraft carriers, the Guadalcanal campaign became an even more bloody struggle on land, air and sea. The Japanese Navy built up and resupplied the Japanese land forces on Guadalcanal in night time sorties colloquially known the 'Tokyo Express'. These, combined with Japanese efforts to harry the Marines from the sea, led to a series of brutal sea engagements. The US Naval forces were now under the inspired leadership of Admiral Halsey and his spirit imbued his subordinate admirals and captains. Battle names such as Blackett Strait, Cape Esperance, Cape St George, Kolombangara, Kula Gulf, Tassafaronga and Vella Lavella became synonymous with sea battles of close quarter ferocity. They are testimony to the tenacity, sacrifice and courage shown by the sailors on both sides.

While the RAN was not a participant in these battles, Hugh MacKenzie and his coastwatchers continued to play a vital role in alerting Admiral Halsey, General Vandegrift and his relief General Alexander Patch[197] to Japanese air and sea movements. Because of their location between Rabaul and Guadalcanal, Jack Read could typically give two and half hours warning of a Japanese raid, Paul Mason two hours and Donald Kennedy forty-five minutes. In some raids all three coastwatchers would report the inbound raid. Once the US fighters were able to operate from the Lunga Point airstrip, now named Henderson Field, they needed at least forty-five minutes warning of a raid to get airborne and be at 30,000 feet for an ideal interception.

Two other coastwatcher roles emerged. The first was to encourage and co-ordinate local guerilla operations with Solomon Islanders attacking the Japanese. This usefully served to provide relatively safe territory in which coastwatchers could operate but then it grew to attack increasingly vulnerable Japanese patrols. The Solomon Islanders proved adept fighters against the Japanese. This was, of course, at variance to the Ferdinand concept but it was one that fitted with Rupert Long's view of taking the fight to the Japanese in unconventional ways. This offensive approach was to prove immensely successful and exponents such as Dalrymple-Hay and Donald Kennedy had in Hugh's words created 'private armies' to attack the Japanese. Hugh reported to Rupert Long and Eric Feldt that this initiative owed much of its success to the peculiar combination of factors in the Solomons where the local population remained loyal to individual coastwatchers who in their turn readily provided either captured Japanese or US weaponry.[198]

The second emergent activity was the rescue and return of downed aviators. The coastwatchers developed local networks that would find and bring them in. A Catalina flying boat could then be requested which would land in a sheltered cove for recovery. These operations were invariably covered by a strong fighter escort. Over a hundred aviators were saved in the campaign. It was through this association that US aviators appreciated the work of the coastwatchers more than most servicemen. This gratitude was reciprocated wherever possible through either providing supply air drops at Hugh MacKenzie's request, or in one case conducting a successful bombing run on a Japanese dog kennel that housed hounds used to track down coastwatchers.[199]

While there were fewer incidents of rescuing sailors in the campaign, coastwatcher Arthur Evans famously recovered the future President John F. Kennedy after his boat *PT 109* was rammed by the Japanese destroyer *Amagiri*, while Henry Joselyn provided succour to 165 survivors from the cruiser *Helena* who got ashore on Vella Lavella after the Battle of Kula Gulf.

The other people Hugh MacKenzie was on the lookout to rescue were the remnants of the expatriate and missionary community that had tried to remain in place in the face of the Japanese occupation. Japanese brutality, combined with tropical disease, wore down even the most strong-willed islander. By late March 1943 Jack Read had found himself with over 50 priests, brothers and nuns as well as Chinese, mixed race and Polynesian men, women and children. Fortuitously Eric Feldt had organized for fresh coastwatchers Jack Keenan and Doug Bedkober and a new rotation of the AIF contingent to be inserted by the submarine *Gato*. Hugh was able to persuade MacArthur's headquarters to allow the women and children to be evacuated. The appointed time for the transfer in Teop Harbour was the evening of 28 March. Earlier in the day a Japanese patrol boat came to anchor and remained overnight before resuming patrol.

Gato remained on the bottom of the harbour and surfaced the following night. The submarine's captain, Lieutenant Commander Bob Foley, to the immense relief of all, agreed to take the all 51 evacuees to safety.

Hugh earned a rebuke from Vandegrift when he organized Horton and some soldiers to recover the malarial Rhoades and Schroeder along with Bishop Aubin, thirteen nuns and a US aviator, using mainly his own resources. Lieutenant Colonel Buckley had first tried to organise two pick-ups of the party but each time arrangements fell through. Hugh thought Buckley was insufficiently seized by their plight and assessed there was a risk that they would be captured before another attempt was made.[200]

This incident was reflective of Hugh's growing estrangement from Buckley and Clemens. Hugh knew from sympathetic members of the US intelligence staff that Buckley wished to exert greater control. One way was through US provided supplies to coastwatchers which had to be approved by Buckley. In one instance Buckley informed Dalrymple-Hay that his next re-supply was on condition that a bottle of whisky be sent down with the native bearers. When they came down without a bottle they were sent back empty handed.[201] This incensed Hugh who had his team provide 'gifts' to the marine quartermasters to ensure the coastwatchers were supplied with essentials. Hugh kept Rupert Long and Eric Feldt apprised of his difficulties and thought as a last resort he should be replaced by a Commander who could be on equal rank terms with Buckley. He wrote:

> I shall hate to have to do this but I fear for the future of our carefully built organization if the inexperienced Buckley and Clemens are to be allowed to control it and introduce the ill-considered plans I feel assured they are now hatching.[202]

Hugh was more critical of Clemens than Buckley and later wrote in a report that:

> To a great extent the trouble could be attributed to the ill-considered advice given to D2 (Buckley) by Captain Clemens in his role as Political Officer at Division HQ. This officer was playing at a game in which he had no training and through ignorance he consistently minimised the

dangers and problems of the watchers and discounted the urgency of their requests for stores.[203]

This assessment appears to be supported by 'Snowy' Rhoades who, along with Schroader after his rescue, briefed Vandegrift and Buckley. Rhoades later wrote:

> We were able to give them a lot of information about terrain with which we were familiar, Schroader having walked practically all over Guadalcanal searching for gold. We were able to rectify some of Clemens inaccuracies.[204]

During Rhoades' time in Guadalcanal before his repatriation, he got to experience the Japanese daytime bomber attacks and night time bombardments from the 'Tokyo Express'. He was impressed by the stoicism of the Marines and later wrote of Hugh:

> The gallant MacKenzie would sometimes walk outside our steel roofed dugout during these bombardments. I am sure to try and steady the nerves of the rest, maybe he suffered from claustrophobia as I did.[205]

As is so often the case with individuals operating in 'pressure cooker' environments a change of personnel can change the situation completely. So it was for Hugh with the arrival of General Patch and his staff to replace General Vandegrift and his men. Patch made it clear from the outset that all he was interested in was results and all coastwatch activities were the responsibility of Hugh. Importantly, Hugh would have direct access to the General and the quartermasters were to ensure that the coastwatchers were adequately resourced. Hugh wrote:

> The strain of continually being on guard to counter the moves to take control by more senior officers, and the well intentioned suggestions of others with impracticable schemes for the improvement of coastwatch was gone. We were free for the first time to concentrate on our work with a feeling of security.[206]

To further ease tensions Martin Clemens had new responsibilities. He was promoted to Major and given command of a British Solomon Islander Service Battalion to undertake guerilla style actions. Over coming months the coastwatch network was further strengthened by the arrival via the faithful *Gato* of Eric Feldt's old friend 'Wobbie' Robinson and Lieutenant

George Stephenson on Bougainville. 'Wobbie' was an ideal choice as he had served with Jack Read on the Sepik back in 1932.

Tragedy however, was regularly mixed with success for the coastwatch enterprise. On 5 March Gordon Train was killed in a Liberator bomber when acting as guide for a mission over Ballale Island. The loss of Hugh's outstanding assistant 'cast a gloom over the whole organization'.[207] In June, Doug Bedkober was captured when his camp was surprised by a Japanese patrol. He refused to leave injured aviators and was taken to Rabaul and there executed.

Throughout 1942 Eric Feldt and Rupert Long corresponded with one another about the sustainment of the coastwatch organization. They were keenly aware of the physical and mental strain on the coastwatchers in the enervating tropical conditions and sounded each other out about suitable replacements and opportunities for insertion.[208] There was one special case and that was Read and Mason. In Eric's opinion the men had 'such a local influence that it was impossible to relieve them'.[209] But even the impossible had to be contemplated over a transition period.

In October 1942 a turf war arose in New Guinea when the General Officer Commanding Port Moresby, Brigadier Ronald Hopkins informed Eric Feldt that the New Guinea Force headquarters would assume control of all teleradios and the associated organizations.[210] Rupert Long was a seasoned campaigner in these matters and knew this idea had not been broached in Melbourne. He therefore told Eric to write a report of the organization and on the achievements of the coastwatch organization and advised him to:

> Keep your temper and use me as your safety valve. As Army have not had the courtesy to tell us of their proposal the next move is up to them.[211]

In early March 1943, from his small office in Townsville Eric discerned a lull in activities. It was time for him to visit the field. In March he flew first to Noumea to call on Admiral Halsey and then to the Solomon Islands. In Guadalcanal Eric called on the General and to his delight found Hugh's operation 'running on ball bearings'.[212] Hugh was now ably assisted by

Wobby Robinson. Also in his staff was radio technician and teetotaller Forbes Robertson who was known as 'Dry Robbie' to differentiate him from Wobby. Eric's week long visit was also to size up the nature of the operation and to select a replacement for the exhausted Hugh, who needed a relief as soon as practicable. At the end of his visit Eric boarded a Kingfisher floatplane for Malaita. An hour into the flight he suffered severe chest pains. Diagnosed with coronary selerosis Eric spent the next three weeks in the US hospital on Tulagi before he was fit enough to fly in a low altitude flying Catalina to Brisbane for convalescence.[213] It was the end of Eric's tenure as head of the coastwatchers.

The unexpected loss of Eric Feldt posed an immediate problem for Rupert Long. His choices for Eric's replacement were Hugh MacKenzie or Commander Eric McManus who was SO(I) Darwin. Hugh was not temperamentally suited nor physically up to the demands of the job. Rupert selected McManus, supported by former coastwatcher Don Macfarlan. The coastwatchers, although unsettled by the loss of Eric, did over time overcome their misgivings that an 'islander' was not in charge. The coastwatch organization continued to prosper under McManus's measured leadership.

After nine months on Guadalcanal Hugh MacKenzie was replaced by Pryce-Jones. Hugh's health was sorely worn and he experienced three bouts of Blackwater fever in short order. Medical science by then knew of the fever's adverse linkage to quinine and so Hugh's days in the tropics were also effectively over.[214]

The Solomons campaign was a brilliant vindication of the coastwatch concept. However, the victory had come at a terrible cost. Admiral Halsey, more than any other senior officer, appreciated the contribution the coastwatchers had made to the campaign. He met as many coastwatchers as he could to personally thank them for their courage and took as keen an interest as Rupert Long to ensure their bravery was recognised. One coastwatcher tellingly showed Halsey a 'guestbook' he kept of rescued aircrew which had thirty precious

Eric Feldt with his Solomon Island Coastwatchers during his March 1943 visit. (AWM)
Front row L to R: *Ashton, LC Noaks, FA Rhoades, Eric Feldt, Hugh MacKenzie, GHR Marsland, H Koch, J Campbell.*
Back row L to R: *M Wright, I Skinner, KT Bridge, R Cambridge, LA Walker, HAF Robertson, CW Seton, L Williams.*

names. It made a deep impression on the hard-bitten Admiral and in his memoirs, Halsey wrote of the coast watchers, 'It was a lonely, desperately dangerous life, and only real men could endure it'.[215] Having said that, Halsey was full of admiration for Ruby Boyle and made a point of flying to Vanikoro to meet the now famous heroine. Later when Ruby fell ill, Halsey directed an aircraft take her for hospital treatment after which she returned to her post.

Soon after his arrival at a Brisbane convalescent hospital, Eric Feldt received a letter from Rupert Long which said:

> I am afraid that you are another example of the 'willing horse' Eric; doing too much for too long was your trouble. We shall have to take more care of you when you are on the job again. My very best wishes old lad, and don't start getting too impatient, there is still plenty of war left.[216]

During his recuperation, Eric at Rupert's encouragement commenced a book on the exploits of his coastwatchers[217] as well as writing an official report of the organization during his tenure. Eric found writing therapeutic and wrote to Hermon Gill on Rupert's staff of his approach to drafting on an old typewriter which he thought 'Noah had used for his

Bill of Loading'.[218] He added:

> Incidentally, I find typing the best thing I can do—it is the only way I can get myself to read it slowly enough to see the grosser and most maladroit expressions with which I conceal my meaning.[219]

Gill was a valuable support to Eric during this period providing advice on combatting writer's block and providing details for the book. The eventual product was always going to be Eric's personalised account rather than the authorised historical record. The first draft, with the assistance of Rupert Long's team in Melbourne, was completed on 18 November 1944. Some were disconcerted by Eric's tone, but not Rupert. From the outset Rupert and Eric envisaged the book to be published both in Australia, Britain and the US with a follow-on Hollywood movie.[220] Rupert, Gill and Paul McGuire did much work to obtain official clearances and secure a publisher.

After the Battle of Savo Island, Admiral Crutchley's depleted Task Group 44 arrived in Noumea to replenish and re-ammunition. In a vote of confidence in Crutchley, he was directed to take his force to join Fletcher's carrier group and command the surface forces of the battleship *North Carolina* and all cruisers against any surface threat. They were part of the protective screen during the Battle of the Eastern Solomons which was fought during 24-25 August 1942. Like the Battle of the Coral Sea it was an action where the aircraft carriers traded blows at great distance. The result was a tactical victory for Fletcher with the Japanese light aircraft carrier *Ryūjō* sunk while *Enterprise* was damaged. Importantly the battle further depleted the Japanese aviator strength which could not be replaced like the US Navy. At the end of the month Task Group 44 was detached and arrived in Brisbane on 3 September. The following day a crucial meeting was held at Ghormley's headquarters in Noumea attended by Admirals Nimitz and Turner as well as General 'Hap' Arnold, head of the US Army Air Forces and General Sutherland, MacArthur's Chief of Staff. MacArthur was concerned that

Japan could attempt another Battle of the Coral Sea style thrust to take Port Moresby and sought more US naval forces for his command. Nimitz assessed that the Japanese would continue to focus their efforts in the Solomons, but was willing to provide Crutchley's Task Force 44 to MacArthur. The die was cast for the employment of the Australian Squadron for the remainder of the war. As was learnt after the war, Nimitz had correctly read the Japanese intent. Only four days before the Noumea conference the Japanese had decided to cease their attempts to capture Milne Bay and threaten Port Moresby and instead concentrate on the Solomons. Nimitz had also formed the view that the most effective means to defeat Japan was through the use of the growing naval strength of aircraft carriers, fast battleships and marines in island hopping assaults in the central Pacific. This was in contrast to MacArthur's northern thrust from New Guinea and onto the Philippines.

The first mission of the newly assigned Task Force 44 was to provide a protective barrier about 150 miles to the south of Port Moresby. For the next twelve months the ships, when not in refit or maintenance would maintain patrols in the Coral Sea area that became known to the sailors as 'the paddock'. This lower tempo of operations provided Crutchley and his staff time to work the ships up to be a more cohesive force that would be battle ready for the demands of MacArthur's inevitable push north.

After the Battle of the Coral Sea Harold Farncomb spoke to the Secretary to the First Naval Member, Captain Bernard Foley about Navy Office's poor handing of media affairs. Foley, while sympathetic, said Navy Office's hand were tied because press releases had to go through MacArthur's headquarters. During the period on barrier patrol, Harold wrote to Rupert Long out of frustration and sought his help to get a change in approach to the press. Harold wrote:

> I know many officers and men feel keenly the fact that their services are very rarely recognized by the public owing to the veil of secrecy, frequently unnecessary, which is cast over every detail of a Naval operation. In our Press, the names of ships, for example, are never mentioned, although the Admiralty very frequently does so in describing some special operation.[221]

In particular Harold was keenly aware of the positive impact on sailors' morale in seeing their ship's names in the press when describing the latest operation. Harold drew Rupert's attention to how the Army and Air Force were much more adept at managing the press and proposed sensible reforms that would have brought the RAN into line with the Admiralty and the other two services. In drafting his letter Harold had his Secretary Trevor Rapke produce an annex listing thirteen recent articles in the press to prove his points. While Rupert tried his best from his end, it was an issue that would continue to energize Harold for the duration of the war.

XI

On the west coast of Australia James Esdaile in *Adelaide* was Commander Task Group 73.4 which, in addition to his ship, included the Dutch cruisers *Tromp* and *Jacob van Heemskerck* and any available smaller escorts. Their role was to escort convoys arriving or departing from that coast.

On 23 November 1942 *Toowoomba*, with a new commanding officer and ship's company, sailed in company with *Cessnock* from Fremantle for service in the British Eastern Fleet. They were also escorting the tanker *Goldmouth*. The following day *Adelaide* led the 4-inch gun armed anti-aircraft cruiser *Jacob van Heemskerck* and three merchant ships[222] from the same port bound for the Persian port of Abadan. On 26 November the two convoys merged and the two cruisers each led a column of merchant ships. Before sailing James Esdaile had discussed with his Dutch counterpart their tactics if they encountered a raider. It was agreed that *Adelaide* with her superior firepower would close the raider while *Jacob van Heemskerck* would use her 32 knot speed to harass the enemy from the flank.[223]

At 2.18 pm on 28 November the lookout high in *Adelaide's* slender foremast first sighted smoke on the horizon and then two masts and a funnel. James Esdaile put his pre-arranged plan into action. He altered course to close the ship. *Jacob van Heemskerck* came up in speed leaving the convoy to the two corvettes. *Adelaide* had a particularly effective camouflage scheme and it was six minutes from *Adelaide's* initial sighting that the mystery ship finally saw the cruisers and altered course away from the convoy. On seeing this change James ordered his men to Action Stations and increased speed to 22 knots. As the two cruisers closed the ship, wireless and visual signals were made for the vessel to identify herself. There was silence. The gun crews who had been closed up for an hour repeatedly peered around their gun shields to see if they would be called to action.

At 3.43 pm the mystery ship was seen to lower two boats and then smoke and then an explosion down aft was observed. On the assumption that the ship was a raider exercising a ruse, both cruisers immediately

HMAS Adelaide *in her final wartime guise modified for convoy escort duties.* (State Library of Victoria)

opened fire. In the brief engagement James altered course to give both *Adelaide's* port and starboard batteries an opportunity to engage the 'raider'. At 3.52 pm the ship suddenly sank stern first. *Adelaide* closed to pick up the survivors whilst *Jacob van Heemskerck* returned to protect the convoy. *Adelaide* recovered 65 Germans, including one Baron, as well as a smattering of Danes, Finns, Norwegians and an Italian. They also took onboard a pig and a dog who paddled alongside the cruiser. The pig joined the menu and the dog became a favourite onboard until *Adelaide* reached Fremantle.[224]

The mystery ship was the German supply ship *Ramses* under the command of Captain Johannes Falke. She had left Germany before the war and had spent some time as a prison ship in Yokohama for merchant sailors captured by German raiders. On 24 October she sailed from Kobe with a cargo of whale, coconut, fish oils and lard. She pulled into Balikpapan for oil but had to divert to Batavia for defect repairs before attempting her return to Europe and the port of Bordeaux. Although *Ramses'* confidential papers were destroyed, one German was found to have a notebook with names and addresses of German couriers in the US. Rupert Long passed this information to American authorities.

In February, off Fremantle, James Esdaile's Task Force 73.4 escorted the most important convoy he would be associated with—the returning 9th Division from the Middle East. Embarked in the *Queen Mary, Aquitania, Ile de France, Nieuw Amsterdam* and *Queen of Bermuda* the thirty thousand troops were escorted across the Indian Ocean by a significant element of the British Eastern Fleet. Across the Bight the escort was joined by *Australia* and the destroyers *Henley, Helm* and *Bagley* under the command of Harold Farncomb. The latter group no doubt welcomed the relief from the uneventful Coral Sea patrols, not to mention the extended visit to Sydney where a new radar was fitted to the cruiser.

XII

After a short time on the naval operations staff in Brisbane, George Armitage was appointed in command of the old converted passenger

James Esdaile (4th from left) with freed merchant navy officers after the sinking of the German supply ship Ramses. *(RAN)*

ferry *Koopa* which he commissioned into the Navy on 10 August 1942. *Koopa* was initially based in Moreton Bay to act as a combined operations training ship and depot ship for Fairmiles with the prospect she would steam north to New Guinea with her small charges.[225] In its training role George oversaw the fitting of a ramp and booms to the side of the ship as well as collapsible boats stored on the top deck. Both Australian and American troops were trained to disembark from *Koopa* to boats.

Initially George Armitage impressed with his performance and enthusiasm for *Koopa's* mission. Physically George was in better condition and his drinking was in moderation.[226] By February 1943 however, Captain Edward Thomas had to report to Navy Office that George's efforts had declined and 'there is reason to believe that this is in some measure due to increasing his consumption of alcohol'.[227] In any case George had to be discharged sick from *Koopa* and was retired from the Navy as physically unfit for naval service on 9 April 1943.[228] George returned to Adelaide and his position in the Taxation Office.

As for *Koopa*, she joined the small and heterogeneous 'navy' of the Naval Officer-in-Charge (NOIC) New Guinea where she was repurposed as a depot ship for the numerous Fairmile or Harbour Defence launches deployed in northern waters.

Another of the Pioneer Class to rejoin only to find the rigours of service too much was Harry Vallentine. In early 1942 he joined the Army and perhaps on the basis of his service in the British Army in World War I quickly rose to the rank of Sergeant. He served in the Army Medical Corps in training depots in Victoria and then Queensland, assisting in the work to rapidly expand the Army for overseas service. However, from early on in his service he suffered from piles and this condition, combined with his age, led to his discharge on 16 May 1944.[229]

In contrast Adrian Watts, who like Harry had served in the Navy and then the Army, had decided in this war to join the RAAF. He did so following Japan's entry into the war, on 23 February 1942 and was soon commissioned as a Flight Lieutenant. Perhaps on the basis of his former Army and fire brigade experience Adrian served as an Airfield Defence Officer. He was attached to Number 25 Squadron which had Wirraways and some hastily acquired, but still obsolescent, Brewster Buffaloes for the defence of Perth. After the danger of attack to city had passed it was re-equipped with Vultee Vengeance dive bombers for more offensive operations. Adrian was responsible for both the security of the base and the airfield fire fighting service. He naturally also provided cartoon and other illustrations for any squadron bulletin that needed enlivening.[230]

Horace Thompson, after leaving the Navy in September 1943, found an unexpected opportunity to use his naval skills. He served in the large fleet of US Army cargo vessels that were employed to support the US Army forces in the south west Pacific. Horace became well regarded as a bridge watchkeeping officer and navigator. In particular he gained a reputation for his navigation skills by regularly making an accurate landfall after an ocean passage.[231]

An Adrian Watts cartoon of his service in No. 25 Squadron. (NLA)

On 28 September 1943 Norman Calder handed over command of *Bungaree* after nearly three years in the minelayer. During that time the ship had performed particularly well in laying defensive minefields in Australian, New Zealand, New Guinea and New Caledonian waters. In the 1943 New Years Honours List Norman was awarded an OBE for his distinguished command.

As the Navy's leading authority on mining Norman was appointed as Deputy Director of Underwater Weapons in Navy Office. He was delighted to find on the staff, now Engineering Commander, 66-year old Archie Creal who had been one of the warrant officers at the Naval College in 1913. In respect to duties Norman found among other things he was the Navy representative of the Executive Committee of the Army Inventions Directorate. The Committee received a large number of suggestions of variable utility from the public to aid the war effort. Among the suggestions was one from Peyton Kimlin who proposed concealing hundreds of microphone near the approaches to vital infrastructure

Norman Calder (3rd from left) with the other members of the Executive Committee of the Army Inventions Directorate.
(*The Argus*/State Library of Victoria)

or own troop positions to give warning of approaching enemy. In a polite letter from the Secretary of the Executive Committee he was thanked for his interest but Peyton was informed his idea 'does not offer sufficient advantages to warrant its adoption'.[232]

Chapter 8
Road to Victory

Into the years that bring, to each one of us,
Measure for measure in pleasure and pain,
Step we unfaltering, sure there is none of us
  Ever would barter his glory for gain.
    Into the Years – A song for the RANC (1913)[1]

I

Since Rear Admiral Crutchley's Task Force had left Guadalcanal at the end of August 1942, the US Navy had lost another three cruisers and many more badly damaged. Nevertheless, US Navy's capacity for renewal, driven by America's industrial might, was gathering pace and it would far outstrip that of the Japanese. Indeed this changing tide would become a tsunami that would overwhelm Japan. In the meantime Admiral Halsey had a short term gap that needed filling and MacArthur offered Crutchley's ships, now redesignated Task Force 74 to fill the deficiency in Halsey's force. On 16 July 1943 Task Force 74 arrived in Espiritu Santo. They were immediately assigned to patrol to the west of the island. On the evening of 20 July, *Australia* leading *Hobart* steamed back to Espiritu Santo with the destroyers *O'Bannon*, *Radford* and *Nicholas* ahead of the cruisers in an anti-submarine screen. All ships zig zagged and were in defence watches. In the fine weather there was excellent visibility.

Unknown to the formation the Japanese submarine *I-11* was on patrol in the area. The submarine had been at sea for a fortnight and her war was one of mixed fortunes. In July 1942 she had sunk three merchant ships off the South Australian and NSW coasts but her captain, Commander Tagami Meiji had also seen her torpedoes miss the US aircraft carrier *Hornet* in September.

I-11 detected Task Force 74 in the afterglow of sunset. Meiji worked *I-11* into an attack position. About 6.30 pm and at a range of 20,000 yards, in now moonless but starry conditions, Meiji fired two torpedoes at the formation. Shortly after the course was altered in the zig-zag which placed *Hobart* in the line of fire. Cook Edward Bunting had just finished supper and had gone for some air on the port side amidships. He glanced aft and, 'saw the foam of the water churning up, and just after that an explosion'.[2] *Hobart* had been struck by one torpedo on the port side aft near the Wardroom and aft 6-inch shell room. Debris and water rose into the air and sailors on the upper deck had to take shelter as it rained down.

Harry Showers was in his sea cabin and had just stood up to return to the bridge. Appreciating that the ship had been torpedoed but not knowing where, he made his way to the bridge and ordered 'Action Stations'. The Oerlikon gun crew atop *Hobart's* forward 6-inch gun just forward of the bridge reported sighting a submarine on the portside and Harry ordered a starshell to be fired. On illumination no enemy could be seen. Now fitted with TBS Harry was able to inform Crutchley and the other ships of the torpedoing and the two destroyers closed the cruiser.

Damage control teams started to report the extent of the damage and effect repairs. At 7 pm the ship was slowly able to get underway. The newly joined Gunnery Officer Lieutenant Commander George Fowle, who Harry Showers had trained at the Naval College, wrote of the impact:

> I happened to be in the Wardroom at the time, sitting next to the Commander James Walton who was severely injured. Others in the

Wardroom were killed or severely injured. I had one of those miraculous escapes, which of course are pretty frequent in a World War!

I eventually made my way to the bridge, and enroute, quickly realized that a very efficient damage control organization was in full operation. All power had gone, and emergency lighting, torches etc., provided some light at the end of the tunnel.

The Captain and Engineer Officer—all hands in fact—did a magnificent job that night. The quarterdeck was hanging on, held by the starboard side plating only. Wire strops were used to hold strength. Power was restored remarkably quickly, and although the rudder had gone, the starboard screws were operative. Through it all Captain Showers was in complete control, displaying a competent, unflappable, efficiency.[3]

Thirteen men were killed and seven seriously injured including some key officers. Fortunately the sea remained calm, indeed in any seaway the quarterdeck would have likely parted from the rest of the ship with potentially catastrophic results. Remarkably *Hobart* could make up to seven knots with an escort of the destroyers *Nicholas* and *O'Bannon*. The following morning the US salvage tugs *Souix* and *Vireo* took *Hobart* in tow and at 2 am on 23 July she limped into port. As dawn broke also to be seen in the harbour were the previously torpedoed cruisers *Leander, Honolulu* and *Saint Louis*. The latter two cruisers were missing their bows. There to assist were three repair ships *Vestal, Medusa* and *Dixie*. *Vestal* was allocated to *Hobart* and, while her engineers commenced taking stock of the damage, Admiral Crutchley directed that Harold Farncomb convene a Board of Inquiry into the torpedoing. The inquiry found that the ship was clearly well organized and the ship's company performed exceedingly well. As became apparent after the war, Harold correctly deduced that the torpedo was fired at long range.

Back in Australia the press got wind of the torpedoing before next of kin were informed. It was suspected by Rupert Long that the leak came from the Prime Minister's Department.[4] Rupert Long drafted the letter that was sent by the Minister for the Navy to the Prime Minister alerting him to the premature release of information.

The heavily damaged HMAS Hobart *in Espiritu Santo.* (RAN)

On 21 August a battered but now seaworthy *Hobart* set sail for Sydney escorted by *Warramunga* and *Arunta*. Remarkably she could steam at 14 knots. In the four weeks since her torpedoing the engineers of *Vestal* had realigned *Hobart's* aft section and more securely attached the two sections of the ship. *Vestal* had performed an impressive job and Lieutenant Commander Fowle later wrote that the repair crews were, 'a lesson in dockyard efficiency and they worked around the clock. The US sailors also organized sporting events and barbecues for *Hobart's* crew'.[5]

Whilst Harold Farncomb and *Australia* remained in the waters off Espiritu Santo a much happier event was taking place in Brisbane. Frank Getting's widow Hazel had through the various commemorations of the loss of *Canberra* met the Commander of US Naval Forces in the South West Pacific, Commodore Robert 'Pug' Coman. Himself a widower, they had fallen in love and on 19 September 1943 they married at St John's Cathedral with Jean Farncomb acting as Matron of Honour.[6]

II

Admiral Crutchely's once again depleted TF 74 reached its lowest ebb when at the beginning of October 1943 it consisted only of *Australia* patrolling off the north Queensland coast. She was operating back under Commander South West Pacific Force, Vice Admiral Arthur 'Chips' Carpenter in General MacArthur's area of operations. Carpenter was a cautious officer but one who knew Australians well having been a junior officer in the Great White Fleet and, more recently, commanded the US submarines in Western Australia.

TF 74 grew steadily in size. First, *Bagley, Warramunga* and *Arunta* joined and then the *Ralph Talbot* arrived with the newly promoted Captain Frank Walker of *Patterson* fame. He was now Commander Destroyer Squadron 4 and had just fought the last sea fight of the Solomons campaign, the Battle of Vella Lavella. In that action the Japanese withdrew the last of their troops and retreated to their Rabaul bastion. By 5 November Crutchely's task force was further greatly strengthened by the arrival of *Shropshire* and the US destroyer *Helm*. It was the first time Harold Farncomb and John Collins had been at sea together since the beginning of the war.

The new-look TF 74 was to support MacArthur's next phase of operations. Australian troops had already conducted a bloody campaign involving the recapture of Buna, Lae, Salamaua and Finschafen along the Rau coast. MacArthur envisaged a series of amphibious landings farther along the coast of northern New Guinea. Before these could occur it was vital to neutralise the threat from Rabaul. To this end the western half of New Britain was secured from the Japanese and Rabaul isolated and pounded by repeated air attacks. The New Britain coastwatchers had the primary role of reporting Japanese aircraft emanating from Rabaul. As MacArthur pushed northwestward they would become increasingly important and this was appreciated by the Japanese. The New Britain operation was called *Dexterity* and involved landings first at Arawe

(Operation *Director*) on the south-west coast and then at Cape Gloucester on the western tip of the island.

Along the New Guinea Rau coast and in western New Britain, Eric Feldt had long sustained coastwatchers and inserted more teams to better report on enemy movements and await the liberation of their areas. But the loss of coastwatchers on the Rau coast and in western New Britain was tragically heavy. Some were killed in circumstances that, perhaps fortunately, were not fully known until some time afterwards. In an incident reported to Eric by coastwatcher Keith McCarthy in March 1943, Warrant Officer Adolph Obst, who was a former missionary Eric had recruited, and Sergeant Bill Butteris were surprised by a Japanese patrol that landed near their observation post near Cape Gloucester. A possibly ill Obst was resting in a hut when a Japanese soldier crawled under the floor and shot him in the groin. He was then captured and tortured with a bayonet. An unarmed Butteris then rushed from the bush and knocked the torturer to the ground. Obst was soon killed and as Butteris was taken away he yelled to the villagers to 'bury him with respect'. The locals who were incensed by the Japanese barbarity duly buried Obst and later showed his grave to Warrant Officer Andrew Kirkwell-Smith who had escaped the Japanese patrol. The brave Sergeant Butteris was later beheaded along with two of his native assistants.[7]

On 7 November 1943, Crutchley's ships arrived in Milne Bay for a period of training and briefings for Operation *Dexterity*. TF 74 was further strengthened towards the end of the month by the US cruisers *Nashville* and *Phoenix*. Each cruiser had an army bombardment liaison team onboard.

TF 74 found that Milne Bay had rapidly developed into an important RAN forward base and the headquarters for the Naval Officer in Charge New Guinea—or 'NOIC' as he was called. On the arrival of Task Force 74 this officer was Harold Farncomb's former Executive Officer in *Australia,* Captain James Armstrong. The base staff provided logistical, engineering, ordnance and sea training support to all ships.

NOIC's staff also coordinated operations along the coast in support of the Army and coastwatchers with a heterogeneous fleet of small ships ranging from cargo vessels to patrol craft known as Motor Launches. Over time a network of naval outposts were spawned under NOIC's command that grew with the Allied advance. At its peak over 100 men were part of the command.

In the first part of the operation Crutchley had Captain Walker take *Ralph Talbot, Helm, Warramunga* and *Arunta* on the evening of 29 November to bombard the Japanese airstrip at Gasmata. On 15 December the US 112th Cavalry Regiment was successfully landed at Arawe with the covering fire from the destroyers. This landing was followed on Boxing Day by the larger Cape Gloucester assault which was supported by an intense bombardment from Crutchley's cruisers. The effectiveness of the support was enhanced by the presence of an army artillery officer on each ship. The Japanese tried to rebuff the landings with two raids each of about 70 aircraft. But with alerts from the coastwatchers and *Shropshire's* tilting air search radar proving its worth in detecting inbound aircraft, only a handful of the enemy were able to get through to the ships. Sixty-four Japanese aircraft were lost on D-Day. One of *Shropshire's* officers, Lieutenant Commander John Alliston later wrote how relaxed John Collins appeared on the bridge during the operation and this confidence exuded through the ship.[8]

An important command position in TF 74 was proving to be the senior Commanding Officer among the destroyers. With the return of Captain Walker to the US, this became Commander Emile Dechaineaux in *Warramunga*. As operations unfolded some, such as at Gasamati, would be undertaken by destroyers alone. Perhaps because Dechaineaux had taken part in the 1940 Dunkirk evacuations, he proved extremely forceful in his support to troops during amphibious bombardments.

The next and final operation to secure the Vitiaz Strait between New Guinea and New Britain was the successful 2 January 1944 landing at Saidor on the New Guinea north coast. Saidor was important to the Allies not only for its airstrip, but also because a foothold there would impede Japanese attempts to evacuate their remaining 12,000 troops in New Guinea. Originally all these operations were to be a precursor to the capture of the now besieged Rabaul. But the Quadrant Conference in Quebec the previous August had wisely decided to by-pass Rabaul with its increasingly fortified 100,000 strong garrison. This decision saved many Allied lives to no strategic disadvantage. The Quadrant Conference also confirmed the dual MacArthur and Nimitz-led advances towards homeland Japan. For the Australian Squadron this would mean supporting landings at Hollandia, Noemfoor Island, Aitape and Morotai before reaching the Philippines. Meanwhile Nimitz's forces would leap frog from the Gilbert, Marshall and Caroline Islands.

After the New Britain operations Crutchley took his cruisers to Milne Bay and there had a meeting with Vice Admiral Thomas Kinkaid, MacArthur's new naval commander. Kinkaid had a well developed appreciation of Australian forces and their fighting spirit. Another veteran of the Great White Fleet, Kinkaid had twice toured the Gallipoli battlefields in the early 1920s with the legendary Colonel Hughes.[9] In this war he had taken part in the Battles of Coral Sea, Midway, the Eastern Solomons and Santa Cruz. Most recently he had commanded the naval forces that helped expel the Japanese from the Aleutian Islands. After the discussion concerning future operations, *Australia* and then *Shropshire* returned to Sydney for leave and maintenance. On 7 February *Shropshire* sailed with Crutchley and the First Naval Member embarked for a tour of the forward bases.

The next strategically important operation was the seizure of the Admiralty Islands. Initially, a reconnaissance in force was staged on 29 February 1944; it was decided to hold ground. The landings were closely supported by Dechaineaux's Australian and US destroyers who hotly engaged enemy artillery at ranges as little as 3,000 yards. Over coming days Crutchley brought cruisers into the fray to finally silence stubborn Japanese resistance. The whole-hearted naval support earned

ROAD TO VICTORY 521

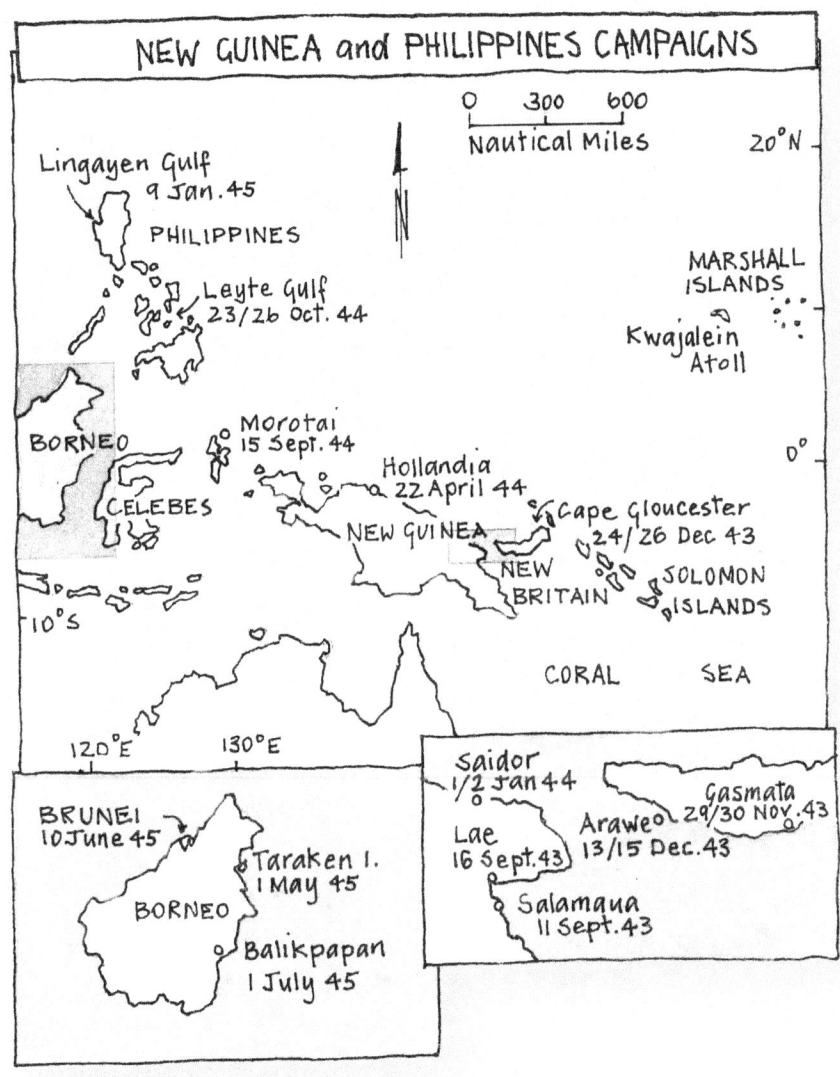

the appreciation of the hard pressed US troops and Marines ashore. The prize was of great strategic significance. Seeadler Harbour on Manus Island, with its large protected anchorage, became the subject of immediate and colossal infrastructure development. A base for over 37,000 personnel was quickly established and a double airstrip constructed. Most critically two 90,000 ton battleship-capable floating docks were towed in sections from the US while repair ships arrived to facilitate even substantial battle damage repair. These facilities provided the springboard for future operations and the forward base for TF 74.

The final operations to neutralise the Japanese XVIII Army in New Guinea were at Hollandia and then on Morotai Island in the Dutch East Indies. It was hoped that the ground beyond the Hollandia landing site would be suitable for heavy bomber airstrips for the Philippines campaign. In order to gain the vital intelligence before the landing, an eleven man coastwatcher team was inserted by the submarine USS *Dace*. The team included RAN and AIF personnel as well as native police and a Dutch Intelligence Officer. It was led by one of Eric Feldt's most trusted men, 'Blue' Harris who had performed so well during the evacuation of New Britain.

On the early morning of 22 April 1944, 158 ships steamed purposefully towards the cloud shrouded coast. In command of the amphibious force was Rear Admiral Daniel Barbey, known to the Australian sailors as 'Uncle Dan' or 'Dan Dan the Amphibious Man'. Among his ships for the first time were the *Kanimbla*, *Manoora* and *Westralia*, now converted to infantry landing ships. Rear Admirals Crutchley and Berkley commanded TF 74 and TF 75 respectively, each with a mix of cruisers and destroyers to support the three simultaneous landings at Aitape, Humbolt Bay and Tanahmerah Bay on a front of about 240 km. The warships opened up an intense bombardment at 6.30 am. Air support was provided by the US 5th Army Air Force. Judging by the Japanese reaction surprise was complete.

As *Shropshire* pounded positions from Tanahmerah Bay a canoe was sighted among some floating logs with the men waving their arms. John Collins directed the destroyer USS *Mullany* to close the canoe.

Onboard was Sergeant Colin Launcelot and four native police from Harris' team. They were soon sent to Admiral Barbey's flagship and gave valuable information about Japanese dispositions and local terrain. They also told how their party had been betrayed to a Japanese patrol. Harris, supported by Trooper Gregory Shortis and Gunner Jack Bunning, held the Japanese at bay for about four hours to allow those not already dead to escape. Harris, wounded three times with his now dead comrades by his side, was captured by the Japanese.[10] Their efforts had allowed six of his men to escape. Unflinchingly, Harris endured interrogation and was finally bayoneted whilst tied to a tree. The news of Blue Harris' death affected the coastwatchers like none other. He was in Eric's words, 'the most colourful personality among a bunch of notable individuals—a man whose vitality was such that his death was, at first, an untenable idea'.[11] On hearing the news of Harris the tough Keith McCarthy went to church for the first time since his marriage.

Even though Hollandia proved unsuitable to build an airstrip for bombers, the operation was a major blow against the enemy. Of the 11,000 Japanese in the area nearly 3,500 were killed and 600 captured.

Captain 'Blue' Harris (back row 3rd from L) and his men in the submarine USS Darter before their insertion prior to the Hollandia landings. (AWM)

In addition to the loss of the coastwatchers, the Allied had about 160 killed. Hollandia was followed in May in similar fashion by landings at Wadke Island and Biak. These operations were TF 74's last under Admiral Crutchley.

4 February 1944 marked a major but unheralded milestone in the development of the RAN. On that day the War Cabinet decided it was time, with the looming end of Crutchley's tenure in command of the Australian Squadron, for an Australian to assume command. John Collins, who had already served as a non-substantive Commodore in the Dutch East Indies and with an outstanding war record, was the logical choice. What is more, the War Cabinet agreed to extend Admiral Royle's tenure as First Naval Member by a further year with the plan for John to be promoted to Rear Admiral and succeed him as professional head of the Navy. The other candidate was Harold Farncomb. Perhaps critically, he was viewed by Crutchley as possessing, 'considerable intellectual ability, but it is more of a critical than of a constructive nature' and only had the potential of becoming, 'a flag officer of average ability'.[12] Crutchley also noted, like others before him, that Harold was a very firm disciplinarian. Indeed some sailors gave him another nickname, 'February Farncomb' because at the Captain's defaulters table sailors knew they would get the maximum 28 days punishment for an offence.[13]

As part of the command changes it was decided that at some point Harold would relieve John Collins in command of the Australian Squadron when John replaced Royle as Chief of Naval Staff. In the meantime, Harold would serve with the RN. The initial plan was for Harold to command a battleship, ideally in the Pacific theatre. This was changed, more usefully for the RAN's future, to be an aircraft carrier although it would be in the Mediterranean.[14]

In implementing this schema, first on 9 March the impressive Emile Dechaineaux took over from Harold in *Australia* when the ship was still alongside at Garden Island. On 6 May John Collins was replaced in *Shropshire* by Harry Showers. On 13 June John, now a Commodore

First Class, became Commodore Commanding Australian Squadron and Commander of TF 74. Importantly the Commodore's staff had grown to about a dozen as a result of war experience. This was important, not only for planning and communications, but also for ensuring engineering and logistics aspects of the Squadron received due attention. This was a far cry from the less than a handful of staff officers embarked with Rear Admiral Crace at the beginning of the war.[15]

These otherwise sound plans had one drawback—Harold Farncomb had been in sea command since 1937. He would be going to command his fifth ship in a row, four of them in wartime. The physical and mental demands on a Captain are cumulatively substantial. Although a strong individual, Harold had turned to alcohol to deal with these pressures. While the war losses of Burnett, Getting and Waller had put greater pressure on the pool of suitable cruiser captains, there was now a younger battle-hardened cohort coming through. It would have been more prudent for the Naval Board to have found Harold a shore position in which to reinvigorate himself, as had been the case for John Collins.

III

In early 1944 another chapter in the *Australia* court martial was played out. Since late 1942 there had been agitation from various quarters for a review of Gordon and Elias' cases. In an attempt to put an end to this matter the Attorney General Dr. Herbert Evatt proposed to the Navy Minister, Norman Makin, that an independent judicial review be conducted on the court martial. The Navy, vexed by the continued agitation, agreed and Justice Allan Maxwell of the NSW Supreme Court held an extensive hearing in February 1944 into the court martial. He was an ideal choice for 'his judgments, laconic and unadorned, went immediately to the heart of the issues'.[16]

At the hearing Rapke was led by Percy Spender KC. On 1 March 1944 Justice Maxwell presented his extremely thorough report to the Attorney General. He went through each area of alleged 'defect' in the court martial, either rejecting them in turn or discounting their materiality. This was until he came to the matter of Harold Farncomb expressing his opinion as to the guilt of the accused. He found this was a substantial defect of the proceedings. Maxwell did however, find that Harold had otherwise performed, 'with dignity and marked ability'.[17] In the end Maxwell did not believe that a miscarriage of justice had occurred. He went on to say having read the transcript as well as other evidence gathered but not presented at the court martial that, 'I have no doubt at all that the prisoners were guilty as charged'.[18] Maxwell also commended Harold's letter of mitigation to the Attorney General when reviewing the sentences.

Later that month Harold Farncomb flew to UK. While attending courses and receiving briefings in London for his new sea command, Harold had the honour of having the Distinguished Service Order for his services in the Solomons campaign presented by King George VI at Buckingham Palace. Harold's new command was to be the three-year old escort carrier HMS *Attacker*, which was provided to Britain by the US under the Lend-Lease Agreement.

About the size of *Australia*, *Attacker*, with a ship's company of nearly 650 men, normally embarked 20 aircraft. The ship, like some other escort carriers, had been modified to support amphibious landings. They were fitted with improved air radars, army communications sets, additional briefing rooms and support equipment to embark either Wildcats, Hellcats or, in the case of *Attacker*, the Seafire. This was the marinised version of the legendary Spitfire. The modified ships were referred to as 'assault carriers.'

The embarked 879 Squadron had a distinctly Commonwealth flavour and was commanded by the experienced South African, Lieutenant Commander DG Carlisle who had cut his teeth flying Fulmars off *Victorious* early in the war. The Seafires were high performance but less than robust aircraft. Their use from assault carriers required skill not only by the pilots but also the bridge team which had to obtain the requisite 24 knots of wind over the deck for launch.

HMS Attacker *under the command of Harold Farncomb was configured as an assault carrier with improved radars, communications and briefing rooms. She embarked 30 Seafires for her Mediterranean deployment.* (RN)

Harold Farncomb joined *Attacker* in Belfast on 12 May 1944. She was in the final preparations for deployment and in addition to her 20 Seafires, she had embarked an additional ten reserve aircraft. Two days later *Attacker* sailed for the Mediterranean with sister ships *Hunter* and *Stalker* escorting convoy KMS.51 enroute. During a short port visit to Gibraltar *Attacker* was berthed alongside the stone detached north mole in the outer harbour. At about 2.15 am on 4 June *Attacker* was rocked by an explosion which caused a loss of power and lighting. The ship had been subjected to a torpedo attack probably from a German submarine that had seen *Attacker's* silhouette but not the stone mole to seaward of her. The torpedo detonated on the mole and *Attacker's* power was restored without damage to the ship. It was a warm German welcome to the Mediterranean.

Attacker joined Task Group 88.1 under the command of Rear Admiral Thomas Troubridge flying his flag in the cruiser *Royalist*. His other carriers were *Emperor*, *Khedive*, *Pursuer* and *Searcher*. Troubridge was very experienced in carrier operations, having commanded two aircraft carriers earlier in the war. Among the carrier Captains in TG 88.1 was a familiar face—Captain Thomas Hilken who had been John Collins' Executive Officer in *Sydney*.

For the next two months *Attacker* undertook convoy escort in the western Mediterranean. Sensibly, Harold Farncomb had at any one time half her aircraft operating from ashore gaining experience in operating in support of the Army.

On 12 August TG 88.1 sailed from Malta for Operation *Dragoon*, the invasion of Southern France. The invasion fleet of nearly 800 ships of all types was under the command of Vice Admiral Henry Hewitt USN. Embarked were US and French troops to be landed on beaches between Toulon and Cannes. TG 88.1 along with TG 88.2—the US carriers *Tulagi* and *Kasaan Bay*—had 166 fighters which provided both air cover and ground support. The latter augmented the bombardments from five battleships and nineteen cruisers.

On the morning of D-Day, 15 August 1944, *Attacker* now with 28 Seafires operational, flew reconnaissance sorties over German positions. On recovery the photographs were quickly developed then flown off in another aircraft and dropped in a waterproof container alongside the Headquarters Ship USS *Catoctin*. The *Dragoon* landings were successful and the assault carriers remained offshore until the end of the month to support the troops as they moved further inland. *Attacker* did particularly well during *Dragoon* and her sortie rates were one of the best of the assault carriers.[19] Over the first week *Attacker's* aircraft flew over 300 sorties attacking German tanks and motor columns, trains, gun emplacements and infantry. Two aircraft were shot down, one pilot evaded capture while the other, although initially captured, managed also to escape. Onboard there were ten landings that resulted in aircraft hitting the crash barrier netting with one Seafire hitting the island. Two of the aircraft had to be jettisoned over the side. This operation was arduous for all concerned, but Harold Farncomb believed that being involved in such a mammoth and historic operation was a great motivator. For his part Harold was Mentioned in Despatches for his distinguished service.[20]

Following their success in France the assault carriers, supported by the 24th Destroyer Flotilla,[21] turned their attention to Crete. On 12 September

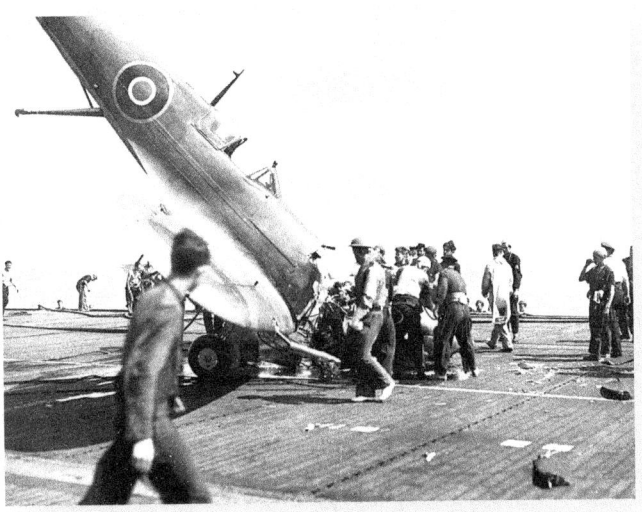

Harold Farncomb's period in command of HMS Attacker *was demanding and eventful. During Operation Dragoon ten Seafires had crash landings on the flight deck (RN).*

they commenced four days of strikes sinking any German ships and small craft in or around the island to prevent the occupiers either being resupplied or escaping. Aircraft also struck the airfields at Maleme and Heraklion further demoralising the marooned Germans. *Attacker* also separately provided air cover for landing parties at the coastal town of Piskopi where a naval landing party unsuccessfully tried to dislodge the German garrison. Flying operations continued to involve incidents, particularly on recovery. On 19 September, one Seafire returned with a bomb that would not drop or release even with vigorous manoeuvring by the pilot. To the consternation of Harold Farncomb and the bridge team, on landing the jolt released the bomb which bounced toward the island.[22] Fortuitously, it was deflected by a deck fitting and instead came to rest four feet from the edge of the flight deck where it was gingerly defused. Harold was watchful about the mental state of his young pilots after such incidents, and after one harrowing recovery he had his outgoing Canadian-born Chaplain Basil Watson[23] take the young pilot down for a calming stiff drink and watch over him until he was in a fit state to go to bed.[24]

After the success of the Crete operation three assault carriers left for the UK whilst *Attacker, Hunter, Stalker* and *Emperor* were directed by the Flag Officer Levant and Eastern Mediterranean, Vice Admiral Bernard Rawlings to enter the Aegean. In Operations *Outing, Cablegram* and *Contempt* they interdicted German shipping, road and rail transport along the coast as well as isolating German island garrisons.

From 3 October the assault carriers made their presence felt, first at Levinthia and Port Laki and then from 8 to 12 October attacking shipping in the Gulf of Salonika. Among their victims were German E-boats as well as military trains. On 13 October *Attacker, Stalker* and *Emperor* were diverted to take part in Operation *Manna*, the reoccupation of Athens and to sink any German shipping along the east coast of Greece and then in the Dodecanese islands. Once again *Attacker's* aircraft interdicted German small craft and motor transport. In some islands the Germans had already left and the reception for a carrier that came to anchor was overwhelming. The reception for the accompanying Greek destroyer *Navarinon* was euphoric.

As a self described 'inveterate tourist,'[25] the well-read Harold Farncomb found the sortie into the Aegean and Dodecanese of immense interest. Where operations allowed, he would steam past or visit islands known from Greek legend. His most memorable visits were to the port of Volos from which Jason and his Argonauts had set sail in search of the Golden Fleece and the mystical island of Patmos where Saint John had written the *Book of Revelations*.[26]

On completion of these operations there were effectively no more German targets left to strike. Harold Farncomb was therefore directed to take *Attacker* along with *Bruiser, Hunter, Stalker, Rajah* and the 24th Destroyer Flotilla back to the UK. After short fuelling stops in Malta and then Gibraltar, they returned to Plymouth on 10 November. Instead of preparing for *Attacker's* refit and then deployment with the East Indies Fleet, Harold left his ship just a week later. Unexpected events in the Pacific required his early return.

A clearly war weary Harold Farncomb with the pilots of 879 Squadron alongside in Algiers. The squadron had a mix of British and Commonwealth pilots with Squadron Commanding Officer, the South African Lieutenant Commander DG Carlisle seated on Harold's right. (RN Research Archive)

Harold Farncomb's professionalism, firmness but underlying good humour and fairness, made him a popular Captain with *Attacker's* ship's company. There was however another side to his time in *Attacker*. Although Harold did not drink at sea, in port he would often become inebriated once alongside. This was to the protective consternation of his officers.[27] Harold's problems with alcohol came to the attention of Troubridge who wrote in Harold's performance report that:

> This officer suffers from one failing, namely a tendency to fortify himself with liquor prior to facing the ordeal of an important social occasion. I am informed that normally he does not over indulge and this is borne out by the efficient manner in which his ship and her aircraft are handled and commanded.[28]

Harold was not alone in dealing with the pressures of sea service through alcohol. Commander John Bower, Eddy Nurse's Captain in the submarine *K12*, perceptively wrote on the strains of sea service during World War I:

Well it does affect people, and there is undoubtedly a great feeling of relief at getting back in harbour safely. In the Navy, where wines and spirits are free of duty, alcohol is cheap and obtainable, and alcohol is a relief from worry and an opiate for tired nerves.[29]

IV

By the middle of 1944 Rupert Long had in place a well developed naval intelligence organization. His efforts were finally recognized by being made an Officer in the Order of the British Empire in the King's Birthday Honours List. Following a visit to Australia, Captain Allan Hillgarth, the Intelligence Officer for the Eastern Fleet[30] wrote a perceptive Top Secret report on his visit to Australia for Winston Churchill via the Director of Naval Intelligence in the Admiralty. In it he wrote of Rupert:

> DNI Melbourne directs Naval Intelligence Division and all its offshoots from Melbourne Navy Office. His industry and astuteness, combined with a flair for organization, have alone enabled him to keep his people together and to avoid extinction. His offices in Melbourne are mainly administrative of the effort in the field, but there is no pie in which he has not at one time or another had his thumb, and in the majority the imprint remains. His principal tools are his Staff Officers (Intelligence) who are everywhere, including all advanced bases, and it is his responsibility to insert in every coastal nook and cranny captured in the operational area. These Port Directors are, generally speaking, accepted readily by the Americans, who have had no luck when trying to produce similar personnel themselves. It is evidently important to get an Australian naval officer put into every new place on the coast as soon as possible. They are provided, incidentally, with nothing—this is no fault of DNI's—and soon learn how to fend for themselves. In several places, with green US troops present, Port Directors have given the (air raid) alert (done by whistle) and then gone off to remove everything they needed from American stores while the Americans took cover.
>
> DNI Melbourne has a useful system by which the Coast Watchers (North East Area) are controlled by Commander McManus, who at the same time controls Staff Officers (Intelligence) and other naval

intelligence personnel in the North East Area <u>but in occupied territory</u>. He then has his ear laid on to both the occupied and the liberated zones. It is difficult to speak of any intelligence entity in Australia or the South West Pacific Area without learning that Commander Long either started it or is still influencing it in the best interests of everybody. Nothing much can happen in Australia without his knowledge, and he has probably a more detailed knowledge of and a more profound view on personalities and events than anyone else in the country. In view of the importance that Americans attach to stripes and to the real importance of Commander Long's work, it is surprising and disconcerting to an outsider to find that he has not been given the acting rank of Captain. Jealousies and possibly the opposition of civil servants acting on red-tape motives can alone explain it.

His relations with the 7th Fleet Intelligence Staff (as with most Americans) are excellent, and he has good working arrangement with Captain McCollum, Fleet Intelligence Officer. But the nature of the US Naval Intelligence organization, with its sharp cleavage between Combat Intelligence and Office of Naval Intelligence, coupled with an increasing reserve where the RAN is concerned, handicap him considerably, and he is forced to have recourse to underground methods to obtain some of the information he must have in order to discharge his job adequately. This is, in my view, entirely the fault of the Americans, who make the fullest use of him and his people but give only a limited trust in return. From what I have seen of his officers, all of whom he has trained himself, they are outstandingly good intelligence personnel with a better grasp of discretion than the Americans possess.

DNI Melbourne has a habit of switching his officers about, so that all the best ones acquire experience in dangerous posts in the operational area. He has offered to take some officers from the Eastern Fleet for training in advanced posts, and this will be implemented as opportunity offers. He is also prepared to supply me with most of the officers I need to fill gaps in the Eastern Fleet Intelligence Staff.[31]

In Britain news of the exploits of the other members of the Pioneer Class had also been read with great interest by three men. They were the now frail Admiral Bertram Chambers, Commander Duncan Grant and their invalid classmate Lloyd Gilling. Admiral Chambers wrote to Naval Instructor Frederick Eldridge of his immense pride in the wartime exploits of members of the Pioneer Class such as John Collins

'His industry and astuteness, combined with a flair for organization, have alone enabled him to keep his people together and to avoid extinction.' Rupert Long in Navy Office late in the war. (RAN)

and Harold Farncomb. Recalling his days at Geelong he said that Frank Larkins was the most impressive of all the Pioneer Class and lamented his early death.³² Chambers did not linger much longer and he died on 27 April 1945 aged 78 years.

Duncan Grant had been back in uniform from the early days of the war and had commanded a coastal radar site before working at the Hydrographic Office. It was there that Grant had a narrow escape when his lodging room was hit by a German bomb in the Bath blitz. Despite a life of physical activity Grant's health was giving way and in 1944 he was discharged from the RN for the last time. He returned to his family and cottage at Haywards Heath.³³

By 1943 Lloyd Gilling's physical state had greatly deteriorated under the ravages of tuberculosis. He had accordingly been admitted to the Newlands Nursing Home at Liss in Hampshire. The establishment was run by the capable Miss Dorothy Finch. There in the twilight of his life Lloyd found love and companionship. For Dorothy at fifty-eight years old and unmarried, this too was an unexpected twist of fate. On 26 July 1944 Lloyd and Dorothy were married at the Church of the Immaculate Conception in Petersfield. Their days together were all too short. On 18 September, Lloyd died at Brompton Hospital in Chelsea with Dorothy's support to the end. Dorothy herself passed away three years later.

V

John Collins' first operation in command of TF 74 was the landing at Noemfoor about 160 km west of Biak. He flew his broad pendant in *Australia* now under the command of Emile Dechaineux whom he had known since the Jervis Bay years of the Naval College. John had more of a hands on approach than Crutchley, best illustrated by him usually operating from the main bridge of *Australia* and not the Admiral's bridge one deck below.[34] Over 70 ships and landing craft embarked 14,000 troops for the Biak assault and easily overwhelmed the opposition. Finally, at the end of the month the last New Guinea landing took place at Cape Sansapor.

In August 1944 another of the Pioneer Class joined the northern operations. James Esdaile became the Deputy Naval Officer in Charge (NOIC) New Guinea Area and after an extensive tour of the expansive NOIC 'empire' became a trusted second in command to Captain James Armstrong. Soon James Esdaile's thoroughness, analytical mind and an

James Esdaile in November 1944 participating in a planning meeting for a proposed airstrip near Palmalmal plantation near Jacquinot Bay, New Britain. The senior officer without the hat is Brigadier Alexander Torr. (AWM)

ability to get on with both the Army and the US Navy showed that he was a good choice for the position. Equally importantly he was able to endure the rigours of the climate and austere accommodation.

Winn Reilly also became a frequent visitor to northern operations. His degaussing organization had established a facility at Manus Island not only to undertake measurements of ships but also to repair defective degaussing sets on Allied naval and merchant ships. As part of this work Winn was seconded for short periods to the US Pacific Fleet at Honolulu and the Admiralty in London to ensure their ships would be adequately protected from magnetic mines in theatre.[35]

In the prelude to the Philippines campaign there was a landing on Morotai Island in the Maluku Islands. Once again the landing was vital to provide airstrips for future operations. This time the airstrips would be important for both the American-led Philippines and Australian-led Borneo campaigns. The opening bombardment by TF 74 on 15 September was accompanied by an eruption of nearby Mount Halmahera which belched smoke. As part of the twin strategy Nimitz's forces were simultaneously landing at Palau. In contrast to Morotai, Palau with its elaborate concealed fortifications was to prove one of the most difficult and bloody landings of the war.

After the Morotai operation Harry Showers' short tenure in command of *Shropshire* came to an end. He had been a popular captain onboard and when he left the cruiser by US PT boat there were three hearty cheers from the ship's company. His relief was Captain Godfrey Nichols, MVO, RN who was a near contemporary of the Pioneer Class and served in the Battle Cruiser Force during the Great War at the same time as half of them. Like Harry, he had first gone into submarines and then specialised in navigation. Nichols became highly regarded and respected onboard.

The reason for Harry Showers' return to Australia was to become Second Naval Member with promotion to Commodore 2nd Class. He would be responsible for personnel issues in the Navy. On assuming the appointment on 15 October Harry became the first Naval College graduate to become a member of the Naval Board. On leaving *Shropshire* he received his performance report from his immediate superior, John Collins who wrote a perceptive picture of his classmate:

> A most loyal and capable Commanding Officer with a high sense of duty and responsibility. Strong physically with plenty of endurance. In action I am sure he would be a courageous leader. Being more the seaman than the diplomat he relies on honesty of purpose and plain speaking, combined with an attractive diffidence rather than personality and conversational ability when senior officers are gathered together. I am sorry to lose him from the Task Force.[36]

On 13 October TF 74 sailed from Hollandia escorting a large convoy towards the first landings in the Philippines. As multiple convoys converged on the landing areas, more than 650 ships dotted the wide expanse of ocean. John Collins and TG 74 remained part of Admiral Kinkaid's 7th Fleet. In his first discussions with Kinkaid, John told him that the Australian Squadron wanted no special consideration and Kinkaid replied that they would be treated as an integral part of his fleet.[37] Most immediately, John came under the command of the Commander Fire Support Group Vice Admiral Jesse Oldendorf, who had held the same command responsibilities in the difficult Palau Operation. Also in support of this vast operation was Admiral Halsey's Third Fleet whose carrier borne air wings had already commenced attacking Japanese positions.

The Australian Squadron's contribution to the Philippines campaign included more than just the cruisers and destroyers. In John Collins' national, but not tactical command were the three landing ships *Kanimbla, Manoora* and *Westralia* and the hydrographic vessels *Gascoyne, Warrego* and *HDML 1074.*

It was anticipated the Japanese response to the operation would be intense. The Japanese High Command saw the Philippines campaign as critical. The Commander-in-Chief of the Imperial Japanese Navy, Admiral Soemu Toyoda said in his post-war interrogation:

> Should we lose in the Philippines operations, even though the fleet should be left, the shipping lane to the south would be completely cut

off so that the fleet, if it should come back to Japanese waters, could not obtain its fuel supply ... There would be no sense in saving the fleet at the expense of the loss of the Philippines.³⁸

The Philippines was also the last opportunity for a 'general decisive battle' and Toyoda's staff had formulated Plan *Sho-Go 1* to concentrate their remaining forces to defeat US naval forces before they reached the Japanese mainland. The likelihood of success with *Sho-Go* was doubtful. Over three days in June during the Battle of the Philippine Sea the Japanese had lost three aircraft carriers but more significantly over 430 carrier-borne and 200 land-based aircraft. The Japanese Navy had been reduced to four naval task forces. In home waters were three aircraft carriers still awaiting replacement aircraft.

The three other task forces that would be involved in the looming battles were two formations to the south west in Brunei and one coming from Formosa (Taiwan). The southern groups were Vice Admiral Takeo Kurita's powerful Central Force of five battleships including the 18-inch gunned behemoths *Yamato* and *Musashi*, twelve cruisers and

Key US naval planners of the Philippines campaign were Vice Admiral Thomas Kinkaid (R) and Rear Admiral Daniel Barbey. The later was known to sailors as 'Dan Dan the Amphibious Man'. Both John Collins and Harold Farncomb forged excellent working relationships with these admirals. (USN)

fifteen destroyers[39] and Vice Admiral Shōji Nishimura's Southern Force comprising the battleships *Yamashiro* and *Fuso*, the heavy cruiser *Mogami* and four destroyers.[40] Vice Admiral Jisaburō Ozawa commanded the Northern Force consisting of the four aircraft carriers *Zuikaku*, *Zuiho*, *Chitose* and *Chiyoda* with the battleships *Ise* and *Hyuga* which had been modified with small flight decks. Importantly Ozawa's force was not fully complemented with aircraft. These three formations would converge on the Philippines to give battle.

The Allied bombardment of Leyte Island began at dawn on 20 October. The battleships, cruisers and destroyers provided a heavy fire with the first wave of landing craft hitting the beach about 9 am. The heavy air cover kept the Japanese aircraft at bay until the afternoon when John Collins saw from *Australia's* bridge a lone Japanese aircraft get through to torpedo the cruiser USS *Honolulu* just forward of her bridge. That afternoon General MacArthur waded ashore at 'Red Beach' and made a brief speech opening with the words 'People of the Philippines, I have returned'.[41]

Early the following morning, the 139th anniversary of the Battle of Trafalgar, *Shropshire's* radar detected a small number of aircraft coming from the west. They were quickly reported on TBS and all ships prepared for the attack. At 6 am *Shropshire* opened fire on a Val dive bomber that passed very close astern of her. At only about 15 metres off the sea the aircraft—which had been hit several times by *Shropshire's* gun crews—appeared to be clearing to the west but then wheeled round and flew towards *Australia*, coming up her stern. A couple of Bofors and Oerlikons scored hits on the Val, but the pilot, in possibly the first suicide attack, continued on and deliberately struck *Australia's* foremast and bridge.[42] Flames shot in the air, and from *Shropshire* the bridge of *Australia* seemed a ball of fire. Watching the scene unfold from less than a mile away on the bridge of his flagship USS *Wasatch* was Admiral Kinkaid. The fire was quickly extinguished. Sailors took John Collins, Captain Dechaineux and other survivors of the attack down below for treatment and then removed the dead from the forward superstructure.

The heavy cruisers Australia *and* Shropshire *at the beginning of the Battle of Leyte Gulf as seen from a US warship.* (USN)

Within an hour of the attack Kinkaid and *Wasatch's* doctor came across to *Australia* by boat to render assistance. The Admiral was distressed to find Collins among the wounded and, 'in great discomfort' lying on the deck of the wardroom.[43]

Dechaineux suffered serious wounds and burns, yet his few words were about the welfare of the other wounded. He passed away later that day. In all thirty men had been killed in the attack. John Collins was lucky to survive. He had however, a broken back, broken ribs, an injured eye, punctured lung, concussion and various 'gunshot' wounds. If he had been on the Admiral's bridge rather than the main bridge he would have likely been uninjured.[44] On initially learning of Collins' injuries, Prime Minister Curtin was reported to have said, 'It may mean the end of our dream of an Australian Navy under an Australian-born Admiral'.[45]

Australia was in no fit state to continue the fight and she and the torpedoed *Honolulu* were ordered by Kinkaid to be escorted to Manus Island. The remaining Commodore's staff transferred to *Shropshire* and Captain Nichols became acting CTG 74. On the passage south the dead were buried at sea.

At Manus Island John Collins and the 63 other wounded were transferred to the US hospital ship *Calamares*. John was accompanied by Chief Steward Connors and Chief Cook Williams of his personal staff who tended their Commodore day and night. Perhaps mercifully his concussion robbed John Collins of the memory of the carnage on *Australia's* bridge. His last memories prior to the attack were of the earlier New Guinea landings.[46]

Australia was able to be repaired at Espiritu Santo. She was joined by a growing casualty list of ships mostly hit by 'suiciders', 'zombies', or 'kamikazes', as they later became known. As a result of Dechaineaux's death, Captain James Armstrong, who had been on leave from NOIC New Guinea, joined *Australia* on Manus Island. James Esdaile became NOIC, a position in which he had been acting for the last month.

Armstrong was known as 'Black Jack' to the old hands who previously served with him in *Australia*. On arrival in the cruiser Armstrong wrote home to say 'what a thrill' it was to return to his old ship as Captain. He said, 'I gather we are to remain the Flagship but who will be the flag officer is still a mystery as John Collins will not be fit for some months to come.'[47]

While *Australia* was absent from the fray the Battle of Leyte Gulf entered its critical phase. On 22 October the Central and Southern Forces sailed from Brunei. The Southern Force shaped course to pass through the Surigao Strait. Admiral Oldendorf received periodic intelligence of Nishimura's progress and indeed the Japanese had been subjected to damaging air attacks during the day.

On the evening of 24 October Oldendorf deployed his forces so that destroyer flotillas would be able to successively attack Nishimura's Southern Force from the flanks as they proceeded through the Strait. Among the destroyers was *Arunta* which would lead a division into the attack. At the northern end of the Strait and ranging across Nishimura's path, would be six battleships and eight cruisers including *Shropshire*.[48] Oldendorf's ships would be able to fire simultaneously but only the lead Japanese could return fire. Nishimura was very conscious of Admiral Toyoda's exhortation to 'Advance counting on Divine Assistance'.[49]

The battered and burnt bridge of HMAS Australia *after the Trafalgar Day 1944 Kamikaze strike.* (RAN)

In the glassy seas the Southern Force steamed through the night at 20 knots. There would be no turning back. As the two forces drew inevitably towards a titanic battle the advances in the war since the Battle of Savo Island were to be starkly drawn. In particular, advanced training and radar technology had now given the US and Australians a decisive edge in night fighting, once the Japanese strength.

At 2.30 am the five ships of Destroyer Squadron 54 launched torpedo attacks from both sides of Nishimura's formation. Through the smoke, starshell and searchlights 47 torpedoes sped towards the Southern Force. Nishimura's flagship *Yamashiro* was struck by one torpedo but continued on. Less fortunate were the destroyer *Michishio* which was stopped and left sinking and *Yamaguma* which blew up, lighting up the horizon for the waiting cruisers and battleships. Unknown to Nishimura, the battleship *Fusō* was also hit by at least one torpedo and capsized within 40 minutes with only ten survivors out of 1,900 men.

The next attack was Destroyer Squadron 24 which again in two divisions launched their attacks. The eastern attack of three destroyers missed their targets. The other division of three destroyers led by Commander Alfred Buchanan in *Arunta* launched 14 torpedoes with one striking *Yamashiro* slowing her down to 5 knots for a short period. In the final destroyer attack, by Destroyer Squadron 56, two more torpedo hits were made on the battleship. At 3.53 am, as the destroyers peeled away Oldendorf's cruisers and then battleships opened a devastating fire. Midshipman Peter Adams wrote in his Journal:

> Now the game was on. When the Admiral gave the 'Open Fire' over the TBS things were still quiet, and it was hard to realise that a Jap Fleet was only 7 miles away ... the Ding-Dong. Blinding Flash ... the sky seems full of tracer. Then an explosion, red and billowing, with great sparks flying high lights up the sea round the Jap ships.[50]

Both *Yamashiro* and *Mogami* sustained fearful punishment. For her part *Shropshire* fired 32 broadsides with hits registering on the beleaguered *Yamashiro* which received a further two torpedo strikes. She rolled over and sank, taking Nishimura with her. The battered *Mogami* retired only to be sunk by carrier aircraft the next day.

The Battle of Surigao Strait was the last engagement in which battleships fought each other. For both *Shropshire* and *Arunta* it was their finest hour. For the RAN some old scores had been settled. Vice Admiral Nishimura was a veteran of the Battle of the Java Sea, while the cruiser *Mogami* had been part of the force that sank *Perth* in the Battle of Sunda Strait.

Meanwhile to the north Kurita's Force had sailed northeast to pass south of Mindoro with the aim of passing through the San Bernadino Strait. Success in this mission would be assisted if the US 3rd Fleet became focused on Ozawa's Force heading south from Formosa. While in part this occurred, Kurita lost the mighty *Musashi* and two cruisers to submarine and air attack. On the morning of 25 October on passing through the San Bernadino Strait, Kurita encountered the escort carrier force of Rear Admiral Thomas Sprague. The Battle of Samar was one of the most remarkable engagements of the war. Kurita with his overwhelming force should have wreaked carnage on Sprague's carriers but was repulsed by the heroic efforts of the destroyer escorts and the hurriedly rearmed carrier aircraft. Sprague lost one escort carrier and three destroyer escorts, while in the repeated air attacks Kurita lost three cruisers.

The Battle of Leyte Gulf was a disaster for Japan. For the Allies there was still more to do to secure the Philippines. Manila was yet to be liberated and airfields in the north had yet to be secured so the US could direct its full might on the Japanese mainland.

VI

The RAN had only one suitable officer to replace John Collins in command of the Australian Squadron and that was Harold Farncomb. After handing over command of *Attacker* he flew home and then joined *Australia*. His return to his old ship was welcomed and to some gave much needed confidence because of his ability to dodge attacking aircraft.[51] The old firm of 'Farncomb and Armstrong' was back.

After Leyte Gulf *Shropshire* had been able to return to Manus Island for rest and maintenance. Her gunnery officer 'Braces' Bracegirdle, armed with two cases of whisky from the Wardroom was able to obtain additional anti-aircraft weapons from the Americans. Twelve 20 mm gun mountings were replaced with thirteen 40 mm guns, which had much greater range and stopping power. Wisely Captain Nichols informed Navy Office of the upgrade as a fait accompli the following month.[52] *Shropshire* had also developed her own methods for dealing with 'suiciders'. This included firing a barrage from her 8-inch guns with the shells fuzed set to explode at a pre-determined time in flight. This created a wall of shrapnel for the pilot to penetrate. 'Braces' also gave gun crews sectors around the ship to automatically open fire on aircraft in what he called 'snap-shooting'. As an old gunnery officer Harold Farncomb appreciated the value of these methods and later wrote to Admiral Kinkaid encouraging their wider use. Harold also approved *Australia's* gunnery officer, Lieutenant Commander Richard Peek, without recourse to Navy Office, to obtain additional 40 mm guns as in *Shropshire*. He also approved mounting radars on the gunnery high angle directors and the use of US Navy 8-inch shells in the Australian cruisers' guns. In the latter matter he had Eddy Nurse's careful supervision of the trial to confirm the US projectiles could be safely fired.[53]

By this time Eddy Nurse's ordnance inspection organization had grown to 15 officers and over 1,200 civilians. They provided technical advice and oversaw the safe production of every type of naval weapon including air and sea launched torpedoes. Eddy in his quietly self-effacing way engendered great loyalty from his staff and had very constructive relations with the various manufacturers. Captain Lance Spooner, RN wrote in 1944 that Eddy:

> ... has resisted the war time tendency to relax production standards at the expense of efficiency. His success may be judged by the fact that he has been responsible for accepting stores to the value of nearly £20 million but no failure has been reported from sea which could be attributed to faulty manufacture. His work has been difficult because Australian manufacturers are inexperienced, and time often necessitates making decisions which an Inspector Naval Officer in England would be able to refer to some experienced authority.[54]

The next amphibious landings were to be directed at the Philippines largest and most important island of Luzon. Instead of a direct landing in Manila Bay to retake the capital, it was decided to land on the central west coast in the relatively lightly defended Lingayen Gulf. There would be two landing sites at the southern end of the Gulf, one near the town of Lingayen and the other near San Fabian. The intent was for the four divisions of the US 6th Army to push south, hopefully securing the good roads south towards Manila.

On 5 January the 875 ship invasion fleet steamed towards Lingayen Gulf. The formation that would assault Lingayen beach was in the van. This included *Shropshire, Arunta, Warramunga, Gascoyne* and *Warrego*. They were followed by the San Fabian group including *Australia*. In the afternoon as the ships steamed passed Manila Bay, Japanese aircraft tried to break through the nearly 60 American fighters that protected the armada. Most aircraft were intercepted, but at 5 pm *Arunta* was missed by a suicider but damaged by its bomb that fell close by. Soon after six Japanese Vals, flying low, evaded American fighters and passed astern of *Australia* with one slamming into the escort carrier USS *Manila Bay*. The fires were extinguished and she would be able to resume flying operations in a couple of days. It was an omen for *Australia* as the carrier had been previously hit by two suiciders on the day *Australia* had received its first hit. And so it proved. Despite concerted anti-aircraft fire, another of the six Vals, after gaining height executed a steep dive and hit portside midships of *Australia*. The aircraft's fuel started a blaze and its bomb also detonated causing death and injury among the gun crews along the port side. *Australia's* third funnel and crane were also damaged. The fire was quickly doused by a hose team led by Stoker Petty Officer Mervyn Evans who went to the seat of the fire despite exploding ammunition.[55] In the attack 25 men were killed, including all of aft portside 4-inch (P2) and eight of the forward (P1) 4-inch gun crews. There were also 30 wounded. To man the guns sailors from some of the smaller calibre guns were moved to P1 and P2 while sailors from the 8-inch magazines backfilled into the smaller calibre guns.

The following day saw the pre-landing bombardment commence within Lingayen Gulf. *Australia* was not assigned specific targets but rather was to respond to any Japanese batteries which opened fire, or new targets of opportunity. One Japanese battery opened fire and was promptly silenced by *Australia*. To the west *Shropshire* was assigned targets on Poro Point. At midday the battleship *New Mexico*, which was steaming ahead of *Shropshire* was attacked by a suicider. Although *Shropshire* managed to take off the aircraft's tail it still struck the battleship's bridge.

It killed 31 men including her Captain and Winston Churchill's liaison officer to General MacArthur, Lieutenant General Herbert Lumsden. Lucky to escape uninjured was the Commander-in-Chief of the newly formed British Pacific Fleet, Admiral Sir Bruce Fraser who was onboard to witness operations. Shortly thereafter *Shropshire* was successively attacked by two low flying Japanese aircraft both of which she shot down within yards of the ship. Less fortunate was the destroyer-transport *Brooks* which was struck by a suicider and *Warramunga* went to her aid.

Throughout the day low flying suiciders came from the coast to attack the ships. At 5.25 am a Val headed towards *Australia* from her starboard quarter. Despite a barrage of fire the suicider struck the starboard side between the two 4-inch guns. Aviation fuel ignited over the deck and the aircraft's bomb exploded. Once again the fire was quickly put out but there was a heavy toll on gun crews. All of the rear starboard 4-inch gun crew (S2) were lost as well as some of those manning S1. In all fourteen were killed. Within a couple of days both 4-inch guns would be made serviceable, but in the meantime *Australia* maintained her station.

The following day both cruisers stood ready to engage any Japanese artillery fire from the shore. *Shropshire* was straddled once and returned fire to silence the shore position. While that day was relatively quiet for air attacks they resumed in earnest on 8 January. After standing offshore overnight the ships steamed into the bay.

Three Val dive bombers, acting as suiciders, flew towards *Shropshire* followed by two American Wildcat fighters. One Val passed down *Shropshire's* starboard side hotly followed by a Wildcat. Both planes were shot down but to the great relief of all the American pilot was safely recovered. Soon after another suicider was engaged and hit the sea 200 yards on the port side of *Shropshire*. This incident and others like it would lead Harold Farncomb after the battle to write to Admiral Kinkaid that:

> Aircraft on occasions did not appear to pay sufficient attention to the need for identifying themselves when closing ships. A small number of irresponsible, though brave young men, continue to cause great inconvenience and discomfort to thousands of personnel in ships.[56]

The battleships USS Mississippi *and* New Mexico *and the heavy cruiser HMAS* Shropshire *open fire on shore positions during the Battle of Lingayen Gulf.* (USN)

The raid was far from complete. Just after the second suicider was destroyed a twin engined Dinah bomber made a run from astern of a line of battleships and cruisers. *Australia,* last in line, opened a concerted fire at the kamikaze. The aircraft was repeatedly struck by fire from *Australia* and a low flying Wildcat. The Dinah hit the water 20 yards from *Australia* but carried on to strike the ship's side. Gun crews down aft were drenched with high octane aviation fuel which fortunately did not ignite. Before these men had time to hose the fuel off their clothes a second Dinah made an almost identical run on *Australia.* It was also hit many times before striking the ship's side below the bridge. Its bomb blew a 14x8 foot hole in the hull and the ensuing ingress of water resulted in a five degree list. One of the aircraft's propellers landed on the upper deck amid other shrapnel but miraculously there were no injuries.[57] Minutes later the escort carrier *Kadashan Bay* also had a hole blown in her side by a suicider.

Harold Farncomb thought *Australia* had become a target in part because of her distinctive three funnels and destroyer USS *Moale* was assigned to ride 'shot gun' on the battered cruiser.[58] Undeterred by repeated strikes *Australia* continued her bombardment duties.

On the morning of 9 January the landings of 68,000 troops took place. *Kanimbla, Manoora* and *Westralia* were among the ships disgorging their precious cargo. Both *Shropshire* and *Australia* took part in further bombardments. Such was the effectiveness of the three previous days of bombardment and air strikes there was virtually no opposition. Suicide air attacks continued however. Just after 1 pm two Ki-61 Judy fighters came in low over land and both were engaged by the warships. The first passed by *Australia* and struck the battleship *Mississippi* at her waterline to little effect. The second flew towards *Australia's* bridge being repeatedly hit as it did so. The suicider narrowly missed the bridge but its wing tip grazed the Type 273 radar and part of the foremast. The fighter then crashed into the top of the forward funnel and passed over into the water. With black humour Armstrong later signalled to Nichols in *Shropshire*, 'We Catch 'em—you shoot 'em'.[59]

Indeed the charmed *Shropshire* was one of only four cruisers or battleships that had not been hit by suicide aircraft.[60] Importantly though, the Army secured the town of Lingayen and its intact airstrip by dusk. At day's end the damaged *Australia* and *Arunta* were ordered to retire south to San Pedro Bay along with other seriously damaged ships. It was clear *Australia* would need to return to Australia. Before she left Harold Farncomb and his staff shifted across to *Arunta* which would take him back to *Shrosphire*. After the action Harold Farncomb wrote to Admiral Royle:

... the suiciders who are rather harassing and who produce a greater psychological effect than the ordinary bomber. The material results they achieve, however, do not compare with that obtained from direct bomb hits ... I consider that her [*Australia's*] ship's company are in urgent need of leave after their shaking experiences in the last two operations. I cannot speak too highly of the courage and efficiency of all hands.[61]

After the Lingayen operation Admiral Fraser later wrote to Admiral Sir Guy Royle of the performance of the Australian Squadron in action:

I watched all their signalling on TBS, their radar reporting to aircraft and their general activities. They were all of the first order, and in the *New Mexico* the Admiral told me he thought the radar reporting of these ships was extremely good.
I thought *Australia*, who seemed to be singled out for attack, dealt with every situation with great courage and determination, and this

fact speaks for itself for, after all the damage she sustained, she carried out her duties until the landing had been completed and her task accomplished. When she was hit in the boiler room she made a signal saying that her speed was reduced to 12 knots and that she was afraid she would lose all steam and be stopped. Fifteen minutes later she made a signal saying she was ready for 22 knots.

I saw your ships firing and they were always quick off the mark, and always seemed prepared and ready for anything. I can assure you that the Americans are loud in their praises.[62]

Indeed Rear Admiral Ingram Sowell from his vantage point of the battleship *West Virginia* signalled to Harold Farncomb:

You and your fine ship can certainly take it. All hands are deserving of commendation. We are proud to be associated with you.[63]

The repeated kamikaze attacks on *Australia* were part of a pattern the US Navy detected where some ships were repeatedly targeted to finally achieve a sinking.[64] The resilience of *Australia* had a positive effect on all the ships of the Australian Squadron. *Gascoyne*, who herself had withstood air attacks to complete her vital surveying duties, signalled to *Australia*, 'We would like to say how proud we are of your stout hearts.'[65] Throughout the suicide attacks Harold Farncomb was a figure of imperturbability on *Australia's* bridge which astounded those around him. It only served to reinforce his 'Fearless Frank' mantle.[66]

The Australian Squadron's deeds in the Philippines campaign represent one of the Navy's finest achievements. Their level of integration with the US Navy was impressive considering their starting point in the Guadalcanal campaign. The resilience and courage of *Australia* captured the national imagination. Less recognized were those of *Shropshire*. Yet she demonstrated a standard of excellence not seen since *Sydney's* feats in the Mediterranean. For his part Harold Farncomb was made a Companion of the Order of the Bath (CB) for services at Lingayen Gulf.[67]

On 22 January Harold Farncomb and his staff joined *Shropshire* in a much quieter Lingayen Gulf. His arrival was inauspicious. Coming up the gangway he tripped. A sailor came down to help him but received a blast for his troubles.[68] It highlighted an unpleasant aspect of Harold's character. His occasional rudeness, whether because of pressure, tiredness or impatience, made him at times an intimidating presence to subordinates. Whether out of shyness or his view of protocol, Harold always maintained a distance as a senior officer. This contrasted to the consideration and even temperedness of Harry Showers and John Collins. Yet the sailors were forgiving of Harold. Leading Seaman 'Nobby' Hall, who as Quartermaster had twice put a drunk Harold to bed after a run ashore, said that while Harold was aloof, 'his troops would follow him anywhere'.[69]

Harold Farncomb's arrival in *Shropshire*, while an impost on accommodation, was eased by the accompanying arrival of mail. In an address to the ship's company Harold told them he was keenly aware of the unsatisfactory state of mail deliveries and outlined his efforts to get improvements back in Australia and along the mail route. Fortunately, he now had Harry Showers as Second Naval Member, with fresh memories of the slow mail, trying to improve matters from Melbourne.[70]

In Lingayen Gulf the air attacks had now largely disappeared and unknown at the time was the relocation of the remaining Kamikaze aircraft to Formosa for homeland defence.[71] As Commander Task Unit 77.3.5 Harold Farncomb had in addition to *Shropshire*, *Arunta* and *Warramunga*; the US heavy cruisers *Portland* and *Minneapolis* and the destroyers *Conway*, *Eaton*, *Braine* and *Frazier*.

On 6 February TU 77.3.5 finally left Lingayen and sailed into Manila Bay. The capital was still being cleared of Japanese who were not finally subdued until 4 March. Dogged fighting was also under way at Corregidor on the tip of the Bataan Peninsula. On 16 February Harold Farncomb's heavy cruisers were called in to assist Admiral Berkey's force in bombarding the Japanese fortified positions. The use of 8-inch semi-armour piercing shells finally had the desired effect on the cliff fortification. At the same time the men had a close view of the historic recapture of Corregidor which included a large scale drop of paratroopers. Also witnessing the event was General MacArthur circling overhead in a B-17.

After five kamikaze hits the battered HMAS Australia *retires from Lingayen Gulf while HMAS* Arunta *comes alongside to embark Harold Farncomb and his staff.* (RAN)

The high level of interoperability now achieved by RAN ships with those of the US Navy enabled individual ships to work readily within US formations where circumstances dictated. During the Philippines campaign it was less common for the RAN ships to operate together, particularly when damage repair and overdue maintenance depleted the force. Harold Farncomb reported to Admiral Colvin that, 'the operation has been an individualistic one for the RAN'.[72] In this changed circumstance Harold saw himself less a tactical commander than the senior RAN officer in theatre orchestrating and maximising national contribution to the operation. He ensured that RAN ships entering theatre were both well prepared in Australia and finally by NOIC New Guinea and that their individual capabilities were understood by receiving US Admirals.[73] Critically, he developed a very productive working relationship with Admiral Kinkaid, Vice Admiral Oldendorf and Rear Admiral Berkey and kept up a regular correspondence with Admiral Royle via Speed Letters.[74] This novel form of communication was a letter sent in telegraphic form very much like a modern email. For his part Royle greatly valued Harold's insights which were particularly useful when briefing the War Cabinet.[75]

Harold Farncomb was conscious of the national importance of maintaining a visible cruiser presence in the final phases of operations against Japan. To that end he strongly encouraged the expeditious repair of *Australia* and the early return of *Hobart* to the fight at the expense of other dockyard work.[76] At the same time he was cognisant of the wearing effect of the operation, with its sustained sea time, 'suiciders' and the tropical heat. His correspondence to Navy Office frequently dealt with the need for sufficient leave once ships returned to Australia. On 27 January Harold wrote:

> I was glad to see that *Australia's* 28 days leave had been approved. It will be very much appreciated. The Ship's Company were getting a bit shaky. Six hits in two operations from the suicide planes were bound to affect their equanimity. Admiral Kinkaid remarked on that morning, that 'anyone who is not frightened by them is dumb!'[77]

An issue of constant attention was the logistic support of the squadron 4,000 miles from Australia. The effort of one dedicated store ship, the old *Merkur*, was insufficient and Harold Farncomb urged enhancements to the organization while at the same time leveraging off the US supply train. Mail was a particular rub and Harold had liaison officers placed in various island hubs to try and accelerate its delivery with frustratingly indifferent results. On 7 March 1945 he proposed to Admiral Royle that an RAN Air Transport Service be created for the purpose of transporting important stores (such as radar spares), mail and personnel. Harold was mindful as the war moved north that the RAN could not continue to rely on the good graces of the USN and had to stand on its own feet. He wrote:

> I am sure that the cost of a <u>fast</u> service, such as I envisage, will, apart from its morale value, be more than paid for by the reduction of man hours lost by personnel in transit to and from the forward bases. *Shropshire's* last draft spent two months in Samar (near Leyte) waiting for transport north.[78]

Harold Farncomb thought also that such an Air Service would, 'be a golden opportunity of starting the thin end of the wedge for an RAN Fleet Air Arm. I have great hopes that the arrival of the British Pacific Fleet with its attendant Air Arm will foster the prospects'.[79] The proposal for an

Air Transport Service did not take off. However, Harold's proposed model for logistic air lift to deployed RAN ships, typically with commercial aircraft, eventually became standard practice later in the century.

After the Corregidor operation *Shropshire* was overdue for a refit in Sydney. She sailed south and Harold Farncomb transferred to the repaired and modernized *Hobart* in Manus on 7 March. Harold was keen to ensure that *Hobart* would be operationally ready for the what lay ahead and delayed *Shropshire*'s return for a couple of days for exercises with the new ship. He rejoined *Shropshire* for passage to Sydney. At the end of the month *Hobart* returned to the fight by bombarding beach positions in the small landing at Cebu.

While the main American effort following the Philippine campaign was to be the landing on Iwo Jima, two other operations were mounted. They were the retaking of Borneo, which would secure oil and rubber supplies and the other was mopping up Japanese positions in New Guinea. These final New Guinea operations would bring members of the Pioneer Class together in war for the last time.

VII

By February 1945 and after six months of light duties at HMAS *Moreton* in Brisbane Eric Feldt was ready to resume active service. Instead of returning to his coastwatch position he became NOIC Torokina and Commanding officer of the new shore base HMAS *Lusair* which was taken over from the US Navy. He was glad to be back in the islands and James Esdaile remarked that Eric was all 'zeal, ability and cooperation'.[80] From a financial perspective it was also a welcome return to service. While Eric had been recuperating in Australia he had lost his Acting Commander rank but under the vigilant eye of Rupert Long, it was returned on taking command of *Lusair*.

Eric first flew from Brisbane to Madang and met James Esdaile at his NOIC New Guinea headquarters for briefings. He then took passage to Bougainville in the sloop *Swan* which had done such good work in the support of the Army along the coast.

Harold Farncomb argued for the highest priority to be given to bringing HMAS Hobart back into service to ensure Australia was providing a meaningful contribution in the final phase of the naval war against Japan. This photograph shows the modernized Hobart. (RAN)

Lusair was on the shores of Empress Augusta Bay in western Bougainville. It was just north of a fighter airstrip that the Americans had built into the jungle. Like many such airfields, with the war moving north, it was only used for emergencies.[81] *Lusair* was one of seventeen naval outposts along northern New Guinea, Bougainville and New Britain. Their roles were logistic support, intelligence and communications. This meant that while James Esdaile had overall command of the network, there were other people such as Rupert Long for intelligence and Jack Newman for communications keenly interested in their performance and output.

From January 1945 James Esdaile had a substantial force that consisted of *Swan*, the old destroyer - now transport *Vendetta*, the frigate *Barcoo*, corvettes *Colac, Cowra, Deloraine, Dubbo* and *Kapunda* as well as a mixed bag of patrol vessels, landing craft and stores ships. In terms of supporting the Army, James worked constructively with Major General Jack Stevens and his 5th and 6th Divisions to assist in their series of landings and coastal

Eric Feldt's last command, the naval base HMAS Lusair *on the shores of Empress Augusta Bay in western Bougainville. This watercolour was painted by Guy Warren then a soldier. As a professional artist Warren would go on to win the 1985 Archibald Prize for portraiture.* (AWM)

drives along the north New Guinea coast. These were demanding operations in more ways than one. The difficult terrain and disease were a given, but the strategic value of the operations compared to the likely losses played on the minds of the troops. Maintaining morale was a constant challenge.

For some of these operations, such as at Wide Bay, Halmahera and Aitape, James Esdaile could provide all the required naval resources. The core of James' force were *Swan,* under the command of Lieutenant Bill Dovers, along with *Dubbo* and *Colac.* Dubbed the Wewak Force they had become adept at working closely with the Army and had General Stevens' confidence. For the Army it was an unexpected boon for Admiral Kinkaid to offer *Hobart, Arunta* and *Warramunga* after the first Borneo landings at Tarakan. Harold Farncomb flew from Sydney to join *Hobart* to command the naval aspects of the operation. Harold had organised with Admiral Sir Bruce Fraser that the British Pacific Fleet cruiser HMS *Newfoundland* would also take part.

As one of the key planners for the Wewak operation James Esdaile determined, based on the operational and environmental considerations, the day for the landings. The code word *Ursula* was used in the operation, which unknown to most was in honour of his daughter.[82]

Harold Farncomb arrived in Hollandia for the dress rehearsal of the landing after first conferring with General Stevens. Harold's late arrival was less than ideal and James Esdaile had acted as the go between with Army planners and the new ships in finalizing the bombardment plan.[83] He spent a day with Harold in *Hobart* to ensure the plan would meet the Army's requirements.

Wewak is situated on a small headland and the proposed landings were to take place to the east of the peninsula. At 7.15 am on 11 May 1945, Harold's ships conducted a concerted bombardment of positions while RAAF Beauforts bombed targets further inshore. There were about 1,700 Japanese troops in the Wewak area and adjacent islands to oppose the Australians. Fortunately, there was only light and sporadic opposition and the Australian troops were expeditiously lodged ashore with nearly 90 Japanese dead at the landing area as a result of the naval bombardment. The Australians moved along the coast and over coming days drove the Japanese from the area. It remained difficult work with Japanese snipers an ever present danger. After the success of the Wewak operation James Esdaile wrote home and captured the mood of the time:

> The successful end of the European war is very satisfactory and it is quite to be hoped that things up here will not be delayed much longer. The Jap is, however, an unpredictable animal and it is not wise to even attempt to forecast his reaction to his present predicament.[84]

The departure of Harold Farncomb and his Squadron out of the area was soon followed by another of the Pioneer Class—Eric Feldt. On 21 May, after only three months at *Lusair*, Eric had to be evacuated with a relapse of his heart condition. He returned to Brisbane for treatment and was assessed as Physically Unfit for Naval Service.[85]

Eric's departure from *Lusair* came as James Esdaile was providing *Colac* and other vessels to him to intercept any watercraft with escaping

Japanese troops around Bougainville. However the main thrust of the war had already moved inexorably north. This meant the work of Eric's beloved coastwatchers was done. Their achievements and scope of their work had exceeded the expectations of even Rupert Long, Eric and Hugh MacKenzie. The Guadalcanal campaign was undoubtedly their finest hour and led Admiral Halsey to famously write, 'They saved Guadalcanal and Guadalcanal saved the South Pacific'.[86] While Eric had envisaged coastwatchers as a fence and trip wire, he did not expect them to be so effective in orchestrating guerilla operations. General MacArthur's headquarters estimated that the coastwatchers accounted for 5,414 enemy killed in the Solomons, New Britain and New Guinea, with 74 Japanese captured. Significantly, they rescued over 500 Allied soldiers and airmen as well as 450 civilians who would have had perilous prospects without the coastwatchers' aid.[87] The personal cost to the coastwatchers was beyond what Rupert and Eric would have imagined at the inception. Thirty-six men gave their lives. Individually and often alone their brutal deaths by sword or bayonet were in the face of an enemy bereft of humanity.

The remarkable achievements of the coastwatchers would not have been possible without outstanding support, particularly from RAAF Catalinas and US Navy submarines. On reflecting on this aspect during his convalescence Eric Feldt wrote:

> It can be stated categorically that not one officer or man in the Ferdinand organization put himself before his duty. This was not advertised but it showed out and its influence permeated to all who came in contact with the coastwatchers and help was rendered when it would not have been forthcoming for any other reason.[88]

VIII

In Borneo the first of the Codename *Oboe* series of landings by Australian troops had already successfully taken place at Tarakan (*Oboe 1*) on 1 May. The next operations would be in the north on Labuan Island with *Oboe 6* near Brunei slated for 10 June involving the Australian 9th

Division and in the south at Balikpapan (*Oboe 2*) programmed for 1 July with the Australian 7th Division.

At the beginning of June *Shropshire* sailed from Sydney to bolster the Australian Squadron for these operations and her shakedown was truncated to ensure she would be able to provide support. On 14 June *Shropshire* joined *Hobart* and *Arunta* in Tawi Tawi in Southern Philippines and Harold Farncomb transferred his flag to the heavy cruiser. After early Allied success on Labuan the Japanese resistance had concentrated and the Squadron steamed to assist the 9th Division. On 18 June Harold went ashore at Labuan and was briefed by the formidable and shrewd Gallipoli veteran Major General George Wootten. That afternoon *Shropshire* closed and fired upon Japanese strongholds to telling effect, killing a hundred Japanese but tragically also two nearby Australian soldiers. Further bombardments took place the following day before Japanese resistance ended.

The Balikpapan landing was destined to be Australia's largest amphibious landing. General 'Ted' Milford[89] who commanded the 7th Division for the operation was in the 1913 Entry at Duntroon and the first graduate from the Military College to become a Major General. He was a specialist in artillery and a meticulous planner. A key issue that arose in the planning for the operation was the selected landing sites. Vice Admiral Barbey and his commander of the Balikpapan Attack Force demurred at the locations selected by Milford as they would be harder to reach and carry more risk in the lodgement phase. The four proposed landing areas were along the Klandasan coast to the south of the Balikpapan township. The Australian General prevailed in the discussions because of the tactical advantage his preferred sites provided to troops once ashore.

At the end of June the Allied amphibious, bombardment and aircraft carriers groups converged on Balikpapan from different ports. On the afternoon of 27 June Harold Farncomb took *Shropshire* and *Hobart,* closed the Klandasan beaches and commenced the initial bombardment whilst his destroyers *Arunta, Hart* and *Metcalf* provided anti-submarine protection to his cruisers. After nearly four hours of deliberate bombardment Harold withdrew his ships into the Makassar Strait. The ships returned each day for further bombardments and to protect the amphibious fleet, which included once again the trio of *Kanimbla, Manoora* and *Westralia*. On the eve of the landing Japanese positions were subject to further Allied air attacks from Liberator bombers as well as Lightning, Kittyhawk and Spitfire fighters operating mainly from bases at Tarakan and southern Philippines.

On the morning of 1 July, with General MacArthur witnessing operations from the cruiser USS *Cleveland*, the 7th Division made their landings. The approach channels, which had been swept for mines, were marked with small buoys and the well practised landing craft were for the most part able to hit the beach such that the troops landed dry shod.[90]

The Japanese resistance was initially light as were the Australian casualties. The warships remained offshore for nine days providing round the clock bombardment support as well as harassing fire to wear down the enemy. During this time Harold Farncomb went ashore to ensure that Milford was being adequately supported. A feature of the Balikpapan operation was the accuracy of the naval gunfire in dealing with Japanese positions and was a testament to the expertise the ships had gained since the beginning of the war. For most ships of the Australian Squadron, 9 July 1945 represented the day they fired their last rounds at the enemy. That evening *Shropshire* weighed anchor and steamed to a well-earned break in the Philippines.

After nearly seven months arduous service on 21 July 1945, Harold Farncomb, after two days of discussions, was replaced by John Collins who had recovered well from his wounds. During their handover both men called on General MacArthur. A worn out Harold was finally to have an appointment ashore as Commodore Training at Flinders Naval Depot.

Harold's tenure in command of the Australian Squadron had been during its most momentous and demanding period. He shone during its greatest challenge and maintained a strategic focus on its war contribution. His immediate American superior in theatre Rear Admiral Oldendorf wrote of Harold:

He showed himself to be a courageous, capable and highly cooperative officer, where ships could always be counted on to do their full share of all assignments and to do them well. He imbued his command with confidence.[91]

Harold Farncomb would later be awarded the US Navy Cross for his 'extraordinary heroism' and 'indomitable fighting spirit'. Lieutenant Commander George Fowle was Harold's Staff Officer Operations for a period and wrote:

> He was a demanding boss, but great to work with in the sense that he had such a quick brain—but was no diplomat, couldn't suffer fools at all, let alone gladly ... An acquired taste HB Farncomb, but once you had it you couldn't miss it. Our lot would have followed him anywhere.[92]

IX

After assuming command of the Australian Squadron John Collins called on Admiral Kinkaid. Among the matters discussed was the Australian Squadron's part in the expected invasion of Japan. The overall campaign was codenamed Operation *Downfall*. It was divided into two large operations, Operation *Olympic*—the invasion of Kyūshū and Operation *Coronet*—the invasion of Honshū. The Australian Squadron would be part of Operation *Olympic* which was set to land its troops ashore on 1 November 1945. To be undertaken by the 3rd Fleet commanded by Admiral 'Bull' Halsey, it would be the largest amphibious operation in history and involve the largest armada ever assembled.

The Australian Squadron would be part of the fleet that would include 17 aircraft carriers, 8 battleships, 20 cruisers and 75 destroyers. John Collins' ships would once again be part of the inshore bombardment force. The defence of Kyūshū was expected to be intense. In addition to the envisaged 9,000 kamikaze aircraft there was also the prospect of attacks from human torpedoes and suicide boats. John, like Harold Farncomb before him, was conscious of the conspicuous appearance of his three funnelled cruisers, which would no doubt draw particular kamikaze attention.[93] Once ashore the US troops would have to face a determined Japanese 16th Army, fighting on their own soil.[94]

To prepare themselves for *Olympic*, the Australian Squadron was based at Subic Bay just to the north of Manila. Fortunately, the Squadron was to be spared the rigours of this final operation. On 6 August the men were astounded to hear that a new bomb of unprecedented destructive power had devastated the Japanese city of Hiroshima. After a call for Japan's surrender went unheeded, a second atomic bomb destroyed Nagasaki on 9 August. Six days later the Japanese announced their unconditional surrender. To John Collins:

> ... the atomic bombs on Hiroshima and Nagasaki, terrible though they were, did in effect save many lives. Without the face-saving excuse the Japanese would have fought to the last man. We, who were to take part, were grateful to our scientists, always remembering that it is no more agreeable to be blown to pieces by high explosive than by an atomic bomb.[95]

John Collins' view was borne out by an audience with Emperor Hirohito in which the Navy Minister, Admiral Mitsumasa Yonai stated:

> ... the atomic bombs and the Soviet entry into the war are, in a sense, divine gifts. This way we don't have to say that we have quit the war because of domestic circumstances.[96]

To the delight of all it was decided the Australian Squadron would be present in Tokyo Bay for the official surrender ceremony. This brought forward the shift from Kinkaid's 7th Fleet to Halsey's 3rd Fleet. John Collins paid farewell calls on both Kinkaid and General MacArthur. The General told John the Squadron's departure from his command was, 'like a death in the family' and presented him with a treasured inscribed framed photograph. In contrast to many who focused on MacArthur's flaws, the General impressed John with his great leadership and contribution to Australia's defence.[97]

John Collins' ships—*Shropshire, Warramunga* and *Bataan*— sailed out of Manila Bay on 25 August passing Corregidor and Bataan at sunset. They then passed Lingayen Gulf where too many men of the Australian Squadron had lost their lives in kamikaze attacks. Clearing the Philippines there were two days of clear blue skies and calm seas as the Squadron relaxed for the first time at sea in five years. After rendezvousing with *Hobart* on passage, on the morning of 31 August, John Collins flying his broad pendant in *Shropshire*, led his ships in line astern into Tokyo Bay. In contrast to the sunny passage the weather was grey and threatening which added to the atmosphere. *Warramunga's* Surgeon Lieutenant Henry Rischbieth wrote:

> A day that will live long in the memory of all the three thousand or so Australians present when the Australian Squadron sailed proudly into Tokyo Bay this morning. All hands, who could possibly be there, were early on deck and one could feel the air of tense expectancy as we eagerly looked for the first sight of land.[98]

As the ships entered port numerous white flags could be seen fluttering from buildings and hill tops. This gave the men their first sense of victory. The desolation of the port, the city and shipping became all too apparent. As the Australian Squadron threaded its way to its assigned anchorage the sailors saw before them the mighty armada of over 250 warships. Overhead there were large formations of aircraft regularly flying over the vanquished city. Among the battleships were Halsey's flagship, *Missouri* where the surrender would take place; *South Dakota*, flying the flag of Admiral Chester Nimitz and HMS *Duke of York* with Admiral Sir Bruce Fraser embarked. Already at the Australian anchorage were the doughty corvettes *Bathurst, Ipswich, Cessnock* and *Pirie*. There were also present the destroyers HMA Ships *Napier* and *Nizam* which were attached to the British Pacific Fleet. There was a sense of great pride among the Australian Squadron sailors at being part of this final act of the war.[99] To the men of *Shropshire*, John Collins later wrote, 'It's a far cry from No.3 Basin, Chatham Dockyard, to Berth D60 in Tokyo Bay, but here we are, and still rather bewildered by the sudden realisation of our dreams'.[100] Having earlier reported to Admiral Halsey for duty by signal John Collins then personally called on 'the old tiger'.[101]

The following day John met the other members of the Australian Delegation for the surrender. It was led by General Sir Thomas Blamey and comprised Lieutenant General Frank Berryman and Air Vice Marshal William Bostock. The Navy was represented by both the Acting First Naval Member Rear Admiral George Moore and John Collins.

'The old tiger'—Admiral 'Bull' Halsey onboard his flagship. He was greatly admired by John Collins, Harold Farncomb and Eric Feldt. (USN)

The day of the Surrender Ceremony was in the words of Surgeon Lieutenant Rischbieth, 'dull and calm, with hardly a breath of air to disturb the profound hush that lay over Tokyo Bay—there was everywhere a suppressed excitement'.[102] From an early hour a steady stream of boats made their way to *Missouri*. The honour of taking MacArthur and Nimitz to the battleship fell to the veteran of Savo Island and many battles after that—the destroyer *Buchanan*. All the time as the dignitaries assembled hundreds of bombers and fighters swept overhead in waves of omnipresent power. When John Collins arrived onboard *Missouri* he was met by her Captain, Stuart 'Sunshine' Murray[103] with whom John had served on Admiral Hart's staff in Surabaya during those dark days of 1942. Also present onboard *Missouri* from that time was Lieutenant-Admiral Helfrich who was the Dutch head of delegation. He warmly welcomed John. Helfrich later wrote:

> I spoke with many friends. British General Percival, who had capitulated at Singapore, the Admirals Nimitz and Halsey USN and their colleagues from the British Navy, Sir Bruce Fraser, the well-

known to me Commodore Collins of the Australian Navy, with whom I had worked so pleasingly on Java. And many others. Handshakes were exchanged. We were all in high spirits. Here there was real Allied military friendship.[104]

In a tribute to the resourcefulness of the Australian sailor, Able Seaman Robert Skinner, who was escorting a journalist and the only RAN sailor onboard *Missouri,* had managed to find a vantage point. He later recalled:

> At 0800h the American Marine band on the quarter-deck played the National Anthem and the Stars and Stripes, as the colours were hoisted to the mast-head, and straight after a prayer was given over the loud-speaker system, giving thanks for this great day and for the deliverance of the Allies. To see all those thousands of men from Generals down to ordinary seamen, standing bare-headed while this prayer was being broadcast, is something one could never forget and it just seemed to be a really fitting start for such a great and historical day as this one was destined to be.[105]

With all the Allies mustered the Japanese delegation arrived led by Foreign Affairs Minister Mr Mamoru Shigemitsu. John Collins then recalled the scene:

> At last MacArthur emerged and, looking every inch the great leader he was, gave his address in telling words, and the signing started.[106]

As the ceremony got underway sailors around the assembled armada listened to proceedings via a radio broadcast. They could hear MacArthur in his distinctive voice act as Master of Ceremonies and call forward each national delegation. The members of each delegation saluted MacArthur and then their head sat down and signed the instrument of surrender. With MacArthur's words, 'These proceedings are now closed', six years of war came to an end. Soon thereafter the sun broke through the diminishing clouds. Privileged to be part of the ceremony John Collins thought, 'It was a pity that every man in the Squadron could not have been there to see the late 'world conquerors' stand so abjectly, waiting to be allowed to sign the surrender document'.[107]

The war had resulted in RAN losses at sea of over 2,100 men and nineteen ships. The Pioneer Class had lost Leigh Watkins, Joe Burnett and Frank Getting as well as forever affecting the lives of most of the others. It was therefore appropriate that a member of their Class was present on deck of *Missouri*. That evening on the quarterdeck of the British battleship *King George V* John Collins attended the large reception for Allied commanders. The event with its free-flowing gin and easy camaraderie, culminated in a ceremonial sunset in which all the Allied flags were lowered. The war was finally over.

'At last MacArthur emerged and, looking every inch the great leader he was, gave his address in telling words'. (State Library of Victoria)

Chapter 9
These Have Been Men

So when the shadow shall fall on the way of us,
Nearing the goal of our threescore and ten,
Happily our sons and their children may say of us
'these have been faithful, these have been Men!'
       Into the Years – A song for the RANC (1913)1

I

After the long years of war the thoughts, hopes and energies of Australians now turned to prospects of a brighter future for themselves and the nation. This was no different for the Pioneer Class. Seven of them—Norman Calder, John Collins, James Esdaile, Harold Farncomb, Hugh MacKenzie, Jack Newman and Eddy Nurse—still saw the Navy as their career for some time to come. For Rupert Long and Winn Reilly the call of private enterprise beckoned. Others such as George Armitage, Horace Thompson, Harry Vallentine and Adrian Watts, had already been released from military service and picked up their earlier civilian lives. They joined Ben Howells, Peyton Kimlin and Jack Lecky who had contributed to the national war effort through other means.

Whilst the war had ended, the responsibilities of Australia's military forces had not, most particularly in Japan where Australia contributed to the British Commonwealth Occupation Force (BCOF). Soon after Japan's formal surrender John Collins, while retaining his command of the Australian Squadron in Japan, moved ashore to a house in the grounds of the British Embassy. He helped coordinate the insertion of BCOF under the Australian Lieutenant General Horace 'Red Robbie' Robertson. During this time John had the opportunity to see first hand the destruction of Hiroshima. Besides the scale of the devastation he was struck by the peculiar aspects of a nuclear explosion—cars compressed into small blocks or unbroken bottles with their sides squeezed by some mysterious force.[2]

Once the Army and Air Force elements were established, John Collins' focus returned to his ships. Typically the Australian task group consisted of two cruisers and two destroyers supported by a small shore base at Kure. In December 1945 John Collins acted as Commander Force T and Senior British Officer Afloat for a month with the departure of Vice Admiral Eric Brind in HMS *Swiftsure* until the arrival of his relief. The work of ships was low key with tasks such as escorting Japanese warships which were used to repatriate Japanese soldiers.[3]

Once the novelty of operating in Japanese waters had worn off it required the skill and leadership of John Collins and his Captains to maintain morale and motivation until the time came for each ship to return home. Many sailors had not known life in a peacetime navy and so the old routines of training, acute attention to a ship's appearance and sport were a new experience. In February 1946 John finally left Japan for Australia.

In the last months of the war Paul Hirst wanted to contribute more directly to the war effort. Accordingly he obtained a commercial Master's Certification to join the US Water Transport and command a Liberty Ship. There was however, not the shortage of Masters that there had been a year before and his application was unsuccessful. So, like Ben Howells and Adrian Watts before him, he joined the Australian Army. On 18 September 1945

Paul was appointed as a Captain and joined the 13th Small Ships Company. The unit had a range of small landing craft and supply vessels which supported the Army in New Guinea. Paul spent most of his service commanding the supply vessel *Emily* operating out of Port Moresby or Bougainville.[4] Paul remained with the 13th Small Ships Company until June 1946. He was discharged in January the following year.

At the end of the war and with the repatriation of the Italian prisoners-of-war who had helped work the property, Evelyn Hirst sold *Ashbourne*. The reunited Hirst family subsequently moved into Launceston with Paul obtaining a position with the Tasmanian Forestry Department. This would prove to be immensely satisfying work, taking him all over Tasmania.

Also returning to sea was Cyril Sadleir. After his discharge from the Navy, he secured a position with Messers JS Lee and Sons of Smithton in northern Tasmania to be Master of the auxiliary trading schooner *Coomonderry*. The 145 tonne ship dated back to 1886 and had traded between Melbourne and the Tasmanian northern ports since 1920. Typically *Coomonderry* would bring cargo such as flour, oats and bricks

Cyril Sadleir was Master of the trading schooner Coomonderry *plying her trade between Melbourne and northern Tasmanian ports.* (State Library of Victoria)

south and return to the mainland with about 65,000 super feet of timber. In the at times brutal weather of Bass Strait, *Coomonderry* had her share of adventures and on one passage took six weeks to reach Melbourne with her crew reduced to eating their cargo of swedes. Yet during Cyril's period of command he had two notable events that took place in port. In April 1947 when the ship was alongside the Wynyard town wharf, a young girl watching the loading of *Coomonderry* fell into the water and started to be swept away with the current. Cyril and his deck hand took to a ship's boat and saved the girl from drowning.[5] The following January when leaving Wynyard the schooner's steering jammed and she went aground on rocks in the Inglis River. After Cyril had her cargo shifted aft *Coomonderry* came free on the evening tide the following day.[6]

Cyril's return to sea was however short-lived. His multiple sclerosis became worse and he developed both blindness in one eye and deafness in one ear. He had to come ashore and obtained a position in the Taxation Office. While there was little satisfaction from this work he did continue to undertake naval reserve service in Melbourne's naval control of shipping cell where his knowledge of the merchant service was valued.

II

The Navy at the end of the war needed to be reduced dramatically in size from its peak of nearly 40,000 men and women and over 330 vessels of all sizes. Most importantly those men and women who had joined only for war service needed to return to civilian life in an expeditious, but ordered manner. To achieve this task the Directorate of Naval Demobilisation was established. It needed an able administrator who had some sense of the extended nature of the Navy's commitments to the north. That officer was James Esdaile. His approach was initially deliberate rather than dramatic. His team established a ranking system whereby all serving officers and sailors were allocated certain points depending on age, years in service and whether they had dependents. The system worked well with the point score for each round of demobilisation being announced across the Navy.[7] Because of continued commitments only 8,000 men and women were released in the first year. This included the disbandment of the entire WRANS organization, to the regret of many. The demobilisation however soon gathered pace as ships were decommissioned and laid up in reserve. By the end of 1948 naval strength had been reduced to just 800 officers and 6,400 sailors.[8]

More broadly the Navy, like the other two services, had to change its orientation and force structure to be relevant for the realities of the post-war world. The advent of the atomic bomb, the demise of the Axis Powers, the decline of Britain and the troubling rise of the Soviet Union were all to be digested and considered.

For the Navy the emergence of the United States as the one true global power had the most portent. While the long and deep bonds with the RN would continue, albeit progressively diminished, there would be growing and deepening links with the US Navy. To some observers this challenge was viewed as a conflict of allegiance and driven by personalities. In July 1945 Captain BF Tompkins, the US Naval Attaché to Australia wrote a series of illuminating sketches for the Chief of Naval Operations Fleet Admiral Ernest King of the key RAN senior officers at war's end. In his covering note he wrote:

> ... it might be worth noting that there appears to be two schools of thought in the RAN. Both recognize the training they have had in the RN schools. One group appears to accept the necessity of the continuation of the RN influence of at least its present level, namely, that there should be an RN officer as First Naval Member of the Australian Commonwealth Naval Board; and that the system of interchanging officers should also continue. The fostering of this idea may be one of the missions of officers loaned by the Admiralty.
> The second group, probably as a result of a cultivated nationalistic feeling, favour an 'all Australian' Naval Board, although they attribute their attitude to the feeling that they get RN officers (for First Member) who are nearing retiring age and that these officers lack the necessary characteristics to stand up to their politicians.[9]

Tompkins then gave his assessments of some of the leading figures in the Navy. Of John Collins he wrote:

> Record bears qualification that he should not be assigned to duty except when a Medical Officer is present. If he fully recovers, is the leading candidate for First Naval Member of the ACNB [Naval Board].[10]

Of Harold Farncomb:

> His fellow officers consider him sounder than the other leading contender (Commodore Collins) for future appointment as First Naval Member of the ACNB. His chances suffer from an argument with the Attorney General, Dr. Evatt, over jurisdiction on a matter of naval discipline [this would have been the HMAS *Australia* court martial].[11]

Of Rupert Long:

> Long, as Director of Naval Intelligence, has been most friendly and cooperative. He has occupied a rather trying position being Director of Naval Intelligence of ACNB and yet not being given intelligence on the highest level. There seems to have been a lot of a feeling he tends to get intelligence by roundabout methods, perhaps a not unnatural result. He is extremely popular with his own staff and is generally well-liked in the RAN, but it is said that he stepped on someone's toes and a result doesn't get promoted. His own staff give him most credit for the coastwatching organisation that did such good work in the Solomons.[12]

Arguably there were neither pro-British nor a pro-American schools. It was more nuanced than this. There were strong links to the RN and for many practical reasons some specialist training and education would still be conducted in UK for many years to come. Both John Collins and Harold Farncomb were representative of a new generation who had been able to fully integrate themselves both into a US command chain and operations more generally. This was to a level of which few of their RN counterparts had little real appreciation or experience.

In February 1946 the cruisers *Australia*, *Shropshire* and *Hobart* were united for the first time since 1944. The ships were in Melbourne and John Collins flew his broad pendant in *Shropshire*. It was a return to the inter-war cycle of exercises and port visits. Large crowds lined up to walk the decks of the war veterans whenever they were open for inspection.

On 2 April it was announced that *Shropshire* would take the Victory Contingent drawn from the three services to England for the Victory Parade. Harry Showers was selected to return to command the cruiser for the deployment. After hasty modifications *Shropshire* sailed from Melbourne on 1 April with an extra 255 men and women onboard. The contingent was commanded by the Major General Kenneth Eather who Harry knew from the New Guinea campaign when he first commanded *Shropshire*. There was a large crowd of well wishers and John Collins in *Hobart* ordered three cheers for *Shropshire* and her contingent. Following the emotional farewell, Bass Strait and then the Great Australian Bight greeted the ship and those onboard to a full running gale.

After embarking the last of the contingent in Fremantle, *Shropshire* sailed for the UK. In a piece of historical symmetry, the cruiser's passage closely followed that of the 1917 voyage of *Omrah* with port visits to Capetown and Freetown before reaching England. On 22 May *Shropshire* arrived in Portsmouth. Among his official visits Harry Showers called on the Commander-in-Chief Portsmouth, Admiral Sir Geoffrey Layton, whom Harry had first met in 1918 when both were in the K Class submarines. Layton was keen to extend a warm welcome to the ship and her Victory Contingent. Earlier that month he had written to the Admiralty seeking adequate funding and wrote, 'In view of lavish entertainments given our ships in Australia I hope this may be assessed on a liberal scale'.[13]

The hospitality during *Shropshire's* one month visit to UK was indeed generous and warm. The highlight was the Victory Parade through the streets of London. Harry Showers sat in the stand adjacent to the dais where King George VI took the salute. For the Contingent the tumultuous reception from the throng that lined the streets would be a life memory— as was seeing Winston Churchill, Admiral Cunningham and other famous leaders seated behind the King and Queen. Leading the naval contingent was Commander Richard Peek. In a reminder of the effects of the Pacific war one of the sailors had to pull out of the contingent as it passed the Embankment due to a bout of malaria.

HMAS Shropshire *under the command of Harry Showers in Port Phillip Bay.* (Green Collection/State Library of Victoria)

On 1 July *Shropshire* sailed for home via the Mediterranean. During a short port visit to Gibraltar Harry Showers called on the Flag Officer Commanding Gibraltar who was Vice Admiral Sir Victor Crutchley. He received a warm welcome from his old Admiral who would finally retire the following year after 41 years of service. After port visits and parades in Fremantle and Adelaide *Shropshire* finally returned to Sydney on 28 August. Once again she became John Collins' flagship.

III

After his 1945 discharge from the Navy Eric Feldt settled once more in Brisbane with Nancy and impatiently awaited the publication of *The Coastwatchers*. It was finally released in 1946 in Australia, Britain and the United States. The Australian edition was the longest with an extended foreword by George Gill, but importantly contained a complete list of the coastwatchers, where they served and their fate. The slimmer US edition benefitted from a generous foreword by General MacArthur who acknowledged the behind the scenes work of 'Captain' Rupert Long and the brilliance of Eric Feldt's leadership. All editions were received to popular and critical acclaim. Importantly, *The Coastwatchers* achieved what Eric Feldt and Rupert Long had hoped for: that the public would for the first time understand the importance of coastwatch operations and

Espions Suicide or Suicide Spies, the cover of the French edition of Eric Feldt's book The Coastwatchers. (Anon)

the astounding bravery of the coastwatchers. On the dust cover of the US Edition is Admiral 'Bull' Halsey's famous quote, 'they saved Guadalcanal, and Guadalcanal saved the South Pacific'. A French translation of Eric's book was published in 1964 under the dramatic title *Espions Suicide* or *Suicide Spies*. Demand was such that a reprint was required in 1967. In Australia there were multiple reprints with *The Coastwatchers* becoming a classic in Australian war literature.

To supplement Eric Feldt's modest income from his naval service, in 1946 and again in 1948 he served for short periods as Secretary of the United Services Club in Brisbane.[14] It was too much for his health however, and in May 1949 Eric applied for a pension with the Department of External Territories based on his New Guinea service. After two years no decision was received so Eric wrote to his old friend Reg Harrigan, who he first met in 1923, and was now Secretary of the Department. Harrigan's pen-note on the Eric's file was, 'Acknowledge personally and advise to expect full advice within a week'.[15] Eric duly received a modest pension. In writing to thank Harrigan for his assistance, Eric summed up his approach to this phase of his life:

> We are living quietly in the old family home, and I do nothing whatever except keep the place tidy, and play bowls. I tried work but found I couldn't stand it, tried to write fiction and couldn't sell it, so I have given it all away. Whenever an urge comes over me to do something, I think of Errol Knox,[16] who had a coronary at the same time as I did. He went back to editing one of the Melbourne newspapers and in three years was Sir Errol Knox; three months later he was the late Sir Errol Knox, so I go on loafing ... Nan is well and does not regret leaving NG [New Guinea] though a boy would be handy for the washing up, a matter in which I concur, with reason. We enjoyed our life up there but are too old for it now.[17]

In 1946 Eddy Nurse became the Director of Naval Ordnance on the return to UK of Captain Lance Spooner. The latter wrote of his deputy:

> This officer has shown exceptional ability as Inspector of Naval Ordnance and the success which has attended the local manufacture of ordnance, torpedoes and mines during the past ten years is largely due to his knowledge and perseverance. I believe it would be difficult to find an equal in the RN Inspection Department.[18]

Two years later, after twelve momentous years in post, Eddy finally left the Directorate of Naval Ordnance. His tenure was one of tremendous achievement for him, his team and Australian industry. High quality munitions of world class standard had been produced in Australia for the first time. His naval ordnance inspection regime had ensured not only the safe manufacture, but also the correct storage and use in RAN and RN ships in the Pacific. Eddy left a significant legacy and foundation that would be of immense importance as the Navy moved into the missile age.

Eddy's considerable expertise was used to positive effect when he became the Australian representative on the UK Ordnance Board. In February 1948 he and his family sailed in *Strathaven* for England for the two year appointment. This would be followed on his return to Australia by two years as the Chief Naval Representative in the Department of Supply.

In 1954 Eddy was to make one final and quite important contribution to the Navy. He was appointed for special duties to the Third Naval Member of the Naval Board, Rear Admiral Charles Clark. He was tasked with introducing planned maintenance into the Navy. This new approach would bring modern maintenance practices into the Navy, reflecting the growing complexity of ship systems and greater focus on the costs associated with through life maintenance.

On 21 November 1956, Eddy Nurse finally retired from the Navy. The *Naval Ordnance Inspection Journal* recorded Eddy's:

> ...clear vision and singleness of purpose, often in the face of determined opposition, which allowed the Branch to reach its present healthy state and we that follow in his footsteps will be forever grateful for the pioneering work that he so ably organized and directed.[19]

Norman Calder also remained in the service after the war. He continued his work as the Deputy Director of Ordnance and Underwater Weapons working closely with Eddy Nurse. On 11 March 1947 he was appointed as Secretary and Comptroller of the Household of His Excellency, the Governor-General, Sir William McKell. In that position he was responsible for the administration of the vice-regal household. Although his previous experience in Government House as an Aide-de-Camp should have boded well for the appointment, Norman was not comfortable in the position and he requested that he return to his former Directorate.

IV

Following an all too brief period in command at HMAS *Cerberus*, Harold Farncomb returned to sea on 9 November 1946 to relieve John Collins as Commodore Commanding the Australian Squadron. The war time losses of officers such as Hec Waller and Joe Burnett who were clearly destined for flag rank were once again felt by John and Harold. With his broad pendant in *Shropshire* and with *Arunta* in company, Harold sailed for Yokohama and occupation duties.

Harold Farncomb as Flag Officer Commanding His Majesty's Australian Fleet. (RAN)

In 1947, as part of the Navy's post-war revamp the Australian Squadron once again become a Fleet and on 8 June 1947 both Harold and John were promoted to Rear Admiral and became the first Naval College graduates to reach flag rank. Because of Harold's earlier promotion to Captain he was the senior of the two on the Navy List.

The Australian Fleet and its men were battle-worn. However they had still to meet operational obligations in the north and south-west Pacific. This was in the context of a desire by many in the Navy to leave the Service which was not helped by comparatively poor pay and conditions for officers and sailors alike. Harold worked to improve the Fleet's operational efficiency and encouraged Navy Office to work harder to improve pay and conditions for officers and sailors.[20] Commander Arthur Storey who commanded *Bataan* whilst Harold was commanding the Fleet wrote of him during this period:

> ... he was a fine Admiral (a bit of a gin drinker but not to excess). Keen on fleet exercises and sport. In summary strict but fair, very good brain, brave and imperturbable. Highly respected by officers and men. In my opinion the best of his product from Jervis Bay.[21]

Notwithstanding Storey's assessment, Harold by this time was heavily dependent on alcohol. His steward Chief Petty Officer Allen Guthrie, who had great respect for Harold, related in later life that his Admiral was a great connoisseur of wine and would often lend him books on fine wines. Guthrie, who had first served as his steward in *Perth,* remained astonished by both Harold's ability to consume large quantities of alcohol which on a typical day alongside consisted of three large bottles of beer (the first at 11 am), half a bottle of gin and a quarter of a bottle of vermouth plus wines. On one occasion when *Australia* was in Melbourne, Harold hosted the State Governor Sir Dallas Brooks to lunch, after which they drank a bottle of whisky between them to remarkably little effect.[22]

Commander Richard Peek, who was then on Harold Farncomb's personal staff recalled one Saturday morning in Fleet Headquarters that he was heading off early to see his young son at Harold's insistence. Before leaving Peek went to see the Admiral in his office. Harold had a glass of neat gin on his desk. Asked if he needed anything Harold good naturedly replied, 'Peek have I ever given you the impression I need you?'[23]

Those close to Harold, such as Harry Showers, linked his battle with alcoholism with his near continuous sea service during the war.[24] The statistics underscore Harry's judgement. Harold spent 78 months of the war in command at sea. This is compared to 54 months for Harry and 38 months for John Collins.

Since Frank Getting's widow Hazel had married Robert Coman, the Farncombs had maintained close contact. In 1949 the Comans, with their four-year old daughter Susan, visited Australia. On a rainy Sunday, 19 June the Comans came onboard the flagship *Australia*, then alongside Garden Island in Sydney for the christening of their daughter. Harold and Jean Farncomb were the proud godparents and in time-honoured tradition Susan's name was inscribed on the inside of the cruiser's bell.[25]

The Comans were destined to see more of the Farncombs for, in early 1950, Harold was appointed to the Australian Embassy in Washington as the Head of its Joint Services Staff. The Ambassador was the former Navy Minister Norman Makin, who Harold knew well. It was in many respects a position which would use both Harold's extensive personal connections, particularly with the US Navy, but also in preparation for him to replace

John Collins as Chief of Naval Staff. On a personal note while the position would allow Harold to potentially regain his health, it was a tremendous challenge for him to control his drinking in the legendary Washington cocktail circuit.

It was decided that Harold Farncomb's tenure in Washington would only be two years and that, based on Admiralty advice, Harold should serve in a policy or naval aviation area of the Admiralty for twelve months. Harold was expected to become Chief of Naval Staff in 1954.[26]

These plans soon went awry. The modest workload combined with the many social engagements saw Harold Farncomb's alcohol consumption increase from its already prodigious level. Harold later said that he was consuming a bottle of gin a day in addition to that consumed as part of official hospitality.[27] Matters came to a head in July 1950 with the arrival of Prime Minister Menzies for an official visit. Harold was among the welcoming delegation at Dulles Airport. The flight was delayed for five hours and during the waiting period Harold fortified himself with gin. When Menzies did arrive, Harold missed his grasp when attempting to shake hands.[28] Whether it was based on that incident or other observations during Menzies' visit, the Prime Minister wanted Harold replaced. On 24 February 1951 it was announced in the press that Harold had retired from the Navy, 'because of his private affairs'.[29] The real reason for Harold's departure was not widely known and Rupert Long wrote of the news that, 'Farncomb's retirement is indeed a blow and I think to Naval prestige. Surely someone could have kept him employed. I hope he has a satisfactory job to go to'.[30] Coincidentally Harold's contribution to the Navy was recognised that month by the citizens of Narooma on the south coast of NSW when they named a new street after him and another after John Collins.[31]

V

While Harold Farncomb was enduring these travails, John Collins' career continued on its upward trajectory. After leaving the Australian Squadron in 1946 he and Phyllis returned to the UK where John attended the Imperial Defence College. This was to prepare him for the most senior positions in the Service but also to help restore his vitality after his war service. Whilst in London, the visiting Queen Wilhelmina of the Netherlands invested John with the Commander Cross of the Order of Oranje Nassau for his service in the Java Campaign.

On 24 February 1948, after his return to Australia, John Collins replaced Admiral Sir Louis Hamilton as the Chief of Naval Staff. At forty-nine years old he was the youngest officer to ever hold that post. Hamilton, while he admired John as a sea officer had misgivings about his selection for the position. He wrote to the First Sea Lord, Admiral Sir John Cunningham (who had succeeded Sir Andrew Cunningham) that he was, 'quite certain he had neither the background or experience to build up a modern Navy from scratch'.[32] Hamilton had advocated to Prime Minister Chifley that a more experienced RN Admiral such as Sir Wilfred Patterson who had commanded the Australian Squadron in 1939 should be selected while John gained further experience in the Admiralty. Hamilton had sensed the strong desire by, 'the wild men in the Cabinet to put in an Australian'[33] while he thought the Secretary of the Defence Department, Sir Frederick Shedden wanted to see the back of troublesome RN Admirals.

John Collins for his part had been also concerned about his relative lack of experience. While attending the Imperial Defence College he had called on Admiral Sir John Cunningham to discuss his situation. Both were keenly aware that one possibility was that if John was not selected then the Australian Government would pick Rear Admiral George Moore, then Flag Officer in Command New South Wales. Because of his age Moore could on promotion potentially serve as First Naval Member for up to seven years—a prospect neither Cunningham nor John relished.[34]

As expected Prime Minister Chifley was insistent that, like the other two services, an Australian should head the Navy.[35] Although John Collins may well have lacked recent Admiralty experience, he had worked there in the 1930s and had been acting Chief of Naval Staff in 1939. In addition, unlike an incoming British Admiral, he understood the Australian defence environment and knew the key men with whom he would have to work. Soon after his appointment *The Argus* wrote of John, 'He has great ability and also a remarkably attractive personality which has won him hosts of admirers both in and outside the service'.[36]

In addition to his concern about his preparation for the post, John Collins was also aware of the financial implications of his early appointment to First Naval Member, noting the retirement age for a flag officer was 60 years of age. This bears explanation. For those of the Pioneer Class remaining in the Navy a key consideration was when could they financially afford to leave the Service. Unlike their British counterparts, who had a pension scheme, RAN officers could instead only defer a proportion of their fortnightly pay to sustain them in retirement. This lump sum would then have to be invested, typically with an insurance company to enable them to receive an annuity. Calculations would have to be made by individuals as to whether they would have enough to sustain themselves for their remaining years. Key factors were the number and age of their children as well as if they had managed to buy their own home during their naval service. If not the latter, then the deposit and loan repayments could absorb a significant portion of the deferred pay.

There was a growing need for a pension scheme if Defence going to be able to have sufficient men and women in peacetime. In 1946, Captain Harry Howden wrote a submission to the Naval Board in which he wrote:

> Many officers—particularly those who come by experience to a realisation of the responsibilities attaching to marriage and the upbringing of a family—are deeply disturbed concerning their future and its relation to the welfare of their wives and families, as they know, as indeed all must know who care to consider the matter, that the deferred pay their wives will receive in the event of death is wholly inadequate to provide housing, food and clothing for a mother and family compatible with their requirements from every reasonable, realistic and practical point of view.[37]

Actuarial analysis revealed that a Captain on retirement, would receive only an annuity of £352 compared to about £1,020 if he was on a pension similar to his RN counterparts.[38] It was also suggested by Howden that the deferred pay scheme had undesirable social side-effects such as naval officers having fewer children[39] and that, 'son after father, generation after generation, has played its special part in adding lustre to the Royal Navy'.[40] While issues such as inter-generational recruitment are complex, it was certainly true that those members of the Pioneer Class who had continued to serve during the interwar period had fewer children than those who had left the Navy. Only the sons of Norman Calder and Joe Burnett joined the Navy.

In 1948 the Defence Force Retirement Benefits (DFRB) Scheme was introduced which finally offered a pension on retirement. Members of the Pioneer Class therefore had the option to transfer to the DFRB and forego their deferred pay. It was not an easy decision for one feature of the DFRB Scheme was that it calculated service only from 21 years of age on the dubious logic that before that men were under training. This was a source of some rancour, particularly in the Navy where some officers and sailors had been under enemy fire from as early as 16 years of age.

Harry Showers as Second Naval Member had been heavily involved in the advocacy for development of the DFRB. He thought it a disgrace that sailors did not have any pension to fall back on. Through his work in helping develop the DFRB, Harry came to greatly admire Prime Minister Chifley for his support of this long overdue reform. On reflecting on his own naval career Harry assessed that his work on the pension scheme was his greatest contribution to the Navy.[41]

Hugh MacKenzie, whose former life in New Britain could not be resumed because of repeated bouts of Blackwater fever and malaria, had remained in the Navy. It was a wrench, for both he and Betty greatly missed their life on their beautiful plantation. By 1948 Hugh was working in the Fleet Headquarters as a watch-keeping staff officer under Captain James 'Copper' Morrow. Hugh had calculated that he would be in a position to retire modestly by 1949. He and Betty had firmed their plans and they decided to remain in Sydney.

On 14 September 1948 Hugh was duty staff officer. This required him to monitor signals from the Fleet at sea and call Morrow or the Admiral if there was anything untoward during the night. As such there was a cabin in the nineteenth century Fleet Headquarters building for the duty officer to retire to of an evening. On that day Hugh had been training his relief Lieutenant Commander Robert Kerruish on the duties and they dined together. They then played dice until about 1.30 am when Kerruish went home. During that time, they each had eight whiskies, although Kerruish assessed that Hugh was none the worse for wear. Hugh then retired to the duty cabin which was located on the first floor of the headquarters above what was originally a ballroom, but since had been used for holding court martials.

Just after 6 am the following morning a sailor found Hugh on the floor of the court martial room in a pool of blood. He had fallen from a small first floor balcony and hit the light fitting during his fall. Hugh was in considerable pain and while awaiting the Garden Island doctor and ambulance he was given a brandy. On arrival Surgeon Lieutenant Francis Archibald found Hugh had suffered a deep laceration to the left side of his forehead and fractured his left forearm, left leg and probably three ribs. In shock but still lucid, Hugh was rushed to Concord Repatriation General Hospital. On examination Hugh had remarkably not sustained a fractured skull or brain damage from the seven metre fall.

During his recovery in hospital Hugh reflected that he must have been sleep-walking and had fallen over the balcony balustrade to the floor below. Although feeling 'lousy' Hugh was soon back to being his optimistic self. He told one of his visitors, 'I am lucky to be alive. I think that I got out of the whole thing lightly'.[42] His doctors told him it would be a slow recovery. On 19 September Hugh unexpectedly had a bout of vomiting and died. A post-mortem and coronial inquest was held. The coroner concluded:

> Effect of injuries accidentally received when he fell or stepped over a balustrade at naval headquarters, Potts Point onto the floor of the court martial room. The evidence adduced does not enable how he came to fall or step over the balustrade but it is probable that he was sleepwalking at the time.[43]

The Coroner's assessment was based on Hugh's statement to Dr. Francis Archibald at Concord Hospital that he had sleep-walked as a youth but had not done so for some years. Archibald noted it was 'typical' that 'after harrowing experiences the sleep-walking may recur'.[44]

The medical cause of Hugh's death was paralytic ileus or paralysis of the small bowel which caused both the bowel and the stomach to swell. The doctor who conducted the post-mortem thought the condition, while not usually resulting from the shock of a fall, was more likely in the case of Hugh, who had repeated instances of Blackwater fever and malaria. It would appear that although the condition was not normally fatal, it unfortunately took some time for the accurate diagnosis to be made and the corresponding treatment given.[45]

For Hugh to die so unexpectedly in this way, after all the dangers he survived in New Britain and Guadacanal, shocked his many friends. Hugh's engaging personality made him a much loved figure within the Pioneer Class and the coast watchers. His fatal accident was perfunctorily reported in *The Sydney Morning Herald* but without noting the significance of the man.[46] Eric Feldt later wrote of 'Hughie':

> The coast watching service was lucky the day it got MacKenzie, for this man, who completely lacked the qualities of salesmanship and showmanship, was to fill brilliantly one of the most dramatic and responsible assignments of the battle for Guadacanal.[47]

VI

On 25 January 1946 Winn Reilly left the Navy. While Winn did not receive any medallic recognition for his outstanding work leading the degaussing organization, he was confirmed in rank as a Commander. This meant much to him. Initially Winn rejoined Australian Iron and Steel but found like many other veterans that men who were his juniors before the war, but did not serve in the forces, were now his seniors. He soon left and joined Clyde Engineering. This again was short lived and in 1948 Winn found professionally rewarding employment in the Non Ferrous Metal Group which was part of that loose confederation of companies controlled from Collins House in Melbourne. Winn went on to become Business Manager of Australia Bronze, which brought him to the attention of Sir Daniel McVey, the Managing Director of the parent company Metal Manufacturers Limited. Winn became Sir Daniel's personal advisor and remained in that position until McVey's retirement in 1962.[48]

Horace Thompson after leaving the service of the US Army secured a position with the NSW Water Board as a draughtsman. Adrian Watts resumed his commercial art profession with commissions such as the Hoyts movie artwork and the Myer catalogues proving to be a mainstay. In the later phase of his working career, when he had lost the facility for finally detailed artwork Adrian took on the coordination of the catalogue.

VII

For those who did not serve in the war the post-war period was also a period of change. Jack Lecky was a thrifty and successful retailer. He sold his general store at Meredin to run a series of businesses. These included a white goods store when refrigerators and washing machines were just entering the market in any numbers. He also ran a West Farmers agency and a hardware store. Jack was a notable figure in the community and for a period was Secretary of the Meredin Agricultural Society.[49] In the late 1950s Jack operated his final store on the main street of Pingelly, 150 km south east of Perth. Then in 1962 Jack's wife Ida was diagnosed with cancer and they moved to South Perth. Ida died on New Year's Eve.

Peyton Kimlin continued to combine his teaching at Manly with his studies at the Conservatorium of Music. Peyton and Myra did not have children and immersed themselves in the music and performing arts scene in Sydney. The post war period was a productive period for them both and it led to work for the Australian Broadcasting Commission (ABC). A number of his scores have survived. They include a Christmas carol called a *Beast's Christmas* and an *Allegro for Strings*.[50] In a highlight for Peyton, the *Allegro* was premiered by the Sydney Symphony Orchestra at an evening concert on 15 December 1950 and broadcast by Radio Station 2BL.

Ben Howells also continued his teaching career at Footscray Tech. In March 1947 his wife Dorothy became President of the Federation of Mothers' Clubs which ran to over 200 affiliated clubs. Under Dorothy's dynamic leadership by 1953 it had grown to 500 clubs representing 45,000 women.[51] The clubs, besides providing support to mothers, also advocated for improvements in education, heath and road safety. Dorothy during her seventeen years as President was an influential opinion maker whose views were regularly reported in the press. Notably she pushed for improved conditions for women and in a 1953 speech said, 'It was high time that mother ceased to be the only member of the family who doesn't get time off' and it was time mothers 'took a stand'.[52] Ben was immensely proud of his wife's achievements and was a valued source of support and assisted in her speech writing. By 1959 the Mothers' Clubs had grown even larger to 850 clubs representing 65,000 women. Dorothy travelled widely in Victoria and in addition to the Mother's Clubs she became Vice President of the Australian Council of Schools Association. Deservedly Dorothy was made an MBE in the 1959 Queen's Birthday Honours List.

VIII

On assuming command of the Navy, John Collins joined his other service counterparts, both 1st AIF Gallipoli veterans, Lieutenant General Sir Vernon Sturdee and Air Marshal George Jones. Because he was a newly promoted Rear Admiral (and one rank junior to the other Service Chiefs) John Collins had to wait until May 1950 when he had the required time in rank to be promoted to Vice Admiral. The Service Chiefs and their departments still remained in Melbourne. This was in contrast to the increasing majority of government departments which had moved to the nation's capital. Bill Riordan was the first of five Navy Ministers John would serve; he had surprised and impressed Admiral Hamilton with his conscientious application to the position.[53] The average tenure of each of these Ministers was just twenty months. But with each Minister John appreciated their challenge to get across such a unique portfolio and he worked to assist them in their role.[54] While nominally a member of the Naval Board, it was rare for the Minister to attend.[55]

The other key figure John Collins had to work with was Sir Frederick Shedden. In post since 1937, he was a formidable public servant who had been heavily relied upon by Menzies, Curtin and Chifley during the war years. Admiral Colvin described Shedden in the following terms:

> ... always had the ear of the Prime Minister and could generally get the Chiefs of Staff's view and wishes overridden. Still ... he was an able and knowledgeable man and though one couldn't trust him personally his views were generally sound.[56]

Admiral Hamilton had a more difficult relationship with Shedden.[57] With the absence of a Chief of Defence Force position, Shedden was well placed to play off the Service Chiefs and from February 1948 he became chair of the Defence Committee.

John Collins well knew that within Navy Office the civilian Secretary of the Department of Navy was a key figure in the Navy's smooth administration. His support was critical to getting many things accomplished. The Secretary on John's arrival was Alfred 'Nanky' Nankervis. The consummate public servant, he had been Secretary since 1939 and had largely been with the Navy since 1915. John had, of course, worked closely with Nankervis at the outbreak of the war when Assistant Chief of Naval Staff. Nankervis' long tenure finally came to end in 1950. He was replaced by the Assistant Secretary Tom Hawkins who had also joined Navy Office in 1915. Like Nankervis, he was an outstanding public servant, his corporate memory was priceless and Hawkins did much for the Navy. Robert Hyslop, that peerless observer of naval administration, wrote:

> Unlike some other Naval officers, Collins was able to see beyond Tom's irascibility with uniformed officers when they made adverse reflections on the civil administration. Collins and Hawkins were both highly competent, Hawkins with long experience in the department and Collins a shrewd reader of the political shifts. They worked effectively together.[58]

In terms of broad Defence policy there was a surprising resurgence in Commonwealth defence planning and cooperation that seemed to belie

John Collins worked constructively with five Navy Ministers. Here he is with his fourth Minister Mr William McMahon at the 1952 Naval College Graduation Ceremony presenting prizes to Cadet Midshipman Peter Hocker.
(*The Argus*/State Library of Victoria)

the eclipse of British power. This development had the strong support of Sir Frederick Shedden among others. For his part John Collins wanted to maintain a close relationship with both US and the UK, each for different but complementary reasons. The US was now unquestionably the pre-eminent naval and military power and the RAN would clearly work as part of an integrated naval force in any future major conflict. On the other hand the UK and its Navy was still the source of ships and training as well as technical and professional advice. In addition, with the reestablishment of Britain in its Pacific colonies there was still an expectation that there would be a significant British presence east of Suez.

It had become a long established practice for the RAN First Naval Member and the RN First Sea Lord to exchange regular private correspondence in which views were exchanged on policy and force structure. When an RN officer was the First Naval Member their letters at times were very critical of the Australian political and defence landscape. In the new paradigm with the First Naval Member now an Australian,

John Collins maintained this correspondence. He wrote twenty-eight letters to three First Sea Lords and it is clear that he still viewed the RN as the 'parent' navy. Gone was any domestic political commentary. Instead John used the correspondence as an effective means to seek information or gain assistance in an expeditious way. The letters also provide an insight into John's approach as the Chief of Naval Staff.

In respect to future defence capabilities, the dominance of the aircraft carrier in the Pacific theatre during World War II had made it imperative for the RAN to embrace this shift away from battleships and cruisers. During Admiral Hamilton's tenure the foundations had been laid for the introduction into service of two light fleet aircraft carriers and the establishment of a Fleet Air Arm. The pair of aircraft carriers—*Sydney* and *Melbourne*—were selected from the clutch of partly built and laid up British ships where work had been halted with the sudden end of World War II. When completed *Sydney* was a cost-effective acquisition with an outlay of only £2.7 million, including aircraft and stores. As the Navy would later learn the real costs lay in updating and maintaining the capability. The Commonwealth vision was for Australia, Canada, India, and possibly even New Zealand, possess task groups built around light fleet carriers and contributing to the post-war stability.

On becoming Chief of Naval Staff John Collins had to steward through the introduction of the most complex warships yet to enter RAN service. Before his time Air Marshal Jones had strongly argued for the RAAF to operate the carriers' air wings but Hamilton, the old naval aviator that he was, had saved the Fleet Air Arm from a still birth. There were therefore many eyes watching the Navy's efforts. John was fortunate in having two senior officers with carrier command experience to help oversee this undertaking. They were Harold Farncomb commanding the Fleet and John's Imperial Defence College classmate Commodore Guy Willoughby, RN who was both Fourth Naval Member and Commodore (Air) responsible for aviation matters and the development of the fledgling Fleet Air Arm.[59]

John Collins worked assiduously to ensure that the introduction of aircraft carriers into the RAN was a success. Here the new HMAS Sydney *visits Melbourne for the first time on 18 May 1949. (The Argus/State Library of Victoria)*

Although the intent was to operate two carriers that would be able to undertake both trade protection and strike against enemy fleets, John Collins soon understood that this would be unattainable. The issue was the complexity of rapidly changing technology. This situation required of him a sophisticated level of engagement with Government and the senior echelons of Defence. While the issues were multifarious, the kernel of the problem was that aircraft carriers now needed to embark jet fighters for them to remain operationally effective. The size of the light fleet carriers made them marginal for these faster, larger and heavier aircraft. While this was less of a problem for the US with their larger aircraft carriers, the UK struggled to both design new aircraft and make them work on smaller flight decks. To make matters worse the likely outcome of the developmental work swung in the balance. On September 1948 John wrote to Admiral Sir Bruce Fraser to say:

> [The letter] of 27th August received here today states 'modernized Majestic' [ie *Melbourne*] will be capable of operating new trade protection type aircraft only. This is such a shattering blow.[60]

In the end a decision was taken to equip *Melbourne* with jet aircraft with associated changes such as an angled flight deck and new launch and landing systems. The ship did not commission until 1955.

Through his correspondence to the First Sea Lord, John Collins was able to obtain the loan of the carrier HMS *Vengeance* to cover the gap. The successful introduction of the aircraft carrier capability into the RAN was an abiding focus for John. In 1948 he wrote:

> ... no war is won on defensive measures alone. We must have offensive weapons to use, particularly in relation to our commitments under the United Nations and as a member of the British Commonwealth. Our Light Fleet Carriers provide the offensive weapon and must retain first priority.[61]

The other major Fleet issue for John Collins was the transition from a fleet of old cruisers, destroyers, frigates and corvettes to a more modern force. Initially he hoped to replace his three cruisers for two new ships, but the RN did not contemplate building any more cruisers for the foreseeable future. Funding constraints and the looming prospect of guided missiles being fitted to such ships made the cruiser issue as opaque as that of aircraft carriers.[62]

In respect to the remainder of the surface fleet the RAN sought a smaller sized flotilla of modern destroyers and frigates able to counter faster jet aircraft and more capable submarines. As the Cold War took shape the contest in the maritime domain would be focused on countering the growing and imposing Russian submarine fleet. Once again John had inherited the start of the program with a pair of Battle Class destroyers, *Anzac* and *Tobruk*, under construction.[63] The new Russian submarines were faster than the German U-boats. In a 1948 Navy Office minute to John he was told:

> It can be seen that the RAN does not possess a single vessel capable of dealing effectively with a submarine with a submerged speed of 16 knots, all destroyers fitted obsolete weapons and equipment. This is considered to be a matter requiring immediate action in view of the fact that Russia has 16 knot submarines, and that the frigates are too slow to deal effectively with such craft.[64]

The short term response by the RAN and Allied navies was to convert some of the younger World War II destroyers into anti-submarine frigates. In the RAN, Q-Class destroyers were modernized into anti-submarine frigates using British plans and in John's assessment they proved a great success.

There was however, a need to place the Navy's new construction program on a firm foundation. John's view was that it was essential to maintain local shipbuilding which had expanded during the war. He was mindful that during the war the majority of anti-submarine escorts had been built locally and the shipbuilding capability had proved invaluable when it came to battle damage repair and modernization. In 1950 John successfully advocated in the Defence Committee to support a local shipbuilding industry. This Defence position was taken to Cabinet.[65] In May 1950 the Menzies Government agreed to continued local construction, not only for warships, but also of coastal and bulk cargo shipping. Menzies recognized the importance of a rolling program and took note of the efficiencies at the Evans Deakin shipyard as a case study:

> Despite considerable increases in wages and material costs over the past three years, the Company has advised it anticipates there will be a saving to the Commonwealth of £16,000. This result was due mainly to the increase of efficiency, methods of construction and improved shipyard facilities, but the greatest single factor contributing to the improvement so far achieved is that the vessels for the first time since the Company was established have been produced quickly because it was able, with orders on hand, to avoid intermittent employment of various shipyard trades.[66]

Despite this success, money was tight and the Navy's long term aspirations for a dozen locally built destroyers would remain unrealised. This was because of competing demands for Government outlays, rising costs associated with increasingly more complex ships and delays in obtaining production drawings from the UK. As such, fewer of the successor *Daring* Class destroyers were built as were fewer old destroyers converted to frigates. In contemplating how to rejuvenate the fleet in a tight fiscal environment John Collins even considered acquiring former US destroyers but thought on balance their adoption would, 'cause tremendous logistic problems'.[67]

The second focus for John Collins during his tenure was personnel. Largely driven by the introduction of the aircraft carrier, the Navy needed

John Collins in his early days as Chief of Naval Staff. He is still a Rear Admiral and with a picture of the new HMAS Sydney *on his desk.* (RAN)

to expand its personnel strength from its 1948 nadir. By 1952 it had to grow to nearly 15,000. In addition, both John and Harold Farncomb were keenly aware that specific expertise was needed, particularly in the area of aviation. Once again John used his direct link with the First Sea Lord to good effect. The RN, which in contrast was having to reduce its personnel strength, was the primary source of this skilled manpower. Over 1,000 men and their families migrated to a new life in Australia. They were joined by aviators from the broader Commonwealth who had emigrated to Australia and wanted to continue flying from carriers.

This influx of skilled officers and sailors was timely, for on 25 June 1950 the North Korean Army, without provocation, invaded South Korea. At that time Australia could provide for the United Nations response forces from the occupation forces in Japan. The quickest to the scene were the

RAAF's 77 Squadron Mustang fighters, the RAN's destroyer *Bataan* and the frigate *Shoalhaven*. For the next three years the Navy provided destroyers and frigates to bombard coastal targets and even those up the navigationally treacherous Han River. The conditions in winter were appalling.

The most notable contribution was the deployment of the aircraft carrier *Sydney* to relieve the British *Glory*. John Collins was initially reluctant for her deployment until the possibility of an escalation of the conflict was better understood. *Sydney's* performance was outstanding, due in large part to the fact that three quarters of her aircrew had World War II service.

The Korean War commitment both energised and severely stretched the Navy. In a welcome move John Collins gained Government approval in July 1950 to reinstitute the WRANS and fortunately the administrative hurdles in their reestablishment were fewer than those experienced by Jack Newman in 1942. The revitalized WRANS, while initially only comprising 300 women, yet again proved themselves to be indispensable to the Navy.

The other major personnel issue John Collins had to deal with was the 1951 introduction of National Service. For the Navy the scheme was a mixed blessing because of the longer upfront training a sailor needed compared to his Army counterpart. John was able to negotiate that for the Navy that naval national servicemen would undertake 124 days initial training compared to 98 days for the Army and then serve for 13 days a year for the next four years compared to 14 days for six years in the Army. To train and employ the National Servicemen, four corvettes were recommissioned.[68]

The third focus for John in his tenure in command was the closer and more formalized cooperation between RAN, USN, RN and RNZN. Usefully in 1948 the British, Australian and New Zealand governments had entered into the ANZAM Pact for the defence of the Malayan area. This included the adjoining sea lines of communication. John was keenly aware of the need to better understand US Navy planning and how best to coordinate efforts. In the same year he visited the Commander-in-Chief Pacific, Admiral DeWitt Ramsey in Honolulu to formulate how the US and the ANZAM navies might delineate, in a geographic sense, their responsibilities for ensuring the free flow of maritime trade. These responsibilities included convoy routing, reconnaissance, anti-submarine warfare and search and rescue. The 1948 meeting commenced discussions and more substantive progress was made in two meetings in 1951 with the new US Commander-in-Chief Pacific, Admiral Arthur Radford. Both men knew each other when they served as part of Halsey's 3rd Fleet at the end of World War II. What is clear from examination of Admiral Radford's papers is that both men developed an excellent rapport and through their personal engagement an agreement for cooperation was developed.[69] It became known as the Radford-Collins Agreement. While there was some concern by Shedden and others that the Agreement should have had greater Defence and Government input, it formed a useful document for the soon to be ratified ANZUS Treaty and remained a foundation document of naval cooperation for generations.

During his extended tenure John and Phyllis experienced some of the greatest high and low points of their married life. In the 1951 New Year's Honours List, John was made a Knight Commander in the Order of the British Empire. He was the first RAN officer to be knighted in seventeen years.[70] Two years later however, Phyllis suffered severe burns when the fumes of a cleaning solvent she was using were ignited by a radiator and a large dish of the solvent caught fire. John also sustained burns to his hands while trying to extinguish the fire.[71] Phyllis' recovery in hospital and then at home was painful and slow. For many months John limited his time away from Melbourne to attend to his wife. It was also during this period that John took up for relaxation the hobby of book binding. The patience and skill required to be proficient made it an absorbing interest. Examples of John's work as well as his monograph, *The Handfinishing Tools as used in Bookbinding*, are held in the New South Wales State Library.[72]

John Collins arriving in Honolulu on 24 February 1951 and met by Admiral Arthur Radford. Their talks built on a strong personal rapport resulted in the strategically important Radford-Collins Agreement. (JA Collins Collection)

Over his nearly seven years in office, John Collins' war service came back to the fore through correspondence or visits from old comrades. Admiral Helfrich commenced the writing of his two volume memoirs and sought out the views of John about the 1942 campaign. In particular the Dutch Admiral was stung by criticism that he had needlessly sacrificed men and ships. In December 1948 John diplomatically and no doubt sincerely replied that:

> Referring to your remarks on the Java Sea Battle, I think the acid test is whether, if one were faced with the same set of circumstances, one would do the same thing. Having put in *Exeter, Perth* and the British destroyers, I naturally have asked myself this question, and after much thought have concluded that I would, and that, had the luck been on our side, far reaching results might have been obtained. It is so easy to be wise after the event.[73]

The anniversary of the victory at the Battle of the Coral Sea became a touchstone for the bond between Australia and the United States. In successive years former senior US military and naval leaders visited

Australia to a warm reception. In 1950 Admiral Radford attended and in the following year John Collins' former commander Admiral Thomas Kinkaid made the journey. The old admiral and his wife were feted in Brisbane, Sydney and Melbourne. Of Kinkaid's Melbourne speech, *The Argus* reported on its front page, 'With all the zest of a refreshing sea breeze an American Admiral blew into Melbourne last night and said bluntly that there was no need for fears about a third world war starting'.[74] While downplaying a possible global conflict, Kinkaid said that naval power would play an important role in any future smaller conflicts in the Pacific.[75] He went on to say that he was delighted to see that the RAN was in the 'safe hands' of his old comrade Vice Admiral Sir John Collins.[76]

The final concern for John Collins was his own relief. With the resignation of Harold Farncomb there were but two options. Extend his own tenure until his now logical successor Roy Dowling was ready, or seek a British admiral for one term. In sounding out the latter option in 1952 John wrote to the then First Sea Lord Admiral Sir Rhoderick McGrigor with a proposal of obtaining on exchange a Vice Admiral with John being offered in return for service with the RN. This would allow him to get closer to his retirement age. In response McGrigor suggested this would be feasible with the post of Commander-in-Chief, East Indies a possibility.[77] The Australian Government was not attracted to this option. Instead John's service was once again extended until 1955 when he was relieved by Roy Dowling. As to his immediate future, John wrote wistfully to Admiral McGrigor:

> For myself I am still in doubt. The only offer that has been made so far is to relieve Rear Admiral Moore as Minister at Manila, which does not appeal to me. If that's the best they can do (remember, we unlike the RN are supposed to serve to our retiring age) then I must get myself discharged and look to big business or such like. I have no desire for the farm and unfortunately no Governorships become vacant for upwards of two years.[78]

As John commenced his last year as Chief of Naval Staff news came of the death of Duncan Grant. The man John considered to be the greatest influence on the Naval College and the Pioneer Class[79] passed away on

5 February 1955 at his home in Haywards Heath with his family by his side. For the past five years he had endured the incapacity of an amputated leg and used a wheelchair for mobility. It was a difficult existence for such a hitherto physically active man. He had a maxim that he instilled into his two sons and young naval officers that they should be proficient at the four basic games for success in life—golf, tennis, bridge and poker.[80] Tragically his son Trevor who had followed in Duncan's footsteps and became a naval physical training instructor took his own life two years after Duncan's death. He was just 31 years of age. They were buried side by side. The shared cross has the inscription under Duncan Grant's name—*He played the Game*.[81]

1955 was also the year that the thirteen-year old entry to the Naval College came to an end. It was a decision that John Collins made with regret. However, the RN had already ended this early age of entry and since 1951 the Naval College had very successfully introduced an Intermediate Entry which took a ready number of 15 to 16 year old boys who had already obtained an Intermediate Certificate.[82]

On the eve of John Collins' retirement as Chief of Naval Staff, Eddy Nurse wrote to John to congratulate him on his success and wishing him well for the future. John replied:

> Dear 'Mum' ... I assure you that the greatest requirement is one over which a person has little control—namely to be in the right spot at the right moment.[83]

Timing had certainly been a fortuitous element of John's career but it of course went beyond this. He continued:

> My basic rule has been what I call 'leading marks'. Know where you are going, select good leading marks and see that you keep them in line—and don't let your attention wander too much. There is the time when a new set of leads are required for the next course. Pick them out in good time and alter course so that they are 'on' when you are on the new course.[84]

Looking to the future, John maintained the navigational theme:

> At the moment however I cannot select my leading marks for I don't know what my next course is, or where I am going! I have been offered one diplomatic post which does not appeal, so I await eventualities.[85]

After refusing the Manila post, that eventuality was to be Australian High Commissioner to New Zealand which he readily accepted. Phyllis' family on her mother's side hailed from New Zealand and John had always enjoyed the country and its people.

IX

Like most of his class mates James Esdaile had to financially secure his future. After overseeing the Navy's demobilization he retired from the service in 1950. James successfully took up egg and poultry farming in Upper Beaconsfield on the eastern outskirts of Melbourne.

Earlier to embark on a second career in private enterprise was Rupert Long. Although an Acting Commander since 1940 Rupert was only made a substantive Commander on his transfer to retirement from the permanent Navy on 4 January 1946. This promotion was on the condition that it did not result any consequential increase in his pay.[86] While a tight cap was kept on promotions, many of Rupert's friends nevertheless considered that as he had performed his duties in such an exemplary manner more generosity should have been shown to him. If there was any consolation for Rupert, it was that there were other officers with extended periods of acting rank who were also not confirmed in the higher rank prior to retirement. To his credit Rupert did not complain and only remarked:

> I must have a crust to chew on in my old age, even if it is only one dipped in water and not very tasty. That is, if I succeed in living to an old age.[87]

Like many Rupert was worn out from the war and this is reflected in a letter to his friend Ted Sayers in October 1945:

> I have spent 33 years in the Navy and the last 12 have not been happy, being solely because I saw war coming and because war was on. I am heartily tired of big organisations and being a small cog in a machine which heaves over so extraordinarily slowly.[88]

He went on to say:

> Australia is in one hell of a mess, but as far as I can see, so is all the world. Two percent of the people in Australia are nasty dirty rats, and eight percent are stupid coots who are out on their own make.

The remaining ninety percent are, without doubt, the cleanest and nicest people in the world and both look it and act like it.

I am leaving Australia probably for its own good, but in any case because I cannot see here the work I want to do in the future. At least I think I must find that work overseas before I can come back here to do it.[89]

Rupert was offered some positions in the post-war intelligence and security organisations but the details remain sketchy. There were also overseas positions including in the US that did not eventuate for a variety of reasons. In 1946 Rupert, with Vera's strong support, decided to enter the business world. While he could probably have found a position in Sir Walter Carpenter's reduced business empire, he elected to strike out on his own. That year he founded RMB Long Engineering with an office in Collins Street in Melbourne. The focus of the business was both engineering consultancy and the provision of industrial, mining and nuclear equipment.

Soon thereafter the Long family moved to Sydney to be, among other things, close to Vera's family. Rupert soon refreshed his many business and political connections in the city. An important connection was Vera's brother-in-law George Proud of the prominent jewellers, Prouds Ltd. George had reputedly helped Rupert in obtaining intelligence in Asia before the war[90] and Rupert agreed to establish a nautical instruments retail division of Prouds Ltd in George Street. This was in addition to his engineering business in which his friend from the Volunteer Coastal Patrol, Harold Nobbs had become a business partner.

Back in the early 1920s Rupert first met Frank de Groot, infamous for cutting the ribbon at the 1932 opening of the Sydney Harbour Bridge ahead of Premier Jack Lange. Long and de Groot remained firm friends and shared similar conservative political views. Both men maintained regular and fulsome correspondence during the 1950s and it is through Rupert's surviving letters that his increasingly wide array of business and political interests can be gleaned.

By 1951 Rupert had joined the Liberal Party and was convinced to nominate for the Federal seat of Barton for the election that year. The French Resistance heroine Nancy Wake, however, was selected to contest the seat against the sitting member Dr. HV Evatt. Rupert also sought but failed to obtain a Liberal endorsement to fill a NSW Senate seat.[91] He later wrote of the experience:

> I had no luck with my attempt at a political career—thank goodness. I nominated because I was asked to and because I felt that it was time I talked more than just around a coffee table about the ills of Australia and the dangerous position in which she stood. From a purely personal point of view I have no desire to be a politician. If I had succeeded in being selected and perhaps in winning my way into Parliament, it would have been at a tremendous personal sacrifice. However the field was much too strong for me and I was saved all that worry.[92]

Later in 1951 an unprecedented 'movement' led by the Chief Justice of Victoria Sir Edmund Herring called 'Call to the Nation' arose involving other judges, church leaders and largely conservative elements of society. Alarmed by what was seen as Cold War dangers abroad and 'moral and intellectual apathy'[93] in Australia the 'Call' issued a declaration for moral renewal entitled, 'A Call to the People of Australia',[94] which exhorted citizens to play more active parts in public affairs. At the behest of his friend Paul McGuire, Rupert became involved and soon was the NSW Secretary. He had initially not wanted to join this 'Cold War Army' but changed his mind after the defeat of the 1951 referendum to ban the Communist Party of Australia. Rupert reasoned that it was not a secret army behind the 'Call' but, 'an army of education'.[95] By February the 'Call' had grown and led Rupert to tell de Groot that:

> The movement is, in fact, rapidly albeit quietly, developing despite the outcries of certain bewildered clerics who can see no reason why their own preaching should not be sufficient.[96]

Rupert's expanding business interests demanded more of his time to ensure their viability. As a result in January 1952 he resigned as State Secretary of the 'Call'.

In addition to his engineering business, Rupert now had a small rutile mining business which he hoped to be able to float on the stock exchange and sought a franchise to manufacture high quality paper pulp from quick-growing plants such as bamboo, kunai and kenaf. Rupert correctly reasoned that in the future there would be a growing Asian market for paper as the region developed. Rupert tried unsuccessfully to form a syndicate to develop pulp operations in Singapore, Borneo and Sarawak as well as persuade Queensland cane growers and British interests to diversify into these plants.[97] His assessment about the potential of these plants proved sound and the three plants would be used for commercial paper production.

Separately, Rupert was hopeful of forming a titanium mining venture with another syndicate. This deal had been in the works for about two years, but like the pulp project it remained elusive. His engineering consultancy and equipment business made more solid progress and he represented some leading UK manufacturers.

During the 1950s one of the limitations, especially for small companies, was access to funds for expansion. The Government maintained particularly tight capital raising regulations. Rupert Long through much exertion was able to secure a few thousand pounds to recommence operations of the Titanium Mining Company. In respect to his rutile venture on 16 miles of beach on the north coast of NSW it was by January 1953 producing a hundred tons a week with a profit of about £25 per ton. Of the Prouds instrument subsidiary Rupert searched for investors to acquire this business. Rupert's plan was to:

> ... create, initially in Sydney, a first-grade servicing workshop for the top types of instruments, geodetic, geophysical, seismographical. No such organisation exists in Australia ... As an example, 30 instruments bought from Germany for the Woomera Range are about to be packed up and sent back to Germany for repair and adjustment ... The workmen to do the job don't exist here but I have lined up the principal world manufacturers who have agreed to send mutually satisfactory workmen out on contract.[98]

If these activities were not enough, Rupert employed up to sixteen geologists in search of tin deposits in the Northern Territory and wrote optimistically to de Groot in July 1953 that scout boring was showing, 'an extraordinary tin concentration. Have to raise more money for more boring before taking the Tin Dredging Company to the stock exchange. Let you know more in the next letter'.[99]

The tin venture did not prove a success and became another drain on Rupert's finances.[100] While he had shed his role in the 'Call' Rupert remained keenly interested in world and national politics. An imperialist to the core, counter to the prevailing view he saw bright prospects for Britain and the Commonwealth countries. Possibly coloured by his first brush with the Bolsheviks in 1919 as a sub-lieutenant, Rupert had an antipathy for Russian communism that was measured and studied. In 1953 he wrote to de Groot that it was clear from 1943 when he observed the activities of the first Russian Legation in Australia and through long talks with William S Wasserman, the head of the US Lease-Lend Mission in Canberra, that the post-war character of the world would tend to become that of two camps. The non-Russian one would tend to be dominated by the dollar. Rupert thought that:

> Nevertheless, it seems to me that the balance of power could be held by the British (the word is used in its widest sense and therefore includes the peoples of Australasia.) It remains my opinion that the extension of South-East Asia, held as a European area, is strategically essential to the non-Russian bloc. One of my jobs in post-war years has therefore been to assist anyone who holds similar views in trying to make the people of this area appreciate the important position into which destiny has thrown them.[101]

Rupert remained critical of the Americans' dislike of the British Empire. He wrote that the late President Franklin Roosevelt, 'was never an Empire administrator, and therefore failed to grasp that disorganised people require more time for tuition to be able to properly manage their own affairs without disturbance to their neighbours'.[102] Of the Russians he wrote to de Groot that:

> You will have noted that the Russian scheme, which is as much to do with true communism as my shoelace, wisely following, in 'colonial' affairs, the British/Roman example of allowing the local people to continue their method of life and their lesser organisations, superimposing

only controlling forces to guide them in the higher flights of internal administration. It is for this reason that one must fear the Russian power to expand and not because they may possess a tank or two or a few bombs more than the rest of the world.[103]

Rupert was equally pragmatic about the resurgent Japanese. Although he could not forgive them for what they had done to so many of his friends, believing that in many respects they remained 'Barbarians', he understood that, 'they do exist in the Pacific, we in Australia need to have them as friends and not enemies'.[104]

Rupert's diverse array of business interests in many respects resembled his intelligence empire of old. Few men could have had so many fingers in so many pies. His core RMB Long Engineering vied to represent leading British, German and Canadian instrument and equipment producers and even entered into local production under license of some equipment. However, Rupert was competing against larger companies. This was at a time when he and other small businessmen were handicapped by the shortage of capital for investment in Australia.[105] In 1955 Rupert wrote to de Groot that, 'although I'm rapidly going white with the strain, I'm getting a great kick out of having my own show'.[106] One of Rupert's business strategies was to stay tuned to international developments and try to be the technological market leader in Australia. In 1957 he wrote:

> It has been clear that as usual Australia is dragging many years behind the rest of the world and that he who gets in first with the new techniques can establish his position. We have done that in our particular lines but there are other lines which need to be added to them to obtain stability and strength.[107]

Never satisfied that he had enough strings to his business bow, Rupert went on to say:

> There is more business offering than we can possibly take care of being limited to having to build on profit. It is a most hazardous game but most interesting and so far the head is just above water. There are many other things I would like to do and if I can make a go of this I propose to do them.[108]

By 1958 however Rupert needed to put his businesses on a sounder and more organised footing and he split his flagship company into specialist parts. The instrument making and instrument selling/servicing each became separate companies leaving his core engineering consultancy. With each arm turning a profit, he remained optimistic. Like Harry Showers, Rupert was an enthusiastic believer in the potential for nuclear energy. There were tangible signs of progress such as the 1958 opening of the first nuclear reactor at Sutherland as a portent of things to come.[109]

In 1959 Rupert, looking to grow his engineering business, wrote to the NSW Premier Joseph Cahill who was about to embark on a trade visit to the US. Rupert had two propositions. The first was the building of a tunnel under the Hunter River to link Newcastle and Stockton using subaqueous tunnel technology developed by the New York engineers Singstad and Baillie. If this came to fruition Rupert hoped for flow on business. He also still hoped to realize the pulping of tropical grasses in the northern rivers area using the latest US technology. Although Cahill met Singstad and Baillie nothing came of both projects.[110]

Between his business and political activities Rupert retained an active interest in two projects that related to his wartime service. The first of which was the mammoth task of writing the RAN's World War II official history which had been commissioned by the Australian War Memorial. It was to be written by George Gill who had been publicity censorship liaison officer in the Naval Intelligence Division. Gill appreciated that Rupert possessed an unrivaled view of the war from his DNI vantage point. He consulted Rupert extensively and sent him draft chapters which Rupert read, 'with diligent scrutiny'.[111] Rupert was greatly touched by being asked to assist. Between 1951 and 1956 Rupert sent over forty letters, as well as red-pencilled corrections to the manuscript. This correspondence, like that with Eric Feldt during the war, contained encouragement and wisdom in Rupert's distinctive turn of phrase. Early in the project Rupert encouraged Gill to show fearlessness:

... it seems to me if history is to be truth, then quite a number of people must, at certain stages, be branded as 'stupid' or worse. I am blowed if I can see why the white-wash pail should be used by a historian although it is clear from the little I have read in the course of my life that it is frequently used, albeit principally by 'historians' writing of a good patron.[112]

Among the corrections were supporting comments such as, 'you have worked into a very smooth way of describing a naval battle'.[113] Gill greatly appreciated the support and wrote that Rupert's, 'sage counsel has been of inestimable benefit'.[114] In 1957 the first volume was published to critical acclaim.[115] The following year it received the Montague Grove Award for history.[116]

The second project was the creation a fitting memorial to Rupert's beloved 'coastwatchers'. In 1948 he suggested to Gordon Laycock, the Director of Lighthouses in New Guinea, that a lighthouse be constructed in the Coastwatchers' memory.[117] Laycock was strongly attracted to the idea and had the old and weak Madang light on Kalibobo Point in mind for replacement. As so often had been the case in the war, Walter Brooksbank (B1) played a major part in realising Rupert's plans. In August 1952 Brooksbank and a dozen of the former coastwatchers met in Rabaul and formed the Coast Watchers Memorial Committee with Walter as the Secretary and the incumbent Director of Naval Intelligence the Chairman. The wheels for another Rupert project were put in motion.

In 1954 the Government had agreed to the erection of the Coast Watchers Memorial Lighthouse. The next step was funding. Rupert Long, Eric Feldt, Walter Brooksbank and the forty or more surviving coastwatchers sought public subscriptions. Donations to the lighthouse came from Australia, New Guinea, New Zealand, the Solomons and the United States. Notable donors were two old Navy men Vice President Richard Nixon, who had come into contact with the coastwatchers when he served in Bougainville, and Fleet Admiral 'Bull' Halsey.

Construction began in early 1959 with the official opening set for 15 August that year. Rupert sought to bring together as many of the surviving coastwatchers as was possible for the occasion and the Memorial Committee set to work. With the same organisational skills as he displayed in the war, Rupert and his 'bunch of thugs' worked to make this a memorable event. Both Movietone and Cinesound newsreel companies sent crews for the opening while Rupert organised for Eric Feldt to record interviews with coastwatchers.[118] In respect to transport, a RAAF VIP Dakota was provided to bring coastwatchers and dignitaries from Australia. In addition, the US Naval Attaché, Captain Clarence White[119] who commanded a fighter squadron on Guadalcanal and had four of his pilots saved by the coastwatchers, also provided space in a US Navy aircraft for attendees. A considerable number of former coastwatchers still worked in New Guinea and the Solomons.

On the eve of the opening a reception was held onboard the frigate *Swan*. On completion everyone adjourned to the Hotel Madang. Roma Bates, the widow of former coastwatcher and Madang District Commissioner Charles Bates recalled:

> I wish I could convey to you the excitement and feeling in the air. They were gathered there en masse and everyone made a great fuss over everyone else. We hurried home to make the wreaths. The atmosphere was terrific and it was so heart-warming and wonderful.[120]

Because of poor weather in the highlands and in the Solomons some of the coastwatchers did not arrive until until hours before the late afternoon opening. As each group entered Hotel Madang there was in 'Wobby' Robinson's words a 'Hollywood arrival'[121] with heartfelt greetings from the growing gathering. They included 'Kassa' Townsend with whom Eric Feldt had first served in 1924. There was particular emotion as small teams from former isolated coastwatching outposts were reunited. The group from Mount Hagen had brought with them pigs for the forty native coastwatchers and Luluais who were accommodated in the nearby native camp. Among them were Paramount Luluai Golpak and Sergeant Yauwiga. Roma Bates wrote:

> ... throughout Saturday the roads were thronged with natives heading towards the Lighthouse and by afternoon all the enclosures were packed, every tree dripped with spectators.[122]

The Coastwatchers Memorial Lighthouse at Madang. (AWM)

Standing proud on the point was the imposing and futuristic white lighthouse. It stood 30 metres high supported by fins on a base of red terrazzo tiles. At 5 pm the opening ceremony commenced with the coastwatchers and their native comrades in pride of place. A guard and contingents drawn from *Swan*, the PNG Division of the RAN, the PNG Volunteer Rifles and the PNG Constabulary were all inspected by Senator John Gorton, the Minister for the Navy. After speeches by Walter Brooksbank and the Administrator Brigadier Sir Donald Cleland, Eric Feldt gave a short but quite emotional address in which he remembered the thirty-six men who gave their lives and then unveiled a plaque with their names at the base of the lighthouse. The lighthouse designer Gordon Laycock then read a poem he had composed about the Coastwatchers. The last line, '*They waited and warned and died that we might live,*' was also inscribed at the lighthouse base.[123]

The ceremony concluded at dusk with Senator Gorton turning on a switch which simultaneously turned on the lighthouse and illuminated it. Coastwatcher Matt Foley described it as, 'a magnificent piece of architecture'.[124] For the coastwatchers there was particular pleasure that the memorial could be of lasting benefit to New Guinea.

Eric Feldt gave an emotional and heartfelt address at the opening of the Coastwatcher's Memorial Light. (RAN)

Coastwatcher Ben Hall said of the event, it was 'a culmination of the efforts of the Coastwatchers and a culmination of the efforts of Eric Feldt'.[125]

Afterwards 'Eric Feldt's gang' as 'Snowy' Rhoades described them, returned to Hotel Madang in a euphoric mood.[126] Jack Gilmore, who was a Coastwatcher in New Britain, foreshadowed 'the dead Japs will be three feet high in the bar tonight'.[127] On a more reflective note he later described the evening as a 'once in a lifetime opportunity. It was so fantastic, we never thought we would see each other again'.[128] Rupert, ever the organiser, passed around a menu for all the veterans to sign to mark the occasion.[129]

Peter Figgis, who earned a Military Cross as a coastwatcher in New Britain summed up the occasion for many. He said he attended for four reasons. To see the light, to see Eric Feldt, to see everyone and in particular to be reunited with his comrades from New Britain. Sorely missed were those coastwatchers who had passed on. In particular, Figgis missed that great individualist Hugh MacKenzie who drove people mad but was greatly loved.[130] For the locals Roma Bates wrote that, 'Madang will never again have a weekend as wonderful as the one just past'.[131]

Of the Madang pilgrimage, Colonel Caleb 'CG' Roberts, who had been Director of Military Intelligence during the war, recalled his traveling companion Rupert Long:

> One of my very happy memories is of the journey to Madang last year. We travelled on the same plane and while there we were quartered together, under conditions which might have led to the small frictions which do occur but which in fact only enhanced my regard and liking for him. My strongest impression of the visit, apart from the pleasure it was to be with him and others I had known, was the sacrifice of his personal interests involved in completing the tape recording of the ceremony and the voices of former coast watchers. I feel that he must have looked upon it as the last act in the drama of which he was the stage manager.[132]

It was indeed the last act for Rupert Long who knew he had lung cancer. Resigned to his fate, he did not go see the doctor until his return from Madang. The doctor gave him three months to live. After telling Vera the news he gathered his three boys and informed them of the prognosis and told his oldest son Robert that he would have to look after his brothers. After surviving Christmas Rupert passed away on 8 January 1960. His old friend Allen Hillgarth wrote:

> What a man he was! Specifically, I've never known anyone with quite his capacity for intrigue combined with a downright honesty that made me ashamed. But he had great gifts in many ways—and not least the quality of friendship, which is by no means ordinary and seldom found in a human being in the degree that came so naturally to him.[133]

An RMB Long Memorial Committee was formed to commission a portrait and have a biography written by Hermon Gill. The response to the appeal for donations and anecdotes was generous and warm. John Collins and Eric Feldt were among the donors who were drawn from around the globe. While a fine portrait was painted, the biography by Gill did not eventuate. Not until 1995 did Barbara Winter complete the appropriately titled biography *Intrigue Master*.[134] Among the letters sent to the committee was a remarkable one from the Guadalcanal veteran Lieutenant Commander Dick Horton who wrote:

> You ask for anecdotes about Cocky and I have something to tell you which is quite extraordinary. Before I go any further I should tell you that what I am going to say is known already to his wife, B1 and Eric Feldt. The background is that I am receiving treatment from a friend

of ours who has the power of healing in her hands and also the power of telepathy etc., for a cataract in my left eye (the result of an ambush in Malaya). Well some little while ago I had a letter from B1 telling me of Cocky's sad and unexpected death and that evening I went for treatment to this friend of ours. At this point I must emphasize that she knows nothing of my background or friends and I had not said anything to her about Cocky on any occasion. Suddenly while I was receiving treatment she said to me, 'Have you had bad news today?' 'Yes', I said. 'Well', she said, 'There is someone who has passed over trying to get through to you.' She then went on to describe Cocky very accurately and what is more his urbane manner and his singular personality. She then told me that he was laughing and waving a bunch of flowers and saying that it was a joke between us. At first I just couldn't see why he should be waving flowers at me—then all of a sudden it struck me—Ferdinand the code name of our CW [Coastwatch] set up—the bull that smelt the flowers. So I told our friend this and she passed on the message. Apparently Cocky was very pleased and very glad to have managed to get in touch with me again. There is no more after that but I'm certain that if a channel such as this friend of ours happens to become available to any of the other Coast Watchers they could get in touch with that disembodied and indomitable spirit we knew in the flesh as 'Cocky' Long.[135]

Just before Anzac Day 1968 the second and final volume of Gill's history of the RAN in World War II was published. In his Preface he lamented:

> In the writing of this volume the author sadly missed the masterly guidance and penetrating comment of the late Commander RMB Long, RAN whose untimely death denied the help so valuable in the preparation of its forerunner.[136]

Throughout John Collins' tenure as Chief of Naval Staff he had the great support of Harry Showers. From 1948 Harry once more became the Second Naval Member and then in May 1950 he was made an Acting Rear Admiral and returned to Sydney as Flag Officer in Charge, Eastern Australia Area (FOICEA). The position was responsible for the support infrastructure, including the naval dockyard and for ships refitting, working up and conducting trials. There was a large social and ceremonial component to FOICEA's role and Harry and his family resided in the waterfront residence *Tresco* complete with a ballroom. In 1951, while still a serving officer, Harry became President of the Royal United Services Institute of New South Wales, a position that he held for three years. In these two positions he mixed widely with Sydney society and this proved invaluable in establishing a working life in the city after the Navy.

At the end of 1954 Harry Showers hauled down his flag and handed over to Rear Admiral Herbert Buchanan. Although never confirmed in the rank of Rear Admiral, John Collins thoughtfully made Harry an Honorary Rear Admiral. This allowed Harry to use the rank in retirement. On 25 January 1955 Harry and Harold Farncomb joined Buchanan in his barge to escort and farewell the old *Australia* out of the harbour.[137] The venerable cruiser was being towed to the UK for scrapping. *Australia* was also escorted by myriad boats and chartered ferries with former *Aussie* sailors and their families embarked. Buchanan later wrote that, 'The harbour echoed with farewells from all ships present'.[138]

Harry Showers was not ready to settle into idle pastimes. He focused his energies to support and grow two organizations. The first was the Navy League in which he was Federal President from 1957 to 1968. In that time the League broadened its reach to the wider community and fostered the expansion of the naval cadets.

The second organization that benefited from the Showers' touch was the Nuclear Research Foundation. Ever since Harry had worked in the remarkably well-equipped workshop in Geelong in 1913 he maintained a keen interest in technology. In 1953 Sydney University established the Nuclear Research Foundation under the energetic leadership of Professor Harry Messel. In 1955 Harry Showers became Secretary of this ground-breaking Foundation which sought financial support from a wide range of sources. In introducing the Foundation newsletter *Nucleus,* Messel wrote in words with which Rupert Long would have agreed:

Australia faces a choice of acting like a grown-up and responsible nation and entering a period of development and prosperity unprecedented; or of being a backward colony in an unfortunate geographical position, eventually to be swallowed up by an expanding Asia.[139]

Although Rupert Long and Messel knew one another no further information on the relationship between Long, Messel and Showers in nuclear matters could be found. The Professor had an entrepreneurial talent for raising money and would seize any opportunity. When two of the Foundation Governors disputed whether it was easier to fall foul of air or sea sickness, Messel organized each proponent to be tested in the other medium. Harry Showers readily agreed to act as the referee for the sailing trip. The end result was £5,000 to the Foundation.[140]

A key milestone in the development of the Nuclear Research Foundation was the building of Australia's second electronic computer.[141] It was called SILLIAC which was the acronym for the Sydney version of the Illinois Automatic Computer. One of Harry Messel's key objectives was to use the Foundation to spearhead the invigoration of science education and SILLIAC was an important element of the program. When Harry Showers joined the Foundation the computer was nearing installation. He brought the family to view the massive and imposing machine. Through his exposure to the cutting edge of science over the next two decades Harry Showers concluded that the greatest technological development in his lifetime was the microchip.

XI

The final members of the Pioneer Class to remain in full or part-time naval service were Jack Newman, Cyril Sadleir and Norman Calder. By war's end Jack retained command of FRUMEL which was an RAN-only activity on a much smaller scale. Because the cloak of secrecy was maintained about the Allied decryption of both German and Japanese codes until 1974, the strategically significant work of the women and men in FRUMEL remained unknown for a generation. Perhaps for this reason the contribution of FRUMEL to the Allied effort has not even today been fully recognised. In the view of Vice Admiral Sir Richard Peek however, Jack Newman probably made as big a contribution as anyone in the RAN to the final victory in World War II.[142] The US Vice Chief of Naval Operations, Vice Admiral Frederick Horne wrote of Jack that his, 'energy, enthusiasm, loyalty, good-will, and tact have contributed to an eminently and satisfying collaboration'.[143]

In June 1949 it was Jack Newman's reputation for technical excellence and for being one who, 'lets very little stand in the way of the attainment of his object'[144] that led to his selection to a new and strategically important endeavour. One of the revolutionary developments in the latter years of World War II was the German V1 and V2 unguided missile program. In the post-war period the US, Soviet Union and Britain all embarked on national rocket programs with considerable energy, urgency and secrecy. In the case of Britain, she sought Australian assistance for access to the latter's vast landmass for range and testing facilities. In 1946 the two nations established the Anglo-Australian Joint Project. The following year an area in central South Australia was selected and a small township was established called Woomera, 500 km from Adelaide. At 270,000 square kilometres, the range was the largest of its kind in the western world.

In June 1949 Jack was appointed the Naval Staff Officer to the Board of Administration in the Department of Supply for the Anglo-Australian Joint Project in Melbourne. Two years later Jack was appointed Superintendent of the Woomera Range and relieved Group Captain George Pither. The facility employed about 700 men and women with a significant number of families living in austere housing. Jack's wife Pamela decided to remain in Melbourne with the family.

Jack soon found that personnel issues were to occupy his time. Like the Jervis Bay community in 1915, Woomera experienced disharmonies over relatively minor issues that were accentuated by its remote location. One such matter was the existence of three different messes that derived from Woomera's military origins. They were based on the

Senior (Officers), Staff (Sergeants) and Junior (other ranks) messes. With the staff composition becoming increasingly civilian, problems and acrimony arose when trying to categorise people for entry into the different messes. To further complicate matters there was a 'Women only' mess based on gender not rank. Pither had made an unsuccessful attempt to categorise people based on salary. Jack called a conference of all concerned to sort out the membership qualifications which he said were at present 'haywire'.[145] This issue bedevilled the harmony of Woomera and was not resolved until a new combined mess was established and the others eventually demolished.

More substantively Jack had to ensure the smooth and safe running of the facility for a series of rocket firings. The major programs during Jack's tenure were the Skylark atmospheric and space research rocket and the Black Knight test launch vehicle. It was planned that Black Knight would eventually lead to the Blue Streak medium-range ballistic missile. Test firings at Woomera began for Skylark in 1957 and Black Knight the following year.

Black Knight firings brought with them concerns about personnel safety. The rocket would take a re-entry head into space which would then return to impact somewhere in an area of 30 km radius, 80 km down range from the launch pad. The impact area took in five properties and four homesteads. Since his arrival at Woomera, Jack had been at pains to explain the relatively low risks to the pastoralists and their families. In 1956 it was decreed for the Black Knights that any potentially exposed personnel had to take shelter in purpose built blast-proof shelters. Once it became known that these shelters were being constructed for Woomera staff, Jack noted that, 'some uneasiness was growing among station owners and managers'.[146] This resulted, after some bureaucratic sucking of teeth and recalculations of the rocket trajectory, in 48 steel framed sandbag shelters being built at the relevant homesteads, outstations and shearing sheds at a cost of £155,000.[147] While initially taking shelter the locals soon became more nonchalant. Pastoralist's wife Mrs Florence Crombie recalled:

Jack Newman (far right) escorting the UK Chief of Defence Staff, Admiral Lord Louis Mountbatten on his 1956 tour of Woomera. (Newman Family)

> They sent us a notice, Black Knight was going up. First it was seventy-two hours, then twenty-four hours, and at last they told us to take shelter. Course, we weren't in it. In fact, the whole household was standing on top of it to get a good look. The rocket went up in the dark but it produced flashes every few seconds so you could see it climbing. It went up and up and everyone was enjoying the show. Then it turned over and began to come down. All the stockhands thought it was falling on them, and it did fall only a few miles away. I turned round to speak to the men and there wasn't a bastard there.[148]

A regular visitor to Woomera, Commander George Fowle recalled Jack Newman's tenure:

> The duties of Superintendent called for man of all seasons ... He was an excellent administrator, a firm captain of his Domain, brooking no interference in the day to day operations either from the Supply Head Office or the Services. All who had to check with him at whatever level had great respect for Captain Jack Newman ... He took a particular interest in and had great sympathy for the aboriginal tribes who wandered about the range from time to time.[149]

By virtue of the high profile of its rocket firings there were frequent VIP visitors from around the world. The hosting of VIPs showed other aspects of Jack's character. He was a stickler for protocol and was at pains to ensure the visits ran smoothly. Jack also spoke French well and was somewhat of a Francophile and gourmet. This was reflected in the high standard of hospitality in the Senior Mess.

On 13 May 1959 Jack Newman celebrated his 60th birthday and had to transfer to the Retired list the following day. He finally left Woomera on 29 June 1959 after five years in the post. Jack was the only Superintendent to serve two terms and appropriately the cricket ground still bears his name. Jack's naval career spanned tremendous changes in technology. As a young officer he had collided with a trading barquentine and it ended being involved in the cutting edge of the missile age.

Also on 29 June Cyril Sadleir's naval reserve service came to end. Even at the close of his career his naval colleagues were unsure of Cyril's medical condition and his Commanding Officer wrote of 'some obscure nervous trouble'.[150] In spite of his condition, Cyril rendered valued service and remained a well regarded member of the local cell which would be responsible for the control of merchant shipping in wartime.

This left only one member of the Pioneer Class still on the Navy's books. Norman Calder had been posted to shore on 6 July 1959 and finally retired from the Navy on his 60th birthday on 17 November 1959 just two months shy of 47 years service. It may have been the end of an era, but it passed without fanfare.

XII

John Collins became Australia's High Commissioner in Wellington in 1956. His tenure spanned seven years, the longest up to that time for an Australian High Commissioner in New Zealand. As was the convention for the period, Australian ambassadors and high commissioners sent regular personal despatches to the Minister for External Affairs regarding the affairs of their host nation. John Collins' despatches were articulate and thoughtful. Over the course of the 1957 election year John sent a series of detailed assessments of New Zealand political parties. Of the smaller parties, he saw no menace in the Communist Party, opining that the New Zealand community, 'is intrinsically conservative, interested mainly in better working conditions, shorter hours, the ownership of their own houses and the doings of the All Blacks'.[151] Of the Social Credit Political League, John was concerned that its 'unthought out monetary theories' would have tragic consequences for the country.[152]

The main New Zealand political parties were the opposition Labour Party and the incumbent National Party. After the Labour Party held its conference John Collins wrote that 'Intellectuals in the New Zealand Labour Party are unknown'[153], and went on to say that:

> Lacking clear objectives, hostile to new ideas, led by an aging oligarchical leadership, Labour's attraction to approximately half of the New Zealand electorate remains a continual source of wonder to an outsider, or, at best, can be explained only by the similarly uninspiring nature of its major opponent.[154]

In respect to the governing National Party, John wrote:

> The New Zealand National Party is a moderate conservative organisation, with a pragmatic approach to the day to day questions of politics, which seems to appeal to the conservative New Zealand temperament ... In office it can point to some steady administrative achievements. Nevertheless the Party's principal weakness would seem to to be lack of any spark to catch the imagination of the electorate in general ... If it should be defeated in November, this will be most probably due to the boredom of the electorate with the Party.[155]

Labour indeed went on to secure a narrow election win. In his reporting of the controversial 1960 All Black tour of South Africa in which the New Zealand Rugby Football Union decided to not select Maori players so that they would not, 'suffer indignities and humiliations'.[156] John Collins displayed a keen understanding of New Zealand's racial issues, while a dispassionate observer he was nonetheless critical of the NZRFU's arrogance and the absence of leadership by Prime Minister Walter Nash on the matter. He concluded his despatch with the observation:

Sir John Collins as High Commissioner. He was an astute and sympathetic observer of New Zealand. (RAN)

The 'Pakehas' (New Zealanders of European descent) are generally tolerant about racial matters although in everyday life they are somewhat indifferent and make no special individual efforts to bring about assimilation of the two races'.[157]

As part of his duties John was also a member of the South Pacific Commission. As such he regularly travelled to the islands, especially those under New Zealand mandate that were edging towards some form of independence. Once again he cast a sympathetic and perceptive eye. John made a point of having private discussions with key figures as well as engaging widely across society. In Samoa where there were four paramount chiefs from each of the dynastic clans, two were to act as joint Heads of State. A third would become Prime Minister. John discussed their nation's future with each in turn. He was most impressed with the one of the prospective Heads of State, Tupua Tamasese Mea'ole, who he thought was, 'a striking personality, undoubtedly the leading figure amongst the Samoans, with a good grip on affairs and balanced attitude to the future'.[158]

However, John was concerned about the calibre of some other leaders. One he assessed 'has less brain power and is more the playboy type' while another, 'is not an outstanding personality and probably would do little harm; he might even do some good'. In January 1962 John led the Australian delegation at Western Samoa's independence ceremonies. Memorably for John and Phyllis, they and some other VIPs were accommodated in the author, Robert Louis Stevenson's residence - *Vailima*. John wrote:

> The old house still carries the aura of RLS and is set in indescribably beautiful grounds. To live in such an historic house and to swim in the waterfall pool built by Stevenson himself amidst tropical trees and flowers was an unforgettable experience.[159]

During the visit John had talks with the new Prime Minister Fiame Mata'afa Faumuina Mulinu'u II and wrote that he possessed, 'great dignity and made an impressive figure'.[160]

Inevitably, John Collins extended tenure in Wellington brought with it in time the mantle of Dean of the Diplomatic Corps[161] which he held for his last five years in country. This enabled him to have a closer view of New Zealand's engagement with other nations. In his final despatch entitled *A Last Look At New Zealand* he wrote a typically thoughtful piece on how Australians could more sensitively engage their New Zealand counterparts and opportunities for shared cooperation and development.[162]

In 1962 John and Phyllis Collins returned to Australia and settled in Sydney. After nearly fifty years of service, John needed both a break and a project. He set about writing his much anticipated memoir. It was published in 1965 and modestly entitled *As Luck Would Have It: The Reminiscences of an Australian Sailor*. The original title of the draft was *It has been fun* and John and the publishers Angus and Robertson wrestled with other options such as *Fifty Years Since* and *As Chance Shall Send*.[163] The final title reflected John Collins' view of the at times tenuous nature of a naval career.

In the year of publishing his memoir John was sounded out by Prime Minister Menzies about becoming Australia's 16th Governor General to replace Lord De L'Isle. John graciously declined. Among his considerations were Phyllis' health, but also the long years of public service he had undertaken. By this time Robert Menzies, John Collins and their wives enjoyed a warm friendship and the Prime Minister fully appreciated the rationale for John's decision.[164]

XIII

As a counterpoint to John Collins success as Chief of Naval Staff, Harold Farncomb's life immediately after leaving the Navy in April 1951 was extremely difficult as he battled alcoholism. This included periods when he was on the streets sleeping rough. Throughout, Jean Farncomb maintained her support and provided succour when he returned home. Help also came from a Salvation Army Officer who encouraged Harold to go to Alcoholics Anonymous.[165] This he did and with its help he turned his life around and gave up alcohol completely. It is unclear for how long Harold was in his nadir—but he appears to have been in recovery by early 1953. In later times Harold provided support and inspiration to others in Alcoholics Anonymous who were dealing with alcoholism.

Needing a new focus in his life, Harold chose his abiding interest in the law and learnt Latin to advance his studies. Harold had throughout his travails maintained a strong Christian faith in the Anglican tradition. During his naval career he had, when in Sydney, been an active parishioner at St Andrews Cathedral and a contributor to diocesan affairs. He watched with dismay as the liturgy and other aspects of the service became less traditional in the pattern of 'Low Church' observance after the arrival of the new Dean of Sydney, Eric Pitt in 1953. This led him to write a series of letters to the Editor in *The Sydney Morning Herald* about the deliberate non-conformity to the rubrics of the 1662 Book of Common Prayer.[166] Specifically, Harold was concerned about changes in terminology, discontinuing the use of some vestments and the shift to the Morning Prayer (or Matins) as the principal service ahead of Holy Communion.[167] The letters show, in the assessment of Professor Tom Frame, one-time Anglican Bishop to the Defence Force, that Harold was, 'a man of Middle or High Anglican temperament who resented the slow and steady movement in Sydney to much 'lower' or less ceremonial church worship'.[168]

In 1956 as he neared the end of his legal studies he served as Clerk to Mr Justice David Roper who was then chief judge in the NSW Equity Court. Harold was admitted to the Bar on 6 June 1958 with Mr (later Justice) David Yeldham moving his admission.[169] Harold joined Denman Chambers and with the support of his sponsor, developed a reasonably busy practice. His briefs included those that went to the Courts of Marine Inquiry where his peerless nautical knowledge was put to telling effect.

His cases included the defence of the Master of the whale-oil tanker *Forso* that grounded off Moreton Bay. Colleagues at court remember Harold to be modest and courteous. He clearly enjoyed both the legal world's mix of formality and camaraderie that was not dissimilar to that of the Navy. In 1963 Denman Chambers closed and, rather than try to find new Chambers as a barrister, Harold transferred from the Bar to become a solicitor with the firm Alfred Rofe and Sons.

Harold Farncomb's most notable case came in 1964 when he was Instructing Solicitor for Captain John Robertson during the first Royal Commission into the *Melbourne-Voyager* collision. Harold knew Robertson well, 'Robbie' had served on his staff when Harold commanded the Australian Squadron in the war. However, Harold's first brush with the *Melbourne-Voyager* tragedy was on the evening of the collision, 10 February 1964. The Commanding Officer of the *Voyager* was Captain Duncan Stevens, son of Major General Sir Jack Stevens, whose troops Harold had supported in the Wewak landings. Sir Jack called Harold on that evening seeking to obtain legal representation for his son. This was before it was known he had in fact drowned that evening along with 81 of his men.

In preparing to adequately represent Captain Robertson before the Royal Commission, Harold first sought to obtain Government assistance for the substantial legal costs for which Robertson would be liable in engaging a Queen's Counsel.[170] The government reluctantly agreed for some support. During the Royal Commission, which was chaired by Judge Sir John Spicer, Chief Justice of the Commonwealth Industrial Court, Harold assisted Robertson's QC, David Hicks, in arguing that Captain Robertson's actions in *Melbourne* were those of a reasonable mariner, noting the experience of Captain Stevens in *Voyager*, whose competence in executing a basic manoeuvre, one was entitled to presume. Of note, John Collins sat in some of the Commission's hearings and later wrote in *The Age* that he, 'had the misfortune to attend some of the more inept meetings of that body'.[171]

In the end the Spicer Royal Commission Report, while apportioning most blame to Stevens was also critical of Robertson. The Report was subjected to substantial criticism and this combined with subsequent allegations about Stevens' dependence on alcohol and persistent ill-health led to an unprecedented Second Royal Commission. Harold Farncomb did not have any formal involvement in this second commission but had the satisfaction of seeing Robertson exonerated. Nevertheless, Robertson's otherwise promising career had been terminally damaged and he resigned in September 1964, refusing to accept a shore posting which he considered a demotion.

In 1969 Harold Farncomb finally retired from the law. As a lawyer, he applied the same penetrating and analytical mind along with the industry and ability which had been his hallmarks in the Navy. He also retained a keen sense of justice. From a religious perspective, Harold had found the legal profession's church and Sydney's second oldest, St James on King Street, much more to his 'High Church' inclinations.

During his legal career Harold had maintained links with the Navy, his old shipmates and returned service organizations. In 1961 in looking back on his war experiences, the memories of friends lost and the world beyond war, Harold said in an Anzac Day address:

> Above all we must keep alive the spirit of those who died; the spirit of self-sacrifice and the spirit of co-operation with our fellow-man in all walks of life; such things must not wait for wars to inspire us. We must seek inspiration in the day to day affairs of our ordinary lives.[172]

Another one of the Pioneer Class working beyond the normal retirement age was Norman Calder. He had elected to remain with the deferred pay arrangements, and without a house of his own, he had to continue to work. Like many former servicemen he tried a succession of jobs. For him these included being a teacher, a laboratory assistant with the Kiwi Polish Company and five years as a clerk with Guardian Royal Exchange Insurance.

In 1966 Norman and his wife Nancie sailed to Japan on holiday. Enroute they visited Noumea where his memories of *Bungaree's* minelaying operations were brought into sharp focus when he saw the wreck of the US merchantman *Yochow* which had strayed into one of his defensive fields and struck a mine. On 26 May of that year, in an ironic twist for his old ship, now the *Eastern Mariner*, she herself struck a mine in the Saigon River.[173]

XIV

Throughout the 1960s more of the surviving Pioneer Class retired from employment. In 1966 Winn Reilly did so and he and his wife Naomi undertook an extended world tour. The timing was fortuitous because, although on return to Australia he was offered various directorships in some of the Collins House subsidiaries, he was not well. After extensive tests which initially drew a blank, Winn was eventually diagnosed with psychotic depression. His final years were spent at Concord Repatriation Hospital where he passed away on 21 June 1978 after a short bout of bronchopneumonia. Although Winn struck out to establish himself in the commercial world, he retained a great bond with the Navy and his old Pioneer Class friends, especially Rupert Long. Some of his family and friends felt Winn, 'bitterly regretted his resignation but would never in any way acknowledge this'.[174] The legacy of the inaugural King's Medallist was his diligent and vital service during the war to help keep hundreds of ships safe from the scourge of magnetic sea mines.

After a professional life engaged in engineering of various forms it was unsurprising to those who knew Eddy Nurse well, that his fertile mind would turn to invention. Indeed in 1944 Captain Spooner wrote that Eddy had, 'a mechanically inventive mind which he could turn to good account if he had leisure'.[175] And so it was that Eddy became a 'gadgeteer'. He wrote in 1969, 'I am interested in all sorts of subjects but mechanical gadgets seem to be my abiding hobby'.[176] Retirement certainly gave full rein to 'gadgeteering' in which his self imposed constraint was that all materials had to be typically found in the back shed. This constraint in Eddy's mind forced him to refine his ideas 'to the limits of simplicity'.[177]

Winn and Naomi Reilly in the USA as part of their 1966 world tour. (WL Reilly Collection)

Eddy wrote that, 'Even in this electronic and space age there is still an almost limitless range for the mechanical gadgeteer'.[178] But within this boundless range Eddy found 'the worst part of gadget-orientated retirement was trying to think of what to think about'.[179]

The Nurse's home was 'riddled with gadgets'[180] from the door bell which rang a cow bell in the main hall, one of the earliest versions of a solar hot water system, a self-propelled garden sprinkler, a reflecting open fireplace, a home cooling system, a dynamic balancer for the laundry spin dryer, a rug making machine and a stereo camera to produce three dimensional photographs. His good humoured wife Marie told a reporter from *The Sun* who wrote a full page story in August 1970 on Eddy's gadgets, 'He's terrific—you never know what is going to happen next'.[181] *The Sun* article had the bannerline, 'Inside the amazing thingamebob whirligig world of Mr Gadgeteer'.[182]

Eddy Nurse like many inventors before him was fascinated by perpetual motion and perhaps his greatest gadgeteering achievement was when he combined this quest with his abiding interest in clocks. The product of his efforts was a 'water-clock' which used water drops to drive a pendulum. It was accurate to one-minute a day and is now part of the Museum of Victoria's collection.[183] The Museum believes that its 'method of drive and the mechanism are unlike anything else in the world'.[184]

Eddy Nurse and Ben Howells maintained their long friendship into retirement. In 1964 after 26 years Ben retired from Footscray Technical College. A farewell speaker said of Ben, he 'had been a boxer,

THESE HAVE BEEN MEN   627

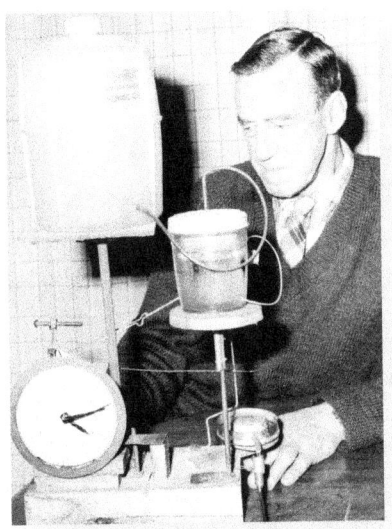

'Unlike anything else in the world':
Eddy Nurse and his Water Clock.
(Mrs Mary Backhouse)

Ben and Dorothy Howells at
Balnarring Beach. (Howells Family)

a rugger player, midshipman, poet and placid conveyor of an appreciation of the English language'.[185] For Ben the school had always been an institution that allowed 'freedom of thought and behaviour in a responsible manner',[186] qualities that he greatly appreciated. In the same year Dorothy retired from the Federation of Mothers' Clubs.

Since the 1930s Ben and the family had regularly gone to Balnarring Beach near Flinders Naval Depot for summer camping holidays. After first being lent a tent by Eddy Nurse, Ben and Dorothy bought a modest holiday home near the beach in 1942. Named *Homeing*, it was a place of great relaxation and creativity. Many of Ben's poems were written at Balnarring and dealt with the wonders of nature that surrounded him. His creativity also extended to improving *Homeing* which would become his and Dorothy's home when their children became adults. Both Ben and Dorothy became engaged in the local Balnarring community with Ben serving as Secretary of the Foreshore Committee.

Like Norman Calder before him, Ben Howells also travelled to the South West Pacific to the places where some of the titanic battles had taken place during the war. In their case Ben and Dorothy visited the Solomon Islands. Ben was struck by the contrast of the quiet beauty of the 'slopes behind Honiara [which] are covered with vivid green grasses that spread outward and upward toward a huge dark mountain, constantly veiled in mist, which dominates the background'[187] and the terrible battles and losses of the war. After viewing Iron-Bottom Sound where his old rugby team mate Frank Getting had been lost, Ben wrote a poem simply entitled *Guadalcanal*,[188]

> Lightnings flick the storm-black mountain,
> Emerald-green enfolds the ground
> Rolling down toward the beaches
> Of black Iron-Bottom Sound.
>
> For the gleam and glare of battle
> From dim shapes in grim array
> Flickered, once, deep in the blackness
> Where a doomed flotilla lay.
>
> And in shrouds of tough sea-tangle
> Warrior bones securely wound
> Silently keep battle stations
> Under Iron-Bottom Sound.
>
> But the flesh and blood that sealed them,
> Resurrected from the tide,
> Breathe enchantment on the grasses
> Growing round the mountain side.

XV

Harry Vallentine's life took an unexpected turn in 1962 when he received a substantial inheritance on the death of an aunt. After decades keeping his distance from his wife Irene, who had raised their three children in Sydney, he re-established contact. After a separation of 30 years Harry took the train to Parramatta and an uncertain reception. Irene was the same beautiful, calm, happy and easy going women he had left. With the words, 'Hello Harry' he was welcomed back into her life. With the inheritance they bought their first home in nearby Harris Park before eventually retiring on the Central Coast near Gosford.[189]

On 19 July 1963 the 50th Anniversary of the Royal Australian Naval College was marked with a graduation parade at Jervis Bay. The Pioneer Class were the guests of honour. Of the eighteen surviving members, seven were able to attend: John Collins, Harold Farncomb, Eddy Nurse, Winn Reilly, Cyril Sadleir, Harry Showers and Horace Thompson. Appropriately, the Governor General was once again in attendance, this time it was Viscount De L'Isle. To the cadet midshipmen on parade some of the seven Pioneers seemed particularly 'wizened' and looked very much the personal link to the dawn of their Navy.[190] When interviewed about the Pioneer Class for the Golden Jubilee commemoration Harold Farncomb said:

> Really there wasn't anything particularly unusual about that Class of '13—just a bunch of bright-eyed lads keen on making the Navy their career.[191]

At the end of the parade the seven men wandered the grounds. To inadvertently demonstrate their humanity, and perhaps harking back to old times, one was spied by some cadet-midshipmen having a pee under the wharf.

In the fifty years since its opening the Naval College had trained over a thousand officers. Of these, sixteen had risen to flag rank of whom three were from the Pioneer Class. During World War II its graduates, and the

Members of the Pioneer Class at the 50th Anniversary parade at Jervis Bay. (RAN)
L to R: *Winn Reilly, Harold Farncomb, Eddy Nurse, Horace Thompson, Harry Showers & John Collins.*

Pioneer Class in particular, had vindicated Sir William Creswell's vision for the Naval College. The conflicts had taken their toll with fifty graduates killed during war. Their losses were not only through the 'violence of the enemy' but also through the 'raging of the sea'. Sadly, these ever present nautical dangers were to become again realised with the 1963 Graduation Class. Four would drown when their whaler capsized in the Great Barrier Reef, while another four were killed in the *Melbourne-Voyager* collision.

XVI

Their lengthening years also saw the remaining members of the Pioneer Class succumbing. The effects of tobacco and alcohol hastened the passing of some. In 1965 Eric Feldt suffered another heart attack. He made a good recovery after a couple of weeks in hospital. Also suffering from heart disease was Peyton Kimlin. He was admitted to Concord Repatriation Hospital but passed away on 17 July 1966. His wife Myra who survived Peyton by another nine years, had inscribed on the plaque to mark where his ashes are interned:

LT PEYTON KIMLIN
RAN 1914-18
SERVED ON HMS 'CANADA'
BELOVED HUSBAND OF MYRA.

Peyton's memorial reflected, like with so many of the Pioneer Class, the central place the Navy had played in their lives and affections, no matter their length of service.

Eric Feldt enjoyed great contentment in his final years. To his extended family Eric was still 'always energetic, kindly, interested and interesting'. He cut a memorable figure by using his old naval sword to trim the bougainvillea in his garden.[192]

Eric continued to take a keen interest in Pacific Island affairs. In 1961 he wrote an article in the *Quadrant* magazine following the publication of Errol Flynn's memoirs *My Wicked, Wicked Ways*.[193] The book included a claim that Flynn had been attacked by natives whilst living in Wau. In the incident Flynn said his servant had been killed and Flynn had been tried before the magistrate for killing one of the attacking natives.[194] Eric as the District Officer and magistrate at the time refuted the story and called Flynn a 'congenital liar'.[195]

An avid reader of the *Pacific Island Monthly*, Eric was particularly concerned that the achievements of the colonial administration were being viewed through increasingly revisionist eyes. This led him in 1967 to write a thoughtful article about the colonial administration between the wars. In it he concluded that:

> Our Administration was admittedly paternal. But I still believe it was the most humane way of governing the country at the time. If we had forced the native into a civilised commercial way of life then, he would have died off in thousands. The other alternative was to have imported Eastern coolie labour, in which case the result would have been worse still.[196]

On 12 March 1968 at his New Farm home, Eric's heart finally gave way. He had let it be known that he wanted 'no fuss' at his funeral. However the chapel overflowed with mourners, chief among them were former coastwatchers to farewell their old leader. The presiding minister Reverend Reuben Foote captured the sentiment of the congregation when he said Eric:

> ... was a courageous person who played a prominent part in the defence of his country. We give thanks to God for such a servant. Australia owes a debt of gratitude to this person. His memory will go down in the history of our land.[197]

Eric's old friend and coastwatcher, Keith McCarthy said:

> Feldt was a farseeing man, and beneath a rather deceptively mild manner there was tremendous drive and determination to get things done. His imagination impelled him to constantly explore new and better ways to do things'.[198]

In reporting his death the *Pacific Island Monthly* wrote:

> He was a graceful writer, and a clear thinker. He was a sincere, competent, fair-minded, reliable, kindly man, who made so many solid friends because he himself was one. His fine memorial is his New Guinea work, both as a pioneering civilian administrator and as a naval commander of great resourcefulness.[199]

Two months later Eric's ashes were scattered by the patrol boat HMAS *Samarai* in the waters off the Coastwatchers Memorial Lighthouse. The final honour was given to his wife Nancy, who on 10 August 1968, launched the new patrol boat HMAS *Madang* at Evans Deakin shipyard in Brisbane. Madang was one of Eric's favourite postings as a District Officer and the location of the Memorial Lighthouse.

Adrian Watts, self portrait.
(Watts Family)

Seven days later Adrian Watts passed away after a protracted battle with prostate and then bowel cancer. A remarkably versatile commercial artist Adrian left a body of artwork and illustrations that are held by the Australian National Library, State Library of Victoria and the Museum of Melbourne.

George Armitage also died in 1968 after some years of coronary artery disease. In 1959 after working at the Taxation Department in Adelaide, he returned to his wife Mabel in Sydney to live out his final years in peace. Despite all his travails, George treasured his service in the Navy, his friendships, in particular with James Esdaile, and remained a 'navy man' to the end. On his death certificate his occupation was listed as Naval Officer.[200]

XVII

In February 1969 Cyril Sadleir contracted bronchopneumonia. For so many sufferers of multiple sclerosis, pneumonia could be fatal and so it was for Cyril who passed away on 3 May. Cyril donated his body to medical science and it was gratefully received by the University of Melbourne.

For Harry Vallentine whose reunion with his wife Irene had been a happy one, their too few years together came to an end on on 3 February 1969 when Irene passed away. The following year Harry himself died of

Cyril & Lauris Sadleir at their daughter's 1965 wedding.
(Sadleir family)

a heart attack. He was remembered by his grandchildren as a kindly old man who would happily play games and had an unusually well-developed facility for card games. To some of the older members of the family Harry's return was a case of a black sheep redeeming himself, while others were less sure. Undoubtedly his return brought immense happiness to Irene in the twilight of her life.

In his retirement Harold Farncomb remained a regular parishioner at St James' Church where he enjoyed the fellowship of his legal friends. On 12 February 1971 Harold passed away at St Vincent's Hospital, finally succumbing to heart disease. He was survived by his devoted wife Jean. She had endured the long separations caused by Harold's sea service and supported him through his many years of battling alcohol. That battle had cost Harold his turn to lead the Navy and the associated trappings such as a knighthood. As the Navy's first aircraft carrier captain it was fitting that Harold's ashes were scattered at sea from the flight deck of his last flagship, the former aircraft carrier *Sydney*. In marking Harold's death the Minister at St James' wrote:

> Admiral Farncomb was greatly honoured as a leader during World War II when he commanded HMAS *Australia*, flagship during the Coral Sea Battle. His achievements at that time were a major factor in the defence of Australia at its most urgent time of need. In addition to his distinguished service in the Royal Australian Navy, we at St. James' Church cherish the memory of one whose wide experience in the legal profession as well as in the Navy, and in various spheres of leadership,

made him a valued parish councillor. But we shall remember him particularly as a devout communicant and a practising Christian of simple dignity and humility.[201]

In 1987 John Collins wrote of Harold Farncomb that he:

> ... had a first class brain, and was almost always in the 'top flight' of his courses. He was much liked by his officers and ships' companies. An excellent officer who stood up outstandingly well under pressure. He was an outstanding officer for whom I had the highest regard.[202]

'Braces' Bracegirdle remembered Harold Farncomb as 'one of the most widely educated Australian senior officers I have met'.[203] For a broader assessment of Harold's naval career there are few who were as well placed as Vice Admiral Sir Richard Peek, who had served with him multiple times during peace and war. He wrote:

> Hal was called 'Fearless Frank' for good reason—he was fearless in command and in dealing with Navy Office. He trusted his subordinates, was loyal to them and in return had their devotion and loyalty. He and Jean went out of their way to entertain and get to know their officers and wives. His success as a naval officer stemmed from his willingness to delegate and trust, from the knowledge that he was personally very capable and wise and from the fact that in Truman's words 'the buck stopped with him'. Not that he accepted sloppiness in the work of his team—on the contrary he could be savage but he accepted any blame from higher authority himself.
>
> He handled *Australia* well but I cannot comment on his ability as a tactician except to say that I was happy to go anywhere with him. Paperwork he disliked but handled brilliantly. He believed in taking responsibility himself and not worrying Navy Office. Some of the things he allowed me to do as gunnery officer on his authority alone are almost unbelievable.
>
> In summary he was a seagoing captain, and admiral in the best of the old traditions, a man whom his people respected and indeed loved, a man who shouldered the vast responsibilities of command at sea in war without running for help to higher authority.
>
> To me he was the greatest of a number of great commanders the RAN had produced and had circumstances been different he would have been a great Chief of Naval Staff. It was an unfeeling stupid administration which did not send him on a long break after the war, and to this omission, I lay the blame for his fall from grace in Washington—

Menzies actions in that case of sacking Hal were a blot on Menzies who after all liked the bottle himself.

I have always thought that of all the officers senior to me Hal had the best brain, not only from the point of view of intelligence but because of his decisiveness. A very great Australian by any measure.[204]

On 3 October 1971 Jack Newman passed away. His beloved wife Pamela had predeceased him by six years. To many WRANS, the Newman marital relationship of 'great mutual respect' left an indelible mark.[205] On Jack's passing the Ex-WRANS Newsletter *Ditty Box* recorded:

> Alas! The encroaching years are leaving their mark when we sigh and yearn for the 'good old days'; but our memories are sacrosanct, and deep in the memories of many of us is the stern but kindly man, assiduous in his work but a gay and stalwart off-duty companion, a splendid example of a true Naval Officer—'our' Commander Newman.[206]

XVIII

Notwithstanding their thinning ranks, some of the Pioneer Class continued to make their mark into the 1970s. In 1971 John Collins wrote his second book, published by the Naval Historical Society of Australia, it was the story of his beloved HMAS *Sydney*.[207] In his introduction he lamented:

> It is sad that there can be so few 'old comrades' of the cruiser *Sydney* of World War II. Only that small number who left the ship before her last battle, when she was lost with all hands, know the details of her story and carry on her memory.
>
> They are mostly in Perth, Western Australia, where she was based at the time. Here each year a small group of '*Ex-Sydneyites*' get together on 19th July, the anniversary of the sinking of the *Bartolomeo Colleoni*, to commemorate their fine ship and her victories and to remember with pride and sorrow the 645 shipmates who made the supreme sacrifice. They exchange telegrams with their old Captain who joins them in remembrance.
>
> As that old Captain, as one of the few, I felt it to be my privilege and obligation towards a magnificent ship and her company to write the story. *Sydney's* loss was a tragic blow to Australia and the Navy, but particularly to me as I knew the fine record of the ship and the great spirit of her company so well.[208]

Towards the end of 1970 Eddy Nurse was diagnosed with lung cancer which was to confine him to home for his last years. Eddy had always been a hospitable host and his martinis were legendary. The free flowing conversations combined with Eddy's genuine interest in others meant that his final years were still filled with visits from friends. In early 1972 Eddy's pain became too much and he was admitted to Heidelberg Repatriation Hospital. Even from his bed Eddy was organizing extra chairs and introducing his many friends to each other and to fellow patients. He impressed the latter with his 'simple wisdom and courage'.[209] Eddy died on 25 March 1972.

Horace Thompson, who like Eddy had attended the Naval College's 50th anniversary celebrations, was also battling cancer. After an operation to stem the spread of bowel cancer, Horace went on a cruise and then stayed with family to recover some health. When he was able Horace returned to Kings Cross where he had a room in a boarding house near his favourite pub. Almost a year to the day from Eddy's death, Horace was found dead in his room. He had been dead for a day or so. The coronial inquest found that Horace had been smoking in bed and that a spilt bottle of rum on the floor nearby had caught fire. Horace had fallen on the floor, perhaps when he tried to extinguish the flames, and suffered serious burns to his left arm and side. He died not from the fire, but from a lethal cocktail of alcohol and the pain killer amylobarbitone. The Coroner assessed these were not ingested by Horace with the intention of taking his own life.[210]

The following month another of the Pioneer Class passed away. Paul Hirst died on 9 April 1973 at Low Head in his beloved Tasmania. His passing recalled to his old *Toowoomba* shipmates his uncanny ability to avoid the bombs from Japanese aircraft. Norm Smith, on hearing the news, wrote that Paul Hirst had, 'brought the ship through several close encounters with the enemy of the time so I and 80 or so others revere his memory in perpetuity'.[211]

On 29 May 1974 Norman Calder started work in his final full-time job. It was with Lloyds agency in the P&O company in Collins Street, Melbourne. He was deliberately vague to his employers about his age but when pressed he gave it as 69 years. It was hard work, but it was the job Norman liked the most since leaving the Navy. Norman later wrote:

> I realised I could not continue to hide my age for very long. I was told very politely that I was becoming a slight embarrassment to P&O as [the] Department of Labour had queried why I was employed at my age'.[212]

Norman finally retired on 9 August 1975. He and Nancie moved to the northern beaches of Sydney and he must have been one of the oldest applicants for a War Service Home Loan.

By 1980 five of the Pioneer Class remained alive. Jack Lecky after a decade of quiet retirement passed away in Perth on 15 June 1981. In that year Ben Howells' life entered a dark place when Dorothy died. But with the support of his family and his poetry he was able to slowly move forward. Ben, who could still recite long passages of Shakespeare and other great poets, assembled 132 of his poems into small thematic booklets. It was a lasting regret for Ben that they did not achieve a greater readership and appreciation. His son John, in assessing his father's output wrote:

> ... at his best Ben is the poet of simple delights—of sunshine, sea and sand; of birds and trees; and of children's laughter and play and make-believe. I am of the opinion that examples of his best deserve to be included in anthology of Australian poetry of the 1940s.[213]

Remarkably in 1983 James Esdaile was still working on his poultry farm in Upper Beaconsfield. After years of drought and a dry and very hot summer however, large bushfires broke out on 16 February. Driven by strong winds they swept across large parts of South Australia and Victoria. One of the worst affected areas was Upper Beaconsfield. Of the 47 Victorians killed in the fires, 21 came from James' district. Among the 3,700 building lost was the Esdaile farmhouse. Although James and his wife survived, most of their possessions did not. True to his character, James had been a meticulous diarist during his naval career and tragically all these papers and naval memorabilia were lost. After the Ash Wednesday fires James and Desiree moved into Melbourne.

Norman Calder enjoyed his retirement and remained quite active through gardening, bowls and bridge. While no longer an active member of a Masonic Lodge he supported its charity work and received a 60-year bar to his 50-year Service Jewel. Like James Esdaile, Norman's retirement was marked by material misfortune. He had always been a keen philatelist with a particular focus on stamps from the British Empire. Devastatingly, Norman's valuable collection was stolen from his home. Totally dispirited, he gave up his hobby. On 9 December 1985, Norman mentioned to his son John that, as he was getting more infirm, he was 'ready to go'. The following morning when Nanette returned to the bedroom with the newspaper and a cup of tea she found her husband had died of a massive heart attack. On Friday 13 December after a ceremony conducted by a naval chaplain, Norman's ashes were scattered off Sydney Heads. He had the distinction of one of the longest naval careers in the RAN's history.

Ben Howell had enjoyed reasonably good health but he too in December 1985 fell ill. Ben contracted an infection in his left ear which led to a palsy down that side of his face. His condition gradually deteriorated and in April 1986 he was admitted to hospital. Four days later, after being read a chapter from his beloved *Pride and Prejudice*, he fell asleep and did not reawaken. In the eulogy for Ben, it was said he was:

> Fond of his family and always gentle, he loved parties and fun, a sing-song round the piano, and recitations. At the same time he found it hard to draw close to others. He worried and fretted over the meaning of existence. He wrestled with God.[214]

The ashes of Dorothy and then Ben were scattered off the rockpools at Balnarring Beach near *Homeing*. In Ben's *Shells in a Rock-Pool*, he wrote:

> Rainbow children of the ocean.
> Torn by water's wild commotion
> You were laid at last, with sighing
> Soft as whispered lullabying
> In the cradle where you sleep.[215]

By 1987 there were three of the Pioneer Class: James Esdaile, Harry Showers and John Collins. In 1987 Harry Showers, still living at home but

Sir John Collins at a 1988 ceremony to remember the loss of HMAS Sydney. *With him are Lieutenant (later Commodore) David Letts, Rear Admiral Tony Horton and the Commanding Officer of the frigate HMAS* Sydney, *Commander (later Vice Admiral) Russ Shalders*. (Letts Collection).

with a daily visiting nurse, wrote in a spidery hand, 'Failing eyesight and lack of ability to read, write or walk are curses.'[216] John Collins also suffered from poor eyesight which precluded reading. His condition was attributed to his injuries at Leyte.[217] Despite this affliction both men regularly caught up for a gin and tonic followed by lunch at the Royal Sydney Golf Club. In May 1989 Harry celebrated his 90th Birthday with a cocktail party and was delighted John Collins could attend.

After a bout of influenza and then pneumonia John Collins passed away peacefully at St. Luke's Hospital in Sydney on 3 September 1989. Fittingly, his funeral was held at St Andrews Cathedral next to Sydney Town Hall where he and *Sydney's* ship's company were feted on 12 February 1941 after their victorious march. It was along George Street, but this time heading back in the direction of the Quay that Sir John Collins' funeral possession made its way. Befitting the man, it was the largest naval funeral ever held in Sydney.[218] One hundred and thirty-eight sailors somberly pulled the gun carriage to the muffled dirge of the Naval band.[219] On either side of the coffin former Chiefs of Naval Staff acted as pall bearers. A large, silent and respectful public observed the procession. Among the crowd were many serving officers and sailors who, without an official role, still wanted to pay their respects to the nation's greatest naval hero. One of them, Lieutenant Commander Mark Shelvey recalled:

> I was in Martin Place to watch the funeral of John Collins ... The drama of the event was very high, the whole length of George Street was lined with sailors on reversed arms. The death march reverberated loudly between the buildings. The sight of the gun carriage being hauled by sailors was such an unusual sight in the modern world that I think all witnesses must have been in awe. As the funeral cortege passed I noticed an elderly lady consoling another very close to me. I offered my handkerchief to the lady who was crying and she accepted the offer. When she had composed herself she apologised for making a fuss and said words to the effect of, 'You have to understand what John Collins meant to us. When we were losing everywhere in the war he gave us our first victory. He gave us hope'.[220]

The sands of time were running out for the Pioneer Class. In one of his last naval events Harry Showers attended the 1990 Reunion of the 1930 Entry to the Naval College. Those men retained a great fondness and respect for Harry for his humane treatment of them as boys at the otherwise austere Flinders Naval Depot and for his genuine interest in them through their careers.

On 31 July 1991 Harry Showers passed away to be followed on 12 October 1993 by James Esdaile, just nine days after his 94th birthday. Before his death the then Chief of Naval Staff, Vice Admiral Ian MacDougall wrote to James expressing the Navy's gratitude to him and the other members of the Pioneer Class for their remarkable contribution to the Navy.

The memory and legacy of John Collins and Harold Farncomb were commemorated by the Navy with the naming of the first two of six Australian built submarines after them. Fittingly, Lady Collins launched *Collins* on 28 August 1993 while Jean Farncomb launched

'He gave us hope.' *A hundred and thirty-eight sailors pull the gun carriage carrying the coffin of Sir John Collins down George Street in Sydney.* (RAN)

Farncomb two years later. Both women epitomised the individual strength of the wives of the Pioneer Class and the support they rendered their husbands through their lives.

By virtue of James Esdaile's contribution to the Navy and the distinction of being the last surviving member of the Pioneer Class, James joined John Collins, Eric Feldt, Harold Farncomb, Rupert Long and Harry Showers as each having an entry in the *Australian Dictionary of Biography*. It is a remarkable collective achievement.

The Pioneer Class were the first and without doubt the greatest class to have graduated from the Royal Australian Naval College. Their mark on the Navy even in the 21st Century is indelible. In 1942 Admiral Colvin wrote in the *London Times* of the first Jervis Bay graduates:

To one who has known them and worked with them there was something out of the ordinary about these sailors of the RAN. Coming from the Australian Naval College they trained for years on their own and with the Royal Navy but they were never mere copyists. They assimilated the knowledge and traditions of the older service, but blended with it something peculiar to themselves and the results was unmistakable and unmistakably good.[221]

On James Esdaile's passing a personal link with origins of Australia's Navy was broken. As Apollonius Rhodius wrote of the original Argonauts in the Third Century BC:

> Farewell, heroic, happy breed of men!
> Your blessing on this lay of mine.
> And as the years go by, may people find it a sweeter
> and yet sweeter song to sing.
> Farewell; for I have come to the glorious finish of your labours.[222]

Endnotes

Preface

1. Collins, As Luck Would Have It, op.cit, pp.50-51.

Chapter 1

1. WR Creswell, *Close to the Wind: The Early Memoirs (1866-1879) of Admiral Sir William Rooke Creswell*, ed. P Thompson, London, Heineman, 1965, p. 200.
2. FB Eldridge, *A History of the Royal Australian Naval College: From its inception in 1913 to the end of World War II in 1945*, Melbourne, Georgian House, Melbourne, 1949, p. 7.
3. AW Jose, *The Official History of Australia in the War of 1914-18 Volume IX: The Royal Australian Navy*, University of Queensland Press, St Lucia, 1981, op.cit. p. lv.
4. Letter from Deakin to Governor General, letter dated 28 August 1906, *Commonwealth Parliamentary Papers* (CPP), 1906, No. 98.
5. JR Reckner, J.R. *Teddy Roosevelt's Great White Fleet*, Annapolis, Naval Institute Press, 2001, p. 97.
6. ibid, p. 100.
7. DM Stevens, D.M. and & J Reeve, J. edited, *Southern Trident: Strategy, History and the Rise of Australian Naval Power*, Crows Nest, Allen and Unwin, Crows Nest, 2000, p. 229.
8. ibid, p. 230.
9. On 10 July 1911 King George V granted the title 'Royal Australian Navy' to the former Commonwealth Naval Force.
10. DM Stevens and & J Reeve, op. cit., p. 221.

11 LF Bates, *Sir Alfred Ewing: A Pioneer in Physics and Engineering*, Longman, London, 1946.

12 EA Hughes, E.A., *The Royal Naval College Dartmouth*, Winchester Publications Ltd, London, 1949, p. 25.

During World War I, Professor Ewing managed the Admiralty's Room 40 which de- de-crypted the German coded signals.

13 CEW Bean, *Flagships Three*, Alston Rivers, London, 1915, p. 303.

14 DC Moore, D.C, *Duntroon: The Royal Military College of Australia 1911-2001*, Canberra, RMC of Australia, Canberra, 2001, pp. 10-21.

15 The Dreadnought Fund was established to contribute to the building of a capital ship for the RN.

16 The sites were Middle Head, Bradley's Head, La Perouse, Mona Vale (Pittwater), Rhodes (Parramatta River), Lugano (Georges River) and Long Bay (Middle Harbour).

17 Vice Admiral B.M. Chambers, Confidential Report, ADM 196/88. (TNA UK). The RN during this period was more forgiving in these matters. Chambers had previously figured in one collision in 1888 and another grounding in 1889.

18 The transfer of the southern part of Jervis Bay to the Commonwealth Government would be achieved through the Jervis Bay Territory Acceptance Act 1915 (the Acceptance Act).

19 Eldridge, op.cit. p.22.

20 Later Sir Austin Chapman.

21 JA Collins, J.A. *As Luck Would Have It: Reminiscences of an Australian Sailor*, Sydney, Angus and Robertson, Sydney, 1965, p. 18.

22 *The Sydney Morning Herald*, 10 August 1914.

23 E Feldt, E., *Reminiscences of Commander Eric Feldt*, transcript of an oral history, Archival No. OH 465, State Library of South Australia, 1966, p. 3.

24 Later Rear Admiral R. C . Boddie, CVO, DSO, RN.

25 Letter from F Brown to FB Eldridge, 12 August 1944, (Eldridge Papers, HMAS *Creswell*).

26 Letter from FW Wheatley to FB Eldridge, 18 July 1944, (Eldridge Papers, HMAS *Creswell*).

27 ibid, p. 1.

28 ibid, p. 2.

29 FW Wheatley, op.cit,ibid, p. 2.

30 http://www.worldlingo.com/ma/enwiki/en/List_of_Old_Dunelmians

31 *The Sydney Morning Herald*, 20 July 1912, p. 3.

32 EA Hughes, op. cit., p. 25.

33 Diary of Captain Edwin Nurse, personal diary.

Chapter 2

1. Royal Australian Naval College Magazine (RANC Magazine), H Thacker Printers, Geelong, 1913, p. 11.
2. FB Eldridge, *A History of the Royal Australian Naval College: From its inception in 1913 to the end of World War II in 1945*, Georgian House, Melbourne, 1949, p. 35.
3. ibid, pp. 35-36.
4. *The Argus*, Melbourne, 5 December 1912, p. 12.
5. ibid, p. 12.
6. FB Eldridge, op. cit., pp. 38-39.
7. *Western Mail*, Perth, 7 July 1899, p. 29.
8. 'Cadet Midshipmen – Naval Officers in the Making', *The Sydney Morning Herald*, 18 July 1914.
9. Letter from Mrs JE Chapman to AW Grazebrook, 1993, (Jones/Grazebrook Papers).
10. JA Collins, *As Luck Would Have It: Reminiscences of an Australian Sailor*, Angus and Robertson, Sydney, 1965, p. 16.
11. AF Feldt, *Gussie's Story*, Unpublished memoirs, 1938, p. 32. (Held by the Feldt family).
12. Captain Edwin Nurse, Diary entry for 2 February, 1913.
13. B Winter, *The Intrigue Master: Commander Long and Naval Intelligence in Australia 1913-1945*, Boolarong Press, Brisbane, 1995, p. 5.
14. *RANC Magazine*, 1913 Edition, op. cit., p. 35.
15. Discussion with Frank Larkin's relative, Captain Gordon Andrews, RAN, March 2010.
16. *RANC Magazine*, 1913 edition, op. cit., p. 8.
17. ibid, p. 8.
18. ibid, p. 8.
19. ibid, p. 8.
20. ibid, p. 8.
21. E Feldt, Reminiscences of Commander Eric Feldt, transcript of an oral history, Archival No. OH 465, State Library of South Australia, 1966, p. 5.
22. The Duncan Grant papers were examined by the author and are held by the Grant family.
23. B Howells' letter, undated.
24. 'Cadet Midshipmen – Naval Officers in the Making', *Sydney Morning Herald*, 18 July 1914.
25. Rear Admiral RC Boddie, CVO, DSO, RN, Unpublished memoirs, p. 58.

26	Handbook of the Royal Australian Naval College, Government Printer, Sydney, 1918, p. 22.
27	JA Collins, op. cit., pp. 16-17.
28	P McGuire & FM McGuire, *The Price of Admiralty*, Oxford University Press, Melbourne, 1944, p. 25.
29	E Nurse, op. cit., p. 5.
30	E Feldt, op. cit., p. 5.
31	'Life in the Royal Australian Naval College', *Catholic Press*, 28 July 1914.
32	*RANC Magazine*, op.cit., 1913 edition, p. 17.
33	ibid, p. 17.
34	ibid, p. 17.
35	*RANC Magazine*, op. cit., 1913 edition, p. 26.
36	ibid, p. 26.
37	ibid, p. 26.
38	ibid, p. 26.
39	ibid, p. 30.
40	The Second XI were known as Dreadnoughts. Letter by JM Armstrong to parents, 6 December 1914. Papers of Captain JM Armstrong, (NLA).
41	*RANC Magazine*, op. cit., 1914 edition, p. 31.
42	*RANC Magazine*, op. cit., 1914 edition, p. 7.
43	E Feldt, op. cit., p. 7.
44	AF Feldt, *Gussie's Story*, op. cit., p. 32.
45	Eric had one brother Gottfried (1883-1906), Mabel (b. 1885), Violet (1888-1899), Emma (1890-1971), Ada (1892-1983) & Minnie (1893-1984).
46	ibid, p. 8.
47	B Howells, Diary entry for 12 February 1914.
48	ibid, Diary entry for 17 February 1914.
49	EC Buley, *Glorious Deeds of Australasians in the Great War*, Andrew Melrose, London, 1915.
50	Captain Mike Calder, Interview, 28 November 2010.
51	Later Captain John Malet Armstrong, CBE, DSO, RAN (1900-1988).
52	Letter by JM Armstrong to parents, 8 March 1914, Papers of Captain JM Armstrong CBE, DSO, RAN (NLA).
53	B Howells, Diary entry for 3 March 1914.
54	E Feldt, op. cit., p. 10.
55	Captain Chambers returned to Britain first to command the old battleship HMS *Illustrious* for a short period and then the armoured cruiser HMS *Roxborough*.
56	BM Chambers, *Salt Junk: Naval Reminiscences, 1881-1906*, Constable & Co. Ltd, London, 1927, p. 37.

57	ibid, p. 1.
58	Original telegrams retained in RANC Historic Collection, HMAS *Creswell*.
59	ibid.
60	District Naval Officer Sydney, A/6/761, dated 19 May 1914.
61	*RANC Magazine*, op. cit., 1960 Edition, p. 26.
62	Letter from Naval Instructor William Atall, RN to Director of Studies, dated 17 April 1913.
63	Director of Studies Report, 2 May 1914.
64	Letter by JM Armstrong to parents, 16 June 1914. Papers of Captain JM Armstrong, (NLA).
65	RANC Minute to Naval Board, (14/4482) dated 9 June 1914 (NAA).
66	ibid.
67	ibid.
68	Commonwealth Naval Board Memorandum and Minute 9 Jun 1914 'Cadet Midshipman, College recommendation for warning given to Watkins, Watts, Lecky and Kelly', (NAA).
69	ibid.
70	RANC Memorandum 29 June 1914 to Naval Secretary, (NAA).
71	ibid.
72	ibid.
73	RANC Memorandum 9 July 1914 from Commander Grant to Naval Secretary, No. 147/C.8 (NAA).
74	Letter from Naval Secretary to Mr JS Watts, 4 July 1914, No. 14/0244/434, (NAA).
75	Commonwealth Naval Board Memorandum and Minute 9 July 1914 'Cadet Midshipman AJB Watts', (NAA).
76	Letter Mr JS Watts to the Naval Secretary 18 July 1914, (NAA).
77	Letter Naval Secretary to Mr JS Watts, 14/0252, dated 24 July 1914, (NAA).
78	RC Boddie, op. cit., p. 62.
79	RC Boddie, op. cit., p. 58.
80	FB Eldridge, op. cit., p. 46.
81	RC Boddie, op. cit., p. 60.
82	Letter by JM Armstrong to parents, 14 August 1914. Papers of Captain JM Armstrong, (NLA).
83	R Hyslop, 'Wheatley, Frederick William' (1871 - 1955), *Australian Dictionary of Biography, Volume 12*, Melbourne University Press, 1990, pp. 452-453.
84	DM Stevens, *In All Respects Ready: Australia's Navy in World War One*, Oxford University Press, South Melbourne, 2014, pp. 57-60.
85	E Feldt, op. cit., p. 10.

86	Letter by JM Armstrong to parents, 16 August 1914. Papers of Captain JM Armstrong, (NLA).	
87	DC Moore, *Duntroon: The Royal Military College of Australia 1911-2001*, Royal Military College of Australia, Canberra, 2001, pp. 44-46.	
88	RC Boddie, op. cit., p. 61.	
89	Letter from JM Armstrong to parents, 20 September 1914. Papers of Captain JM Armstrong, (NLA).	
90	Letter from JM Armstrong to parents, 6 December 1914. Papers of Captain JM Armstrong, (NLA).	
91	Service record of Able Seaman HP Hollywood, Series A6770, Accession Number 4553276, (NAA).	
92	Letter from Naval Secretary to Mr G Watkins, 3 December 1914, No. 14/0219/391, (NAA).	
93	Letter from Naval Secretary to Mr JS Watts, 3 December 1914, No. 14/0404, (NAA).	
94	Study Corporal James Brigande Condor, Unpublished Memoirs, SPC-A.	
95	Naval Board Minutes, 31 December 1914 (NAA).	
96	Naval Board Minutes, 26 January 1915 (NAA).	
97	Naval Board Minutes, 28 January 1915 (NAA).	
98	Sir Adrian Knox, King's Counsel, later Sir Adrian Knox the Second Chief Justice of the High Court.	
99	Naval Board Minutes, 3 October 1916 (NAA).	
100	Letter from F Brown to FB Eldridge, 12 August 1944, (held in Eldridge Papers HMAS *Creswell*).	
101	Letter from Mr JS Watt to the Naval Secretary, 5 January 1915, (NAA).	
102	Letter from the Naval Secretary to Mr JS Watts, 10 February 1915, (NAA)	
103	ibid.	

Chapter 3

1	*Royal Australian Naval College Magazine (RANC Magazine)*, H Thacker Printers, Geelong, 1917 Edition, p. 53.	
2	*RANC Magazine*, 1915 Edition, p. 3.	
3	JE Hewitt, *The Black One*, Langate Publishing, South Yarra, 1984, p. 12.	
4	JC Howells, *Ben and Dorothy: A Portrait of My Parents,* Published Privately, Camberwell, 2012, p. 31.	
5	RC Boddie, op. cit., p. 68.	
6	FB Eldridge, op. cit., p. 94.	
7	RC Boddie, op. cit., p. 65.	

8	Study Corporal James Brigande Condor, Extract from unpublished Memoirs, RAN Sea Power Centre.
9	'Visit to the Naval College', *The Mail*, Adelaide, 18 March 1916, p. 12.
10	Letter from JM Armstrong to parents, 9 May 1915. Papers of Captain JM Armstrong, NLA.
11	E Feldt, *Reminiscences of Commander Eric Feldt,* transcript on an oral history, Archival No. OH 465, State Library of South Australia, 1966, p. 12.
12	'A Brief Outline of the History of the Naval College', anon, undated, p. 2.
13	RC Boddie, op. cit., p. 61.
14	RC Boddie, ibid, p. 64.
15	Service Record of Vice Admiral CH Morgan, RN, ADM 196/42/275.
16	ibid.
17	RC Boddie, op. cit., p. 70.
18	Unreferenced newspaper article in the journal of Mrs CH Morgan held at the RAN Sea Power Centre.
19	*RANC Magazine,* 1916 Edition, p. 6.
20	Letter by JM Armstrong to parents, 10 October 1915. Papers of Captain JM Armstrong, NLA.
21	*RANC Magazine*, 1915 Edition, p. 31.
22	E Feldt, op. cit., p. 15.
23	JA Collins, op. cit., p. 17.
24	E Feldt, op. cit., p. 16.
25	JE Hewitt, op. cit., p. 20.
26	FB Eldridge, op. cit., p. 94.
27	ibid, p. 94.
28	P McGuire & FM McGuire, *The Price of Admiralty*, Oxford University Press, Melbourne, 1944, p. 23.
29	ibid, p. 24.
30	W Crouch, *Daily Telegraph - Admirals on Parade*, Sydney, 19 July 1963, p. 34.
31	O Frewen, *Sailor's Soliloquy*, London, Hutchinson and Company, 1961, p. 40.
32	Oral History of Vice Admiral Sir Richard Peek, (TRC532), May-June 1977, National Library of Australia.
33	ibid, p. 26.
34	DC Moore, *Duntroon: The Royal Military College of Australia 1911-2001,* Royal Military College of Australia, Canberra, 2001, pp. 29-30.
35	Royal Military College Provisional Standing Orders, June 1911, p. 4.
36	DC Moore, op. cit., p. 348.
37	Letter from Mr JS Armitage to AW Grazebrook, 2 February 1993.

38 Brian Larkins had been discharged from an Alexandria hospital just a couple of weeks before the landing after complaining of chest pains. After a month on the peninsula serving in the 1st Division, Brian was admitted to hospital on Lemnos Island with pleurisy. At Heliopolis he was diagnosed with heart disease and would return to Australia for discharge. See Service Records of Private BL Larkins, 5426 (NAA).

39 Letter from JM Armstrong to parents, 17 October 1915. Papers of Captain JM Armstrong, (NLA).

40 Harry Vallentine's older brother was Private Joseph Osborne Vallentine who was twice wounded and gassed and contracted TB whilst on the Western Front.

41 HMAT *Miltiades* (gross tonnage 7814 t) G Thompson & Co Ltd, London chartered by the Commonwealth Line.

42 AJB Watts, Army Records, Regimental Number 21140.

43 *RANC Magazine*, 1917 Edition, p. 40.

44 RC Boddie, op. cit., p. 69.

45 *RANC Magazine*, 1917 Edition, p. 41.

46 Letter from Mrs JE Chapman, undated, p. 2.

47 Letter from Miss Frances Lecky to Captain Morgan, 18 August 1915.

48 *RANC Magazine,* 1916 Edition, p. 6.

49 The cruiser HMAS *Adelaide* was eventually built but did not enter service until after the conclusion of World War I. The two super-dreadnoughts were not ordered.

50 *The Mercury*, Hobart, 4 October 1915, p. 4

51 *The Argus*, Melbourne, 1 October 1915, p. 6.

52 *The Advertiser*, Adelaide, 2 October 1915, p. 14.

53 *The Argus*, op. cit., p. 6.

54 John Valentine Stuart Lecky Record of Service card.

55 Naval Board letter 15/0131.683 dated 20 December 1915.

56 Letter from Captain Morgan to Naval Secretary 13 December 1915.

57 Letter from Mr F Parsons to Captain Morgan, 31 January 1916. (NAA)

58 Letter from Captain Morgan to Mr F Parsons, 3 February 1916. (NAA)

59 ibid, p. 5.

60 Letter by Captain Morgan to the Naval Secretary 16/106, 20 February 1916. (NAA)

61 Minutes of a Court of Inquiry held at Navy Office, Melbourne, 22 February 1916, to investigate certain circumstances at Royal Australian Naval College, Jervis Bay, NSW, p. 7, (NAA)

62 ibid, p. 5.

63 ibid, p. 7.

64 ibid, p. 7.
65 ibid, p. 7.
66 ibid, p. 7.
67 ibid, p. 7.
68 ibid, p. 2.
69 ibid, p. 3.
70 ibid, p. 3.
71 ibid, p. 3.
72 ibid, p. 3.
73 Deposition by Lieutenant C Cotton-Stapleton RNR 20 February 1916.
74 Letter from Second Naval Member to Naval Secretary 22 February 1916, pp. 1-2, (NAA).
75 ibid, p. 2.
76 Letter from Captain Morgan to the Naval Secretary, 18 March 1916.
77 *RANC Magazine,* 1917 Edition, p. 7.
78 Calder Family history, p. 2.
79 *Australian Dictionary of Biography* entry for John Charles Wright (1861-1933).
80 *RANC Magazine,* 1917 Edition, p. 10.
81 Letter from H Lambert, Secretary of State Colonial Office to the Secretary to the Admiralty, 10 June 1916.
82 Letter from the Governor General (No. 369) to Secretary of State for the Colonies 20 September 1916.
83 Letter to AW Grazebrook from Mr FWS Grant, 7 December 1992.
84 ibid, p. 40.
85 ibid, p. 40.
86 ibid, p. 41.
87 'The Naval College – Officers in the Making', *The Sydney Morning Herald,* October 1917.
88 Unreferenced newspaper article in the journal of Mrs CH Morgan held at the RAN Sea Power Centre, Canberra.
89 Sub-Lieutenant James Macleod went on to become a Lieutenant Commander. In World War II he was appointed Mechanical Engineering Officer of the destroyer HMS *Glowworm*. He was lost with many of her crew when in the ship's heroic action against the German heavy cruiser *Hipper* off Norway on 8 April 1940. His Commanding Officer, Lieutenant Commander GB Roope, RN was awarded the posthumous Victoria Cross.
90 RC Boddie, op. cit., p. 72.
91 Letter from JM Armstrong to parents, 12 March 1914. Papers of Captain JM Armstrong, (NLA).

92	ibid, p. 72.
93	RC Brown, op. cit.
94	ibid.
95	Naval Service records of Dominick Healy (5195) and John Hennigan (2576), (NAA).
96	*The Advertiser,* Adelaide, 21 March 1916, p. 6.
97	ibid. Erle Boyd would continue to serve in the RAN through to the end of World War II and eventually become a Chief Petty Officer.
98	*RANC Magazine,* 1917 Edition, p. 8.
99	*Referee* magazine, 6 September 1916.
100	E Nurse, op. cit., entry for June 1916.
101	*Royal Military College Journal*, November 1916, p. 30.
102	*The Sydney Morning Herald,* 30 October 1916, p. 6.
103	JC Howells, *Ben and Dorothy: A Portrait of My Parents,* Published Privately, Camberwell, 2012, p. 30.
104	ibid, p. 37.
105	NK Calder, Diary entry, 6 December 1916.
106	Commanding Officer RAN College letter to the Naval Secretary 16/322 dated 14 August 1916.
107	ibid.
108	ibid, 10 December 1916.
109	*RANC Magazine,* 1917 Edition, p. 10.
110	'The Naval College – Australian Sea Officers', *The Sydney Morning Herald,* 18 December 1916, p. 8.
111	ibid, p. 8.
112	ibid, p. 8.
113	*RANC Magazine,* 1917 Edition, p. 10.
114	JE Hewitt, op. cit., p. 20.
115	*The Sydney Morning Herald*, 13 December 1916, p. 10.
116	GP Gilbert, *Australian Naval Personalities*, Papers in Australian Maritime Affairs No.17, Sea Power Centre, Canberra, 2006, p. 56.
117	*RANC Magazine,* 1917 Edition, p. 11.
118	Discussion with author and AW Grazebrook, December 1999.
119	*RANC Magazine*, 1917 Edition, p. 12.
120	NK Calder, op. cit., 12 December 1916.
121	A charabanc was an open motor car typically with four to five rows of seats. Popular up to the 1920s. They were replaced by motor coaches.
122	*The Sydney Morning Herald*, 13 December 1916, p. 10.
123	ibid.

Chapter 4

1. FB Eldridge, *A History of the Royal Australian Naval College: From its inception in 1913 to the end of World War II in 1945,* Georgian House, Melbourne, 1949, p. vi.
2. Email to author from John Howells, 10 February 2011.
3. ibid.
4. Letter from Midshipman Frank Larkins to Ben Howells, 8 January 1917 (Held by Mr JC Howells).
5. Eight Midshipmen embarked in Sydney, 12 in Melbourne and two in Fremantle. Navy Office Minute 'Embarkation of Midshipmen in RMS *Omrah*', dated 18 December 1916.
6. Naval Secretary letter 16/9658 to the Naval Representative London dated February 1917.
7. Machine Gun Company 3, Reinforcement 10.
8. Captain AH Cobby, DSC, DFC & 2 Bars. He had 29 aircraft kills and also destroyed 13 balloons. He later become an Air Commodore in the RAAF.
9. NK Calder, op. cit., Diary entry for 16 January 1917.
10. ibid, Diary entry for 16 January 1917.
11. Minutes of the Naval Board, 27 January 1917, p. 1, (NAA).
12. ibid, Entry for 6 February 1917.
13. ibid, Entry for 10 February 1917.
14. E Feldt, op. cit., p. 22.
15. ibid, p. 21.
16. RAN College letter 16/322 to Naval Secretary dated 7 July 1916.
17. *Appointment of Midshipmen RAN to Seagoing Ships in the Grand Fleet*. Extract from Naval Representative's 98th Report (Captain Francis F. Haworth-Booth, CMG, RN retired) dated 25 March 1917, MP1049/1.
18. E Feldt, op. cit., p. 22.
19. The collision between the French ammunition ship SS *Mont Blanc* and the Norwegian SS *Imo* resulted in the then world's largest man-made detonation which killed about 2,000 people and devastated the city and port. Bertram Chambers retired as a Vice Admiral in 1922.
20. *RANC Magazine*, 1916 Edition, pp. 18-20.
21. NK Calder, op. cit., Diary entry for 6 April 1917.
22. E Nurse, op. cit., Entry for 8 April 1917.
23. E Feldt, op. cit., p. 23.
24. ibid, p. 33.
25. *Encyclopedia of Canadiana*, Volume 6, The Grolier Society of Canada, Toronto, 1966, p. 311.

26 Vice Admiral JA Collins, Oral History, Merrill Legal Solutions, undated, p. 7.
27 Later Vice Admiral Sir John Crace, KBE, CB, RN.
28 Later Commodore Sir Phillip *Bowyer-Smyth* RN.
29 Later Admiral James Clement Ley, CB, CVO, RN.
30 E Feldt, op. cit., p. 33.
31 Later Admiral Sir William Nicholson KCB, RN.
32 Captain Adolphus Williamson, CMG, MVO, RN.
33 JA Collins, *As Luck Would Have It*, op. cit., p. 3.
34 ibid, p. 3.
35 E Feldt, op. cit., p. 37.
36 ibid, pp. 5-6.
37 ibid, p. 7.
38 Death certificate for AH Williamson available at Yarmouth, Volume 4B, September 1918, p. 5.
39 E Feldt, op. cit., p. 33.
40 ibid, p. 39. Captain Watson was later Sir Hugh Dudley Richards Watson, KCB, CVO, CBE, RN.
41 A Creswick, *Australians at War* entry, www.australiansatwar.gov.au.
42 ibid.
43 *UB-32* sank ten more ships before being lost with all hands after herself being attacked by a Royal Naval Air Service aircraft on 17 November 1917 in the English Channel.
44 Letter to AW Grazebrook from Mr S Armitage, 2 February 1993.
45 C Hocking, *Dictionary Of Disasters At Sea During The Age Of Steam: Including sailing ships and ships of war lost in action, 1824-1962*, Volume 1, London : Lloyd's Register of Shipping, 1969.
46 Letter from Lord Stamfordam to GA Steel Private Secretary to the First Lord of the Admiralty 12 December 1916.
47 NK Calder, op. cit., Diary entry 27 May 1917.
48 E Nurse, op. cit., Diary entry for 8 April 1917.
49 Letter from Peyton Kimlin to Ben Howells, February 1918, Howells Family Papers.
50 E Feldt, op. cit., p. 35.
51 AW Jose, *The Official History of Australia in the War of 1914-18 Volume IX: The Royal Australian Navy*, University of Queensland Press, St Lucia, 1981, p. 298.
52 Report of the Court of Enquiry into the Circumstances, attending the loss of HMS *Vanguard* on 9 July 1917. Held onboard HMS *Emperor of India*, 30 July 1917. ADM 137/3681, Public Record Office.
53 These ships were battleship HMS *Bulwark*, the cruiser HMS *Natal*, the minelayer

	HMS *Princes Irene* and the monitor HMS *Glatton*.
54	Letter from E Feldt to P Feldt, 20 June 1917.
55	Letter from E Felt to P Feldt, 11 November, 17.
56	Letter from Midshipman Norman Calder to his mother, 25 September 1917 (AWM).
57	Letter from Midshipman Eddy Nurse to Ben Howells, 5 October 1917.
58	NK Calder, op. cit., Entries for 22 and 23 August 1917.
59	Letter from Mrs Janet Getting to Major Lean, 10 February 1918.
60	Australian War Memorial 145 Roll of Honour cards, 1914-1918 War.
61	Service Record of Sergeant WH Burnett, 2912, (NAA).
62	JS Corbett, Naval Operations, *Naval Operations, Volume V*, Longmans, Green and Co., London, p. 169.
63	E Nurse, op. cit., Entry for 16 November 1917.
64	NK Calder, op. cit., Entry for 17 November 1917.
65	ibid, Entry for 16 November 1917.
66	ibid, Entry for 17 November 1917.
67	Later Admiral Sir Walter Henry Cowan, 1st Baron of the Baltic, KCB, DSO*, MVO (1871–1956).
68	British cruiser casualties were *Caledon:* five ratings killed, *Calypso:* one officer, eight ratings killed. One additional rating died of wounds. *Cardiff:* six ratings killed and one additional rating died of wounds.
69	*The London Gazette*, No. 30687, 17 May 1918.
70	German damage and casualties in the battle was *Königsberg*: one 4-inch hit in the shield of starboard No. 1 gun, no damage and one 15-inch', three funnels pierced, explosion in a filled coal bunker, one boiler out of action, speed reduced to 24 knots, nine killed, three severally wounded, nine slightly wounded. *Pillau*: one15-inch hit in the port No. 1 gun without explosion, gun put out of action, one killed, two blown overboard, six slightly wounded. *Frankfurt*: two 6-inch hits in the superstructure, four killed, two blown overboard, eight seriously wounded, nine slightly wounded. *Nűrnberg*: No direct hits, four killed, six slightly wounded.
71	E Nurse, Diary Entry for 17 November 1917.
72	*Argus*, Melbourne, 8 February 1918, p. 8.
73	E Feldt, op. cit., p. 36.
74	*Argus*, Melbourne, 8 February 1918, p. 8.
75	D Everitt, *The K Boats*, New English Library, London, 1972, p. 29.
76	Letter from Vice Admiral Sir John Jellicoe, Second Sea Lord to Lord Fisher, former First Sea Lord, 1 June 1913; D Everitt, *The K Boats*, New English Library, London, 1972, p. 9.
77	ibid, p. 69.

78 As the Midshipmen were still officially posted to HMS *Glorious*, the source of which K class they were serving in is the diary of Captain Nurse. There is one discrepancy. The Showers family believe Harry Showers served in the *K14* and suffered from exposure to Chlorine gas. (see E Crouch, *Obituary Rear Admiral Henry Arthur Showers*, Naval Historical Review, 1992, p. 29) As it is possible for Harry to have been still exposed in the *K22* I have relied on the Nurse Diary for boat assignment.

79 Interview with George Kimber with AW Grazebrook, 1 August 1985.

80 E Nurse, op. cit., Diary entry for 26 January 1918.

81 D Everitt, *K Boats: Steam-powered submarines in World War I*, Airlife Publishing, Bridgend, 1999 (first published by George C Harrap & Company Ltd in 1963), p. 79.

82 The distance was six cables astern of HMS *Courageous*. Letter from Commander EW Leir, DSO, RN Commanding Officer HMS *Ithuriel* to Vice Admiral Commanding Battle Cruiser Force, 2 February 1918.

83 Letter from Commander TCB Harbottle, RN Commanding Officer HM Submarine *K14* to Commander EW Leir, DSO, RN Commanding Officer HMS *Ithuriel*, 2 February 1918.

84 Letter from Lieutenant Commander C De Burgh, RN Commanding Officer HM Submarine *K22* to Commander EW Leir, DSO, RN Commanding Officer HMS *Ithuriel*, 1 February 1918.

85 Letter from Commander TCB Harbottle, RN Commanding Officer HM Submarine *K14* to Commander EW Leir, DSO, RN Commanding Officer HMS *Ithuriel*, 2 February 1918.

86 Able Seaman GV Knell later joined the RAN and came to Australia in HMAS *Oxley*. Details of the incident from an undated *Tingira Boys Association Newsletter*.

87 E Crouch, *Obituary Rear Admiral Henry Arthur Showers*, Naval Historical Review, 1992, p. 29

88 Report into the Loss of K Class Submarines, No. 453/HF. 1100, 19 February 1918, (RAN Sea Power Centre).

89 E Nurse, op. cit., Diary entry for 26 January 1918.

90 Interview with George Kimber with AW Grazebrook, 1 August 1985.

91 D Everitt, op.cit.

92 *Collisions Involving HM Ships Inflexible and Fearless and HM Submarines K14, K22, K17 and K6*, ADM 156/86, (TNA UK).

93 Nurse, op.cit., Entry for 26 January 1918.

94 Report into the Loss of K Class Submarines, No. 453/HF. 1100, 19 February 1918. (RAN Sea Power Centre).

95 Result of Court Martial of Commander EW Leir, DSO, RN, Held in HMS *Crescent*, 22 March 1918, (RAN Sea Power Centre).

96 NK Calder, Diary entry for 9 February 1918.

97	Letter from Midshipman PJ Kimlin to Ben Howells, undated but 1917.
98	Letter from Mr WJ Cunningham to Naval Secretary, Navy Office, 8 March 1919, National Archives MP1049/1/0/1918/036.
99	Navy Office Telegram No. 15998 from Naval Representative, London, dated received 30 March 1919.
100	E Nurse, op. cit., Entry for 16 February 1918.
101	E Nurse, op. cit., Entry for 19 February 1918.
102	Service Record Warrant Officer TL Dix, ADM 196/166/49, (TNA UK).
103	Report on Destruction of German Fishing Trawlers by HMS *Vega* in the Kattegat 16 April 1918, ADM 137/2132. (TNA UK). The trawlers were, *Odin, Kriegschiffe III, Hornsriff, Wien, Odin, Fritz Busse, Schelligh, Wega Heindrich, Diestal* and *Senator*.
104	*RAN Personnel - Midshipman RMB Long, WL Reilly & J Burnett*, 8724669, (AWM).
105	Letter from Mrs Mary Backhouse, undated, (held by author).
106	*The Argus*, 'Successful Midshipmen', 29 October 1918, p. 4.
107	Letter from Commander RM Dalglish, RN to Commanding Officer RAN College, undated. An extract held in the papers of Lieutenant Commander Percy Ferguson Dash (3DRL/7696) held at Australian War Memorial.
108	Report 'Midshipman RAN' Rear Admiral Commanding HM Australian Fleet by Captain HL Mawbey, RN (Commanding Officer HMS *Agincourt*), 14 September 1918 (NAA). Later Admiral Henry Lancelot Mawbey, CB, CVO RN (1870–1933).
109	Sub Lieutenant F Getting RAN, S-206, 11 January 1918, (NAA).
110	While the particulars of S-206 changed over time the officer reporting system remained unchanged in the RAN until the advent of the Freedom of Information Act in 1982. An 'open' system of reporting was introduced and officers could receive their 'closed' reports.
111	Form. 12E Report on Lieutenant ES Nurse, 30 September 1922, HMS *Dauntless*.
112	NK Calder, op. cit., Diary entry for the 26 October 1918.
113	ibid, Entry for the 11 November 1918.
114	E Feldt, op. cit., p. 42.
115	ibid.
116	The destroyers were HMA Ships *Huon, Parramatta, Swan, Torrens, Yarra* and *Warrego*.
117	JS Armitage, Letter to AW Grazebrook, 2 February 1992.
118	The Allied naval forces were from the Australian, British, French, Greek and Italian navies.
119	JS Armitage, Letter to AW Grazebrook, 2 February 1992.

120 Due to the loss of British Army records in German World War II air raids, it is unknown when Harry Vallentine joined the British Army.
121 W Werner, *Rifle Brigade Chronicle for 1919,* John Bale & Sons, London, 1920, pp. 178-179.
122 E Nurse, op. cit., Entry for 13 February 1919.
123 HM Submarine *J6* had been sunk by a British Q-Ship in error during World War I.
124 MWD White, *Australian Submarines: A History,* Canberra, AGPS, 1992, p. 86.
125 They included Lieutenant Claude Barry who was awarded a DSO for his sinking of *UB72* while in command of HM Submarine *D4.*
126 ibid, pp. 87-88.
127 *RAN Navy List,* April 1919, p. 31.
128 Report of Collision, HMA Submarine *J5,* 14 April 1919, Navy Office records file MP 525, File No. 13/5/25.
129 ibid.
130 Report of Court of Enquiry held in HMAS *Brisbane,* 18 June 1919.
131 Australian Commonwealth Naval Board, letter 19/4609 dated 29 July 1919.
132 Secretary of the Australian Commonwealth Naval Board letter to the Treasury, 11 May 1922.
133 TM Jones, *Watchdogs of the Deep : Life in a submarine during the Great War, 1914-1918,* Pinnacle Press, 1944, p. 197.
134 ibid, p. 197.
135 *The Argus,* 'Australian Navy: Warships Returning', 14 April 1919, p. 6; and *The Advertiser,* 5 April 1919, p. 11.
136 Letter from His Majesty King George V dated 15 April 1919.
137 MHD White, op. cit., p. 91.
138 *The Sydney Morning Herald,* 31 May 1919, p. 18.
139 For more details see *The Royal Australian Navy,* op. cit., p. 56.
140 *The Sydney Morning Herald,* 17 June 1919, p. 7.
141 TM Jones, op. cit., p. 202.
142 *RANC Magazine,* 1919 Edition, p. 10.
143 Melbourne Church of England Grammar School Magazine, 15 May 1917, p. 93.
144 RANC Magazine, 1919 Edition.
145 Melbourne Church of England Grammar School Magazine, 15 May 1917, p. 93.
146 TM Jones, op. cit., p. 208.
147 *The Sydney Morning Herald,* 21 July 1919, p. 10.
148 *The Sydney Morning Herald,* 21 July 1919, p. 9.
149 ibid, p. 9.
150 JA Collins, op. cit., p. 21.

Chapter 5

1. WH Ross, *Lucky Ross: The Autobiography of an RAN Officer 1934-1951,* Hesperian Press, Carlisle, 1994, p. 129.
2. Australian War Memorial www.awm.gov.au/research/infosheets/war_casualties.asp
3. ibid.
4. Naval Board Minutes, 26 November 1918, (NAA).
5. Naval Board Minutes, 28 November 1918, (NAA).
6. Naval Board Minutes 2 December 1918, (NAA).
7. Charles Childers left the Navy in 1922 as part of the naval reductions. He rejoined the Royal Navy Volunteer Reserve and commanded the naval trawlers HMS *Burra* and HMS *Bern* during World War II.
8. 'Navy Breaking: The Minister's Blow at Discipline', *Queensland Courier,*
9. *Evening News,* 14 July 1919.
10. Captain DW Grant service record, ADM 196/142/551, (TNA UK).
11. *The Advertiser,* Federal Parliament, 1 August 1919, p. 10.
12. *The Queenslander,* Discipline in the Navy, 9 August 1919, p. 20.
13. ibid.
14. *The Brisbane Courier,* 4 August 1919, p. 7.
15. *The Sydney Morning Herald,* 8 December 1919, p. 4.
16. Email from Mrs Catherine Grant, 12 December 2010.
17. Details obtained from the Grant family.
18. Conversation with Captain Michael Calder RAN (Retired), 28 November 2010.
19. Lieutenant ES Nurse AS.206, 1 October 1919, (NAA).
20. HMAS *Suva* letter to Naval Secretary, 'Special Report on Sub-Lieutenant Peyton J Kimlin', RAN, 4 August 1919, (NAA).
21. Those embarked were Armitage, Burnett, Gilling, Kimlin, Long, Newman, Nurse, Reilly, Sadleir, Showers and Watkins.
22. PR Burnett, *Captain Joseph Burnett,* RAN, *Naval Historical Review,* Sydney, December 1973, pp. 3-9.
23. *Royal Naval College: Session 1919-20 Final Examination, Officers of the Royal Australian Navy,* June 1920, ADM 203/42, 122712, (TNA UK).
24. Captain, Naval Representative Australia House, letter 1147/2, NR 9580, dated 7 July 1920, (NAA).
25. Captain, Naval Representative Australia House, letter 1147/4, NR10567, dated 17 February 1921, (NAA).
26. The Lower Deck is a collective term for sailors who in the days of sail lived in the lower decks.

27   Commanding Officer, HMAS *Brisbane* letter to Commodore Commanding HM Fleet, D578, 13 June 1921, (NAA).
28   ibid.
29   Commodore Commanding HM Australian Fleet letter to the Naval Secretary 839/AF 255 dated 17 June 1921, (NAA).
30   *The Argus*, Melbourne, 12 January 1922, p. 8.
31   *The Sydney Morning Herald,* 12 December 1924, p. 5.
32   G Blaikie, *Remember Smith's Weekly*, Rigby Ltd, Sydney, 1966, p. 18.
33   For examples see *Aussie* Magazine, No. 67 (15 September 1924), No. 70 (15 December 1924) & No. 74 (15 April 1925).
34   CL White, *Art That Pays*, Leyshon White Commercial Art School, booklet, two editions 1930s, 1193743, (State Library of Victoria).
35   MWD White, *Australian Submarines: A History*, AGPS, Canberra, 1992, p. 106.
36   Norman Calder was to remain a Freemason for over 60 years. He was admitted to the Third Degree on 21 June 1923 in the Needlemakers Lodge No. 4343 in England, and to the Second Degree in the vicinity of Hampton Court, in the mid 1920s and his 50 Year Service Jewel was awarded in 1972 followed by the 60-year Bar, in 1982.
37   GAH Gordon, *The Rules of the Game: Jutland and British Naval Command*, London: John Murray, 1996, p. 336.
38   JA Collins, AS 206 Report, 29 July 1922, (NAA).
39   *The Navy League Journal*, The Magazine of the Navy League, NSW Branch, Volume 3, No. 8, August 1940, Sydney, p. 7.
40   E Feldt, op. cit., p. 45.
41   ibid, p. 45.
42   *Medical Report on a Case for Survey - Sub Lieutenant HA MacKenzie*, 17 December 1919, Series B3476, Barcode 410670, (NAA).
43   The Four Power Treaty on the Limitations of Naval Armaments. The signatory nations were France, Great Britain, Japan and the United States.
44   Letter from Naval Representative, Australia House to Lieutenant ES Nurse, RAN (N1634/2) dated 10 July 1922.
45   Letter from Mr P Reilly to AW Grazebrook 22 July 1992, p. 2. (Jones/Grazebrook Papers).
46   ibid, p. 2.
47   Australian Commonwealth Naval Board Minutes No. 402, 1922, NAA (ACT): A2585/1.
48   E Feldt, op. cit., p. 51.
49   ibid, p. 51.
50   E Feldt, op. cit., p. 54.
51   Letter from EA Feldt to Senator Sir George Pearce, 1 August 1923 contained in *EA Feldt - Pensioner - Former New Guinea Officer*, A452, 3554676, (NAA).

52	Brigadier General EA Wisdom, CB, CMG, DSO (1869-1945).
53	James Reginald Halligan, OBE (1894-1968); See the on-line *Australian Dictionary of Biography*.
54	Penscript on Memorandum for Secretary Home and Territories Department from the Administrator of New Guinea, 22 September 1923, *EA Feldt - Pensioner - Former New Guinea Officer*, A452, 3554676, (NAA).
55	P Biskup, B Jinks, and H Nelson, *A Short History of New Guinea*, Angus and Robertson, Sydney, 1968, pp. 87-88.
56	*New Guinea Gazette*, Permanent Staff List, No. 90, 25 July 1924.
57	*New Guinea Gazette*, No. 74, 15 December 1923, p. 437.
58	*New Guinea Gazette*, Permanent Staff List, No. 90, 25 July 1924.
59	Letter from Secretary Home and Territories Department to EA Feldt dated 1 November 1923, *EA Feldt - Pensioner - Former New Guinea Officer*, A452, 3554676, (NAA).
60	Lieutenant Colonel John Wolstab, DSO (1885-1957).
61	George Wilfred Lambert Townsend.
62	John Keith McCarthy (1905-1976); See the on-line *Australian Dictionary of Biography*.
63	JK McCarthy, *Patrol Into Yesterday*, FW Cheshire, Melbourne, 1963, p. 50.
64	Sleeping baskets are a woven cocoon-like 'tent' supported by cane hoops for an entire family to sleep in at night to avoid the Sepik mosquitoes.
65	ML Townsend, *District Officer*, Pacific Publications, Sydney, 1968, p. 98.
66	E Feldt, op. cit., p. 64.
67	ibid, p. 107.
68	ibid, pp. 107-8.
69	E Feldt, op. cit., p. 71.
70	Brigadier General Evan Alexander Wisdom, CB, CMG, DSO (1869–1945).
71	E Feldt, op. cit., pp. 79-80.
72	The ED Robinson photographic collection is in Australian Museum.
73	E Feldt, op. cit., p. 72.
74	ES Nurse, Diary entry for 7 July 1925.
75	HMS *Excellent* Form 206 on Lieutenant JA Collins, RAN dated 15 August 1924.
76	Cuthbert Quinlan Dale Collins (1897–1956) (see *Australian Dictionary of Biography* entry for details).
77	Lieutenant HB Farncomb, RAN, Special Notation in Record, SC 2021/8/25 dated 26 October 1922. Attached to Confidential Reports.
78	DM Stevens, *The Royal Australian Navy in World War II*, 2nd edn., Allen and Unwin, Crows Nest, 2005, p. 73.
79	Oral History of Vice Admiral Sir Richard Peek, (TRC532), May-June 1977, (NLA).

80 Extract from the Flimsey Log held at the Royal Navy Submarine Museum, Gosport.
81 Later Vice-Admiral Wilfred Tomkinson CB, MVO.
82 Abstract of the certificates of Lieutenant Commander LF Gilling (Form S-1353). Contained in the HMAS *Canberra* Grounding Lieutenant Commander LF Gilling Court Martial documents (NAA).
83 Lieutenant Commander LF Gilling AS. 206 Report 30 March 1926.
84 ibid.
85 ES Nurse, op. cit., Diary entry, 1925.
86 WJL Wharton, *Hydrographical Surveying: A description of the means employed in constructing marine charts,* originally published 1888 and updated by AM Field, 1922, p. 194.
87 Form S-206 on Lieutenant AD Conder by Commander P Maxwell, RN dated 13 March 1924.
88 Form S-206 on Lieutenant AD Conder by Commander CH Knowles, RN dated 28 March 1925.
89 ibid.
90 Vice Admiral Sir John Edgell, KBE, CB, FRS, RN.
91 Discussions with CAR Sadleir's daughter Ms Deni McKenzie, June 2013.
92 Lieutenant JCD Esdaile, S206 Report from HMS *Osprey,* 9 November 1924.
93 *Requirements of Minesweeping and Auxiliary anti-submarine Vessels at various Empire Ports in the event of War in the East,* 12 March 1925, Committee on Imperial Defence, AWM 124, pp. 3-132.
94 Letter from Mr P Reilly to AW Grazebrook, 22 July 1992, pp. 2-6.
95 Letter from GS Kimlin to AW Grazebrook, 20 August 1992.
96 Copyright Lodgement document for *Carnival,* 9 January 1928 Series Number A1336, Control Symbol 16996 (NAA).
97 *Coolamon School Administration File 1923-1939,* 5/15496.1 (NSW SA).
98 Copyright Lodgement document for *A Foxtrot,* 27 May 1931, Series Number A1336, Item 21188, Control Symbol 3498756 (NAA).
99 *New South Wales Police Gazette,* 3 Jul 1929, p. 484.
100 Lieutenant GWT Armitage AS 206 dated 14 March 1926.
101 Interview with Warrant Officer Steward Allen Guthrie (retired) 19 July 2013.
102 Minutes of Proceedings at a Court Martial onboard HMAS *Platypus* in Hobart on 12 February 1926 for the trial of Lieutenant GWT Armitage, AF 165/401/4, (NAA).
103 Lieutenant GWT Armitage AS 206, dated 8 April 1927.
104 Papers of Commander Norman Calder OBE, Life Summary, PR0323, (AWM).
105 E Feldt, op. cit., p. 100.

106 Kiap was a pigeon English word derived from the German käpitan for to describe a district or patrol officer.
107 E Feldt, op. cit., p. 100.
108 *The Brisbane Courier*, '£20 Bail Forfeited', 17 December 1927, p. 11.
109 In *Melbourne's* place on the Australia Station was HMS *Dehli*.
110 JA Collins, op. cit., pp. 35-36.
111 ibid, p. 36.
112 ibid, pp. 37-38.
113 ibid, p. 39.
114 'Canberra Ceremony: Historic Scene', *The Argus*, 10 May 1927, pp. 19-21.
115 *The Sydney Morning Herald*, 21 November 1927, p. 4.
116 HA Showers, *Recollections of HMAS Sydney*, undated, (Showers Family Papers).
117 Australian Archives MT856/1: Item 559/206/915 Lieutenant Commander RB Long.
118 File note SC 2026/8/27 in Commander RBM Long, Confidential Reports.
119 *The Hobart Mercury*, 2 May 1928, p. 15.
120 'Australia's Navy: Graduates of Jervis Bay', *The Sydney Morning Herald*, 21 June 1928, p. 11
121 'HMAS Australia: Launching Ceremony', *The Advertiser*, 19 March 1927, p. 15.
122 Sonar systems were called ASDIC sets until US sonar term gained wide currency towards the end of World War II.
123 Creswell was promoted to Vice Admiral in September 1922.
124 'HMAS Australia: Leaving Tomorrow: Portsmouth Function', *The Canberra Times*, 20 July 1928, p. 6.
125 JA Collins, op. cit., p. 45.
126 *The West Australian*, 'HMAS Australia: New Yorkers Welcome', 1 September 1928, p. 19.
127 *The Argus*, 11 October 1928, p. 10.
128 'HMAS Australia: Inspected by Mr Bruce', *The Argus*, 17 October 1928, p. 10.
129 *The Sydney Morning Herald*, 29 October 1928, p. 14.
130 *The Advertiser*, Adelaide, 23 May 1929, p. 12.
131 ES Mayo, *The Visit to the Submarines, Royal Australian Naval College Magazine,* 1929 Edition, Sydney, p. 28.
132 ibid, p. 28.
133 Lieutenant Commander FE Getting AS 206 Report, 1930, (NAA).
134 HMS *Osprey* Form 206 on Lieutenant Commander JCD Esdaile, RAN dated 30 September 1930.
135 Letter from Commanding Officer HMS *Douglas* to Naval Representative, Australia House, 14 April 1930.

136 Conversation AW Grazebrook and Mrs JR Farncomb, 9 June 1988.
137 Imperial Defence College Report on Lieutenant Commander HB Farncomb, RAN, 559/204/369 dated 7 January 1931. Contained in Confidential Reports of HB Farncomb, (NAA).
138 E Feldt, op. cit., p. 102.
139 IL Idriess, *Gold-dust and ashes: the romantic story of the New Guinea goldfields*. Angus and Robertson. Sydney, 1933, p. 113.
140 E Feldt, op. cit., p. 106.
141 E Felt, *Errol Flynn at Salamaua*, Quadrant, Spring, 1961, Volume 5 (4), pp 81-88.
142 E Feldt, ibid, p. 116.
143 http://en.wikipedia.org/wiki/Blackwater_fever.
144 IL Idriess, *Gold-dust and ashes*, op. cit., p. 229.
145 John Lawrence Baird, 1st Viscount Stonehaven, GCMG, DSO, PC, JP, DL (27 April 1874 – 20 August 1941).
146 Luluais were government appointed headmen and were assisted in keeping the village records by younger Tultuls who would likely become a Luluai. The medical Tultuls received basic medical training.
147 Annual Report 1928-29, p. 83, cited in LP Mair, *Australia in New Guinea*, Christophers, Melbourne, 1948, p. 107.
148 *The Queenslander*, 5 September 1929, p. 49.
149 The Marriage Certificate of AD Conder and EKM Kerwin, No. 6631, dated 28 August 1929.
150 *Australia* and *Canberra* alternated as Squadron flagship depending on which ship was in refit.
151 Later Admiral Sir Edward Ratcliffe Garth Russell Evans, 1st Baron Mountevans, KCB, DSO.
152 C Choules, *Claude Choules: His Autobiography, The Last of the Last*, Hesperian Press, Carlisle, 2009, p. 80.
153 Minutes of Proceedings at a Court Martial onboard HMAS *Canberra* at Jervis Bay on 25 November 1929 for the trial of Lieutenant Commander Lloyd Falconer Gilling, RAN of HMAS *Canberra*, NAA Files A471, Item 22468, p. 9.
154 Choules, op. cit., p. 80.
155 ibid, p. 28.
156 ibid, p. 81.
157 Minutes of Proceedings at a Court Martial onboard HMAS *Canberra* at Jervis Bay on 25 November 1929 for the trial of Captain GL Massey, RN of HMAS *Canberra*, NAA Files A471, Item 22468, p. 45.
158 Minutes of Proceedings of Court Martial onboard HMAS *Canberra* on 25 November 1929, op. cit., p. 34.
159 ibid, p. 47.

160 ibid, p. 42.
161 ibid, p. 49.
162 Lieutenant Commander LF Gilling AS.206, 26 November 1929, (NAA).
163 ibid.
164 Incoming Passenger List SS *Moldavia,* 10 January 1930.
165 Promotion Summary Sheet in confidential report file of LF Gilling, 311631, (NAA).
166 Lieutenant Commander HA Showers, AS 206 Report, 6 August 1931.
167 JA Collins, op. cit., p. 49.
168 Lieutenant Commander JA Collins, S206 Report, dated 31 March 1930.
169 Lieutenant Commander PH Hirst, AS.450, 10 April 1930, (NAA).
170 Lieutenant Commander PH Hirst, AS 206, 10 April 1930 (NAA).
171 ibid, p. 50.
172 Lieutenant Commander JA Collins S206 Report, dated 18 Oct 1930.
173 Lieutenant Commander JCD Esdaile, Form AS 450 from Rear Admiral ERGR Evans, 15 April 1931.
174 Lieutenant Commander JCD Esdaile, Form AS 206, dated 14 October 1933.
175 Captain Geoffrey RS Watkins, DSO, RN (later Rear Admiral).
176 Lieutenant Commander J Burnett, RAN S.206 Report dated 1 January 1932, (NAA).
177 Promotion Recommendation for Lieutenant Commanders J Burnett and JA Collins from the Director RNSC Greenwich, 30 April 1932, (NAA).
178 Commander RBM Long Confidential Reports (NAA).
179 Lieutenant Commander GWT Armitage Record of Service Card annotation (NAA).
180 *The Mercury*, 24 March 1934, p. 7
181 C Simpson, *Plumes and Arrows: Inside New Guinea,* Angus and Robertson, Sydney, 1962, p. 10.
182 ibid, p. 24.
183 ibid, p. 24.
184 ibid, pp. 24-25.
185 ibid, p. 25.
186 There was and remains a high incidence of mouth cancer as a result of betel nut chewing.
187 ibid, p. 26.
188 SJ Chinnery, *Malaguna Road: The Papua and New Guinea Diaries of Sarah Chinnery*, NLA, Canberra, 1998, p. 114.
189 ibid, p. 65.
190 *The North West Courier*, 13 August 1934, p. 3.

191   *The Advertiser*, Adelaide, 29 August 1934, p. 7.

192   HMS *Curlew* Medical Officers Report 1933, Entry 9a, (RN NHB).

193   ibid.

194   SF Dudley, Pulmonary Tuberculosis in the Royal Navy and the Use of Mass Miniature Radiography in its Control, *Proceedings of the Royal Society of Medicine*, Volume XXXIV, 28 March 1941, p. 402.

195   GH Gill, *Royal Australian Navy 1939-1942*, Melbourne, Collins, 1985, p. 15.

196   *War Memorandum (Eastern) Sections A-E, Admiralty,* 19 September 1933, ADM 116/3475, p. 8 (RN NHB).

197   T Wildenberg, *All the Factors of Victory: Admiral Joseph Mason Reeves and the Origins of Carrier Airpower*, Potomac Books Inc., Washington, 2003, pp. 180-195.

198   JVP Goldrick, *Buying Time: British Submarine Capability in the Far East, 1919-1940*, Global War Studies, 2015.

199   *War Memorandum (Eastern) Sections A-E, Admiralty*, op. cit., p. 9.

200   Letter from Admiralty to the Australian Commonwealth Naval Board, M.02799/31, 19 April 1932, NAA: MP 1049/9.

201   Naval Staff Meeting - Summary of Discussion, dated 19 October 1932.

202   ibid, p. 1.

203   ibid, p. 2.

204   Report, *Seaward Defence of Australian Ports*, Australia's Submission No. 290/196/, 7 February 1933, (SPC-A).

205   Commander HB Farncomb, S206 Report from Rear Admiral Hyde, 18 May 1932, (NAA).

206   Letter from Commander AS Storey to AW Grazebrook, 9 June 1992.

207   Commander HB Farncomb, S206 Report, 31 March 1935, (NAA).

208   Lieutenant Commander HA Showers AS206, 14 April 1933, (NAA).

209   Letter from Commander LR Brooks to AW Grazebrook, 24 September 1993.

210   IJ Cunningham, *Work Hard Play Hard, The Royal Australian Naval College 1913-1988*, AGPS, Canberra, 1988, p. 23.

211   Commander HA Showers, AS206 dated 4 June 1934.

212   Papers of Commander NK Calder OBE, PR0323, (AWM).

213   Mrs B Crouch, interview with AW Grazebrook, 10 June 1992.

214   Commander HA Showers S206, dated 10 September 1936, (NAA).

215   Commander J Burnett, S206 Reports 14 April 1937 and 14 October 1936.

216   Commander JCD Esdaile, AS 206, 3 December 1934, (NAA).

217   *The Argus*, 4 December 1934, p. 5.

218   RMB Long letter to GH Gill, 3 April 1952, AWM 69 (AWM), p. 2.

219   Mr Peter Long, interview with author, 1 September 2010.

220   Lieutenant Commander RBM Long, S206, 14 December 1932, (NAA).

221 Lieutenant Commander RBM Long, S206, 18 October 1933, (NAA).
222 Lieutenant Commander RBM Long, S206, 10 May 1935, (NAA).
223 Lieutenant Commander RBM Long, S206, 5 November 1935, (NAA).
224 RMB Long letter to GH Gill, 3 April 1952, AWM 69 (AWM), p. 2.
225 Lieutenant HWG Nobbs, RANVR.
226 Lieutenant Commander RBM Long S206, dated 22 May 1936, (NAA).
227 *RAN Navy List*, January 1936, (RAN Sea Power Centre).
228 ibid.
229 George Lionel Macandie, CBE (1877-1968) see *Australian Dictionary of Biography*.
230 GP Gilbert, edited, *Australian Naval Personalities: Lives from the Australian Dictionary of Biography*, SPC-A, Canberra, 2006, p. 130.
231 An extract of the Testimonial on Parchment and the Looe Lifeguard report are attached to JA Collins Confidential Reports, (NAA).
232 *The West Australian*, Perth, 6 April 1935, p.18; *The Advertiser*, Adelaide, 6 April 1935, p. 13.
233 Commander JA Collins, S206, 14 January 1935, (NAA).
234 JA Collins, *HMAS Sydney*, The Naval Historical Society of Australia, Garden Island, 1971, p. 1.
235 HMAS *Sydney's* Asdic was a Type 125 fitted in a retractable dome. It was normally fitted to destroyers. It was fitted with a mechanical distance finder and was gyro-stabilized and electrically trained.
236 *The Courier-Mail*, Brisbane, 4 October 1935, p. 14.
237 Captain JUP Fitzgerald, CB, RN. He was lost at sea while serving as a Convoy Commodore.
238 JA Collins, *As Luck Would Have It: Reminiscences of an Australian Sailor*, Sydney, Angus and Robertson, 1965, p. 59.
239 ibid, p. 60.
240 RR Moore, *The Life and Time of Robert Ralph Moore (1919-1985)*, p. 25.
241 JA Collins, *As Luck Would Have It: Reminiscences of an Australian Sailor*, Sydney, Angus and Robertson, 1965 (the paragraph related to this incident can be found in the original manuscript kept in the National Library of Australia).
242 WH Ross, op. cit., p. 107.
243 JA Collins, op. cit., p. 66.
244 *The Sydney Morning Herald*, 3 August 1936, p. 9.
245 *The Sydney Morning Herald*, 26 November 1934, p. 12.
246 *The Sydney Morning Herald* 24 September 1936, p. 1; Letter from Mr DL Dowam, General Manager in Australia, Orient Steam Navigation Company to Secretary, Naval Board, 443/202/62 dated 26 September 1936.

247 Mr Cyril John Sadleir, telephone discussion with the author, 1 July 2013.
248 *The West Australian*, 2 July 1937, p. 13.
249 Captain HB Farncomb, S206 Report from Rear Admiral Custance, 11 November 1938, (NAA).
250 *The Sydney Morning Herald*, 20 August 1937, p. 4.
251 Lieutenant Commander JB Newman, S206 Report, 15 April 1935.
252 A Nelson, *HMAS Harman 1943-2003,* Canberra, RAN, 2003, pp. 1-2.
253 Minute, *Trawler A/S Outfit - Allocation and Stowage*, MP/1049/5/0, 21 January 1938, (NAA); Minute, *Anti-Submarine Equipment*, 2026/5/162, dated 18 January 1938, (NAA).
254 Thomas Joseph Hawkins (1898-1976), Australian Dictionary of Biography, Volume 14, 1996.
255 Letter from RMB Long to GH Gill, 5 July 1950, AWM 69 (AWM), p. 1.
256 Minute from Commander Esdaile to CNS, June 1938, MP 1049/5, 2026/2/152, (NAA).
257 Letter from RMB Long to GH Gill, 3 April 1952, AWM 69 (AWM), p. 2.
258 Letter from RMB Long to GH Gill, February 1952, AWM 69 (AWM), p. 2.
259 *Naval Ordnance Inspection and Design Branch: Branch History 1911-1949*, Directorate of Naval Ordnance Inspection, 1 August 1985, p. 3.
260 His Excellency Brigadier General The Rt Hon The Lord Gowrie, VC, GCMG, CB, DSO & Bar, PC.
261 Minute from DNI (Collins) to CNS, *Proposal for the Creation of a Naval Intelligence Centre at Port Moresby*, 5 May 1939, Series B34476, p. 2.
262 Letter from Mrs JE Chapman to AW Grazebrook, 1993, (Jones/Grazebrook Papers).
263 *The Sydney Morning Herald*, 13 June 1939, p. 17.
264 Commander HA Showers, AS206, dated 1 May 1939, (NAA).
265 Letter from Mr Jim Nicholson to AW Grazebrook, 12 October 1992.
266 *The Sydney Morning Herald*, 3 June 1939, p. 17.
267 *The Mercury,* Hobart, 16 May 1939, p. 2.
268 *The Argus*, Melbourne, 10 March 1939, p. 12.
269 BG Hayler, *The Bygone Years: My Life in War and Peace*, 2010, Held by SPC-A, p. 14.
270 Later Rear Admiral William Leslie Graham Adams, RN.
271 BG Hayler, op. cit., p. 16.
272 *The Canberra Times*, 12 July 1939, p. 4.
273 Later Commander WS Bracegirdle, DSC**, RAN.
274 Letter from Commander CR Reid RAN (retired) to AW Grazebrook, dated 6 January 1989.

275 *The Courier Mail*, Brisbane, 7 August 1939, p. 1.
276 *The Courier Mail*, Brisbane, 7 August 1939, p.
277 Commander US Third Naval District, Press Release, 1 August 1939.
278 Indeed the popular and capable Custance would be dead by the year's end, passing away on the passage home to England; *The Sydney Morning Herald*, 30 December 1939, p. 16.
279 Oral History of Vice Admiral Sir John Collins (1899-1989), Mel Pratt Collection, 27 August 1975, NLA.

CHAPTER 6

1 A Gordon, *The Rules of the Game: Jutland and British Naval Command*, Naval Institute Press, Anapolis, 1996, p. xii.
2 RG Menzies, *Afternoon Light: Some Memories of Men and Events*, Cassell, Melbourne, 1967, p. 15.
3 Letter from Mr Alan Zammit to AW Grazebrook, 18 May 1989, (AW Grazebrook Collection). There are different occasions where he is said to earned the nickname, such as the Battle of the Coral Sea, but this is its earliest mention.
4 Commander JCD Esdaile, AS206 Report, 20 November 1939.
5 T Detmers, *The Raider Kormoran*, Tandem Publishing, London, 1973, p. 13.
6 GH Gill, *Royal Australian Navy 1939-1942*, Collins, Melbourne, 1985, p. 78.
7 GH Gill, op. cit., p. 64.
8 Barbara Poniewierski (nee Winter). See B Winter, *The Intrigue Master: Commander Long and Naval Intelligence in Australia, 1913-1945*, Boolarong Press, Brisbane, 1995.
9 Letter from W Brooksbank to Lieutenant AWG Nobbs, 16 July 1960, RMB Long Papers (AWM).
10 B Winter, op. cit., p. 44.
11 *Description of Papua, New Guinea and Solomon Islands*, undated, p. 2.
12 Staff Officer (Intelligence) Port Moresby Report to Director Naval Intelligence, *Report on Coast Watching Organization (3)*, 19 December 1939.
13 AHP Freund, *Missionary Turns Spy: Pastor APH Freund's Story of His Service with the New Guinea Coast Watchers in the War Against Japan, 1942 - 1943*, Lutheran Homes Incorporated, Adelaide, 1989, p. 42.
14 J Griffin, *Papua New Guinea Portraits: The Expatriate* Experience (ed), Australian National University Press, Canberra, 1978, p. 138.
15 Letter from EA Feldt to Mr Manning, 31 February 1962, *Coastwatchers*, Series B34476, (NAA).
16 ibid, p. 43.
17 EA Feldt, *The Coast Watchers*, Nelson Doubleday, New York, 1979, p. 4.

18	Letter from Director Naval Intelligence to Staff Officer (Intelligence) Port Moresby, 30 July 1940, (NAA).	
19	Letter from Lieutenant Commander EA Feldt to Commander RMB Long, 6 August 1940, Series B34476.	
20	Letter from Commander EA Feldt to Commander RMB Long, 19 June 1941, Series B34476, (NAA).	
21	Letter from Director Naval Intelligence to Staff Officer (Intelligence) Port Moresby, 30 July 1940, (NAA).	
22	Staff Officer (Intelligence) Port Moresby Report to Director Naval Intelligence, 2 August 1940 (NAA).	
23	Letter from Commander RMB Long to Commander EA Feldt, 12 October 1942, Series B34476, (NAA).	
24	Letter from Commander RMB Long to Lieutenant Commander EA Feldt, 13 January 1940, Series B34476, (NAA).	
25	Minute from Lieutenant Commander EA Feldt to the Controller AIB, *Activities of Section C AIB while under the command of Lieutenant Commander Feldt*, 1943, Series B34476, (NAA).	
26	Letter from Lieutenant Commander EA Feldt to Commander RMB Long to, 1 March 1941, Series B34476, (NAA).	
27	B Winter, op. cit., p. 49.	
28	Notes on Defence Committee Agendum 104/41 *Special Intelligence Organization*, 18 November 1941, (NAA).	
29	*Establishment of a Cryptographic Organization in Australia*, Report MP 1185/8 Item 1937/2/415 (NAA).	
30	EA Feldt, op. cit., p. 4.	
31	Letter from RMB Long to GH Gill, 3 April 1952, AWM 69 (AWM), p. 4.	
32	The long term reservists included members of the RAFR.	
33	Captain JA Collins, S206 Report, 15 November 1939.	
34	HMS *Kanimbla* Letter of Proceedings, November-December 1939, p. 2 (AWM78).	
35	Note from Lady Collins to T MacDougall, undated, (Collins Papers).	
36	Captain TJN Hilken DSC, RN, THN 1, Diary entry for 15 November 1940, Personal papers (IWM).	
37	TJN Hilken, op. cit., Diary entry for 14 December 1940.	
38	TJN Hilken, op. cit., Diary entry for 13 January 1940.	
39	Anon, *Huddart Parker Limited: 1939-1945*, John D. Harris & Co, Melbourne, 1951, pp. 27-28.	
40	Service Summary of Lieutenant Commander HJH Thompson (NAA).	
41	TJN Hilken, op.cit., Diary entry for 30 January 1940.	
42	TJN Hilken, op.cit., p. 50.	

43 ibid, p. 17.
44 ibid, Appendix 1.
45 ibid, p. 3.
46 Admiral Sir Percy Noble, GBE, KCB, CVO, RN (1880-1955).
47 HMS *Kanimbla* Letter of Proceedings, November-December 1939, Appendix 1, p. 3 (AWM78).
48 The interception occurred 56 km from the coast of Niijima on January 21, 1940. HMS *Liverpool* removed 21 of *Asama Maru's* German passengers believed to be survivors of the scuttled German liner *Columbus*.
49 Captain CD Dykes, interview with author, 1 April 2012.
50 CD Dykes, *A Mariner of the Twentieth Century: The Life Story of Captain Cecil Donald Dykes, RD, FAIN,* , p. 7, (SPC-A).
51 HMS *Kanimbla* Letter of Proceedings, 26 April-17 May 1940, (AWM 78).
52 *Vladimir Mayakovsky* (ex *Bela Khun*), built in 1929 at 3,972 tonnes.
53 HMS *Kanimbla* Letter of Proceedings, 26 April-17 May 1940, Appendix 1, p. 8 (AWM 78).
54 Captain CD Dykes, interview with author, 1 April 2012.
55 HMS *Kanimbla* Letter of Proceedings, 15-31 July 1940, p. 6, (AWM 78).
56 *The Sun*, Sydney, 1 April 1940.
57 Captain Rupert Clare Garsia, RAN (1887-1954).
58 Papers of Admiral Sir John Crace RN, 69/18/3, Entry for 1 June 1940, (IWM).
59 J Crace, op. cit., Entry for 2 June 1940.
60 J Crace, op. cit., Entry for 6 June 1940.
61 Letter from Commander CR Reid RAN (retired) to AW Grazebrook, 6 January 1989.
62 Letter from Commander WS Bracegirdle to AW Grazebrook, 14 February 1989, (Jones/Grazebrook Papers).
63 *War Cabinet Minutes,* Nos 1027-1227, 9 May 1941 - 18 July 1941, Volume 7, A5954, 689417, pp. 873-874 (NAA).
64 The 10th Destroyer Flotilla comprised of HMA Ships *Stuart, Vampire, Vendetta, Voyager* & *Waterhen*.
65 RG Menzies, *Afternoon Light: Some Memories of Men and Events*, Cassell, Melbourne, 1967, p. 24.
66 A Lambert, *Admirals: The Naval Commanders who Made Britain Great*, Faber & Faber, London, 2008, p. 386.
67 JA Collins, op. cit., p. 84.
68 Photograph Album of Stoker EC Evans, DSM, (AWM).
69 GH Johnston, *Grey Gladiator,* Angus and Robertson, Sydney, 1941, p. 20.
70 ibid, p. 21.

71 Stoker EC Evans, Diary entry, DSM, PR 00811, (AWM).
72 TJN Hilken, op. cit., p. 76.
73 TJN Hilken, op. cit., p. 77.
74 ibid, Entry for 26 June 1940.
75 ibid.
76 ibid, p. 39.
77 JA Collins, *HMAS Sydney*, op. cit., p. 14.
78 RR Moore, op. cit., p. 28.
79 TJN Hilken, op. cit., p. 80.
80 M Stille, *Italian Battleships of World War II*, Osprey Publishing, Colchester, 2011, p. 8.
81 The modernized 15 inch guns had a range of 32,000 yards.
82 The unmodernised 15 inch guns had a range of 23,500 yards.
83 TJN Hilken, op. cit., p. 87.
84 M Simpson, *The Cunningham Papers, Volume I - The Mediterranean Fleet 1939-1942*, ed., The Navy Records Society, Aldershot, 1999, p. 99.
85 EC Evans, op. cit., Diary entries for 10-11 July 1940.
86 EC Evans, op. cit., Diary entries for 10-11 July 1940.
87 G Ciano, *Ciano's Diary 1939-1943*, ed. H Gibson, Howard Fertig, New York, 1973, pp. 275-276.
88 JA Collins, op. cit., p. 82.
89 M Simpson, op. cit., p. 99.
90 Report on *The Naval Action of the 19th Instant*, Vice Admiral F Casardi, 23 July 1940, NID 1900/48.
91 TJN Hilken, op. cit., p. 95.
92 Report from HMAS *Sydney* to Rear Admiral Commanding 7th Cruiser Squadron, 30 July 1940, p. 1, (NAA).
93 CB 04027 - *The Fighting Instructions,* 1939 Article 4.82. (ADM 239/261).
94 EC Evans, op. cit., Diary entry for 19 July 1940.
95 TM Jones, & IL Idriess, *The Silent Service: Action Stories of the Anzac Navy*, Sydney, Angus and Robertson, 1944, p. 35.
96 GH Gill, op. cit., p. 188.
97 F Casardi, op. cit., p. 5.
98 Oral History of Signalman Artemio Ettore Torselli, *Memories of an Italian Naval Signalman*, Bedford Museum, Article ID: A5815776, 19 September 2005.
99 EC Evans, op. cit., Entry for 19 July 1940.
100 Gunnery Narrative contained in the Report on *HMAS Sydney - Action on 19 July 1940*, C-in-C of Mediterranean, Med 0903/0710/30/2, 21 September 1940.

101 AB Cunningham, *A Sailor's Odyssey,* Hutchinson and Company, London, 1951, p. 266.
102 EC Evans, op. cit., Entry for 20 July 1940.
103 WH Ross, *Lucky Ross: The Autobiography of an RAN Officer 1934-1951*, Carlisle, Hesperian Press, 1994.p. 169.
104 EC Evans, op. cit., Entry for 20 July 1940.
105 JA Collins, *As Luck Would Have It,* op.cit., p. 88.
106 TJN Hilken, op. cit., p. 101.
107 Report on *HMAS Sydney - Action on 19 July 1940,* Commander-in-Chief Mediterranean, Med 0903/0710/30/2 dated 21 September 1940, pp. 1-2.
108 G Ciano, *Ciano's Diary 1939-1943,* ed. H Gibson, Howard Fertig, New York, 1973, p. 278.
109 *The Times,* 22 July 1940, p. 5.
110 *The Canberra Times,* 24 July 1940, p. 2.
111 *Supplement to The London Gazette,* Number 35025, 27 December 1940, p. 7279.
112 *The Canberra Times,* 22 July 1940, p. 1.
113 *The Mercury,* Hobart, 30 July 1940, p. 3.
114 *The Age,* Melbourne, 22 July 1940, p. 5.
115 *The Argus,* Melbourne, 23 July 1940, p. 5.
116 ibid.
117 *The Canberra Times,* 22 July 1940, p. 1.
118 Letter from Lieutenant Commander HAL Hall to author, 12 April 2012.
119 GN Galuppini, *Un Insolito Funerale Di Guerra*, Bollettino D'Archivo Dell Ufficio Storico Della Marina Militare, Year 6, March 1992, pp. 283-294.
120 Signal from Naval Attaché, Athens to Commander-in-Chief Mediterranean, 31 July 1940.
121 G Ciano, *Ciano's Diary 1939-1943*, Weidenfeld & Nicolson History, London, 2002, Entry for 12 October 1940.
122 The Headquarters were established on August 20, 1940 by *Supermarina* Order Number 3474. It was called the Command *Supermarina* Higher Traffic Albania - Maritrafalba.
123 C Peluso, *The torpedo boat 'Nicola Fabrizi' in the Adriatic and the escort of convoys for Greece,* Newsletter Archive Historical Office of the Navy - June 2012, p. 45.
124 HMAS *Sydney*, Letter of Proceedings, November 1940, 1 December 1940, 191/8945, (AWM), p. 2.
125 *Antonio Locatelli,* 5691 tonnes (GRT), built 1920; *Premuda* 4427 tonnes, built 1907; *Cape Vado,* 4391 tonnes, built 1906; *Catalans* motor vessel 2429 tonnes, built 1928.

126	HMAS *Sydney*, Letter of Proceedings, November 1940, 1 December 1940, 191/8945, (AWM), pp. 2-3.
127	The cruisers were *Muzio Attendolo*, *Eugenio di Savoia*, *Emanuele Filiberto Duca d'Aosta*, *Duca degli Abruzzi* and *Guiseppe Garibaldi*.
128	G Fioravanzo, *Action in the Strait of Otranto. Examination Comparative Relations Officers*, April 1954 (in Italian).
129	Lieutenant General WGS Dobbie, CB, CMG, DSO (1879-1964).
130	HMAS *Sydney* Report of Proceedings January 1941, dated 1 February 1941, p. 3.
131	ibid.
132	GH Johnston, op. cit., p. 145.
133	Captain JA Collins, S206 Report, 7 April 1941.
134	ibid.
135	*The Sydney Morning Herald*, 12 February 1941, p. 5.
136	Report on Pacific Ocean Raiders (*Manyo Maru*, *Narvik* and *Tokyo Maru*), Naval Intelligence Division, Navy Office, Melbourne, March 1941, Series Number B6121, Barcode 453332, (NAA), p. 11.
137	ibid.
138	Advisory War Council Minutes (Original Set) Volume 1. Meeting 2 December 1940. Agendum 10/1540, A5954, 310381, (NAA).
139	J Crace, op. cit., Diary entry for 10 February 1941.
140	*The Sydney Morning Herald*, 10 February 1941, p. 10.
141	*The Mercury*, Hobart, 12 February 1941, p. 2.
142	ibid.
143	ibid.
144	J Crace, op. cit., Diary entry for 10 February 1941.
145	ibid.
146	*The Sydney Morning Herald*, 12 February 1941, p. 11.
147	K Weyler & HJ Ehtlich, *The Black Raider*, London, Elek Books, 1955, p. 92.
148	ibid.
149	Convoy US.4 comprised of *Mauretania*, *Empress of Japan* and *Orcades* from New Zealand and *Aquitania* from Sydney.
150	Papers of Professor Sir John Madsen, Basser Library, (Australian Academy of Science).
151	Interview with PR Burnett with AW Grazebrook 11 June 1992.
152	D Mellor, *Australia in the War of 1939-1945*, Series 4 - Civil, Volume V – *The Role of Science and Industry*, Australian War Memorial, Canberra, 1958, pp. 464-465.
153	See Series MP 150/1 in National Archives of Australia.
154	Oral History of Mr BC Ballard, (NLA).

155 WG Burchett, *Pacific Treasure Island: New Caledonia; voyage through its land and wealth, the story of its people and past*, David MacKay Company, Philadelphia, 1944, pp. 200-201.
156 Bertram Charles Ballard (1903-1981), for more details on his life see the *Australian Dictionary of Biography*.
157 Oral History of Mr BC Ballard, (NLA).
158 Note from A Stirling to SM Bruce, 9 September 1940, CRS A 2937, New Caledonia, (NAA).
159 *Letter of Proceeding HMAS Adelaide* September 1940, 2026/7.185, (NAA).
160 This view also held by Rear Admiral Crace; see J Crace, op.cit., Diary entry for 3 September 1940.
161 Report on Legal Action Shaw Savill and Albion Company Ltd versus The Commonwealth, 521/201/239, (NAA).
162 B Winter, op. cit., p. 59.
163 HMAS *Adelaide* Letter of Proceeding, September 1940, op. cit., p. 1.
164 HA Showers & M Simington, interview, 23 December 1974.
165 Oral History of Mr BC Ballard, (NLA).
166 ibid.
167 Annex of Events from HMAS *Adelaide* Letter of proceedings, September 1940, op. cit.
168 Mr BC Ballard, Oral history, (NLA).
169 ibid.
170 WG Burchett, op. cit., p. 211.
171 Mr BC Ballard, Oral history, (NLA).
172 H Sautot, *Grandeur et Decadence du Gaullisme le Pacifique*, FW Cheshire, Melbourne, 1949, p. 43.
173 ibid, p. 44.
174 ibid.
175 ibid, p. 3.
176 ibid, p. 3.
177 Cable 248/CE 51W 492, 3 October 1940, Barcode 179272, (NAA).
178 Cablegram from BC Ballard, No. 24, 24 September 1940, Barcode 179272, (NAA).
179 HMAS *Adelaide* Letter of Proceeding, September 1940, op. cit., p. 8.
180 Statement Made by Captain HA Showers, RAN to Governor Sautot and the de Gaullist Committee at Government House, Noumea in the presence British Consul and the Australian Government Representative at 1545, Local Time, Friday 27 September, 1940, p. 2 (NAA).
181 ibid, p. 8.

182   Prime Minister Cablegram O.7109 dated 28 September 1940, Barcode 179272, p. 2 (NAA).

183   J Lacouture, *De Gaulle: The Rebel 1890-1944*, New York, WW Norton and Company, 1993, p. 270.

184   Secretary of State for Dominion Affairs cable to Prime Minister of Australia, 2 October 1940, Barcode 179272, (NAA).

185   Letter M Sautot to Commanding Officer HMAS *Adelaide*, 4 October 1940, (NAA).

186   Telegrams BC Ballard, 3 October and 5 October 1940, Barcode 179272.

187   B Winter, *The Intrigue Master: Commander Long and Naval Intelligence in Australia, 1913-1945*, Boolarong Press, Brisbane, 1995, p. 62.

188   HMAS *Adelaide* Letter of Proceedings, op. cit., p. 9; Henri Camille Sautot (1885-1963) would after a difficult tenure as Governor serve as Mayor of Noumea 1947-53 and be buried in Noumea.

189   Naval Board letter to Flag Officer Commanding His Majesty's Australian Squadron, 2026/7/185, dated 20 October 1940, MP 1049/5 Barcode 408800, (NAA).

190   Memorandum from the Secretary Department of External Affairs to Secretary department of the Navy, dated 23 October 1940, MP 1049/5 Barcode 408800, (NAA).

191   DM Stevens, *The Royal Australian Navy in World War II* (ed.), 2nd edn, Allen and Unwin, Crows Nest, 2005, p. 21.

192   The convoy was the US.6 comprising *Aquitania* (Commodore), *Queen Mary* and *Mauretania*. In charge of the escort was RACAS in *Perth*.

193   GH Gill, op. cit., p. 275.

194   Letter from EW Dingle to Captain HB Farncomb, 27 November 1940.

195   Report on Pacific Ocean Raiders (*Manyo Maru*, *Narvik* and *Tokyo Maru*), Naval Intelligence Division, Navy Office, Melbourne, March 1941, Series Number B6121, Barcode 453332, (NAA).

196   There were sailors and passengers including the Chief Justice of Tonga and his wife. They were from N*otou*, *Turakina*, *Ringwood*, *Holmwood*, *Rangitane*, *Triona*, *Vinni*, *Triadic*, *Triaster* and *Komata*.

197   The set, long sought by Eric Feldt, would eventually arrive on 6 January.

198   R Eyssen, *HKS Komet: Kaperfahrt auf Allen Meeren*, Koehlers, Herford, 1960, p. 107.

199   Report from HMAS *Canberra* 2026/3/416 (*Ketty Brøvig* Action) dated 9 March 1941 (NAA).

200   GH Gill, op. cit., p. 369.

201   GH Gill, op. cit., p. 458.

202   *Thor*, in one remarkable cruise bettered three Armed Merchant Cruisers. They were HMS *Alcantara* (28 July 1940), then HMS *Carnarvon Castle* (5 December 1940) and sinking HMS *Voltaire* (4 April 1941).

203 CB 3081(5), *Battle Summary Number 13: Actions with Enemy Disguised Raiders 1940-1941*, Admiralty, London, 1942, p. 6.

204 ibid, p. 10.

205 AS 206 for Lieutenant Commander CAR Sadleir, 28 July 1941, (NAA).

206 Lieutenant Commander GWT Armitage, AS 206, 9 July 1942 (NAA).

207 Letter from Secretary of Navy to NOIC Brisbane, 559/222/1102, 30 July 1942, contained in 11206558, (NAA).

208 JC Howells, *Ben and Dorothy: A Portrait of My Parents,* Camberwell, 2012, pp. 93-94.

209 *The Sydney Morning Herald*, 5 June 1940, p.9.

210 EH Pask, *Enter the Colonies, Dancing: A History of Dance in Australia, 1835-1940*, Oxford University Press, Melbourne, 1979, p. 138.

211 From concert program contained in Mischa Burlakov Papers, MS 9501, (NLA).

212 Letter from GS Kimlin to AW Grazebrook, 20 August 1992.

213 GH Gill, op. cit., pp. 419-420.

214 FB Eldridge, *A History of the Royal Australian Naval College: From its inception in 1913 to the end of World War II in 1945*, Georgian House, Melbourne, 1949, p. 336.

215 NK Calder, *HMAS Bungaree - Minelayer*, undated, p. 7.

216 ibid, p. 2.

217 ibid, p. 3.

218 ibid, p. 13.

219 NK Calder, op. cit., p. 15.

220 NK Calder, ibid, p. 27.

221 Examiner, Launceston, 16 April 1941, p. 1.

222 A Nelson, *A History of HMAS Harman,* 1943-1993, Navy Publications, 1993, p. 26.

223 S Fenton Huie, *Ships Belles: The story of the Women's Royal Australian Naval Service 1941-1985,* Sydney, Watermark Press, 2000, p. 21.

224 J Hemstock, *Women of the Royal Australian Navy- Part 1,* Instant Colour Press, Belconnen, 2013, p. 39.

225 GH Gill, *Royal Australian Navy 1939-1942*, op. cit., p. 414.

226 Mr DY Syme (1844-1932) see *Australian Dictionary of Biography*.

227 Reg would later be Secretary of Navy House in Melbourne, *Bay of Plenty Times*, 8 December 1950.

228 GH Gill, *Royal Australian Navy 1939-1942*, op. cit., p. 415.

229 B Donoghue, *In Retrospect, Ex-WRANS Ditty Box,* August 1972, p. 3.

230 B Donoghue, ibid p. 5.

231 J Hemstock, *Women of the Royal Australian Navy- Part 1.* Instant Colour Press, Belconnen, 2013, p. 196.

232 GH Gill, *Royal Australian Navy 1939-1942*, Collins, Melbourne, 1985, p. 250.
233 FE McMurtrie, *Jane's Fighting Ships 1942*, Sampson Low, London, 1942, pp. 287-297.
234 J Leutze, *A Different Kind of Victory: A Biography of Admiral Thomas C. Hart*, Naval Institute Press, Annapolis, 1981, p. 179.
235 RG Menzies, *Afternoon Light: Some Memories of Men and Events*, Cassell, Melbourne, 1967, p. 20.
236 GH Gill, op. cit., p. 269.
237 ibid, p. 269.
238 Menzies, op. cit., p. 20.
239 *Fuehrer Conferences on Naval Affairs 1941*, Admiralty, London, 1947; Meeting on 18 March 1941.
240 GH Gill, *Royal Australian Navy 1939-1942*, op. cit., p. 424.
241 Menzies, op.cit, p. 21.
242 ibid, p. 21.
243 ibid, p. 22.
244 ibid, p. 22.
245 ibid, p. 32.
246 GH Gill, *Royal Australian Navy 1939-1942*, op. cit., p. 427.
247 Plan Rainbow 3 (WPL 44).
248 *War Cabinet Minutes,* Numbers 874-1026, 5 March-4 May 1941, Volume 6, A5954, 689294, p. 665, (NAA).
249 ibid, p. 665.
250 ibid, p. 665.
251 J Leutze, op. cit., p. 194.
252 *War Cabinet Minutes,* Volume 6, op. cit., p. 716.
253 HMAS *Sydney* was in Singapore 19-22 April 1941.
254 Letter from Lieutenant Commander EA Feldt to Commander RMB Long, 16 June 1941, (NAA).
255 *War Cabinet Minutes,* Volume 6, op. cit., p. 783.
256 ibid, p. 783.
257 J Leutze, op. cit., pp. 212-214.
258 ibid, p. 164.
259 Admiral Hart letter to Admiral Stark, 29 April 1941.
260 Oral History of Admiral TC Hart, USN, Operational Archives, p. 143. (USNHHC).
261 Admiral TC Hart, USN, Diary entry for 2 April 1941, (USNHHC).
262 J Leutze, op. cit., p. 210.
263 ibid.

264 J Leutze. op. cit., pp. 188-189.
265 Admiral Hart letter to Admiral Stark, 29 April 1941.
266 DM Stevens, *The Royal Australian Navy in World War II* (ed.), Allen and Unwin, Crows Nest, 2005, p. 254.
267 RMB Long letter to GH Gill, 15 January 1952, AWM 69 (AWM), pp. 1-2.
268 RMB Long letter to GH Gill, 20 February 1956, AWM 69 (AWM), p. 4.
269 Lieutenant Admiral is the equivalent rank to Vice Admiral.
270 Admiral TC Hart, USN, Diary entry for 2 November 1941, (USNHHC).
271 JA Collins, *As Luck Would Have It,* op. cit., p. 100.
272 J Leutze, op. cit., pp. 58-60.
273 ibid, p. 74.
274 Admiral TC Hart, USN, Diary entry for 3 November 1941, (USNHHC).
275 Chief of Naval Operations despatch to Commander-in-Chief Asiatic Fleet, 13 September 1941.
276 *Operations Matador and Sandwich*, WO 106/2506, August-November 1941, (TNA UK).
277 M Tsuji, *Singapore The Japanese Version*, Ure Smith, Sydney, 1960, p. 24.
278 Admiralty signal to Commander-in-Chief China 993 & ACNB sent 1403Z, dated 6 October 1941 (SPC-A)
279 Commander-in-Chief China signal to Admiralty 402 sent 0837Z, dated 7 October 1941 (SPC-A).
280 Admiralty signal to Commander-in-Chief China & ACNB sent 0746Z dated 8 October 1941 (SPC-A)
281 *War Cabinet Minutes,* Volume 7, op. cit., p. 872.
282 ibid, p. 874.
283 RMB Long letter to GH Gill, 5 July 1950, AWM 69 (AWM), p. 3.
284 Minute Central War Room and Joint Planning, 1940, MP729/6 Item 15/401/342, (NAA).
285 *War Cabinet Minutes,* Volume 6, op. cit., Supplement to Agendum 74/1941.
286 Letter from B Wurbath to Lieutenant AW Nobbs, 15 October 1960, RMB Long Papers, (AWM).
287 Captain J Burnett, RAN AS 206 dated 12 May 1941. His scores were Initiative 9, Judgement 8, Zeal and Energy 9, Reliability 8, Administrative ability 8 and Professional ability 9.
288 TR Frame, *HMAS Sydney: Loss and Controversy*, Hodder & Stoughton, Sydney, 1993, p. 33.
289 T Detmers, op. cit., p. 119.
290 The maximum range of the German 5.9-inch gun was 25,000 yards but the effective range would have been shorter.
291 T Detmers, *The Raider Kormoran*, Tandem Publishing, London, 1973, p. 17.

292   The Germans referred to three Australian light cruisers as Perth Class. They were also known as Modified Leander Class.

293   T Detmers, *The Raider Kormoran*, Tandem Publishing, London, 1973, pp. 184-185.

294   TRH Cole, *The Loss of HMAS Sydney II Inquiry,* Volume 1, Canberra, 2009, p. 29, Paragraph 2.34.

295   DL Mearns, *The Search for the Sydney: How Australia's Greatest Maritime Mystery was Solved*, Harper Collins, Sydney, 2009, p. 194.

296   T Detmers, op. cit., p. 186.

297   T Detmers, op. cit., p. 191.

298   J Crace, op. cit., Diary entry for 24 November 1941.

299   T Detmers, *The Raider Kormoran*, Tandem Publishing, London, 1973, p. 202.

300   T Detmers, ibid, p. 203.

301   Prime Ministerial Statement No. 78, 20 November 1941, A5954 2400/21, (NAA).

302   *The Canberra Times*, 1 December 1941, p. 1.

303   ibid, pp. 1-2.

304   ibid, p. 1.

305   ibid, p. 2.

306   Minutes of the Naval Board 15 January 1942, A2585, (NAA).

307   ibid, p. 208.

308   M Buckland, SM Cannon, L De Yong, GI Gamble, JC Jeremy, T Lyon, P McCarthy, B Morris, RA Neill, MB Seen, B Suendermann &T Turner, *HMAS Sydney II Commission of Inquiry: Report on Technical Aspects of HMAS Sydney and HSK Kormoran,* DSTO, DSTO-GD-0559, 2009, p. ii.

309   ibid.

310   ibid, p. iv.

311   JA Collins, *HMAS Sydney*, Garden Island, The Naval Historical Society of Australia, 1971, p. 47.

312   ibid, p. 47.

313   GH Gill, op. cit., p. 458.

314   Letter from LAC K Homard to his parents, 7 October 1941.

315   Letter from KJ Cumisky to GH Gill, 10 July 1958, AWM 69 (AWM).

316   CB 3081(5), *Battle Summary Number 13: Actions with Enemy Disguised Raiders 1940-1941*, op. cit., p. 22.

317   PR Burnett, *Captain Joseph Burnett*, RAN, *Naval Historical Review*, Sydney, December 1973, p. 7.

318   JA Collins, *As Luck Would Have It*, op. cit., p. 98.

319   ibid

320   Letter from Vice Admiral JA Collins to GH Gill, 16 July 1958, AWM 69, (AWM).

321   The letter was found in the Gill Papers by the author in January 2016.

322   GH Johnston, *Lioness of the Seas,* Victor Gollancz Ltd, London, 1941, p. 13.

Chapter 7

1. AWR McNicoll, *Sea Voices*, from the poem Sea Voices, pages not numbered, printed in HMAS *Canberra*, 1932.
2. PLENAPS - Plans for the Employment of Naval and Air Forces of the Associated Powers.
3. JA Collins, *As Luck Would Have It: Reminiscences of an Australian Sailor*, Angus and Robertson, Sydney, 1965, p. 101.
4. Admiral TC Hart, USN, Diary entry for 6 December, 1941, (USNHHC).
5. J Leutze, *A Different Kind of Victory: A Biography of Admiral Thomas C. Hart*, Naval Institute Press, Annapolis, 1981, p. 224.
6. The Kota Bharu Invasion Force was under the command of Rear-Admiral Shintaro Hashimoto. It comprised the light cruiser *Sendai* and destroyers *Ayanami, Isonami, Shikanami* & *Uranami*.
7. Letter from WH Brookbank to HWG Nobbs, 16 July 1960, (RMB Long Papers).
8. ibid.
9. JI Holwitt, *Execute Against Japan: The US Decision to Conduct Unrestricted Submarine Warfare*, Williams-Ford Texas A&M University, 2013, pp. 162-166.
10. J Curtin, National Address: Japan Enters Second World War.
11. JA Collins, *As Luck Would Have It*, op. cit., p. 102.
12. SW Roskill, *Churchill and the Admirals*, Pen & Sword Military Classics, Barnley, 2004, p. 199.
13. ibid, p. 199.
14. The Japanese ships consisted of the battleships *Kongō & Haruna*, three Takao-Class cruisers & eight destroyers. They were strengthened by Cruiser Division 7 (four Mogami Class cruisers of & one light cruiser) & Destroyer Squadron 3 (four ships).
15. JA Collins, *As Luck Would Have It*, op. cit., p. 104.
16. WS Churchill, *The Second World War, Volume III: The Grand Alliance*, Penguin, London, 2005, p. 551.
17. JA Collins, *As Luck Would Have It*, op. cit., p. 104.
18. GH Gill, *Royal Australian Navy 1939-1942*, op. cit., pp. 492-493.
19. ibid, p. 105.
20. JL Carpenter, *HMAS Toowoomba - J157*, undated, p. 2.
21. ibid, p. 100.
22. The destroyers were *Stewart, Alden, Bulmer, Whipple* and *Edsall*.
23. Admiral TC Hart, USN, Diary entry for 4 January, 1942, (USNHHC).
24. J Leutze, op. cit., pp. 267-268.
25. Admiral TC Hart, USN, Diary entry for 27 January, 1942, (USNHHC).
26. ibid.

27	Commodore JA Collins RAN, *China Force War Diary*, ADM 1/12190, Entry for 5 February, 1942.
28	JL Carpenter, *HMAS Toowoomba - J157*, undated, p. 4.
29	ibid, p. 5.
30	ibid, p. 5.
31	Letter from Commander Paul Hirst to his wife, 7 February 1942.
32	Admiral TC Hart, USN, Diary entry for 31 January, 1942.
33	ibid, Diary entry for 8 February, 1942.
34	Letter from Commander Paul Hirst to his wife, 7 February 1942.
35	Able Seaman N Smith, *Last Stop Tjilitjap (S.E. Java 2 March 1942)*, Papers and poems of Able Seaman N Smith retired, (Held by author).
36	Commander-in-Chief to Commander in Chief US Asiatic Fleet, despatch dated 5 February, 1942, (USNHHC).
37	Admiral TC Hart, USN, Diary entry for 16 February, 1942.
38	'World Battlefronts: Dutchman's Chance', *Time Magazine*, 23 February 1942.
39	*The Age*, 20 November 1965, p. 24.
40	JL Carpenter, op. cit., p. 11.
41	*HMAS Perth War Diary*, 1932/2/200, 1 October 1945, Diary entry for 22 February, 1942; GH Gill, Volume I, op. cit., p. 580.
42	JKW Mathieson, *The Memoirs of Chaplain JKW Mathieson 14/2/42 - 8/10/42*, 1948, p. 7.
43	Paymaster Lieutenant Commander POL 'Polo' Owen.
44	ibid, p. 7.
45	The Japanese destroyers were *Amatsukaze, Asagumo, Harusame, Hatsukaze, Kawakaze, Minegumo, Murasame, Samidare, Sazanami, Tokitsukaze, Ushio, Yudachi & Yukikaze*.
46	GH Gill, *Royal Australian Navy 1939-1942*, op. cit., p. 611.
47	ibid, p. 3939.
48	ibid, p. 3940.
49	ibid, p. 3940.
50	JA Collins, *As Luck Would Have It*, op. cit., p. 116.
51	Admiral TC Hart, USN, Oral history transcript, p. 180.
52	The 5th Destroyer Flotilla consisted of *Natori, Harukaze, Hatakaze, Asakaze, Fubuki, Hatsuyuki, Shirayuki, Shirakumo* and *Murakumo*.
53	GH Gill, *Royal Australian Navy 1939-1942*, op. cit., p. 621.
54	The poem was *Vision 4*, see JC Howells, op. cit., p. 34.
55	KL Spurling, *Cruel Conflict: The triumph and tragedy of HMAS Perth*, New Holland Press, Sydney, 2008, pp. 161-2.
56	Letter Mr TJ Roberts to AW Grazebrook, 17 July 1992.

57　Commodore JA Collins RAN, *China Force War Diary*, Entry for 2 March 1942, ADM 1/12190.

58　The battleships were *Hiyei and Kirishima* and the aircraft carriers *Kaga, Hiryu* and *Soryu*.

59　GH Gill, *Royal Australian Navy 1939-1942*, op. cit., p. 631.

60　JA Collins, S.206 Report 8 December 1941, Contained in Confidential reports. A3978, 11230575, (NAA).

61　JA Collins, Citation contained in Confidential reports. A3978, 11230575, (NAA).

62　RMB Long letter to GH Gill, 20 February 1956, AWM 69 (AWM), p. 4.

63　Admiral TC Hart, USN, Oral history transcript, p. 172.

64　RMB Long letters to GH Gill, 20 February 1956, p. 5; 3 September 1956, pp. 4-5, AWM 69 (AWM).

65　Letter from Commander JCR Proud to AW Nobbs, dated 19 November 2014, contained in RMB Long Papers, (AWM).

66　JL Carpenter, op. cit., Entry for 16 July 1942.

67　Item 101 in the Minutes of the Naval Board, 8 July 1942, Series A2585, (NAA).

68　Interview with Signalman DR Fraser with the author on 28 March 2012.

69　ibid.

70　ibid, Entry for 25 July 1942.

71　Letter from Mr TJ Roberts to AW Grazebrook, 17 July 1992.

72　Letter from Commander JCR Proud to AW Nobbs, 3 November 1960 contained in RMB Long papers.

73　JCH Gill, *The Last Days of Rabaul: December 13, 1941 to January 23, 1942,* Paper to The Royal Historical Society of Queensland, 23 March 1961, p. 663.

74　ibid, p. 665.

75　EA Feldt, *The Coast Watchers*, op. cit., p. 44.

76　Lieutenant Commander H MacKenzie, RAN, *Report of Events Following the Fall of Rabaul*, 29 April 1942, Series Number B6121, Barcode 646443, Appendix I, (NAA).

77　EA Feldt, *The Coast Watchers*, op. cit., p. 52.

78　Letter from Commander RMB Long to Commander EA Feldt, 12 October 1942, Series B34476, (NAA).

79　M Leaf, *The Story of Ferdinand,* Viking Press, New York, 1936.

80　EA Feldt, *The Coast Watchers*, Nelson Doubleday, New York, 1979, p. 2.

81　Letter from Commander EA Feldt to Commander RMB Long, 4 February 1942, Series B34476, (NAA).

82　Griffin, op. cit., p. 141.

83　Letter from Commander JCR Proud to AW Nobbs, 3 November 1960, op. cit., pp. 1-2.

84　LR Silver, *The Heroes of Rimau: Unravelling the mystery of one of World War II's most daring raids*, Birchgrove, Sally Milner Publishing, 1990, p. 70.

85   *Australia - Royal Australian Navy - Personality Sketches*, Naval Attaché, 12 July 1945, Serial 45-R-45, Monograph Index Guide Number 901, (US National Archives).

86   Captain RT Fabian, Oral History 09-83, 4 May 1983, Center for Cryptographic History, p. 17,(US National Security Agency).

87   They were Professor TG Room, RJ Lyons, Professor AD Trendall and AP Treweek.

88   Letter from GT Brookbank to HWG Nobbs, 15 August 1960. Commander RMB Long papers, (AWM).

89   Captain RT Fabian, Oral History 09-83, 4 May 1983, Center for Cryptographic History, (US National Security Agency).

90   ibid, pp.78-79.

91   Captain DL Whitlock, USN, Oral History 05-83, Center for Cryptographic History, pp. 107-108.

92   ibid, p. 102.

93   Admiral Sir John Crace RN, Diary entries for September-October 1942, Papers of Admiral Sir John Crace RN, 69/18/3, (IWM).

94   The cruisers were *Indianapolis, Minneapolis, Pensacola* and *San Francisco*.

95   Regulation 439(3) - 'It is the duty of the Captain of the ship to which the accused belongs in ordinary cases to act as Prosecutor, but if for any reason it is undesirable or impossible for the Captain or Executive Officer of that ship to conduct the Prosecution the convening authority shall appoint a competent person to undertake the duty.'

96   Letter from Commanding Officer HMAS *Australia* to Rear Admiral Commanding HM Australian Squadron, 7 April 1942 contained in Series Number B6121, Barcode 399541, (NAA).

97   Admiral Sir John Crace, Diary entry for 12 March 1942, Papers of Admiral Sir John Crace RN, 69/18/3, (IWM).

98   Testimony of Surgeon Lieutenant MJL Stenning, RANR contained in Series Number B6121, Barcode 399541, (NAA).

99   Letter from Commander JM Armstrong to Captain HB Farncomb, 21 March 1942, contained in Series Number B6121, Barcode 399541, (NAA).

100   ibid.

101   Cause of death was general peritonitis, following a penetrating wound of the abdominal cavity, a perforating wound of the small intestine, penetrating wounds of the right pleural cavity, laceration of the right lung, a penetrating wound in the liver and perforation of the diaphragm, severe blood loss and shock.

102   Letter from Commanding Officer HMAS *Australia* to Rear Admiral Commanding HM Australian Squadron, 7 April 1942 contained in Series Number B6121, Barcode 399541, (NAA).

103   Regulation 439(3) see above.

104   The other officers were Commander SW Roskill, RN (who later wrote the official history of the RN in World War II), Acting Commander JF Rayment RAN, Lieutenant Commander FH Mansell, RN & Lieutenant Commander JL Bath, RAN.

105 Report of Court Martial, p. 86, contained in Series Number B6121, Barcode 399541, (NAA).
106 Report of Court Martial, p. 150, contained in Series Number B6121, Barcode 399541, (NAA).
107 Letter from Paymaster Lieutenant T. Rapke, RANVR to CO HMAS *Australia* dated 20 April 1942. (Contained in B6121, op. cit.)
108 ibid.
109 Letter from Commanding Officer HMAS *Australia* to Rear Admiral Commanding HM Australian Squadron, 20 April 1942 contained in Series Number B6121, Barcode 399541, (NAA).
110 *FRUMEL Records of communications intelligence to the Coral Sea Battle,* Series B5555, Barcode 856345, (NAA).
111 KH Dalrymple-Hay, *Coastwatching in Fight for the Solomons,* Preface.
112 *The Sydney Morning Herald,* 5 May 1992, p. 3.
113 Oral History of Leading Seaman RB Walker, S00708, 28 June 1989, transcript p. 6 (AWM).
114 Letter from Mrs Jean Farncomb to AW Grazebrook, 25 October 1987.
115 Able Seaman RE Scrivener, Transcript of oral history, 10 February 1989, S00535, p. 21, (AWM) and Oral History of Petty Officer GJ Glansford, January 1989, S00516, transcript p. 20, (AWM).
116 *FRUMEL Records of communications intelligence to the Coral Sea Battle,* Series B5555, Barcode 856345, (NAA).
117 *The Argus,* Melbourne, 15 May 1942, p. 3.
118 *The Canberra Times,* 11 May 1942, p. 2.
119 Letter from Lieutenant FS Sharp RANVR to AW Grazebrook, 18 January 1993.
120 Letter from Lieutenant FS Sharp to AW Grazebrook, 16 December 1992.
121 The midget submarines were of the Ko-hyoteki Class.
122 GH Gill, *Royal Australian Navy 1942-1945,* op. cit., pp. 62-63.
123 ibid, p. 65.
124 Report from Commanding Officer HMAS *Yandra* to NOC Sydney, 3 June 1942 contained in *Japanese Midget Submarine Attack on Sydney Harbour,* May 31st-June 1st 1942, Series Number SP338/1, Barcode 318205, (NAA).
125 Letter from Rear Admiral in Charge HMA Establishments Sydney to First Naval Member, 22 June 1942 contained Series Number SP338/1, Barcode 318205, (NAA).
126 Letter from Lieutenant FS Sharp RANVR to AW Grazebrook, 18 January 1993, (Jones/Grazebrook Papers).
127 Report from Commanding Officer USS *Perkins* to The Commander Southwest Pacific Forces, 2 June 1942 contained in Series Number SP338/1, Barcode 318205, (NAA).

128   Letter from Lieutenant Commander HAL Hall to author, 12 April 2012, (Jones/Grazebrook Papers).
129   *HMAS Hobart War Diary 1-31 January 1942*, 2 Feb 1942, p. 10, (AWM).
130   Oral History of Able Seaman RE Scrivener, 10 February 1089, S00535, transcript p. 15, (AWM).
131   LJ Lind & MA Payne, *HMAS Hobart: The Story of the 6-inch Cruiser 1938-1962*, The Naval Historical Society of Australia, Garden Island, 1971, p. iii.
132   Captain WLG Adams, RN.
133   Temporary Engineering Commander JSD McGuffog, OBE, RANR.
134   Captain CD Dykes, interview with author, 1 April 2012.
135   Lieutenant Commander MJ Gregory RAN, interview with author, 28 March 2012.
136   ibid.
137   T Ohmae, *The Battle of Savo Island*, US Naval Institute Proceedings, 83/12, December 1957, p. 1263.
138   *FRUMEL Records of communications intelligence to the Midway Battle*, Series B5555, Barcode 856346, (NAA).
139   The Japanese aircraft carriers lost were *Akagi, Kaga, Soryu* and *Hiryu*.
140   Lieutenant Commander M Gregory, interview with author, 28 March 2012.
141   NK Calder, *HMAS Bungaree - Minelayer*, undated, p. 30.
142   MB Twining, *No Bended Knee: The Battle for Guadalcanal*, Presidio Press, Novato, 1996, p. 38.
143   GGO Gatacre, *Report of Proceedings*, Manly, Nautical Press, 1982, p. 157.
144   MB Twining, *No Bended Knee: The Battle for Guadalcanal*, op. cit., p. 45.
145   ibid, p. 46.
146   Contained in SE Morrison Papers, Box 27, (USNCCC).
147   GH Gill, *Royal Australian Navy 1939-1942*, op. cit., p. 127.
148   B Loxton & C Coulthard-Clark, *The Shame of Savo: Anatomy of a naval disaster*, Allen and Unwin, St Leonards, 1994, p. xxii.
149   Sub-Lieutenant KH Dalrymple Hay, 'Report on Guadalcanal', contained in *Reports on Activities in New Britain (North East Area)*, B3476, Barcode 411541, p. 2, (NAA).
150   ibid, p. xxiii.
151   T Ohmae, op. cit.
152   *HMAS Australia Report of Proceedings*, August 1942 (NAA).
153   The Japanese accounts of their actions were detailed in time zone GMT +10 whereas the Allied forces were using the time zone GMT +12. Therefore Japanese times have been brought forward two hours.
154   T Ohmae, op. cit.
155   GH Gill, *Royal Australian Navy 1942-1945*, op. cit., p. 138.

156 *Lessons learned from loss of HMAS Canberra,* MP 1049/5, Barcode 399876, Contains Rear Admiral Crutchley's post action report (NAA).
157 *Minute from Executive Officer HMAS Canberra to Rear Admiral Commanding Task Force 44*, 12 August 1942, Barcode 399876 (NAA).
158 MB Twining, *No Bended Knee: The Battle for Guadalcanal*, op. cit., p. 63.
159 *Lessons learned from loss of HMAS Canberra,* op. cit., Contains Rear Admiral Cruthley's post action report. (NAA).
160 T Ohmae, op. cit.
161 MB Twining, *No Bended Knee: The Battle for Guadalcanal*, op. cit., p. 64.
162 Navy Week Address by Lieutenant Commander Mackenzie Gregory, Melbourne Shrine of Remembrance, 26 August 2008.
163 ibid.
164 *Minute from Executive Officer HMAS Canberra to Rear Admiral Commanding Task Force 44*, 12 August 1942, Barcode 399876 (NAA). There is some conjecture about whether *Canberra* was torpedoed. The RAN Board of Inquiry judged she had not been but Walsh, Crutchley and Collins believe she was. The *Shame of Salvo* makes a persuasive case to support the ship being torpedoed.
165 T Ohmae, op. cit.
166 Minute from Commanding Officer HMAS *Hobart* to Commander Task Force 62.6, 15 August 1942, p. 1.
167 Vice Admiral Sir Richard Peek, interview with author, 18 June 2010.
168 Navy Week Address by Lieutenant Commander Mackenzie Gregory, op. cit.
169 Letter from Lieutenant Commander HAL Hall to author, 12 April 2012, (Jones/Grazebrook Papers). Frank Getting was buried at sea on 10 August.
170 B Loxton, & C Coulthard-Clark, *The Shame of Savo: Anatomy of a naval disaster*, Allen and Unwin, St Leonards, 1994, pp. 251-252.
171 T Ohmae, op. cit.
172 *The Argus*, 21 August 1942, p. 5.
173 JH Adams, *Ships in Battledress*, The Currawong Publishing Company, Sydney, 1944, p. 117.
174 Letter from Commander EA Feldt to Commander RMB Long, 23 August 1942, Series B34476, (NAA).
175 *The Times* (London), 22 August 1942, p. 41.
176 *Lessons learned from loss of HMAS Canberra,* MP 1049/5, Barcode 399876, (NAA).
177 *BR 1736(14) Battle Summary No.21. Naval Operations in the Campaign for Guadalcanal - August 1942*, Admiralty, London, 1949.
178 *The Battle of Savo Island: August 9th 1942*, Strategic & Tactical Analysis, US Naval War College, 1950.
179 GGO Gatacre, *Report of Proceedings*, Nautical Press, Manly, 1982, p. 179.

180   Minute from Captain JA Collins to Chief of Naval Staff, 'Remarks on the Loss of HMAS *Canberra*', 10 November 1942.

181   RF Newcomb, *Savo: The Incredible Naval Débâcle off Guadalcanal*, Ure Smith, Sydney, 1963.

182   B Loxton, & C Coulthard-Clark, *The Shame of Savo: Anatomy of a naval disaster*, Allen and Unwin, St Leonards, 1994.

183   RF Newcomb, *Savo: The Incredible Naval Débâcle off Guadalcanal*, op. cit., pp. ix-xv.

184   Letter from Commanding Officer HMAS *Australia* to Commander Task Force 44, Barcode 399876 (NAA), p. 5.

185   Rear Admiral Turner did suggest to Rear Admiral Crutchley that he shift his flag to the *Chicago* which was fitted with a better radar.

186   Letter from Commanding Officer HMAS *Australia* to Commander Task Force 44, op. cit., p. 7.

187   Minute from Commanding Officer HMAS *Hobart* to Commander Task Force 62.6, 15 August 1942, op. cit.

188   Navy Week Address by Lieutenant Commander Mackenzie Gregory, Melbourne Shrine of Remembrance, 26 August 2008.

189   USS *Saratoga* was torpedoed on 31 August 1942.

190   Cablegram from Secretary of State for Dominion Affairs cablegram to Prime Minister of Commonwealth of Australia 29 August 1942, A5954, 424581, (NAA).

191   Telegram from Private Secretary to the King to the Governor General of Australia 12 September 1942, A5954, 424581, (NAA).

192   *The Melbourne Age*, 8 October 1943.

193   S Nicholls, *HMAS Shropshire*, The Naval Historical Society of Australia, Sydney, 1989, p. xvii.

194   JM Alliston, *Destroyer Man*, Greenhouse Publications, Richmond, 1985, pp. 124-125.

195   W Lord, *Lonely Vigil: Coastwatchers of the Solomons*, Naval Institute Press, Annapolis, 2006, p. 56.

196   Letter from Lieutenant Commander HA MacKenzie to Commander RMB Long, 24 October 1942, Series B34476, (NAA).

197   General Patch assumed command in Guadalcanal in October 1942 when the US Army replaced the Marines.

198   *Report by Lieutenant Commander HA MacKenzie RAN (DSIO North East Area) on Coastwatch in South West Pacific 1 June 1942-21 April 1943*, p. 29, Series B34476, (NAA).

199   WF Halsey, & J Bryan, *Admiral Halsey's Story*, Zenger Publishing Co. Inc, Washington, 1947, p. 150.

200   M Clemens, *Alone in Guadalcanal: A Coastwatchers Story*, op. cit., pp. 239-241; *Report by Lieutenant Commander HA MacKenzie RAN (DSIO North East Area)*

	on Coastwatch in South West Pacific 1 June 1942-21 April 1943, op. cit., p. 18.
201	Report by Lieutenant Commander HA MacKenzie RAN (DSIO North East Area) on Coastwatch in South West Pacific 1 June 1942-21 April 1943, op. cit., p. 20.
202	Letter from Lieutenant Commander HA MacKenzie to Commander RMB Long & Commander EA Feldt, 6 October 1942, Series B34476, (NAA).
203	Report by Lieutenant Commander HA MacKenzie RAN (DSIO North East Area) on Coastwatch in South West Pacific 1 June 1942-21 April 1943, op. cit., p. 21.
204	FA Rhoades, *Diary of a Coastwatcher in the Solomons*, The Nimitz Foundation, Fredericksburg, 1982, p. 29.
205	ibid, p. 30.
206	ibid, p. 27.
207	ibid, p. 29.
208	Letter from Commander EA Feldt to Commander RMB Long, 26 October 1942, Series B34476, (NAA).
209	Minute from Lieutenant Commander EA Feldt to the Controller AIB, *Activities of Section C AIB while under the command of Lieutenant Commander Feldt*, 1943, p. 9, Series B34476, (NAA).
210	Letter from Commander RMB Long to Commander EA Feldt, 12 October 1942, Series B34476, (NAA).
211	Letter from Commander RMB Long to Commander EA Feldt, 10 September 1942, Series B34476, (NAA).
212	EA Feldt, *The Coast Watchers*, op. cit., p. 136.
213	Final Medical Board Report, 31 July 1945 contained in *EA Feldt - Pensioner - Former New Guinea Officer*, A452, 3554676, (NAA).
214	*Inquest File for HA MacKenzie*, 19/3793,1377/1948, 15 October 1948 (NSW SA).
215	WF Halsey & J Bryan, *Admiral Halsey's Story*, Zenger Publishing Co. Inc., Washington, 1947, p. 150.
216	Letter from Commander RMB Long to Commander EA Feldt, 20 April 1943, Series B34476, (NAA).
217	Letter from Commander EA Feldt to Commander RMB Long, 12 September 1942, Series B34476, (NAA).
218	Letter from Commander EA Feldt to Mr G Gill, 29 August 1944, Series B34476, (NAA).
219	ibid.
220	A motion picture entitled *Mother Goose* was produced in 1964 about a coastwatcher but was based not on Eric's book but on the book by *A Place of Dragons* by SH Barnett.
221	Letter from Captain HB Farncomb to Commander RMB Long, 25 September 1945, (SPC-A).
222	The merchant ships were *Tarakan*, *Tatra* and *Agovi Prince*.

223   *Sinking of German Ship 'Ramses' by 'Adelaide'*, Report S68/2/42 dated 7 December 1942, p. 5.

224   The crew composition was 65 German, 10 Finns, 10 Norwegians, 3 Danes & 1 Italian. The Baron was Reinhold Stäl von Holstein & interview by author with Lieutenant Commander MJ Gregory, 28 March 2012.

225   I Nesdale, *Small Ships at War: They Joined the RAN*, Underdale, Adelaide, 1984, p. 75.

226   Lieutenant Commander GWT Armitage AS 206 dated 15 November 1942, 11206558 (NAA).

227   Lieutenant Commander GWT Armitage AS 206 dated 17 February 1942, 11206558 (NAA).

228   Health grounds were with exhaustion neurosis and portal cirrhosis.

229   Service Record for HB Vallentine, V80315, (NAA).

230   Interview with Mr Howard Watts by the author, 1 March 2013.

231   Letter from Lieutenant FS Sharp RANVR to AW Grazebrook, 16 December 1992 (Jones/Grazebrook Papers).

232   Letter from DH Merry to J Kimlin, 16 July 1942 contained in *J Kimlin: Detection of Enemy Movements by Means of a Listening Post*, MP 76/1, 2406, Barcode 4335596, (NAA).

Chapter 8

1   *Royal Australian Naval College Magazine*, H Thacker Printers, Geelong, 1913, p. 11.

2   Board of Inquiry Report, p.10 (Contained in *HMAS Hobart Torpedoing of off Espiritu Santo*, A5954, 518/27) (NAA).

3   Letter from GL Fowle to AW Grazebrook, dated 2 November, 1992.

4   Minute from Director Naval Intelligence to Chief of Naval Staff, *HMAS Hobart – leak of information 22 July 1943 in Hobart damage report*, A5954, 518/27, (NAA).

5   Letter from GL Fowle to AW Grazebrook, dated 2 November 1992.

6   *The Sydney Morning Herald*, 20 September 1943, p. 7.

7   Minute from Captain JK McCarthy to Commander EA Feldt, A/Sergeant WAH Butteris, 3 March 1943 contained in B3476, Barcode 411499, (NAA).

8   JM Alliston, *Destroyer Man*, Greenhouse Publications, Richmond, 1985, p. 128.

9   TC Kinkaid, ABC Broadcast 29 April 1951, Sydney, Transcript p. 2. Kinkaid Papers, (USNHHC).

10   The three men were Mentioned in Despatches.

11   EA Feldt, *The Coast Watchers* (The Australian Edition), Currey O'Neil, South Yarra, 1975, p. 373

12   Captain HB Farncomb, S206 dated 9 March 1944, (NAA).

13 Interview by author with Lieutenant Commander MJ Gregory, 28 March 2012.
14 *War Cabinet Minutes,* Numbers 2989-3331, 6 September 1943-4 February 1944, Volume 14, A5954, 689725, (NAA).
15 Based on an examination of *RAN Navy Lists,* April 1939-January 1945, (RAN Sea Power Centre).
16 JK McLaughlin, *Maxwell, Allan Victor (1887–1975), Australian Dictionary of Biography,* Volume 15, 2000, National Centre of Biography, Australian National University.
17 Commissioner's Report to the Attorney General dated 1 March 1944 in Series Number B6121, 399541, (NAA).
18 ibid, p. 24.
19 Directorate of Naval Operational Analysis Studies - Report No. 67/45 *Analysis of the Flying Effort of British assault carriers in Operation DRAGOON,* ADM/219/269 (TNA UK).
20 *London Gazette,* 27 March 1945.
21 24th Destroyer Flotilla at the time consisted of *Troubridge, Teazer, Termagant* and *Tenacious.*
22 Sub Lieutenant AW Clarke, (A) RNVR, Diary entries for September 1944 (see www.royalnavyresearcharchive.org.uk)
23 Reverend BA Watson (1916-2004) later Vicar of the Guild Church of St Lawrence Jewry-next-Guildhall.
24 Sub Lieutenant AW Clarke, Diary entries, op. cit.
25 HB Farncomb, *Aircraft Carrier Operations in the Aegean, September-October 1944,* undated, p. 10.
26 ibid.
27 Letters from Commander AG Leatham, RN to AW Grazebrook, 20 November 1987 and 26 January 1988, he was Lieutenant Commander (Air) in HMS *Attacker,* (Jones/Grazebrook Papers).
28 Captain HB Farncomb, S206 dated 6 October 1944, (NAA).
29 JG Bower (*Klaxon*), *The Story of our Submarines,* Blackwood & sons, 1919, p.76.
30 Captain AH Hillgarth, CMG, OBE, RN (1899-1978).
31 *Captain Hillgarth's report on visit to Australia,* May-September 1944, PREM 3/159/10 (TNA UK).
32 Letter from Admiral BM Chambers to FB Eldridge, 9 November 1944.
33 Letter from FWS Grant to AW Grazebrook, 7 December 1992.
34 D Hamer, *Memories of My Life,* South Wind, Singapore, 2002, p. 176.
35 Eldridge, op. cit., p. 406.
36 Captain HA Showers, AS206, 25 September 1944, (NAA).
37 TC Kinkaid, ABC Broadcast 29 April 1951, Sydney, Transcript p. 5. Kinkaid Papers, (USNHHC).

38   Admiral Soemu Toyota, Interrogation transcript, OPNAV-P-030I00, p. 317.

39   The battleships were *Yamato, Musashi, Nagato, Kongo* & *Haruna*. The cruisers were *Atago, Maya, Takao, Chokai, Myoko, Haguro, Kumano, Suzuya, Tone, Chikuma, Noshiro* & *Yahagi*.

40   The destroyers were *Michishio, Yamagumo, Asagumo* and *Shigure*.

41   Gill, 1942-1945, op. cit., p. 509.

42   There is debate about whether *Australia* was the first victim of a kamikaze attack. The Val that attacked the cruiser was from the 6th Flying Brigade, Imperial Japanese Army Air Force and did not come from the newly formed dedicated Imperial Japanese Navy Special Attack Unit. It appears that the pilot, perhaps believing his damaged aircraft would not reach base, decided to conduct a suicide attack on *Australia*.

43   TC Kinkaid, ABC Broadcast 29 April 1951, Sydney, Transcript p. 5. Kinkaid Papers, (USNHHC).

44   D Hamer, *Memories of My Life*, op. cit., p. 178.

45   DM Horner, *High Command: Australia & Allied Strategy 1939-1945*, Allen & Unwin, Sydney, 1982, p. 364.

46   JA Collins, *As Luck Would Have It: Reminiscences of an Australian Sailor*, op. cit., p. 153.

47   Letter from Captain JM Armstrong to Mrs EJ Armstrong, November 1944, JM Armstrong Papers (NLA).

48   Oldendorf's battleships were *Maryland, Mississippi, Tennessee, California, Pennsylvania* & *West Virginia*. His cruisers were *Louisville* (flagship), *Portland, Minneapolis, Shropshire, Denver, Columbia, Pheonix* & *Boise*.

49   Admiral Soemu Toyota, Interrogation transcript, op. cit., p. 317.

50   Entry for 25 October 1944, Journal of Midshipman PW Adams contained in Papers of Lieutenant PW Adams.

51   Oral History of Leading Seaman RB Walker, S00708, 28 June 1989, transcript p. 6 (AWM).

52   Commanding Officer HMAS *Shropshire* to Commander Task Group 77.2, *HMAS Shropshire Action Report 1-18 January 1945*, 24 January 1945.

53   Letter from Vice Admiral Sir Richard Peek to AW Grazebrook, 22 January 1988 and Commander ES Nurse AS 206 dated 15 October 1945.

54   Commander ES Nurse, AS 206, 8 May 1944, 311631, (NAA).

55   Stoker Petty Officer Mervyn Evans was later awarded a Distinguished Service Medal.

56   Letter from Commodore Commanding HMA Squadron to Commander 7th Fleet, 7 February 1945.

57   Anon, *The Cruiser and the Kamikazes: The Story of Japanese Suicide Attacks on HMAS Australia at Lingayen Gulf, Luzon 4th-9th January 1945*, JM Armstrong Papers.

58   Speed Letter from Commodore Commanding HMA Squadron to ACNB, 27

January 1945. A Speed Letter was essentially a letter sent via signal. Farncomb generally sent Personal for the First Naval Member letters by Speed Letter.
59 Letter from Commander WS Bracegirdle to AW Grazebrook, 14 February 1989.
60 The other ships were the battleships *Pennsylvania* & *West Virginia* & the cruiser *Portland*.
61 Speed Letter from Commodore Commanding HMA Squadron to ACNB, 12 January 1945.
62 Contained in a letter from Secretary of Naval Board to Secretary of the Admiralty, 448/201/2003, February 1945.
63 Annex to Commanding Officer HMAS *Australia* to Commodore Commanding His Majesty's Australian Squadron, *Action Report - Operation Mike 1*, 22 January 1945.
64 *Suicide Weapons and Tactics: Know Your Enemy, CinCPac Bulletin 126-45,* 28 May 1945, p. 5.
65 ibid.
66 Letter from Commander AS Storey to AW Grazebrook, 9 June 1992.
67 *London Gazette*, 1 May 1945.
68 Mattiske, op. cit., pp. 185-186.
69 Lieutenant Commander H Hall, Letter to the author, 12 April 2012.
70 ibid, p. 594.
71 GH Gill, 1942-1945, op. cit., p. 593.
72 Speed Letter Commodore Commanding HMA Squadron to ACNB, 12 January 1945.
73 Speed Letter from Commodore Commanding HMA Squadron to ACNB, 27 January 1945.
74 Speed Letter from Commodore Commanding HMA Squadron to ACNB, 27 January 1945.
75 Signal from First Naval Member to Commodore Commanding Australian Squadron 150910Z FEB 45.
76 Speed Letter Commodore Commanding HMA Squadron to ACNB, 24 January 1945.
77 Speed Letter Commodore Commanding HMA Squadron to ACNB, 27 January 1945.
78 Speed Letter from Commodore Commanding HMA Squadron to ACNB, 7 March 1945.
79 Speed Letter from Commodore Commanding HMA Squadron to ACNB, 7 March 1945.
80 Acting Commander EA Feldt, AS 206, 19 July 1945, (NAA).
81 Letter and map from Mr AJ 'Sandy' Pearson to PD Jones, 26 May 2012.
82 Letter from Captain James Esdaile to his wife, 13 May 1945, (Esdaile Family).

83 G Long, *Australia in the War of 1939-45 Series One: Volume 7: The Final Campaigns*, Canberra, Australian War Memorial, 1963, p. 350.
84 ibid.
85 Eric Feldt was finally discharged on 28 September 1945.
86 EA Feldt, *The Coast Watchers*, op. cit., p. 1.
87 ibid, p. ix.
88 Minute from Lieutenant Commander E Feldt to the Controller AIB, *Activities of Section C AIB while under the command of Lieutenant Commander Feldt*, Section C, p. 12.
89 Major General Edward James Milford (1894-1972).
90 Report Commanding Officer HMAS *Manoora* to Commander Task Unit 78.2.2, 1 July 1945, Operation OBOE Two Operations, Report of Wave Leader, Wave 7, contained in HMAS *Manoora* Report of Proceedings (AWM).
91 Letter from Commander Battleship Division Two to Commander Seventh Fleet, *Commodore HB Farncomb, RAN - Report on Fitness*, 27 January 1945, contained in HB Farncomb confidential report file (NAA).
92 Letter from Lieutenant Commander GL Fowle, DSC, RAN to AW Grazebrook dated 9 November 1992.
93 JA Collins, *As Luck Would Have It*: Reminiscences of an Australian Sailor, Angus and Robertson, Sydney, p. 155.
94 WA Silkett, *Downfall: The Invasion That Never Was*, US Army War College Quarterly - *Parameters*, 5 September 2012, pp. 114-115.
95 JA Collins, *As Luck Would Have It*, op. cit., p.155.
96 RB Frank, *Downfall: The End of the Imperial Japanese Empire*, New York, Penguin, 1999, p. 310.
97 ibid, p. 156.
98 Letter from Surgeon Lieutenant HG Rischbieth, RANR, 31 August 1945, p. 5.
99 ibid.
100 Anon, *Porthole: Souvenir of HMAS Shropshire*, John Sands Printers, Sydney, 1946, p. iii.
101 JA Collins, *As Luck Would Have It*, op. cit., p. 156.
102 Letter from Surgeon Lieutenant HG Rischbieth, RANR, 1 September 1945, p. 5.
103 Captain SS Murray, USN (1898-1980).
104 CEL Helfrich, *Memoires*, Volume 2, Amsterdam, Elsevier, 1950, p. 224 (translated from Dutch).
105 http://www.ww2australia.gov.au/vevp/surrender.html
106 JA Collins, *As Luck Would Have It*, op. cit., p. 157.
107 Anon, Porthole: Souvenir of HMAS *Shropshire*, op. cit., p. iii.

Chapter 9

1. *Royal Australian Naval College Magazine*, Geelong, H Thacker Printers, 1913, p. 11.
2. JA Collins, *As Luck Would Have It: Reminiscences of an Australian Sailor*, Angus and Robertson, Sydney, p. 162.
3. Letter of Proceedings 6 December-23 December 1945 from Commodore JA Collins to Commander-in-Chief British Pacific Fleet, 24 December 1945, contained in HMAS *Hobart* Reports of Proceedings for 1945, (AWM).
4. *Emily* (AY2075).
5. *Advocate*, Burnie, 24 April 1947 p. 4.
6. *Advocate*, Burnie, 19 January 1948, p. 5.
7. Mr Phillips, Paper titled '*Demobilisation of the RAN*', AWM 69, Series 23/44, (AWM).
8. DM Stevens, *The Australian Centenary History of Defence Volume III: The Royal Australian Navy*, op. cit., p. 156.
9. *Australia - Royal Australian Navy - Personality Sketches*, Naval Attaché, 12 July 1945, Serial 45-R-45, Monograph Index Guide Number 901, pp.1-2 (US National Archives).
10. ibid.
11. ibid.
12. ibid.
13. Minute from C-in-C Portsmouth to the Admiralty, 15 May 1946, ADM 1/9568, (TNA UK).
14. Manager of United Services Club Queensland, email to author, 16 October 2015.
15. Letter from EA Feldt to R Harrigan dated 20 August 1951 contained in *EA Feldt - Pensioner - Former New Guinea Officer*, A452, 3554676, (NAA).
16. Sir Errol Galbraith Knox (1889-1949) see *Australian Dictionary of Biography*.
17. Letter EA Feldt to R Harrigan dated 13 March 1951 contained in *EA Feldt - Pensioner - Former New Guinea Officer*, A452, 3554676, (NAA).
18. Acting Captain ES Nurse, AS 206 20 May 1946, (NAA).
19. Anon, *Naval Ordnance Inspection Journal*, No. 27, March 1957, pp. 75-77.
20. Letters from Rear Admiral WDH Graham to AW Grazebrook, 12 October 1987 & 21 March 1989.
21. Letter from Commander AS Storey to AW Grazebrook, 9 June 1992.
22. Interview with Warrant Officer Allen Guthrie by author, 20 July 2013.
23. Interview with Vice Admiral Sir Richard Peek, 18 June 2010.
24. Letter from Rear Admiral HA Showers to AW Grazebrook, 19 December 1987 (Jones/Grazebrook Papers).

25	*The Sydney Morning Herald*, 16 June 1949, p. 7.
26	Letter from Chief of Naval Staff (Collins) to First Sea Lord (Fraser), 5 August 1949 contained in S Rose, *The Naval Miscellany* (ed), *Volume 7*, The Naval Records Society, Aldershot, 2008, p. 552.
27	Based on account of conversation between HB Farncomb and Commodore 'Toz' Dadswell. Interview with Commodore 'Toz' Dadswell with author, 11 September 2015.
28	Commodore 'Toz' Dadswell, interview with the author, 7 October 2010.
29	*The Sydney Morning Herald*, 24 February 1951, p. 1.
30	Letter from RMB Long to GH Gill, 8 March 1951, p. 1, AWM 69 (AWM).
31	*The Sydney Morning Herald*, 3 February 1951, p. 1
32	Letter from Chief of Naval Staff (Hamilton) to First Sea Lord (Cunningham), 3 February 1947 contained in S Rose, (ed), *The Naval Miscellany, Volume 7*, op. cit., p. 521.
33	ibid.
34	Letter from First Sea Lord (Cunningham) to Chief of Naval Staff (Hamilton), 30 May 1947 contained in S Rose, (ed), *The Naval Miscellany, Volume 7*, op. cit., p. 525.
35	JA Collins, *As Luck Would Have It*, op. cit., p. 166.
36	*The Argus* (Melbourne), 6 March 1948, p. 2.
37	Letter from Commanding Officer HMAS *Penguin*, *RAN Officers - Deferred Pay and Child Allowance* to Secretary Naval Board, circa 1946, 186/1/11, p. 1, contained in Captain HL Howden Papers, (AWM).
38	ibid, p. 2.
39	ibid, p. 2.
40	ibid, p. 3.
41	Mrs B Crouch, interview with PD Jones, 14 September 2015.
42	*Inquest File for HA MacKenzie*, 19/3793,1377/1948, 15 October 1948 (State Archives of NSW).
43	*Death Certificate of Hugh Alexander MacKenzie*, 1948/027275, (State Archives of NSW).
44	*Inquest File for HA MacKenzie, op. cit.*
45	ibid.
46	*The Sydney Morning Herald*, 20 September 1948, p. 3.
47	EA Feldt, *The Coast Watchers*, op. cit., p. 13.
48	Letter from Commander AS Storey to AW Grazebrook, 10 September 1992, (Jones/Grazebrook Papers).
49	*The West Australian*, 6 January 1951, p. 7.
50	PJ Kimlin, Sheet Music, *Beast's Christmas, Allegro for Strings*, 190989, (NLA).

51 *The Argus*, Melbourne, 11 March 1953, p. 6.
52 *The Argus*, Melbourne, 7 July 1953, p. 9.
53 Letter from Chief of Naval Staff (Hamilton) to First Sea Lord (Cunningham), 3 February 1947, op. cit., p. 519.
54 Oral History of Vice Admiral Sir John Collins interviewed by Robert Hyslop, S046522, March 1988, (AWM).
55 During the 1950-52 when there were 37 meetings of the Naval Board, the Minister attended once.
56 Sir Frederick Shedden entry contained in the *Australian Dictionary of Biography*.
57 ibid.
58 R Hyslop, *A Very Civil Servant: An Australian Memoir*, Clarion Editions, Binalong, 1998, p. 100.
59 R Hyslop, *Aye, Aye, Minister: Australian Naval Administration, 1939-59*, AGPS Press, Canberra, 1990, p. 54.
60 Letter from Chief of Naval Staff (Collins) to First Sea Lord (Fraser), 7 September 1948, contained in S Rose, (ed), *The Naval Miscellany, Volume 7*, op. cit.
61 Minute from Chief of Naval Staff to Deputy Chief of Naval Staff, *A/S Warfare*, 1 November 1948.
62 Letter from Chief of Naval Staff (Collins) to First Sea Lord (Fraser), 22 June 1951, contained in S Rose, (ed), *The Naval Miscellany, Volume 7*, op. cit.
63 In part because John Collins had commanded the first *Anzac*, his wife Phyllis launched HMAS *Anzac* (II) soon after he became Chief of Naval Staff.
64 Minute from DTSR to CNS, *Anti-Submarine Warfare - Review of Present Position*, 4 October 1948, p. 3.
65 Minutes from Naval Board Meeting 3 May 1950 contained in Naval Board Minutes, 1950-1953, 4269885 & Cabinet Submission *Australian Shipbuilding*, March 1950, A4639, 5104159, (NAA).
66 Cabinet Submission *Australian Shipbuilding*, op. cit., p. 4.
67 Letter from Chief of Naval Staff (Collins) to First Sea Lord (Fraser), 2 April 1951 contained in S Rose, *The Naval Miscellany* (ed) *Volume 7*, op. cit.
68 They were HMA Ships *Colac, Cowra, Gladstone* & *Latrobe*.
69 Papers of Admiral AW Radford, USN, (USNHHC).
70 Admiral George Hyde was made a Knight Commander of the Order of the Bath on 1 January 1934.
71 *Townsville Daily Bulletin*, 4 May 1953, p. 1.
72 JA Collins, *The Handfinishing Tools as used in bookbinding*, undated. I31061758, (NSW State Library).
73 Translated from Dutch, CEL Helfrich, *Memoires*, 2 volumes, Amsterdam, Elsevier, 1950, pp. 55-56.
74 *The Argus*, Melbourne, 2 May 1951, p. 1.

75 ibid.
76 TC Kinkaid, ABC Broadcast 29 April 1951, Sydney, Transcript, Kinkaid Papers, (USNHHC).
77 Letter from First Sea Lord (McGrigor) to Chief of Naval Staff (Collins), 22 April 1955 contained in S Rose, *The Naval Miscellany* (ed.), *Volume 7*, op. cit.
78 Letter from Chief of Naval Staff (Collins) to First Sea Lord (McGrigor), 27 January 1955 contained in S Rose, *The Naval Miscellany* (ed.), *Volume 7*, op. cit., p. 620.
79 Oral Histories of Vice Admiral Sir John Collins, 27 August 1975 & March 1988.
80 Letter from FWS Grant to AW Grazebrook, 7 December 1992.
81 Details obtained from the Grant family.
82 IJ Cunningham, *Work Hard Play Hard, The Royal Australian Naval College 1913-1988*, AGPS, Canberra, 1988, p. 49.
83 Letter from Vice Admiral JA Collins to Captain ES Nurse, 10 February 1955, (Jones/Grazebrook Papers).
84 ibid.
85 ibid.
86 Notation on Commander RMB Long's Record of Service, (NAA).
87 Letter from RMB Long to FE de Groot, 27 September 1951, p. 2.
88 Letter to CE Sayers from Commander RMB Long, 18 October 1945.
89 Letter to CE Sayers from Commander RMB Long, 18 October 1945.
90 B Winter, *The Intrigue Master*, op. cit., Boolarong Press, 1995, p. 95.
91 Letter from RMB Long to FE de Groot, dated 3 May 1951.
92 Letter from RMB Long to GH Gill, 3 April 1951, AWM 69, (AWM), p. 1.
93 *The Sydney Morning Herald*, 12 November 1951, p. 1.
94 *A Call to the People of Australia*, picture, H34151, (State Library of Victoria).
95 Letter from RMB Long to FE de Groot, dated 27 September 1951, p. 2.
96 Letter from RMB Long to FE de Groot, dated 20 February 1952, p. 2.
97 Letter from RMB Long to FE de Groot, dated 20 August 1952.
98 Letter from RMB Long to FE de Groot, dated 6 March 1953, p. 3.
99 Letter from RMB Long to FE de Groot, dated 24 July 1953.
100 Mr Robert Cliff, interview, 1 April 2015.
101 Letter from RMB Long to FE de Groot, dated 13 July 1953.
102 Letter from RMB Long to FE de Groot, dated 12 April 1958, p. 2.
103 ibid.
104 Letter from RMB Long to FE de Groot, dated 2 June 1959, p. 3.
105 Letter from RMB Long to FE de Groot, dated 18 March 1957.
106 Letter from RMB Long to FE de Groot, dated 13 June 1955.

ENDNOTES 699

107 Letter from RMB Long to FE de Groot, dated 18 March 1957, p. 6.
108 ibid.
109 Letter from RMB Long to FE de Groot, dated 26 March 1958.
110 Letter from RMB Long to FE de Groot, dated 29 July 1959.
111 GH Gill, *Royal Australian Navy 1939-1942*, Collins, Melbourne, 1957, p. xv.
112 Letter from RMB Long to GH Gill, 31 January 1952, AWM 69, p. 1.
113 Letter from RMB Long to GH Gill, 23 May 1952, AWM 69, p. 1.
114 ibid.
115 GH Gill, *Royal Australian Navy 1939-1942*, Collins, Melbourne, 1957.
116 Awarded by the International PEN Club.
117 *The Coastwatchers*, audio tape, Madang, New Guinea, 15 August 1959, 238264, (National Film & Sound Archive).
118 Letter from RMB Long to Irwin Hunter Esq, 4 September 1959. The recording is *The Coastwatchers*, audio tape, Madang New Guinea, 15 August 1959, 238264, (National Film and Sound Archive).
119 Captain Clarence Marbury White, Jr (1910-1963).
120 *Una Voce,* Journal of the Papua New Guinea Association of Australia, September 1999.
121 *The Coastwatchers*, audio tape, op. cit.
122 *Una Voce,* Journal of the Papua New Guinea Association of Australia, September 1999.
123 *The Coastwatchers*, audio tape, op. cit.
124 *The Coastwatchers*, audio tape, op. cit.
125 Lieutenant BWG Hall MC, AIF, *The Coastwatchers*, audio tape, op. cit.
126 Lieutenant Commander FA Rhoades, RANR, *The Coastwatchers*, audio tape, op. cit.
127 ibid.
128 ibid.
129 This document was given to Tony Grazebrook during the course of his research into the Pioneer Class and presented by the author to the Sea Power Centre-Australia for posterity.
130 Major PE Figgis, MC, AIF, *The Coastwatchers*, audio tape, op. cit.
131 *Una Voce,* Journal of the Papua New Guinea Association of Australia, September 1999.
132 Letter from Colonel GG Roberts to AWG Nobbs, 22 July 1960, RMB Long papers, op. cit, (AWM).
133 Letter from Captain AH Hillgarth to AWG Nobbs, 20 Jan 1960, RMB Long papers, op. cit.
134 B Winter, *The Intrigue Master: Commander Long and Naval Intelligence in Australia, 1913-194*5, Boolarong Press, Brisbane, 1995.

135 Letter from Lieutenant Commander RC Horton to AWG Nobbs, 14 September 1960, RMB Long papers, op. cit.

136 GH Gill, *Royal Australian Navy 1942-1945*, Melbourne, Collins, 1968, p. xv.

137 D Hamer, *Memories of My Life*, South Wind, Singapore, 2002, p. 296.

138 Flag Officer in Charge East Australian Area Reports of Proceedings November-March 1954-55, p. 3 (AWM).

139 *Nucleus,* Volume 1, September 1954, p. 12.

140 *Nucleus,* Volume 1, July 1955, p. 4.

141 Australia's first electronic computer was CSIRAC (Council for Scientific & Industrial Research Automatic Computer). It was originally known as the CSIR Mk 1.

142 Interview with Vice Admiral Sir Richard Peek with AW Grazebrook, 3 June 1992, (Jones/Grazebrook Papers).

143 Excerpt contained in Letter from Secretary of Naval Board to Secretary of Department of Defence. Confidential File of Commander JB Newman, (NAA).

144 Commander JB Newman, AS 206 Performance Report, 10 October 1945.

145 P Morton, *Fire Across the Desert: Woomera and the Anglo-Australian Joint Project 1946-1980*, AGPS, Canberra, 1989, p. 242.

146 Memorandum from Superintendent Range to Controller Weapons Research Establishment, 29 August 1956, File 5411/8/1 Part 1 (NAA).

147 P Morton, *Fire Across the Desert: Woomera and the Anglo-Australian Joint Project 1946-1980*, op. cit., p. 65.

148 ibid, p. 66.

149 Letter from Lieutenant Commander GL Fowle to AW Grazebrook, 9 February 1992. (Jones/Grazebrook Papers).

150 Lieutenant Commander CAR Sadleir, AS 206 Report, 30 November 1956, (NAA).

151 Australian High Commission, Wellington, Despatch 10/1957 - *The New Zealand Communist Party*, 1171196, 16 October 1957, p. 7, (NAA).

152 Australian High Commission, Wellington, Despatch 9/1957 - *The New Zealand Social Credit Political League*, 1171196, 2 September 1957, p. 5, (NAA).

153 Australian High Commission, Wellington, Despatch 5/1957 - *The New Zealand Labour Party*, 1171196, 5 July 1957, p. 4, (NAA).

154 ibid, p. 6.

155 Australian High Commission, Wellington, Despatch 6/1957 - *The New Zealand National Party*, 1171196, 9 August 1957, p. 5, (NAA).

156 Australian High Commissioner to New Zealand, Despatch No. 3, 20 August 1959, p. 2.

157 ibid, p. 4.

158 Australian High Commissioner to New Zealand, Despatch No. 2, 8 July 1959, p. 2.

159 Australian High Commission, Wellington, Despatch 1/1962 - *Western Samoan Independence Celebrations*, 10 January 1962, p. 1, 742236, (NAA).

160 ibid, p. 4.
161 The Dean or doyen of the Diplomatic Corps is the senior diplomatic representative who has served the longest in a country. Seniority depends on the date of arrival in the capital coupled with the official presentation of credentials. The duties are chiefly ceremonial in nature.
162 Australian High Commission, Wellington, Despatch 3/1962 - *A Last Look at New Zealand*, 742236, 28 August 1962, (NAA).
163 The original draft for the John Collins memoir is held by the National Library of Australia and the different titles appear on the cover sheet.
164 Letter from Prime Minister RG Menzies to Vice Admiral JA Collins, 4 September 1965 (Collins Papers).
165 Commodore 'Toz' Dadswell, interview with the author, 7 October 2010.
166 *The Sydney Morning Herald*, 15 June 1953, p. 2.
167 Professor TR Frame, email to PD Jones, 10 May 2015.
168 ibid.
169 *The Age*, 7 June 1958.
170 TR Frame, *Where Fate Calls*, Coronet Books, Rydalmere, 1993, pp. 12-50.
171 *The Age*, 20 November 1965, p. 24.
172 HB Farncomb, *Anzac Address to Dapto Returned Service League*, 23 April 1961, Farncomb Papers (RAN).
173 NK Calder, op. cit., p. 27. The ex-*Bungaree* was salvaged by a Japanese company, renamed the *Kitagawa Maru* before finally being scrapped in 1968.
174 Letter from Mr P Reilly to AW Grazebrook 22 July 1992, p. 5.
175 Commander ES Nurse, AS 206, 8 May 1944, 311631, (NAA).
176 Letter from ES Nurse to Mr Lowy, 19 May 1969, (Museum of Melbourne).
177 ibid.
178 ibid.
179 *The Sun*, 15 August 1970, p. 8.
180 ibid.
181 ibid.
182 ibid.
183 Item ST 29857 in the Museum of Victoria collection.
184 http://collections.museumvictoria.com.au/items/386336.
185 JC Howells, *Ben and Dorothy: A Portrait of My Parents,* Published Privately, Camberwell, 2012, p. 95.
186 ibid.
187 Introduction to Ben Howell's poem *Guadalcanal* (Howells Family).
188 EB Howells, *Guadalcanal*, unpublished, (Howells Family).
189 Mrs Barbara Willingham, email to the author, 2 November 2011.

190 Rear Admiral CSH Harrington, email to the author, 14 November 2014.
191 W Crouch, 'Admirals on Parade', *Daily Telegraph*, Sydney, 19 July 1963, p. 34.
192 Letter from Mrs P Tait to PD Jones, 9 August 2015, (Jones/Grazebrook Papers).
193 E Flynn, *My Wicked, Wicked Ways*, G.P. Putnam's sons, New York, 1959.
194 ibid, pp. 91-93.
195 E Felt, *Errol Flynn at Salamaua*, Quadrant, Spring, 1961, Volume 5 (4), pp. 81-88.
196 EA Feldt, *New Guinea's Between-Wars Administration is too Frequently Misunderstood*, Pacific Island Monthly, May 1967, pp. 58-60.
197 *The Courier Mail*, Brisbane, 15 March 1965, p. 9.
198 Undated newspaper article from Biographical Cuttings for Commander EA Feldt, 42651783, (NLA).
199 Anon, 'Death of Eric Feldt', *Pacific Island Monthly*, April 1968, p. 133.
200 Letter from Mr JS Armitage to AW Grazebrook, 8 March 1993.
201 *Parish Messenger*, St James Church (Sydney), Volume 56, Number 11, February/March 1971, p. 2.
202 Letter from Lady Collins to AW Grazebrook, 20 November 1987.
203 Letter from Commander WS Bracegirdle to AW Grazebrook, 14 February 1989, (Jones/Grazebrook Papers).
204 Letter from Vice Admiral Sir Richard Peek to AW Grazebrook, 22 January 1988 (Jones/Grazebrook Papers).
205 B Donoghue, *In Retrospect, Ex-WRANS Ditty Box*, August 1972, p. 5.
206 ibid, p. 6.
207 JA Collins, *HMAS Sydney*, The Naval Historical Society of Australia, Garden Island, 1971.
208 ibid, 1971, p. ii.
209 E-mail from Mrs Mary Backhouse to author 17 November 2015.
210 Inquest into the death of HJH Thompson, 24 September 1973, NSW Coroners Court, Glebe.

Amylobarbitone is a hypnotic-sedative barbiturate that was probably prescribed to Horace for insomnia. When mixed with alcohol it could have severe side effects including loss of consciousness and seizures.

211 Papers and poems of Able Seaman N Smith retired, (Jones/Grazebrook Papers).
212 Papers of Commander NK Calder, RAN (Captain M Calder).
213 ibid, p. 111.
214 ibid, p. 112.
215 ibid, p. 123 from Ben Howell's poem *Shells in a Rock-Pool*.
216 Letter from Rear Admiral HA Showers to AW Grazebrook, 19 December 1987 (Jones/Grazebrook Papers).
217 Letter from Lady Collins to AW Grazebrook, 20 November 1987, (Jones/Grazebrook Papers).

218 *The Canberra Times*, 9 September 1989, p. 2.
219 For details of the funeral carriage see BR 1834 *Royal Naval Handbook of Ceremonial & Drill*.
220 Email from Lieutenant Commander M Shelvey, 27 June 27 2013.
221 *The Times*, London, 22 August 1942, p. 41.
222 Apollonius Rhodius, *The Voyage of the Argo*, Translated by EV Rieu, Penguin Classics, London, 1971, p. 195.

Bibliography

Articles, Artwork, Journals & Speeches

Anon, The Cruiser and the Kamikazes: The Story of Japanese Suicide Attacks on HMAS Australia at Lingayen Gulf, Luzon 4th-9th January 1945, J.M. Armstrong Papers, (NLA).

Anon, *Naval Ordnance Inspection Journal*, No.27, March 1957, pp. 75-77.

Anon, Death of Eric Feldt, *Pacific Island Monthly*, April 1968, p.22 & p.133.

Anon, *Parish Messenger*, St James Church (Sydney), Volume 56, Number 11, February/March 1971.

Bennett, J.A., Fears and Aspirations: US military Intelligence Operations in the South Pacific, 1941-1945, *The Journal of Pacific History*, Volume 39, No. 3, 2004, pp. 283-307.

Burnett, P.R., Captain Joseph Burnett, RAN, *Naval Historical Review*, Sydney, December 1973, pp.3-9.

Carpenter, J.L, *HMAS Toowoomba - J157*, undated.

Clark, C, The Statute of Westminster and the murder in HMAS *Australia*, 1942, *Australian Defence Force Journal*, Issue 179, 2009, pp. 18-28.

Crotty, J, Ballet and the Australian Way of Life: the Development of a National Dance Repertoire 1951-1961, *Acta Musicological*, 1 January 2010, Volume 82 (2), pp. 305-340.

Crouch, E, Obituary Rear Admiral Henry Arthur Showers, *Naval Historical Review*, 1992, p.29.

Creswick, A, *Australians at War* entry, www.australiansatwar.gov.au.

Daily Telegraph (UK), Obituary of Mrs Suzanne Kyrle-Pope, 6 February 2015.

Donoghue, B, In Retrospect, Ex-WRANS *Ditty Box*, August 1972, pp 3-6.

Dudley, S.F., Pulmonary Tuberculosis in the Royal Navy and the Use of Mass Miniature Radiography in its Control, *Proceedings of the Royal Society of Medicine*, Volume XXXIV, 28 March 1941, pp.401-406.

Farncomb, H.B., Aircraft Carrier Operations in the Aegean, September-October 1944, undated, Farncomb Papers (RAN Seapower Centre).

Farncomb, H.B., Particulars of Allied Landings in South of France on 15 August 1944, undated, Farncomb Papers (RAN Seapower Centre).

Farncomb, H.B., Anzac Address to Dapto Returned Service League, 23 April 1961, Farncomb Papers (RAN Seapower Centre).

Fioravanzo, G, Action in the Strait of Otranto. Examination Comparative Relations Officers, April 1954 (in Italian).

Felt, E, Errol Flynn at Salamaua, *Quadrant*, Spring, 1961, Volume 5 (4). pp 81-88.

Feldt, E.A. The Coastwatchers, *Journal of the Historical Society of Queensland*, Volume 6, Number 4, 1961-62, pp. 762-778.

Feldt, E.A., New Guinea's Between-Wars Administration is too Frequently Misunderstood, *Pacific Island Monthly*, May 1967, pp. 58-60.

Flint, E.A. The Formation and Operation of the US Army Small Ships in World War II, *United Service*, Volume 55, No. 4, March 2005, pp. 15-20.

Galuppini, G.N. Un Insolito Funerale Di Guerra (An Unusual Funeral Of War), *Bollettino D'Archivo Dell Ufficio Storico Della Marina Militare* (Newsletter Archive of the Navy Historic Office), Year 6, March 1992, pp. 283-294.

Gill, J.C.H. The Last Days of Rabaul: December 13, 1941 to January 23, 1942, Paper to The Royal Historical Society of Queensland, 23 March 1961.

Goldrick, J.V. P., The Australia Court Martial of 1942, M.Litt. thesis, Armidale: University of New England, 1984.

Goldrick, J.V.P., Buying Time: British Submarine Capability in the Far East, 1919-1940, *Global War Studies*, 2015.

Howells, J.C, *The Colours Cap of Ben Howells*, unpublished.

Jeffery, V, Frank Getting - A Forgotten Submariner, *The Navy*, Volume 65, No.3 , pp.19-21.

Kimbell, G.T.W. Over and Under: My Experienced while serving in HM Submarine K17, Part of the Papers of Commander ER Dodd, RN, 87/3/1 (IWM).

Maude, H.E. and Terrell, J, Bibliography of Current Publications, *The Journal of Pacific History*, Volume 3, 1968, pp. 193-209.

McLaughlin, J.K., Maxwell, Allan Victor (1887–1975), *Australian Dictionary of Biography*, Volume 15, 2000, National Centre of Biography, Australian National University.

Melbourne Church of England Grammar School Magazine, 15 May 1917.

Milner, S.L., The Coastwatchers, *Military Affairs*, Volume 11, No.3, Autumn 1947, pp 188-189, Society of Military Affairs.

Nelson, H., Fighting for Her Gates and Waterways: Changing Perceptions of New New Guinea in Australian Defence, Discussion Paper 2005/3, State, Society and Governance in Melanesia, The Australian National University, Research School of Pacific and Asian Studies.

Nichols, R, The Great Depression and the Navy, *Naval Historical Review*, June 2011, pp. 23-27.
Nucleus, The Newsletter of The Nuclear Research Foundation, Sydney, University of Sydney, 1955-1979.
Ohmae, T, The Battle of Savo Island, US Naval Institute Proceedings, 83/12, December 1957. Also available at http://www.navalhistory.org/2012/08/09/the-battle-of-savo-island .
Peluso, C, The torpedo boat 'Nicola Fabrizi' in the Adriatic and the escort of convoys for Greece, *Newsletter Archive Historical Office of the Navy - June 2012* (translated from Italian).
Proud, J.C.R., The Navy's Secret War in the Pacific, *Naval Historical Review*, December 1971.
Radford, R, Burning the Spears: A 'Peace Movement' in the Eastern Highlands of New Guinea 1936-37, *The Journal of Pacific History*, Volume 12, No.1, 1977, pp. 40-54.
The Navy League Journal, The Magazine of the Navy League of Australia, Editions from 1922-1994.
Silkett, W.A. Downfall: The Invasion That Never Was, US Army War College Quarterly - *Parameters*, 5 September 2012, pp.111-120.
Simington, M, Australia and the New Caledonia Coup d'etat, *Australia Outlook*, 1976, Volume 30, No.1, pp. 73-92.
Slattery, M.J, H. B. *"Fearless" Farncomb: Barrister and Commander*, 21 March 2012.
Swinden, G.J., Australian Naval Forces and Commonwealth Naval Forces, *Naval Historical Review*, June 2011.
Swinden, G.J., Midshipman Armitage and the loss of the Ballarat, *Sabretache*: The Journal of the military Collectors Society of Australia, 2008, Volume 49, edition 3, pp. 36-39.
Una Voce, Journal of the Papua New Guinea Association of Australia, September 1999.
Watts, A.J.B. *Aussie* Magazine, No. 67 (15 September 1924), No. 70 (15 December 1924) & No. 74 (15 April 1925), Artwork contained in these editions.
White C.L., *Art That Pays*, Leyshon White Commercial Art School, booklet, two editions 1930s, 1193743, (State Library of Victoria).
Whitlock, D.L. Station C and Fleet Radio Unit Melbourne (FRUMEL) Revisited, Address to Third Cryptologic History Symposium, National Security Agency, 28 October 1992.

Books

Adams, J.H., *Ships in Battledress*, The Currawong Publishing Company, Sydney, 1944.
Allen, L, *Singapore 1941-1942*, London, Davis-Poynter, 1977.
Alliston, J.M, *Destroyer Man*, Greenhouse Publications, Richmond, 1985.
Anon, *Huddart Parker Limited: 1939-1945*, Melbourne, John D. Harris & Co, 1951.

Anon, *The Book of the Ballarat: Left Australia, 19 February, Torpedoed Anzac Day, 25 April,1917, With Few Laughs In Between*, London, Wightman, 1917.

Anon, Australian Army Amphibious Operations in the South-West Pacific 1942-45, Papers 1994 Australian Army History Conference, Army Doctrine Centre, Canberra, 1995.

Anon, *Porthole: Souvenir of HMAS Shropshire*, John Sands Printers, Sydney, 1946.

Anon, *With the Diggers 1914-18, Songbook of Fourth Division Army Medical Corps Association*, 1934.

Apollonius Rhodius, *The Voyage of the Argo* (aka *The Argonautica*), translated by E.V. Rieu, Penguin Classics, London, 1971.

Armstrong, J.G., *The Halifax explosion and the Royal Canadian Navy: Inquiry and Intrigue*, University of British Colombia Press, Vancouver, 2003.

Australian Dictionary of Biography, Australian National University Press, Canberra, various entries.

Bates, L. F. *Sir Alfred Ewing: A Pioneer in Physics and Engineering*, London, Longmans, 1946.

Bayliss, P.J. *The Forgotten Fleet, Australian Army Small Ships*, ebook from 32 Small Ship Squadron RAE Association, www.32smallshipsqn.org.au.

Bean, C.E.W., *Flagships Three*, Alston Rivers, London, 1915.

Bennett, G, *The Loss of the Prince of Wales and Repulse*, London, Ian Allen Ltd, 1973.

Biskup, P., Jinks, B. and Nelson, H. *A Short History of New Guinea*, Angus and Robertson, Sydney, 1968.

Biskup, P., Jinks, B. and Nelson, H. *Readings in New Guinea History*, Angus and Robertson, Sydney, 1973.

Blaikie, G, *Remember Smith's Weekly*, Rigby Ltd, Sydney, 1966.

Bond, B & Tachikawa, K edited, *British and Japanese Military Leadership in the Far Eastern War, 1941-1945*, London, Frank Cass, 2004.

Booth, D.R, *Mountains, Gold and Cannibals*, Eagle Press, Sydney, 1929.

Bower, J.G., *The British Submarine Service: The Royal Navy and the Submersible War 1914-1918*, Leonaur, 2010.

Brescia, M, *Mussolini's Navy: A Reference Guide to the Regia Marina 1930-1945*, Barnsley, Seaforth Publishing, 2012.

Buley, E.C, *Glorious Deeds of Australasians in the Great War*, London, Andrew Melrose, 1915.

Burchett, W.G, *Pacific Treasure Island: New Caledonia; Voyage through its land and wealth, the story of its people and past*, David MacKay Company, Philadelphia, 1944.

Calder, N.K. and Vickerage, G.L.W. *HMAS Bungaree: Australia's Only Minelayer*, Monograph 179, Sydney, Naval Historical Society of Australia, 2001.

Carruthers, S.L. *Japanese Submarine Raiders 1942: A Maritime Mystery*, Narrabeen, Casper Publications, revised 2006.

Chambers, B.M., *Salt Junk: Naval Reminiscences, 1881-1906*, London, Constable & Co.

Ltd, 1927.

Chinnery, S.J., *Malaguna Road: The Papua and New Guinea Diaries of Sarah Chinnery*, National Library of Australia, Canberra, 1998, p.114.

Choules, C, *Claude Choules: His Autobiography, The Last of the Last*, Hesperian Press, Carlisle, 2009.

Churchill, W.S. *The Second World War, Volume III: The Grand Alliance*, London, Penguin, 2005.

Ciano, G, *Ciano's Diary 1939-1943*, Edited Gibson, H, Howard Fertig, New York, 1973.

Clemens, M, *Alone in Guadalcanal: A Coastwatchers Story*, Naval Institute Press, Annapolis, 1998.

Clarke, H.V. & Yamashita, T. *To Sydney by Stealth*, Sydney, Horwitz Publications Inc, 1966.

Coleridge, E.P, *The Argonautica of Apollonius Rhodius*, George Bell and Sons, Covent Garden, 1889.

Collins, D. *Bright Vista*, Jenkins, London, 1946.

Collins, D. *Ordeal*, Cornstalk Publishing Company, Sydney, 1924.

Collins, J.A., *As Luck Would Have It: Reminiscences of an Australian Sailor*, Sydney, Angus and Robertson, 1965.

Collins, J.A., *HMAS Sydney, Garden Island*, The Naval Historical Society of Australia, 1971.

Collins, J.A. *The Handfinishing Tools as used in bookbinding*, undated. I31061758, (New South Wales State Library).

Connor, J, *Anzac and Empire: George Foster Pearce and the Foundation of Australian Defence*, Port Melbourne, Cambridge University Press, 2011.

Corbett, J.S. *Naval Operations, Naval Operations, Volume I*. Longmans, Green and Company. London.

Creswell, W.R. *Close to the Wind: The Early Memoirs (1866-1879) of Admiral Sir William Rooke Creswell*, edited by P. Thompson, London, Heineman, 1965.

Cunningham, A.B. *A Sailor's Odyssey*, Hutchinson and Company, London, 1951.

Cunningham, I.J., *Work Hard Play Hard, The Royal Australian Naval College 1913-1988*, AGPS, Canberra, 1988.

Curtis-Otter, *WRANS: The Women's Royal Australian Naval Service*, Sydney, The Naval Historical Society of Australia, 1975.

Dalrymple-Hay, K.H. *Coastwatching in Fight for the Solomons, MS 1943*, Unpublished Manuscript, 1943 (NLA).

Day, D, *Reluctant Nation: Australia and the Allied Defeat of Japan 1942-45*, Melbourne, Oxford University Press, 1992.

De Gaulle, C., *Discours et Messages, Pendant La Guerre Juin 1940 - Janvier 1946*, Plon, Paris, 1970.

Detmars,T, *The Raider Kormoran*, Tandem Publishing, London, 1973.

Dorling, T, *Endless Story: Being an Account of the Work of the Destroyers, Flotilla-Leaders,*

Torpedo-Boats and Patrol-Boats in the Great War, Hodder and Stoughton, London, 1936.

Encyclopedia of Canadiana, The Grolier Society of Canada, Toronto, 1966.

Eldridge, F.B. *A History of the Royal Australian Naval College: From its inception in 1913 to the end of World War II in 1945*, Melbourne, Georgian House, 1949.

Everitt, D, *K Boats: Steam-powered submarines in World War I*, Airlife Publishing, Bridgend, 1999 (first published by George C Harrap & Company Ltd in 1963).

Eyssen, R, HKS *Komet: Kaperfahrt auf Allen Meeren*, Koehlers, Herford, 1960.

Feakes, H.J. *White Ensign – Southern Cross: A Story of the King's Ships of Australia's Navy*, Ure Smith, Sydney, 1951.

Feldt, E.A, *The Coast Watchers*, Currey O'Neil, South Yarra, 1975 (Australian Edition).

Feldt, E.A, *The Coast Watchers*, Nelson Doubleday, New York, 1979, (US Edition)

Fenton Huie, S, *Ships Belles: The story of the Women's Royal Australian Naval Service 1941-1985*, Sydney, Watermark Press, 2000.

Frame, T.R. *HMAS Sydney: Loss and Controversy*, Hodder & Stoughton, Sydney, 1993.

Frame, T.R. *No Pleasure Cruise: The Story of the Royal Australian Navy*, Crows Nest, Allen and Unwin, 2004.

Frame, T.R. *Pacific Partners: A History of Australian-American Naval Relations*, Hodder & Stoughton, Rydalmere, 1992.

Frame, T.R. *Where Fate Calls*, Coronet Books, Rydalmere, 1993.

Frank, R.B, *Downfall: The End of the Imperial Japanese Empire*, New York, Penguin, 1999.

Freund, A.H.P., *Missionary Turns Spy: Pastor A. P. H. Freund's Story of His Service with the New Guinea Coast Watchers in the War Against Japan, 1942 - 1943*, Adelaide, Lutheran Homes Incorporated, 1989.

Frewen, O, *Sailor's Soliloquy*, London, Hutchinson and Company, 1961.

Gatacre, G.G.O. *Report of Proceedings*, Manly, Nautical Press, 1982.

Gilbert, G.P. edited, *Australian Naval Personalities: Lives from the Australian Dictionary of Biography*, RAN Seapower Centre, Canberra, 2006.

Gill, G.H., *Royal Australian Navy 1939-1942*, Collins, Melbourne, 1985.

Gill, G.H., *Royal Australian Navy 1942-1945*, Collins, Melbourne, 1968.

Gordon, A., *The Rules of the Game: Jutland and British Naval Command*, Naval Institute Press, Annapolis, 1996.

Gordon, O.L. *Fight it Out*, Kimber, London, 1961.

Greene, J & Massignani, A, *The Naval war in the Mediterranean 1940-1943*, Chatham Publishing, Rochester, 1998.

Griffin, J., edited, *Papua New Guinea Portraits: The Expatriate Experience*, Australian National University Press, Canberra, 1978.

Halsey, W.F. & Bryan, J, *Admiral Halsey's Story*, Zenger Publishing Company Inc, Washington, 1947.

Hamer, D, *Memories of My Life*, South Wind, Singapore, 2002.

Helfrich, C.E.L., *Memoires, 2 volumes*, Elsevier, Amsterdam, 1950 (In Dutch).

Hemstock, J., *Women of the Royal Australian Navy- Part 1*. Instant Colour Press, Belconnen, 2013.

Hewitt, J.E. *The Black One*, Langate Publishing, South Yarra, 1984.

Hocking,C., *Dictionary Of Disasters At Sea During The Age Of Steam: Including sailing ships and ships of war lost in action, 1824-1962, Volume 1*, London: Lloyd's Register of Shipping, 1969.

Hogan, G., *Parliament House 6 Canberra, 1927: Records Relating to the Design, Construction and Opening of the Provisional Parliament House*, National Archives of Australia, 1997.

Holwitt, J.I, *Execute Against Japan: The US Decision to Conduct Unrestricted Submarine Warfare*, Williams-Ford Texas A&M University, 2013.

Hordern, M.C, *A Merciful Journey: Recollections of a World War II Patrol Boat Man*, The Miegunyah Press, Melbourne, 2005.

Hore, P, *Sydney: Cipher and Search: Solving the Last Great Naval Mystery of the Second World War*, Readlesham, Seafarer Books, 2009.

Howells, J.C., *Ben and Dorothy: A Portrait of My Parents*, Camberwell, Published Privately, 2012.

Hughes, E.A., *The Royal Naval College Dartmouth*, Winchester Publications Ltd, London, 1949.

Hyslop, R., *A Very Civil Servant: An Australian Memoir*, Clarion Editions, Binalong, 1998.

Idriess, IL., *Gold-Dust and Ashes: The Romantic Story of the New Guinea Goldfields*. Angus and Robertson. Sydney, 1933.

Ind, C, *Allied Intelligence Bureau: Our Secret Weapon in the War Against Japan*, New York, Curtis Books, 1958.

Johnston, G.H., *Grey Gladiator*, Angus and Robertson, Sydney, 1941.

Johnston, G.H., *Lioness of the Seas*, Victor Gollancz Ltd, London, 1941.

Jones, T.M., *Watchdogs of the Deep : Life in a submarine during the Great War, 1914-1918*, Pinnacle Press, 1944.

Jones, T.M. & Idriess, I.L. *The Silent Service: Action Stories of the Anzac Navy*, Sydney, Angus and Robertson, 1944.

Jose, A.W. T*he Official History of Australia in the War of 1914-18 Volume IX: The Royal Australian Navy*, University of Queensland Press, St Lucia, 1981.

Lacouture, J, *De Gaulle: The Rebel 1890-1944*, New York, W.W. Norton and Company, 1993.

Lambert, A, *Admirals: The Naval Commanders who Made Britain Great*, Faber & Faber, London, 2008.

Laurie, E.A.H, *Australia in New Guinea*, Current Book Distributors, Sydney 1944.

Leaf, M, *The Story of Ferdinand*, Viking Press, New York, 1936.

Lenton, H.T., *Navies of the Second World War: Royal Netherlands Navy*, London, MacDonald & Company, 1968.

Leutze, J, *A Different Kind of Victory: A Biography of Admiral Thomas C. Hart*, Annapolis, Naval Institute Press, 1981.

Lind, L.J. & Payne, M.A. *H.M.A.S. Hobart: The Story of the 6-inch Cruiser 1938-1962*, Garden Island, The Naval Historical Society of Australia, 1971.

Lind, L.J, *The Midget Submarine Attack on Sydney*, Sydney, Bellrope Press, 1990.

Long, G, *Australia in the War of 1939-45 Series One: Volume 7: The Final Campaigns*, Canberra, Australian War Memorial, 1963.

Lord, W. *Lonely Vigil: Coastwatchers of the Solomons*, Naval Institute Press, Annapolis, 2006.

Loxton, B & Coulthard-Clark, C, *The Shame of Savo: Anatomy of a naval disaster*, St Leonards, Allen and Unwin, 1994.

Lunney, W. & Finch, F, *Forgotton Fleet: A History of the part played by Australian men and ships in the US Army Small Ships Section in New Guinea*, 1942-45, Forfleet Publishing, Medowie, 1995.

MacDonnell, J.E. *Valiant Occasions*, London, Constable and Company Ltd, 1952.

Macintyre, D. *The Battle for the Pacific*, Sydney, Angus and Robertson, 1966.

Mair, L.P. *Australia in New Guinea*, Christophers, Melbourne, 1948.

Mattiske, D, *Fire Across the Pacific*, self-published, Runaway Bay, 2000.

McCarthy, J.K., *Patrol Into Yesterday: My New Guinea Years*, F.W. Cheshire, Melbourne, 1963.

McGuire, F.M. *The Royal Australian Navy: Its Origins, Development and Organization*, Melbourne, Oxford University Press, 1948.

McGuire, P. & McGuire, F.M., *The Price of Admiralty*, Melbourne, Oxford University Press, 1944.

McMurtrie, F.E. *Jane's Fighting Ships 1942*, Sampson Low, London, 1942.

McNicoll, A.W.R., *Sea Voices*, Printed onboard HMAS Canberra, 1932. (copy held at ADFA Library).

Mearns, D.L. *The Search for the Sydney: How Australia's Greatest Maritime Mystery was Solved*, Harper Collins, Sydney, 2009.

Mellor, D, *Australia in the War of 1939-1945, Series 4 - Civil, Volume V – The Role of Science and Industry*, Australian War Memorial, Canberra, 1958.

Menzies, R.G., *Afternoon Light: Some Memories of Men and Events*, Cassell, Melbourne, 1967.

Moore, D.C, *Duntroon: The Royal Military College of Australia 1911-2001*, Canberra, Royal Military College of Australia, 2001.

Morton, P, *Fire Across the Desert: Woomera and the Anglo-Australian Joint Project 1946-1980*, Australian Government Publishing Service, Canberra, 1989.

Nash, N S (2009) *K boat catastrophe: eight ships and five collisions. The full story of the*

'Battle of the Isle of May', Barnsley: Pen & Sword Maritime, 2009.

Nelson, A, *HMAS Harman 1943-2003*, Canberra, RAN, 2003.

Nesdale, I, *Spin Me A Dit: Tales of the Royal Australian Navy*, Gillingham, Adelaide, 1984.

Nesdale, I, *Small Ships at War: They Joined the RAN*, Underdale, Adelaide, 1984.

Newcomb, R.F, *Savo: The Incredible Naval Débâcle off Guadacanal*, Sydney, Ure Smith, 1963.

Nichols, B, *War to War: Australia's Navy 1919-1939*, Draft held by Sea Power Centre Australia, 2010.

Nicholls, S, *HMAS Shropshire*, Naval Historical Society of Australia, Sydney, 1989.

Olsen, W, *Bitter Victory: The Death of HMAS Sydney*, Nedlands, University of Western Australia Press, 2000.

Parry, A.F. *HMAS Yarra 1936-1942*, Sydney, Naval Historical Society of Australia, 2000.

Pask, E.H. *Enter the Colonies, Dancing: A History of Dance in Australia, 1835-1940*, Melbourne, Oxford University Press, 1979.

Payne, M.A, *HMAS Australia 1928-1955*, Sydney, Naval Historical Society of Australia, 2000.

Payne, M.A, *HMAS Canberra*, Sydney, Naval Historical Society of Australia, 1973.

Payne, M.A and Lind, I.J., *HMAS Hobart*, Sydney, Naval Historical Society of Australia, 1979.

Pfennigwerth, I, *Missing Pieces: The Intelligence Jigsaw and RAN Operations from 1939-71*, Papers in Australian Maritime Affairs Number 25, Canberra, Sea Power Centre – Australia, 2008.

Phillips, S, *Secret Mission to Melbourne, November, 1941*, Manhattan, Kansas, Sunflower University Press, 1992.

Plowman, P. *Across the Sea to War: Australian and New Zealand troop convoys from 1865 through Two World Wars to Korea and Vietnam*, Dural, Rosenberg Publishing. 2003.

Reckner, J.R. T*eddy Roosevelt's Great White Fleet*, Annapolis, Naval Institute Press, 2001.

Reid, R, *Australia under Attack: Sydney and the Midget Submarines 1942*, Canberra, Department of Veteran Affairs, 2007.

Rhoades, F.A. *Diary of a Coastwatcher in the Solomons*, The Nimitz Foundation, Fredericksburg, 1982.

Roberts, R.G. *Age Shall Not Weary Them: The Story of HMAS Perth*, Patersons Printing Press, Perth, 1942.

Rose, S (edited)., *The Naval Miscellany, Volume 7*, The Naval Records Society, Aldershot, 2008.

Roskill, S.W., *Churchill and the Admirals*, London, Collins, 1977.

Roskill, S.W., *The Navy at War 1939-1945*, Ware, Wordsworth Editions Limited, 1998.

Ross, W.H. *Lucky Ross: The Autobiography of an RAN Officer 1934-1951*, Carlisle, Hesperian Press, 1994.

Sadkovich, J.L. *The Italian Navy in World War II*, Westport, Greenwood Press, 1994.

Sautot, H, *Grandeur et Decadence du Gaullisme le Pacifique*, Melbourne, F.W. Cheshire, 1949.

Scott, G, *HMAS Sydney*, Sydney, Horwitz Publications Inc, 1962.

Silver, L.R. *The Heroes of Rimau: Unravelling the mystery of one of Wolrd War II's most daring raids*, Birchgrove, Sally Milner Publishing, 1990.

Simpson, C, *Plumes and Arrows: Inside New Guinea*, Sydney, Angus and Robertson, 1962.

Simpson, M, edited, *The Cunningham Papers, (Admiral of the Fleet Viscount Cunningham of Hyndhope, OM, KT, GCB, DSO**), Volume I - The Mediterranean Fleet 1939-1942*, Ashgate for The Navy Records Society, Aldershot, 1999.

Simpson, M, edited, *The Cunningham Papers, (Admiral of the Fleet Viscount Cunningham of Hyndhope, OM, KT, GCB, DSO**, Volume II - The Triumph of Allied Seapower 1942-1946*, Ashgate for The Navy Records Society, Aldershot, 1999.

Smith, N.C. *Men of the Ballarat : the sinking of the Australian Imperial Force Troopship Ballarat*, Brighton, Mostly Unsung Military History Research and Publications, 2006.

Smith, P.C, *British Battle Cruisers*, New Malden, Almark Publications, 1972.

Spurling, K.L. *Cruel Conflict: The triumph and tragedy of HMAS Perth*, Sydney, New Holland Press, 2008.

Stevens, D.M. and Reeve, J. edited, *Southern Trident: Strategy, History and the Rise of Australian Naval Power*, Crows Nest, Allen and Unwin, 2000.

Stevens, D.M., *The Australian Centenary History of Defence Volume III: The Royal Australian Navy*, Melbourne, Oxford University Press, 2001.

Stevens, D.M., *A Critical Vulnerability: The impact of the submarine threat on Australia's maritime defence 1915-1954*, Canberra, RAN Seapower Centre, 2005.

Stevens, D.M. edited, *The Royal Australian Navy in World War II*, Crows Nest, Allen and Unwin, 2005, (Second Edition).

Stevens, D.M. *In All Respects Ready: Australia's Navy in World War One*, South Melbourne, Oxford University Press, 2014.

Stille, M, *Italian Battleships of World War II*, Osprey Publishing, Colchester, 2011.

Strachan, H. edited, *Military Lives*, Oxford University Press, Oxford, 2002.

Swindon, G, *HMAS Adelaide 1922-1946 A Short History of the Cruiser*, Garden Island, The Naval Historical Society of Australia, 1996.

Townsend, M.L., *District Officer*, Pacific Publications, Sydney, 1968.

Tsuji, M, *Singapore The Japanese Version*, Sydney, Ure Smith, 1960.

Twining, M.B., *No Bended Knee: The Battle for Guadalcanal*, Novato, Presidio Press, 1996.

Veale, L, *The Wewak Mission: Coastwatchers at War in New Guinea*, Ashmore, Thai Watana Panich Press, 1996.

Walhert, G, edited *Australian Army Amphibious Operations in the South-West Pacific:1942-45*, Sydney, Southwood Press, 1994.

Washington, J, *William (Bill) Menzies: Able Seaman HMAS Sydney II*, Nelson Bay, Menzies Family, 2010.
Werner, W, *Rifle Brigade Chronicle for 1919*, London, John Bale & Sons, 1920.
Weyler, K & Ehtlich, H.J. *The Black Raider*, London, Elek Books, 1955.
Wheeler, G. E., *Kinkaid of the Seventh Fleet*, Annapolis, Naval Institute Press, 1996.
White, M.W.D., *Australian Submarines: A History*, Canberra, AGPS, 1992.
White, M., *We Were Cadet Midshipmen: RANC Entrants 50 Years On*, Queanbeyan, Grinkle Press, 2006.
Whiting, B, *Ship of Courage: The Epic Story of HMAS Perth and Her Crew*, St Leonards, Allen and Unwin, 1994.
Wildenberg, T. *All The Factors of Victory: Admiral Joseph Mason Reeves and the origins of Carrier Seapower*, Potomac Books Inc, Washington, 2003.
Winter, B., *The Intrigue Master: Commander Long and Naval Intelligence in Australia, 1913-1945*, Brisbane, Boolarong Press, 1995.

CORRESPONDENCE

Cablegram from Secretary of State for Dominion Affairs cablegram to Prime Minister of Commonwealth of Australia 29 August 1942, contained in Loss of HMAS *Canberra* - and allocation of HMS *Shropshire* - 17/8/42 - 23/12/46, A5954, 424581, (NAA).
Letter from Captain Morgan to Naval Secretary, 13 December 1915, (NAA).
Letter from Mr F. Parsons to Captain Morgan, 31 January 1916, (NAA).
Letter from Captain Morgan to Mr F. Parsons, 3 February 1916, (NAA).
Letter from Captain Morgan to the Naval Secretary No. 16/106, 20 February 1916, (NAA).
Letter from Second Naval Member to Naval Secretary, 22 February 1916, (NAA).
Letter from Captain Morgan to the Naval Secretary, 18 March 1916, (NAA).
Letter from H. Lambert, Secretary of State, Colonial Office to the Secretary to the Admiralty, 10 June 1916, (NAA).
Letter from the Governor General (No. 369) to Secretary of State for the Colonies, 20 September 1916, (NAA).
Letter from Lord Stamfordam to G.A. Steel Private Secretary to the First Lord of the Admiralty, 12 December 1916, (SPC-A).
Letter from Midshipman Frank Larkins to Ben Howells, 8 January 1917, (Held by Mr J.C. Howells).
Letter from Midshipman Norman Calder to his mother Mrs Mary Calder, 25 September 1917, (AWM).
Letter from Midshipman Edwin Nurse to Ben Howells, 5 October 1917, (Held by Mr J.C. Howells).

Letter from Lieutenant Commander C. De Burgh, RN Commanding Officer HM Submarine *K.22* to Commander E.W. Leir, DSO, RN Commanding Officer HMS *Ithuriel*, 1 February 1918. (SPC-A).

Letter from Commander T.C.B. Harbottle, RN Commanding Officer HM Submarine *K.14* to Commander E.W. Leir, DSO, RN Commanding Officer HMS *Ithuriel*, 2 February 1918. (SPC-A).

Letter from Commander E.W. Leir, DSO, RN Commanding Officer HMS *Ithuriel* to Vice Admiral Commanding Battle Cruiser Force, 2 February 1918. (SPC-A).

Letter from Captain O. Backhouse, RN, Commanding Officer HMAS *Australia* to Rear Admiral Commanding 2nd Battle Cruiser Squadron, 28 February 1918, (SPC-A).

HMAS Suva letter to Naval Secretary, 4 August 1919, Special Report on Sub-Lieutenant Peyton J. Kimlin, RAN (NAA).

Naval Secretary letter to Commodore Commanding HM Australian Fleet, 9 August 1919 (NAA).

Commanding Officer, HMAS *Brisbane* letter to Commodore Commanding HM Fleet, D578, 13 June 1921, (NAA).

Commodore Commanding HM Australian Fleet letter to the Naval Secretary 839/AF 255, 17 June 1921, (NAA).

Letter, Admiralty to the Australian Commonwealth Naval Board, M.02799/31, 19 April 1932, MP 1049/9, (NAA).

Letter from Commander R.M.B. Long to Lieutenant Commander E.A. Feldt, 13 January 1940, Series B34476, (NAA).

Letter from Director Naval Intelligence to Staff Officer (Intelligence) Port Moresby, 30 July 1940, (NAA).

Letter from Lieutenant Commander E.A. Feldt to Commander R.M.B. Long, 2 August 1940, Series B34476, (NAA).

Letter from Lieutenant Commander E.A. Feldt to Commander R.M.B. Long, 6 August 1940, Series B34476, (NAA).

Letter M. H. Sautot to Commanding Officer HMAS *Adelaide*, 4 October 1940, (NAA).

Letter from the Naval Board to Flag Officer Commanding His Majesty's Australian Squadron, 2026/7/185, dated 20 October 1940, MP 1049/5 Barcode 408800, (NAA).

Letter from E.W. Dingle to Captain H.B. Farncomb, 27 November 1940, (Farncomb Papers–SPC-A).

Letter from Lieutenant Commander E.A. Feldt to Commander R.M.B. Long to, 1 March 1941, Series B34476, (NAA).

Letter from Lieutenant Commander E.A. Feldt to Commander R.M.B. Long to, 16 June 1941, Series B34476, (NAA).

Letter from Commander E.A. Feldt to Commander R.M.B. Long, 19 June 1941, Series B34476, (NAA).

Letter from LAC K. Homard to his parents, 7 October 1941 (SPC-A).

Letter from Commander E.A. Feldt to Commander R.M.B. Long, 4 February 1942, Series

B34476, (NAA).

Letter from Lieutenant Commander Paul Hirst to his wife, 7 February 1942, (Hirst Family).

Letter from Commanding Officer HMAS *Australia* to Rear Admiral Commanding HM Australian Squadron, 7 April 1942 contained in Series Number B6121, Barcode 399541, (NAA).

Letter from Commanding Officer HMAS *Australia* to Rear Admiral Commanding HM Australian Squadron, 20 April 1942 contained in Series Number B6121, Barcode 399541, (NAA).

Letter from Paymaster Lieutenant T. Rapke, RANVR to CO HMAS *Australia* dated 20 April 1942, Series Number B6121, Barcode 399541, (NAA).

Letter from Rear Admiral in Charge HMA Establishments Sydney to First Naval Member, 22 June 1942, Series Number SP338/1, Barcode 318205, (NAA).

Letter from D.H. Merry to J. Kimlin, 16 July 1942 contained in J. Kimlin: Detection of Enemy Movements by Means of a Listening Post, MP 76/1, 2406, Barcode 4335596, (NAA).

Letter from Secretary of Navy to NOIC Brisbane, 559/222/1102, 30 July 1942, contained in 11206558, (NAA).

Letter from Commander E.A. Feldt to Commander R.M.B. Long, 23 August 1942, Series B34476, (NAA).

Letter from Commander R.M.B. Long to Commander E.A. Feldt, 10 September 1942, Series B34476, (NAA).

Letter from Commander E.A. Feldt to Commander R.M.B. Long, 12 September 1942, Series B34476, (NAA).

Telegram from Private Secretary to the King to the Governor General of Australia 12 September 1942, contained in Loss of HMAS *Canberra* - and allocation of HMS *Shropshire* - 17/8/42 - 23/12/46, A5954, 424581, (NAA).

Letter from Captain H.B. Farncomb to Commander R.M.B. Long, 25 September 1945, (SPC-A).

Letter from Commander E.A. Feldt to Commander R.M.B. Long, 4 October 1942, Series B34476, (NAA).

Letter from Lieutenant Commander H.A. MacKenzie to Commander R.M.B. Long & Commander E.A. Feldt, 6 October 1942, Series B34476, (NAA).

Letter from Commander R.M.B. Long to Commander E.A. Feldt, 12 October 1942, Series B34476, (NAA).

Letter from Lieutenant Commander H.A. MacKenzie to Commander R.M.B. Long, 24 October 1942, Series B34476, (NAA).

Letter from Commander E. A. Feldt to Commander R.M.B. Long, 26 October 1942, Series B34476, (NAA).

Letter from Commanding Officer HMAS *Australia* to Commander Task Force 44, 1942, Barcode 399876 (NAA).

Letter from Commander E. A. Feldt to Commander R.M.B. Long, 12 March 1943, Series

B34476, (NAA).

Letter from Commander R.M.B. Long to Commander E.A. Feldt, 20 April 1943, Series B34476, (NAA).

Letter from Commander E.A. Feldt to Commander R.M.B. Long, 25 April 1943, Series B34476, (NAA).

Letter from Commander E.A. Feldt to Mr G. Gill, 29 August 1944, Series B34476, (NAA).

Letter from Admiral B.M. Chambers to F.B. Eldridge, 9 November 1944, Eldridge Papers, (HMAS Creswell).

Letter from Captain J.M. Armstrong to Mrs E.J. Armstrong, November 1944, J.M. Armstrong Papers (NLA).

Speed Letter from Commodore Commanding HMA Squadron to Australian Commonwealth Naval Board, 12 January 1945, (SPC-A).

Speed Letter from Commodore Commanding HMA Squadron to Australian Commonwealth Naval Board, 24 January 1945, (SPC-A).

Speed Letter from Commodore Commanding HMA Squadron to Australian Commonwealth Naval Board, 27 January 1945, (SPC-A).

Letter from Commodore Commanding HMA Squadron to Commander 7th Fleet, 7 February 1945, (SPC-A).

Letter from Secretary of Naval Board to Secretary of the Admiralty, 448/201/2003, February 1945, (SPC-A).

Letter from Commander Battleship Division Two to Commander Seventh Fleet, Commodore H.B. Farncomb, RAN - Report on Fitness, 27 January 1945, contained in H.B. Farncomb confidential report file (NAA).

Speed Letter from Commodore Commanding HMA Squadron to Australian Commonwealth Naval Board, 7 March 1945, (SPC-A).

Letter from Mr G. Gill to Commander R.M.B. Long, 20 April 1945, Series B34476, (NAA).

Letter from Commander R.M.B. Long to Commander E.A. Feldt, 26 April 1945, Series B34476, (NAA).

Speed Letter from Commodore Commanding HMA Squadron to Australian Commonwealth Naval Board, 16 May 1945, (SPC-A).

Letter from Commander R.M.B. Long to Commander E.A. Feldt, 23 May 1945, Series B34476, (NAA).

Letter from Captain James Esdaile to his wife, 13 May 1945, (Esdaile Family).

Speed Letter from Commodore Commanding HMA Squadron to Australian Commonwealth Naval Board, 14 June 1945, (SPC-A).

Speed Letter from Commodore Commanding HMA Squadron to Australian Commonwealth Naval Board, 24 June 1945, (SPC-A).

Report Commanding Officer HMAS *Manoora* to Commander Task Unit 78.2.2, 1 July 1945, Operation OBOE Two Operations, Report of Wave Leader, Wave 7, contained in HMAS *Manoora* Report of Proceedings (AWM).

Speed Letter from Commodore Commanding HMA Squadron to Australian Commonwealth Naval Board, 11 July 1945, (SPC-A).

Letter from Commander E.A. Feldt to Mr G. Gill, 13 September 1945, Series B34476, (NAA).

Letter from Commander E.A. Feldt to Mr G. Gill, 29 September 1945, Series B34476, (NAA).

Letter from Surgeon Lieutenant H.G. Rischbieth, RANR, 31 August 1945, Rischbieth Papers, PR 00795, (AWM).

Letter from Surgeon Lieutenant H.G. Rischbieth, RANR, 1 September 1945, Rischbieth Papers, PR 00795, (AWM).

Letter from Commander R.M.B. Long dated 18 October 1945 (held by author).

Letter of Proceedings 6 December -23 December 1945 from Commodore J.A. Collins to Commander-in-Chief British Pacific Fleet, 24 December 1945, contained in HMAS *Hobart* Reports of Proceedings for 1945, (AWM).

Letter from Commanding Officer HMAS *Penguin*, RAN Officers - Deferred Pay and Child Allowance to Secretary Naval Board, circa 1946, 186/1/11, contained in Captain H.L. Howden Papers, PR 86/145, (AWM).

Letter from Chief of Naval Staff (Collins) to First Sea Lord (Fraser), 7 September 1948, (TNA UK).

Letter from Chief of Naval Staff (Collins) to First Sea Lord (Fraser), 22 June 1951, (TNA UK).

Letters from R.M.B. Long to G.H. Gill, 1951-1959, AWM 69, (AWM).

Letters from R.M.B. Long to F.E. de Groot, 1951-1959, (Long-Cliff Family).

Letter from Vice Admiral J.A. Collins to Captain E.S. Nurse, 10 February 1955, (Jones/Grazebrook Papers).

Letter from K.J. Cumisky to G.H. Gill, 10 July 1958, AWM 69 (AWM).

Letter from Vice Admiral J.A. Collins to G.H.Gill, 16 July 1958, AWM 69 (AWM).

Letter from R.M.B. Long to Irwin Hunter Esq, 4 September 1959, (Jones/Grazebrook Papers).

Letter from W.H. Brookbank to H.W.G. Nobbs, 16 July 1960, (R.M.B. Long Papers- AWM).

Letter from Colonel G.G. Roberts to A.W.G. Nobbs, 22 July 1960, (R.M.B. Long Papers - AWM).

Letter from E.A. Feldt to Mr Manning, 31 February 1962, Coastwatchers, Series B34476, (NAA).

Letter from Prime Minister R.G. Menzies to Vice Admiral J.A.Collins, 4 September 1965 (Collins Papers).

Letter from E.S. Nurse to Mr Lowy, 19 May 1969, (Museum of Melbourne).

Letter from Mr Jim Nicholson to A.W. Grazebrook, 12 October 1992, (Jones/Grazebrook Papers).

Letter from Mrs Jean Farncomb to A.W. Grazebrook, 25 October 1987, (Jones/Grazebrook Papers).

Letter from Commander A.G. Leatham, RN to A.W. Grazebrook, 20 November 1987, (Jones/Grazebrook Papers).

Letter from Lady Collins to A.W. Grazebrook, 20 November 1987, (Jones/Grazebrook Papers).

Letter from Rear Admiral H.A. Showers to A.W. Grazebrook, 19 December 1987, (A.W. Grazebrook).

Letter from Vice Admiral Sir Richard Peek to A.W. Grazebrook, 22 January 1988, (Jones/Grazebrook Papers).

Letter from Commander A.G. Leatham, RN to A.W. Grazebrook, 26 January 1988, (Jones/Grazebrook Papers).

Letter from Commander C.R. Reid to A.W. Grazebrook, 6 January 1989, (Jones/Grazebrook Papers).

Letter from Commander W.S. Bracegirdle to A.W. Grazebrook, 14 February 1989, (Jones/Grazebrook Papers).

Letters from Rear Admiral W.D.H. Graham to A.W. Grazebrook, 12 October 1987 & 21 March 1989, (Grazebrook Papers).

Letter from Mr Alan Zammit to A.W. Grazebrook, 18 May 1989, (Jones/Grazebrook Papers).

Letter from Lieutenant Commander G.L. Fowle to A.W. Grazebrook, 9 February 1992. (Jones/Grazebrook Papers).

Letter from Mr T.J. Roberts to A.W. Grazebrook, 17 July 1992, (Jones/Grazebrook Papers).

Letter from Mr P. Reilly to A.W. Grazebrook, 22 July 1992, (Jones/Grazebrook Papers).

Letter from Mr F.W.S. Grant to A.W. Grazebrook, 7 December 1992, (Jones/Grazebrook Papers).

Letter from Vice Admiral R.I. Peek to A.W. Grazebrook, 4 April 1992, (Jones/Grazebrook Papers).

Letter from Commander A.S. Storey to A.W. Grazebrook, 9 June 1992, (Jones/Grazebrook Papers).

Letter from Commander A.S. Storey to A.W. Grazebrook, 10 September 1992, (Jones/Grazebrook Papers).

Letter from Lieutenant Commander G.L. Fowle to A.W. Grazebrook, 2 November 1992. (Jones/Grazebrook Papers).

Letter from Lieutenant Commander G.L. Fowle to A.W. Grazebrook, 9 November 1992 (Jones/Grazebrook Papers).

Letter from Lieutenant F.S. Sharp RANVR to A.W. Grazebrook, 16 December 1992 (Jones/Grazebrook Papers).

Letter from Mrs J.E. Chapman to A.W. Grazebrook, 1993, (Jones/Grazebrook Papers).

Letter from Lieutenant F.S. Sharp RANVR to A.W. Grazebrook, 18 January 1993

(Jones/Grazebrook Papers).

Letter from Mr J.S. Armitage to A.W. Grazebrook, 8 March 1993, (Jones/Grazebrook Papers).

Letter from Commander L.R. Brooks to A.W. Grazebrook, 24 September 1993, (Jones/Grazebrook Papers).

Letter from Lieutenant Commander H.A.L. Hall to P.D. Jones, 12 April 2012, (Jones/Grazebrook Papers).

Letter and map from Mr A.J. 'Sandy' Pearson to P.D. Jones, 26 May 2012, (Jones/Grazebrook Papers).

Letter from Mrs P. Tait to P.D. Jones, 9 August 2015, (Jones/Grazebrook Papers).

Email from Professor T. R. Frame to P.D. Jones 10 May 2015.

Documents, Reports and Signals

Actions with the Enemy (3), including Battle of Calabria, ADM 1/20008, (TNA UK).

Arrangements for Repair of HMAS *Australia* and loan of HMS Sussex, ADM 1/18667, (TNA UK).

Australia - Royal Australian Navy - Personality Sketches, Naval Attaché, 12 July 1945, Serial 45-R-45, Monograph Index Guide Number 901, (US National Archives).

Australian Commonwealth Naval Board cable to Admiralty, 8 December 1941, Raider No.41 Interim Report of Interrogation of Survivors, included in War Diary (Naval), Admiralty 1941 (RN NHB).

Australian High Commission, New Zealand - Despatches, 1956-1962 , A4231, 1171189, 1171188, 1171194, 1171195, 1171196 & 742236 (NAA).

Australian Shipbuilding Industry, August-December 1950, A4639, 5104162, (NAA).

Australian Shipbuilding, March 1950, A4639, 5104159, (NAA).

Awards of US Decorations to RAN and AMF officers - Feldt and 4 others; A816, 171615, (NAA).

Battle Cruiser Force War Records, ADM 137/2131 to ADM 137/2134, (TNA UK).

Battle of the Java Sea, 27th February 1942, Supplement to *The London Gazette,* 7 July 1948, Number 38346, pp.3937-3947.

BR 1736(1) Battle Summaries No.2, Action off Cape Spada, Admiralty, London, 1957, (SPC-A).

BR 1736(14) Battle Summary No.21. Naval Operations in the Campaign for Guadacanal - August 1942, Admiralty, London, 1949. (SPC-A).

BR 1736(28) Battle Summary No.34. Naval Strategy in the Pacific - February 1943 - August 1945, Admiralty, London, 1946. (SPC-A).

BR 1736 (36) Battle Summary. Invasion of the South of France - Operation Dragoon, Admiralty, London, 1949. ADM 186/796, (TNA UK).

BR 1736(38) Battle Summaries Numbers 1,6,7 & 19 No.21. Selected Bombardment (Mediterranean) 1940-1941, Admiralty, London, 1954, (SPC-A).

BR 1736(14/49) Battle Summary No.21. Naval Operations in the Campaign for Guadalcanal August 1942-February 1943. Admiralty, London, 1949, (SPC-A).

Calder, N.K., HMAS *Bungaree* - Minelayer, draft undated, (Calder Family).

Captain, Naval Representative Australia House, letter 1147/2, NR 9580, 7 July 1920, (NAA).

Captain, Naval Representative Australia House, letter 1147/4, NR10567, 17 February 1921, (NAA).

China Force War Diary submitted by Commodore J.A. Collins RAN, ADM 1/12190, (TNA UK).

Captain Hillgarth's Report on visit to Australia, May-September 1944, PREM 3/159/10 (TNA UK).

Captain Getting - Recommendation for Post-Humous Award, A5954, 678237, (NAA).

CB 04027 -The Fighting Instructions, 1939 - Article 4.82. (ADM 239/261).

CB 3081(5), Battle Summary Number 13: Actions with Enemy Disguised Raiders 1940-1941, Admiralty, London, 1942.

Coastwatchers, Series B34476, (NAA).

Coles, T.R.H. The Loss of HMAS *Sydney II*, Volumes 1-3, Canberra, 2009.

Collisions Involving HM Ships *Inflexible* and *Fearless* and HM Submarines *K14*, *K22*, *K17* and *K6*, ADM 156/86, (TNA UK).

Coolamon School Administration File 1923-1939, 5/15496.1 (NSW SA).

Commander-in-Chief Mediterranean War Diaries 1944, ADM 199/1430-1433, (TNA UK).

Commanding Officer HMAS *Australia* to Commodore Commanding His Majesty's Australian Squadron, Action Report - Operation Mike 1, 22 January 1945, (SPC-A).

Commanding Officer HMAS *Shropshire* to Commander Task Group 77.2, HMAS Shropshire Action Report 1-18 January 1945, 24 January 1945, (SPC-A).

Commander Task Group 74.1 to Commander 7th Fleet, Report of Proceedings: 1-31 January 1945, 5 February 1945, (SPC-A).

Commander Task Group 74.1 to Commander 7th Fleet, Report of Proceedings: February 1945, 4 March 1945, (SPC-A).

Copyright Lodgement document for Carnival, 9 January 1928 Series Number A1336, Control Symbol 16996 (NAA).

Copyright Lodgement document for A Foxtrot, 27 May 1931, Series Number A1336, Item 21188, Control Symbol 3498756 (NAA).

Death Certificate of Hugh Alexander MacKenzie, 1948/027275, (State Archives of NSW).

Decorations: United States Awards to Australian Nationals: Newman, Commander J.B, A1067, 192296, (NAA).

Demobilisation of the RAN, Paper by Mr Phillips, AWM 69, Series 23/44, (AWM).

Deposition by Lieutenant C. Cotton-Stapleton RNR, 20 February 1916 (NAA).

Description of Papua, New Guinea and Solomon Islands, undated, p.2, (NAA).
Development of RAN Intelligence Organisation in Wartime, 8 January 1944, Director of Naval Intelligence, (NAA).
Directorate of Naval operational Analysis Studies - Report No. 67/45 Analysis of the Flying Effort of British assault carriers in Operation DRAGOON, ADM/219/269 (TNA UK)
E.A. Feldt - Pensioner - Former New Guinea Officer, A452, 3554676, (NAA).
Exchange and Loan of RAN and RN Officers, ADM 116/213, (TNA UK).
Extension of Naval shipbuilding facilities in Australia, 1948, A5799, 524297, (NAA).
First Sea Lord Record and Correspondence, 1948, ADM 205/69, (TNA UK).
Flag Officer Commanding Second Battle Squadron letter dated 9 February 1918, Findings of Court of Inquiry, ADM 156/86 (TNA UK).
Foreign Vessels - Damage and Loss of Italian Cruiser *Bartolomeo Colleoni*, ADM 1/11178, (TNA UK).
FRUMEL Records of communications intelligence to the Coral Sea Battle, Series B5555, Barcode 856345, (NAA).
FRUMEL Records of communications intelligence to the Midway Battle, Series B5555, Barcode 856346, (NAA).
FRUMEL World War II Diplomatic Intercept (German/Japan), Series A10909, Barcode 3256744, (NAA).
Government policy on shipping and shipbuilding - Decision 215, October 1951, A4905, 4687952, (NAA).
Grand Fleet Report of Proceedings 1917, ADM 137/875 and ADM 137/876, (TNA UK).
HMAS *Canberra*: 8 August 1942: Sunk by Enemy Action, ADM 358/3126, (TNA UK).
HMAS *Hobart* Torpedoing of off Espiritu Santo, A5954, 518/27, (NAA).
HMAS *Hobart* War Diary 1-31 January 1942, 2 Feb 1942, (AWM).
HMAS *Perth* War Diary, 1932/2/200, 1 October 1945 (SPC-A).
HMAS *Shropshire*: Visit to UK, ADM 1/19568, (TNA UK).
HMAS *Sydney*, ADM 267/77, (TNA UK).
HMAS *Sydney* Sinking - German Newspaper Report, ADM 1/19442, (TNA UK).
HMS *Attacker* Ship's Logs 1944, ADM 53/118929 to ADM 53/118934, (TNA UK).
HM Submarine *K 17* Ships Log for November 1917, ADM 173/6677, (TNA UK).
HMS *Vega* Ship's Logs February-June 1918, ADM 53/66963 and ADM 53/66964, (TNA UK).
Inquest File for H.A. MacKenzie, 19/3793,1377/1948, 15 October 1948 (NSW SA).
Japanese Midget Submarine Attack on Sydney Harbour, May 31st June 1st 1942, Series Number SP338/1, Barcode 318205, (NAA).
Kimlin, P.J, Sheet Music, *Beast's Christmas*, Allegro for Strings, Bib 190989, (NLA).
Kimlin, P.J. Invention for Listening Device, Number 4335596,16 July 1942, (NAA).

Lessons learned from loss of HMAS *Canberra*, MP 1049/5, Barcode 399876, (NAA).

Loss of HMAS Voyager after collision with HMAS *Melbourne* - 10th February 1964: Report of Royal Commission, A5954, 1916/1 (NAA).

Loss of H.M. Ships *Prince of Wales* and *Repulse*, Supplement to *The London Gazette*, 20 February 1948, Number 38214, pp.1237-1244.

Medical Report on a Case for Survey -Sub Lieutenant H.A. MacKenzie, 17 December 1919, contained in MacKenzie Report, Series B3476, Barcode 410670, (NAA).

Memorandum from Secretary Department of External Affairs to Secretary Department of the Navy, 23 October 1940, MP 1049/5 Barcode 408800, (NAA).

Memorandum from Superintendent Range to Controller Weapons Research Establishment, 29 August 1956, File 5411/8/1 Part 1 (NAA).

Midget submarine attack on Sydney Harbour, MP1049/5, 2026/21/79, Barcode 413209, (NAA).

Minutes of a Court of Inquiry held at Navy Office, Melbourne, 22 February 1916, to investigate certain circumstances at Royal Australian Naval College, Jervis Bay, N.S.W. (NAA).

Minutes of Proceedings at a Court Martial onboard HMAS Platypus in Hobart on 12 February 1926 for the trial of Lieutenant G.W.T. Armitage, AF 165/401/4, (NAA).

Minutes of Proceedings at a Court Martial onboard HMAS *Canberra* at Jervis Bay on 25 November 1929 for the trial of Lieutenant Commander Lloyd Falconer Gilling, RAN of HMAS *Canberra*, Files A471, Item 22468, (NAA).

Minutes of Proceedings at a Court Martial onboard HMAS *Canberra* at Jervis Bay on 25 November 1929 for the trial of Captain George Lawrence Massey, RN of HMAS *Canberra*, Item 441631, (NAA).

Minute, Anti-Submarine Equipment, 2026/5/162 dated 18 January 1938, (NAA).

Minute, Trawler A/S Outfit - Allocation and Stowage, MP/1049/5/0 dated 21 January 1938, (NAA).

Minute from ACNS to CNS, A Plea for Smaller Sloops in Lager Numbers, February 1938, (SPC-A).

Minute from Commander Esdaile to CNS, June 1938, MP 1049/5, 2026/2/152, (NAA).

Minute from DNI (Collins) to CNS, Proposal for the Creation of a Naval Intelligence Centre at Port Moresby, 5 May 1939, Series B34476, (NAA).

Minute from Staff Officer (Intelligence) Port Moresby to DNI, 17 August 1940, Series B34476, (NAA).

Advisory War Council Minutes (Original Set) Volume 1. Meetings 29 Oct 1940 to 14 Feb 1941. Minute Nos 1 to 149B, A5954, 310381, (NAA).

Minutes of the Naval Board, 8 July 1942, Series A2585, (NAA).

Minute from Executive Officer HMAS *Canberra* to Rear Admiral Commanding Task Force 44, 12 August 1942, Barcode 399876 (NAA).

Minute from Commanding Officer HMAS *Hobart* to Commander Task Force 62.6, 15

August 1942, Barcode 399876 (NAA).

Minute from Commander Task Group 44 to Secretary of Naval Board, 8 November 1942, Barcode 399876 (NAA).

Minute from Captain J.A. Collins to Chief of Naval Staff, Remarks on the Loss of HMAS *Canberra*, 10 November 1942, Barcode 399876 (NAA).

Minute from Lieutenant Commander E. Feldt to the Controller AIB, Activities of Section C AIB while under the command of Lieutenant Commander Feldt, 1943, Series B34476, (NAA).

Minute from Captain J.K. McCarthy to Commander E.A. Feldt, A/Sergeant W.A.H. Butteris, 3 March 1943 contained in Reports from Coastwatchers in New Guinea, New Britain, New Ireland Areas, B3476, Barcode 411499, (NAA).

Minutes of the Board of Enquiry into the Circumstances Attending The Damage to HMAS *Hobart* by Enemy Torpedo Attack on 20th July 1943, (NAA).

Minute from Director Naval Intelligence to Chief of Naval Staff, HMAS *Hobart* – leak of information 22 July 1943 in Hobart damage report, A5954, 518/27, (NAA).

Minute from Commodore Commanding HMA Squadron to Secretary of Naval Board, Honours and Awards, 22 January 1945, (SPC-A).

Minute from Commander-in-Chief Portsmouth to the Admiralty, 15 May 1946, ADM 1/9568, (TNA UK).

Minute from Director Training and Staff Requirements to Chief of Naval Staff, Anti-Submarine Warfare - Review of Present Position, 4 October 1948 (SPC-A).

Minute from Chief of Naval Staff to Deputy Chief of Naval Staff A/S Warfare, 1 November 1948, (SPC-A).

Minute from Fourth Naval Member to Chief of Naval Staff, Balanced RAN, 5 April 1949, (SPC-A).

Murder of Stoker John Joseph RILEY o/n 23239 onboard HMAS *Australia*. Court martial proceedings regarding Edward Joseph ELIAS o/n 20975 and Albert Ronald GORDON o/n 20871, Series Number B6121, Barcode 399541, (NAA).

Naval Board Minutes, 1950-1953, Series A2585, Barcode 4269885, (NAA).

Naval Operations in the Mediterranean, ADM 199/445, (TNA UK).

Naval Ordnance Inspection and Design Branch: Branch History 1911-1949, Directorate of Naval Ordnance Inspection, 1 August 1985.

Naval Staff Meeting - Summary of Discussion dated 19 October 1932, (SPC-A).

New Guinea Gazette (1923-1938), Harry William Hamilton, Government Printer, Rabaul, (NLA).

New South Wales Police Gazette, Harry Bertram Vallentine, 3 July 1929, p. 484, (Archives NSW).

Notes on Defence Committee Agendum 104/41 Special Intelligence Organisation, 18 November 1941, (NAA).

Operation Dragoon Reports, ADM 199/911-912, (TNA UK).

Operations Matador and Sandwich, WO 106/2506, August-November 1941, (TNA UK).

Prime Ministerial Statement No. 78, 20 November 1941, A5954 2400/21, (NAA).

RAN and RN Officers - Interchangeability, ADM 116/2389, (TNA UK).

RAN Personnel - Midshipman R.B.M. Long, W.L. Reilly & J.Burnett, 8724669, (AWM).

Rear Admiral Farncomb - Civil Honour, A463, 1847470, (NAA).

Rear Admiral in Charge HMA Naval establishments, Sydney Report, Midget submarine attack on Sydney Harbour May31st-June 1st, 1942, 16 July 1942, contained in MP1049/5, 2026/21/79, Barcode 413209, (NAA).

Report on the Royal Australian Naval College for 1916, 25 July 1917, (NAA).

Report of the Court of Enquiry into the Circumstances, attending the loss of HMS *Vanguard* on 9 July 1917. Held onboard HMS *Emperor of India*, 30 July 1917. ADM 137/3681, (TNA UK).

Report Midshipman R.A.N, Rear Admiral Commanding H.M. Australian Fleet by Captain M.L. Mawbey, RN (Commanding Officer HMS *Agincourt*), 14 September 1918 (NAA).

Report into the Loss of K Class Submarines, No. 453/HF. 1100, 19 February 1918. (SPC-A).

Report on Seaward Defence of Australian Ports, Australia's Submission No. 290/196/1 dated 7 February 1933, (SPC-A).

Report on Establishment of a Cryptographic Organization in Australia, MP 1185/8 Item 1937/2/415 (NAA).

Report on The Naval Action of the 19th Instant, Vice Admiral F. Casardi, 23 July 1940, NID 1900/48, (NAA).

Report from Commander (D) 2nd Destroyer Flotilla to Vice Admiral (D), Mediterranean, 25 July 1940 (dealing with observations from *Bartolomeo Colleoni* survivor), (SPC-A).

Report from HMAS *Sydney* to Rear Admiral Commanding 7th Cruiser Squadron, 30 July 1940, (NAA).

Report on HMAS *Sydney* - Action on 19 July 1940, Commander-in-Chief Mediterranean, Med 0903/0710/30/2 dated 21 September 1940 (SPC-A).

Report from HMAS *Canberra* 2026/3/416 (Ketty Brøvig Action) dated 9 March 1941 (NAA).

Report on Pacific Ocean Raiders (Manyo Maru, Narvik and Tokyo Maru), Naval Intelligence Division, Navy Office, Melbourne, March 1941, Series Number B6121, Barcode 453332, (NAA).

Report by Lieutenant Commander H. MacKenzie RAN of Events Following the Fall of Rabaul, 29 April 1942, Series No. B6121, Barcode 646443, (NAA).

Report by Lieutenant Commander H.A. MacKenzie RAN (DSIO North East Area) on Coastwatch in South West Pacific 1 June 1942-21 April 1943, Series B34476, (NAA).

Reports from Coastwatchers in New Guinea, New Britain, New Ireland Areas, B3476, Barcode 411499, (NAA).

Reports on Activities in New Britain (North East Area), B3476, Barcode 411541, (NAA).

Report of an Action with the Italian Fleet off Calabria, 9 July 1940. Supplement to The London Gazette, 27 April 1948, pp. 2643-2649.

Report from Commanding Officer HMAS Adelaide- Letter of Proceeding HMAS *Adelaide* September 1940, 2026/7.185, (NAA).

Report on Legal Action Shaw Savill and Albion Company Ltd versus The Commonwealth, 521/201/239, (NAA).

Report from Australian Commonwealth Naval Board on operations leading up to the loss of HMAS *Canberra*, August 1942, Barcode 399876 (NAA).

Result of Court Martial of Commander E.W. Leir, DSO, RN, Held in HMS *Crescent*, 22 March 1918, (SPC-A).

Return of Duke of Gloucester in HMAS *Australia*, ADM 1/8827, (TNA UK).

HMAS *Sydney II* Commission of Inquiry: Report on Technical Aspects of HMAS *Sydney* and HSK *Kormoran*, DSTO, by M. Buckland, S.M. cannon, L. De Yong, G.I. Gamble, J.C. Jeremy, T. Lyon, P. McCarthy, B. Morris, R.A. Neill, M.B. Seen, B. Suendermann and T. Turner. DSTO-GD-0559, 2009.

Requirements of Minesweeping and Auxiliary anti-submarine Vessels at various Empire Ports in the event of War in the East, 12 March 1925, Committee on Imperial Defence, AWM 124, 3-132, (AWM).

Royal Australian Naval College Magazine, Geelong, H.Thacker Printers, 1913-1920.

Royal Australian Navy Lists, 1912-1960.(available on-line at www.navy.gov.au).

Royal Military College Provisional Standing Orders, June 1911.

Royal Naval College: Session 1919-20 Final Examination, Officers of the Royal Australian Navy, June 1920, ADM 203/42, 122712, (TNA UK).

Appointment of Midshipmen RAN to Seagoing Ships in the Grand Fleet. Extract from Naval Representative's 98th Report dated 25 March 1917. MP1049/1, (NAA).

Service Records and Confidential Reports of all members of the Pioneer Class, (NAA).

Service Records of RN Officers, ADM 196/46 series, (TNA UK).

Staff Officer (Intelligence) Port Moresby Report to Director Naval Intelligence, Report on Coast Watching Organization (3), 19 December 1939 (NAA).

Staff Officer (Intelligence) Port Moresby Report to Director Naval Intelligence, 2 August 1940 (NAA).

Shipping and shipbuilding - Decision 11, May 1951, A4905, 4687951, (NAA).

Shipping and Shipbuilding, 1951, A5104, 6/3/3 Part 1, 3209189, (NAA).

Ships and shipbuilding - Naval conference on naval construction, 1950, MP370/7, 1084253, (NAA).

Signal from Naval Attache, Athens to Commander-in-Chief Mediterranean, 31 July 1940, (SPC-A).

Signal from First Naval Member to Commodore Commanding Australian Squadron 150910Z FEB 45, (SPC-A).

CTG 51.4 Report to CTF 51, Report Sinking of German Ship *Ramses*, 2 December 1942, B6121, 399242, (NAA).

Sinking of German Ship '*Ramses*' by '*Adelaide*', S68/2/42 dated 7 December 1942, (SPC-A).

Statement on shipbuilding and shipping industries, 1951, A816, 3360694, (NAA).

Suicide Weapons and Tactics: Know Your Enemy, CinCPac Bulletin 126-45, 28 May 1945.

The Battle of Savo Island: August 9th 1942, Strategic & Tactical Analysis, US Naval War College, 1950.

UK Ordnance Board Minutes, SUPP 6/855, (TNA UK).

War Book Sub-committee - Working Party on Policy in Respect of Shipbuilding or Ship Repairs, 1950, A816, 3365138, (NAA).

War Cabinet Minutes, Numbers 676-873, 27 January-27 February 1941, Volume 5, A5954, 689282, (NAA).

War Cabinet Minutes, Numbers 874-1026, 5 March -4 May 1941, Volume 6, A5954, 689294, (NAA).

War Cabinet Minutes, Numbers 1027-1227, 9 May-18 July 1941, Volume 7, A5954, 689417, (NAA).

War Cabinet Minutes, Numbers 1456-1643, 30 October-30 December 1941, Volume 9, A2673, 12031205, (NAA).

War Cabinet Minutes, Numbers 2989-3331, 6 September 1943-4 February 1944, Volume 14, A5954, 689725, (NAA).

War Diary (Naval), Admiralty 1939-1945. (RN NHB).

War Memorandum (Eastern) Sections A-E, Admiralty, 19 September 1933. ADM 116/3475, (RN NHB).

Diaries, Film, Interviews, Oral History, Speeches, Personal Papers and Memoirs

Papers of Lieutenant P.W. Adams, PR00174.002, (AWM).

Diary of Able Seaman A.J. Andrews, PR 83/162, (AWM).

Papers of Captain J.M. Armstrong CBE, DSO, RAN, (NLA).

Papers of Commander B. Boase, RN (1899-1926), Accession Number 1991/89, (Royal Navy Manuscript Collection).

Oral History and Papers of Mr B.C. Ballard, (NLA).

Diary of Rear Admiral R.C. Boddie, CVO, DSO, RN. 1914-17, contained in his private papers, Documents 6442, (IWM).

Papers of Mischa Burlakov, MS 9501, (NLA).

Unpublished family history, Captain P. Burnett, RAN Retired (Held by family).

Diary of Midshipman N.K. Calder, RAN (Captain M. Calder).

Papers of Commander Norman Keith Calder OBE, PR0323, (AWM).
Papers of Sub-Lieutenant J.E.N. Carter RNR 92/45/1, (IWM).
Diary of Sub Lieutenant A.W. Clarke, (A) RNVR, (www.royalnavyresearcharchive.org.uk)
Oral History of Vice Admiral Sir John Collins, Mel Pratt Collection, 27 August 1975, (NLA).
Oral History of Vice Admiral Sir John Collins interviewed by Robert Hyslop, S046522, March 1988, (AWM).
Papers of Vice Admiral Sir John Collins (Held by family).
Memoirs of Study Corporal James Brigande Condor, (SPC-A).
Oral History 38-86, Rear Admiral R.E. Cook, USN, Center for Cryptographic History, (NSA).
Papers of Admiral Sir John Crace RN, 69/18/3, (IWM).
Papers of Vice Admiral W.R. Creswell, (SPC-A).
Recollections of Commodore D.H.D. Smyth, http://www.pacificwar.org.au/CoralSea/theyserved/DacreSmyth.html
Papers of Lieutenant Commander P.F. Dash RAN, 3DRL/7696, (AWM).
Papers of Commander E.R. Dodd, RN, 87/3/1, (IWM).
Dykes, C.D., A Mariner of the Twentieth Century: The Life Story of Captain Cecil Donald Dykes, RD, FAIN,(SPC-A).
Diary and photographs of Stoker E.C. Evans, DSM, PR 00811, (AWM).
Oral History 09-83, Captain R.T. Fabian, 4 May 1983, Center for Cryptographic History, (NSA).
Papers of Rear Admiral H.B. Farncomb, (SPC-A).
Oral History of Commander Feldt, E.A, Reminiscences of Commander Eric Feldt, Transcript of an oral history, Archival Number OH 465, 1966, (State Library of South Australia).
Papers of Commander E.A. Feldt (State Library of Queensland).
Memoirs of Mrs A.F. Feldt, Gussie's Story, 1938. (Held by the Feldt family).
Oral History of Petty Officer G.J. Glansford, January 1989, S00516, (AWM).
Navy Week Address by Lieutenant Commander Mackenzie Gregory, Melbourne Shrine of Remembrance, 26 August 2008.
Papers of the HMAS *Assault* Association, PR00631, (AWM).
Diary of Lieutenant Henry Hackworth, RN, 1940, 1998/36/1, (Royal Naval Museum).
Oral History of Admiral T.C. Hart, USN, Operational Archives, (US Navy Yard, Washington).
Hayler, B.G., The Bygone Years: My Life in War and Peace, 2010, (SPC-A).
Papers of Captain T.J.N. Hilken DSC, RN, THN 1, (IWM).
Papers of Captain H. L. Howden, PR86/145, (AWM).
Diary of Cadet Midshipman E.B. Howells, RAN, (Howells Family).

Papers of the Commander R.M.B. Long Memorial Fund, 3DRL/6906, (AWM).

Papers of Professor Sir John Madsen, MS 072, Basser Library, (Australian Academy of Science).

Mathieson, J.K.W., The Memoirs of Chaplain J.K.W. Mathieson 14/2/42 - 8/10/42, 1948, (SPC-A).

Moore, R.R., The Life and Time of Robert Ralph Moore (1919-1985), (SPC-A).

Papers of Vice Admiral Sir Trevylyan Napier RN, 99/34/1-4, (IWM).

Diary of Captain E.S. Nurse, RAN (Nurse Family Papers).

Oral History of Able Seaman H.G.S. Peacock, 27 February 1989, S00525, (AWM).

Oral History of Vice Admiral Sir Richard Peek, May-June 1977, (NLA).

Papers of Surgeon Lieutenant H.G. Rischbieth, RANR, PR 00795, (AWM).

Oral History of Sub-Lieutenant R.T. Slatyer, 25 May 2005, S03756 (AWM).

Oral History of Able Seaman R.E. Scrivener, 10 February 1089, S00535, (AWM).

Showers,. H.A. Recollections of HMAS *Sydney*, undated, (Showers Family Papers).

Papers and poems of Able Seaman N. Smith, (Held by author).

Papers of Major General J.E.S. Stevens, 3 DRL 3561, (AWM).

Oral History of Mr. Artemio Ettore Torselli, Memories of an Italian Naval Signalman, Article ID: A5815776, 19 September 2005, (Bedford Museum).

Interrogation of Admiral Soemu Toyoda, OPNAV-P-030I00, Naval Analysis Division, 13-14 November 1945, Interrogation 75, USSBS 378 //www.ibiblio.org/hyperwar/AAF/USSBS/IJO/IJO-75.html

Papers of Arthur Hubert. Turner, 96/22/1, (IWM).

Oral History of Leading Seaman R.B. Walker, S00708, 28 June 1989, (AWM).

Oral History 05-83, Captain D.L. Whitlock, USN, Center for Cryptographic History, (NSA).

Oral History of Lieutenant W.F. Wreford, S00526 (F2786/21), 23 February 1989, (AWM).

Papers of Allan Zammit, (Australian Defence Force Academy Library).

Interviews with Mrs Mary Backhouse, Commander Peter Burnett, Mrs Barbara Crouch, Commodore 'Toz' Dadswell (retired), Captain Donald Dykes (retired), Mr D. Fraser, Lieutenant Commander Mackenzie Gregory, Warrant Officer Allen Guthrie, Lieutenant Commander Henry Hall, Vice Admiral Sir Richard Peek, Mr Sandy Pearson, Commodore Ian Pfennigwerth, Rear Admiral Andrew Robertson, Lieutenant Commander Mark Shelvey, Commander Graham Wright, Lieutenant Commander Ian Wrigley and other extended family members of the Pioneer Class.

Photographs and Film

A Call to the People of Australia, Picture, H34151, (State Library of Victoria).

Captain P. Burnett Collection (held by the Burnett family).

Vice Admiral Sir Collins Collection (copies held by SPC-A).
Rear Admiral H.B. Farncomb Collection (held by SPC-A).
Captain Duncan Grant Collection (held by the Grant family).
Cadet Midshipman E.B. Howells Collection (held by the Howells family).
Sub Lieutenant P.J. Kimlin Collection (held by the Kimlin family).
Captain J.B. Newman Collection (Held by family).
Captain E.S. Nurse Collection (Held by family).
Commander W.L. Reilly Collection (held SPC-A).
Lieutenant Commander C.A.R. Sadleir Collection (held by family).
Cadet Midshipmen H.B. Vallentine Collection (held by family).
SPC-A Photography Collection.
Memorial Light for Coast Watchers, Madang New Guinea, Film contained in 59216, Cinesound Review, No. 1451, August 1959, 1272080, (National Film and Sound Archive).
Memorial Light to the Coast Watchers, Madang New Guinea, Film contained in 61893, Movietone News, No. A1696, A1697, August 1959, 127869, (National Film and Sound Archive).
The Coastwatchers, audio tape, Madang New Guinea, 15 August 1959, 238264, (National Film and Sound Archive).

Abbreviations

AWM	Australian War Memorial, Canberra.
IWM	Imperial War Museum, London.
NAA	National Archives of Australia (Canberra, Sydney and Melbourne).
NLA	National Library of Australia, Canberra.
NSA	National Security Agency, Washington.
NSW SA	State Archives of New South Wales, Kingswood.
RN NHB	Royal Navy Naval Historical Branch, Portsmouth.
SPC-A	Sea Power Centre - Australia
TNA UK	The National Archives United Kingdom, Kew.

Index

1st Battle Squadron, 220, 232
1st Light Cruiser Squadron, 125
2nd Battle Cruiser Squadron, 103, 107, 135
2nd Destroyer Flotilla, 313, 315
2nd Italian Cruiser Division, 313
5th Battle Squadron, 132
5th Destroyer Flotilla, 422
6th Light Cruiser Squadron, 125, 127
7th Cruiser Squadron, 303, 305, 308–310, 322, 325, 327
7th Japanese Cruiser Division, 422
10th Destroyer Flotilla, 303
12th Submarine Flotilla, 130, 132, 137–138
13th Destroyer Flotilla, 142
13th Submarine Flotilla, 130, 132, 135, 137
24th Destroyer Flotilla, 528, 530

A

ABDACOM, see American-British-Dutch-Australian Command
Abruzzi, 310
Achilles, 339, 446
Adams, Captain William, 471
Adams, James, 489
Adams, Midshipman Peter, 543
Adelaide, 70, 180, 194–195, 208, 212, 231, 268–269, 294, 343, 357, 369, 372, 390, 418, 430, 462, 469, 471
 collision with *Coptic*, 344–345
 convoy protection duties, 300–302, 336
 operations against *Jacob van Heemskerck*, 506–508
 recommissioned, 275
 support to Free French transition, Noumea, 345–353
Adele, 62
Admiral Charnier, 345, 348–350, 352
Admiral Scheer, 361
Admiralty Islands, seizure of, 520–522
Adventure, 216
AE2, 153
Agincourt, 146
AIB, see Allied Intelligence Bureau
Ajax, 120, 328
Akagi, 430–431
Albert, Frank, 22, 42–43, 62
Albert, Otto, 5, 22–23, 25, 34–35, 42–44, 91, 93, 167

Alden, 412, 419
Alexander-Sinclair, Rear Admiral Edwyn, 125
Allied Intelligence Bureau, 429, 445
Aloha, 185–186, 188
Alston's Seamanship, 95
Amagiri, 498
American-British-Dutch-Australian Command, 410
Amphion, 269
Anchises, 100
Anderson, Warrant Officer Herbert, 466
Andresen, Andy, 455
Andrewes, Bill, 109–110
Angora, 142
Anking, 411, 424
anti-submarine capabilities, Australian, 200–201, 244, 264
Antonio Locatelli, 328, 330
Anzac, 160, 178–179, 211, 234, 244, 414, 592
Anzac Squadron, 446
Aoba, 479
Aosta, 310
Aquitania, 336, 395–396, 508, 519
Arashi, 425
Archibald, Surgeon Lieutenant Francis, 584–585
Arethusa, 247
Ariadne, 61
Armitage, Captain Harold, 67
Armitage, George, 21–22, 25, 67, 96, 103, 113–115, 148–150, 152, 178, 204–206, 236, 249, 275, 365, 509, 567, 632
Armstrong, Captain James, 518, 535, 541

Armstrong, Commander John, 23, 41, 49, 51, 62, 448–449, 544, 549
Arnold, General, 504
Arunta, 464, 516–517, 519, 541, 543, 546, 549, 551–552, 556, 577
Asagumo, 420–421
Asama Maru, 297
asdic, 200–201, 244, 255, 262, 264, 428, 464
Aspinall, Archie, 241
Astoria, 448, 477–478, 481, 486, 488
Atago, 425
Atlantis, 333, 336, 354–355, 361
Attacker, 526–531, 544
Attendolo, 310
Aubin, Bishop, 499
Australia, 31, 37, 41, 43, 89, 101, 103, 116, 118, 142–143, 145, 147–149, 152, 154–156, 159, 172, 177, 216–218, 230, 233–234, 244–245, 248, 257–259, 270, 278, 301, 361, 397, 446, 458, 493, 508, 513, 516–518, 524, 535, 540–542, 544, 547, 553, 572, 579, 613, 633–634
  Battle of May Island, 129, 132, 135, 137
  building and launch, 211–213, 215
  collision with *New Zealand*, 107
  Gordon and Elias incident, 448–453, 525–526
  Guadacanal, battle for, 473, 475, 477–479, 481, 486, 490–492
  kamikaze attack, 454, 539, 546, 548–550, 552
  mutiny, 157, 166
  paid off, 178
  scuttled off Sydney Heads, 180

Australian Commonwealth Naval
    Board, 4
Australian Fleet, 37, 154, 180
    birth of, 7–8
Australian New Guinea Administrative
    Unit, 433
Autolycus, 268–270, 520
Automedon, 354
Auxiliary Service, 266–267

B

Backhouse, Captain Oliver, 136, 139
Bacon, Lieutenant Commander Jack,
    305
Badminton, 193
Bagley, 491, 508, 517, 545
Ballarat, 96, 412, 415, 422, 425
    sinking of, 113–115
Ballard, Bertram, 342–344, 346–351,
    353
Ban, Lieutenant Katsuhisa, 466–467
Banckert, 412
Bande Nere, 315, 317–318, 320
Barbey, Rear Admiral Daniel, 522–
    523, 538, 559
Barbiano, 310
Barbini, Lieutenant Giovanni, 328–331
Barcoo, 555
Barham, 131, 147, 155
Barnett, 488
Baroni, Captain Enrico, 305–306, 308,
    335
Bartholomew, General, 221
Bartolomeo Colleoni, 313, 318, 320,
    323, 325, 332, 384
Basilisk, 258
Bataan, 551, 562, 578, 595
Bates, Charles, 608
Bates, Roma, 608, 610

Bathurst, 563
Battle of Jutland, 108–109, 279
BCOF, see British Commonwealth
    Occupation Force
Bean, Charles, 9
Beatty, Admiral Sir David, 107–108,
    120, 123, 125, 131
Bedkober, Doug, 498, 501
Belconnen, 262
Bell, Captain LH, 426
Beltana, 212
Benavon, 339
Benbow, 147
Bendigo, 412, 415, 422, 424
Benham, Greg, 433, 436–437
Bennett, Major General Gordon, 412
Berkey, Rear Admiral Russell, 551–552
Berryman, Lieutenant General Frank,
    563
Bevan, Captain Robert, 450–451
Bidwell, Admiral Roger, 110
Bingera, 464
Birdwood, General Sir William, 155
Bismarck, 279
Blackwood, Captain Maurice, 253
Blamey, General Sir Thomas, 563
Blandy, HR, 343, 345–346, 353
Bloemfontein, 410
Blue, 480
Board of Inquiry
    Terreneuvien Yolande incident, 154
    Vanguard incident, 119
Boddie, Engineer Lieutenant
    Commander Ronald, 13, 32, 38, 47,
    49, 51, 58, 60–61, 69, 74, 103
Bode, Captain Howard, 466, 481, 490
Bolzano, 311
Bombay, 462, 468
Borneo operations, 558–561

Bostock, Air Vice Marshal William, 563
Bower, Commander John, 131, 137, 531
Bowyer-Smyth, Captain Sir Philip, 110, 301
Boxer Rebellion, 3
Boyce, Captain Hector, 205
Boyd, Able Seaman Erle, 82
Boyle, Commander Edward, 153
Boyle, Ruby, 440, 503
Bracegirdle, Lieutenant Commander 'Braces,' 271, 302, 495, 544, 634
Bradshaw, Commander George, 130
Braine, 551
Brand, Brigadier General Charles, 210
Brereton, Major General Lewis, 405
Bridge, KT, 503
Bridges, Brigadier General William, 10, 51
Brind, Vice Admiral Eric, 568
Brisbane, 69–70, 155, 157, 172, 174, 178–179, 202, 208, 239, 344, 353, 398
Britannia Naval College, 42, 66
British Commonwealth Occupation Force, 568
Brodie, Engineer Lieutenant Commander Bernard, 369
Brooke-Popham, Air Chief Marshal Sir Alan, 379–380, 382–383, 409
Brooks, Governor Sir Dallas, 579
Brooks, Sub-Lieutenant Leslie, 246
Brooksbank, Lieutenant Gilbert, 281, 443
Brooksbank, Walter, 252, 281, 286, 405, 607, 609
Brown, Betty, 239
Brown, Frederick, 13–15, 37, 52
Brown, Vice Admiral Wilson, 446, 454
Brownlow, Frederick, 43

Bruce, Prime Minister Stanley, 191, 193, 210, 218, 269
Bruiser, 530
Buchanan, 543, 564
Buchanan, Rear Admiral Herbert, 613
Buckley, Lieutenant Colonel Edmund, 499
Buka, Sergeant, 523
Bulwark, 11
Bungaree, 368–373, 462, 469, 473, 511, 624
Bunning, Gunner Jack, 523
Bunting, Cook Edward, 514
Burlakov, Mischa, 367
Burnaby, Reverend Arthur, 96
Burnett, Joseph, 103, 121, 135, 142, 147, 154, 157, 169, 171–172, 194, 212, 216, 219, 228, 232, 235, 249, 290–291, 293, 378, 387–388, 525, 565, 577, 583
  commands *Sydney*, 383, 389
  Kormoran engagement, 390, 393, 395, 399–401
  marries Enid Ward, 195
  Naval College, 21–23, 25, 64–65, 68, 84
Burnett, William, 121
Burnie, 412, 424–426
Burrows, Commander William, 169
Butteris, Sergeant Bill, 518

C

Cahill, Premier Joseph, 606
Calabria, battle, 309–312
Calamares, 541
Calder, Norman, 97–98, 100, 103–104, 116, 119, 121–122, 141, 147–148, 153, 169, 177–178, 190, 206, 212, 219, 228, 247, 567, 583, 614, 624, 627, 636, 638

Aide-de-Camp to the Governor General, 266
commands *Bungaree*, 368, 370–373, 462, 469, 473, 511
Deputy Director of Underwater Weapons, 511
District Naval Officer, Sydney, 278
marries Nancie Dixon, 232
Naval College, 21, 23, 25, 32, 40, 68, 77–78, 88, 92
retires from Navy, 618
Secretary and Comptroller to the Governor-General, 577
Calder, William, 98
Caledon, 125, 128
Calvert, Commander Thomas, 132
Calypso, 125, 127
Cambridge, 340
Cambridge, R, 503
Campbell, J, 503
Campbell-Bannerman, Sir Henry, 4
Campioni, Vice Admiral Inigo, 310–311
Canada, 103–104, 106, 109–110, 112, 115, 118–119, 122, 128, 145, 234, 310
Canadian Cruiser, 361
Canadian Royal Military College, 10
Canberra, 216, 218, 227–228, 232, 244, 248, 260–262, 278, 292, 301–302, 309, 336, 339, 390, 445–446, 462, 471, 491, 493–494, 516
building and launch, 211–213
German raider operations, 354–357, 361–364
grounding, 229–231
Guadacanal, battle for, 475–476, 478–479, 481, 484
sinking of, 485–488
Canning, Frances, 73

Cantanni, Luigi, 307
Cantile, Commander Colin, 192
Cape Spada, battle, 313–323
Capetown, 301, 361
Capo Vado, 328, 330
Caradoc, 125
Cardiff, 125, 127
Cargill, James, 466
Carless, Ordinary Seaman John, 128
Carlisle, Lieutenant Commander DG, 526, 531
Carpenter, Signalman James, 413, 428, 517
Carpenter, Sir Walter, 261
Carpenter, Vice Admiral Arthur, 517
Carter, Alexander, 82–83
Carter, Ida, 226
Casardi, Rear Admiral Ferdinando, 313, 315–318
CAST, see Station C, cryptanalysis unit at Corregidor
Catalani, 328, 330
Catoctin, 528
Centaur, 396
Cerberus, 3, 9, 195, 577
Ceres, 125
Cessnock, 506, 563
Chambers, Admiral Bertram, 11–16, 19–22, 26, 29, 40–42, 45–46, 61, 63, 104, 146, 168, 533–534
Chambers, Ken, 433
Chapman, Austin, 11
Chatfield, Admiral Sir Ernle, 249, 251
Chicago, 446, 455, 458, 460, 462, 464–468, 475, 478, 481–482, 484, 486, 488
Chifley, Prime Minister Ben, 581, 583, 588
Chikuma, 425
Childers, Midshipman Charles, 164

China Force, 411–415, 426
Chinnery, Sarah, 239–240
Chitose, 539
Chiyoda, 539
Chokai, 479, 484–486
Choules, Petty Officer Claude, 229
Chuma, Lieutenant Kenshi, 466
Churchill, Winston, 303, 323, 377–379, 407, 409, 462, 532, 547, 573
City of Rayville, 340
Clairmont, 410
Clark, Rear Admiral Charles, 577
Clarke, Lieutenant Henry, 127
Cleland, Brigadier Sir Donald, 609
Clemens, Captain Martin, 165, 440, 496, 499–500
Cleveland, 560
coastwatch operations, 251, 285–288, 291, 338, 357, 429–445, 456, 462, 474, 478–479, 494–504, 517–519, 523–524, 558, 574–575, 607–610, 631
  establishment of, 282–284
  Memorial Lighthouse, 607–610
Coates, Prime Minister Joseph, 217
Cobby, Lieutenant Arthur, 96
Coburg, 363
Cockman, Captain GW, 115
COIC, see Combined Operational Intelligence Centre
Colac, 555–557
Collins, 640
Collins, Lady, 640
Collins, Mrs Esther, 12
Collins, John, 103, 110–112, 148–149, 151, 160–161, 169, 172, 178–179, 182, 208–211, 216, 234, 248, 256–259, 264–265, 267, 273, 275, 290, 295, 300, 333–337, 362, 373, 376, 381, 389, 393, 395, 399, 401–403, 406–410, 428–429, 463, 490, 517, 519, 522, 524, 527, 533, 539, 544, 551, 560, 567, 572–574, 577, 579, 586, 599, 611–613, 623, 625, 629, 634–635, 639–641
  Assistant Chief of Naval Staff and Director of Naval Intelligence, 263
  Assistant Chief of Staff to Admiral Layton, 383–386, 388
  British Commonwealth Occupation Force, 568
  Chief of Naval Staff, 581–583, 587–598
  Commander *TF 74*, 525, 535, 537–538
  commands *Shropshire*, 494
  commands *Sydney*, 293
  Commodore Commanding Australian Squadron, 525
  Commodore Commanding Fremantle, 427
  Commodore Commanding the China Force, 411–426
  Executive Officer, *Sydney*, 254–255
  High Commissioner, Wellington, 618–621
  honours and awards, 91, 190, 254, 426
  Imperial Defence College, UK, 580–581
  marries Phyllis McLachlan, 233
  Mediterranean operations, 303–310, 312, 315–318, 320–328, 330–332
  Naval College, 12, 22–24, 33, 39, 43, 48, 63, 71, 78, 80, 84, 87, 93

Senior Naval Officer, Western
   Australia, 427
Staff Course, Greenwich, 235
surrender of Japan, 561–566
wounded, 540–541
Colville, Admiral The Honourable
   Sir Stanley, 102
Colvin, Vice Admiral Sir Stanley,
   102, 263–265, 273, 278, 289–
   290, 293, 301–302, 333–334, 378,
   381, 386, 388, 400, 446, 489, 552,
   588, 638, 641
Coman, Commodore Robert, 516, 579
Combined Operational Intelligence
   Centre, 387–388, 408, 442
Commissaire Ramel, 354
Commonwealth Naval Force, 3, 6,
   215
Conder, Alfred, 22–23, 25, 32, 37,
   58, 103, 135, 145, 153, 169, 196,
   198, 226, 232, 240–241, 383
Condor, James, 58
Congressional Medal of Honour, 423
Conti di Cavour, 309, 311
Conway, 551
Cook, Captain James, 196
Cook, Sir Joseph, 11, 154
Coomonderry, 569–570
Coonawarra, 262
Coptic, 344–345
Coral Sea, battle of, 453–462
Cornwall, 364, 467
Cotton-Stapleton, Lieutenant
   Campbell, 60, 74, 77
Courageous, 104, 123–125, 131–132,
   137
Courts of Inquiry
   Hall Affair, 75–77
   May Island incident, 139

Cowan, Commodore Walter, 125
Cowra, 555
Cowrie, Second Officer Joan, 447
Crace, Rear Admiral Jack, 110, 278,
   301–302, 334, 380, 395, 397,
   445–449, 451–452, 455–458,
   460–461, 473, 475, 525
Creal, Archie, 13, 511
Cream, Sergeant, 523
Creswell, 90
Creswell, Admiral Sir William Rooke,
   2–4, 7–10, 14–15, 20, 26, 29, 45,
   78, 89–90, 145, 168, 253, 263, 475
Creswick, Private Arthur, 114
Crombie, Florence, 616
Cross, Stan, 176
crossing-the-line ceremony, 100
Crutchley, Vice Admiral Sir Victor,
   473, 475–478, 480–483, 486,
   490–492, 504–505, 513–515,
   518–520, 522, 524, 535, 574
cryptanalysis, 289–290, 378, 404,
   442–443, 456
Culblean, 132
Cunningham, Admiral Sir Andrew,
   303–305, 308–312, 315–316,
   321–323, 325–327, 330–332,
   334–335, 573
Cunningham, Admiral Sir John, 581
Cunningham, Dick, 21–23, 25, 43,
   58, 72, 80, 87, 104, 108, 120,
   129–130, 162, 210
   death of, 139, 141
Curlew, 241
Curtatone, 330
Curtin, Prime Minister John, 333,
   356, 359, 386, 397, 406, 461–462,
   494, 540, 588
Custance, Rear Admiral Wilfred,

119, 261, 273

D

Dace, 522
Dalglish, Rear Admiral Robin, 110–112, 145, 235, 245
Dalrymple-Hay, Ken, 455, 478, 497
Dalton, Commander Lionel, 323
Danae, 411, 419
Darter, 523
Dauntless, 196
De Angelis, Commander Francesco, 328, 331
De Burgh, Commander Charles, 134
de Chair, Governor Admiral Sir Dudley, 167
de Gaulle, General Charles, 341–343, 345–346, 352–353
de Groot, Frank, 601–605
De L'Isle, Lord, 621, 629
de Quievrecourt, Capitaine de Frégate Pierre Toussaint, 344, 346, 350–351, 353
De Ruyter, 412, 419–421
Deakin, Prime Minister Alfred, 2, 4–8
Dechaineux, Captain Emile, 202, 519–520, 524, 535, 539–541
Defence Force Retirement Benefits Scheme, 582
Defence Science and Technology Organisation, 398
degaussing, 340–341, 536, 585
Deloraine, 555
Demonsthenes, 171
Denis, Lieutenant Colonel Maurice, 345, 347
Denman, Governor General Lord, 25–27, 29
Destroyer Division 7, 404, 407
Destroyer Squadron 4, 517
Destroyer Squadron 24, 543
Detmers, Korvettenkapitän Theodor, 337, 389–396, 398–399, 401
Dexterity, Operation, 517–520
DFRB, see Defence Force Retirement Benefits Scheme
Dingle, Second Officer, 355–356
Dix, Warrant Officer Thomas, 13, 62, 68, 88–89, 142, 206
Dixie, 515
Dobbie, Lieutenant General William, 331
Dobbin, 462
Dominion Monarch, 408
Doomba, 468
Doorman, Admiral Karel, 408, 411, 414, 419–421
Douglas, 220–221
Douglas, Vice Admiral Percy, 240
Dovers, Lieutenant Bill, 556
Dowling, Vice Admiral Sir Roy, 598
Downward, Surgeon Commander Charles, 485, 488
Dragon, 410–411, 419
Dryad, 220
Dubbo, 555–556
Dudley, Rear Admiral Sheldon, 242
Duggan, Sir Winston, 441
Duke of York, 563
Dumaresq, Commodore John, 154, 156–157, 166, 170, 172–174
Dumont D'Urville, 343–344, 347–353
Dunera, 300
Duntroon, 51, 84–85, 92, 294, 559
Duntroon, 254
Durban, 300, 389–390, 412, 416
Durnford, Commander John, 234
Dutch East Indies, naval operations, 416–427

Dutton, Henry, 62

E

E14, 153
E42, 131
Eagle, 309
Eather, Major General Kenneth, 573
Eaton, 551
Echlin, Nancy, 239
Edsall, 425
Edward VII, King, 7
Edwards, 412
Edwards, Captain Herbert, 127
Edwards, Murray, 433
Eldridge, Frank, 15, 64, 82, 91, 246, 533
Electra, 406, 412, 419–421, 424
Elias, Stoker Edward, 448–453, 525
Ellet, 488
Elwell, First Lieutenant Charles, 12–13, 45, 48–50
Emden, 50, 97, 157, 164, 216, 301, 323, 332, 396
Emerald, 361
Emily, 569
Emperor, 527, 530
Emperor of India, 128
Encounter, 8, 12, 16, 31, 35–36, 157, 412, 419–420
Enterprise, 474, 504
Esdaile, James, 98, 103, 135, 143, 147, 160, 169, 172, 178, 191, 199–201, 211, 220, 232, 234–235, 244, 248–249, 263–265, 278, 373, 462–463, 632, 637–638, 640–642
  commands *Adelaide*, 469, 471, 506, 508
  Deputy Naval Officer in Charge, New Guinea Area, 535, 541, 554–557, 567
  Directorate of Naval Demobilisation, 570
  Naval College, 21, 23, 25, 37, 43, 72, 87, 91
  retires from Navy, 600
Espero, 305–308, 316, 332, 335
Espero convoy, battle, 305–308
Ettrick, 300
Euripides, 196
Evans, Admiral Sir Edward, 227, 230, 233, 324
Evans, Stoker Eric, 307
Evans, Stoker Petty Officer Mervyn, 546
Evan-Thomas, Vice Admiral Hugh, 131, 137
Evatt, Dr. Herbert, 525, 572, 602
Evertsen, 422
Ewen, Flying Officer Francis, 210
Ewing, Professor James, 9, 107
Excellent, 102, 190
Exeter, 411, 419–420, 597
Express, 406, 412
Eyers, Lieutenant Harold, 466
Eyssen, Kapitän Robert, 357–358

F

Fabian, Lieutenant Commander Rudolph, 442–443, 445, 546
Fadden, Acting Prime Minister Arthur, 381, 386
fagging, 65, 67, 109
Falke, Captain Johannes, 508
Fantome, 197
Far East Combined Bureau, 289–290, 383, 404, 443
Far East Liaison Office, 440, 445

Farncomb, 641
Farncomb, Harold, 102–103, 143,
  160–161, 169–170, 178, 191,
  195–196, 211, 244–246, 248, 300,
  396, 399, 517–518, 524–525, 538,
  590, 594, 598, 613, 629, 633–634,
  640–641
  Board of Inquiry, *Hobart*
    torpedoing, 515
  Chief of Staff to Rear Admiral
    Crace, 445–446
  commands *Attacker*, 526–531
  commands *Australia*, 446–516
  commands Australian Squadron,
    544–578
  commands *Canberra*, 301, 336,
    339, 354, 356, 362, 364
  commands *Perth*, 268–272, 276–277
  commands *Yarra*, 261
  Gordon and Elias incident,
    448–453
  Head Joint Services Staff,
    Washington, 579–580
  honours and awards, 526, 550, 561
  law practice, 621–624
  marries Jean Nott, 221
  Naval College, 21–23, 25, 43, 66,
    72, 87, 90–91
Farncomb, Jean, 516, 621, 640
Fearless, 130, 132, 137–138
FECB, see Far East Combined Bureau
Feldt, Eric, 102–104, 109, 112–113, 119,
  128, 148, 160–161, 178–179, 261,
  522, 558, 564, 585, 606–611, 641
  appointed Staff Officer
    Intelligence Port Moresby, 282
  assigned to Buka Island,
    Bougainville, 189
  assigned to Namatanai, New
    Ireland, 206–208
  assigned to Salamaua, 221–225
  clerk in Rabaul, 183–184
  coastwatch operations, 283–284,
    290–291, 381, 405, 429, 433,
    435, 437–438, 440, 445,
    455, 462, 474–475, 479, 489,
    494–495, 497–499, 501, 518
  The Coastwatchers (book), 574–
    576
  commands *Lusair*, 554, 556
  health issues, 502–503, 557, 630
  Naval College, 21–25, 30, 34, 38,
    41, 48, 50, 59, 63, 65, 72, 80,
    83, 87
  patrol officer, PNG, 184–189
  post-war, 631
  rejoins Navy, 267
  takes naval redundancy, 181
  tracking murderers, 236–239
FELO, see Far East Combined Bureau
Ferguson, Governor General Sir
  Ronald Munro, 160, 166
Field, Vice Admiral Sir Frederick, 194
Figgis, Lieutenant Peter, 434–435,
  610
Finch, Admiral Aubrey, 456–457
Finch, Cecil, 248
Finch, Desiree Ursula, 248
Finch, Miss Dorothy, 534
Fisher, Admiral Jackie, 7–9, 16, 258
Fisher, Mrs Jane, 70
Fisher, Prime Minister Andrew, 6–7,
  10–11, 25, 27, 29, 70
Fisher, Vice Admiral Sir William, 232, 258
Fitzgerald, Captain JUP, 255–257, 259
Fleet Radio Unit, Melbourne,
  443–445, 447, 453–454, 456, 464,
  472, 614–615

Fleet Unit Concept, 7
Fletcher, Vice Admiral Frank, 447, 456, 461, 474, 476–478, 481, 493, 496
flimsy, 146–147
Flinders, Matthew, 196
Flowers, William, 82–83
Foley, Captain Bernard, 505
Foley, Captain James, 263
Foley, Commander Bob, 499
Foley, Matt, 609
Foote, Reverend Reuben, 631
Force Z, 403, 405–407
Ford, 412
Ford, Rear Admiral Wilbraham, 247
Fowle, Commander George, 617
Fowle, Lieutenant Commander George, 514, 516, 561
Foxton, Colonel JF, 7–8
Frame, Professor Tom, 622
Francol, 424
Frankfurt, 125
Franklin, 62–64, 69–70, 81, 188, 202
Franklin, Charles, 15, 59, 63, 82
Fraser, Admiral Sir Bruce, 549, 556, 564, 591
Frazier, 551
Free Masons, 178, 266, 638
Freud, Reverend, 434
Freund, Reverend Harold, 284
Frewen, Oswald, 66
FRUMEL, see Fleet Radio Unit, Melbourne
Furutaka, 479
Fuso, 539, 543

G

Gabriel, 135–136
Galatea, 125
Gale, Lieutenant Commander D'Arcy 'Tommy,' 369
Gallipoli, 67–68, 150, 258–259, 303
Garibaldi, 310
Garvey, Reverend Brother Thomas, 324
Gascoyne, 537, 546, 550
Gatacre, Commander Galfrey, 475, 490
Gato, 498–499, 501
Gaze, Harold, 266
Geelong, 462, 467
George, Prime Minister Lloyd, 303
George F Elliott, 480
George VI, King, 494, 526, 573
Geosounder, 398
Geranium, 179, 198–199
German raider operations, 336–341, 354–364, 387–402
Getting, Frank, 22, 104, 108, 116, 130, 141, 146–148, 152–153, 155, 158, 169, 213, 220, 278, 292–293, 369, 387, 490, 493, 516, 525, 566, 579, 628
  Assistant Navy Chief of Staff, 388
  boxing, 120–121
  commands *Canberra*, 471–489
  commands *H47*, 193
  commands *Kanimbla*, 295–300
  commands *Oxley*, 214
  divorced, 219
  fatally wounded, 485, 488–489
  marries Emma Forsayth, 192
  Naval College, 21, 23, 25, 48, 72, 80, 84
Getting, George, 121
Getting, Hazel, 489, 579
Ghormley, Vice Admiral Robert, 474, 476, 493, 504
Gieves, James, 102, 115

Giles, William, 253
Gill, George, 574, 606–607, 611–612
Gill, Hermon, 503–504
Gill, Ordinary Seaman Telegraphist James, 287
Gill, Sub Lieutenant John, 431–432, 434
Gilling, Lloyd, 21, 23, 103, 147–148, 155, 157, 169, 172, 180, 194–196, 212, 219, 228–232, 241–242, 258, 533–534
Gilmore, Jack, 610
Giovanni delle Bande Nere, 313
Giulio Cesare, 309–311
Glasgow, 361
Glorious, 104, 108, 122–125, 129–131, 141–142, 146, 153
Glory, 595
Glossop, Commodore John, 157, 166
Gloucester, 303, 317
Godfroy, Vice Admiral René-Émile, 305
Golpak, Paramount Luluai, 608
Good, Percy, 439
Goodwin, Sir John, 227
Gordon, Leading Stoker Albert, 448–453
Goshawk, 101
Goto, Rear Admiral Aritomo, 109, 455, 477
Gough, Steward George, 449
Goulburn, 412, 422, 425, 427
Gould, Gordon, 72, 85, 467
Gowrie, Lord, 266
Grant, Captain Duncan, 14–15, 29–30, 36–37, 40–41, 43–46, 49–51, 57–58, 61, 63–64, 66–67, 73–75, 78–80, 82–83, 85–88, 104, 121, 142, 146, 158, 168, 246, 367, 533, 598

commands Naval College, 42
discharged from Royal Navy, 534
Executive Officer, Naval College, 12
resigns from Naval College, 164–167
Grant, Rear Admiral Sir Percy, 166
Gravener, Lieutenant Commander Sam, 139
Great White Fleet, 5–6, 217, 517, 520
Gregory, Sub-Lieutenant MacKenzie, 471, 484
Grieve, Lilias, 202
Guadacanal, battle for, see also Savo Island, battle of
Guadacanal, battle of, 474–491
Guilio Cesare, 311–312
Guissano, 310
Gul Djemal, 153
Guthrie, Chief Petty Officer Allen, 578

H

H27, 193
H47, 193
Haes, Commander Edmund Mount, 299
Hagan, Leading Signalman, 449
Haguro, 419, 421
Hall, Able Seaman Henry 'Nobby,' 488, 551
Hall, Ben, 610
Hall, Reverend William, 14–15, 29, 46, 50, 52, 60, 62, 73–78
Halligan, Reginald, 183–184
Halsey, Admiral 'Bull,' 454, 493–494, 497, 501–503, 513, 537, 558, 561–564, 575, 596, 607
Hamilton, Admiral Sir Louis, 581,

587–588, 590
Hammond, Chief Petty Officer
  Edward, 179
Hara, Rear Admiral Kenzaburo, 422
Harbottle, Commander Tom, 132–135,
  139
Hardie, Reverend Andrew, 88, 96, 208,
  210
Harefield, Chief Petty Officer, 13
Harman, 262, 290, 375
Harrigan, Reg, 575–576
Harris, Captain Gwynne 'Blue,' 434,
  522–523
Harry Ludenbach, 410
Hart, Admiral, 404, 410–411, 414–
  416, 421, 427, 442, 444, 479, 559,
  564
Harukaze, 422
Harvey, Commander Neville, 262
Hasty, 313
Havock, 312, 315–317, 320–321
Hawkins, 263, 361
Hawkins, Thomas, 263
Hawkins, Tom, 588
Haworth-Booth, Captain Francis, 103
Hayler, Ordinary Seaman Basil, 269
Healy, Dominick, 82–83
Hearn, Commander Henry, 132, 138
Helena, 498
Helfrich, Admiral Conrad, 384, 411,
  414–416, 421, 424, 427, 564, 597
Heligoland Blight, Second Battle of,
  122–129
Helm, 508, 517, 519
Henderson, Admiral Sir Reginald, 6–7,
  9, 11, 243, 497
Henderson, Captain Denys, 199
Henderson Report, 6–7
Henley, 508

Hennigan, John, 82–83
Hero, 313
Herring, Sir Edmund, 602
Hewitt, Joe, 56, 64, 90
Hewitt, Vice Admiral Henry, 528
Heyen, Lieutenant Gerhard, 292
Hicks, David, 623
Hilken, Captain Thomas, 293–295,
  306–307, 322–323, 325, 527
Hill, Lieutenant Commander Cyril,
  205
Hillgarth, Captain Allan, 532, 611
Hindenburg, 148
Hindenburg, President Paul, 253
Hine, Commander Gordon, 214, 219
'Hints to Cadets Passing Out', 104–106
Hirohito, Emperor, 453, 562
Hirst, Evelyn, 569
Hirst, Paul, 103, 160, 178, 636
  commands *Success*, 226, 234–235
  commands *Toowoomba*, 373–374,
    409–410, 412–416, 424,
    427–428
  discharged from Navy, 429
  First Lieutenant at Flinders Naval
    Depot, 267
  marries Eve Carruthers, 226
  Naval College, 21–23, 25
  post-war, 568–569
  resigns from Navy, 236
Hobart, 70, 235, 255, 302, 411,
  417–419, 455, 458, 470–471, 475,
  478, 481, 486, 488, 493, 513–516,
  553–557, 559, 562, 572–573
Hodgson, W R, 353
Holbrook, 410
Hole, Lieutenant Commander Donald,
  362, 485
Hollandia, operations, 522–523

Hollywood, Able Seaman Hugh, 51
Holmwood, 359
Holt, Stoker Kenneth, 449
Honey, Galie, 240
Honolulu, 515, 539–540
Hood, 194–195
Hopkins, Brigadier Ronald, 501
Horne, Vice Admiral Frederick, 615
Hornet, 514
Horton, Lieutenant Commander Dick, 438, 611
Horton, Rear Admiral Tony, 639
Houston, 410, 412, 419–424
Howden, Captain Harry, 411, 458, 470–471, 582–583
Howells, Ben, 117, 120–121, 141, 174, 202, 228, 365, 367, 423, 567–568, 626, 637
   discharged from Navy, 95
   marries Dorothy Hicks, 226
   Naval College, 21–23, 25, 27, 30, 32, 34, 40–41, 48, 51, 56, 68, 80, 86
   post-war, 587, 627–628
Howells, Dorothy, 587
Howells, John, 95
Huáscar, 13
Hughes, Lieutenant Colonel Cyril, 258
Hughes, Prime Minister Billy, 86, 154, 180, 191, 334, 355, 374
Hughes-Onslow, Captain Constantine, 20
Huhs, Dorthy, 226, 228
Hunter, 530
Huon, 148–149, 178
Hyde, Admiral Sir Francis, 168, 170, 172–173, 196, 201, 215–217, 220, 244–245, 248

hydrography capabilities, Australian, 196–199, 240
Hyperion, 313, 315, 317, 320
HYPO, Station, 456, 472
Hyslop, Robert, 588
Hyuga, 539

I

I-11, 514
I-21, 464–465
I-22, 464
I-24, 464
I-27, 464
I-29, 464
I-65, 407
Ile de France, 508
Ilex, 313, 315, 320, 326
Illustrious, 325, 327–328
Imamura, Lieutenant General Hitoshi, 422–423
Imperial Conferences, 3–4, 7, 180, 191
Inconstant, 125
Indefatigable, 107
Indomitable, 132, 135, 386
Inflexible, 132, 135–136
Inoue, Admiral Shigeyoshi, 430, 453–455, 458,
intelligence capabilities, naval, Australian, 211, 249–253, 265–266
Invincible, 107
Ipswich, 563
Ise, 539
Ithuriel, 130, 132, 134–137, 141

J

J1, 152–153, 177
J2, 152–155, 158, 177

INDEX   747

J3, 152–153, 177
J4, 152–153, 177
J5, 152–155, 177
J7, 152–153, 177
Jacob van Heemskerck, 506–507
Jandakot, 262
Japanese 4th Fleet, 430
Japanese surrender, 562–566
Jarvis, 475, 480
Java, 412, 419, 421
Java Sea, battle of, 420–421
JAYWICK, Operation, 441
Jeffries, Commissioned Gunner (T) Henry, 369
Jellicoe, Admiral Sir John, 107–108, 120, 130, 170, 178, 180, 216, 266
Jensen, Mr Jens, 54, 70, 88
Jervis, Cecil, 433
Jervis Bay, 336
Jeune, Private, 523
Jintsu, 419–420
John D Edwards, 419
John D Ford, 419
Johnston, WA, 347
Jones, Air Marshal George, 587
Jones, Leading Seaman 'Taffy,' 154,
Joselyn, Henry, 498
Josselyn, Harry, 438, 478
Jumna, 412, 424
Jupiter, 412, 419, 421, 424
Jutland, Battle of, 107–108

K

K3, 132, 138
K4, 132, 138, 140, 383
K6, 132, 138–140, 383
K7, 132, 138–139
K9, 462, 467
K11, 130, 132, 141

K12, 130–133, 137, 141–142, 531
K13, 129–131
K14, 130, 132–134, 139
K15, 130
K17, 130, 132, 137–139, 141
K22, 130–136
Kadashan Bay, 548
Kaga, 430–431
Kaiser, 123, 127
Kaiserin, 123, 127
Kako, 479
Kanimbla, 292–300, 369–370, 462, 468, 471, 522, 537, 548, 560
Kapunda, 555
Kasaan Bay, 528
Kato, 489
K-boats, 129, 131, 139, 142, 153
Keenan, Jack, 498
Kehdingen, 125
Kennedy, Major Donald, 440, 455–456, 497
Kennedy, President John F, 498,
Kennett, Major, 151
Kerruish, Lieutenant Commander Robert, 584
Kerschbaum, Father, 188
Kerwin, Dr PE, 227
Kerwin, Eleanor, 227
Ketty Brøvig, 361, 363, 399
Keyes, Admiral Sir Roger, 209
Khedive, 527
Killeen, Stoker Kenneth, 468
Kimber, Dick, 130
Kimlin, Peyton J, 100–101, 103, 112, 117, 141, 143–145, 170, 172, 174, 203–204, 215, 259, 367, 512, 567, 630
    Naval College, 21–23, 25, 37, 62, 80

post-war, 586
King, Admiral Ernest, 411, 416, 454, 474, 477, 493–494, 571
King, Phillip Parker, 196
King, Stoker Tom, 414
King Alfred, 101
King George V, 566
Kinkaid, Vice Admiral Thomas, 520, 537–540, 545, 547, 552–553, 556, 561–562
Kinugasa, 479, 486
Kirkwell-Smith, Warrant Officer Andrew, 518
kite balloon, 149
Knell, Able Seaman George, 134
Knight, Signal Yeoman George, 432
Knox, Sir Errol, 576
Koch, H, 503
Kofuku Maru, 441
Komata, 356–357
Komet, 336, 356–359
Konigsberg, 125, 128
Koolinda, 396
Koopa, 509
Kormoran, 279, 291, 337, 339, 389–399
Kortenaer, Dutch destroyer, 412, 419–420
Krait, 441
Krasnoff, General Pyotr, 150
Kreigsmarine capabilities, 279–280
Krüder, Captain Ernst-Felix, 355
Kulmerland, 356–357, 359, 389, 394
Kurita, Vice Admiral Takeo, 422, 538, 543–544
Kuroki, Tokitaro, 351
Kuttabul, 462, 467–468
Kyle, Bill, 433

L

L21, 192
La Guardia, Fiorello, 270
La Motte Picquet, 299
Lady Betty, 224, 239
Laird, Captain James, 338–339, 435
Lamson, 446
Lancelot, Sergeant, 523
Lange, Premier Jack, 601
Lark Force, 430–434
Larkins, Frank, 21, 23, 25, 36, 38, 43, 48, 62–65, 67–68, 80, 83–85, 96, 103, 116, 120, 147, 153, 158–159, 162, 218, 423, 534
Launaro, Midshipman, 320
Launcelot, Sergeant Colin, 523
Laurabada, 435
Lauriana, 467
Laws, David, 285, 435
Laycock, Gordon, 609
Layton, Admiral Sir Geoffrey, 381–385, 408, 410, 426, 573
Leach, Captain John, 403, 407
Leander, 257, 294, 303, 359, 361–362, 364, 400, 446, 450, 491, 515
Leary, Vice Admiral Herbert, 445–446, 469
Leatham, Admiral Sir Ralph, 302, 361, 363–364
Lecky, Francis, 72
Lecky, Jack, 21–23, 44, 69, 72, 225, 267, 567, 586, 637
Lecky, William, 23
Leir, Commander Ernest, 130, 135, 136–137, 139
Letts, Lieutenant David, 639
Levant, Flag Officer, 530
Leveson, Rear Admiral Arthur, 103, 135–137

Lexington, 446, 454, 461
Ley, Captain Jimmy, 110
Lion, 123, 127, 143
Little, Captain Charles, 130, 137
Liverpool, 297, 322
Lolita, 365, 466–467
Long, Rupert, 103, 116, 135, 142–143, 145, 148–149, 152, 169, 211, 217, 235, 251–252, 263, 267, 344, 359, 426–427, 429, 440–443, 474, 503–505, 515, 533–534, 555, 558, 572, 580, 613–614, 625, 641
    coastwatch operations, 437–438, 445, 462, 495–497, 499, 501–502, 574
    Director Combined Operational Intelligence Centre, 387–388, 405, 408
    Director Naval Intelligence, 274, 280, 282, 290–291, 295
    District Intelligence Officer, Sydney, 249
    honours and awards, 532
    marries Vera Cliff, 261
    Naval College, 22–23, 25, 48, 65
    post-war, 567, 600–612
Lookout, 114
Lorraine, 304
Loxton, Midshipman Bruce, 485, 491
Luke, Sir Harry, 343
Lumsden, Lieutenant General Herbert, 547
Lusair, 554–557
Lyon, Captain Ivan, 441

M

M-22, 467–468, 470
M-24, 466, 468
M-27, 466

Macandie, George, 253
MacArthur, General Douglas, 382, 404–405, 441–445, 461, 467, 498, 505, 513, 517, 520, 539, 547, 551, 558, 560, 562, 564–566, 574
MacDougall, Vice Admiral Ian, 640
Macfarlan, Don, 478, 502
MacFarlan, Lieutenant Don, 440, 455–456
MacKenzie, Betty, 240
MacKenzie, Eric, 558
MacKenzie, Hugh, 104, 120, 130, 134, 143–144, 261, 287, 585, 610
    coastwatch operations, 289, 291, 358–359, 430–432, 434–435, 438, 474, 495–498, 500, 502–503, 558
    marries Betty Brown, 239
    Naval College, 21–23, 25, 34, 48
    post-war, 567, 583–585
    rejoins Navy, 288
    resigns from Navy, 179
    trader in New Guinea, 189, 224
Mackie, Lieutenant James, 438
MacLeod, Captain William, 245
Macleod, Sub-Lieutenant, 81
Madang, 607, 609–610, 632
Madsen, Professor Sir John, 340
Maimoa, 354–355
Mainguy, Admiral Edmund Rollo, 109
Mainwaring, Captain PCW, 364
Mair, Premier Alexander, 323
Makin, Norman, 396, 525, 579
Malaita, 431
Malaya, 191, 195, 308–309, 311, 390
Malleson, Lieutenant Claud, 361–362
Mandasor, 333
Manisty, Paymaster-in-Chief Eldon, 20

Manoora, 295, 357, 372, 522, 537, 548, 560
Manyo Maru, 357
Marblehead, 412
Marchant, William, 440
Mareeba, 389–390
Mariba, Private, 523
Marlborough, 220
Marrack, Commander Hugh, 214
Marsden, Mr, 13
Marshall, Irene, 202
Marsland, GHR, 503
Martin, Rayman, 496
Maryborough, 412
Mas, Sergeant, 523
Mascot, 435
Mason, Cecil, 437, 501
Mason, Lieutenant Commander 'Rosie,' 442–443
Mason, Paul, 438, 479, 497
Mason, Pilot Officer Cecil, 436
Massey, Captain George, 196, 229–230
Mathieson, Chaplain, 417–418
Matsuo, Lieutenant Keiu, 467–468, 470
Mauretania, 336
Mawbey, Captain Henry, 146
Mawson, Sir Douglas, 15, 365
Maxwell, Commander Patrick, 197
Maxwell, Justice Allan, 525–526
May Island incident, 129–142
Maya, 425
Mayo, Lieutenant Eric, 219
McCarthy, Keith, 433, 523, 631
McCarthy, keith, 518
McCawley, 481
McCollum, Captain, 533
McDonald, John, 436

McGrigor, Admiral Sir Rhoderick, 598
McGuffog, Commander James, 471
McGuire, Paul, 504, 602
McIntosh, Hugh, 93
McKell, Sir William, 577
McKenzie, Florence Violet, 374
McLachlan, Phyllis, 233
McMahon, William, 589
McManus, Commander Eric, 502, 532
McNeil, Rear Admiral Percival, 264
McNichol, Able Seaman, 523
McVey, Sir Daniel, 586
Mea'ole, Tupua Tamasese, 620
Mearns, David, 398
Medina, 73–75, 77, 185
Medusa, 515
Meiji, Commander Tagami, 514
Meiyo Maru, 479
Melba, Dame Nellie, 210
Melbourne, 35–37, 88, 149, 152, 179, 182–183, 191, 199, 206, 208–210, 212, 215, 220, 398, 590–591, 623, 630
Melusia, 183–184
Melville, Lieutenant Harry, 199
Melville, Lieutenant Jack, 207
Menzies, Prime Minister Robert, 273–274, 277, 289–290, 295, 303, 342–343, 378–379, 386, 580, 588, 593, 621, 635
Merula, 415
Mesley, Lieutenant Commander Jack, 484
Messel, Professor Harry, 613–614
Metaxas, Prime Minister Ioannis, 327
Metcalf, 559
Michishio, 542
Mikawa, Vice Admiral Gunichi, 477–480, 483, 485–486, 489–490, 492

Milford, General 'Ted,' 559, 560, 559–560
Miller, Captain Charles, 108, 128, 146
Miltiades, 68, 100, 449
minefields, defensive, 368–373
Minneapolis, 551
Mississippi, 385, 548–549
Missouri, 563–566
MMS.51, 424
Moale, 548
Mogami, 422, 539, 543
Mohawk, 328–329
Monash, General Sir John, 152, 174
Monk, Engineer Lieutenant Commander William, 13
Montecuccoli, 310
Montgomery, Lieutenant Commander Clive, 293
Moore, Rear Admiral George, 563, 581, 598
Moresby, 198, 226, 371
Moreton, 554
Moreton Bay, 299
Morgan, Captain Charles, 49, 61–64, 69, 72–77, 83, 88, 90, 92, 103
Morgan, Constance, 61–62
Morotai Islands, operations, 536
Morrison, Leonard, 15
Morrow, Captain James 'Copper,' 583–584
Mount Stewart, 215
Mountbatten, Admiral Lord Louis, 130, 617
Moyes, Commander Morton, 15, 60, 206, 208, 245, 365
Muirhead-Gould, Acting Rear Admiral Gerard, 464–469
Mullany, 522

Munro-Ferguson, Governor General Sir Ronald, 70, 88
Munson, Lieutenant Commander Henry, 479–480
Murray, Captain, Stuart 'Sunshine,' 564
Murray-Lyon, Major General David, 409
Musashi, 538, 543
Mussolini, Benito, 312, 323, 326
Myers, Dr David, 340

N

Nachi, 419, 421
Nagano, Admiral Osami, 472, 479
Nagumo, Vice Admiral Chuichi, 425
Nankervis, Alfred 'Nanky,' 588
Napier, 563
Napier, Acting Vice Admiral Trevylyan, 123, 125, 127
Nashville, 518
Naval Inspection Branch, 266
Navarinon, 530
Nave, Commander Eric, 290
Nellore, 358
Neosho, 457–458
Neptune, 257, 303–304, 310–311
Nestor, 121
Neuralia, 300
Nevasa, 301
New Mexico, 546, 548–549
New Zealand, 103, 107, 123, 132, 135, 159, 180, 373
Newfoundland, 556
Newman, Jack, 112, 153, 159, 169, 173, 177, 215, 253, 261–262, 267, 285, 444, 447, 474, 555, 635
Director of Signal Communications, 290–291, 293, 295, 374–376, 380, 442–443

Naval College, 21–23, 25, 37, 48, 51, 65, 80, 84
  post-war, 567, 595, 614–618
Newman, John, 103
Newman, Sub-Lieutenant Jack, 154
Niagara, 291–292, 336
Nicholas, 513, 515
Nichols, Captain Godfrey, 536, 540
Nicholson, Captain William, 110, 119, 313, 320–321
Nicola Fabrizi, 328–330
Nicolson, Commander Hugh St. L, 313, 315–316, 323
Nieuw Amsterdam, 508
Nimbin, 340
Nimitz, Admiral, 442–444, 454, 477, 493, 504–505, 520, 536, 563–564
Nishimura, Vice Admiral Shoji, 539, 541–544
Nixon, Vice President Richard, 607
Nizam, 563
Noaks, LC, 503
Nobbs, Harold, 251, 253
Norden, 345–348
Nordvard, 339
North Carolina, 474, 504
North King, 132
Notou, 338, 343, 359
Nottingham, 108
Noumea, Free French transition, 341–353
Novaro, Captain Umberto, 318, 320, 324
Nowaki, 425
Nubian, 328
Number 1 Squadron, RAAF, 406
Nürnberg, 125
Nurse, Eddy, 96, 100, 104, 108, 116, 120, 122, 124, 128, 130, 137, 139, 141, 143–144, 147, 151–152, 161, 171, 190, 196, 210, 228, 371, 373, 531, 567, 599, 629, 636
  Director of Naval Ordnance, 576–577
  Naval College, 17, 21, 23, 25, 33–34, 48, 56, 72, 84–85, 87
  ordnance inspection, 545
  post-war, 625–627
  transfer to Auxiliary Service, 266
  transfer to Engineering Branch, 169

O

O'Bannon, 513, 515
Oberon, 214
Obst, Warrant Officer Adolph, 518
Ohmae, Commander Toshikazu, 486
Oldendorf, Vice Admiral Jesse, 537, 541, 543, 552, 560
Ole Jacob, 354
Omrah, 113, 208, 294, 573
  passage to UK, 96–101
Onslow, 109
Orcoma, 100
Orion, 257, 273, 291, 303–304, 326, 328, 336, 338–339, 341, 343, 356–357
Orlando, 61
Ormode, 197
Ormonde, 240, 260
Orsova, 240, 247
Osborne House, see Royal Australian Naval College
Osprey, 199, 220
Osterley, 75, 167, 234, 328–329
Ostro, 305
Otway, 214
Ourmori, Petty Officer Takeshi, 468
Ovens, 215

Owen, Major Bill, 434
Oxley, 214–215, 220
Ozawa, Vice Admiral Jisaburo, 539, 543

P

Page, Cornelius, 431, 435–436
Page, Dr Earle, 12
Paige, Sax, 203
Paine, Beatrice, 167
Pakenham, Rear Admiral William, 107–108, 123, 125, 127–128, 172
Palliser, Rear Admiral Arthur, 407, 411
Palmer, Major Edward, 434
parachute jumps, 149
Parker, Lauris, 276
Parnell, Major General John, 83, 85
Parramatta, 26, 36, 68, 148–149, 152, 264
Patch, General Alexander, 497, 500
Pato, 239
Patterson, 475, 482, 484, 488, 517
Patterson, Captain Julian, 206, 301
Patterson, Captain Wilfred, 278
Paul Jones, 412, 419
Peace Procession (1919), 159–160
Pearce, Senator Sir George, 1, 14, 20–21, 27, 29, 52, 70, 145, 154, 183, 191
Pearl Harbor, 405–406, 430, 443, 453, 477, 489
Pearman, Chief Steward, 35
Peek, Vice Admiral Sir Richard, 471, 488, 573, 579, 615, 634
Peirse, Air Chief Marshal Sir Richard, 410
Peirson, Lieutenant JR, 154
Pélicier, Governor Georges, 342, 344–345
Pelly, Sub Lieutenant Denis, 101

Penglase, Nick, 238
Penguin, 278
Percival, General Arthur, 564
Perkins, 446, 462, 464, 466, 468–469
Perry, Paymaster Commander Patrick, 450
Perth, 70, 255, 268–269, 277, 300–301, 331, 333, 339, 357, 417–422, 424, 493–494, 543, 578, 597
  sinking of, 423
  at World Fair, New York, 270–272
Pétain, Marshal Philippe, 341
Phelps, 461
Philippines campaign, 537–554
Phillips, Admiral Sir Tom, 403–407
Phoenix, 114, 308, 518
Pierre Lotti, 350, 352–353
Pillau, 125
Pinguin, 336, 339, 354–356, 363–364
Pirie, 563
Pither, Group Captain George, 615–616
Pitt, Eric, 622
Plans for the Employment of Naval and Air Forces of the Associated Powers, 384–385
Platte, 446
Platypus, 153, 156, 158, 177, 201, 205–206, 218, 234
Playfair system, 285, 288
PLENAPS, see Plans for the Employment of Naval and Air Forces of the Associated Powers
Plunkett-Cole, Lieutenant Commander John, 485
Pognon, Monsieur Raymond, 346–347, 352
Polacchini, Captain Romulus, 331
Poore, Vice Admiral Sir Richard, 10

Poorten, Lieutenant General Heinter, 410
Pope, 412
Pope, Captain Cuthbert, 13, 50, 103, 205, 250–252
Port Bowen, 232
Port Brisbane, 354–356
Port Dunedin, 232
Port Hobart, 232
Portland, 551
Pound, Admiral Sir Dudley, 259, 404
Pownall, Lieutenant General Sir Henry, 409
Poynton, Alexander, 156, 164–167
Premuda, 328–330
Price, Flight Lieutenant Tom, 304
Pridham-Whippell, Vice Admiral, 328–330, 332
Prince of Wales, 386, 403, 406–408
Princess Margaret, 142
Princess Royal, 123
Protector, 2–3, 41
Proud, Commander John, 411, 427, 429, 441
Proud, George, 601
Pryce-Jones, Lieutenant Commander Ira, 436, 502
PT 109, 498
Purnell, Captain William, 380
Pursuer, 527

Q

Queen Elizabeth, 139
Queen Mary, 107, 269, 336, 341, 508
Queen of Bermuda, 508
Queensland Naval Forces, 2
Quincy, 477–478, 481, 486, 488

R

R4, 192
Rabinovitch, Dr, 59
Radford, 513
Radford, Admiral Arthur, 596–598
Rajah, 530
Ralph, 475
Ralph Talbot, 481, 517, 519
Ramb I, 361, 364, 400
Ramb III, 328–331
Ramillies, 300, 469
Ramses, 508
Ramsey, Admiral DeWitt, 596
Rangitane, 358–359
Rankin, Lieutenant Commander Robert, 425
Rapke, Paymaster Lieutenant Trevor, 450–451, 453, 506, 525
Raranga, 160
Rawlings, Vice Admiral Bernard, 530
Read, Jack, 438, 497–498, 501
Reilly, Winn, 103, 135, 142, 145, 147–148, 154, 157, 169–171, 202, 211, 254, 261, 340, 536, 567, 629
 awarded Goodenough Medal, 172–173
 awarded King's Medal, 115–116
 Naval College, 21–23, 25, 48, 65
 post-war, 585–586, 625
 rejoins Navy, 268
 resigns from Navy, 181
Renown, 209–211
Repulse, 123, 128, 194, 221, 403, 406–408, 467
Resolution, 220, 232, 241
Revenge, 232
Rhoades, Ashton 'Snowy,' 440, 455, 499–500, 503
Riefkohl, Captain Frederick, 481–482, 486, 491

Riley, Reverend Frederick, 74–75, 80, 448, 450–451
Riley, Stoker John, 386, 448–451
Riordan, Bill, 587
Rischbieth, Surgeon Lieutenant Henry, 563–564
Roberts, Colonel Caleb 'CG,' 610
Robertson, Captain John, 623–624
Robertson, Forbes, 502
Robertson, HAF, 503
Robertson, Lieutenant General Horace 'Red Robbie,' 568, 623
Robinson, Eric, 189
Robinson, 'Wobbie,' 501–502
Rockwell, Rear Admiral Francis, 436
Rooks, Captain Albert, 410, 421, 423
Roosevelt, President Franklin, 604
Roosevelt, President Theodore, 5
Roper, Justice David, 622
Roskill, Captain Stephen, 407, 491, 493
Ross, Lieutenant John, 322
Roxborough, 104
Royal Australian Naval College, 172, 177
   academics, 31–32
   daily routine, 30, 33, 66–67
   discipline, 33, 64–66
   fagging, 65
   formal warnings at, 44–47
   formation of, 8–17
   induction into, 24–25
   Jervis Bay, 51–52, 55–94
   moves to Flinders Naval Depot, 246
   official opening, 25–29
   Osborne House, Geelong, 12, 19–54
   Passing-Out Parade, 88–93

proposed locations, 11
resignation of Captain Grant, 164–166
seining, 59
selection process, 19–23
sport, 32–33, 36–38, 40–41, 51, 57–58, 71–72, 79–80, 83–85
tragedies, 81–83
Royal Military College, Duntroon, 50, 67, 83, 85
Royal Naval Air Service, 143
Royal Oak, 118, 464
Royal Sovereign, 103–104, 106, 109, 122, 128, 308–310
Royalist, 125, 127, 527
Royle, Vice Admiral Sir Guy, 387, 396, 441, 446, 469, 490, 524, 549, 552–553
Rushcutter, 278, 294, 373, 463
Rycroft, Lieutenant Commander James, 396
Ryojo, 504
Ryujo Maru, 422

S

S38, 479
S43, 437
S44, 489
S-206 Officers Report, 146
Sadleir, Cyril, 21, 98, 103, 135, 145, 153, 169, 196, 198, 241, 614, 618, 629, 632–633
   divorced, 233
   Flinders Naval Depot, 365
   health, 199, 260
   invalided from Navy, 199
   marries Lauris Parker, 276
   marries Phyllis Wheatley, 202
   Naval College, 22–23, 25, 32, 43,

58, 71
Naval Reserve Depot, Melbourne, 268
post-war, 569–570
Saint Louis, 515
Sakura Maru, 422
Salt Lake City, 475
Samarai, 632
San Juan, 478, 481, 486
Sanderson, Midshipman Noel, 485
Saratoga, 474, 493
Saumarez, Lieutenant Commander Philip, 326
Saunders, Carrie, 74
Sautot, Henri, 342–343, 345–353, 372
Savo Island, battle of, 483–491, see also Guadalcanal, battle of
Savoia, 310
Sayers, Ted, 600
Scanlan, Lieutenant Colonel, 430–432
Scheer, Vice Admiral Reinhard, 108, 336, 359, 361
School of Military Science, Sydney University, 9–10
Schroader, Lafe, 440, 500
Schroeder, 456, 499
Scorpion, 303
Scott, Rear Admiral Norman, 481, 491
Scout, 412, 419
Sea Mist, 468
Seamanship examination, 144–145
Searcher, 527
Selfridge, 488
Seton, CW, 503
Shah, 13
Shalders, Commander Russ, 639
Shamrock, 359

Shark, 410
Shaw, Norman, 213
Shedden, Sir Frederick, 581, 588–589, 596
Shelvey, Lieutenant Commander Mark, 640
Shigemitsu, Mr Mamoru, 565
shipbuilding, Australia, 70, 374, 593
Shoalhaven, 595
Shoho, 455–456, 458
Shokaku, 455, 460
Shortis, Trooper Gregory, 523
Showers, Rear Admiral Harry, 104, 120–121, 129–131, 133–134, 147, 153, 169, 171, 177, 193, 198, 220, 245, 260, 294, 369, 372, 551, 579, 606, 613–614, 629, 638–641
  commands *Adelaide*, 275, 300–301, 336, 343–353, 430, 448, 462, 469
  commands *Hobart*, 470–471, 474, 488, 493, 514–515
  commands Naval College, 246
  commands *Shropshire*, 524, 536, 573–574
  commands *Swan*, 268
  Defence Force Retirement Benefits Scheme, 583
  marries Jean Cunningham, 210
  Master Attendant, Sydney, 233
  Naval College, 21–23, 25, 36, 44, 48, 84, 91
  post-war, 612–614
Shropshire, 493–495, 517, 519–520, 522, 524, 536–537, 539–541, 543–551, 553–554, 559–560, 562–563, 572–574, 577
Siassi, 284
Simons, Charles, 182

Sims, 457–458
Singapore and Malaya, battle for, 405–416
Singapore Conference (1940), 378–382
Singapore strategy, 180, 191, 243, 377–382
'sJacob, Dutch tanker, 418
Skinner, I, 503
Slade, Evelyn, 74
Smith, Captain Gordon, 75, 77
Smith, Norm, 636
Smith, Seaman Norm, 415
Smith, Stanley, 15
Solferino, 330
Somerville, Admiral Sir James, 410, 443
Souix, 515
Special Intelligence Bureau, 290
Special Service Squadron, 175, 194–195
Spencer, 149, 151
Spender, Percy, 525
Speybank, 361
Spicer, Judge Sir John, 623–624
Spooner, Captain Lance, 545, 576, 625
Sprague, Rear Admiral Thomas, 544
Spurgeon, Commander Arthur, 258
Spurgeon, Commander Stanley, 244
Stackouwer, Governor General Jonkheer Alidius van Starkenborgh, 379
Stalker, 527, 530
Stalwart, 160, 178, 191, 204–205
Stamatios G. Embricos, 389
Station C, cryptanalysis unit at Corregidor, 404, 411, 442–443
Steady Hour, 468
Steele, Captain, 355

Stephenson, Lieutenant George, 501
Stevens, Captain Duncan, 623
Stevens, Major General Sir Jack, 555, 623
Stevenson, Captain John, 179, 194, 230
Stevenson, Robert Louis, 620
Stoke, 214
Stokes, John Lort, 196
Stonehaven, Lord, 224
Storey, Commander Arthur, 245, 578
Storstad, 339, 355
Straat Malakka, 391
Strait of Otranto, battle, 328–330
Strathaird, 300
Strathaven, 576
Strathella, 132
Strathmore, 301
Stronghold, 412, 424–425
Stuart, 244, 308, 310–311, 331
Sturdee, Lieutenant General Sir Vernon, 587
submarine capabilities, Australian, 193
H class, 193
J class, 77–78, 152–159
O class, 218–220
Success, 160, 204–205, 226, 234–236
Sussex, 235
Sutherland, Major General Richard, 442, 505
Suva, 170, 215
Svent Istfan, 149
Swan, 150, 169, 255, 264, 268, 275, 372, 554–556, 608–609
Swiftsure, 568
Swordsman, 160, 177–178
Sydney, 50, 69, 97, 118, 149, 154, 157, 170, 201, 205, 210, 212, 254–260,

278, 293–295, 300–302, 333–335, 381, 383, 388, 493–494, 527, 590–591, 594–595, 635, 639
Calabria, battle of, 309–312
Cape Spada, battle of, 313–323
Espero convoy, battle of, 305–308
Mediterranean operations, 303–332
sinking of, 390–402
Strait of Otranto, battle of, 328–330
Sydney harbour attack, 464–469
Syme, David York, 376

T

Takagi, Rear Admiral Takeo, 419–420, 455–458, 460–461
Takao, 425
Talbot, 475
Talmage, Jack, 435
Tamerlane, 364
Tanda, 353
Taplin, Lieutenant James, 467
Task Force 44, 475–477, 505
Task Force 73.4, 508
Task Force 74, 513–514, 518
Task Group 44, 504
Task Group 73.4, 506
Task Group 88.1, 527
Tasmania, 160–161
Tattoo, 160
Taylor, Sir Allen, 10
Teleradio 3B, 285, 288
Tenedos, 406, 412, 419
Tennenfels, 361
Terreneuvien Yolande, 153–154
TF 74, 517–519, 522, 524–525, 535–537
TG 88.1, 527–528
TG 88.2, 528

The Coastwatchers (book), 574–575
Thomas, Captain Edward, 509
Thompson, Horace, 103, 143, 160–161, 198, 274, 278, 294, 510, 567, 586, 629
commands *Franklin*, 202
discharged from Navy, 469
health issues, 636
marries, 202
Naval College, 22–23, 25, 43, 48, 72
Sydney harbour attack, 463, 466, 468–470
Thor, 336, 364, 389
Thring, Captain Hugh, 172
Tickell, Captain Frederick, 9–10
Tiger, 123
Tirpitz, 279
Tobruk, 592
Tomkinson, Captain John Wilfred, 194
Tompkins, Captain BF, 571–572
Toowoomba, 373, 409–410, 412–413, 415–416, 418, 422, 424–425, 427–428, 506, 636
Torr, Brigadier Alexander, 535
Torrens, 148–149, 204
Torselli, Signalman Artemio, 320
Tovey, Vice Admiral Sir John, 303, 305, 310–313, 322
Townsend, GWL 'Kaasa,' 185, 189, 225, 433
Toyoda, Admiral Soemu, 537–538, 541
Train, Lieutenant Gordon, 496
training, UK, 168–173, 192, 199
Triadic, 356–357
Triaster, 356–357
Trienza, 356

Triona, 356, 358
Trisaster, 356
Trocas, 395
Tromp, 464, 473, 506
Troubridge, Rear Admiral Thomas, 527, 531
Tulagi, 440, 453–456, 474, 476, 478, 483, 502, 528
Tulloh, Chaplain Alexander, 158
Turakina, 338–339, 359
Turner, Rear Admiral Kelly, 474, 476, 481, 504
Tweedmouth, Lord, 5
Twining, Lieutenant Colonel Merrill, 474–475, 484

U

UB-32, 114–115
Ulimaroa, 100
Ulster, 142
University of Melbourne, 9
University of Sydney, 9, 340, 370, 443

V

Valiant, 325
Vallentine, Harry, 21, 23, 32, 44–45, 68, 150, 160, 202, 204, 291, 509, 567, 628, 632
Vampire, 244, 278, 406, 412
Vandegrift, Major General Archie, 474, 476–477, 481–484, 494, 496–497, 499–500
Vanguard, 118–119
Vega, 142–143
Velebit, 389
Vendetta, 244, 555
Venetian, 139
Vengeance, 592

Vernon, 235
Vesper, 142
Vestal, 515–516
Victoria Cross, 109, 128, 153
Victorious, 526
Victory, 269
Victory Parade, 573
Viebeg, Oberleutnant zur See Max, 114
Vimera, 143
Vincennes, 477–478, 481–482, 486, 488, 490
Vinni, 356–357
Vireo, 515
Vladimir Mayakovsky, 298–299
Voltaire, 364
Volunteer Coastal Patrol, 253, 601
Volunteer Defence Patrol, 464
Von Der Hey, Constance, 61
von Reuter, Rear Admiral Ludwig, 123, 125, 127–128, 148
von Spee, Vice Admiral Maximilian, 50
Voyager, 244, 278, 623, 630

W

Waddel, Nick, 438
Waitamata, 100, 294
Wake, Nancy, 602
Walcott, Commander John, 2
Walker, Captain Frank, 517
Walker, LA, 503
Wallace, 232, 235
Waller, Hec, 247, 303, 332, 418, 420–423, 491, 525, 577
Walmar Castle, 100
Walsh, Commander John, 485
Walter, Commander Philip, 252
Walton, Commander James, 514

War Sirdar, 418
Warramunga, 398, 516–517, 519, 546–547, 551, 556, 562–563
Warrego, 26, 36, 68–69, 151–152, 264, 373, 537, 546
Warren, Guy, 556
Warrnambool, 265
Warspite, 304, 308–312, 316, 321, 460, 473
Wasatch, 539
Washington Naval Conference, 180
Wasp, 474
Wasserman, William S, 604
Watchtower, Operation, 474–475, 492
Waterhen, 244
Watkins, Leigh, 22–23, 25, 44–45, 48, 52, 103–104, 120, 143, 147, 153, 171, 181, 278, 365, 417–419, 422–423, 565
Watson, Chaplain Basil, 529
Watson, Lalla, 47
Watts, Adrian, 17, 21–23, 44–47, 52, 68, 121, 151, 160, 174–176, 202, 227, 240, 510, 567–568, 586, 632
Watts, James, 17, 174–175, 510
Watts, John, 52–54
Wavell, General Archibald, 410, 415
Webber, Lieutenant, 523
Wellen, Russian merchantman, 464–465
WESC, see Women's Emergency Signalling Corps
West Point, US Military College, 10
West Virginia, 550
Western Striking Force, 419
Westralia, 274, 294, 333, 462–463, 522, 537, 548, 560
Wewak operation, 557
Weyher, Korvettenkapitän Kurt, 338–339, 357
Wharton, Sir William, 196
Wheatley, Dr Frederick, 13–15, 49–50, 52–53, 59, 75–77, 81–82, 202, 246, 289, 373
Wheatley, Vivian, 81
White, Captain Clarence, 608
White, General Sir Brudenell, 239
Whitlock, Ensign Duane, 444
Whyalla, 462, 468
Willard A., 410
Willes, Midshipman Charles, 164–165
Williams, L, 503
Williamson, Captain Adolphus, 110–111, 113
Williamson, JC, 240
Willoughby, Colonel Charles, 442, 445
Willoughby, Commodore Guy, 590
Wilson, Captain Alexander, 262
Wisdom, Brigadier General Evan, 183
Witt de With, 412, 419
Wollongong, 409–410, 412, 415
Wolstab, Lieutenant Colonel John, 185, 188
Women's Emergency Signalling Corps, 374–375
Women's Royal Australian Naval Service, 375–376, 443, 447, 571, 595, 635
Woodroffe, Leading Seaman John, 437
Woomera, 603, 615–618
Wootten, Major General George, 559
WRANS, see Women's Royal Australian Naval Service
Wright, M, 503
Wright, Most Reverend John, 78

Wyngerie, 465–466
Wyrallah, 396

Y

Yali, Sergeant, 523
Yamaguma, 543
Yamamoto, Admiral Isoroku, 472
Yamashiro, 539, 542–543
Yamato, 538
Yandra, 464, 467–468
Yarooma, 466, 468
Yarra, 26, 36, 68, 149, 152, 261, 264, 412, 424–425
Yauwiga, Sergeant, 608
Yochow, 625
Yonai, Admiral Mitsumasa, 562
Yorktown, 447, 454, 456, 461, 472
Yuawike, Sergeant, 438
Yubari, 454, 479, 488
Yunagi, 479, 483

Z

Zealandia, 390, 430
Zeffiro, 305
Zuiho, 539
Zuikaku, 455, 460, 539

www.ingramcontent.com/pod-product-compliance
Lightning Source LLC
Chambersburg PA
CBHW070745230426
43665CB00017B/2257